The Behavioral Sciences and Health Care

The Behavioral Sciences and Health Care

2nd revised and updated edition

Edited by

OLLE JANE Z. SAHLER, MD

Professor of Pediatrics, Psychiatry, Medical Humanities, and Oncology
University of Rochester School of Medicine and Dentistry
Rochester, NY

and

JOHN E. CARR, PhD

Professor of Psychiatry & Behavioral Sciences and Psychology
University of Washington School of Medicine
Seattle, WA

Library of Congress Cataloging in Publication

is available via the Library of Congress Marc Database under the
LC Control Number 2006938796

Library and Archives Canada Cataloguing in Publication

The behavioral sciences and health care / edited by Olle Jane Z. Sahler and
John E. Carr. – 2nd rev. and updated ed.

Includes bibliographical references and index.
ISBN 978-0-88937-307-5

     1. Medicine and psychology. 2. Social medicine. 3. Psychology, Pathological.
I. Sahler, Olle Jane Z., 1944- II. Carr, John E.

R726.5.B452 2007   616.001'9   C2007-900326-5

PUBLISHING OFFICES
USA: Hogrefe & Huber Publishers, 875 Massachusetts Avenue, 7th Floor,
              Cambridge, MA 02139
              Phone (866) 823-4726, Fax (617) 354-6875; E-mail info@hhpub.com
EUROPE: Hogrefe & Huber Publishers, Rohnsweg 25, 37085 Göttingen, Germany
              Phone +49 551 49609-0, Fax +49 551 49609-88, E-mail hh@hhpub.com

SALES & DISTRIBUTION
USA: Hogrefe & Huber Publishers, Customer Services Department,
              30 Amberwood Parkway, Ashland, OH 44805
              Phone (800) 228-3749, Fax (419) 281-6883, E-mail custserv@hhpub.com
EUROPE: Hogrefe & Huber Publishers, Rohnsweg 25, 37085 Göttingen, Germany
              Phone +49 551 49609-0, Fax +49 551 49609-88, E-mail hh@hhpub.com

OTHER OFFICES
CANADA: Hogrefe & Huber Publishers, 1543 Bayview Avenue, Toronto, Ontario M4G 3B5
SWITZERLAND: Hogrefe & Huber Publishers, Länggass-Strasse 76, CH-3000 Bern 9

Hogrefe & Huber Publishers
Incorporated and registered in the State of Washington, USA, and in Göttingen, Lower Saxony, Germany

Printed and bound in the USA
ISBN 978-0-88937-307-5

About the Editors

Olle Jane Z. Sahler, MD is currently Professor of Pediatrics, Psychiatry, Medical Humanities, and Oncology at the University of Rochester School of Medicine and Dentistry. She is a behavioral pediatrician with a special interest in the care of chronically and terminally ill children and their families. Her foundation- and federally-funded research over the years has focused on siblings and mothers of children with cancer. She has also been funded by the National Center for Complementary and Alternative Medicine of the National Institutes of Health to study the effects of using music therapy in the management of patients undergoing bone marrow or stem cell transplantation on symptom control and immune reconstitution.

As an educator, she was the Director of the Pediatric Clerkship at the University of Rochester School of Medicine for 17 years and the Director of the Department of Education at the American Academy of Pediatrics in 1995–1996. She was also the founding president of the Council on Medical Student Education in Pediatrics in 1991–1992. As President of the Association for the Behavioral Sciences and Medical Education (ABSAME) in 1992–1993, she began a project to develop a comprehensive curriculum guide for medical student and resident education in the behavioral sciences that was published in 1995. An updated version of this curriculum guide, reflecting the many advances in the behavioral sciences that occurred around the turn of the century, forms the foundation for this book. The authors and editors who contributed to this text represent the diverse experience and expertise of ABSAME's membership, working in conjunction with other expert professionals dedicated to excellence in education.

John E. Carr, PhD is currently Professor Emeritus in the Departments of Psychiatry & Behavioral Sciences and Psychology at the University of Washington where he has played a principal role in developing behavioral science curricula for the School of Medicine. He has written extensively about the need for an "Integrated Sciences Model" for the behavioral and biological sciences in medical education. He has served as a consultant to the World Health Organization on Behavioral Sciences in Health Care Training and recently co-coordinated a cooperative venture between the Association for the Behavioral Sciences and Medical Education, the Association of Medical School Psychologists, and the International Union of Psychological Societies to develop behavioral science training modules for WHO.

He holds Diplomates in Clinical and Health Psychology from the American Board of Professional Psychology. He is a Fellow of the American Psychological Association, Association of Psychological Science, Society of Behavioral Medicine, and the Academy of Behavioral Medicine Research. He has served on the National Board of Medical Examiners Behavioral Sciences Test Committee, and is a founding member and two-time Past President of the Association of Psychologists in Academic Health Centers. His promotion of an integrated sciences model in medical education reflects his biobehavioral orientation and a career-long research program focused upon identifying the mechanisms of biobehavioral interaction in stress, anxiety, and depression.

Contributors

Albano, Anne Marie, PhD, ABPP
(Anxiety Disorders)
Associate Professor of Clinical Psychology (in Psychiatry)
Division of Child and Adolescent Psychiatry
Columbia University/NYSPI
New York, NY

Anderson, Arne J., MD, CDR, MC, USN
(Pregnancy and Infancy)
Department Head, Pediatrics
National Naval Medical Center
Bethesda, MD

Baxley, Elizabeth G., MD
(The Health Care System)
Professor and Chair, Department of Family and Preventive Medicine
University of South Carolina School of Medicine
Columbia, SC

Bennett, Forrest C., MD
(Pregnancy and Infancy, Toddlerhood and Preschool Years)
Professor, Department of Pediatrics
University of Washington School of Medicine
Seattle, WA

Bogdewic, Stephen P., PhD
(The Health Care System)
Executive Associate Dean for Faculty Affairs & Professional Development
George W. Copeland Professor and Associate Chair of Family Medicine
Indiana University School of Medicine
Indianapolis, IN

Borkan, Jeffrey M., MD, PhD
(Culture and Ethnicity)
Professor and Chair, Department of Family Medicine
Brown Medical School and
Memorial Hospital of Rhode Island
Pawtucket, RI

Botelho, Richard, MD
(Changing Risk Behavior)
Professor, Department of Family Medicine
University of Rochester School of Medicine
Rochester, NY

Buckley, Robert H., MD, FAAP, CDR, USMC
(Toddlerhood and Preschool Years)
Head, Developmental Pediatrics
U.S. Naval Hospital
Yokosuka, Japan

Calderón, José L., MD
(Health Literacy)
Assistant Professor, Ophthalmology/Biomedical Research Center-RCMI
Director, Drew University Center for Cross Cultural Epidemiologic Studies (DUCES)
The Charles R. Drew University of Medicine & Science
Los Angeles, CA

Campbell, James D., PhD
(Social Behavior and Groups)
Professor and Research Director, Family and Community Medicine
University of Missouri-Columbia School of Medicine
Columbia, MO

Carr, John E., PhD
(Co-Editor; The Clinical Decision-Making Process; Cognition and Emotion; Complementary and Integrative Medicine; Evolving Models of Health Care; Health Care in Minority and Majority Populations; Learning Processes; Predisposition; Social Behavior and Groups; Stress, Adaptation, and Illness)
Professor of Psychiatry & Behavioral Sciences and Psychology
University of Washington School of Medicine
Seattle, WA

Castellani, Brian, PhD
(Theories of Social Relations)
Assistant Professor, Department of Sociology
Kent State University
Ashtabula, OH

Culhane-Pera, Kathleen A., MD, MA
(Culture and Ethnicity)
Assistant Professor, Department of Family
Practice and Community Health
University of Minnesota
Minneapolis, MN
and
Associate Medical Director,
West Side Community Health Services
St. Paul, MN

Daugherty, Steven R., PhD
(Epidemiology; Biostatistics; Practice USMLE Exam)
Director, Education and Testing
Kaplan Medical
Chicago, IL

Doerr, Hans O., PhD
(Selected Theories of Development)
Professor Emeritus, Department of Psychiatry &
Behavioral Sciences
University of Washington School of Medicine
Seattle, WA

Eklund, Nancy, MD
(Human Sexuality and Sexual Disorders)
Volunteer Faculty, Family Medicine
Miller School of Medicine
University of Miami
Miami, FL
and
Founder and Medical Director,
Miami Center for Holistic Healing
Miami, FL

Ellwood, Amy L. MSW, LCSW
(Health Literacy)
Professor of Family Medicine & Psychiatry
University of Nevada School of Medicine
Las Vegas, NV

Farrow, James A., MD
(Pregnancy and Infancy; Adult Years; School Years)
Professor, Medicine & Pediatrics
and
Director, Student Health
Tulane University School of Medicine
New Orleans, LA

Felix, Steven, MD
(Pregnancy and Infancy; Toddlerhood and Preschool Years; School Years; Adult Years)
Clinical Assistant Professor of Pediatrics
Carilion Neurodevelopment Clinic
University of Virginia School of Medicine
Roanoke, VA

Flipse, Ann R., MD
(Societal Health Problems; Social Behavior and Groups; The Medical Encounter)
Director (retired),
Office of Teaching and Learning
Miller School of Medicine, University of Miami
Miami, FL

Frank, Julia, MD
(Practice USMLE Exam)
Associate Professor of Psychiatry
George Washington University MFA
Washington, DC

Frisina, Susan, RN
(Complementary Medicine)
Research Coordinator, ENT Division
University of Rochester Medical Center
Rochester, NY

Glew, Gwen, MD, MPH
(Pregnancy and Infancy; Toddlerhood and Preschool Years)
Fellow, Developmental Pediatrics
University of Washington School of Medicine
Seattle, WA

Glovinsky, Paul B., PhD
(Chronobiology and Sleep)
Director, Capital Region Sleep Wake Disorders
Center
Albany, NY

Gómez, Maria Fernanda, MD
(Substance Abuse)
Associate Professor of Clinical Psychiatry and
Behavioral Sciences
and
Associate Director, Psychosomatic Medicine
Montefiore Medical Center
Department of Psychiatry and Behavioral
Sciences
Albert Einstein College of Medicine
Yeshiva University
Bronx, NY

Greer, Pedro J., Jr., MD
(Poverty and Homelessness)
Associate Dean for Homeless Education
Mercy Hospital
University of Miami School of Medicine
Miami, FL

Guttmacher, Laurence B., MD
(Anxiety Disorders; Principles of Psychopharmacology)
Associate Clinical Professor of Psychiatry
and Medical Humanities and Associate Dean,
University of Rochester School of Medicine
and
Acting Clinical Director and Chief of Psychiatry
Rochester Psychiatric Center
Rochester, NY

Hafferty, Frederic W., PhD
(Theories of Social Relations; Competencies in Medical Education)
Professor, Department of Behavioral Sciences
University of Minnesota Medical School-Duluth
Duluth, MN

Haldeman, Douglas C., PhD
(Health Care Issues Facing Gay, Lesbian, Bisexual, and Transgender Individuals)
Clinical Instructor, Psychology
University of Washington School of Medicine
Seattle, WA

Hicks, Lanis L., PhD
(The Health Care System)
Professor and Program Director, Health Services
Management
Department of Health Management & Informatics
University of Missouri-Columbia School of
Medicine
Columbia, MO

Hosokawa, Michael C., EdD
(Health Care in Minority and Majority Populations; Social Behavior and Groups; Poverty and Homelessness)
Associate Dean and Professor, Department of
Family and Community Medicine
and
Adjunct Professor, Department of Educational
Leadership and Policy Analysis
College of Education
University of Missouri-Columbia
Columbia, MO

Houghtalen, Rory P., MD
(Dissociative Disorders and Cognitive Disorders; Eating Disorders; Human Sexuality and Sexual Disorders; Introduction to Psychopathology; Major Mood Disorders; Schizophrenia and Other Psychotic Disorders)
Medical Director for Adult Mental Health
Ambulatory Services
Department of Psychiatry
Unity Health System
and
Clinical Associate Professor of Psychiatry
University of Rochester School of Medicine
Rochester, NY

Jacoby, Liva, PhD, MPH
(Adult Years)
Associate Professor of Medicine
Alden March Bioethics Institute
Albany Medical College
Albany, NY

Kappes, Bruno M., PhD
(Cognition and Emotion; Sensation; Stress, Adaptation, and Illness)
Professor of Psychology & Health Science
Department of Psychology
University of Alaska
Anchorage, Alaska

Klingbeil, Karil S., MSW
(Interpersonal Violence)
Clinical Associate Professor, School of Social
Work
University of Washington School of Medicine
and
Director of Social Work (retired)
Harborview Medical Center
Seattle, WA

Larsen, Lars C., MD
(The Clinical Decision-Making Process; The Medical Encounter; The Physician-Patient Relationship)
Professor, Family Medicine
and
Associate Dean for Academic and Faculty
Development
Brody School of Medicine
East Carolina University
Greenville, NC

Lee, Elizabeth A., RN, MSPH
(The Health Care System)
Director, Indiana Patient Safety Center
Indiana Hospital & Health Association
Indianapolis, IN

Lenahan, Patricia M., LCSW, LMFT
(Geriatric Health and Successful Aging)
Associate Professor, Department of Family
Medicine
University of California-Irvine School of Medicine
Irvine, CA

Levenkron, Jeffrey C., PhD
(Introduction to Psychopathology)
Clinical Associate Professor of Psychiatry
(Psychology)
University of Rochester School of Medicine
Rochester, NY

Llorente, Maria D., MD
(Suicide)
Professor, Department of Psychiatry
Division of Geriatric Psychiatry
Department of Psychiatry & Behavioral Sciences
Miller School of Medicine, University of Miami
and
Chief of Psychiatry
Miami VA Healthcare Systems
Miami, FL

Maiuro, Roland D., PhD
(Interpersonal Violence)
Adjunct Research Scientist
Moss Rehabilitation Research Institute
Albert Einstein Health Care Network
University of Washington School of Medicine
Seattle, WA

Martell, Christopher R., PhD, ABPP
*(Health Care Issues Facing Gay, Lesbian,
Bisexual, and Transgender Individuals)*
Clinical Associate Professor, Department of
Psychiatry & Behavioral Sciences
University of Washington School of Medicine
Seattle, WA

May, Harold J., PhD
*(The Clinical Decision-Making Process; The
Medical Encounter; The Physician-Patient
Relationship)*
Clinical Professor of Family Medicine
Brody School of Medicine
East Carolina University
Greenville, NC

McBride, J. LeBron, PhD, MPH
(The Family)
Director of Behavioral Medicine
Floyd Medical Center
and
Associate Clinical Professor
Mercer University School of Medicine
Macon, GA

McCauley, Elizabeth, PhD, ABPP
(School Years)
Professor, Psychiatry & Behavioral Sciences
University of Washington School of Medicine
Children's Hospital and Regional Medical Center
Seattle, WA

Moore, Les, ND, MSOM, LAc
(Complementary Medicine)
Director, Integrative Medicine
Clifton Springs Hospital
Clifton Springs, NY

Nunes, João, MD
*(Adjustment Disorders and Somatoform
Disorders; Brain Structures and Their Functions;
Chronobiology and Sleep; Cognition and
Emotion; Disorders of Infancy, Childhood, and
Adolescence; Learning Processes; Neuronal
Structures and Functions; Predisposition;
Introduction to Psychopathology; Sensation;
Substance Abuse)*
Chairman, Department of Behavioral Medicine
Sophie Davis School of Biomedical Education
City College of the University of New York
New York, NY

Pakpreo, Ponrat, MD
(Obesity)
Adolescent Medicine
Sacred Heart Children's Hospital
Spokane, WA

Pantalone, David, PhD
*(Health Care Issues Facing Gay, Lesbian,
Bisexual, and Transgender Individuals)*
Department of Psychology
University of Washington School of Medicine
Seattle, WA

Parmelee, Dean X., MD
(Neuronal Structures and Functions)
Associate Dean for Academic Affairs
Boonshoft School of Medicine
Wright State University
Dayton, OH

Parson, Elvin B., MD
(Substance Abuse)
Chief, Addiction Clinic
Metropolitan Hospital Center
Department of Psychiatry
New York Medical College
New York, NY

Patten, Sonia, PhD
(Culture and Ethnicity)
Visiting Assistant Professor, Department of
Anthropology
Macalester College
St. Paul, MN

Plastow, Rosemary, PhD
(Introduction to Psychopathology)
Psychology Intern
University of Windsor
Windsor, ON, Canada

Pleak, Richard R., MD
*(Disorders of Infancy, Childhood, and
Adolescence)*
Associate Professor of Clinical Psychiatry and
Behavioral Sciences
Director of Education in Child & Adolescent
Psychiatry
Long Island Jewish Medical Center
Albert Einstein College of Medicine
New Hyde Park, NY

Privitera, Michael R., MD, MS
(Major Mood Disorders)
Director, Psychiatry Consultation/Liaison Service
Director, Mood Disorders Consultation Clinic
Associate Professor of Clinical Psychiatry
Department of Psychiatry
University of Rochester School of Medicine
Rochester, NY

Quill, Timothy E., MD
(Palliative Care)
Professor of Medicine, Psychiatry and Medical
Humanities
Director, Center for Humanities, Ethics and
Palliative Care
University of Rochester School of Medicine
Rochester, NY

Raffield, Troy J., MA
(Anxiety Disorders)
Associate Director of Psychology
Pinecrest Developmental Center
Pineville, LA

Rediess, Sharilyn, PhD
(Introduction to Psychopathology)
Scientific Affairs Liaison
Ortho-McNeil Janssen Scientific Affairs, LLC
Johnson & Johnson
Rochester, NY

Sahler, Olle Jane Z., MD
*(Co-Editor; Complementary and Integrative
Medicine; Disorders of Infancy, Childhood, and
Adolescence; Evolving Models of Health Care;
Obesity; Practice USMLE Exam)*
Professor of Pediatrics, Psychiatry, Medical
Humanities, and Oncology
University of Rochester School of Medicine
Rochester, NY
and
Medical Director, Integrated Complementary
Medicine Program
Thompson Health, Inc.
Canandaigua, NY

San Miguel, Xavier, MD
*(Adjustment Disorders and Somatoform
Disorders)*
Assistant Clinical Professor, Department of
Psychiatry
Mount Sinai Hospital School of Medicine
New York, NY

Sawchuk, Craig N., PhD
(Learning Processes)
Assistant Professor, Psychiatry & Behavioral
Sciences
University of Washington School of Medicine
Seattle, WA

Scott, Valerie D., EdD
(Biostatistics; Introduction to Psychopathology)
Professor and Director, Graduate Program in
Counseling Psychology
MAC Project Director
Department of Psychology
College of Saint Elizabeth
Morristown, NJ

Seitz, Frank C., PhD, ABPP
(The Clinical Decision-Making Process)
Adjunct Professor, Department of Psychiatry &
Behavioral Sciences
Division of Medical Science
University of Washington School of Medicine
Seattle, WA

and
Montana State University
Bozeman, MT

Shah, Mindy S., MD
(Palliative Care)
Departmental Fellow and Clinical Instructor in Medicine
University of Rochester School of Medicine
Rochester, NY

Silverman, Joel J., MD
(Neuronal Structures and Functions)
Professor and Chair, Department of Psychiatry
Virginia Commonwealth University School of Medicine
Richmond, VA

Smith, Sandra A., MPH, CHES
(Health Literacy)
Health Education Specialist
Department of Health Services
Center for Health Education & Research
University of Washington
Seattle, WA

Spielman, Arthur J., PhD
(Chronobiology and Sleep)
Professor, Department of Psychology
Sophie Davis School of Biomedical Education
City College of the University of New York
New York, NY
and
Associate Director, Center for Sleep Disorders Medicine and Research
New York Methodist Hospital
Brooklyn, NY

Spike, Jeffrey P., PhD
(Ethical and Legal Issues in Patient Care)
Associate Professor of Medical Humanities and Social Sciences
Florida State University College of Medicine
Tallahassee, FL

Stangl, Susan, MD, MSEd
(The Clinical Decision-Making Process; The Medical Encounter; The Physician-Patient Relationship)
Associate Professor, Family Medicine
David Geffen School of Medicine at UCLA
Los Angeles, CA

Stuber, Margaret L., MD
(The Clinical Decision-Making Process; The Medical Encounter; The Physician-Patient Relationship)
Jane and Marc Nathanson Professor
Director of Medical Student Education
Department of Psychiatry & Biobehavioral Science
Semel Institute for Neuroscience and Human Behavior at UCLA
Los Angeles, CA

Talbot, Nancy, PhD
(Dissociative Disorders & Cognitive Disorders)
Associate Professor of Psychiatry (Psychology)
Department of Psychiatry
University of Rochester School of Medicine
Rochester, NY

Tantillo, Mary D., PhD, RN, CS, FAED
(Eating Disorders)
Clinical Associate Professor, Psychiatry & Behavioral Health
University of Rochester School of Medicine
and
Director, Eating Disorders Program
Unity Health System
Rochester, NY

Wallace, Jeffrey I., MD, MPH
(Adult Years)
Associate Professor, Department of Medicine
Division of Geriatrics
University of Colorado Health Sciences Center
Denver, CO

Womack, William M., MD
(Adult Years)
Associate Professor Emeritus, Department of Child Psychiatry & Behavioral Sciences
Division of Child and Adolescent Psychiatry
Children's Hospital and Regional Medical Center
University of Washington School of Medicine
Seattle, WA

Wood, Isaac K., MD, FAACAP
(Biological Mediators of Behavior; Brain Structures and Their Functions; Chronobiology and Sleep; Neuronal Structures and Functions)
Associate Dean of Student Affairs
Associate Professor of Psychiatry and Pediatrics
Director, Undergraduate Medical Education in Psychiatry
Virginia Commonwealth University School of Medicine
Richmond, VA

Worthington, Ralph C., Jr., PhD
(The Clinical Decision-Making Process; The Medical Encounter; The Physician-Patient Relationship)
Retired
Ayden, NC

Yang, Chien-Ming, PhD
(Chronobiology and Sleep)
Associate Professor, Department of Psychology
National Chengchi University
Taipei, Taiwan
Republic of China

Yu, Wan-Hua Amy, PhD
(Brain Structures and Their Functions; Neuronal Structures and Functions)
Professor, Department of Cell Biology and Anatomical Sciences
Sophie Davis School of Biomedical Education
City College of the University of New York
New York, NY

Zollinger, Terrell W., DrPH
(The Health Care System)
Professor, Department of Family Medicine
Indiana University School of Medicine
Indianapolis, IN

Table of Contents

About the Editors v

Contributors vii

Table of Contents xv

Section I   **The Behavioral Sciences and Health** 1
                   Introduction and How to Use this Book 3
            1   Evolving Models of Health Care 5

Section II   **Biological Mediators of Behavior** 15
            2   Neuronal Structures and Functions 17
            3   Brain Structures and Their Functions. 26
            4   Chronobiology and Sleep. 33
            5   Predisposition. 40

Section III   **Individual-Environment Interaction** 47
            6   Sensation 49
            7   Stress, Adaptation, and Illness 55
            8   Learning Processes. 63
            9   Cognition and Emotion 73

Section IV   **Development Through the Life Cycle** 79
          10   Pregnancy and Infancy. 81
          11   Toddlerhood and Preschool Years 87
          12   School Years. 94
          13   Adult Years. 101
          14   Selected Theories of Development. 109

Section V   **Social and Cultural Determinants** 117
          15   Social Behavior and Groups. 119
          16   Theories of Social Relations. 123
          17   Culture and Ethnicity 130
          18   Health Care in Minority and Majority Populations 140
          19   The Family 147

Section VI   **Societal and Behavioral Health Challenges** 157
          20   Obesity 159
          21   Substance Abuse. 163

22 Interpersonal Violence 170
23 Poverty and Homelessness. 178
24 Suicide 183
25 Geriatric Health and Successful Aging 189
26 Human Sexuality and Sexual Disorders. 198
27 Health Care Issues Facing Gay, Lesbian, Bisexual, and
     Transgender Individuals 210

Section VII   The Health Care System, Policy, and Economics 217
28 The Health Care System. 219
29 Complementary and Integrative Medicine. 230
30 Palliative Care 240
31 Competencies in Medical Education 251
32 Ethical and Legal Issues in Patient Care 256

Section VIII   The Physician-Patient Interaction 267
33 Health Literacy. 269
34 The Physician-Patient Relationship 276
35 The Medical Encounter 281
36 The Clinical Decision-Making Process 287
37 Changing Risk Behavior 294

Section IX   Psychopathology 303
38 Introduction to Psychopathology 305
39 Eating Disorders 314
40 Adjustment Disorders and Somatoform Disorders 320
41 Anxiety Disorders. 326
42 Major Mood Disorders 333
43 Dissociative Disorders and Cognitive Disorders 344
44 Schizophrenia and Other Psychotic Disorders 349
45 Personality Disorders and Impulse Control Disorders 355
46 Disorders of Infancy, Childhood, and Adolescence. 362
47 Principles of Psychopharmacology 373

Appendices
Appendix A: Epidemiology. 379
Appendix B: Biostatistics 385

Review Questions – Answer Key. 393

Practice USMLE Exam
Questions 395
Answers 440

Subject Index 485

Section I

The Behavioral Sciences and Health

Introduction and How to Use This Book

Over time, health care has evolved from a spiritually based healing art to a scientifically based technical profession, reflecting advances in our knowledge of the biologic functioning of the human body. Prior to World War II, the focus of most health care scientists was concentrated on such exciting – indeed, revolutionary – discoveries as the role of antibiotics in curing previously fatal infections. The impact of World War II and its horrors for so many thousands of returning soldiers forced medical scientists to focus on the role of the mind, memory, and perceptions of the world around us in sustaining health and, even more importantly, illness and disability. In the 60s and 70s, physicians began to refer to a "Biopsychosocial Model", which proposed that psychosocial variables were equally as important as biological variables in determining health status. Although a major step forward in our realization of the complexity of the underpinnings and consequences of health and illness, the model did not explain how these distinctly different sets of variables actually interact.

In the last years of the 20th century, the Integrated Sciences Model (ISM) was introduced. The ISM postulates that not only do the biological, behavioral, cognitive, sociocultural and environmental variables underlying health status interact, but they are also interdependent. Furthermore, to conduct the kind of research required to define how and under what circumstances these interdependencies occur, the principles and research methods of the behavioral, social, and biological sciences must be integrated: that is, we can no longer work in discipline-specific isolation. The time has definitely come to put mind-body dualism to rest.

In 2004, the Institute of Medicine (IOM) affirmed this principle, urging the integration of the behavioral and social sciences into medical school curricula throughout all four years of undergraduate education, throughout all years of residency training, and, by extension, throughout the entire career of the practicing physician. To make its recommendations clear, the IOM recommended prioritized attention to several specific areas: mind-body interactions; patient behavior; physician role and behavior; physician-patient interactions; social and cultural issues in health care; and health policy and economics.

In designing this book, we have grouped chapters to highlight the themes the IOM has identified as key to optimizing medical education.

In Section I, we briefly trace the evolution of health care practices and models, the development of contemporary medical practice, and the historical events leading to the development of the Integrated Sciences Model as background to contemporary health issues.

In Section II, Biological Mediators of Behavior, we review the biologic basis for behavior in the context of neuroanatomy and physiology, chronobiology and sleep, and predisposition or the roles of genetics and environment in determining human nature.

In Section III, Individual-Environment Interaction, we particularly focus on how the person receives, processes and interprets information from the environment and how, through learning, responses to stress can promote either health or illness.

In Section IV, Development Through the Life Cycle, we review human development from before birth to old age from the perspectives of Freud, Erickson, Piaget, and Social Learning Theory. Taken together, these theorists provide a rich picture of the many different perspectives through which an infant becomes an elder.

In Section V, Social and Cultural Determinants, we learn first how the individual, in general, behaves in the context of others, including the family. We then examine how specific groupings such as culture or ethnicity, minority status, or sexual orientation influence how health care is delivered and received.

In Section VI, Societal and Behavioral Health Challenges, we explore a variety of issues confronting contemporary medical practitioners.

In Section VII, The Health Care System, Policy, and Economics, we examine the health care system, the emerging role of Complementary Medicine as it evolves into Integrative Medicine, the expanding role of palliative care, legal and ethical issues, and the increasing need for practitioners to communicate effectively with patients.

In Section VIII, The Physician-Patient Interaction, we focus on the basic elements of physician behavior toward patients and, in keeping with the Art of Medicine, how the physician can effect behavior change in patients to maximize health.

In Section IX, we review the more common psychiatric illnesses that it is important all physicians can identify so that appropriate referral can be made.

In our Appendices, we review the principles of Epidemiology and Biostatistics, subjects included in the Behavioral Sciences course offerings at many medical schools.

Finally, we provide a challenging series of questions patterned after the USMLE multiple-choice question examinations. Each question is accompanied by a full explanation. Some of these questions reinforce material within the text; many cover topics not included in the text to provide supplemental learning.

Reviewing the IOM recommendations, coverage is provided as follows: mind-body interactions (Sections II and III); patient behavior (Sections III, IV, and VIII); physician role and behavior and physician-patient interactions (Section VIII); social and cultural issues in health care (Sections V and VI); and health policy and economics (Section VII).

We hope that you find this text informative and useful.

Olle Jane Z. Sahler, MD
John E. Carr, PhD

1 Evolving Models of Health Care

- What is the World Health Organization definition of health?
- How do disease, sickness and illness differ?
- What is the difference between direct and indirect risks to health?
- How does primary prevention differ from secondary prevention?
- How have traditional medical systems influenced modern health care beliefs and practices?
- What was the significance of the *Flexner Report*?
- What is the biopsychosocial model?
- What is the integrated sciences model?

Health, Illness, Sickness, and Disease

What is the World Health Organization definition of health?

The most fundamental definition of **health** is "the absence of disease or disability." The World Health Organization (WHO) defines health as a state of complete physical, social, and mental well-being. Health is measured by the patient's ability to cope with everyday activities and function fully physically, socially, and emotionally. At its optimal level, good health provides for a quality of life marked by spiritual serenity, zestful activity, a sense of competence, and psychological well-being.

How do disease, sickness and illness differ?

Disease is defined by its etiology; that is, as a process that is caused by environmental trauma, biologic malfunction, or an identifiable agent or substance (e.g., pneumonia that is caused by a virus or bacterium). Disease may be due to a structural defect, such as an aortic aneurysm, or a functional impairment, such as an underactive thyroid gland (hypothyroidism). In each of these examples, medical intervention aimed at the causative agent would be considered not only necessary, but also sufficient, to produce health.

Sickness is different from having a disease. An individual can look and feel sick, yet have no identifiable disease such as an infection, defective organ, or impaired physiologic functioning. Conversely, a person can have a disease for any or all of these reasons but not feel or act sick. Being perceived as sick by others or feeling sick oneself implies assuming a **sick role** that is defined within relationships, families, the workplace, or the community. It frees a person from the obligation to perform the tasks of everyday living without blame ("I just feel too sick today to go to work"). There are, however, certain obligations that the sick person must fulfill: (1) rely on experience or seek professional assistance to find ways to get better, and (2) adhere to culturally or professionally prescribed regimens that will facilitate a return to health reasonably quickly.

Illness represents the totality of how the patient behaves and feels, how the patient perceives the disease, and how the family and community respond to these perceptions. Illness behavior varies according to the person's place within the family or community. For example, it may reflect the person's attempts to gain attention. From the community's point of view, it may be seen as retribution for past misdeeds, as a chance occurrence, a burden imposed to test will, or belief in a higher power. The patient's explanation of how or why the illness occurred **(explanatory model),** and the course the illness takes, determines how the patient behaves and how the larger community will respond.

Disease, sickness, and illness can, but do not necessarily, coexist in a patient. For example, a patient can have a disease, be seen as sick, and yet act well. This may reflect resiliance or denial or, as in the case of early asymptomatic phases of some diseases, may reflect reality. A person can have a disease, not be seen as sick by others, and yet act ill. This may reflect a need for support, or acknowledgment of some real or perceived malfunctioning and is often encountered in individuals who have a "hidden" condition (e.g., spinal stenosis). In these instances, except for the patient's **sick role** or **illness behavior,** the condition would not be apparent to and, therefore, acknowledged by others. A person also may have no identifiable physiologic pathology but feel sick. This is common in persons experiencing stress. The individual may manifest the stress response by behaving ill, focusing upon the physical symptoms rather than the sources of the stress. Indeed, in all of these different cases, assuming the sick role or displaying illness behavior may help to rally external support for the individual's coping efforts. Thus, assuming the sick role and engaging in illness behavior, under certain circumstances, can be the first step toward health.

> What is the difference between direct and indirect risks to health?

Action may be taken in response to direct or indirect risks to health. **Direct risks to health** are practices that endanger good health (e.g., reckless driving, excessive alcohol or caffeine consumption). **Indirect risks to health** are lower risk practices or prevention failures (e.g., driving without a seat belt, not exercising). Most risk factors are related to a person's lifestyle and are, therefore, modifiable. Some risk factors, such as age, race, gender, or genetic makeup, cannot be modified by the individual. Other risk factors, such as social class, religious practices, and cultural traditions, relate to health status in complex ways and may or may not be modifiable.

Thus, the concept of health care has broadened from the treatment of disease to the prevention of disease, injury, sickness, and illness and the promotion of health. To achieve these goals, health care professionals not only apply medical treatments, but also seek to change patient behaviors, beliefs, social and cultural practices, and environmental conditions. To do so successfully requires knowledge of the ways these factors affect patient health and the methods by which they can be effectively modified.

Health Promotion and Maintenance

> How does primary prevention differ from secondary prevention?

The health of individuals and populations is maintained by measures that promote primary and secondary prevention. **Primary prevention** involves practices to protect, promote, and maintain health, such as exercising regularly, maintaining a normal weight, and eating nutritional foods. It also involves avoidance of activities that jeopardize health, such as smoking or substance abuse. **Secondary prevention** involves practices that enhance resistance to disease, such as immunization, medical surveillance, and health screening.

Primary prevention programs may focus on individuals or communities. Community programs include education (e.g., about general health, school safety, violence prevention, or safe sexual practices); government programs include maintaining good sanitation or eliminating environmental hazards (e.g., eradicating mosquito breeding areas), and universal immunization programs.

Evolving Approaches to Health Care

Medicine likely had its earliest origins in primitive health care practices that began about 30,000 years ago, but knowledge of the human body and theories of health care began to emerge in more systematic form recorded by the Babylonians 6,000 years ago. The Code of Hammurabi defined surgical operations to be performed, scale of fees, and penalties for malpractice. Five-thousand-year-old Egyptian records describe symptoms of abdominal, eye and heart disorders, treatment of wounds, fractures and dislocations, and an understanding that brain lesions were associated with paralysis of the opposite side of the body.

How have traditional medicine systems influenced modern health care beliefs and practices?

Major systems of traditional **Chinese, Ayurvedic, and Greek medicine** began to evolve between 1500 and 500 B.C., and became the bases for traditional health care systems currently practiced in many parts of the world. Despite their cultural and geographic differences, there is evidence that there was a vigorous exchange of knowledge, likely through trade and conquest, resulting in common doctrines fundamental to all of these systems:

1. The world is viewed as an integrated whole, subject to universal laws, governing all phenomena including human behavior and health;
2. The individual is a unified system of physical, mental, cultural and spiritual aspects of life;
3. Health is a state of "balance" (homeostasis) between the individual and the universe and among elements, humors, and forces within the individual;
4. All living things are endowed with a "life force" composed of male/female or other oppositional forces;
5. Disease results from disruption of the life force or imbalance among humors, bodily functions, and external forces;
6. Symptoms are manifestations of the body's efforts to restore balance and health;
7. The healer's role is to aid the body's efforts to restore balance via treatments based on universal principles.

These early conceptualizations of disease and health, rooted in indigenous cultural beliefs, constitute the subject matter of ethnomedicine (see Chapter 17, Culture and Ethnicity). While seemingly primitive, they reflect a budding awareness of the complex relationships among **etiologic factors**, the principle of **homeostasis** and the influence of **stress** conditions as well as insight into the role of the healer. Thus, it is not surprising that these concepts are prevalent and continue to influence health care practices throughout the world today.

Modern medicine has its roots in the traditions of **Hippocrates** (b. 460 B.C.), credited with establishing the first school dedicated to the sci-entific study of medicine and formulating the first principles for professional conduct. Hippocratic medicine was the definitive standard for medical knowledge until **Galen**, in the second century A.D., who began anatomical and physiological investigations. Based on animal dissection, many of his findings proved to be in error, but there was a beginning understanding of the respiratory, circulatory, digestive, and neural systems.

Galen laid the foundations for what would come to be called **allopathic medicine** by asserting that organic lesions led to dysfunctions, thereby establishing the principle that treatment of biological pathology was the primary concern of the physician. Treatments were based on the **law of opposites**, i.e., diseases were treated with medicines or interventions intended to create the opposite effect of the symptom. Galenic medicine had a profound impact on the development of medicine. With all its shortcomings as well as merits, it became the unchallenged authority in medical dogma for 1400 years, with the result that its dispersal worldwide influenced indigenous medical systems while stifling scientific advancement. The law of opposites was loosely interpreted leading to the indiscriminate use of enemas, bloodletting, purging, and other toxic and invasive procedures.

The resurgence of rationality, critical discourse, and experimental investigation that marked the **Renaissance** led to important advances in the development of medicine. By the 17th century, developments in the natural sciences stimulated increasing research into the physical, mechanical, and chemical functions of the body. By the 18th century, challenges to Galenic or Allopathic medicine and treatments based on the law of opposites led to a reaffirmation of the physician's role in assisting the body's healing efforts. This led to the development of homeopathic, osteopathic, naturopathic, and chiropractic approaches to medicine. (see Chapter 29, Complementary and Integrative Medicine).

What was the significance of the *Flexner Report*?

By the end of the 19th century, medicine was beginning to acquire a more scientific foundation and clinical techniques became more sophisticated and disease specific. Advances in microbiology showed that microorganisms contributed to disease and could be controlled by sterilization, antiseptics and immunization.

At the same time, the quality of medical training was being scrutinized. The *Flexner Report,* published in 1910, called for the establishment of higher standards for U.S. medical education and defined **biomedicine** as firmly grounded in the basic biologic sciences and scientific methodology. Public support for research and training increased, leading to the provision of enormous financial and technological resources. However, by defining scientific medicine as solely biological and ignoring the contributions of other sciences, the broader context of health care became obscure in post Flexnerian medical education and practice.

The limitations of **biomedicine** became evident during WW II when the treatment of injured soldiers suffering "shell shock" (posttraumatic stress disorder) raised awareness of the influence of **psychosocial factors** on a patient's illness and treatment outcome. This awareness led to the development of **psychosomatic medicine**

and a proliferation of psychologic and sociocultural models of health care as alternatives to pure biomedicine. But these models were flawed in the same way as biomedicine – too narrowly psychological or too narrowly sociocultural, emphasizing the importance of their specific factors but failing to take into account how these factors interacted with biologic factors. By the mid 1970s there was increasing recognition that a more comprehensive approach to health care was needed.

What is the biopsychosocial model?

In 1977, an internist at the University of Rochester, **George Engel**, published an article in *Science,* which proclaimed "The Need for a New Medical Model: A Challenge for Biomedicine." Engel asserted that in this new **biopsychosocial model** (1) there are multiple determinants in the development of disease and the resultant illness process; and (2) there is a hierarchical organization of biologic and social systems that contribute to the disease and illness experience. Each system is a component of a higher, more abstract system, and any changes in one system will change other systems, especially those most closely linked to it within the hierarchy (see Figure 1.1.). It follows that (3) the psychologic and social sciences are equally as important as the natural sciences in understanding the determinants of illness.

During the early 1970s, behavioral research was already generating convincing data supporting what was to become known as the biopsychosocial model, including the importance of cognition, learning, society, culture and the environment, as well as biology, in determining health and illness. The Canadian government's *Lalonde Report of 1974* and the *U.S. Surgeon General's Report of 1979* concluded that most major health problems confronting North Americans had their origins in individual behavior. The field of **behavioral medicine** emerged as an interdisciplinary research effort to define the empirical linkages between the behavioral and biomedical sciences. What was needed was a blueprint, a theoretical/conceptual framework, to guide this interdisciplinary effort. The biopsychosocial model needed to be moved beyond the notion of an amalgamation of distinct sciences to the notion that medicine is really the product of the integration of these distinct sciences.

Clinical Application of the Biopsychosocial Model

A person can function normally physiologically with only one kidney. Therefore, after recovery, an individual who has served as a kidney donor can have normal renal functioning. In the biomedical model, this person has returned to a fully healthy state. However, in the biopsychosocial model, attention would be paid to the psychosocial parameters of the patient's condition as well as the biologic state of health. Recovery may be facilitated if the donor knows the recipient was helped by the donation, the community applauds the donor for the gift, and the donor believes that full and rapid recovery is expected. On the other hand, the donor may feel damaged or otherwise impaired, or may feel that insufficient gratitude was expressed. These latter perceptions may slow or prohibit full functional recovery (i.e., a return to life as it was experienced preoperatively).

In the case of the kidney donor, no biologic intervention beyond appropriate postoperative care is required. However, the biopsychosocial model recognizes that education about the physiology of renal functioning is essential to reassure the patient of his/her biologic integrity; information about the benefits to the recipient will reinforce the donor's sense of self worth by acknowledging his/her altruism; the support of family and the community can be useful in permitting a period of recovery followed by graded reintegration to full activity.

Figure 1.1. Biopsychosocial model

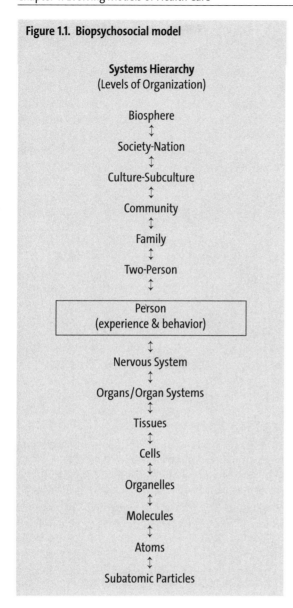

Systems Hierarchy
(Levels of Organization)

Biosphere
↕
Society-Nation
↕
Culture-Subculture
↕
Community
↕
Family
↕
Two-Person
↕
Person
(experience & behavior)
↕
Nervous System
↕
Organs/Organ Systems
↕
Tissues
↕
Cells
↕
Organelles
↕
Molecules
↕
Atoms
↕
Subatomic Particles

The Integrated Sciences Model of Health Care

What is the Integrated Sciences Model?

In the **Integrated Sciences Model** (ISM), psychosocial phenomena are functionally connected to biological phenomena in accord with common universal principles such as homeostasis, stress adaptation, learning and development. According to this model, each patient is a complex but integrated system of many interacting variables that can be organized under five domains: **biological, behavioral, cognitive, sociocultural, and environmental** (see Figure 1.2.). Each domain represents a category of information that is critical to the evaluation of the patient. The variables within each domain are constantly interacting with variables in all the other domains such that any change in one effects a change in all the others. Like all systems in all sciences, the human system strives to maintain an optimal balance, not only within each of the domains but between them. Hence, the concept of **homeostasis** applies to psychosocial as well as biologic phenomena and defines one of the universal integrating principles.

Any challenge to homeostasis is regarded as **stress.** This is not the popular, narrow notion of situational stress but rather the universal principle that describes any "system under strain." Of course, stress or challenge is not the problem, per se. First, the degree of stress determines, in part, the nature and intensity of the response. Every college student is familiar with the "inverted U" shaped curve describing the relationship between stress and productivity. Too little challenge (stress) is poorly motivating, hence poor performance. Too much challenge (stress) can impair performance. Moderate challenge (stress) appears to be optimal, i.e., enough to motivate and inspire, but not overwhelming.

Second, it is the stress response, or more specifically, its failure in enabling the individual to successfully cope with, adapt to, and resolve the stressful condition, that defines the individual's health vs. illness. It is the breakdown or dysfunction of the stress response that constitutes disease or disorder. Ironically, it is also the successful functioning of the stress response that can sometimes contribute to disease and disorder, as in autoimmune diseases where an "overzealous" immune system begins to attack its own host body.

The stress response is composed of biological reactivity (physical symptoms), as well as behavioral, cognitive, and sociocultural reactivity, each domain influenced by genetic determinates, learning processes and past experience. Biological reactivity reflects the complex interplay of the body's "life support" systems and their genetically predetermined response to homeostatic challenge, manifested as the physical "symptoms" commonly associated with the stress response (see Chapter 7, Stress, Adaptation, and Illness).

Figure 1.2. Integrated Sciences Model

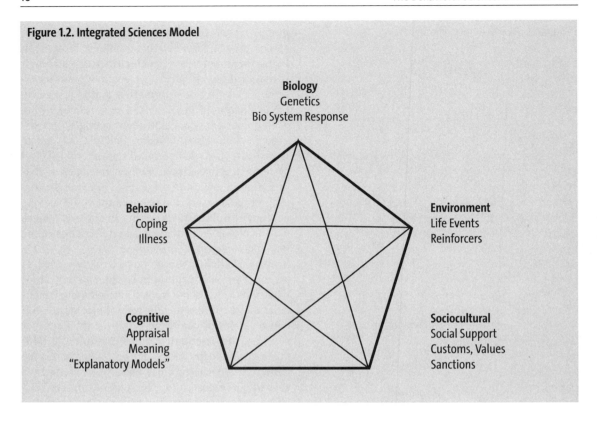

In every individual, any challenge (stress) to any domain destabilizes the entire interdependent system and results in a multivariate response throughout all domains. This destabilization is not necessarily problematic since the patient may be able to cope, i.e. adapt quite well in all domains. For example, biological challenge (disease) can necessitate behavioral adaptation (take medicine), cognitive adaptation ("I can't work and need someone to cover for me"), sociocultural change (let mom take care of me) and environmental change (move to a healthier climate).

The system is **evolutionary,** that is, continually subject to adaptive change. As a person encounters new experiences, stressful challenges or changes in one domain, responses in other domains are induced. This complex interaction of domains contributes to the health condition of the patient at all ages and developmental levels from "womb to tomb." For example, caught up in change and experimentation, adolescents engage in behaviors that may become health threatening. Attitudes and patterns related to diet, physical activity, tobacco, alcohol and substance abuse, safety and sexual behavior may persist from adolescence into young

adulthood, setting the stage for potential major health care problems later in life. As another example, healthy diet (e.g., low fat, low salt, low cholesterol), no use of tobacco, illegal substances or alcohol, and healthy physical activity, as well as healthy stress response patterns (e.g., reducing the Type A response) aid in preventing high blood pressure, coronary heart disease, diabetes and certain cancers in adults. Thus, establishing and maintaining healthy lifestyle patterns early in life are essential for continued good health in later years.

How variables in the five domains interact over the life span of the individual is a product of **adaptive experience.** The basic process underlying this adaptive experience is **learning** in all its forms, from the most fundamental reflexive act to the most complex abstract conceptual formulation. No other process is sufficient to account for the myriad connections that have been demonstrated to exist among variables in the domains. The lines of the pentagram in Figure 1.2. represent the acquired or learned connections between these variables. It is understanding the mechanisms underlying these interactions that is the focus of behavioral medicine research.

Diagnostic Assessment

The accurate **assessment** of the differential and interactive contributions of biological, behavioral, cognitive, cultural and environmental risk factors and etiologic agents is essential to determining the most efficacious treatment interventions or strategies. Thus, comprehensive evaluation of every patient should involve a detailed exploration of the variables within each of the five domains. By so doing, the physician determines the nature of the problem, identified not only in terms of biologic symptoms and etiology, but also where it occurs (environment), what the patient was doing at the time (behavior), what the patient was thinking, saying, interpreting (cognition) in what setting, with whom, under what circumstances, and with what consequences (sociocultural). Having this comprehensive information informs the physician about the complex biobehavioral interactions that contribute to the particular disorder and so provides the information required to design an effective treatment plan.

The model illustrates the complexity of factors contributing to this major health risk, and why treatments that focus only on one domain (e.g., change smokers' cognitions) or one variable (e.g.,

stop cigarette advertisements) are likely to fail. Health behaviors are complexly determined and the probability of change is maximized only if treatments address *all* of the contributing factors. Thus, the ISM demonstrates that optimal treatment must be multimodal. In our example, a **multimodal approach** might involve the following:

- *Biological*: Nicotine patches to counter nicotine dependence
- *Behavioral*: alternative work breaks such as exercise; social gatherings in nonsmoking venues; stress management training
- *Cognitive:* require patient to explain to others (e.g., young people) how smoking is harmful; expose to high-profile, high-status nonsmokers as models
- *Cultural*: encourage family to reinforce not smoking; limit smoking to inconvenient and uncomfortable places; encourage patient to join a "smokers anonymous" group
- *Environmental*: make smoking materials less accessible, e.g., raise taxes, restrict access; promote nonsmoking social and recreational areas (note link with Culture)

Not all interventions will be feasible but a multimodal approach is more likely to be successful than a single intervention that targets a non-responsive variable. Extrapolating beyond the individual patient, the same principles apply to **community, regional, and global health programs**. For example, by identifying the treatment goal of a public health initiative, e.g., reduced incidence of dengue fever (biological domain), a health care researcher can identify factors that contribute to the problem: (1) *behavioral factors* – no one takes responsibility for draining or treating standing water; (2) *cognitive factors* – no public awareness about how to treat the problem; (3) *cultural factors* – lack of community coordination of efforts (house construction, social and personal habits contributing to infection risk); and (4) *environmental variables* – poor drainage is a known problem in swampy land. Thus, any effort, regardless of magnitude, that targets a single variable will be less successful than a multimodal approach targeting multiple variables.

Even though a specific biobehavioral factor is important in the etiology of a condition, it does not always play an equally important role in treatment (i.e., biologic causes do not always require biologic treatments). For example, in cases of CNS damage, behavioral rehabilitation

---

Clinical Application of the Integrated Sciences Model

A patient has been advised by his doctor to give up smoking because of chronic obstructive pulmonary disease (COPD). Reduced smoking behavior is the treatment goal. We review the domains in Figure 1.2. and the variables that influence smoking using (-) after a variable if it discourages smoking, and (+) if it encourages smoking:

Biological: COPD (-), nicotine dependence (+), genetic factors (+/-)

Behavioral: peers smoke (+), social gatherings (+), social censure (-), stress reduction (+), "cool" image (+).

Cognitive: knowledge of smoking risks (-), belief "I'm invulnerable, and can quit anytime" (+),

Cultural: value systems (+/-), gender models (+), social sanctions (+), roles in interaction (+/-)

Environmental: accessible (+), relatively inexpensive (+), reinforcing advertisements (+)

is the best approach to reestablishing lost function by programming other areas of the brain to perform that function. Although new drugs have significantly improved the survival statistics for HIV and AIDS patients, behavioral management of the psychological and social consequences of the disease and its spread is still a major focus of disease management. Insulin-dependent diabetes also reflects the complex interaction of biologic (administering insulin) with behavioral factors (diet, exercise, monitoring). Dysmenorrhea and premenstrual tension are clinical phenomena that derive from a biologic basis but may be precipitated by and manifested as complex, multidimensional biobehavioral conditions. Thus, optimally effective treatment will often involve **combinations** of biological/pharmacological and behavioral approaches.

As the name implies, the **Integrated Sciences Model** attempts to account for all the possible variables and processes that determine the etiology and

---

Integrated Sciences Model

1. Stress in the form of challenges or change (disruption of homeostasis) in the biological, behavioral, cognitive, sociocultural and/or environmental condition of the patient initiates responses in all domains (to restore homeostasis).
2. The system is constantly evolving. Challenges to the organism are ongoing and the system is continuously adapting to the stresses of everyday life and experiences.
3. Disease is a byproduct of the individual's efforts to adapt to biological, behavioral, cognitive, cultural and environmental stressors. Therefore, accurately assessing the differential role of each of these risk factor domains is essential to determining the best treatment strategy. Treatment strategies may address an etiologic factor directly or indirectly (i.e., biologic causes do not always require biologic treatments).
4. The treatment, itself, will have direct biological, behavioral and cognitive effects on the patient, as well as cultural and environmental impacts (side effects).
5. Thus, the treatment response may require additional intervention in any or all of the domains (e.g., combined biologic and behavioral therapies for stroke patients).

---

course of a disease, and the patient's responses to both the disease and its treatment. Specific genetic, neuroendocrine, biologic, behavioral, cognitive, sociocultural, or environmental models have been proposed to explain specific disease states or health conditions. While highly circumscribed, these models should not be dismissed but rather should be included within the broader context of the ISM.

Recommended Reading

Carr JE. Proposal for an Integrated Sciences Curriculum in Medical Education. *Teaching and Learning in Medicine* 1999; 10:3–7.

Cuff PA, Vanselow NA (Eds.). *Improving Medical Education: Enhancing the Behavioral and Social Science Content of Medical School Curricula.* Washington, DC: National Academies Press; 2004.

Engel GL. The need for a new medical model: A challenge for biomedicine. *Science* 1977; 196:129–136.

Kandel ER. *In Search of Memory: The Emergence of a New Science of Mind.* New York: Norton; 2006.

Porter R. *The Greatest Benefit to Mankind: A Medical History of Humanity.* New York: Norton; 1997.

World Health Organization. *The World Health Report 1997: Conquering suffering, enriching humanity.* Geneva, Switzerland: World Health Organization; 1997.

Review Questions

1. A process that is caused by environmental trauma, biologic malfunction, or an identifiable agent or substance is defined by which of the following concepts?
    A. Disease
    B. Illness
    C. Injury
    D. Sick Role
    E. Sickness

2. Scientific standards for modern biomedicine and educational standards for modern medical education are associated with which of the following?
    A. The Biopsychosocial Model
    B. The Explanatory Model

   C. The Integrated Sciences Model
   D. The 1910 *Flexner Report*
   E. The 1979 *Surgeon General's Report*

3. Defining all the variables and processes that contribute to health, disease, sickness and illness, and the complexity of biobehavioral mechanisms by which they interact and are interdependent defines which of the following models?
   A. Behavioral Model
   B. Biomedical Model
   C. Biopsychosocial Model
   D. Integrated Sciences Model
   E. Sociocultural Model

Key to review questions: p. 393

Section II

Biological Mediators of Behavior

2 Neuronal Structures and Functions

- What role do neurons play in brain function?
- How do neurons develop?
- What is an action potential?
- What is neurotransmission?
- Why do SSRIs have so many side effects?

At birth, the human brain provides genetically determined, survival-oriented reflexive behaviors. Through interaction with the environment, the brain learns, i.e., acquires and stores information, solves problems, and evolves highly complex and specific behaviors to maintain the integrity of the internal milieu (homeostasis) while responding to ever changing environmental demands.

Neurons

What role do neurons play in brain function?

Neurons are the structural and functional units of the central and peripheral nervous systems (CNS and PNS, respectively). Neurons are specialized cells capable of transmitting information from the environment as well as from within the body, and eliciting appropriate responses for the survival of individuals. The brain contains about 100 billion neurons, ranging from 0.01 mm to 0.08 mm in diameter. Neurons are classified based on the number of processes emerging from their cell bodies, length of the axon, what the axon connects to, or the type of neurotransmitter released. A neuron with one process is **unipolar**; with two processes, **bipolar;** and with more than two processes, **multipolar.** The multipolar neuron is the most abundant type in the brain. Neurons with long axons projecting to distant targets are **projection** neu-

Basic Components of a Neuron

Soma (cell body): contains the cell nucleus and cytoplasmic organelles. The soma is the site of protein synthesis, including enzymes that synthesize neurotransmitters, and of most proteins destined for the axon and dendrites.

Dendrites: are neuronal processes specialized for receiving neurotransmission from other neurons. The membrane of dendrites has specific receptors that bind with neurotransmitters.

Axon: is a neuronal process that propagates electrical signals (action potentials), and transports molecules to and from its distal end, or axon terminal. Neurons typically have only one axon, whose length ranges from less than a millimeter to over a meter. The velocity of signal propagation depends on the diameter of the axon and thickness of the myelin sheath that covers it. Neurotransmitters, except for the peptide type, are synthesized and stored locally in synaptic vesicles at the terminal.

Synapse: is the cellular junction. It specializes in transferring electrical signals in a polarized fashion from the presynaptic axon to the postsynaptic cell (e.g., another neuron or effector cells, such as muscle and glandular cells). Signal transfer at the synapse is accomplished by the release of neurotransmitters from the presynaptic axon terminal into the synaptic cleft. Neurotransmitters bind to their receptors in the postsynaptic cell membrane, thus evoking postsynaptic electrical responses. Neuron-to-neuron synapses may be axodendritic, axosomatic, or axoaxonic, depending on the portion of the receiving neuron with which the transmitting axon connects.

rons. Neurons with short axons that form local circuits within a region are **interneurons**. Neurons making connections with sensory receptors in the body are **sensory neurons**, while neurons innervating muscle cells are **motor neurons**. Neurons are also classified based on the neurotransmitter they use. Thus **cholinergic, norepinephrinergic,** and **serotonergic neurons** use the neurotransmitter acetylcholine, norepinephrine or serotonin, respectively.

GLIA

Glia are non-neuronal cells that support neuronal function in a variety of ways. The CNS has four types of glial cells: **astrocytes**, **oligodendrocytes**, **microglial cells** and **ependymal cells**. Astrocytes maintain an appropriate chemical and ionic environment for neuronal signaling, inactivate certain neurotransmitters, and form scar tissue after CNS injury. Oligodendrocytes provide and maintain myelin sheaths. Microglial cells remove dead cells and cellular debris, and defend against infection. Ependymal cells form the lining of the fluid-filled brain ventricles.

Neuronal Development

How do neurons develop?

The **neural tube**, from which the CNS develops, is formed about 22 days after conception in humans. Neuroepithelial cells in the neural tube give rise to CNS neurons and glial cells (except microglial cells). Schwann cells (the peripheral counterparts of oligodendrocytes) and neurons whose cell bodies are in the PNS derive from the **neural crest**, the bits of neural ectoderm that are pinched off during the formation of the neural tube.

Neurons of both the CNS and PNS go through three major stages: cell proliferation, cell migration, and cell differentiation. Consider the building of the six-layer neocortex as an example. In humans, the vast majority of neocortical neurons are born in the ventricular zone of the neural tube between the fifth week and the fifth month of gestation. Radial glial cells provide the scaffolding

that supports building the cortex by spanning their processes from the ventricular zone to the pia. **Neuroblasts** (immature neurons) migrate along radial glial cell processes. Each wave of neuroblasts migrates past the preceding ones, thereby creating horizontal cortical plates in an inside-out fashion.

Once appropriately positioned in the cortex, neuroblasts start to differentiate by sprouting off neurites, which ultimately become axon and dendrites. Axonal elongation depends on the presence of appropriate cell-adhesion and extracellular matrix molecules. The direction of axonal growth requires environmental **guidance cues**, including **chemoattractants** secreted by target cells. When the axon comes in contact with its target cell, a synapse is formed. In some regions of the brain, early synaptic connections are stable and maintained into adult life. In other regions, initial synaptic contacts are later reorganized, and some are eventually eliminated.

The development of neurons and glial cells follows a **genetically determined** course. The establishment of brain circuitry occurs mostly before birth, and is guided by physical cell-to-cell communication and by chemical signals. The final refinement of synaptic connections, influenced by the sensory environment, occurs during **critical periods** of infancy and early childhood. However, experience-dependent synaptic plasticity that modifies brain function persists throughout life.

Action Potentials and Neurotransmission

What is an action potential?

Direct electrical stimulation or activation of ion channels such as (1) ligand-gated channels that respond to chemical signals (most common), (2) voltage-gated channels that react to changes in the membrane potential, and (3) ion channels specifically sensitive to heat or mechanical distortion of the membrane can cause a transient state of depolarization or diminution in the strength of the charge across the neuronal membrane. Depolarization is accomplished by the opening of sodium channels in the membrane, which allows

The **membrane potential** is the voltage across the cell membrane at any given time. Ions diffuse through a fully permeable membrane from higher to lower concentration until reaching equilibrium, which produces a membrane potential of 0 millivolts. Because neuronal membrane is semi-permeable, its typical potential at rest is polarized at about -65 millivolts. Thus, neuronal cytosol is negatively charged with respect to the extracellular fluid.

Negative membrane potential of a resting neuron is an absolute prerequisite for a functioning nervous system. The resting potential of neurons is the result of unequal concentrations of positively and negatively charged ions on either side of the membrane. The two ion pumps, the sodium-potassium pump and the calcium pump, actively exchange external Na^+ for internal K^+, and transport Ca^{++} out of the cytosol across the cell membrane, respectively. In addition, because it contains a large number of potassium ion channels, the resting neuronal membrane is highly permeable to K^+. Consequently, the neuron at rest has a *higher* concentration of K^+ and a *lower* concentration of Na^+ and Ca^{++} in the cytosol compared to the extracellular fluid.

the influx of Na^+ into the cell. In this process, the cytosol side of the membrane becomes less negative compared to the extracellular fluid than it is in its resting state. If this depolarization process proceeds beyond a critical level (**threshold**), an all-or-nothing electrical event called an **action potential** is generated and is propagated along the neuronal membrane.

What is neurotransmission?

When the action potential propagating along the axon reaches the axon terminal, neurotransmitters are released from the synaptic vesicles into the synaptic cleft. Neurotransmitters then bind to their specific receptors in the postsynaptic cell membrane, which leads to opening or closing of ion channels in the postsynaptic cell membrane, resulting in depolarization (excitation) or hyperpolarization (inhibition) of the postsynaptic cells. Thus, propagation of a message in the nervous system consists of a series of electrical-chemical reactions.

Receptors for neurotransmitters can be classified into two broad categories: **transmitter-gated ion channels** and **G-protein-coupled receptors**. When a neurotransmitter binds to transmitter-gated ion channels, the ion channels directly open or close, which produces the fastest and briefest type of postsynaptic responses. G-protein-coupled receptors act through G-proteins, which either alter ion channel activity, or activate second messenger cascades. Prominent second messengers include cyclic nucleotides, Ca^{++}, and inositol triphosphate (IP_3). Activating the second messenger system leads to phosphorylation of ion channels, which in turn changes the functional state of ion channels. Neurotransmission via G-protein-coupled receptors typically produces slower and longer-lasting postsynaptic responses.

Once neurotransmission has taken place, the neurotransmitter activity is terminated through (1) **diffusion**, the neurotransmitter is flushed away from the synaptic cleft, (2) **degradation**, enzymes break down the neurotransmitter at the synaptic cleft, or (3) **reuptake**, the neurotransmitter is taken back through active transport into the presynaptic terminal, where it is either reloaded into synaptic vesicles for future use or degraded enzymatically. The **glial cell membrane** also has neurotransmitter transporters to assist in neurotransmitter removal from the synaptic cleft.

Neurotransmitters can be divided, based on size, into two broad categories: small- and large-molecule neurotransmitters. **Small-molecule neurotransmitters** include amino acids, monoamines, and acetylcholine. **Large-molecule neurotransmitters** constitute a group of neuroactive peptides.

To be considered a neurotransmitter, a molecule has to meet the following criteria:
1. be synthesized and stored in the presynaptic neuron
2. be released from the presynaptic axon terminal upon depolarization in a Ca^{++}-dependent manner
3. bind with high affinity to its receptor in the postsynaptic cell membrane, and elicit electrical responses in the postsynaptic cell
4. be inactivated or removed from the site of action through specific mechanisms

Types of Neurotransmitters and Their Actions

Neurotransmitter	Site of action	Action
A. Amino acid	Throughout CNS	
Glutamate	Cerebellar granular cells, thalamocortical and corticostriatal projections, cortical pyramids, hippocampus, entorhinal cortex	Excitatory. Opens Na+, K+, and Ca++ channels. N-methyl-D-aspartate (NMDA) receptor aids in learning and memory; role in psychopathology
Gamma aminobutyric acid (GABA)	Midbrain & diencephalon; less in hemispheres, pons and medulla. Does not cross blood-brain barrier	Inhibitory. May suppress mania, anxiety, seizures. Receptors mediate inhibitory feedback loops; have sites for benzodiazepines and barbiturates
GABA$_A$		Most abundant. Antagonists cause seizures
GABA$_B$		G-protein associated receptor. Agonist (baclofen) useful to treat spasticity
GABA$_C$		Opens Cl channels directly; like GABA$_A$
B. Monoamine		
Dopamine	Nigrostriatal tract	Initiates and coordinates movement
	Mesolimbic-mesocortical tract	Affects cognition, emotion, operant learning
	Tuberoinfundibular tract	Inhibits prolactin release
Norepinephrine	Locus ceruleus, wide CNS projections; adrenal medulla; PNMT converts NE to E	Regulates arousal, attention, perception, mood, sleep-wake cycle, organ function, BP, cardiac function, adipose tissue metabolism, bronchial contraction
Epinephrine	Secreted by adrenal medulla	Affects peripheral neurotransmission
Serotonin	Raphe nuclei —> throughout CNS/PNS	Suppresses arousal, sexual interest, aggression, pursuit of goal-directed tasks Regulates sleep, anxiety, obsessive-compulsive behavior, depression
Histamine	Hypothalamus —> throughout CNS/PNS	
H$_1$		Increases IP$_3$. Reduces pain perception
H$_2$		Increases cAMP
H$_3$		Unknown (may regulate vascular tone)
C. Acetylcholine	Reticular formation; basal forebrain (nucleus basalis of Meynert), striatum. Voluntary, smooth, heart muscles	Facilitates memory in frontal cortex, modulates sleep & arousal, coordinates movement
D. Neuropeptide	Coexists with other neurotransmitters	
Enkephalin	Hypothalamus, pons, hippocampus, midbrain; widespread projections	Decreases pain perception
Endorphin	Same as above	Affects behavior, pain perception
Oxytocin & vasopressin	Hypothalamus	Affect attention; regulate mood
Substance P	Afferent sensory areas, nigrostriatal tract	Opens K+ channels (excitatory); pain perception
Cholecystokinin		Produces anxiety & panic attacks
E. Unconventional		
Nitric oxide	Selective neurons throughout CNS/PNS	Retrograde signaling and synaptic plasticity

Amino Acid Neurotransmitters

Major amino acid neurotransmitters include **glutamate, γ aminobutyric acid (GABA)**, and **glycine**. About 70 % of the synapses in the brain are either glutamatergic or GABAergic.

Glutamate is synthesized enzymatically from glucose. Glutamate is the neurotransmitter that most excitatory neurons in the CNS use. There are three types of glutamate receptors: **AMPA, NMDA,** and **kainate receptors**. Each of these is a transmitter-gated ion channel, and mediates fast excitatory synaptic transmission by admitting sodium ions into the cell, resulting in a rapid and large depolarization.

GABA and **glycine** mediate most synaptic inhibition in the CNS. GABA is synthesized from glutamate by glutamic acid decarboxylase. Glycine, like glutamate, is synthesized enzymatically from glucose.

Three types of GABA receptors – $GABA_A$, $GABA_B$, and $GABA_C$ – have been identified. $GABA_A$, $GABA_C$ and glycine receptors are transmitter-gated ion channels, whereas the $GABA_B$ receptor is a G-protein-coupled receptor. Binding to $GABA_A$, $GABA_C$ or glycine receptors opens chloride channels, causing an influx of negatively charged chloride ions. Binding to $GABA_B$ causes efflux of positively charged potassium ions. Chloride influx or potassium efflux **hyperpolarizes** and **stabilizes** the cell membrane, thereby inhibiting the postsynaptic cell from firing off an action potential.

> Benzodiazepines, among the most effective drugs in treating generalized anxiety, bind to a specific site in the $GABA_A$ receptor. While benzodiazepines by themselves have very little effect, in the presence of GABA, they increase the efficacy of the inhibitory effect of GABA.

Amine Neurotransmitters

About 5–10% of the synapses in the CNS are aminergic. Major amine neurotransmitters include:
- **catecholamines (dopamine, nor-epinephrine,** and **epinephrine)**
- **serotonin**
- **histamine**

Catecholamines are monoamines whose synthesis starts with action of the enzyme tyrosine hydroxylase on the amino acid, tyrosine.

Dopamine (DA) is made first in the pathway of catecholamine biosynthesis. DA-containing neurons in the brain are localized primarily in the substantia nigra, ventral tegmental area, and the arcuate nucleus of the hypothalamus. Projections from these neurons form several dopaminergic tracts in the brain.

1. **Nigrostriatal tract** – which participates in the control of volitional movement; it is affected in Parkinson's disease and other movement disorders.
2. **Mesolimbic-mesocortical tract** – which is involved with emotion especially pleasure, motivation, and operant reinforcement of learning; it is affected in schizophrenia.
3. **Tuberoinfundibular tract** – which inhibits prolactin release.

The effects of DA are mediated exclusively by G-protein-coupled receptors. Seven types of DA receptors have been identified. Activation of one of them in the medulla inhibits vomiting. Antagonists to this particular receptor are used to induce vomiting after poisoning or drug ingestion-overdose. DA activity is terminated by reuptake. DA is degraded by monoamine oxidase (MAO) and catechol O-methyl-transferase (COMT).

Norepinephrine (NE) is formed as the enzyme dopamine-β-hydroxylase produces hydroxylation of the side chain of dopamine. NE-containing fibers project diffusely from the **locus ceruleus** in the brainstem to a variety of targets in the brain and spinal cord. Noradrenergic neurons are nearly silent electrically during sleep, somewhat active during wakefulness, and most active in watchfulness and startle situations. Thus, NE appears to play a role in attention, perception, mood states, arousal, and the sleep-wake cycle.

Epinephrine is converted from NE by the enzyme phentolamine N-methyltransferase. Epinephrine-containing neurons in the CNS, fewer in number than other catecholaminergic neurons, are primarily found in the lateral tegmental area and medulla, and project to the hypothalamus and thalamus. The function of these epinephrine-secreting neurons in the brain is not known. NE and epinephrine act on α- and β-**adrenergic receptors**, both of which are G-protein-coupled receptors. Two subtypes of α- and three subtypes of β-adrenergic receptors are known. Activation of $\alpha1$ receptors causes depolarization, while activation of α2 receptors elicits hyperpolarization. Two subtypes of β receptors are expressed in many types of neurons. Peripherally, β receptors regulate blood pressure, cardiac function, bronchial muscle contraction and adipose tissue catabolism. NE and epinephrine syntheses are controlled by the availability of the precursor dopamine, auto-regulation via α2 receptors, and end-product inhibition. NE and epinephrine, like DA, are degraded by MAO and COMT.

Serotonin (5-hydroxytryptamine, or 5HT**)**, an indolamine, is synthesized from the essential amino acid, tryptophan, by the enzyme tryptophan hydroxylase. Serotoninergic neurons, fewer than other aminergic neurons, are found in the **raphe nuclei** in the brainstem, and project diffusely throughout the brain and spinal cord. Serotoninergic neurons regulate the level of sexual interest, aggression, and sleep, and suppress arousal. The serotonin metabolite, 5-hydroxyindoleacetic acid, was found to be decreased in the CSF of murderers and rapists. Serotonin is involved in people's ability to pursue goal-directed tasks, in anxiety and depression, and in obsessive-compulsive behavior. In the spinal cord, in association with endogenous opioid peptides, serotonin reduces the perception of pain. A large number of serotonin receptors, most of which are G-protein-coupled, have been identified in the brain and throughout the body. Serotonin is removed by special transport reuptake, and degraded by MAO.

Histamine, an imidazolamine, is produced from histidine by the enzyme histidine decarboxylase, and is metabolized by the combined actions of histamine methyl-transferase and MAO. Histamine is widely distributed in the body, and, like serotonin, is much more prevalent elsewhere than in the brain. It is often released in response to trauma and allergic reactions causing pain and producing burning and itching sensations. All of the histaminergic neurons in the brain are located in the hypothalamus. These neurons project diffusely to virtually all regions of the brain and spinal cord. The central histamine projections mediate arousal and attention, in similar fashion to central acetylcholine and NE projections. Histamine also controls the reactivity of the vestibular system. There are *three types of histamine receptors:* H_1, H_2, and H_3, all of which are G-protein-coupled receptors. H_1 and H_2 act, respectively, through the second messenger systems IP_3 and cyclic AMP. H_3 may regulate vascular tone. The mechanism for the well

known sedative effect of antihistamine medications used for the treatment of allergy is their interference with the role of histamine in CNS arousal.

Why do SSRIs have so many side effects?

Monoamine Hypothesis of Depression

The monoamine hypothesis postulates that depression is associated with insufficient amounts of 5-HT or NE in the synaptic cleft. Antidepressant medications named selective serotonin reuptake inhibitors (SSRI's) ameliorate depression by increasing neurotransmitter availability in the synaptic cleft. They block neurotransmitter reuptake, which is often followed by degradation by MAO.

Clinical Application

A 52-year-old woman has been taking a selective serotonin reuptake inhibitor for two weeks. She complains of abdominal cramping, diarrhea and headache. How would you explain these symptoms to her?

Fourteen types of **serotonin receptors** are found in the body, including the stomach, intestinal tract, sympathetic nervous system, cerebral cortex, and dorsal raphe nuclei. Thus, an antidepressant medication that acts through serotonin reuptake inhibition may produce unwanted **side effects.**
- Serotonin-receptor binding in the **gastrointestinal system** causes smooth muscle contraction. Increased serotonin may produce abdominal cramps and diarrhea.
- Increased serotonin in the **area postrema** (the vomiting center) may cause nausea and vomiting.
- Serotonin-receptor binding in the cranial blood **vessels** causes vessel dilation, hence, headaches.
- Binding in the **limbic system** causes anxiety.
- Binding in the **basal ganglia** causes agitation and akathisia (extreme anxiety with restlessness).

Acetylcholine

Most neurotransmitters are either amino acids, or derived or constructed from amino acids. **Acetylcholine** (ACh), however, is not made from amino acids, but is synthesized from choline and acetyl coenzyme A (CoA) in a reaction catalyzed by choline acetyltransferase. The amount of ACh formed is determined by the firing rate of cholinergic neurons and the degree of saturation of the high-affinity choline transporter system. ACh actions are terminated by the enzyme acetylcholinesterase, which is highly concentrated in the synaptic cleft. Much of the choline released from ACh hydrolysis is taken up by axon terminals and reused for ACh synthesis.

In the brain, cholinergic neurons are found in the pontine tegmentum and basal forebrain. The tegmental cholinergic neurons provide a major cholinergic innervation to the reticular formation and thalamus to modulate wake-sleep cycles and arousal. Among the groups of basal forebrain cholinergic neurons, the **nucleus basalis of Meynert** draws much more attention since it sends cholinergic innervation to the entire cerebral cortex, including the hippocampus and amygdala. These projections are thought to be necessary for memory, and are among specific areas in the brains of persons with Alzheimer's disease in which abnormality and destruction occur.

Among cholinergic neurons are also interneurons in the striatum where they exert inhibitory influence on DA-mediated motor effects. In the PNS, ACh is the neurotransmitter for motor neurons innervating voluntary and cardiac muscles, and smooth muscles in the iris and the intestinal tract. There are two types of ACh receptors: **nicotinic** and **muscarinic**. Nicotinic receptors are transmitter-gated ion channels, best known in the neuromuscular junction of voluntary muscles. Muscarinic receptors are G-protein coupled, and mediate most of the ACh effects in the brain. Muscarinic ACh receptors are highly expressed in the striatum and various other forebrain regions.

Peptide Neurotransmitters

Peptides are molecules composed of 3–36 amino acids; many peptides serve as hormones and as neurotransmitters. They differ from small-molecule neurotransmitters in several ways:

Peptide neurotransmitters are synthesized in the neuronal soma under the direction of mRNA and transported to the axon terminal.

Peptide neurotransmitters require high frequency stimulation for release.

Peptide neurotransmitters are usually co-released with amino acid or amine neurotransmitters.

Peptide neurotransmitters can be grouped into five categories according to tissue localization: the **brain/gut peptides** (e.g., substance P, chole-cystokinin); **opioid peptides** (e.g., enkephalin, endorphins); **pituitary peptides** (e.g., vasopressin, oxytocin); **hypothalamic releasing hormones**; and **miscellaneous peptides** (e.g., neurotensin, neuropeptide-γ). Some neuropeptides are involved in complex behaviors (e.g., opioid in sexual attraction and aggressive/submissive behaviors), while others appear to have only limited roles (e.g., oxytocin and vasopressin in influencing attention; neuropeptide-γ in feeding behavior leading to satiety or obesity). Neuropeptides initiate their effects by activating G-protein-coupled receptors.

Substance P is an excitatory neuropeptide that opens K^+ channels; it is present in high concentrations in the hippocampus, striatum and neocortex. It is released from small afferent fibers in the peripheral nerves that convey information about pain and temperature.

Neurotensin and **cholecystokinin** are peptide neurotransmitterers that coexist with DA in some axon terminals, and may play a role in the pathophysiology of schizophrenia. Cholecystokinin is anxiogenic, producing panic attacks in persons with panic disorder.

Unconventional Neurotransmitters

Neuronal signaling also utilizes some unconventional molecules as neurotransmitters. These molecules are not stored in synaptic vesicles, need not be released from presynaptic terminals, and may even transmit from the postsynaptic cells back to presynaptic terminals in a "retrograde" signaling fashion. One example of such neurotransmitters is **nitric oxide** (NO).

NO is a gaseous molecule generated simultaneously in the conversion of the amino acid arginine into its metabolite citrulline by the enzyme **nitric oxide synthase** (NOS). NOS is found in a variety of cells in the body, including certain populations of neurons in the CNS and PNS. The biological activity of NO is cell specific. For example, NO generated by macrophages kills bacteria. NO released from the endothelium regulates blood flow by relaxing smooth muscle cells in the vessel walls. NO acts in neurons as a retrograde signal that regulates transmitter release from presynaptic terminals. Once NO is produced, it diffuses across the plasma membrane much more freely than most other neurotransmitter molecules.

Thus, NO can act on nearby neurons in a range well beyond its site of release before it is degraded by reacting with oxygen to become inactive nitrogen oxides. This free diffusion property allows NO to coordinate the activities of multiple neurons in a localized region, and may mediate certain forms of synaptic plasticity within small networks of neurons. The best known actions of NO are mediated by the activation of the enzyme guanylyl cyclase, which in turn produces the second messenger cGMP in the target cells.

Recommended Reading

Beatty J. *The Human Brain.* Thousand Oaks, CA: Sage Publications; 2000.

Harris JC. *DevelopmentalNeuropsychiatry, Volume I: Fundamentals.* New York: Oxford University Press; 1998.

Kandel ER, Schwartz JH, Jessell TM. *Principles of Neural Science.* New York: McGraw-Hill; 2000.

Purves D, Augustin GJ, Fitzpatrick D, Katz LC, Lamantia A-S, McNamara JO (Eds.). *Neuroscience.* Sutherland, MA: Sinauer Associates Inc; 2005.

Review Questions

1. A medical researcher has developed a new drug that inhibits the biogenic amine neurotransmitter system, but does not affect the amino acid neurotransmitter system. The most likely site of action of this drug is the
   A. calcium channel
   B. mitochondrium
   C. postsynaptic membrane
   D. presynaptic neuron
   E. second messenger system

2. The adenylate cyclase and phosphoinositide second messenger systems are alike in that they both
   A. activate adenylate cyclase

   B. are activated by amino acid neurotransmitters
   C. cause the release of sodium from the neuron
   D. increase intraneuronal potassium levels
   E. inhibit G-protein activated enzymes

3. Following the administration of a psychoactive medication, a woman begins lactating. The medication being taken by this woman is most likely a
   A. cholinergic agonist
   B. cholinergic antagonist
   C. dopamine agonist
   D. dopamine antagonist
   E. selective serotonin reuptake inhibitor

4. A 23-year-old man is arrested after a series of vicious murders in which he strangled, raped and mutilated his victims. He has a history of violent behavior as a child and teenager. An analysis of his cerebrospinal fluid is most likely to show decreased
   A. choline
   B. homovanillic acid
   C. 5-hydroxyindoleacetic acid
   D. 3-methoxy-4-hydroxymandellic acid
   E. uroporphrynogen-1-synthetase

5. Mr. Morris, who is 72, has been losing his memory, especially for recent events, for the past 2 years. He often does not remember at noon what he had for breakfast. Recently he was lost overnight trying to find his way home after going out for a stroll in the park located three blocks from his house. The police found him in a neighboring town. On examination, Mr. Morris is alert, oriented as to person but disoriented as to time and place. He has short-term memory defects, labile affect, and poor judgment. Mr. Morris's memory deficits are best explained by a shortage of which of the following brain neurotransmitters?
   A. Acetylcholine
   B. GABA
   C. Glutamate
   D. Histamine
   E. Serotonin

6. Mr. Morris became agitated, pacing around, flailing his arms frantically, and was deemed to be in danger of hurting himself or others.

Because Mr. Morris could not cooperate and take oral medicines, the examining physician ordered an intramuscular injection of a benzodiazepine. The medication has its effects by acting on a receptor of which one of the following neurotransmitters?

A. Acetylcholine
B. GABA
C. Glutamate
D. Histamine
E. Serotonin

Directions: The items below consist of lettered headings followed by numbered descriptions. For each numbered description choose the *one* lettered heading to which it is *most* closely associated. Each letter heading may be used *once, more than once,* or *not at all.*

Serotonin receptors are present throughout the body. Therefore, antidepressant medications that act on serotonin receptors could produce unwanted side effects. Match the site of action with the possible side effect.

A. Area postrema of the brainstem
B. Basal ganglia
C. Cranial vessels
D. Gastrointestinal tract
E. Limbic system

7. Headaches
8. Smooth muscle contraction
9. Cramps, diarrhea
10. Nausea and vomiting
11. Anxiety

12. A prominent biological hypothesis about the etiology of schizophrenia suggests the disorder is caused by increased amounts of a certain neurotransmitter in the synapse. What is the neurotransmitter?

A. Acetylcholine
B. Dopamine
C. Histamine
D. Norepinephrine
E. Serotonin

13. Several hypotheses have been postulated to explain depression. One such hypothesis involves which one of the following biogenic amine neurotransmitters?

A. 5-hydroxy-indolacetic acid
B. 5-hydroxy-triptamine
C. Acetylcholine
D. Glutamate

Key to review questions: p. 393

3 Brain Structures and Their Functions

- What structures form the brainstem?
- Why might the diencephalon be considered the "seat of emotion"?
- What functions are associated with the frontal, parietal, occipital, and temporal lobes?
- How are connections made between the cerebrum and the peripheral nervous systems?
- What is hemispheric dominance?
- What is the difference between structural and functional imaging?
- What is an evoked potential?
- What do tachistoscopic viewing and dichotic listening reveal about brain functioning?

The brain consists of three major parts: **forebrain** (cerebrum), **midbrain** and **hindbrain**. The forebrain and hindbrain have several subdivisions, with distinct anatomical features. The forebrain is composed of the **diencephalon** and two **cerebral hemispheres**. The midbrain, due to its location and function, is studied as part of the brainstem. The hindbrain consists of the **pons**, **medulla oblongata**, and the **cerebellum**.

Brainstem

What structures form the brainstem?

The **brainstem**, the functional unit that connects the forebrain with the spinal cord, is composed of the midbrain, pons, and medulla oblongata. The brainstem has conduit and integrative functions, and is the site of cranial nerve nuclei. Information from sensory receptors throughout the body and its extremities, including exteroception, proprioception, and enteroception, is transmitted from the spinal cord to the cerebrum and cerebellum via a series of ascending tracts, coursing through the brainstem. After processing, messages are referred back via descending tracts, also within the brainstem, through the spinal cord to appropriate ana-

tomical structures (e.g., muscle groups) initiating a physiological (e.g., motor) response. In addition, the brainstem integrates and regulates a number of vital functions, such as respiration, cardiovascular activity, and consciousness. Thus, one can survive damage to the cerebrum and cerebellum, but damage to the brainstem can lead to rapid death.

The Forebrain

The Diencephalon

Why might the diencephalon be considered the "seat of emotion"?

The **diencephalon** includes the thalamus and hypothalamus. Activities of the diencephalon promote information processing, define and regulate emotions, and contribute to adaptability, flexibility, and creativity.

The **thalamus** consists of a group of nuclei that reciprocally connect with practically all parts of the cerebral cortex. Fiber bundles making thalamus-cortex and cortex-thalamus connections are known as **thalamic radiations**, and constitute large portions of the **internal capsule**. The thalamus is the gateway to the cerebral cortex since all sensory information, with the exception of olfaction, must pass through it before reaching the cerebral cortex. The thalamus relays circuits of the basal ganglia and cerebellum to the cerebral cortex to execute smooth and coordinated motor responses, and links limbic structures with the cortex for cognitive functions, memory, and emotional expression.

The **hypothalamus** is the activating nucleus for the autonomic nervous system. Anterior and medial hypothalamic areas control parasympathetic activity. Lateral and posterior areas control sympathetic activity. The hypothalamus mediates complex neuroendocrine autonomic and somatic responses to stress (challenge, need, threat), initiating coping behaviors (e.g., feeding, drinking, fight or flight, inhibition) and associated emotional reactions (e.g., pleasure, displeasure, fear, rage, aversion).

The Cerebral Hemispheres

Each **cerebral hemisphere** is composed of the basal ganglia and cerebral cortex.

The **basal ganglia** include four nuclei that lie deep within the cerebral hemisphere: **caudate**, **putamen**, **globus pallidus**, and the **subthalamic nucleus**, and one midbrain structure, the **substantia nigra**. The basal ganglia provide subcortical input to the cerebral cortex via the thalamus and, in turn, are targets of cortical projections. Thus, the basal ganglia are the central structures in three parallel loops that carry out motor and non-motor brain functions. The putamen receives cortical inputs from sensorimotor areas and projects to the motor and premotor cortices, forming the **motor loop** that facilitates the initiation of willed movement. The caudate receives cortical inputs from association areas, and projects to the prefrontal cortex, forming the **executive loop** that is involved in cognitive functions. The **nucleus accumbens** (the region of continuity of the caudate nucleus with the putamen) both receives inputs from the limbic lobe and projects back to the limbic lobe, constituting the **limbic loop** to regulate emotional behaviors.

The **cerebral cortex** is anatomically divided into four lobes: **frontal**, **parietal**, **temporal**, and **occipital**. The limbic lobe, the cortical component of the limbic structure, consists of a strip of cortex that encircles the corpus callosum and part of the medial surface of the temporal lobe. Each anatom-

ical lobe has a primary sensory or motor cortex surrounded by much larger association cortices. Lobes within the same and opposite hemispheres are connected anatomically and functionally by association and commissure fibers.

Frontal Lobe

What functions are associated with the frontal lobe?

The **frontal lobe,** which makes up about half the area and volume of the cerebral cortex, has three functional regions: (1) the primary motor cortex, (2) the premotor cortex, and (3) the prefrontal cortex.

The **primary motor cortex** is located in the precentral gyrus. Its output contributes to about 40% of the corticospinal tract, which makes monosynaptic and polysynaptic connections with motor neurons in the spinal cord. Monosynaptic connections are primarily for movement of individual fingers for skillful tasks, whereas the polysynaptic connections are for movement of limbs in such behaviors as reaching for an object and walking.

The **premotor cortex** is primarily responsible for planning and selecting movements. It lies rostral to the primary motor cortex, and contributes to about 30% of the corticospinal tract.

The **prefrontal cortex,** which comprises the rest of the frontal cortex, has three main regions: (1) the dorsal prefrontal association area, (2) the ventral orbitofrontal cortex, and (3) the medial prefrontal cortex.

The **dorsal prefrontal association area** (the anterior association area) integrates multimodal sensory information from the posterior association area located in the parietal and temporal lobes. The highly processed information is then trans-

Broca's speech area and the frontal eye field are two examples of the sensory motor integration that occurs in the dorsal prefrontal association area. Broca's speech area receives input from sensorimotor and visual cortices and from Wernike's area that comprehends verbal input, and initiates a motor response in the form of speech. The frontal eye field is involved in the initiation of saccadic eye movement. Through its connections with several cortical and brainstem structures, the frontal eye field moves the eyes toward objects of interest, and coordinates eye-head movements.

formed into judgment, movement planning and programming for implementation by the premotor and motor cortices.

The **ventral orbitofrontal cortex** and **medial prefrontal cortex** represent the prefrontal limbic cortex. The two cortices have direct connections with other limbic structures.

> The **orbitofrontal** cortex modulates arousal. Electrical stimulation of the region can affect respiration; alter blood pressure; and cause a hungry animal to stop eating and fall into slow-wave sleep. The **medial prefrontal cortex** maintains homeostatic modulation of motor and limbic activities while the organism is interacting with the external environment.

Parietal Lobe

What functions are associated with the parietal lobe?

The parietal lobe processes and integrates somatosensory information with information from the visual system for visuospatial localization, language, attention, and learning tasks requiring coordination of the body in space. The parietal lobes have three functional regions: (1) the primary somatosensory cortex, (2) the somatosensory unimodal association area, and (3) the multimodal sensory association area.

The **primary somatosensory cortex** is located in the postcentral gyrus. It is the initial site for receiving and interpreting the somesthetic information coming to the cortex from the contralateral part of the body.

The **somatosensory unimodal association area**, located immediately posterior to the primary somatosensory cortex, further processses somesthetic information. For example, it allows one to recognize a key in the pocket based solely on tactile recognition of its size and shape, texture, and weight.

The **multimodal sensory association area** (the parietal portion of the posterior association area) receives and integrates convergent projections from highly processed somesthetic, visual, auditory, and movement-related information from several association cortices. Thus, this area discerns the three-dimensional position of objects in space, body image and the space in which the body moves, direction of movement, and sound location. The left inferior parietal lobule is thought to integrate sensorimotor information for the perception and production of written language, and for performance of skilled, temporally sequential motor acts, and arithmetic calculations.

Occipital Lobes

What functions are associated with the occipital lobe?

The **occipital lobe** consists of two functional regions: (1) the primary visual cortex located along the bank of the calcarine fissure for the initial processing of visual information relayed by the thalamus, and (2) the visual unimodal association area for processing visual information coming from the primary visual cortex. This association area extends beyond the anatomical boundaries of the occipital lobe to occupy the inferiolateral surfaces not only of the occipital but also the temporal lobe.

Temporal Lobes

What functions are associated with the temporal lobe?

The temporal lobe processes auditory stimuli, as well as gustatory, visceral, and olfactory sensations. The inferior temporal cortex allows facial recognition. The temporal lobe has several functional regions: (1) the primary auditory cortex, (2) the auditory unimodal association cortex, (3) the visual unimodal association cortex, (4) the multimodal sensory association area (the temporal portion of the posterior association area), (5) the limbic association area, and (6) the amygdala and hippocampus.

The Limbic System

The **limbic system** is a collection of structures and their connections that mediate memory and learning and the feelings and emotional states associated with these processes. Limbic structures include the limbic lobe (cingulate gyrus and parahippocampal gyrus), the prefrontal limbic cortex, and deep structures of the temporal lobe, and the amygdala and hippocampus, two central components of the limbic system.

The **amygdala** is a complex of nuclei that mediates highly processed information of every sensory modality, including all types of visceral inputs. Interconnections within the amygdala allow the integration of information from different sensory modalities. Sensory stimuli passing through the amygdala can evoke a strong immediate autonomic response due to amygdala projections to hypothalamic and brainstem centers that regulate autonomic function. The amydgada also connects with cortical areas associated with the **interpretation or meaning** of stimuli (the frontal and cingulate cortices), and with memory (hippocampus). Thus, the amygdala shapes the initial interpretation of a sensory stimulus using the memory of past events. The amygdala circuitry that processes fear and aggression has been the focus of much research.

The **hippocampus** is located in the lower medial wall of the temporal lobe behind the amygdala. The hippocampus interacts with the hypothalamus, amygdala, and neocortex to refine and provide **temporal and spatial context** to incoming information, and promote learning and memory. In association with the right amygdala, the hippocampus participates in dream production by contributing images, words, and ideas.

The **septal nucleus** is located anterior to the third ventricle, near the hypothalamus. It inhibits extreme emotion and arousal in order to preserve quiescence and readiness for action. In particular, the septal nucleus modulates the activity of the amygdala, preventing excessive interpersonal attachment and socialization, and suppresses hypothalamus-induced rage reactions.

Cerebrospinal Connections

How are connections made between the cerebrum and the peripheral nervous system?

A number of ascending and descending tracts relay information between the cerebrum and the peripheral nervous system via the brainstem and spinal cord.

Long ascending tracts starting from the spinal cord include the dorsal column-medial lemniscal and the anteriolateral pathways for general somatic sensory information originating from the body. The former transmits tactile and vibratory senses, whereas the latter conveys pain and temperature.

At the brainstem, pathways for hearing and taste, together with that for general sensory modalities from the face, merge with the spinal sensory pathways to form the **lemniscal system.** Lemniscal system information reaches the cerebral cortex via the thalamus for the conscious perception of pain, temperature, touch, taste, hearing, discriminative touch, and the appreciation of form, weight, and texture. The conscious experience of these sensations is mediated by the reticular system.

The **reticular system** originates in the spinal cord as the reticular formation, courses through the brainstem, hypothalamus and thalamus, and terminates in the frontal lobes. The reticular system organizes patterns of visceromotor activity (e.g., gastric motility, and respiratory and cardiovascular activities), and is elemental in arousal, consciousness and attention.

Incoming sensory information that demands action (e.g., muscle activity) triggers motor cortex commands that travel via the descending tracts to the skeletal muscles. The descending tracts that reach the spinal cord consist of the lateral and ventromedial pathways. The lateral pathways control voluntary movement of the distal musculature, and are under the direct control of the cerebral cortex (e.g., the corticospinal tract). The ventromedial pathways control the musculature in the trunk for posture and locomotion. These pathways originate in the brainstem motor centers, and are under the indirect control of the cortex.

The **cerebellum** receives inputs from the cerebral cortex, spinal cord, and vestibular system. The cerebellar cortex integrates the information, and relays the information back to the motor cortex and brainstem motor centers. The lower motor neurons turn cerebellum-modulated motor commands into precise, smooth, and coordinated motor activity.

Hemispheric Dominance

What is hemispheric dominance?

At birth, the left and right cerebral hemispheres are functionally disconnected because the **corpus callosum**, and **anterior and posterior commissures** are not yet myelinated. Myelination of these tracts is completed at about five years of age.

> **Hemispheric dominance** is defined in terms of the **laterality of functions** or functional specialization of one hemisphere over the other. The left hemisphere is dominant for language in up to 99% of right-handed people, and in up to 70% of left-handed people. The right hemisphere is dominant for spatial location and orientation, although not to the same degree as the left hemisphere dominance in language.

Left hemisphere functions include verbal comprehension and differentiation, identification, and linguistic labeling of visual, auditory, and somesthetic information.

Right hemisphere functions include nonverbal awareness of the environment, visual-spatial perception, facial recognition, body image, voice tone, melody and rhythm perception, and various aspects of emotionality.

Lateralization, though more pronounced in the neocortex, is also observed in limbic structures. For example, the right amygdala/hippocampal complex processes visual/spatial memory, while the left amygdala/hippocampal complex processes verbal memory.

Methods for Evaluating Brain-Behavior Associations

Imaging Techniques

> What is the difference between structural and functional imaging?

Computed tomography (CT) produces an image of a slice of living brain. An x-ray source, rotating around the subject's head within the plane of the desired cross section, releases beams from different angles. As the x-ray beams pass through tissue, density gradient profiles are established as a result of differential resistance to x-rays. The information is fed to a computer to reconstruct the image of the brain. CT non-invasively reveals the gross organization of gray and white matter, and the position of the ventricles.

Magnetic resonance imaging (MRI) manipulates and records changes in tissue electromagnetic forces, which are then used to construct computer-

enhanced images of the tissues. Elements that are abundant in tissue (e.g., hydrogen) generate a magnetic moment (i.e., a magnetic field with strength, orientation, and random directions). The MRI scanner sets up an external magnetic field that aligns all magnetic moments. Thus organized, the magnetic moments "hum" at a given frequency, which is enhanced through application of an external radio signal. When the external radio signal is stopped the hydrogen atoms "relax" and lose energy. The strength of the energy loss is captured as a shade of gray, which produces a computer-enhanced MRI image. MRI produces higher resolution than CT and is free of bone artifacts.

> **Functional imaging**
>
> When an area of the brain is stimulated, blood flow increases carrying more glucose and oxygen to support metabolism at that site. Imaging cerebral blood flow and metabolism at rest establishes a baseline for comparison with changes resulting from a task that increases brain activity. Since both excitatory and inhibitory neuronal activity increase metabolism and blood flow, increased activity reflects increased synaptic activity within a brain region.

Nontomographic regional cerebral blood flow (RCBF), the first technique devised for *in vivo* functional imaging, is performed by inhalation of ^{133}Xenon. Sensors placed on the scalp measure gamma rays emitted by the decaying ^{133}Xenon to construct an image. The rate at which the tracer is cleared from tissue is used as a measure of function. Since tracer clearance is four times faster in gray matter than in white matter, RCBF techniques are used primarily to collect data from gray matter.

Tomographic functional imaging produces three-dimensional images from two-dimensional information, using projection reconstruction. A tracer compound is administered systemically and then monitored until it is consumed or cleared.

PET scanning uses radiolabeled compounds, or radiopharmaceuticals, that emit two simultaneous gamma rays traveling in opposite directions. This technique enhances sensitivity to measurements of subtle functional changes, especially in deep brain structures. In contrast, SPECT scanning uses radiopharmaceuticals that emit a unidirectional gamma ray. Although SPECT scanning is less sensitive than PET scanning, especially in deep brain structures, the radiopharmaceuticals required are more stable, routinely available in the average nuclear medicine department, and, thus, less costly.

Functional magnetic resonance imaging (fMRI) assesses functioning of brain regions directly by imaging metabolic changes such as glucose or oxygen utilization, and indirectly by imaging changes in blood flow, which carries oxygen and glucose to areas of high activity.

Electroencephalography

Brain electrical activity can be recorded through electrodes placed strategically on the scalp. The recorded signal is amplified and transformed into a visual analog (e.g., a tracing on paper or a computer screen). The tracing represents "brain waves," which vary in form and amplitude depending on the particular area and activity of the brain. Taken collectively and organized according to a standard convention that is used by all laboratories, brain waves form the **electroencephalogram** (EEG).

What is an evoked potential?

Evoked potentials are brain wave changes in response to a visual or auditory stimulus. The patient's brain response to sensory stimuli can be followed from the brainstem to the cortex, and across the corpus callosum. This image is compared to images obtained from a normative group. Evoked potentials are useful in the diagnosis of demyelinating diseases, such as multiple sclerosis.

Computerized EEG

Computerized EEG entails no radiation exposure, is noninvasive, and is comparatively inexpensive. Thus, serial measurements may be obtained from the same patient (e.g., pre- and post-institution of pharmacologic treatment) to monitor effect or other changes over time. Because measurements of electrical brain activity can be done in less than a millisecond, computerized EEG has the best temporal resolution of all functional imaging techniques (see below). Disadvantages include limit-

ed spatial resolution and artifacts from eye movement, muscle activity, or any other electrical activity that exceeds the normal range of the human EEG (1–50 Hertz).

Functional imaging is obtained through computerized manipulation of a multichannel EEG that produces a topographic map of the brain's electrical activity. Specific EEG parameters, corresponding to specific electrode placements, are assigned numeric values. Numeric values are also interpolated for areas located between electrodes. Each numeric value is then assigned a color within a preset scale to form a graphic representation of cerebral electrical activity. Although this is not a truly anatomic image of the brain, it approximates it.

Tests for Laterality and Dominance

What do tachistoscopic viewing and dichotic listening reveal about brain functioning?

Tachistoscopic viewing and **dichotic listening** are methods used to explore the relationship between perceptual laterality and cerebral dominance. Perceptual laterality is the tendency to perceive input from sensory receptors located on one side of the body more accurately than input from sensory receptors located on the other side.

In **tachistoscopic viewing,** the clinician presents stimuli in the left and right visual fields. Stimuli presented in the right visual field are projected to the left hemisphere, and stimuli presented to the left visual field are projected to the right hemisphere. Right-handed people more accurately perceive written language material presented in the right visual field, and spatial visual tasks (e.g., localization of dots in space) in the left visual field. Thus, right-handed people are said to display **right** visual field superiority for verbal visual stimuli and **left** visual field superiority for spatial visual tasks.

Dichotic listening involves the simultaneous presentation of different auditory stimuli to each ear. Although what is heard in one ear is referred to both hemispheres, up to 65% of what is heard is referred to the contralateral side. Right-handed people most accurately perceive verbal (speech) material presented to the right ear (left hemisphere), and nonverbal sounds (e.g., music) presented to the left ear (right hemisphere).

Neuropsychological Assessment

Neuropsychology is the study of relationships between brain function and behavior. Neuropsychological tests are most useful in describing and quantifying the effects of localized brain dysfunction, disease or other stressors on a patient's performance of a wide range of sensory, motor, perceptual, conceptual, and problem-solving tasks (see Psychological Testing in Chapter 38, Introduction to Psychopathology).

Recommended Reading

Adel A, Bergman RA. *Functional Neuroanatomy: Text and Atlas.* New York: McGraw-Hill; 1997.

Kandel ER, Schwartz JH, Jessell TM, *Principles of Neural Science.* (4th ed.). New York: McGraw-Hill; 2000.

Mesulam MM. *Principles of Behavioral and Cognitive Neurology.* New York: Oxford University Press; 2000.

Review Questions

1. As part of the examination of a newborn, the underside of the infant's foot is stroked resulting in flaring of the toes with the great toe hyperextended. This activity is being mediated through the
    A. diencephalon
    B. mesencephalon
    C. prosencephalon
    D. rhombencephalon
    E. telencephalon

2. Following a viral illness, a 6-year-old girl develops excessive appetite and thirst with a 40-pound weight gain, extreme emotionality with outbursts of anger, and hyponatremia. These findings are most consistant with viral encephalitis that has destroyed all or part of the
    A. amygdala
    B. hippocampus
    C. lateral hypothalamus
    D. medial hypothalamus
    E. septal nucleus

3. The principle underlying functional imaging is based on blood flow and
    A. build up of lactic acid
    B. changes in vessel diameter
    C. electrolyte balance
    D. glucose metabolism
    E. secretion of neurotransmitter

Key to review questions: p. 393

4 Chronobiology and Sleep

- What is circadian rhythm?
- How does circadian rhythm affect organ system functioning?
- What is the difference between REM and non-REM sleep?
- How do the sleep patterns of infants, mid-age adults, and the elderly differ?
- What steps should a person take to have consistently good sleep?
- Why is it easier to accommodate to a flight from Boston to Los Angeles than from Los Angeles to Boston?
- What are the potential outcomes of severe obstructive sleep apnea?
- What are the differences between nightmares and night terrors?

Some physiologic functions have predictable temporal fluctuations in their sensitivity to environmental factors. **Chronobiology** is the discipline that studies the effect of time on living systems.

Circadian Rhythm

What is circadian rhythm?

The fluctuations of certain physiological functions, such as core body temperature and serum cortisol level, over repetitive 24-hour cycles, are called **circadian rhythms.** These cycles are responsive to environmental rhythms **(zeitgebers)** such as the light-dark cycle and ambient temperature changes. For example, environmental light changes induce

Control of the Sleep-Wake Cycle

The endogenous biological clock that controls the sleep-wake cycle is located in the suprachiasmatic nucleus (SCN) of the hypothalamus. The SCN induces pineal gland secretion of melatonin when environmental light decreases (sunset) and inhibits secretion when environmental light increases (sunrise).

or inhibit sleep by regulating melatonin secretion from the pineal gland.

Restricting rest and activity to specific times of day in synchrony with environmental day-night cycles is beneficial to survival in most organisms. The process of adjusting circadian rhythms to environmental rhythms is called **entrainment.**

Circadian Rhythm and Organ System Functioning

How does circadian rhythm affect organ system functioning?

Various physiological activities, such as body temperature, urine production, hormone secretion, sensory processing and cognitive performance, demonstrate circadian rhythmicity. Similarly, some disorders appear to be related to effects of circadian periodicity on organ systems.

Cardiac contractility shows daytime activity peaks, nighttime inactivity troughs, and graded changes over 24 hours. Generally there is a trough in the early morning before typical wake-up time; a rising phase just prior to wake-up time; a peak in the early afternoon or evening; a fall before bedtime; and a steep decline at sleep onset continuing into the sleep period. The incidence of cerebral vascular accidents, myocardial infarction, and sudden death is increased between 6 AM and noon. The association of typical chronophysiologic patterns of cardiac contractility with adverse cardiac events suggests that imbalance between cardiac demand and myocardial oxygen supply is most likely to occur in the morning.

Respiratory changes occur during sleep. Changes in the CO_2 chemoreceptor increase the CO_2 threshold (the concentration of CO_2 that triggers breathing), which decreases the ventilatory drive. This produces a decrease in minute ventilation (the volume of air breathed per minute) during sleep. In addition, there is decreased respiratory accessory muscle tone and increased bronchoconstriction.

> Chemical and mechanical challenges to breathing during sleep contribute to nocturnal hypoxemia and hypercapnia.

Gastrointestinal motor activity, such as gastric emptying rates, slows during the evening and overnight. Many drugs taken by mouth in the evening are absorbed more slowly, possibly delaying their onset of action. Fasting gastric acid secretion is markedly elevated between 9 PM and midnight consistent with the observation that gastrointestinal symptoms often worsen around midnight.

> Evening administration of antacids provides protection during the period of greatest vulnerability.

The **musculoskeletal system** is also susceptible to the effects of time of day. Morning joint swelling and stiffness, diagnostic hallmarks of rheumatoid arthritis, appear to be associated with the rhythmic nocturnal fall in circulating endogenous corticosteriods.

In the **immune system,** allergen skin testing shows a greater response if done in late evening compared to the morning. Results from tests done in the morning should be viewed cautiously to avoid false-negatives. In contrast to skin reactivity, hay fever symptoms are more pronounced upon awakening. Total T lymphocyte and CD4 T lym-

phocyte concentrations peak around 4 AM, about the same time that kidney transplant rejection is most likely to occur.

> Immunosuppressant treatment to avoid tissue rejection should be most beneficial when administered at night.

The efficacy and rate of adverse effects of platinum and other agents used to treat ovarian cancer are influenced by time of day. Similarly, maintenance chemotherapy for acute lymphoblastic leukemia administered in the evening appears to be more effective.

Sleep

> What is the difference between REM and non-REM sleep?

Sleep is divided into **rapid-eye-movement (REM) sleep** and four levels of **non-REM sleep** (stage 1 or light sleep to stage 4 or deep sleep).

During REM sleep, the brain is highly active and is driven by spontaneous neural discharges originating primarily in the pontine reticular formation. However, the neural pathways associated with sensory input and motor output are inhibited. Thus, vivid dreaming and decreased perception of the environment are characteristic of REM sleep. Because the brain is isolated from its sensory input and motor output channels during REM sleep, information transmitted from the sensory organs to the cortex is attenuated, and the motor neurons of the muscles are inhibited.

> During REM sleep, the brain may activate cortical areas normally involved in visual perception and motor movements, leading the individual to perceive that he or she is seeing objects and making movements, but actually doing neither.

In contrast, during non-REM sleep, the brain is less activated, and there is less cognitive activity. Stages 3 and 4, the deep sleep stages, are called

slow-wave sleep (SWS). Throughout the night, non-REM sleep and REM sleep alternate in approximately 90-minute cycles. SWS typically occurs during the earlier portion of the night, and REM sleep predominates in the last third of the night.

Sleep Patterns and Architecture

How do the sleep patterns of infants, mid-age adults, and the elderly differ?

Sleep and waking appear to be regulated by homeostasis and circadian rhythms. **Sleep patterns** vary across age groups. Average daily total sleep time decreases from up to 18 hours during infancy to about 10 hours in early childhood to about 8 hours in adulthood. Among the elderly, nighttime sleep is diminished but daytime napping is increased; as a result, total sleep time is similar to that of mid-age adults.

Sleep architecture also changes with age. Newborn infants spend about 50% of their sleep time in REM sleep and 50% in non-REM sleep with predominantly slow-wave activity. Infant sleep is polyphasic and occurs in 3- to 4-hour cycles. Children develop a diurnal pattern of sleep during the second year of life that includes a long episode of nocturnal sleep and a brief nap during the afternoon. As children mature, the percentages of REM sleep and SWS decrease. For example, the time spent in REM sleep decreases to about 20–25% by late adolescence and remains stable until older age. The percentage of SWS, however, diminishes gradually throughout life. Complaints of difficulty maintaining sleep are more common among older people. These sleep difficulties may be due to an underlying health condition, medication or sleep disorders that are more prevalent among the elderly (e.g., breathing disturbances, periodic limb movements).

Sleep Hygiene

What steps should a person take to have consistently good sleep?

A set of simple guidelines collectively called **sleep hygiene** is often used in the clinical setting to help persons who have sleep difficulties regain consistent sleep.

1. Use the bed for sleep and sex only (e.g., not for eating, reading, or watching television).
2. Limit time in bed to that present before the sleep difficulty.
3. Go to bed only when sleepy.
4. If not asleep after 20 minutes, do some drowsing activity in another room. Return to bed when sleepy.
5. Sleep only the right amount to feel refreshed, roughly the same amount every night (no sleeping in).
6. Maintain sleep conditions close to ideal, and avoid excessive ambient warmth or cold.
7. Go to bed and wake up around the same time each day.
8. Exercise regularly but not close to bedtime.
9. Avoid napping.
10. Avoid stimulating substances (alcohol, tobacco, caffeine) near bedtime.
11. Limit use of sedatives.
12. If eating near bedtime, eat lightly.
13. Practice relaxation.
14. A body temperature-raising 20-minute hot bath near bedtime may be helpful.

Assessment

Like that of any disorder, the assessment of sleep disorders relies on thorough history, sleep-related history, mental status, review of systems, physical and ancillary exams. It is important to keep in mind that such thorough assessment is warranted since sleep disorders may be primary or secondary to other medical disorders, including psychiatric disorders. Care must be exercised for the evaluation to constitute a valid basis for effective treatment. The subjective and objective behavioral aspects of sleep must be assessed and recorded accurately, and referred to a sleep disorders center for polysomnography when the diagnosis is not clear or patients need special help (e.g., specific diagnosis, sleep staging, determination of severity of the disorder, precise determination of daytime sleepiness, fitting of mask for continuous positive air pressure therapy).

Sleep-Wake Schedule Disorders

Sleep disorders can arise either from a defect in the **circadian oscillator** (the suprachiasmatic nucleus, the endogenous timing system) or from the limited capacity of the internal timing system to adjust to changes in external clock time. The shifting capacity of the human circadian rhythm is 2 hours per day or less. Therefore, sleep difficulties can occur whenever the sleep-wake schedule is shifted outside an individual's range of entrainment.

Disorders of the sleep-wake schedule, also known as **circadian rhythm disorders,** result from disturbances in the timing of actual sleep-wake behavior relative to the person's circadian sleep-wake rhythm. Such disturbances can be transient (e.g., jet-lag or work shift changes) or more persistent (e.g., delayed sleep phase syndrome, advanced sleep phase syndrome, permanent rotating shift-work). Affected individuals simply cannot either stay awake or stay asleep when it is necessary or desired to do so.

Jet Lag

> Why is it easier to accommodate to a flight from Boston to Los Angeles than from Los Angeles to Boston?

Jet lag results from rapid changes in time zone due to transmeridian travel. Symptoms include insomnia, fatigue, and gastrointestinal complaints. Westbound travel is generally less disruptive than eastbound travel because delaying the sleep-wake cycle (to adjust to the prevailing clock time after westbound travel) is easier to accomplish than advancing the sleep-wake cycle. Sleep disruption can persist for up to 8 days after travel but jet lag usually requires no treatment. Adhering to the clock time of the original time zone minimizes jet lag during brief trips.

Shift Work

Shift work, or any acute change in work schedule, can desynchronize sleep within the circadian cycle. The problem is transient if the worker remains on the new work schedule; however, it can become a persistent disorder if the worker is required to rotate shifts continually. Insomnia, mood changes, and gastrointestinal symptoms are common side effects. The shift worker who is required to work at night and sleep during the day also must contend with lower levels of arousal at night, which can cause perfor-

mance deficits, as well as with higher levels of arousal during the day, which can impair the ability to sleep.

Delayed Sleep Phase Syndrome

Delayed sleep phase syndrome (DSPS) is the inability to both fall asleep and wake up at desired times consistent with societal norms. The individual will have essentially normal sleep if allowed to go to sleep and wake up late. Individuals with this syndrome often suffer from **sleep-onset insomnia** if they attempt to fall asleep earlier to obtain an adequate amount of sleep before arising at the time required for school or work. Allowing themselves to sleep on a delayed schedule on weekends or vacations reinforces their habit of a delayed sleep time. Symptoms include grogginess in the morning, and irritability. Best functioning is in the early evening.

Advanced Sleep Phase Syndrome

Advanced sleep phase syndrome (ASPS) is the inability to stay awake in the evening and stay asleep in the early morning. Individuals with this syndrome often complain of **sleep-maintenance insomnia** because they are unable to sleep past the early morning hours. When affected individuals are allowed to sleep from the evening to the early morning, their sleep is normal. They may become sleep deprived from postponing their bedtime while still being unable to sleep later in the morning.

Treatment of Sleep Phase Disorders

Transient sleep disorders (e.g., jet lag) usually require no treatment if the dyssynchrony is isolated. However, short-acting hypnotics and melatonin can improve alertness and promote sleep following abrupt changes in the sleep-wake schedule.

ASPS has been treated successfully using a **chronotherapy** technique that delays the individual's bedtime by up to 3 hours every 2 days until the required bedtime is attained. This, in turn, will gradually extend the individual's sleep period so that it lasts until later in the morning.

DSPS is more difficult to treat than ASPS. This is due in part to the endogenous cycle being longer than 24 hours; that is, advancing bedtime to an earlier time requires shortening the wake phase. Chronotherapy for DSPS requires up to 2 weeks before the desired bedtime is achieved.

> The use of bright light to promote a phase shift has been shown to be helpful in the treatment of sleep-wake cycle or circadian rhythm disorders.

Narcolepsy Syndrome

Narcolepsy has been conceptualized as an abnormal intrusion of components of REM sleep into wakefulness. It is a chronic neurologic disorder characterized by four major symptoms:

(1) excessive daytime sleepiness
(2) cataplexy
(3) sleep paralysis
(4) hypnagogic hallucinations

Excessive daytime sleepiness may be relatively continuous or episodic. Severity varies from a mild desire to sleep to an irresistible "sleep attack." Daytime sleep bouts vary from seconds of nodding to short naps of 20 minutes. Patients with narcolepsy usually awaken feeling refreshed.

Cataplexy is sudden loss of muscle tone triggered by strong emotions. The patient is awake during cataplexy, which typically lasts seconds to minutes. The muscle weakness may be localized or affect all postural muscles. The loss of muscle tone during cataplexy is the result of the same neural mechanisms that produce the active inhibition of the musculature typical of REM sleep.

Sleep paralysis is the inability to move at sleep onset or upon awakening. It is a manifestation of REM sleep muscle inhibition.

Hypnagogic hallucination, or dreaming while still awake, is the result of a normal component of REM sleep occurring during wakefulness.

The diagnosis of narcolepsy is confirmed using the **Multiple Sleep Latency Test (MSLT),** which consists of four or five naps spaced 2 hours apart. The patient is placed in a quiet, dark bedroom and monitored by polysomnography (PSG). The time from "lights out" to sleep onset (sleep latency) is measured for each nap, and the appearance of REM sleep within 15 minutes, called a sleep-onset REM period, is noted. Findings consistent

with narcolepsy include an average sleep latency of 6 minutes or less, which documents pathologic sleepiness, and the appearance of at least two sleep-onset REM periods.

Treatment consists of stimulant medications, good nocturnal sleep, and prophylactic naps. Cataplexy, sleep paralysis, and hypnagogic hallucinations are responsive to tricyclic and some selective serotonin reuptake inhibitor antidepressants.

Mechanical/Structural Sleep Disorders
Sleep-Disordered Breathing

Sleep-disordered breathing results when respiratory control is adversely affected by chemical information (chemoreceptor changes in PaO_2, $PaCO_2$, and pH), behavioral information derived from cortical activity, and mechanical feedback via stretch receptors in the chest wall, upper airway, and lung. Arousal from sleep is produced by low oxygen levels (hypoxemic response), high levels of carbon dioxide (hypercapnic response), or occlusion or obstruction to airflow. The arousal threshold to these stimuli is state-related; awakening is more difficult from REM sleep than from non-REM sleep.

> Benzodiazepines, barbiturates, sedating antidepressants, antihistamines, antipsychotics, narcotics, and alcohol can all depress ventilation. A careful drug history is essential when screening for sleep-disordered breathing.

Obstructive Sleep Apnea

> What are the potential outcomes of severe obstructive sleep apnea?

Obstructive sleep apnea syndrome affects 2–4% of the general population overall, but is especially prominent in middle-aged men and postmenopausal women. The condition consists of temporary but recurrent obstruction of the upper airway during sleep that produces **apnea** (cessation of the airflow for 10 seconds or more). The most common sites of occlusion are the soft palate or the base of the tongue.

During an episode of obstructive apnea, chest and abdominal movements are ineffective in moving air. A brief period of electrocortical arousal follows the episode and is accompanied by deep gasping resuscitative breathing and loud snoring. In severe cases, up to 500 episodes of apnea can occur each night producing abnormal hemodynamics, blood gas changes, cognitive deficits, disrupted sleep, and daytime sleepiness. Some cases are fatal.

> In addition to age and gender, risk factors for sleep apnea include obesity, diastolic hypertension, large neck circumference, and structural abnormalities of the upper airway.

Treatment options include mechanical devices, behavioral interventions, and surgery. The most common treatment for moderate and severe cases is **continuous positive airway pressure (CPAP)** via the nose. In milder cases, an oral appliance, which advances the mandible and frees up space in the oropharynx, is worn during sleep. Behavioral therapy includes weight loss and avoiding the supine sleeping position, alcohol, and sedating medications. Surgical options include uvulopalatophar angioplasty, tonsillectomy-adenoidectomy, and a variety of mandibulomaxillary advancement procedures. Tracheostomy may be necessary in extreme cases associated with life-threatening cardiopulmonary complications.

Central Sleep Apnea

Central sleep apnea syndrome is an uncommon sleep disorder manifested by insomnia, gasping for air, arousals from sleep, and either mild or absent snoring. In this form of apnea, the absence of ventilatory effort results in the cessation of airflow. Cardiac, neurologic, and cerebrovascular disease play a role in the pathophysiology of this disorder.

Cheyne-Stokes Respiration

Cheyne-Stokes respiration with central sleep apnea is a form of periodic breathing character-

ized by recurrent cessation of breathing alternating with increased airflow (hyperpnea) in a crescendo-decrescendo pattern. The condition is seen most commonly in patients with congestive heart failure and central nervous system disease. The reduced circulatory time from alveolar unit to chemoreceptor and the length of the crescendo-decrescendo cycle have been implicated in the etiology of this breathing pattern.

Treatment of central sleep apnea with or without Cheyne-Stokes respiration can be difficult. Nasal CPAP, oxygen, respiratory stimulants such as acetazolamide or theophylline, and mechanical ventilation all have specific risks and benefits.

Insomnia

Insomnia, the most common sleep disorder, has a significant negative effect on quality of life, mood, cognitive functioning, performance capacity, and alertness. In addition to psychiatric disorders that interfere with adequate sleep, the etiology of insomnia includes conditions such as sleep-related breathing dysfunction, periodic limb movements, circadian rhythm dysregulation, worry about sleeplessness, late night exercise, caffeine ingestion, daytime napping, and medical conditions.

General treatments include better sleep hygiene, such as setting a regular wake up time; eliminating napping, alcohol, and caffeine; and relaxing before bedtime with a ritual to reduce physiologic hyperarousal. In addition, patients should be instructed to get out of bed if they do not fall asleep in 15–20 minutes. Cognitive approaches target arousing, worrisome, and self-defeating thoughts that sustain insomnia. A variety of rapid-acting hypnotic drugs are safe when taken alone, and can help induce and maintain sleep

Nightmares and Night Terrors

> What are the differences between nightmares and night terrors?

A **nightmare** is a terrifying dream that awakens the dreamer from REM sleep. Nightmares tend to occur during the early morning when REM periods are naturally more intense. They are common in children and decrease with age. Nightmares may be induced by stress or represent a reaction to a traumatic event.

Nightmares can be caused by certain medications such as L-dopamine and beta blockers. Alcohol and other drugs have a REM-suppressing effect. When these drugs are discontinued, an increase in the amount and intensity of REM sleep (rebound) occurs causing especially emotional and frightening dreams.

Night terrors, unlike nightmares, occur during slow-wave sleep, in the first half of the night. They are characterized by a confused arousal in which the person appears to be terrified, often crying out in horror. Attempts to rouse or calm the person are futile. Unlike the person who has nightmares, the person who has night terrors cannot recall details about what was going through his or her mind. In fact, in the morning, the person usually has forgotten the event altogether. Night terrors are common in children less than 10, and uncommon in adults.

Recommended Reading

Damasio AR. Remembering when. *Scientific American* 2002; 287:66–73.

Palmer JD. *The Living Clock.* Oxford, UK: Oxford University Press; 2002.

Wright K. Times of our lives. *Scientific American* 2002; 287:58–65.

Smallwood P, Stern TA. Patients with disordered sleep. In Stern TA, Fricchione GL, Cassem NH, Jellineck MS, Rosenbaum, JF (Eds.). *Massachusetts General Hospital Handbook of General Hospital Psychiatry.* (5th ed.). St. Louis: Mosby; 2004, pp. 531–546

Review Questions

Directions: The items below consist of lettered headings followed by numbered descriptions. For each numbered description choose the one lettered heading with which it is *most* closely associated. Each lettered heading may be used *once, more than once,* or *not at all.*

Match the sleep stage with the numbered descriptions.

A. REM sleep
B. Stage 1 non-REM
C. Stage 2 non-REM
D. Stage 3 non-REM
E. Stage 4 non-REM

1. Peter dreams a lot. He keeps a pad and pencil by his bed because he often wakes up in the morning from a dream and wants to record it. He aspires to become a best-selling author and believes that his dreams give him good ideas for plots and imagery. Which is Peter's favorite sleep stage?
2. During this sleep stage, Isabel is oblivious to all but the greatest disruptions. If awakened from this stage, she will not be able to report dream imagery.
3. During this sleep stage, a patient is most quickly and easily aroused.
4. During this sleep stage, information transmitted form the sensory organs to the cortex is attenuated and the motor neurons of the muscles are inhibited.

Key to review questions: p. 393

5 Predisposition

- What is the human karyotype?
- How is genotype distinguished from phenotype?
- What information is provided by a twin study?
- What information is provided by a pedigree study?
- How does organism-environment transaction differ from organism-environment interaction?
- How does personality contribute to illness vulnerability?

Genetic Predisposition

The central nervous system (CNS) provides the mechanisms for the human organism to interact with the environment and to adapt to changing environmental demands, drawing upon accumulated experience. Because the CNS of the newborn has not yet accumulated experience, it must rely on genetically programmed reflexive responses to insure survival until its learning processes accrue sufficient information for adaptive problem solving. The ability to produce reflexive responses is inherited from the parents along with physical, biochemical, physiological and personal characteristics.

What is the human karyotype?

The totality of genetically transmitted information is contained in 46 **chromosomes** (23 pairs) that constitute the human **karyotype.** Each chromosome contains **DNA, RNA,** and **proteins.** Each somatic cell contains 22 pairs of similar chromosomes (autosomes) and a pair of sex chromosomes that are either XX (female) or XY (male).

How is genotype distinguished from phenotype?

Genes come in pairs of **alleles** (one from each parent). A person with a pair of identical alleles is **homozygotic,** while one with a pair of different alleles is **heterozygotic.** The expression of the entire complement of genetic material a person possesses, the **genotype,** into the discernible biological characteristics that distinguish a particular individual is referred to as the **phenotype.** Each personal characteristic is called a **trait;** traits can be determined by either **dominant** or **recessive** genes. Dominant genes express themselves phenotypically even when the person is heterozygous; in contrast, recessive genes express themselves phenotypically only if the person is homozygous. Mendelian law assumes genetic transmission through a single gene with two alleles, resulting in three genotypes: recessive/recessive; recessive/dominant; and dominant/dominant.

Genes **determine** species, gender, structure, function, and capacity of body organs. Genes **influence** behavior (personality, cognition, language, intelligence, temperament and mental state). While it is not entirely clear how genes influence behavior, a combination of the following mechanisms provides a partial answer.

1. Genes directly code for proteins, including structural proteins and enzymes. In the CNS, even minor structural alterations can have behavioral consequences. Also, since neurotransmitters are synthesized through enzymatic action, genes can affect neurotransmission and, therefore, behavior.
2. Genes determine the chemical organizers that mediate cell migration in embryonic brain

cortex formation and, thus, influence behavior.

3. Genetically determined deviations can create biological vulnerabilities, which may be anatomic-structural, physiological, or biochemical. Their exact mode of transmission is not yet known.

Research Designs to Separate Genetic from Environmental Determination

Family Risk Studies

Family risk studies determine the rate of occurrence of a condition or trait in **first-degree relatives** (those who share 50% of their genetic material, e.g., parents, siblings, children) and more distant relatives of an affected person (**proband**). These rates are then compared with rates for the general population. A genetic component is suggested if the rates for probands and their first-degree relatives have highest **concordance** (rate values are closest) followed by other relatives' rates and by lowest concordance with rates in the general population.

Twin Studies

What information is provided by a twin study?

Monozygotic (identical) twins share 100% of their genetic material; dizygotic (fraternal) twins share 50% of their genetic material. If both twins present with the same particular trait or condition, they are said to be 100% concordant for the trait or condition.

The concept of **heritability** is derived from comparisons of concordance rates between monozygotic twins and dizygotic twins. Higher concordance rates between monozygotic twins suggest that genetic factors are determining the condition. However, higher concordance rates among monozygotic twins can result from sharing one placenta, developing together, or being treated equally, all of which are nongenetic factors. To increase **specific-**

ity and diminish the influence of rearing in determining the presence of a trait or disorder, studies of twins reared apart from birth are conducted.

Adoption Studies

Non-twin adoption studies are useful to:
1. Determine the risk of having the trait or disorder for biologic and adoptive relatives compared with controls. If the risk is higher among biological relatives, a genetic factor is likely. If the risk is higher among adopted relatives, environmental factors are suspected.
2. Determine the risk of having the trait/ disorder for adopted children whose biologic parents have the trait/disorder compared with controls. Higher risk among adoptees whose biological relatives are affected suggests genetic transmission.
3. Determine the risk of having the trait/ disorder for adoptees whose adoptive parents are normal but who have a biological parent who has the trait/disorder, and compare it with the risk for adoptees whose biological parents are normal but who are raised by an affected adoptive parent ("cross-fostering" studies). Such comparisons help identify both genetic and environmental influences.

Pedigree Studies

What information is provided by a pedigree study?

Pedigree (ancestral line or lineage) studies rely on the construction of a family tree, beginning with an individual who manifests the trait or disorder. Evidence of the trait or disorder in a large number of relatives spanning many generations suggests a genetic component and may enable the investigator to determine if the mode of inheritance is recessive or dominant.

Pedigree studies are strengthened by **linkage** studies. These studies seek to associate a trait with another gene called a **marker,** which has a **Mendelian** mode of inheritance and whose chromosomal position (locus) is known. If the trait under study and the marker are neighbors on the same chromosome, they are likely to be inherited together, or linked. Traditional markers include human leukocyte antigens (HLA), blood groups, and color blindness. To be conclusive, linkage studies depend on a large pedigree (a large number of relatives) whose condition is known or who are willing to be studied, usually through blood or tissue testing. Linkage studies have been enhanced through the use of molecular genetics techniques.

DNA Markers

DNA markers can be used to identify the chromosomal locations of genes responsible for several disorders. Among those already mapped are:
- some forms of Alzheimer's disease, an autosomal dominant condition arising from genes on chromosomes 14, 19, and 21
- Huntington's disorder, an autosomal dominant condition arising from a gene on chromosome 4

The inheritance of behavioral traits and disorders does not conform to Mendelian law. Rather, behavioral traits and disorders arise from genetic-environmental interactions that produce the phenotype.

1. **Incomplete penetrance:** An individual's genotype may have incomplete phenotypic expression due to interaction with other genetic and environmental factors.
2. **Phenocopy:** An individual may not carry the genotype, but has the phenotypical expression of a trait or disorder due to the action of other genetic or environmental factors.
3. **Polygenic action:** An individual has several genes that contribute modestly to the phenotype, which is also influenced by environmental factors.
4. **Mixed model of inheritance:** An individual may have a primary single gene that is modified by several other genes, all interacting with the environment.

Temperament

The human newborn has observable genetically determined patterns of personal attributes and behavioral tendencies that are stable and develop into distinctive personality and behavioral characteristics. Differences in these tendencies contribute to differences in infant reaction patterns.

Temperamental traits are perceived as positive or negative and lead to parental perceptions that a child is "easy," "slow-to-warm-up," or "difficult." Such perceptions are based on how the child responds to various environmental stimuli and on the ease with which the child achieves contentment.

Nine Elements of Temperament

1. Activity level
2. Rhythmicity
3. Approach
4. Adaptability
5. Intensity of reaction
6. Threshold of responsiveness
7. Mood
8. Distractibility
9. Attention span/persistence

Contemporary concepts of temperament emphasize psychophysiological reactivity and self-regulation of emotion. Inhibited children have higher sustained heart rates and more widely dilated pupils than uninhibited children. These physiological differences are readily seen when children are stressed, but also may be present when no stress is discernible. Differences in temperament may be modified by environmental experiences that foster or inhibit certain behaviors, e.g., parental intervention (acclimating the inhibited child to peer interactions by inviting a friend to a sleepover) or age-related expectation ("I'm too old to be afraid of the dark.") Physiological responses can be moderated through biofeedback or pharmacological interventions.

Genetic-Environmental Interactions

How does organism-environment transaction differ from organism-environment interaction?

Genetic characteristics **predispose** the individual to react to or be influenced by certain environmental conditions. Genetic determinants are present at birth. Some are activated only by specific interactions between the organism and the environment during specific **critical periods. Imprinting** in animals, **bonding,** and language development in humans are examples of time-specific environmental-organism interactions. As the organism evolves, the organism and environment interact in three ways:

1. **Organism-Environment Interaction.**
   Individuals react differently to the same environmental conditions. This differential reactivity may be genetically influenced and/or modified by the effects of experience.
2. **Organism-Environment Covariance.**
   Individuals with differing characteristics elicit different responses from the environment, thus creating a covariant interaction between the environment and the organism.
3. **Organism-Environment Transaction.**
   The organism and the environment have a mutual effect on each other over time. Organism-Environment Transaction encompasses Organism-Environment Covariance, but carries it further over time. The organism influences the environment which influences the organism and so on in a series of reciprocal changes. Thus, transaction refers to an ongoing process of adaptation between the organism and the environment.

Developmental changes in the nature of learning reflect a temporal transaction process. At birth, in response to a survival imperative, genetic influences are manifested in reflexive responses to environmental stimuli. As development progresses, genetic predisposition requires specific environmental stimuli during critical periods to activate certain survival responses (e.g., **imprinting, bonding**). With further development, the organism begins to respond to experience, but only instantaneously **(one-trial learning)**. Increasingly, experience plays a more important role in learning (e.g., **classical conditioning, operant conditioning, modeling, social learning** (see Chapter 8, Learning Processes).

Diathesis-Stress Transactions

Researchers have increasingly broadened the concept of predisposition. For example, the field of behavioral genetics focuses on the role that genes and post-conception biological, social and environmental events play in determining individual dif-

ferences. These cognitive, behavioral, sociocultural, and environmental as well as genetic and biological predispositions determine an individual's **diatheses** or vulnerabilities to particular stressors and subsequently define their temperament, personality, and coping.

Diathesis-Stress Transaction and Depression

Cognitive and familial diatheses predispose certain individuals to be vulnerable to loss (e.g., of a valued person, role, self-esteem), to perceive events negatively, and to engage in behavior that further increases their vulnerability to stressors. This can result in behaviors and cognitions (e.g., reduced initiative, avoidant behavior, self-criticism, anticipated bad outcomes) that contribute to depression.

Personality

Personality is the distinctive and consistent set of characteristics that predicts how an individual will respond in a variety of situations. It is the developmentally advanced version of temperament and, therefore, an important influence on illness and health care.

Unlike childhood temperament, which is fairly stable regardless of context, adults' response patterns, which we term personality, result from a greater interaction between the predisposition to respond (the personality characteristic) and a specific situation. Thus, a personality characteristic defines a response tendency in one situation but does not necessarily have predictive value in all situations.

Research on **change in personality traits** show a pattern of normative change across the life span. Social vitality and openness increase during adolescence, but decrease during old age. There is an increase in social dominance, conscientiousness, and emotional stability, especially in early adulthood.

Personality assessment is, in part, a function of the observer's **implicit personality theory.** While a personality characteristic may be observable, how it gets labeled is in the **eye of the beholder.** A personality characteristic is typically labeled a **"trait"** i.e., it is unique, distinctive, and enduring, rather than a **"state,"** or a situation-specific response.

Personality and Illness Vulnerability

How does personality contribute to illness vulnerability?

As a result of personality characteristics, early socialization, and life experiences, some people are "resilient" while others are "vulnerable." Opposite to what happens to resilient people, when vulnerable people encounter stressors, they are at risk for illness and premature death. This constitutes a psychological risk factor that contributes to all causes of mortality and is comparable to other health risks, such as high blood pressure or elevated serum cholesterol. For example, there is evidence of a response style often called **Type A personality or response style** that puts the individual at risk for **cardiovascular disease.** Type A individuals are hard driving, time-urgent, and hostile, the opposite of Type B individuals, who are easy-going, patient, and soft-spoken. While, at first, Type A personality was said to double the risk for angina, silent and overt heart attacks, and coronary death, today a central core of the behavioral style composed of cynicism, hostility, anger, and suspiciousness has been identified as a predictor for heart disease. A plausible pathophysiological hypothesis suggests that, faced with persistent stressors, Type A individuals may generate an excessive and sustained rise and fall of catecholamines, thus increasing plaque development.

Although explanatory hypotheses do exist, linkages between personality characteristics and illness are not yet definitively clear.

Most current models assume a complex set of interrelationships between genetic-based predisposition, psychosocial stressors, behavior, and disease. For example, some people show a genetic predisposition for depressive personality traits, which result in a catastrophic view of the world and one's personal competence. Such individuals show higher vulnerability to significant losses and bereavement to which they respond with suppressed immune system functioning. Excessively negative perceptions leave such individuals vulnerable to discouraging or failed life experiences manifested as an acquired avoidant response pattern akin to what was called **learned helpless-** ness in an animal model. Such individuals are at risk for developing eating and sleeping disorders, impaired social relations, and substance abuse.

Resilience and Psychological Well-Being

Certain personality characteristics are associated with **resilience**, increased resistance to stressors including illness. Resilient children come from households with stable value systems and communities that provide various sources of counsel and emotional support and are characterized by:
– good ability to **cope** with adverse conditions,
– close **bonding with a competent role model** attuned to the child's needs, and
– qualities that **elicit positive responses** from a wide range of caregivers.

Resilient children are active, affectionate, and good-natured. By preschool age, they demonstrate coping abilities, autonomy, and the ability to ask for help when needed. In elementary school, they become impressive problem solvers and communicators. By adolescence, they have an identified talent, and are confident, autonomous, and emotionally sensitive. Across gender and ethnic lines, at major life transition points (e.g., adolescence, early adulthood), these individuals seize alternative opportunities to rebound from obstacles, negative experiences, and setbacks.

Recommended Readings

Feldman MD, Christensen JF. *Behvioral Medicine in Primary Care, A Practical Guide.* (2nd ed.). New York: Lange Medical Books/McGraw Hill; 2003.

Lippa RA. *Gender, Nature and Nurture.* Mahwah, NJ: Lawrence Erlbaum Associates; 2002.

Pinker S. *The Blank Slate: The Modern Denial of Human Nature.* New York: Penguin; 2002.

Plomin R, DeFries JC, McClean GE, Rutter M. *Behavioral Genetics.* (3rd ed.). New York: WH Freeman; 1997.

Roberts WR, Walton KE, Viechtbauer W. Patterns of mean-level change in personality traits across the life course: A meta-analysis of longitudinal studies. *Psychological Bulletin* 2006; 132:1–15.

Zuckerman M. *Vulnerability to Psychopathology.* Washington, DC: American Psychological Association; 1999.

Review Questions

Directions: The items below consist of lettered headings followed by numbered descriptions. For each numbered description choose the one lettered heading to which it is *most* closely associated. Each lettered heading may be used *once, more than once,* or *not at all.*

Match the study design with the numbered description.
A. Adoption
B. Family risk
C. Linkage
D. Pedigree
E. Twin

1. Look for trait and disease within families by connecting trait and marker.
2. Use a family tree as a major tool.
3. Investigate how often a disease occurs in family members of a proband compared with how often it occurs in the general population.
4. In monozygotic twins reared apart, attempt to distinguish genetic from environmental factors in disease production.

Key to review questions: p. 393

Section III

Individual-Environment Interaction

6 Sensation

- What role does sensation play in survival?
- How does the central nervous system process incoming sensory information?
- How do nocioception, pain, suffering, and pain behavior differ?
- How does the brain integrate information from various senses?
- What is the difference between sensation and perception?

What role does sensation play in survival?

The ability of an individual to interact with the environment and to discern internal states is mediated by three essential functions of the central nervous system:

1. **sensation** or the reception of survival-relevant sensory input from the organism and from the environment;
2. **learning** or the relatively permanent behavioral change resulting from experience that entails recording, storage, and retrieval of information from the environment relevant to adaptation and survival; and
3. **cognition** or the processing and integration of information necessary for problem solving, creativity, and sociocultural activities.

Sensation results from the functioning of sensory receptor organs that detect environmental (e.g., light, heat, vibration, sound, smell) and internally generated stimuli. These receptor organs, composed of highly specialized nerve cells that respond to discrete stimuli, constitute the basic senses. For example, the somatosensory and vestibular systems detect mechanical stimuli and position sense; vision and audition detect stimuli whose sources are distant from the receptors; and olfaction and gustation detect chemical stimuli. Despite these differences and the specificity of both peripheral and central pathways for each sensory modality, the brain handles information from the senses in a uniform manner.

The energy of stimuli (e.g., photons, sound waves, mechanical forces) acts upon sensory receptor organs and is perceived, encoded, transduced, and transformed into bioelectrochemical energy that is then transmitted to modality-specific sensory association areas of the brain. In these areas, neurons interpret the information qualitatively and quantitatively, and relay it to multimodal association areas for interactions of greater complexity. The brain then relies on the information it receives to make and execute suitable action plans.

Sensory systems have a **threshold** (the minimum strength at which a stimulus provokes a response), can **habituate** (lose sensitivity or become tolerant to a stimulus) and **adapt** (become accustomed to a stimulus and no longer respond to small variations in its intensity).

Once a stimulus rises above threshold, the organism "understands" that *something* new has happened. The specific sensory modality identifies the **nature** of this *something*, and the frequency of receptor cell firing determines its *intensity*. The location of the firing receptors determines the *site* of the event on the body surface, since the information goes to the corresponding (**somatotopic**) areas of the somatosensory cortex. Because sensory systems synapse with motor systems, action often follows. Thus, the characteristics of the information may provoke differential responses that are at or between extremes. For example, a person's hand accidentally touching an unusually hot surface can provoke an instant reflex reaction as the person withdraws the hand and is aroused to a state of vigilance or fight-or-flight behavior. On the other hand, a person may quietly, deliberately, and dispassionately collect, analyze, and store stimuli for future reference, relying more on cognitive functions.

Disorders of sensation involve varying degrees of sensory loss or hyperexcitability. Examples of the former include hearing and visual deficits, and anosmia while examples of hyperexcitability include hyperesthesia and hyperalgesia. Paresthesia, another disorder of sensation, is experienced as the feeling of "pins and needles," e.g., when a foot "goes to sleep," and suggests compromise somewhere in the nerve pathway from the periphery to the CNS.

> How does the central nervous system process incoming sensory information?

Somatosensory System

The **somatosensory system** has two major subsystems of **cutaneous** and **subcutaneous** receptors. One detects mechanical stimuli, e.g., light touch, vibration, and pressure. The other provides information about pain and temperature. Cutaneous and subcutaneous receptors are classified into **mechanoceptors**, **thermoceptors**, and **nociceptors**, and can be free or encapsulated nerve endings. Receptors gather information, which they then relay to the CNS, which interprets, appraises, and acts upon it as required. Receptors are distributed in widely variable densities in different areas of the body. For example, the density of tactile receptors varies from 1,300 receptors per square inch on the hand to fewer than 100 receptors per square inch on the back. Additional receptors, called **proprioceptors**, provide information about internal forces, and are located in deeper structures such as muscles, tendons, and joints. All receptors act together so animals can identify shapes and textures and monitor internal and external forces that impinge upon the organism. Animals can thus detect and understand situational changes, whether innocuous or potentially harmful.

There are **six somatosensory modalities**: light touch, pressure, pain, temperature, vibration, and position sense or proprioception. Axons carry information from the receptors in the periphery to the spinal cord. In the spinal cord, these nerve fibers are organized into three tracts. In the first tract, the fibers synapse within one or two spinal cord segments, concentrating the signal, leaving out non-essential elements, and, thus, further refining the sensory information. The second tract, the fibers of which cross the midline and ascend on the spinothalamic tract, carries information for the conscious perception of touch and temperature. Information for the perception of discrete acute pain travels on the lateral spinothalamic tract, while information for the perception of diffuse chronic pain travels on the medial spinothalamic tract and on the spinal-reticulo-thalamic tract. The third tract ascends without crossing the midline, forming the posterior columns of the spinal cord, and carries information for the conscious perception of touch, vibration, and proprioception.

In 1937, Penfield discovered that the human somatosensory cortex is somatropic, i.e., its organization corresponds spatially to the location of receptor networks on the body. Penfield considered this somatosensory organization to be invariable, but modern evidence indicates that considerable developmental variation can occur in response to individual experience, adaptive learning, and brain plasticity. For example, shifts in somatosensory function to intact cortical tissue can occur when stroke or injury damages its prior location.

Somatosensory information from any given area of the body is bundled together with other information from that same area. It is then forwarded to the thalamus for integration with other sensory information, and finally to the parietal cortex, Brodmann areas 1, 2, and 3.

> How do nociception, pain, suffering, and pain behavior differ?

Nociception is the detection of thermal, chemical or mechanical energy impinging on specialized nerve endings in the skin **(cutaneous nociceptors)** or in the walls of viscera **(visceral nociceptors).** Nociceptive stimuli are carried as far as the spinal cord.

Pain is the alarm response of the CNS to tissue damage caused by thermal, chemical or mechanical stimuli detected by nociceptors but is not necessarily coincident with the nocioception.

Suffering is the cognitive interpretation and associated emotional distress that occurs in response to the experience of pain.

Pain behavior is the observable activity that occurs in response to nociception, pain, and suffering. Pain behavior is influenced by biology, cognition, the environment, sociocultural expectations, and, like any behavior, by its consequences. Pain behavior can therefore be learned (see Operant Conditioning, Chapter 8, Learning Processes). Pain, suffering, and complex pain behavior require an intact and functional cerebral cortex.

Sharp, well localized nociception travels to the spinal cord on small lightly myelinated nerve fibers. Dull, diffuse nociception travels on non-myelinated nerve fibers. For instance, if a person inadvertently pierces the skin of the hand on a pointy object, the following sequence occurs: a sharp sensation, a withdrawal reflex, and then, dull pain. The reflexive part of this nociceptive reaction may include changes in facial expression, posture, and other movement; endocrine changes; and changes in heart rate and blood pressure. This chain reaction depends on an intact spinal cord and does not reach the cerebral cortex. Thus, it can be seen in people who fall into a comatose state.

In the dorsal horn of the spinal cord, axons carrying nociception synapse with inhibitory and excitatory interneurons and with projection neurons. The latter cross the midline to form the antero-lateral fasciculus that sends connections to the brainstem reticular formation, tectum, and thalamus. The pain and touch systems only become integrated in the somatosensory cortex. Further integration takes place with other cortical areas to complete the perception in true-to-life complexity.

Pain is classified by duration as either acute or chronic. **Acute pain** lasts up to 6 months, typically has a single cause, is accompanied by distress, and is effectively managed with analgesics or relaxation techniques. **Chronic pain**, which lasts more than 6 months, is less responsive to analgesics, and is often associated with pain behaviors and maladaptive patterns of social interactions with family, friends, and coworkers.

The **gate control** theory of pain asserts that there is extensive pain modulation in the dorsal horn of the spinal cord. Interaction between the touch-pressure system and pain sensation takes place when axons enter the dorsal horn of the spinal cord. Afferent activity in large, well myelinated fibers can diminish the intensity of pain signals,

> Psychogenic pain is a term frequently applied where there is the experience of pain but the absence of any known physical cause. Psychogenic pain often becomes chronic, when inadvertent reinforcement of acute pain behaviors perpetuates them, although the original insult has healed.

perhaps, but not yet confirmed, through stimulation of inhibitory interneurons. It is as if the signals pass through a hypothetical "gate" one at a time. Thus, strong afferent activity seems to close the "gate" preventing painful stimuli from entering, being perceived in the cerebral cortex as pain and suffering, and generating pain behaviors. This would explain why the sharp pain of an injury diminishes if the area is rubbed. Dull reactivity in response to the rubbing blocks or reduces the sharp, intense pain of the injury. It also explains how intermittent, tolerable cutaneous electric stimulation can relieve certain cases of chronic pain, and why diseases of myelinated nerves often generate chronic neuropathic pain: they keep the "gate" open.

The **vestibular system** has its peripheral portion in the inner ear. In the vertical and horizontal planes, translation is primarily sensed by otolith organs while rotation is primarily sensed by the semicircular canals. These organs continually report on position and motion of head and body. The information is then relayed to cerebellar and brainstem centers that analyze and integrate its various parts. The functioning of the vestibular system, which governs postural reflexes, balance, orientation of the body and its parts in space, and eye movements, takes place unconsciously. Injury or disease in any part of the system will impair vestibular functioning. Because vestibular pathways course through large parts of the brainstem, signs of vestibular malfunctioning should alert one to possible brainstem damage.

Vision

Light in wavelengths between 390 and 770 nanometers is reflected off objects and enters the **cornea** where it is gathered, reflected and refracted. It then passes through the **iris**, which regulates the amount of light entering, and crosses the **lens** to reach the **retina**, which contains **rods** (receptor cells exquisitely sensitive to light across the visual spectrum) and **cones** (color-sensitive receptor cells, also responsible for fine spatial resolution in the central 10 degrees of vision). The retinal **macula** contains the highest concentration of cones. Cones generate neural impulses that travel via the optic nerve to the geniculate body and then to the calcarine cortex. The 10 degrees of central vision they initiate covers about half of the visual field, yet takse up as much anatomic space as the entire rest of the visual field. **Central vision** allows the person to determine what he/she is looking at.

Peripheral vision begins in the outer areas of the retina where there is the greatest concentration of rods. Their impulses travel to the geniculate body and then to the calcarine cortex and join central vision information to complete the visual map of the world. There are connections between the peripheral retina and the midbrain tectum that project to the parietal cortex to direct eyes and body toward new stimuli. Thus, once a new stimulus reaches peripheral vision, eyes and body turn so the stimulus falls on central vision.

Each cell column of the calcarine cortex responds to a different angle and orientation of incoming visual stimuli. Complex cell columns, largely in **Brodmann's area 18,** organize the information from the simple cells into a rudimentary perception of form. Hypercomplex cells in **Brodmann's areas 18 and 19** then analyze discontinuity, angles, corners, movement, position, and orientation to discern complex geometric forms. Binocular input to these hypercomplex cells results in stereoscopic vision that provides information about distance and depth. The visual association area is linked to the parietal and temporal visual areas permitting object recognition and perception of object distance and position.

Visual impairment is due to peripheral disorders of the eyeball, CNS lesions, or more complex systemic disease processes. Ophthalmologists treat primarily intrinsic eyeball disorders such as refraction errors, e.g., myopia and hyperopia. Neurologists and, occasionally, neurosurgeons help patients with nerve- and CNS-related visual disorders. Internal medicine specialists concern themselves with systemic disorders that affect vision.

Myopia (nearsightedness): The eyeball is longer than normal, causing light to converge before reaching the retina. Images are clear if objects are near and blurred if they are far.

Hyperopia (farsightedness): The eyeball is shorter than normal, so that light reaches the retina before converging. Images are clear if objects are far and blurred if they are near.

Central visual acuity losses (unilaterally or bilaterally) are caused by disorders that affect structures between – and including – the cornea and the optic chiasm.

Peripheral visual acuity losses are caused by lesions beyond the optic chiasm, in the contralateral optic radiation in the temporal and occipital lobes. There are additional extra-striate visual areas (25 in primates, including humans). Rather than ending in the calcarine cortex, they project to temporal and parietal cortices and to the limbic system, and provide additional visual information. Disruption produces problems such as faulty color discrimination and faulty identification of faces.

Audition

The human auditory system processes sound frequencies ranging from 20 to 20,000 Hertz (cycles per second). Most speech and environmental sounds are in the range of 400–3,000 Hertz. Sounds produce variation in air pressure, which causes the tympanic membrane to vibrate. The vibration is then communicated to the **ossicles** (malleus, incus, and stapes) and from there to the cochlear fluid where hair cells translate sound frequencies into electrical potentials that are ordered in similar fashion to the tones represented on a piano keyboard. These electrical potentials travel on the cochlear nerve to the brainstem's **cochlear nuclei.** The nerve impulses are then relayed through the lateral lemniscus to the inferior colliculi, from where they reach the medial geniculate nucleus (MGN) of the thalamus. MGN neurons connect with neurons in the primary **auditory cortex** located in the posterior aspect of the temporal lobe **(Brodmann's areas 41 and 42 or Heschl's gyri).** Each component of the primary auditory cortex processes a different sound frequency. The primary auditory cortex retains sound for up to one second permitting temporal sequencing, location of sounds in space, and recognition of nonverbal sounds such as animal noises, rainfall, prosodic-melodic nuances, and various aspects of music.

Auditory sensation is relayed to **Brodmann's association area 22** where it is combined with somesthetic and visual sensory information for more complex processing. Final decoding of auditory sensation takes place in the left temporal lobe, which includes part of **Wernicke's area,** the primary center for understanding speech, and the right auditory association area, the primary center for recognizing components of music such as timbre, pitch, tone, and melody.

Clarity of sounds is determined by its intensity and frequency. Therefore, the severity of hearing impairment depends on which components of sound perception are affected and to what extent.

Hearing impairment may be temporary or permanent and is caused by pathology affecting the ear structures proper or those that lay beyond the ear. These include the external ear canal (obstruction, trauma); middle ear (otitis media, trauma, otosclerosis); inner ear (Meniere's disease, trauma, and presbycusis, or age-related hearing loss); nerve damage (trauma, infection, acoustic neurofibroma); brain matter disorders (demyelinating diseases such as multiple sclerosis); and vascular disorders (stroke).

Although end-organ disease often leads to bilateral hearing impairment, brain matter disorders lead most frequently to unilateral impairment.

Hearing and visual impairments are most common in the elderly. Because of their nature, these sensory impairments can contribute to a heightened sense of isolation and mimic cognitive and emotional disorders; and paranoid-like feelings can occur. For example, a person who is hard of hearing may be convinced that people holding a conversation are actually whispering bad things about him or her.

Olfaction

Olfaction requires receptor-cell contact with **odorants,** or volatile chemical cues. Odorants enter the nose, dissolve in mucus and bind to receptors on the membrane surface of specialized neurons located in the mucosa. Humans have approximately 10 million such receptor cells. Constant replenishment is essential since they have an average lifespan of 8 weeks. There are many hundreds of different receptors, but each neuron has a specific receptor for a specific odor. Neurons of the same type are randomly arranged in the olfactory mucosa. Humans detect an estimated 10,000 odors.

The olfactory information carried by receptor cell axons crosses the cribriform plate to the olfactory bulb. There it reaches 2,000–3,000 processing units, called glomeruli, establishing a unique spatial pattern that permits the person to identify specific odors. The intensity of olfactory stimuli is determined by the number of molecules bound to receptors, which, in turn, determines the neuronal firing rate. The pattern or location of neuronal firing determines the scent. Current understanding of central projections of olfactory bulb neurons is sketchy. Olfactory signals are not relayed to the thalamus but project onto the frontal cortex and limbic system (amygdala, hippocampus, and pyriform cortex), which correlates with the observation that smells may evoke strong emotions and memories. Olfaction is phylogenetically older than other senses and is strongly connected with reproductive activities.

Pheromones

The vomeronasal organ, a structure related to the olfactory system, detects pheromones, or chemical cues that provoke stereotypical responses, especially regarding sex and reproduction in non-human animals. In some animals, early ablation of the vomeronasal organ prevents the onset of puberty.

Recent evidence suggests the existence of some human responsiveness to such molecules, which varies with menstrual cycle phases. However, it is not clear if or to what extent pheromones influence human behavior. A major difficulty in cross species comparisons that include humans is that, in the latter, higher olfactory processing structures of non-human animals correspond to discrete limbic structures thought to be responsible for more differentiated emotional and memory functions.

Gustation

Taste requires that substances be dissolved in saliva and kept in contact with the surface of the tongue, which is lined with **papillae.** Papillae direct molecules to any of the 10,000 **taste buds,** each of which contains about 150 **taste cells.** Taste cells, which have an average life span of 10 days, are in a constant process of replacement.

Taste cells are the receptor cells through which the tongue recognizes the four primary taste sensations: bitter, posterior section; sweet, anterior section; sour, mid and posterior sections bilaterally; and salty, lateral strips along both sides of the tongue. Since a unique set of receptor cells mediates each modality, taste information is organized into discrete patterns that travel on the gustatory nerves, formed by the axons of taste cells, to the nucleus solitarius in the brainstem. Although in final analysis the medial temporal lobe is activated by taste sensations, the complete mechanism is not yet understood.

Flavor

Taste sensations involve the perception of flavors, which arise from the complex combination of taste, smell, touch, vision and hearing. Many foods are difficult to identify if their smell is absent. Thus, the temporary or permanent loss of the sense of smell (anosmia) or any illness that compromises the functioning of the nasal passages (e.g., a cold) alters the sense of taste by impairing the sense of smell. Visual and hearing cues and cultural or social factors also influence the perception of taste through previous experiences with particular foods and drinks.

How does the brain integrate information from the various senses?

In general, input signals from the various senses converge on the **thalamus** where they are integrated and forwarded to respective sensory association areas in the cortex. There they are evaluated against stored memories and interpreted (perceived).

What is the difference between sensation and perception?

Perception is the cognitive process of interpreting and assigning meaning to sensory information. Perception matures throughout childhood. A **unitary perception** is not possible until adolescence when sensory association areas become fully myelinated. While **sensory systems** are structurally and

functionally similar in all people, **perception** is specifically tied to the individual's store of cortical information that is accumulated through individual life experiences. Thus, any sensory experience can be perceived (interpreted) differently by different people based on their own past experience.

Recommended Reading

Beatty J. *The Human Brain: Essentials of Behavioral Neuroscience.* Thousand Oaks, CA: Sage Publications; 2001.

Kalat JW. *Biological Psychology.* (7th ed.). Belmont, CA: Wadsworth-Thompson Learning; 2001.

Kandel E, Schwartz JH, Jessell TM. *Principles of Neural Science.* (4th ed.). New York: McGraw-Hill; 2000.

Purves D, Augustin GJ, Fitzpatrick D, Katz LC, Lamantia A-S, McNamara JO (Eds.) *Neuroscience.* Sutherland, MA: Sinauer Associates, Inc.; 2005.

Review Questions

1. Incoming visual sensations are organized into visual perceptions by which of the following areas of the brain?
    A. Brodmann's areas 18 and 19
    B. Brodmann's area 22
    C. Brodmann's areas 41 and 42
    D. Heschl's gyri
    E. Wernicke's area

2. The detection of thermal, chemical, or mechanical energy impinging upon special nerve endings in the skin is called
    A. kinesthesis
    B. nociception
    C. pain
    D. perception
    E. suffering

Key to review questions: p. 393

7 Stress, Adaptation, and Illness

- What is the origin of most illnesses seen by primary care physicians?
- What are the components of the stress response?
- How does stress promote learning?
- How does the acute stress response differ from the chronic stress response?
- What role do the glucocorticoids play in the etiology of stress disorders?
- How does learning contribute to the development of stress disorders?
- What role does cognition play in the development of the stress response?

Stress and Adaptation

What is the origin of most illnesses seen by primary care physicians?

The majority of illnesses seen by physicians are by-products of the body's attempts to adapt to **stress**. Derived from physics, the concept originally referred to forces causing structural or systemic strain. Applied to medicine, the concept of **stress** refers to any challenge to the integrity or survival of the organism and includes the complex *interaction of biological, behavioral, cognitive, sociocultural, and environmental changes that can disrupt homeostasis.* Any such challenge will trigger "strains" within the body's systems and activate a **stress response**, setting into motion an array of adaptive and defensive mechanisms within each of these systems. Disease and dysfunction typically occur in response to the body's maladaptive responses, but can occur as the result of successful adaptive responses as well. Thus, many of the illnesses that physicians treat are **stress disorders** and can best be understood by studying the nature of the body's **stress response**, the mechanisms involved in its function, and the consequences of their actions.

The stress response is the result of an evolutionary process that began millions of years ago with single-celled organisms having no nuclei (prokaryotes). Since their DNA consisted mainly of gene encoding proteins, they were limited in their ability to adapt or develop. Over time, a dramatic genetic shift occurred with the appearance of multicellular organisms whose cells contained nuclei (eukaryotes). These cells possessed a regulatory system of RNA that produced unique DNA sequences, interspersed with "introns", bits of DNA that had the ability to insert themselves into host genomes and splice themselves out in the form of RNA. This gave the intron the ability to proliferate, mutate, and evolve innovative changes in cell structure and function. This genetic capability for adaptation set the stage for the development of complex life support systems (e.g., respiration, circulation, digestion, elimination, immunity). Each system became homeostatically regulated and centrally coordinated (nervous system), enabling the organism to adapt to and survive in a hostile/challenging stressful environment. A recently discovered genetic process by which RNA sequences change at specific sites has been found to be unique to primates and particularly active in the brain. This suggests that the appearance of this process in primates led to a new level of complexity in RNA processing, and the subsequent development of the brain structure and function that made possible a quantum leap in human adaptive learning and cognition.

The Stress Response

The **stress response** involves a complex set of physiological, cognitive, and behavioral reactions that physiologist Walter Cannon called the **fight or flight** response. Physiologist Hans Selye believed the response to be uniform regardless of the nature of the stressor. However, subsequent research showed that the response varies with the intensity and duration of the stressor. Selye distinguished between **eustress**, meaning healthy stress, and **distress** or unhealthy stress. Eustress represented the **optimal degree of arousal** required to perform well or learn, generally in response to moderate stress or challenge. Distress occured when arousal impeded performance, generally in instances of high stress.

The **Yerkes-Dodson Law** (see Figure 7.1.) states that, in general, performance and adaptive learning are optimal under moderate rather than either high or low stress (arousal) conditions. High stress may impede performance, as evidenced by overly anxious college students who cannot concentrate on an exam. Low stress (arousal) may fail to stimulate adequately, leading to a lackluster performance. Two important corollaries to the Yerkes-Dodson Law apply to specific learning situations. (1) Learning new or difficult tasks is optimal under low to moderate stress conditions (recall how difficult it is to learn new material when anxious). (2) Performance of well-learned tasks is optimal under high stress conditions (e.g., the track star who runs fastest when "pumped").

Chronic vs. Acute Stress

Selye noted that, whereas the stress response was designed to protect and "heal" the body, under conditions of sustained or **chronic stress**, the body's adaptive mechanisms could break down, resulting in disease and dysfunction. In other words, in response to chronic stress, the cure could be worse than the disease. In his **General Adaptation Syndrome (GAS)** model, Selye referred to the initial stage of the stress response as the **alarm stage**. This was followed by a **resistance stage**, during which the organism attempted to cope with or adapt to continued challenges utilizing available resources. During this stage, the individual became susceptible to **diseases of adaptation** (e.g., arterial hypertension). The final **exhaustion**

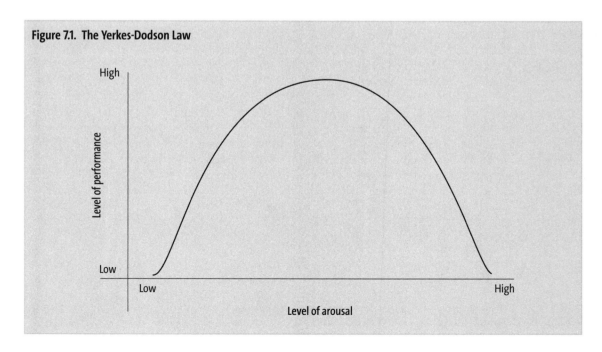

Figure 7.1. The Yerkes-Dodson Law

stage occurred when demand exceeded available resources. During this stage, the individual was increasingly susceptible to illnesses in general.

Thus, the effects of stress depend not only on the nature and intensity of the stressor, but also on its duration or **chronicity**. Being able to adapt to **chronic** as well as **acute stress** requires two types of stress response. First, there is an **immediate nervous system response** for acute stress situations. After receiving sensory input indicating a stressor condition, the response focuses upon **emergency functions** in keeping with the organism's survival imperative. Energy is mobilized from storage sites while further storage is temporarily halted; muscles are fueled with glucose, simple fats, proteins and oxygen for fight or flight; and there is rapid delivery of oxygen and fuel to muscles via increased heart rate, blood pressure,

and respiration. Simultaneously, non-critical functions are put on hold (e.g., digestion, growth, and reproduction).

Stress and the Neuroendocrine Systems

Incoming sensory information is collected by the thalamus, then simultaneously forwarded to the amygdala, hippocampus and cortical association areas (see Figure 7.2.). Analogous to a "first response team," the **amygdala** initiates an **emergent reaction (fight or flight),** initially arousing and mobilizing the organism via the **sympatho-adrenomedullary (SAM) axis**, which trig-

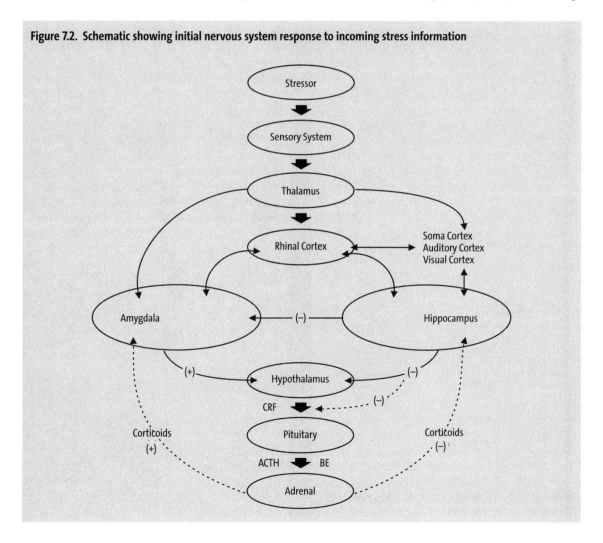

Figure 7.2. Schematic showing initial nervous system response to incoming stress information

Figure 7.3. Schematic showing initial nervous system response to incoming stress information

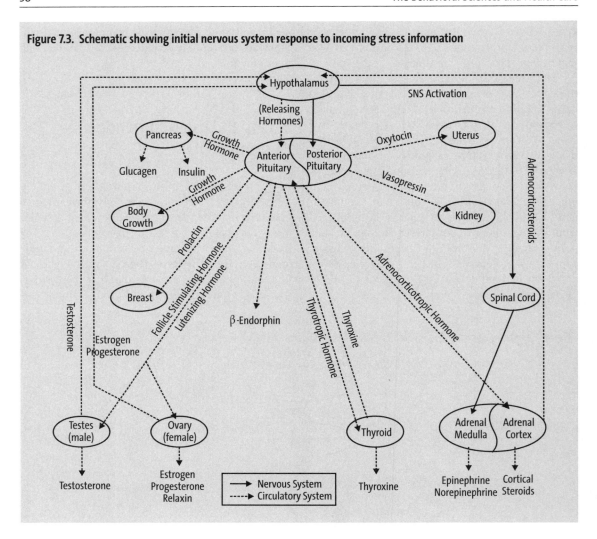

gers release of catecholamines through activation of the hypothalamus, pituitary, and adrenal (HPA) axis. The amygdala's response is mitigated by the **hippocampus,** analogous to an "intelligence gathering network," which obtains relevant analyses from the cortex as to the import, meaning and past experience relevant to the incoming information. If judged to be a potential high stress condition, the emergent response continues. If judged of lesser import or non-threatening, the response is mitigated, changed or terminated. Thus, the function of the hippocampus is to modulate the amygdala in gearing up the neuroendocrine system and the stress response.

How does the acute stress response differ from the chronic stress response?

While the "first response" of the nervous system addresses the body's most emergent survival needs, it cannot sustain the response at such a high level in the face of prolonged stress. Relying on circulatory system transport of hormonal messengers, the **endocrine system** initiates a more sustained highly complex response by activating

In response to perceived stress, sympathetic neural pathways, originating in the hypothalamus, trigger release of **epinephrine** at these synapses and from the adrenal medulla. Concurrently, **norepinephrine** is released at all other sympathetic synapses in the body to act on postsynaptic receptors of end organs. The two **catecholamines** promote generalized sympathetic arousal.

a system of glands that, in turn, activate an extensive array of distant target glands and organs (see Figure 7.3. for a simplified schematic).

Once the stress ceases, parasympathetic pathways originating in the hypothalamus activate **cholinergic** neurons in the same end organs. This dissipates the state of arousal. Thus, the body's initial reaction to a stress condition is an immediate but brief autonomic nervous system-initiated response.

> **What role do the glucocorticoids play in the etiology of stress disorders?**

Every time the stress response is activated, nerve impulses fire, hormones are secreted and target organs, tissues and cells are triggered. The patient momentarily feels aroused, pumped up, on edge, or even anxious. With **acute stress,** the response shuts down quickly whereas with **chronic stress,** hormones remain activated, and **glucocorticoids** flood the blood stream, impairing the ability of the hippocampus to suppress the amygdala and terminate the stress response. Overtime, adaptive systems begin to break down.

> The hypothalamus secretes **corticotrophin-releasing hormone (CRH)**, which is transported to the pituitary via hypothalamic-pituitary-portal circulation. The anterior pituitary secretes **adrenocorticotropic hormone (ACTH)** into the blood stream. The ACTH is transported to the adrenal cortex and stimulates **glucocorticoid** secretion into the circulatory system. In the stress response, glucocorticoids inhibit protein synthesis and accelerate protein catabolism, increase lipolysis, and decrease peripheral glucose utilization.

Stress and the Immune System

While acute stress activates the **immune system,** chronic stress and the resultant excess levels of glucocorticoids in the blood stream impair immune system functioning by damaging or destroying T cells and inducing premature migration of T cells from the thymus, resulting in thymus shrinkage. Thus, patients under chronic stress are more susceptible to diseases associated with **immune system suppression.** Ironically, chronic stress can also effect a **heightened immune system response** where organs or tissues in the host body are attacked. These **autoimmune disorders** include multiple sclerosis, pernicious anemia, rheumatoid arthritis, juvenile diabetes, and various allergies. Autoimmune diseases can be **organ specific**, where the antigenic response focuses upon a specific tissue or organ, like Hashimoto's thyroiditis (thyroid) or multiple sclerosis (nerve cell myelin sheaths). Autoimmune diseases can also be **non-organ specific**, where the antigen is universal, attacking parts of every cell, as in systemic lupus erythematosus (onset believed precipitated by viral infections) or forms of rheumatoid arthritis (onset believed precipitated by bacterial infections).

Stress and Cancer

As noted earlier, chronic stress can impair normal cell processes, like **apoptosis** (cell death and recycling). As a result, cells can become "immortal" resulting in rapid, seemingly endless cell division. In addition, **regulatory genes** can be mutated by carcinogens, such as UV rays or toxic chemicals, impairing cell growth processes. Because chronic stress can impair the ability of the immune system to mobilize defenses against invading tumor cells, it can also inadvertently enhance their growth, facilitating **angiogenesis** (increased capillary growth) and nutrient feeding of the tumor cells. Thus, especially with tumors that are viral in origin, *stress may enhance their growth, but not necessarily contribute to their origin.*

Stress and Growth Processes

While moderate stress can facilitate growth processes, chronic stress can have impact on normal growth and development. It can also inhibit **growth hormone** release (due in part to excess levels of glucocorticoids), reducing target cell sensitivity and the synthesis of new proteins and DNA in cell division.

Stress and Metabolic Processes

While acute stress triggers an emergent response (shunting of stored nutrients to muscle and organ sites, shutting down of digestion and other non-emergent functions), chronic stress causes this process to turn on and off repeatedly. As a result, **nutrient stores** are depleted faster than they are replaced and the body begins to catabolize muscle tissue to make up for the loss. The stressors driving this process can be serendipitous or purposeful (e.g., stressful exercise or weight management programs) and, if not well managed, can lead to **eating disorders** such as **anorexia** or **bulimia** (see Chapter 39 for a more detailed discussion of Eating Disorders).

In some individuals, the excess **glucocorticoids** resulting from chronic stress can impair the cell's ability to respond to insulin, resulting in increased **glucose** and **fat** in the blood stream, impeding oxygen flow and organ efficiency. This process can lead to adult onset Type II or **Non-Insulin Dependent Diabetes Mellitus (NIDDM)**, a major health problem among aging overweight individuals (see Chapter 20, Obesity, and Chapter 25, Geriatric Health and Successful Aging for a further discussion of health problems in an aging population). Some individuals may suffer from Type I or **Insulin Dependent Diabetes Mellitus (IDDM)** due to a genetically influenced shortage of insulin. The onset of this disease may be triggered by a pancreatic viral infection that initiates an autoimmune response in which the insulin-producing cells of the pancreas are attacked.

Stress and Reproductive Processes

High levels of chronic stress can result in glucocorticoid inhibition of hypothalamic release of **lutinizing hormone** (LH) and **follicle stimulating hormone** (FSH). The effect is to inhibit **testosterone** release and **sperm production** in males, and **estrogen** release and **egg production** in females. Stress can also impede the parasympathetic activation required for male penile erections resulting in **impotence** or **premature ejaculation**. Stress-induced fat cell consumption in females can impede **estrogen** production, resulting in a relative buildup of male hormone that contributes to **amenorrhea**. The lowering of **progester-** one levels combined with glucocorticoid blockade of bone recalcification can lead to **osteoporosis**. Other consequences may include **atherosclerosis**, and impaired uterine wall nutrition increasing the risk of spontaneous abortion. Table 7.1. lists other common stress disorders that are consequences of chronic stress-induced system breakdowns.

Table 7.1. Common disorders resulting from chronic stress-induced system failures

- **Gastrointestinal:** peptic ulcer, ulcerative colitis, irritable bowel syndrome, esophageal reflux
- **Cardiovascular:** essential hypertension, migraine headache, Raynaud's disease
- **Respiratory:** asthma, hyperventilation
- **Dermatologic:** eczema, acne, psoriasis, alopecia
- **Musculoskeletal:** muscle strain, tendonitis, tension headache, low back pain
- **Cognitive:** low self-esteem and self-efficacy, pessimistic expectancy, learned helplessness
- **Emotional:** affective and adjustment disorders, posttraumatic stress disorder, reactive psychosis

Learning, Cognition and the Stress Response

Lazarus and Folkman proposed a stress model that attempted to go beyond the physiological mechanisms of the stress response and explain the role that **learning and cognition** play in influencing the individual's stress response. They proposed that the impact of a stressor is determined or mediated by the individual's ability to accurately **appraise** the stressor, i.e., to evaluate or assign meaning based on past learning, experience, and memory (cognition). The stress response is also influenced by the individual's **vulnerabilities**. For example, a patient can be genetically vulnerable (sickle cell anemia), cognitively vulnerable (depressive, defeatist beliefs), behaviorally vulnerable (a smoker or drinker), or socioculturally vulnerable (poor, undernourished, denied health care or economic opportunities). **Coping skills** reflect the individual's adaptive abilities in the form of behavioral skills, cognitive strategies, sense of efficacy based on past successes, as well as motivated effort. **Social support** refers to the validation, support and assurance of assistance that the individual can count on from others. Other **resources** include material, financial, educational, intellectual, cognitive, health, creative, and social skills and benefits the individual can call upon.

The process of symptom acquisition and its **conditioning** to multiple psychosocial triggers and reinforcers begins with the stress response. Over the life span of the individual, the homeostatic process of adapting to stress involves the **learning** of complex interactions among biologic, behavioral, sociocultural, cognitive, and environmental experiences. As a result, the **biologic symptoms** of the stress response become **conditioned** to beliefs, emotions, behaviors and events, all of which then acquire the ability to **trigger, reinforce and maintain** these symptoms. (See Chapter 8, Learning Processes, for further discussion of the learning processes that play such an important role in stress adaptation and health care.)

Research shows that the intensity and duration of a stressor may be **perceived** differently by various individuals as a result of **life experiences, beliefs** and **memories** that are part of the **cognitive structure** that influences subsequent perceptions and behaviors. In other words, "stress is in the eye of the beholder," and one person's severe stressor may only be another person's mild challenge. (See Chapter 9 for a further discussion of how cognition influences perception of stress, disease, and health care.)

Psychological Consequences

Chronic stress, which induces continued emotional arousal, can have serious psychological consequences. Conditions leading to an excessive fear response can result in chronic **anticipatory anxiety**, a learned sensitivity to fear-inducing situations. Similarly, continuous exposure to

loss or coping can lead to depression and a sense of **learned helplessness**. In addition, emotional responses can become conditioned to specific cognitions, such as memories or self-statements. These cognitions then serve as cues for activating these same emotional states (e.g., "every time I fail, I get depressed").

Sudden, traumatic, life-threatening events during which the individual exhibits intense feelings of helplessness and powerlessness can lead to the development of a **posttraumatic stress disorder** (PTSD). The precipitating event, per se, is not responsible for PTSD; rather PTSD is the result of a stress response so severe that the emergent function of the amygdala overwhelms the ability of the hippocampus to act as modulator (to analyze past relevant contextual experience, learn, and offer an adaptive response). As a result, the emotional consequences of the stressor event are not anchored in any identifiable contextual memory (cognition). This results in nightmares and "flashbacks" (reliving the event as if it is actually happening), as well as insomnia, heightened physiologic arousal, and emotional hypervigilance. (See Chapter 8 for a further discussion of the impact of stress on cognition, and Chapter 41 for a further discussion of PTSD and other anxiety disorders.)

Moderators of the Stress Response

An individual's stress response is idiosyncratic, i.e., influenced by **personal experiences** that define the nature and intensity of any stressor condition, and the individual's **self-efficacy** or self confidence in his/her ability to cope with the stressor. Thus, a person's stress response can be moderated by interventions that modify the individual's predisposing **vulnerabilities** (biologic, cognitive,

Medication, meditation and relaxation can limit physiological arousal and re-establish psychophysiological homeostasis. Optimally effective long-term treatment, however, should also include cognitive-behavioral or other psychotherapy interventions (see Chapter 9) plus psycho-educational training in accurate stress appraisal, adaptive coping and problem-solving strategies, recruiting social support, and utilizing available resources.

behavioral, sociocultural), stress **appraisal abilities** (cognitive), **coping skills**, and **social support** and other **resources**. Stress is a naturally and continuously occurring phenomenon. Thus, learning to effectively manage stress is a more realistic goal than trying to eliminate it.

Recommended Reading

Beatty J. *The Human Brain: Essentials of Behavioral Neuroscience.* Thousand Oaks, CA: Sage Publications; 2001.

Carr JE. Stress and Illness. In Wedding D, Stuber M (Eds.). *Behavior and Medicine.* (4th ed.). Cambridge, MA: Hogrefe & Huber; 2006.

Kandel E, Schwarz J, Jessell T. *Principles of Neural Science.* (4th ed.). New York: McGraw-Hill; 2000

LeDoux J. *The Synaptic Self.* New York: Viking Press; 2002.

Mattick JS. The hidden genetic program of complex organisms. *Scientific American* 2004; 291:60–67.

Zimmer C. Great mysteries of evolution: New discoveries rewrite the book on who we are and where we came from. *Discover: Science, Technology and Medicine* 2003; 24:34–42.

Review Questions

1. The concept of stress refers to any challenge to the homeostasis or integrity of the organism. Stress disorders have their origins from stressors in which of the following domains?
    A. Biological
    B. Cognitive-behavioral
    C. Environmental
    D. Sociocultural
    E. All of the above

2. Among the following, which brain structure modulates the stress response based upon past experience relevant to incoming sensory information?
    A. Amygdala
    B. Hippocampus
    C. Hypothalamus
    D. Pituitary
    E. Thalamus

3. Which of the following is a true statement about the effect of chronic stress on the immune system?
    A. Chronic stress can suppress but not heighten immune system responses.
    B. Chronic stress contributes to non-organ specific but not organ specific autoimmune disorders.
    C. Chronic stress induces migration of T cells into the thymus resulting in thymus swelling.
    D. Excess levels of circulating glucocorticoids damage or destroy T cells.

4. Intense chronic stress debilitates the body resulting in various medical disorders. This effect is mediated by the
    A. cardiovascular system
    B. endocrine system
    C. hematopoietic system
    D. immune system
    E. sensory system

Key to review questions: p. 393

8 Learning Processes

- What role does learning play in evolution?
- How do the brain and CNS learn?
- What is the difference between implicit and explicit learning?
- What is the developmental significance of the various kinds of learning?
- How does reinforcement influence behavior?
- What is the Premack Principle?
- How are complex social associations learned?
- What is cognitive-behavioral therapy?

What role does learning play in evolution?

Learning is possible because the brain and CNS associate and store sequences and patterns of events in time and space. This capability leads to **adaptability** and contributes to the **evolution** of behaviors, traits, and physical characteristics that are most successful in overcoming environmental challenges. Successful adaptations are then passed on to offspring through **natural selection.** Thus, the current genome is the result of an accumulation of interactions between heredity and learned adaptations that promote survival. However, the genetic contribution to this evolutionary process is not *what was learned* but rather the *ability to learn.*

Learning enables the organism to modify immediate behavior, future goals and incentives. **Behavior modification** involves altering behavior associated with events contiguous in time and space. **Incentive modification** involves anticipating outcomes and altering future goals based on "lessons learned" from past experience. Incentive modification may also involve learning how to delay or inhibit certain responses in order to achieve desired outcomes.

Principle of Association

The **principle of association** refers to the ability of organisms to "record" relationships between environmental events, biologic responses, cognitions, or behaviors and their consequences. Associations range from simple sequential connections (*if* I push the button, *then* the horn will honk) to more complex associations incorporating information about temporal, spatial, and causal relationships, contextual cues, and consequences (if I honk the horn during rush hour [temporal] on the freeway [spatial], I may get an angry response [past experience]). Learning experiences occur in context. **Contextual cues** play an important role in guiding attention, encoding, and memory retrieval, thereby influencing subsequent behavior. **Time** is an especially important contextual cue because the passage of time constantly changes the context.

Biological Basis of Learning

How do the brain and CNS learn?

Stimulus characteristics are stored in memory in the form of **individual nerve cell responses** and associated via **synaptic links** between nerve cells. Association between nerve cells is facilitated by neurotransmission. The extensive **dendritic tree** of a single vertebrate neuron can form 100,000–200,000 receptive synaptic contacts with other neurons, thus providing an extraordinary array of potential associative networks.

> **What is the difference between implicit and explicit learning?**

There are two types of learning based on the complexity of the neurologic mechanisms involved.
1. **Implicit learning** is the association of immediately sequential sensory and motor system responses via lower levels of cortical mediation. The information stored is limited to predictive relationships between events. Implicit learning tends to be slow, automatic, reflexive, and cumulative over time, often without the conscious participation of the individual.
2. **Explicit learning** involves more concrete associations between diverse stimuli and events that vary across time and space. Explicit learning tends to be rapid, intentional, and typically requires more active participation by the individual. Explicit learning outcomes may be more immediate (e.g., instantaneous "insight") or delayed (e.g., extended "reflection").

Implicit Learning

During **implicit learning,** excitation of a sensory neuron stimulates release of the neurotransmitter, **serotonin.** Serotonin then initiates a series of biochemical changes, including activation of a protein **kinase** that prolongs the action potential, thereby allowing more neurotransmitter to be released at the synaptic junction. Sequential stimulation of two adjacent neurons results in the convergence of two different signals on the synaptic junction. The first signal sensitizes the synapse, which **potentiates** or amplifies the effect of the second signal and enhances the associative link between the two neurons. Through this mechanism, the organism records information in the form of sensory memories derived from environmental interactions. These sensory memories are short-lived due to the limited time span of synaptic firing. This pro-

cess can be enhanced and made more durable by repeated associations with other sensory or motor signals occurring in connection with the same stimulus event.

Explicit Learning

Explicit learning requires activation and coordination of structures in the cortex, especially the temporal lobe, and other mediating brain networks for the longer-term processing, coding, and storing of complex information. The **limbic system** (hippocampus, amygdala, basal forebrain, and thalamus) receives and integrates incoming sensory information. The diverse sensory inputs of an event (e.g., time, space, contextual cues) are collated by the **thalamus,** and then referred on to the **amygdala** which records its "emotional" significance, and the **hippocampus** which assigns it a temporal and spatial context. These contextual cues facilitate learning by enabling the limbic system to reference the new information to related memories in the cortex.

Although memories are dispersed throughout the brain, memories that are related to each other are clustered together because they share direct synaptic connections to relevant sensory organs and contribute similar types of information for storage. For example, visual memories are stored in the occipital and adjacent temporal regions; auditory and verbal memories are stored in the parietal and adjacent temporal regions; motor skill memories are stored in the brainstem.

The hippocampus and its associated structures in the limbic system serve as a central switchboard, connecting the various storage sites distributed throughout the cortex to form combined memories. When learning new information occurs, these connections constitute **temporary memory** and are easily lost or reorganized as additional and ongoing information is received. However, over time, as some memories are repeatedly activated and continue to have predictive value, they are eventually forwarded by the hippocampus to the **neocortex** to become part of **long-term or permanent memory.**

Major neural pathways of the hippocampus use the excitatory amino acid, glutamate, as the neurotransmitter. After neuronal excitation, **glutamate** binds with two types of protein receptors on the cell membrane of the postsynaptic neuron: (1) **NMDA receptors** (named after the chemical *N*-methyl D-aspartate, which also binds to these receptors), and (2) all other or **non-NMDA receptors.** The response of NMDA receptors is blocked by magnesium ions until the cell is unblocked by depolarization due to the stimulation of non-NMDA receptors. The intensity of the stimulus will determine the magnitude of the depolarization and, therefore, the intensity of the cell response.

The convergence of NMDA and non-NMDA receptor activation produces a slow, long lasting, and efficient synaptic response. In complex learning situations (i.e., those requiring multiple stimulus associations), the repeated convergence of these excitatory changes on two or more neurons serves to both potentiate and prolong the sensitivity of the synaptic link. This **long-term potentiation** (LTP) effect, however, requires that the two signals – glutamate binding to the receptor and depolarization of the postsynaptic cell – take place simultaneously, thus providing the associative linkage.

Learning and Developmental Demands

> What is the developmental significance of the various kinds of learning?

Reflex Learning

Reflexive behavior, the most fundamental form of implicit learning, is present at birth. The **reflex** represents the cumulative result of ancestral learn-

> From birth to maturity, humans must adapt to increasingly demanding interactions between the environment and the organism. Progressively more complex and sophisticated learning processes occur in a developmentally-appropriate manner: (1) Reflex Learning; (2) Critical Period Learning; (3) One-trial Learning; (4) Classical Conditioning, (5) Operant Conditioning; and, (6) Social Learning

ing that has been genetically programmed into the organism. Reflexes (e.g., distress cries, nursing reflexes) ensure the organism's survival during early life, before it has had time to learn based on its own experience. Reflexes require minimal interaction with the environment and function to satisfy immediate basic needs (e.g., comfort, nurturance).

Critical Period Learning

Critical period learning is also the result of genetic programming but requires a beginning interaction with the environment. **Imprinting** and **bonding,** for instance, occur in response to specific stimulus cues in the environment (e.g., nurturing or "maternal" figures) that are essential to the continued survival of the organism (e.g., establishing protective social relationships). Critical period learning, however, is time limited; that is, the organism is most responsive and amenable to the stimulus for only a brief time.

One-Trial Learning

One-trial learning behaviors are also reflexive in their survival value but are increasingly dependent on direct experience and interaction with the environment. The strength or durability of learning depends on the intensity of the stimulus, the intensity of the subsequent biologic or emotional response, and the biological relevance to the organism's survival. Examples of more durable one-trial learning episodes include severe pain from touching a hot stove or becoming intensely nauseated after ingesting a particular substance.

Classical Conditioning

Classical conditioning, an implicit form of learning, reflects the ability of the organism to learn from increasingly complex interactions with the environment. It involves the association of two sequential events (A and B) such that one event (B) acquires the ability to elicit responses (R) formerly associated with the other event (A). For instance, Pavlov observed that presenting a dog with food (A) normally causes it to salivate (R). If a ringing bell (B) was repeatedly paired with the presentation of food (A), over time, the bell (B) would acquire the ability to cause salivation (R), even in the absence of food.

> After repeated trips to the hospital for chemotherapy (unconditioned stimulus, US), the side effects of which include nausea (unconditioned response, UR), a patient may begin to experience nausea (conditioned response, CR) as soon as the hospital (conditioned stimulus, CS) comes into view. Thus, through an associative learning process, the hospital acquires the ability to induce feelings of nausea.

Stimulus Generalization

Stimulus generalization is a process by which additional stimuli acquire the ability to elicit a specific conditioned response. Stimuli that share characteristics similar to the original conditioned stimulus are the most amenable to this conditioning process. Stimulus generalization explains why a long time smoker may find it difficult to stop when smoking behavior has been conditioned to an array of contextual cues, all of which can trigger the smoking response (e.g., coffee breaks, parties, specific locations).

Response generalization is a comparable process that explains why responses similar to the original response can be conditioned to the original stimulus. **Generalization** is adaptive in enabling the individual to build complex associative links, but it can become problematic. For example, if two individuals have many similar characteristics (e.g., are twins), others may become confused and make identical responses to both.

Survival ultimately requires the capacity for **stimulus discrimination,** the process of learning to respond differentially to stimuli that are similar but have significant, albeit subtle, differences. Stress tends to increase when responses are contingent upon making fine-grained distinctions between similar stimuli. This capacity is critical to physicians distinguishing between diseases that have similar symptoms, but require different treatments.

Operant Conditioning

Operant conditioning is an advanced form of learning that makes it possible for the individ-

ual to learn from the positive or negative consequences of interactions with the environment, thus becoming more effective in adapting to and coping with stressful challenges. The **Law of Effect** assumes that if a certain behavior is followed by positive consequences that behavior will increase over time. Conversely, if a certain behavior is followed by negative consequences, that behavior will decrease over time.

> A patient complains of pain and receives over-the-counter medication and affectionate attention from loved ones. Over time, the patient complains more frequently of increased pain. The pain reduction associated with taking medication and the attention received from family actually reinforces the pain complaints and increases their frequency. In addition, they can also increase the perceived intensity of the pain. The patient's physician orders "time contingent" medication doses and counsels the family to be judicious in their attention to the patient's needs. Why did the physician make that recommendation?

> How does reinforcement influence behavior?

> A reinforcer is any biological, behavioral, cognitive, sociocultural or environmental event that leads to an increase in behavior by reducing stress and restoring homeostasis (e.g., eating, resting, drinking, sex, financial achievement, power, authority, praise, fame, "luck").

Having a rewarding experience is **positively reinforcing,** while avoiding an unpleasant or punishing experience is **negatively reinforcing.** In both cases, the behavior is **reinforced** and therefore, will continue or increase over time. **Negative reinforcement** explains several aspects of human behavior, such as studying to *avoid* failing or obeying the speed limit to *avoid* getting a ticket. It also explains why many patients *avoid* or delay going to the doctor due to fears of experiencing pain (e.g., injections and blood draws), undergoing unpleasant examinations (e.g., prostate or pelvic examinations), hearing bad news (e.g., laboratory results suggestive of malignant cancer), or being faced with undertaking unpleasant treatment regimens (e.g., dietary changes, abstinence from alcohol, smoking cessation). Although the avoidance behavior leads to a temporary reduction in distress (negative reinforcement), the patient is at greater risk for more tertiary health problems that may require invasive procedures if certain medical conditions remain unmanaged.

Primary reinforcers maintain homeostasis and gratify basic survival needs such as food, water, and social relations. **Secondary reinforcers** acquire value through association with a primary need (e.g., money, attention, status, power). Reinforcement value can change in response to supply and demand. Thus, today's reinforcer may not be a reinforcer tomorrow. Reinforcers motivate behavior. If certain reinforcers are applied too liberally, the organism may become satiated and, thus, less responsive or motivated to obtain the reinforcer. In these cases, the behavior will decline.

Reinforcement and the Dopamine System

As incoming sensory information is processed by the brain, the dopamine neurotransmitter system enables the CNS to compare the reward value of new experiences with the reward value of stored memories. If the new experience is less rewarding than comparable past experience, then the new information is less likely to be retained and the new behavior less likely to be pursued. If the event is more rewarding, the association is likely to be strengthened, the memory added to future expectancies, and the behavior likely to be pursued.

The Premack Principle

What is the Premack Principle?

If an individual engages repeatedly in an activity, it is because it is desirable (reinforcing). Based on this observation, psychologist David Premack proposed that: *A highly valued or frequently performed behavior (reward) can be used as a reinforcer for a less valued or lower frequency behavior (target)*. A mother invokes this principle when she tells her 6-year-old, "If you pick up your toys, you can watch your favorite TV show".

Extinction is the decrease in or disappearance of conditioned responses when reinforcement ends. Extinction can be used as a treatment tool to reduce unhealthy behavior by eliminating or

limiting opportunities for reinforcers (e.g., posting "no smoking" signs in rest rooms). Occasionally, a behavior that has been extinguished will reappear for no apparent reason. A patient who has given up smoking suddenly experiences a craving and "lights up." This **spontaneous recovery** may take place without the individual's awareness, and occurs when the stimulus cues or reinforcers of a previously extinguished response are sufficiently strong to initiate the response and overcome the **extinction threshold** (the tendency to not respond). Spontaneous recovery is evidence that learning experiences are durable and conditioned associations are never completely "extinguished."

The manner in which reinforcement is delivered (**reinforcement schedule**) influences how quickly something is learned and how well it is retained. The **reinforcement schedule** can **be continuous** (rewarded each time) or **intermittent** (not rewarded each time). With **continuous reinforcement,** a behavior is acquired more rapidly, but will also extinguish quickly when the reward ceases. If a person is playing a slot machine and wins every time, the association, "if I pull the handle, then I will win" is learned quickly. As soon as the machine stops paying, however, the person stops playing, realizing that the previously learned association no longer applies. With **intermittent reinforcement,** a behavior is acquired gradually, but will extinguish more slowly. If the machine only pays off occasionally, the individual is more likely to persist in playing for some time, even though un-reinforced, because of uncertainty about how frequently the machine will pay off.

Schedules of Reinforcement

	Ratio	Interval
Fixed	Buy 5, get 1 free	Weekly paycheck
Variable	Choose a checkout line	Slot machine payoff

Social Learning

Social learning represents the further adaptation of human learning to environmental demands, especially the complexities of social relationships. In social learning, behavior is acquired in response to reinforcement from other people collectively or individually, depending on the nature of their role (e.g., status, authority), relationship (e.g., parent, spouse, child), or perceived similarity to the individual.

While much is learned through direct instruction, learning can also be **vicarious or observational.** For example, **imitation** of parents and significant others who **model** behavior, provides the child with social and coping skills. Reinforcement in these situations is usually secondary (e.g., money, a hug and kiss, social support, praise). Since **information is reinforcing,** an important element of social learning is evaluative **feedback** about how well the behaviors are being learned. Desired behaviors that are more complex often require **shaping**. Shaping is the process in which successive approximations (e.g., body orientation, eye contact, approach) of the goal behavior (e.g., initiating conversation) are reinforced. Degree of success helps determine the individual's sense of efficacy, and subsequent expectations about personal ability to cope and function well.

Clinical Applications

Since illness behaviors, emotional responses, and health-related beliefs are learned (i.e., conditioned to biologic stress response symptoms), clinical strategies using learning principles were developed to assist patients to unlearn maladaptive responses and learn more adaptive and healthy behaviors. Similarly, providers have become increasingly aware of contextual and environmental factors that influence illness, health care, and behavior change. An array of **behavior therapy (BT)** techniques have been shown to be especially effective in the treatment of many stress-induced disorders.

Conditioning therapy is based on classical conditioning principles (e.g., pairing a weaker stimulus with a stronger stimulus to elicit a desirable response). This technique has been applied in the treatment of cancer where certain chemotherapies have severely noxious delayed side effects. By repeatedly pairing the treatment with a pleasant odor (benign stimulus), the odor acquires the

ability to elicit the treatment effect but with fewer of the noxious side effects of the chemotherapy.

Aversive conditioning is conditioning a noxious stimulus to an undesired response, thereby leading to the extinction of the undesired response. This approach has been used in alcohol treatment programs by conditioning noxious substances (e.g., antabuse) to the drinking behavior.

Exposure therapy extinguishes conditioned fear reactions and avoidant responses. The patient is exposed to stimuli that trigger undesirable symptoms (e.g., anxiety), but under conditions that minimize reinforcement (e.g., sympathy) or maladaptive responses (e.g., avoidance). To control the intensity of the response, exposure therapies can be applied via imagery (i.e., imagining a stressful situation), virtual reality situations, or *in vivo* (i.e., real life/real time). The patient can be exposed gradually from minimal to more intense stimuli (systematic **desensitization)** or in a sin-

A diabetic patient refuses to test her own blood glucose levels because she is phobic about needles. These fears date to a traumatic childhood injury and a frightening visit to the emergency room. The patient is referred for "systematic desensitization," progressive exposure of the patient to the avoided object.

How Does Exposure Therapy Work?

It has been hypothecized that exposure, imaginal or real, triggers the stress response including the simultaneous release of adrenocorticotropic hormone (ACTH), which has excitatory effects, and beta endorphin (BE), which has analgesic and anxiolytic effects. The ACTH contributes to the "fight or flight" response to the "stressor" (needle) and, because it is antagonistic to BE, momentarily blockades BE receptor sites. Within minutes, however, the ACTH decays biochemically; the BE, which has a longer half-life, moves into the receptor sites, producing an anxiolytic effect.

Clinically, the patient reports an initial heightened arousal (stress hormones including ACTH), followed, in minutes, by a reduction in anxiety (due to BE). The patient has confronted the feared object, tolerated the stress, and been rewarded by biologically mediated anxiety reduction, which reinforces coping behavior and increases a sense of self-control.

gle "flooded" exposure **(immersion).** Systematic desensitization is usually associated with more positive and longer-lasting treatment outcomes in comparison to immersion techniques.

Contingency management is selectively manipulating the consequences of a behavior to

- increase desired behaviors (via positive reinforcement)
- decrease undesirable behaviors (via extinction)
- avoid undesirable consequences (via negative reinforcement).

Contingency management can be effective in the treatment of patients with chronic pain complaints without a physiologic basis. Reinforcers of pain-related complaining behavior (e.g., attention, financial compensation) are identified and eliminated or gradually reduced **(fading)** leading to the eventual extinction of this undesirable behavior. The approach can also be used to progressively develop desirable health behaviors through **shaping** (i.e., progressively reinforcing each advancement in a behavioral repertoire such as a physical therapy routine or a diet program).

Stimulus control involves the manipulation of anticipatory cues to guide behavior toward more rewarding consequences. If a child sees reminders to brush her teeth when entering the bathroom in the morning, this behavior is more likely to occur and can then be reinforced by the parent ("What sparkling teeth you have!").

In addition to rewarding desirable behavior, undesirable behavior can be extinguished by removing the opportunity for reinforcement **(time out),** or forfeiture of positive reinforcers **(response cost). Response cost** is frequently incorporated into **token economy** programs where children are rewarded with tokens for appropriate behaviors (e.g., a sticker for feeding the dog) and removal of these tokens for inappropriate behaviors (e.g., stickers taken away when the child acts destructively).

Feedback, based on the principle that information is reinforcing, involves communicating clearly to the patient information that enables **self-monitoring** and adaptive change. **Biofeedback,** utilizing electronic physiologic monitors, provides the patient with information about autonomic, neuroendocrine, and other biologic system responses to stress. Training in relaxation skills, for instance, can lead to a reduction in sympathetic nervous system activation. Direct feedback from physio-

logical indices regarding progress can be reinforcing, and thus will increase the likelihood that these skills will be utilized in the future. Maintaining **behavioral records** of eliciting events, symptom frequency, associated cognitions, behaviors, and outcomes (e.g., reinforcers) is the most useful and fundamental feedback technique. Health-related behaviors, such as diet, activity level, and substance abuse, are choices individuals make in response to a range of variables (e.g., situational demands, access to alternative choices, and reinforcing consequences). In order to make informed choices over adaptive behavioral changes that will maximize a sense of self-control, the patient must have continuing access to necessary information (feedback) to learn which factors are influencing their behavior, the reliability of these triggers, how they characteristically respond, and what the associated outcomes are.

What is cognitive-behavioral therapy?

Cognitive-Behavior Therapy (CBT) involves the application of behavior therapy techniques together with the recognition that the patient's cognition has a profound influence on how the patient interprets or defines a stressor condition, resulting illness, and the efficacy of prescribed treatments. Biological symptoms of the stress response are conditioned to the patient's cognition, as well as behavior, environmental events, and broader socioculture influences. Thus, cognitions, like behaviors, can be maladaptive, contributing to the disease-illness process. CBT strategies are developed to modify patients' maladaptive belief systems (cognitions) as well as their maladaptive behaviors. By restructuring cognitions, teaching more effective coping skills, and learning about the nature of the stress response, CBT interventions increase the patient's ability to more effec-

A 35-year-old man with no history of cardiac risk factors has visited the emergency room several times over the last six months with complaints of "strange sensations in my chest." He initially presents with elevated heart rate, sweating, dizziness, and shortness of breath. Cardiac function tests appear normal and these symptoms dissipate after an hour of monitoring in the hospital.

tively problem solve and adapt to stressor conditions and environmental changes.

Cognitive restructuring refers to the modification of the patient's perceived significance of bodily sensations, self-esteem, self-efficacy (coping effectiveness), nature and severity of illness, effectiveness of treatments, competence of health professionals, prognosis, and other perceptions that influence health and health care. In the above case example, this patient may be interpreting a twinge in his chest as a sign of an impending heart attack. A catastrophic belief such as this initiates the stress response, which, in turn, produces even more sympathetic nervous system activation. A cognitive restructuring intervention might therefore involve teaching the patient to challenge his initial catastrophic belief by considering supportive evidence (e.g., no personal or familial risk factors; previous cardiac testing has yielded normal findings), and developing alternative explanations (e.g., stress, heartburn).

Relaxation and breathing training refer to exercises designed to teach patients how to modulate key physical symptoms of the stress response (e.g., muscle tension, hyperventilation) that can contribute to or complicate illnesses. Relaxation training is often used in conjunction with biofeedback techniques. Through self-monitoring, the patient might learn that once he notices atypical chest sensations and interprets them as dangerous, he immediately starts hyperventilating. The patient could then learn to regulate his breathing under these circumstances and, in effect, offset the cycle of sympathetic nervous system arousal.

Interoceptive exposure refers to exercises that encourage the patient to gradually experience the bodily sensations of the stress response, induced under controlled conditions. *The primary goal of interoceptive exposures is to assist the patient to better understand the mechanisms that induce these stress-response symptoms, improve tolerance, and learn how to control them.* The patient in our case example may be instructed to hyperventilate, climb stairs, and spin on a chair repeatedly to induce feared sensations and notice how they gradually dissipate without having to seek medical attention or reassurance.

Imaginal exposure refers to exercises that encourage the patient to recall stressful events or conditions, thereby generating (cognitively induced) stress response symptoms. The goal, as in all exposure exercises, is to enable the patient to better understand the stress response mechanisms that produce the symptoms and thereby increase tolerance and control of them. Gradual and repeated exposures to these scenarios in imagination will eventually lead to associated reductions in the fear response when thinking about or actually participating in a feared behavior (flying in a plane, riding a horse, giving a recital).

In vivo **exposure** refers to exercises carried out in real time/real life situations with the same goals in mind – to assist the patient in better understanding the stressor-stress response mechanism to increase tolerance and control. For example, the patient may have started to avoid driving his car on busy streets due to fears of having a heart attack and losing control of the vehicle. *In vivo* exposure exercises would involve having him drive in progressively more dense traffic situations on busier roadways. Teaching individuals to approach previously avoided situations is a powerful learning experience as, in many cases, individuals are provided with corrective information (i.e., the feared event or consequence does not happen).

Recent technological advances have begun exploring the delivery of *in vivo* exposure through the use of **virtual reality** simulations. Experimental studies suggest that this approach can be especially effective as an intermediary treatment step between imaginal and *in vivo* exposure approaches.

The efficacy of CBT is directly dependent on:

1. Accurate identification of the target behavior or cognition to be learned or unlearned;
2. A behavioral analysis of stimulus and reinforcing conditions that perpetuate or inhibit the behavior or cognition;
3. An assessment of the changes in schedules of reinforcement that are realistic and will be effective in the given situation; and,
4. A final treatment plan for modifying the behavior or cognition.

Motivational Interviewing

Developed by William Miller as a strategy for motivating behavioral change in problem drinkers, **Motivational Interviewing** (MI) is a directive client-centered intervention designed to help patients explore and resolve their ambivalence about behavior change. It is based upon five basic principles: (1) *accurate empathy* (understanding the patient's viewpoint and communicating that to the patient); (2) *expressing respect* for, and acceptance and affirmation of the patient and his/her issues; (3) *eliciting and selectively reinforcing* the patient's problem recognition, desire to change, and self-efficacy; (4) monitoring the patient's readiness to change and "rolling with the resistance" until the patient resolves it and is ready to change; and (5) *affirming the patient's control* of decision making and behavior change.

While Miller is not explicit about the theoretical basis of MI, discerning practitioners recognize the clinical application of a melding of behavioral science principles from research on communication and attitude change in social and cognitive psychology with the more familiar learning principles of cognitive behavioral therapies. The approach has proven to be especially efficacious in the treatment of those leading causes of mortality in which patient behavior is a principle contributing factor (see Chapter 37, Changing Risk Behavior).

Efficacy of Cognitive-Behavioral Treatments

The Institute of Medicine reports more than three decades of mounting empirical evidence of the effectiveness of Cognitive-Behavioral and other psychological treatments for medical and psychiatric disorders (Cuff & Vanselow, 2004; see Recommended Reading). The application of these treatments has given rise to the fields of Health Psychology, Behavioral Medicine, and associated disciplines. Increasingly, health care practitioners recognize the effectiveness of combined biomedical and behavioral treatments to ensure effective intervention, follow-up, and prevention.

Recommended Reading

Beatty J. *The Human Brain: Essentials of Behavioral Neuroscience*. Thousand Oaks, CA: Sage Publications; 2001.

Carr JE. Neuroendocrine and behavioral interaction in exposure treatment of phobic avoidance. *Clinical Psychology Review* 1996; 16:1–15.

Cuff PA, Vanselow NA (Eds.). *Improving Medical Education: Enhancing the Behavioral and Social Sciences in Medical School Curricula*. Washington, DC: National Academies Press; 2004.

Lieberman DA. *Learning: Behavior and Cognition*. Belmont, CA: Wadsworth-Thompson Learning; 2000.

Kandel ER, Schwartz JH, Jessell TM. *Principles of Neural Science*. (4th ed.). New York: McGraw-Hill; 2000.

Kandel ER. *In Search of Memory: The Emergence of a New Science of Mind*. New York: WW Norton; 2006.

Review Questions

1. The acquisition of associations between diverse stimuli and events that vary in time and space requires conscious participation, and can occur over a period of time is called
    A. conditioning
    B. explicit learning
    C. implicit learning
    D. operant learning
    E. social learning

2. Which brain structure serves as a central switch board and assigns temporal and spatial context to incoming sensory information?
    A. Amygdala
    B. Hippocampus
    C. Limbic system
    D. Neocortex
    E. Thalamus

3. After repeated trips to the hospital for chemotherapy, the side effects of which include nausea, a cancer patient begins to experience nausea as soon as the hospital comes into view. The patient is manifesting the effects of
    A. imprinting
    B. reflux
    C. response generalization
    D. social reinforcement
    E. stimulus generalization

4. An elderly patient refuses to go to the doctor for his routine checkup because he "always gets bad news." This kind of reinforcement is called
   A. continuous
   B. intermittent
   C. negative
   D. positive
   E. primary

5. The neurotransmitter system that appears to be most involved in the reinforcement of new experiences is
   A. dopamine
   B. epinephrine
   C. glutamate
   D. norepinephrine
   E. serotonin

6. Most human health-related behaviors are reinforced under which of the following schedules
   A. Continuous
   B. Fixed interval
   C. Fixed ratio
   D. Variable interval
   E. Variable ratio

7. A CBT technique that includes in its objectives encouraging the patient to gradually experience bodily sensations of the stress response under controlled conditions is
   A. imaginal exposure
   B. interoceptive exposure
   C. *in vivo* exposure
   D. virtual reality exposure
   E. all of the above

Key to review questions: p. 393

9 Cognition and Emotion

- What is cognition and what processes does it include?
- What evidence suggests that language is biologically determined by the structure and function of the brain?
- What is the relationship between arousal, cognition, and emotion?

Stress triggers adaptive cognitive responses as the individual attempts to problem solve and resolve the challenge to homeostasis. **Cognition** is an extension of the learning process. The brain identifies and records not only sensory information but also commonalties among stimuli (concepts), and sequences of operations or behaviors (schemas) as a means of organizing information. The storage of this information involves memory.

Cognition

What is cognition and what processes does it include?

Cognition is the set of processes by which information is acquired through sensation and learning, is analyzed, forwarded to appropriate cortical centers, organized and stored in memory for future retrieval, and used in problem solving. Cognitive processes include

– **consciousness**	**(system arousal)**
– **alertness**	**(system arousa)l**
– **attention**	**(system arousal)**
– **memory**	**(info storage)**
– **concept formation**	**(info organization)**
– **perception**	**(utilization)**
– **thinking**	**(utilization)**
– **intelligence**	**(utilization)**
– **language**	**(utilization)**

Consciousness, Alertness, Attention

Consciousness is the state of being "powered up." Activation of the CNS results in awareness of self and the environment.

Alertness is the level of awareness or responsivity to the environment. Typically, maximal alertness occurs at times of stress or challenge.

Attention is the ability to focus selectively on relevant stimuli and is characterized by intensity, selectivity, and voluntary control. **Intensity** refers to the level of arousal. **Selectivity** is the ability to attend to the most immediate and relevant stimuli (e.g., threatening, painful, rewarding), while screening out irrelevant or unimportant stimuli. **Voluntary control** is the ability to direct or focus attention. **Concentration** is the ability to sustain focused effort on a task.

Memory

Memory is the reception, retention, storage and retrieval of information. There are two general types of memory that, like the two types of learning, are defined in terms of their neural operations.

(1) Implicit Memory: Sensory memory is the storage of incoming sensory information. Information of low interest may be retained for a few minutes in **short-term memory** areas such as the prefrontal cortex. **Procedural memory** is acquisition and retrieval of motor sequences (tying shoe laces) and cognitive sequences (organizing a schedule).

(2) Explicit Memory: More stimulating, challenging, or critical information or complex associations are transmitted via the hippocampus to cortical areas for storage as **long-term memory.**

Consolidation of long-term memory is the time required for memory to become sufficiently permanent that it cannot be erased or altered by pharmacologic or electrical interventions. In humans, **consolidation** that is resistant to pharmacologic erasure may take only a few hours. Electroconvulsive therapy (ECT) may produce temporary loss of both **anterograde** and **retrograde** memory, but memory loss is usually restricted to hours or days. Semantic and episodic memory are sometimes referred to as declarative memory. **Semantic memory** is retention and retrieval of abstract information (e.g., concepts, theories, formulae) or events and their time sequences (e.g., the landing of humans on the moon). **Episodic or personal memory** involves the retention and retrieval of recollections of personal experiences.

Implicit Memory

Sensory – incoming information
Short-term – immediate, short retention
Procedural – basic sequences

Explicit Memory

Long-term – challenging, complex
Semantic – concepts, schemas
Episodic – personal experience

Amnesia

People with amnesia can acquire and retrieve information regarding motor and cognitive sequences (i.e., procedural memory is intact), but they do not know they have such information because declarative memory is impaired. This suggests that there are different mechanisms for different types of long-term memory.

The amnestic syndrome results from conditions that disrupt communication between the hippocampus, fornix, septum, mamillary bodies, and thalamus (e.g., thiamine deficiency, head injury, and encephalopathy).

Concept Formation

The brain records basic stimulus-response associative links enabling the individual to "perceive" relations between events. Because the number of associations the individual can experience is virtually limitless, the brain identifies and records commonalties among classes of stimuli (e.g., objects, places, events) and sorts them into categories **(concepts)** that share the same features. Conceptualizations of operations (e.g., how to bake a cake, conduct a war, repair a motor) are called **schemas**. Concepts and schemas are learned as the individual attempts to adapt to life challenges. As new challenges are experienced, these new events are compared to the memory of past experiences through **hypothesis testing.** If the hypothesis is confirmed, it is retained. If disconfirmed, it is discarded, changed, or disconfirming evidence ignored (see Defense Mechanisms below).

Types of Memory and Associated Brain Structures

Procedural	Cerebellum
Evaluative	Amygdala
Episodic/Contexual	Hippocampus
Features	Neocortex
Semantrics (concepts)	Neocortex

Concept formation is a highly advanced form of learning process and is essential for human survival. It enables vast quantities of highly complex information, diverse in time and context, to be processed and categorized. It is essential for such activities as abstract thinking, complex problem solving, and predicting and controlling future outcomes.

Personal Memory

– Rare before age 2, linked to maturation of hippocampus.
– No clear evidence personal memory exists before this.
– Thus, efforts to "uncover hidden memories" can lead to creating false memories.

Thinking refers to the application of stored information, concepts, schemas and strategies to solve problems and assess experiences.

Intelligence

Intelligence is not a cognitive process per se but rather refers to the individual's *capacity to learn from and adapt to new experiences* and is determined by both heredity and experience. It is usually defined in terms of **verbal ability** and **problem-solving** skills, but cultural definitions vary. In Western cultures, speed of processing information is valued. In other cultures, cautious introspection may be more highly valued. All cultures make some reference to social judgment or "social appropriateness" as a measure of intelligence, but differ widely with regard to specific behaviors.

> It is generally agreed that there are no significant differences in intelligence across populations distinguished by race, ethnicity, or culture. Studies that claim to identify such differences have been faulted on the basis of linguistic, ethnic, and cultural bias of the measuring instruments.

Intelligence usually reflects **convergent thinking** (i.e., the individual responds with typical solutions to a problem). This is in contrast to **divergent thinking** (i.e., the individual responds with alternative solutions to a problem). Divergent thinking is more **creative** (i.e., events are perceived in unusual ways that generate novel solutions to problems). Creativity appears to be determined by unique learning experiences or associative links.

Perception

Perception is the cognitive process of interpreting and assigning meaning to new incoming sensory information based upon the concepts and schemas developed from past experience. As experience accumulate, perception develops throughout childhood. This early learning prompts neurogenesis, and grey matter increases in the frontal lobes up to around age 11–12. With continuing experience and trial and error learning, the brain begins to "prune" incorrect or maladaptive information. Correct and adaptive stored information is reinforced and progressively insulated within a myelin sheath. Thus, a complex integrated cognitive structure, capable of mature perception and judg-

> **Memory, Coping, and Stress**
>
> Neurogenesis and learning are promoted by moderate levels of acute stress and challenge, but are impaired by chronic and severe stress due to increased glucocorticoid in the blood stream, which
> - stimulates amygdala functions and
> - impairs hippocampus functions, which
> - impairs explicit learning/memory and thereby
> - impairs adaptive response to stress, which
> - results in futility, learned helplessness, and depression (see Chapter 42).

ment, becomes available only in late adolescence or early adulthood.

Language

The ability of humans to communicate was the result of a remarkable evolutionary change in brain structure that appears to have occurred over 100,000 years ago. A mutation of the FoxP2 gene enabled the brain to learn, remember and conceptualize auditory representations of experience. Thus, while the first human communications were gestural responses to visual events, in time, gestures and events became associated with specific sounds, that acquired specific situational or object meaning. This association between observed events, gestures, and vocal expression suggests that the biologic basis for language occurred when neural connections between visual association areas, auditory association areas, and speech production areas were established.

There is debate about whether the genetic change leading to language occurred at about the same time and perhaps facilitated the "out of Africa" migration of *homo erectus*. This hypothesis suggests that increased ability to communicate enabled proto humans to plan and coordinate more complex group actions.

> What evidence suggests that language is biologically determined by the structure and function of the brain?

All human languages are composed of the same basic structural elements:

Phonemes: basic sound units

Morphemes: basic meaning units (the smallest number of sounds that will produce a meaning)

Syntax: rules for combining words into phrases and sentences (grammar)

Semantics: meaning associated with words and sentences

Prosody: vocal intonation that modifies the meaning of words and sentences

The universality of language structure suggests that language is biologically determined by the structure and function of the brain. By 3–6 months of age, there is evidence of a biological readiness to develop language. This readiness includes an inherent mechanism for imposing language structure on whatever language the child learns.

Because language is a byproduct of human interaction with the environment, language structure is influenced by the **ecology** in which it develops, and in turn influences **perception** of the environment. For example, the multiple specific words used by Alaska Natives to describe ice and snow would be incomprehensible to Bedouins. In contrast, because trade languages evolve to facilitate communication and understanding among peoples from widely varying cultures, they tend to be more general and have less ecological specificity.

Cognitive Style

Cognitive style is the individual's unique manner in which a new experience is perceived, interpreted and organized, ultimately producing a predictable **coping response.** One cognitive style is **locus of control** (generalized expectations about whether rewards are brought about through one's own efforts [internal], or are due to factors outside one's control [external]). Individuals with an internal locus of control believe they exert significant self-control over themselves and their environment. Other cognitive styles include **learned helplessness** (a self-defeating cognitive style), **hardiness** or **resiliency** (a sense of "toughness" in which stress is viewed as a challenge rather than as a threat), **self-efficacy** (the individual's level of confidence about successfully coping with a challenging situation), and the **Type A personality,** characterized by excessive competitiveness, impatience, time urgency, and hostility that has been linked to high rates of coronary artery disease.

Defense Mechanisms

The concept of **defense mechanism** was derived from psychoanalytic theory and refers to cognitive processes that influence the various ways individuals perceive, interpret, assign meaning to and respond to situations and events that challenge cognitive, psychologic, or biologic homeostasis. Among the more common defense mechanisms are:

Denial: incoming information that is threatening or contradictory to stored memory is perceived, evaluated, and rejected.

Repression: a more extreme cognitive refutation than denial by which perceptions of events that are threatening or contradictory to past experiences are neither recognized nor recorded.

Intellectualization: an event or memory is reconceptualized in sufficiently abstract terms to "distance" it from its original referent and associated conditioned emotional responses.

Projection: an idea, feeling, or behavior, viewed as inconsistent with one's self-concept, is attributed to another person.

Regression: stress is responded to using developmentally earlier cognitive processes associated with periods of less stressful coping.

These cognitive processes may lead to **cognitive distortions,** erroneous or maladaptive interpretations of experience. These can include **catastrophizing** (magnifying consequences into disastrous proportions), **overgeneralizing** (sweeping conclusions based on a single example), **personalization** (making oneself the cause of other people's actions), **mind reading** (making assumptions about others' motives without evidence), and **unsubstantiated expectations** of others' behaviors and motives without basis in fact.

Clinical Applications

Commonly used cognitive therapy (CT) interventions incorporated into Cognitive-Behavioral treatments (CBT) include:

Problem Solving: developing skills for resolving stressful situations and enhancing self-esteem. The five major steps of problem solving include (1) identifying the problem, (2) generating possible solutions, (3) choosing plausible solutions, (4) implementing solutions, and (5) evaluating the outcome.

Self-control Contracting: identification of goals with rewards or reinforcing consequences for the attainment of each goal.

Cognitive Restructuring: Replacing maladaptive cognitions with more adaptive cognitions that are then reinforced.

Cognitive Rehearsal: Rehearsal of anxiety inducing situations to practice new skills, accommodate to anxiety, and restructure cognitive responses (self statements, strategies).

Emotion

Emotion, feeling, and affect describe *a complex subjective state resulting from the interaction of physiologic, cognitive, environmental, sociocultural, and behavioral responses to stress.* A specific emotional state begins with a condition of physiologic **arousal** in response to any stressor that disturbs homeostasis. Regardless of the source of the stress, the **limbic system** consolidates the incoming sensory information, refers it to the association areas of the cortex for evaluation and formulation of an action plan, and then activates the hypothalamus and autonomic nervous system to carry out the response.

> The limbic system is the source of arousal, the "powering up" of the organism's emotional as well as coping response to any challenge.

Initial emotions in the newborn are genetically programmed expressions of distress designed to generate caregiving behaviors in parents. The most basic emotion is pleasure-displeasure, which differentiates into other primary emotions (e.g., joy, sadness, fear, anger, interest, surprise, disgust). Certain emotions appear to be universal, suggesting a survival value, and may be biologically determined.

> What is the relationship between arousal, cognition, and emotion?

An **emotion** begins with a state of physiological **arousal** occurring in a specific **situational context** that is assigned meaning based on an individual's **cognitive interpretations** derived from **past experiences.** The defining emotional label for a specific arousal state and the appropriate behavioral response will vary as a function of the particular defining context even though various states of arousal may be indistinguishable physiologically. For example, arousal in the context of the death of a loved one would be defined differently from arousal in the context of winning the lottery, although the physiologic manifestations of these two states may be quite similar.

The meaning of emotions is **culturally influenced** (See Chapter 17, Culture and Ethnicity) and expression is governed by **display rules** that define when, where, and how emotions are shown. Some emotions, like shame and guilt, develop in response to social interaction between the individual and others, especially family and culture. **Guilt** refers to feelings about behaviors or thoughts that have harmed others; **shame** refers to a feeling of personal inadequacy, defectiveness, or failure.

Gender and Emotion

Males and females use the same emotional expressions, report similar emotional experiences, and use similar emotional language to describe their experiences. Both genders are equal in their expression of love or anger, happiness or sadness, and confidence or anxiety. When challenged, men are more likely to show anger towards others, especially males, and to be aggressive. This expression of anger-aggression is associated with the release of testosterone during the male stress response. It is also a common display rule for males in many cultures, suggesting an *evolutionary interaction between heredity and sociocultural sanction.*

Women are more likely than men to express fear and sadness especially within the context of interpersonal relationships (e.g., family and friends).

Both genders tend to accept the stereotype that men conceal their feelings more than women. However, women can be equally as inhibited as men with regard to emotional expression, and men can be equally as emotional as women.

> Gender role stereotypes for emotional expression reflect long-standing sociocultural influences on how and to whom specific emotions are expressed.

Recommended Reading

Beatty J. *The Human Brain: Essentials of Behavioral Neuroscience.* Thousand Oaks, CA: Sage Publications; 2001.

Elfenbein HA, Ambody N. On the universality and cultural specificity of emotion recognition: A meta-analysis. *Psychological Bulletin* 2002; 128:203–235.

Kandel ER, Schwartz JH, Jessell TM. *Principles of Neural Science.* (4th ed.). New York: McGraw-Hill; 2000.

Wade N. Early voices: The leap to language. *New York Times (Science Times)*, July 15, 2004, D1 and D4.

Review Questions

1. The retention and retrieval of abstract information involves what kind of memory?
   A. Declarative
   B. Episodic
   C. Procedural
   D. Semantic
   E. Sensory

2. People with amnesia acquire and retrieve information regarding motor and cognitive sequences but do not know they have such information because of impaired
   A. consolidated memory
   B. declarative memory
   C. procedural memory
   D. sensory memory
   E. short-term memory

3. The cognitive representation of an operation (e.g., how to apply for a job) is called a(n)
   A. cognitive style
   B. concept
   C. hypothesis
   D. problem solution
   E. schema

4. The labeling of an emotion requires which of the following combinations?
   A. Arousal, situational context, cognitive interpretation
   B. Situational context, concept formation, operational schema
   C. Situational context, cultural norms, social sanctions
   D. Stimulus, response, reinforcement
   E. Stress, arousal, stress response

5. Which of the following statements about gender and emotion are true?
   A. Males and females use the same emotional expressions
   B. Males and females use similar emotional language to describe their experiences
   C. Males and females are equal in their expression of love or anger, happiness or sadness, confidence or anxiety
   D. Males are more likely than females to show anger toward others, especially males, when challenged
   E. All of the above

Key to review questions: p. 393

Section IV

Development Through the Life Cycle

10 Pregnancy and Infancy

- What effects do maternal health and lifestyle have on the developing fetus?
- What does the Apgar Score assess?
- How do growth parameters change during infancy?
- What changes in motor skill and response to stimuli occur during infancy?
- What is object permanence?
- What is the difference between bonding and attachment?

Developmental change takes place throughout the entire life cycle and is punctuated by **stages** and intervening **transition periods.** Stage-appropriate expectations, or **developmental milestones,** have been identified to serve as guidelines for assessing a person's developmental stage. Culture, heredity, environment, and physical and mental abilities influence not only when but also which behaviors and skills are learned.

Prenatal – Perinatal Period

The mature human fetus is delivered between 38 and 42 weeks of gestational age. **Premature or preterm** and **postmature or postterm** refer to births occurring before or after this period of normal gestation. Average birthweight (ABW) is about 3,500 gm (7 1/2 lb). Low birthweight refers to less than 2,500 gm (5 1/2 lb); very low birthweight refers to less than 1,500 gm (3 1/2 lb); extremely low birthweight consistent with gestational age refers to less than 1,000 gm (2 1/2 lb). Because they have had less time to grow in utero, most premature infants have low birthweight. Although the prematurity rate in the U.S. continues to be about 10% of live births, survival at 23–25 weeks gestational age is common; the survival rate at 28 weeks is about 90%. Advances in care during the **perinatal** (surrounding birth) and **neonatal** (first 30 days of life) periods have dramatically reduced the neonatal mortality rate for preterm infants.

Preterm infants are at risk for **neurodevelopmental and neurobehavioral disorders.** These disorders are due to the interruption of normal fetal developmental processes caused by preterm delivery or specific complications (e.g., hypoxia, ischemia, intracranial hemorrhage, infection) associated with prematurity.

Major adverse outcomes include cerebral palsy, mental retardation, and sensory deficits that usually are apparent in the first two to three years of life.

Minor adverse outcomes can include borderline intelligence, language and learning disabilities, fine motor dysfunction, perceptual problems, social and emotional immaturity, and attention deficit disorders.

The smaller and more vulnerable the infant, the more likely it is that some of these difficulties will become manifest. Also, if the home environment is compromised by poverty, inadequate parenting, or maltreatment, the risks of impaired development, behavior, and school function are increased further.

Genetic or chromosomal bases for intrinsic deviations in brain and central nervous system development during early gestation account for more chronic childhood disability than all of the acquired extrinsic brain insults combined. These disorders include cerebral palsy, mental retardation, autism, and developmental language disorders.

Maternal Disease or Infection

What effects do maternal health and lifestyle have on the developing fetus?

Maternal diabetes mellitus (particularly the insulin-dependent or Type I form) increases the likelihood of both major congenital malformations (e.g., sacral agenesis, spina bifida, congenital heart disease, cleft lip/palate) and impaired neurodevelopmental performance. These complications can be minimized by optimizing maternal diabetic control throughout pregnancy.

Persistent **maternal hypertension** can produce progressive uteroplacental insufficiency, leading to **intrauterine growth retardation** (IUGR) and asphyxia resulting in neurodevelopmental impairment. Certain chronic maternal illnesses, such as **systemic inflammatory conditions,** also can impair fetal well-being. Elevated serum phenylalanine levels in the mother who has **phenylketonuria** can disrupt fetal brain development, producing a permanent encephalopathy, even if the fetus itself does not have the disorder.

Several **maternal infections,** including some which are asymptomatic, have a deleterious effect on the fetus. **Cytomegalovirus (CMV)** infection is caused by a neurotropic DNA herpesvirus that frequently produces only a mild respiratory illness in the mother. However, in 40% of cases of primary maternal CMV infection during pregnancy, the fetus becomes infected and has a 10–20% chance of sensorineural hearing impairment and delayed development. About 5% of infected infants are more severely affected. The severe form of CMV can be fatal.

Neonatal herpes simplex virus (HSV) infection can result from transmission of maternal infection to the fetus during delivery through the birth canal. Pregnancies complicated by primary genital herpes are at increased risk of spontaneous abortion, preterm birth, and IUGR. Neonates infected with herpes simplex virus can develop disseminated disease involving many organs, (liver and lung predominantly), localized CNS disease, or disease located to skin, eyes, and mouth. A neonate infected with HSV is rarely, if ever asymptomatic.

Maternal human immunodeficiency virus (HIV) infection can be transmitted to the fetus either through the placenta or through breast feeding producing health, growth, and neurodevelop-

mental disorders, or even death. **Pediatric AIDS** remains one of the leading causes of death among children 2–5 years of age in many large urban areas.

Maternal Ingestions

Maternal ingestion of alcohol during pregnancy may be responsible for more neurodevelopmental and neurobehavioral dysfunction among children than any other single, identifiable cause. **Fetal alcohol syndrome (FAS)** affects approximately one in 750 live births in the U.S. Diagnostic features of FAS include facial dysmorphology, organ malformations, growth retardation, and intellectual impairment. The incomplete syndrome, **fetal alcohol effects (FAE),** includes language delay, socioemotional incompetence, learning disabilities, and attention deficit disorder. Individual differences in maternal/fetal susceptibility to the effects of alcohol clearly exist; no absolutely safe maternal dose has been determined.

Maternal tobacco consumption can result in fetal growth retardation. The amount of exposure to tobacco during fetal life is positively correlated with decreases in birthweight in a dose-response manner. Fetal brain growth, as measured by fetal head circumference, is adversely affected by heavy maternal smoking.

Certain **controlled substances** such as opiates, cocaine, methamphetamine, and marijuana produce varying combinations of neonatal symptomatology and long-term developmental or behavioral dysfunction. Opiates such as heroin and methadone can cause **neonatal addiction.** Withdrawal symptoms such as jitteriness and irritability are referred to as the **neonatal abstinence syndrome.** Maternal use of **cocaine** usually does not produce an acute withdrawal syndrome in the newborn. The neurobehavioral problems and academic and social difficulties experienced by the children of cocaine-addicted mothers may be the result of subtle neurophysiologic changes in the child, the typically impoverished and socially disruptive environment in which the child is raised or both.

Maternal use of certain **prescribed medications,** such as commonly used anticonvulsants (e.g., hydantoin, valproic acid, carbamazepine, trimethadione), have been linked to isolated birth defects or specific malformation syndromes.

Individual susceptibility to these agents varies. Psychotropic medications (e.g., lithium), antineoplastic agents (e.g., methotrexate), and dermatologic medications (e.g., retinoic acid) are associated with combinations of birth defects.

Birth Complications

Fetal distress from **asphyxia** can result from uteroplacental insufficiency, umbilical cord compression, and placental abruption. The asphyxia syndrome includes components of hypoxia, ischemia, hypotension, and impaired perfusion of multiple organs, particularly the brain. If brain damage occurs before the infant is delivered and adequately resuscitated, any of a wide range of neurodevelopmental disabilities such as cerebral palsy, mental retardation, epilepsy, and learning and behavioral problems can occur.

Trauma at birth can be the result of malpresentation (e.g., breech, transverse lie), an exceptionally large infant (e.g., infant of a diabetic mother), or poor descent requiring assisted delivery with instrumentation. Sequelae include intracranial contusion or hemorrhage, fractures, spinal cord injury, and peripheral nerve damage such as a brachial plexus traction injury known as an Erb's palsy.

After birth, an extremely common complication is **hyperbilirubinemia** or jaundice. Jaundice is yellowish discoloration of the skin caused by excessive bilirubin (hyperbilirubinemia) in the bloodstream and is easily treated by natural light or phototherapy if detected early enough. In the typical newborn delivered at term, the enzyme glucuronyltransferase develops by day 5 of life and begins, at that time, to break down bilirubin. At that point, bilirubin can be removed from the bloodstream naturally. When an infant is born early, the infant spends a large number of days without glucuronyltransferase. During that time, bilirubin accumulates. If levels in the bloodstream reach a critical level, kernicterus can result. **Kernicterus** is bilirubin toxicity affecting the basal ganglia and brainstem, parts of the brain responsible for balance and motor coordination. Damage from kernicterus is permanent and can be manifested by a choreoathetoid movement disorder and gaze and auditory abnormalities.

Assessment of the Newborn

What does the Apgar Score assess?

The **Apgar Score,** a numerical rating of the adequacy of neurophysiologic transition in the newborn infant, is the standard method of postdelivery assessment. Its principal utility is assessment of current status, which serves as an indicator of the potential need for neonatal resuscitation. The score is typically assigned and recorded at one and five minutes of life; the score can also be determined at 10, 15, or 20 minutes of life, if there are problems in newborn adaptation. One-minute scores of 8–10 indicate no CNS depression; 5–7 indicate some depression; and 0–4 indicate severe depression that may require resusitation.

The **Dubowitz** and **Ballard neonatal examinations** are used to estimate gestational age (time since conception) and determine the adequacy of intrauterine growth. These examinations are particularly useful when the length of the pregnancy is uncertain and are as helpful as birthweight in assessing for potential problems.

The **Brazelton Neonatal Behavioral Assessment Scale** provides a neurobehavioral assessment of such characteristics as visual attention, alertness, auditory responsivity, and habitation. The scale can be administered serially to provide an objective measure of change over time; it also can be used to investigate relationships between newborn characteristics and later behavioral outcomes.

The Apgar Score

Sign	Score		
	0	1 point	2 points
Heart rate	None	< 100	>100
Respiratory effort	None	Weak	Cry
Muscle tone	Flaccid	Some flexion	Well flexed
Reflex irritability	No response	Grimace	Cough
Color	Blue, pale	Trunk pink, extremities blue	Pink

Infancy (Birth to 12 months)

Infancy is marked by rapid growth and development. Whereas a newborn infant weighs 3.5 kg and spends virtually the entire day sleeping, crying, taking in food, and eliminating waste, the 12-month-old child weighs 10 kg, has a distinct personality, can crawl or walk, feed himself, and communicate with gestures and a few words. Infant development is influenced by biologic and environmental factors. Biologic factors include genetic make-up, temperament, and state of health. Significant environmental factors affecting the infant are the child's parents and their attitudes, and the culture and socioeconomic status of the family.

How do growth parameters change during infancy?

Birthweight is doubled by 4–5 months of age and tripled by 12 months. The infant's **length** grows 25 cm during the first year of life. The **head** grows 6 cm during the first 3 months and an additional 6 cm over the next 9 months. The volume of the newborn infant's **brain** is about 25% of adult volume; by 12 months, it is about 75% of adult volume. **Physiologic changes** that occur during infancy include improvement in respiratory pattern, coordination of sucking and swallowing, and temperature control. Changes in the **respiratory pattern** include a gradual decline in respiratory rate from 30–50 breaths per minute at birth to 25–35 breaths per minute at 12 months. By 12 months of age, the infant has progressed from taking only liquid food to being able to personally put solid food into the mouth, and then chew and swallow it without difficulty. **Temperature regulation** is established during the first few days of life so that the infant is able to maintain a core temperature of 37°C under normal ambient conditions.

What changes in motor skill and response to stimuli occur during infancy?

Gross motor skills rely on large muscles active in posture and locomotion, i.e., sitting, walking, running. Infants progress from having no independent means of locomotion to walking from place to place. **Visual-motor or fine motor skills** refer to hand manipulative abilities and eye-hand coordination. The infant progresses from being a

From Reflex to Learned Intentional Action

The infant is born with involuntary nuturance-seeking reflexes that are critical for early survival. These reflexes, mediated by the brainstem and elicited by specific stimuli, include the Moro or startle reflex (when startled, the infant's arms are thrown outward and the neck extends), rooting or nursing reflex (when stroked on the cheek, the head turns in that direction), and palmar grasp (when the palm is stroked, the infant grasps).

During the first year, reflexes fade and are replaced by learned intentional actions. During learning, synaptic links are formed in response to experience and strengthened by repeated stimulation (synaptogenesis).

Synapses that are not stimulated wither through a process called pruning. Synaptogenesis and pruning underlie the learning of adaptive skills and the extinction of maladaptive skills.

newborn with clenched hands to a 12-month-old capable of picking up small objects between the tips of the index finger and thumb and putting these objects into the mouth. At birth, an infant has **visual perception** and the eyes will briefly follow a moving object. At 1 month, the infant tracks an object to midline; at 2 months, the infant tracks past midline. At 3–6 months, coordination of the extraocular muscles permits binocular vision; at 6–8 months, there is evidence of depth perception.

At birth, an infant can **hear** and will be alert to sounds. At 3 months, the infant turns to the side of the sound, then at 4 months, the eyes will look toward the sound as the head turns. At 5–6 months, the head is turned to one side and then upwards, if the sound is made above the ear. Shortly afterward the infant will look upwards if the sound is made above the ear. At 8–10 months, the infant will turn diagonally and directly to the sound, and at 12 months, the child's ability to localize a sound source approaches that of an adult.

Cognitive Development

Piaget postulated four stages of cognitive development by observing what children do and how they do it. The first, or **sensorimotor stage,** occurs from birth to 18 months of age. Piaget suggested that at this stage the intelligence of the infant is manifested by actions. Because an infant cannot take a typical intelligence test, his level of intelligence can only be inferred by observation. Thus, the child's cognitive status at this age is associated with exploratory behaviors and interactions with the envi -ronment. During the first several months, major change occurs as the infant's behavior develops from reflexive responses to learned intentional activities such as reaching.

What is object permanence?

At about 7–9 months of age, the child develops **object permanence.** Prior to this time, the very young infant will not seek a desired object unless it is in view. That is, if an object cannot be seen, it does not exist.

> As the hippocampus, which coordinates memory storage, becomes fully functional, the infant is able to form explicit memories of people and objects.

When object permanence develops, the child has learned that objects still exist even when they are not visible. If the object is hidden while the infant observes, the infant will search for it even though it is not in sight.

Psychosocial Development

What is the difference between bonding and attachment?

Bonding and **attachment** describe the affectional relationships that develop between primary caregivers (usually, the parents) and infants. **Bonding** begins immediately or shortly after birth and reflects the feeling of the parents toward the newborn. **Attachment** involves reciprocal feelings between parent and infant and develops gradually over the first year. The infant is an active participant in the development of attachment.

By 10 days of age, infants can distinguish the smell of their own mother's breast milk from that of other women. At about 5–6 weeks of life, the infant becomes able to recognize individuals, and will show preference for a primary caregiver by smiling and vocalizing. Parents respond to the infant's "social smile" with mutual gaze, friendly facial expressions, "parentese" (high-pitched, vowel-rich verbal messages), and touching and caressing. The child follows the parents intently, first with the eyes and later by crawling after them. Although the mother is usually the primary attachment figure because she is the person most constantly present, infants will form an attachment to anyone who is consistently responsive to them. In fact, most infants form multiple attachments, which helps protect them in the event of absence or loss of their primary caretaker.

Stranger anxiety develops at about 5–6 months of age when the infant becomes fretful at the sight of a stranger and seeks parental comfort and reassurance. Such behaviors reinforce the parent's protectiveness and the infant's signaling of potential danger.

Separation anxiety becomes apparent at 6–9 months. The child begins to understand simple cause-and-effect relationships and anticipate separations (e.g., seeing mother putting on her coat). When the mother actually leaves the child's presence, the child will cry and actively look for her. This behavior persists to about 2 ½ to 3 years of age when, through experience, the child learns the mother will return and no longer fears her going. However, if the primary caretaker(s) never leave the child with others, the child may have difficulty passing through this stage, particularly if the child is shy, fearful, or anxious in temperament.

Bonding, attachment, stranger anxiety, and separation anxiety are tasks to be mastered during Erikson's first psychosocial stage, **trust vs. mistrust.** Trust is the belief that there are people who will provide nurturance and comfort. Healthy mistrust is the realization that there are exceptions to this rule; others do exist who should be regarded with caution.

Gender identity, the sense of being male or female, begins to be established as soon as the parents discover the sex of their child. Thus, biologic, genetic, and environmental factors play a significant role as the child is given a sex assignment and is named, dressed, and played with accordingly. **Parental attitudes** (e.g., activity in boys and docility in girls), and learning what kinds of behaviors elicit favor or disfavor, further influence the establishment of gender identity.

Recommended Reading

American Academy of Pediatrics. *Your Baby's First Year.* Elk Grove Village, IL: American Academy of Pediatrics; 1998.

Bennett FC. Developmental Outcome. In MacDonald MG, Mullett MD, Seisha MMK (Eds.). *Avery's Neonatology: Pathology and Management of the Newborn.* (6th ed.). Philadelphia: Lippincott, Williams & Wilkins; 2005.

Brazelton TB. *Infants and Mothers: Differences in Development.* New York: Dell Publishing; 1969.

Gopnick A, Meltzoff AN, Kuhl PK. *The Scientist in the Crib.* New York: Harper Collins; 1999.

Review Questions

1. The prematurity rate in the United States is approximately
   A. 1%
   B. 5%
   C. 10%
   D. 15%
   E. 20%

2. The current survival rate at 28 weeks gestational age is approximately
   A. 25%
   B. 33%
   C. 50%
   D. 75%
   E. 90%

3. A pregnant woman's use of which of the following substances is responsible for the greatest number of cases of neurodevelopmental dysfunction in childhood?
   A. Alcohol
   B. Cocaine
   C. Heroin
   D. LSD
   E. Tobacco

4. By which of the following ages has a child learned object permanence, or that objects still exist even when you cannot see them?
   A. 1–3 months
   B. 4–6 months
   C. 7–9 months
   D. 10–12 months
   E. 13–15 months

5. According to Piaget, the first stage of development that occurs from birth to 18 months and infers intelligence from action is called
   A. activity vs. inactivity
   B. exploratory stage
   C. oral stage
   D. sensorimotor stage
   E. trust vs. mistrust

Key to review questions: p. 393

11

Toddlerhood and Preschool Years

- When is a child ready for toilet training?
- How does language evolve between 12 and 36 months?
- How does a child's play change between 12 and 36 months?
- How does egocentrism affect how a child sees the world?
- How do young children assign guilt and blame?
- Why do young children have fears?

Toddlerhood (1 to 3 Years)

Early in the second year of life, children complete the transition from crawling to walking. Multiple factors are involved in the process of walking, including the development of an upright posture and the ability to shift weight, alternate leg movements, and process sensory information while moving. Most 1-year-old children walk with a wide-based gait and short, toddling steps that have given rise to the term **"toddler."**

The average age for taking the first independent steps is 12 months. Most children are not only walking but also pushing or pulling a toy while

Selected Developmental Milestones from 12 Months to 36 Months

Age (months)	Gross motor	Fine motor	Language
12	Wide-based independent walking	Rolls a ball Pincer grasps	"mama", "dada" and 2 other words
15	Push/pull toy while walking	Imitates a vertical line	3–6 words
18	Walks up stairs holding on	Brushes teeth with help	20 words
20	Kicks ball forward	Builds tower of 4 cubes	Points to two pictures
24	Jumps Walks up and down stairs independently	Turns book pages one at a time Spontaneous scribbling Builds tower of 5 blocks	50–250 words Points to 6–8 body parts Names pictures of well known objects Combines words ("go car") Uses pronouns
30	Throws ball overhand	Builds tower of 8 blocks	Speech is half understandable
36	Heel-to-toe gait Turns and changes direction Gallops Stands on one foot briefly Pedals tricycle	Snips with scissors Copies circle	3–4 word "sentences" 50–75% intelligibility to strangers

walking by 15 months. However, some otherwise normal infants may not begin walking until 18 months. Most children can walk up stairs holding a person's hand by 18 months. By 20 months, most children can kick a ball forward. By 24 months, they are beginning to jump and some can walk up and down stairs by themselves.

By age 36 months, most children have an adult-like heel-to-toe gait; they are able to run and change direction with agility; they like to try new types of movements such as galloping; and they are able to stand on one foot briefly. Many children can pedal a tricycle at 36 months of age.

One-year-old children can roll a ball; by 30 months they can throw it overhand. Children also progress from finger feeding to self-feeding with a fork and spoon and they are able to turn the pages of a book one at a time (24 months), unscrew lids (26 months), build a tower of eight blocks (30 months), and snip with scissors (36 months). This progression parallels the child's ability to recognize objects and associate them with their functions. Thus, the child begins to use objects rather than just mouthing and banging them.

When is a child ready for toilet training?

Before **voluntary bladder and bowel control** can occur, the sensory pathways from the bladder and bowel must be mature enough to transmit signals to the cortex of the brain that indicate bladder or bowel fullness. Children must then learn to associate these signals with the need to (1) eliminate, followed by the need to (2) tighten the sphincter to prevent immediate elimination, and finally, after tightening, the need to (3) loosen the sphincter to permit elimination, but only when properly seated on or standing by the toilet or potty chair. In addition, the child must have the fine motor skill to remove clothing quickly and reliably before urinating or defecating. Children typically are not able to voluntarily postpone elimination until they are at least 15 months of age. By 2 years of age, some children are able to remain dry during the day although many children wear diapers until 3 years of age. Most children are not bowel trained until they are 4 years old. In general, girls develop toileting skills earlier than boys do.

Cognitive Development

Beginning at about 7–9 months and extending into the second year of life, the child learns that an object exists even when it is not present by developing a mental image **(object permanence).** During the second year, children will quickly look for an object that they observed being moved through a series of displacements. Between 18 and 24 months, children begin to search for a hidden object even if it was moved while they were not looking; furthermore, they will check several possible locations in an attempt to find it.

At the end of the second year, children begin to base their actions on internal mental symbols or **representations** (e.g., mental images or words). In addition, their improving memory skills allow them to make **associations,** such as matching a place at the table with one person. In fact, they get upset if someone else sits in that place.

Children in the third year of life continue to develop the ability to represent reality to themselves through the use of **words and symbols,** including gestures. They can solve simple problems, understand ordination (one book, two books) and classification (a dog is an animal), and sort by color and shape. Their thinking is called **preoperational,** indicating that it is not logical but rather rich with fantasy. **Egocentrism,** the belief that they are the center and initiator of all activity and the inability to put themselves in the place of others, is a prominent feature of children's thinking at this age.

Language Development

How does language evolve between 12 and 36 months?

At 12 months, use of specific words is limited to "mama" and "dada" for their parents and about three other words. **"Jargoning,"** utterances that sound like statements but contain no real words, is common.

During the second year, a child's repertoire of words accumulates slowly and then increases dramatically. Children will know approximately 20 words at 18 months and 50–250 words by 2 years. By 2 years, most children will also be able to point to 6–8 body parts as well as name pictures of well-known objects. Most early words label things or classes of things such as "doggie" or "ball" or are closely associated with an action the child can perform, such as "run." At 2 years, children also begin to combine words. The earliest word combinations are actually phrases ("go bye-bye") or labels ("baby baby") that the child perceives and uses as a single entity.

By the end of the third year, utterances are typically three to four words long and are increasingly grammatically correct; the plural form is used occasionally. Children this age can name several pictures instead of just pointing to an object that has been named for them. They also know and can say the name of at least one color as well as the action of several objects. The speech of most 3-year-olds is 50–75% intelligible to a stranger. In addition to having imperfect diction, many children stutter. These speech-related problems are common and are known as **developmental disfluencies.**

Because **receptive language** (what a child is able to understand) generally precedes the development of **expressive language** (what a child is able to communicate), children can point to pictures before they can name them. Similarly, they can follow two- or three-part commands before they are able to express such commands themselves and, when asked, can pick up blocks of particular colors before they can name the colors.

Affective Development

During the second and third years, children become increasingly mobile. As object permanence develops, the toddler can form a stable image of the parent even when the parent is not present; this provides reassurance and diminishes the child's need to be anxious. Now the mother can become a secure base from which the child can make exploratory excursions. The child may even go into a different room where there is no direct visual contact with the mother, although contact is renewed from time to time. Children also use these contacts as opportunities to be guided in their behavior by a nod or frown **(social referencing).** With repeated experience, a firm **reciprocal emotional relationship** between child and caregiver develops, allowing the child to feel secure even during lengthy periods of separation (e.g., attending school).

Emotional Development

During the first year of life, children are believed to experience and communicate **primary emotions** including: distress, joy, anxiety, fear, anger, surprise, sadness, and disgust. Between 12 and 24 months of age, children begin to experience learned **secondary emotions** of embarrassment, jealousy, pride, shame, guilt, and envy. These secondary emotions do not appear until children are able to think about and evaluate themselves in terms of some social standard, rule, or desired goal. Thus, secondary emotions can be considered **social emotions** because they involve either challenge to or enhancement of the child's sense of self.

Social Development

Social development is the process through which children acquire the standards, values, and knowledge of society (become **socialized).** They also become differentiated as distinct individuals with a unique **personality.**

Early childhood is the time when children learn to initiate their own activities, enjoy their accomplishments, and develop a sense of competence. This is also an age when children ask questions, experiment, and explore in order to learn what behaviors are acceptable and to discover how much power and influence they wield over adults. If adults over-regulate them or act as if their ideas are unworthy of adult approval, children are less likely to strive for independence. A lack of limits, however, can result in poor socialization and lack of self control.

Recognition of Self and Social Relations

Walking and using language promote new forms of **social relations** as children learn that they can share experiences and compare reactions. The process of developing a **sense of self** leads to a new awareness of their own ability to create plans or do things independently. This increasing competence is the basis for the emerging sense of **autonomy** characteristic of this stage.

Autonomy
A child's sense of autonomy is also accompanied by a strong desire to see personal wishes fulfilled. Given that children this age lack the ability to

think logically and rationally, they cannot understand logical and rational arguments provided by their parents. They are also unable to understand postponement of their immediate desires, and so are in frequent conflict with others. Because they lack sufficient language skills to express their disappointment or frustration, they demonstrate these feelings be-haviorally through **tantrums,** the hallmark of the **"terrible two's."**

Sense of Self
During the second year of life, children's sense of self also allows them to respond to others' distress. For example, during the first year of life, infants often cry at the sound of another infant crying. They may then seek to comfort themselves by holding on more firmly to a parent's finger or sucking more vigorously on a pacifier. This response is due to the infant's inability to distinguish who is hurting or unhappy. During the second year, however, when confronted with the distress of someone else, children are capable of understanding that the distress is affecting another person and not themselves. They may even try to comfort the other person.

Play

> How does a child's play change between 12 and 36 months?

Play is an important aspect of social development and reflects increasing mental abilities. During the first year of life, play is sensorimotor (e.g., touching, mouthing, banging).

At 12 months, children begin to use objects in play (e.g., banging a spoon). Later, they begin to use the object functionally (e.g., pretending to eat with the spoon).

In the next stage, the child uses a toy to represent a real action (e.g., using a toy telephone to "call Daddy"). These later activities are known as **symbolic play** (one object [toy] stands for another [telephone]).

Symbolic play becomes increasingly complex until, at approximately 24–30 months, the child uses toys in real actions in which dolls or other inanimate objects participate (e.g., having a doll eat from the spoon held to the doll's mouth).

Later, the child may have a "mother" doll feed a "baby" doll. This marks the beginning of **imaginary play.**

When children are placed side by side, they typically amuse themselves with little interaction or joint play. This behavior is called **parallel play.** Between 2 and 3 years of age, **joint or associative play** develops. Two or three children cooperate in a game or project, take turns, and observe and imitate the actions of others. Learning to share is a major milestone that requires understanding ownership, taking turns, and delaying gratification.

Gender Identity

Increasing autonomy and sense of self enhance the development of **gender identity.** By 2 years of age, children are able to discriminate whether a playmate is male or female. This identification of gender is based on anatomical inspection as well as an understanding of core gender identity. By 3 years of age, children know their own identity as male or female. Although in their fantasy life there may be mixtures of male and female elements in how they see themselves, children will nonetheless be protective of their gender identity and protest vigorously when an adult playfully states that they are of the opposite gender.

Health Risks

Diet
Although toddlers eat a variety of foods, it is common to go through periods when they will eat only certain foods (e.g., peanut butter and jelly sandwiches every day). Despite their idiosyncrasies, toddlers virtually always take in what they need to grow appropriately. In fact, research has shown that children are responsive to the energy content of their diets. Routine monitoring of growth is mandatory, however, and each child should have growth parameters entered onto an appropriate growth chart to verify adequate growth.

Injury
The significant risk of injury during toddlerhood is a function of the child's increasing motor ability and desire to explore. During this period, accidental injury, poisoning, and drowning are ajor concerns because an energetic 2-year-old can get into trouble quickly. Health care for children at this age should include parental guidance in accident prevention.

Early Childhood (3 to 6 Years)

Physical development progresses from walking, jumping, hopping, and skipping to skilled bike riding with the ability to independently explore the environment. The use of **symbols** changes understanding of the world from a sensorimotor perspective to that of elaborate fantasy. Growth in language explodes from use of a limited vocabulary and simple sentences to the ability to tell a complex story and communicate with significant mastery of the complicated rules of grammar. The egocentric toddler who fears separation from the primary caregiver becomes a social child who enjoys interactions with peers in **cooperative play** and group activities.

During this period, children grow only 6–8 cm and gain only about 2 kg each year. Decreased appetite coupled with increased physical activity produce the leaner body of the preschooler as compared to the pudgy body of the toddler. By the end of early childhood, the brain has attained 90% of its adult weight. In addition, significant myelinization and neuronal connections have developed. Connections between the temporal, occipital, and parietal lobes enhance **information processing** needed for continued cognitive and language development. Additional connections between the cerebellum and the cerebral cortex enhance control of **voluntary motor movements,** such as those needed to write.

Cognitive Development

According to Piaget's stages of cognitive development, the **preoperational stage** occurs between 2 and 6 years of age. During this stage, children are able to use symbols, and objects and events need not be physically present to be thought about in problem solving. Children also become less egocentric and understand that others may have a different perspective from their own. Their thinking is, however, still **magical** ("If I think something will happen, it will"), **prelogical,** and **precausal** (the juxtaposition of two unrelated events in time are interpreted as causal). They also exhibit **centering** (attending to a single obvious feature of an object to the exclusion of others).

> How does egocentrism affect how a child sees the world?

> **Egocentrism**
>
> In Piaget's classic demonstration of egocentrism, a child is shown a large three-dimensional diorama of three mountains, each with a different size, shape, and distinctive landmark. The child is asked to walk around the diorama.
> Once familiar with the diorama, the child is seated at one side and shown a doll. The doll is placed on the opposite side of the diorama.
> The child is then shown pictures of the different sides of the diorama and asked which one the doll is seeing. Children at the prelogical stage of development almost always choose the picture corresponding to their point of view and not that of the doll.

Concepts begin to emerge during early childhood as children seek to organize and understand their world. The initial concepts are simplistic and often limited to a single obvious characteristic or feature (e.g., all four-legged animals are "doggies"). **Logic** and **cause-and-effect relations** tend to be concrete and egocentric. A child may believe he caused his mother to cut her finger while chopping vegetables because he was angry with her for not giving him a cookie before dinner. Asked why the sky is blue, a child may answer that it was painted.

Moral Development

> How do young children assign guilt and blame?

Within cognitive development, **moral judgment** refers to a child's ability to understand moral concepts. **Moral behavior** refers to the child's actual behavior regardless of whether or not it is congruent with his moral judgment. Four-year-old children can understand what promises are but do not always keep them. Similarly, they can recognize the difference between truth and fantasy but do not always tell the truth.

Children in this stage apply the concepts of morality independently of what is right or wrong, and their primary motivation for good behavior is to **avoid punishment.** Thus, they obey adult rules even though they do not understand why the rules exist. They have little understanding of **intent** or motive behind a particular behavior because (1) they still have difficulty understanding another

---

If you were a 5-year-old, who would you say was naughtier?

"John is running around in the kitchen and spills a little milk on the floor. Paul is carrying his glass of milk to the table for supper and drops the glass."
When children of this age are asked which child was naughtier, they reply that Paul was because he made the larger spill.

---

person's perspective, and (2) they cannot focus on more than one characteristic of an object or event at a time (amount of damage done vs. intent). As a result, the degree of **guilt or blame** a child typically ascribes is associated with the degree of damage.

Gender Role Identification

Gender role identification evolves through **observation, imitation, and reinforcement** given by parents for gender role-appropriate behaviors. As the child's concept of gender identity forms, children become adept at labeling themselves as a boy or a girl. Soon they develop a **gender role schema** for boy and girl and are able to identify objects and behaviors that are associated with each gender role. As they are reinforced socially, they increasingly value those things associated with their gender role and imitate them.

Sexual play among preschool children is a natural consequence of the child's cognitive, emotional, and social development. Children are interested in "private parts" and in what distinguishes "boys" from "girls." They are fascinated with toileting and the function of "private parts." Preschoolers may participate in games of "mommy and daddy" or "doctor" in order to further explore gender differences.

Sexual play is common and does not predict fixation on these behaviors as an adult. However, children should be educated about "good touch" and "bad touch" and that no one has permission to touch them in their "private parts."

Childhood Fears

Why do young children have fears?

Learning to cope with stress is important to healthy emotional and cognitive growth. However, the

child's **stress response** may be manifested as **fear.** Children at this age still believe their parents can protect them from their fears. Thus, the parents' most important role is to offer reassurance, explanation, and safety. Arguments over the irrationality of preschoolers' fears are not helpful and can lead to a feeling that the parent does not understand the fear and is, therefore, not able to protect them.

Many fears during childhood are based on a lack of understanding (sometimes due to faulty cause-and-effect reasoning) which should be explained and corrected simply and clearly. Reassurance that the parent will use "great power" (e.g., a special monster spray) is particularly appealing to the younger child's magical thinking; giggling rather than crying is the desired outcome.

Children's increasing cognitive ability to fantasize can lead to undue worrying about both real and imagined dangers. **Nightmares,** like fantasies, are a way for children to work through normal fears about growing up. Nightmares are most prevalent between 4 and 6 years of age. Children also signal their fears in other nonverbal ways such as sleep refusal, increased visual or auditory vigilance, and nonspecific irritability

Health Risks

Trauma is the greatest health risk during early childhood. Increasing mobility, independence, and interest in exploration can result in accidents or poisoning. In addition, caregivers often have difficulty containing the child's willfulness and limit testing. As a result, children are at increased risk for excessive physical or emotional **punishment** (child maltreatment). Because children of this age often attend childcare or preschool, exposure to **communicable infectious diseases** is another common health concern.

Recommended Reading

Capute AJ, Accardo PJ. *Developmental Disabilities in Infancy and Childhood.* (2nd ed.). Baltimore, MD: Paul H. Brooks; 1996.

Goswami U (Ed.). *Blackwell Handbook of Childhood Cognitive Development.* Oxford, UK: Blackwell Publishing; 2002.

Siegel DJ. *The Developing Mind*. New York: Guilford Press; 2002.

Smith P, Hart C. (Eds.). *Blackwell Handbook of Childhood Social Development*. Oxford, UK: Blackwell Publishing; 2002.

Review Questions

1. In the preoperational stage, children
   A. are able to use symbols to represent reality
   B. can generate hypothetical answers to questions
   C. explore their environment by physical manipulation of objects
   D. have sophisticated mental processes but are inflexible in their thinking
   E. rely on the presence of an event to think about it

2. Piaget's three mountains experiment demonstrates the concept of
   A. categorical reasoning
   B. centering
   C. egocentrism
   D. precausal reasoning
   E. seriation

3. A child's tendency to see life in non-living objects and assign them human feelings and motives is
   A. animism
   B. artificialism
   C. conservation
   D. magical thinking

4. The stable conceptualization of being either a male or female despite superficial features such as dress or mannerism is
   A. gender identity
   B. sex role stereotype
   C. sex role schema
   D. sexual orientation
   E. sexual preference

Key to review questions: p. 393

12 School Years

- Why is thinking during middle childhood called "concrete operational"?
- What are the characteristics of peer groups during middle childhood?
- What motivates a 10-year-old to "do the right thing"?
- What are the major health concerns of middle childhood?
- What are the three major identity issues of adolescence?
- How does timing of pubertal development influence self-concept?
- How do different "developmental trajectories" manifest themselves during adolescence?
- Why might an adolescent experience problems feeling close to someone?

Middle Childhood (6 to 12 Years)

Although **middle childhood** is a period of significant physical, cognitive, social, and emotional development, changes are more gradual and subtle than those that accompany the dramatic growth surges found during the infancy/preschool and the adolescent years.

From the age of 6 years until the adolescent growth spurt, children grow about 6 cm and gain approximately 3 kg each year. As early as age 7, production of **adrenal steroids** increases in both boys and girls; this is followed by increases in **estrogen** and then **androgen** production. As a result, fat is deposited in subcutaneous tissues beginning at approximately age 8 in girls and age 10 in boys.

In many girls, the first **pubertal changes** of breast budding followed by pubic and ancillary hair growth occur during middle childhood. **Menarche** (onset of menses) occurs after the growth spurt. In girls, the growth rate begins to accelerate as early as 10 years of age, with most girls experiencing their major growth spurt between 11 and 13 years.

Boys typically develop later than girls; their major growth spurt is between 13 and 15 years.

Bone and muscle growth results in enhanced physical coordination and more complex motor skills. Whereas the 5-year-old can run, ride a tricycle, print his name, and throw a ball, most 10-year-olds have mastered a two-wheel bike, can run and dribble a ball simultaneously, and write in cursive.

Permanent teeth begin erupting during the early elementary school period. Loss of the primary or deciduous (baby) teeth occurs at a rate of about four teeth per year, from age 6–14.

Neurological changes result in important cognitive developments. Continued **myelinization of the cortex** is manifested by increased numbers and density of dendrites and synaptic connections. Brain cell genesis, nerve myelination, and dendrite pruning, particularly in the frontal cortex, increases during late childhood and early adolescence and continues into young adult life. During childhood, the thickness of the cerebral cortex varies with periods of thickening and thinning and the cortical fissures become more prominent. Electroencephalographic (EEG) activity transitions from primarily delta wave (frequency: 3–5/sec) to predominantly alpha wave (frequency: 8–13/sec) activity after age 6. EEG activity becomes increasingly stable, localized, and function-specific depending on the task the child is doing.

Cognitive Development

Why is thinking during middle childhood called "concrete operational"?

By the age of 7, most children can consider more than one characteristic of an object or issue simultaneously and understand that an object does not change merely because its appearance varies. Piaget termed this phenomenon **conservation.** Thus, the child recognizes that the amount of liquid remains the same even if poured from a tall container into a shorter but wider container.

Other important skills learned at this time include **seriation,** or the ability to conceptualize quantifiable differences (e.g., Jane is taller than Sue), and **transivity,** or the ability to infer the relations among elements in a serial order (e.g., if I am taller than Jane, and Jane is taller than Sue, then I am taller than Sue). These new mental skills allow children to perform simple mathematical functions. These skills also enhance the child's conception of **time** so that waiting for a turn, anticipating a holiday, and planning ahead become possible.

Memory also improves as children learn to use rehearsal or categorizing to help them organize daily living tasks. These skills are, however, still connected to the physical world (i.e., things the child can see, feel, or manipulate). Thus, this stage is termed the **concrete operational stage** of thinking. It is not until adolescence that the cognitive ability to manipulate ideas, possibilities, or abstract concepts emerges.

Cognitive structure and problem-solving skills evolve during middle childhood through complex **fantasy play** and following **rules.** The elementary school-aged child typically enjoys board games and team sports. A major developmental step is the transition from the need to interpret rules strictly and rigidly to the ability to negotiate changes in the rules, and the ability to apply rules from one situation to another similar situation **(generalization).** These skills are learned by trial-and-error and repetition.

Social Cognition

Social cognition refers to skills that reflect a person's sense of self and how that person relates to others.

> During middle childhood, children become able to appreciate increasingly complex qualities in themselves and others.

At age 6–7, children compare their personal qualities with those of others but are bound to observable physical attributes, such as who runs the fastest or counts the highest. At age 8–10, children begin to notice and include **psychological attributes** such as fairness or generosity. Late middle childhood children can evaluate traits such as shyness or reliability. Despite this progress, they remain tied to concrete representations of these behaviors, and cannot yet understand that differing social or emotional situations may elicit different behavior patterns without changing the basic characteristic (e.g., a generous person may withhold a donation at the end of the month).

As children develop a more complex sense of self and others, they demonstrate increased ability to **take another person's perspective.** Between ages 8 and 10, children are able to begin to consider another person's point of view but cannot consider two points of view (theirs and the other person's) simultaneously. By age 12, however, almost all children can consider multiple perspectives simultaneously as long as the issue is tied to the concrete world (e.g., discussion of how a parent, teacher, and child might react differently to a rule-breaking situation). At this point, as children are moving into early adolescence they begin to understand that ability is a stable trait and to infer that repeated failures may represent a lack of ability rather than a chance occurrence.

> What are the characteristics of peer groups during middle childhood?

During elementary school, boys and girls belong primarily to same-sex **peer groups.** These groups are more formalized than previously, and selection of friends is based on common interests or personality traits rather than merely living close by or being in the same classroom. Members of a peer group interact on a regular basis and have a shared set of **norms** and a clear sense of belonging to the group. Gradually, **roles** emerge with particular members becoming leaders or followers. As the child matures, peers become less interchangeable, allowing lasting friendships to become established. The importance of peers and the amount of time spent with them increase steadily throughout middle childhood.

Personal and Social Competence

According to Erikson, the major task for the child during middle childhood is developing a sense of **personal competence** by mastering the many new physical, cognitive, and social skills introduced by school and community activities.

> School work, athletic activities, and hobby groups all focus on practice, motivation, and **accomplishment.**

Children who do not find areas of success and accomplishment, even in doing chores around the house, develop a sense of inferiority and failure that can lead to decreased self-esteem and reluctance to take on new challenges and responsibilities.

Children who have poor **social skills** (e.g., inaccurate sense of personal space, inadequate hygiene, clinging or demanding behavior, little sense of role or personal skills) have difficulty maintaining social relationships despite a strong desire for companionship. They are usually bewildered by their lack of acceptance because their behaviors result from not perceiving the subtle intricacies of relationships rather than any conscious rudeness or disrespect. "She just doesn't get it" is a perfect description. For some children, intentional buffoonery or antisocial behavior becomes the only means of peer "acceptance."

Moral Development

> What motivates a 10-year-old to "do the right thing"?

At the beginning of middle childhood, children still remain strongly focused on **punishment** as the major determinant of behavior. Thus, for the 6- to 7-year-old, goodness or badness is determined by the consequences of an act. By 8–9 years of age, children become fascinated with **rules.** They establish elaborate **rituals** which must be followed in their games. They continue to see the world as black or white, right or wrong. Good behavior is a way to gain rewards. Kohlberg describes this behavior as **native hedonism,** which operates within a moral frame of "You help me, I'll help you."

By about age 10, children begin to consider intent in understanding their own and others'

behavior. The cognitive process underlying moral judgments shifts to a desire to behave in ways that gain **social approval.**

Gender Identity and Sex Role Development

By middle childhood, gender-related behavioral patterns are well-established and children are clear about "boy" versus "girl" behaviors, although they are more rigid in their expectations for boys. For example, boys are teased if they play with dolls or cry openly, whereas girls who are sports minded or "tomboyish" are generally accepted.

Open curiosity about other children's bodies and bodily functions is less common during middle childhood than it was at earlier ages. Many children are modest about their body and want privacy while bathing or toileting. Bedwetting is still common among 6- to 8-year-olds and may interfere with social activities that involve an overnight stay away from home. Jokes about embarrassing bodily functions are common, but given the strong taboos against sexual play in Western culture, most sexual interactions become covert during middle childhood. Many children engage in some same-sex sexual play, consisting primarily of comparing genitalia and some touching.

> Practicing boy-girl social relationship roles is common during middle childhood. In the primary grades, boys and girls engage in chasing and teasing games; later, many children experience their first real crush. Many gay and lesbian adults report knowing they had "different" romantic interests as early as middle childhood, even before having a clear cognitive understanding of sexual orientation.

Health Risks

> What are the major health concerns of middle childhood?

The major health concerns arising during middle childhood fall into three categories: (1) the presentation of a chronic medical or developmental condition such as diabetes or asthma; (2) the management of injuries associated with the child's increasing involvement in more demanding physical activities; and (3) learning disability, or attention deficit disorder.

It is critical that children who have a chronic medical condition be treated within the context of their overall developmental needs. This means encouraging the child and family to normalize the child's life as much as possible by encouraging appropriate school and peer activities. Because children of this age are forming their sense of self, it is essential that they, and their families, do not define themselves in terms of the child's medical or behavioral condition. The physician can assess and reinforce this sense of balance by including questions about school, athletic, and social participation as part of every health care visit.

Adolescence (12 to 19 Years)

Adolescence is the developmental period from the appearance of secondary sex characteristics to the cessation of somatic growth. Individuals can begin pubertal development as early as age 8 in girls (breast budding) and age 10 in boys (testicular enlargement).

Phases of Adolescence

	Age	Sexual maturity rating
Early	12–13	1–2
Middle	14–16	3–5
Late	17+	5

What are the three major identity issues of adolescence?

After the neonatal period, adolescence is the time of most dramatic physical and psychological change. These changes generate three major identity issues: Who am I physically? Who am I sexually? Who am I vocationally?

During adolescence, the final 25% of adult height and 50% of adult weight are attained. Such significant visible changes focus the teenager's attention on the self and heighten concern about **body image.**

The pubertal growth spurt occurs earlier in females than in males.

On average, 12-year-old girls are taller than 12-year-old boys although there is marked normal variability. When boys do begin to grow, their spurt is longer and of greater magnitude than that of girls. Given the considerable variation in the timing of pubertal change, most young people need reassurance that they are normal. Any concerns they have related to body changes must be taken seriously and explained in sufficient detail to allay unnecessary anxiety.

Neurological changes result in more mature brain functioning. As noted in the beginning of this chapter, adolescence is now known to mark a second period of marked brain development with increased cell genesis, nerve myelination, and dendrite pruning, particularly in the frontal cortex.

Biochemical Mechanisms of Puberty

The onset and course of pubertal events are organized around a feedback mechanism that involves the integration of protein peptide hormones released by the **hypothalamus** and **pituitary** with steroid hormones secreted by the gonads. **Gonadotropin releasing hormone (GnRH)** is synthesized and stored in the hypothalamus. When released, this small peptide regulates the production and release of two anterior pituitary hormones, or gonadotropins, **luteinizing hormone (LH),** and **follicle stimulating hormone (FSH).** The two primary sex steroids produced by the gonads, **estradiol** and **testosterone,** act on peripheral target organs and tissues and also act within a negative feedback loop to suppress hypothalamic release of GnRH. The notable exception to this negative feedback loop is the regulation of **ovulation;** in this instance, positive feedback of ovarian steroid ultimately produces an LH surge and ovulation.

The **hypothalamus** acts as a central common pathway for impulses from the cortex, limbic system, and pineal gland and is sensitive to **catecholamine** and **indolamine** stimulation. Neuroendocrine response to stress and nutritional status influence such pubertal manifestations as linear growth and regular menstruation.

Cognitive Development

The ability to use abstract thought, consider theoretical notions, devise hypotheses, examine cause-and-effect relationships, and make judgments based on future considerations begins to emerge during adolescence. This stage of **formal operations** can occur as early as 12 years and is achieved by about 35% of 16- to 17-years-olds. However, not all individuals fully develop these abilities and may reach adulthood with only a limited ability to deal with such abstract concepts as religion, morality, philosophy, and ethics. Many adolescents can think more abstractly when considering topics such as political issues but are less flexible in their thinking when it comes to more personal social or emotional issues. Especially during this period, regression in cognitive processing to a more concrete stage of thinking is common in the face of physical or emotional stress.

Cognitive development during the three stages of adolescence focuses on the search for **personal identity** or that sense of self that combines the person's diverse and often conflicting social roles (e.g., child, friend, student, athlete), talents (artistic, musical, analytical), values, and attitudes.

Early adolescents are preoccupied with the **physical changes** associated with puberty. Although early adolescents engage in role experimentation and seek independence via close relationships with peers, family relationships and parental approval remain important.

Middle adolescents are preoccupied with their **social role** and are intensely aware of how they appear to and are judged by their peers. They begin experimenting with risk-taking behaviors and asserting their independence from family.

Older adolescents are preoccupied with decisions about **work and career.** Family influences become less important as **intimate relationships** are established. Some older adolescents postpone physical and financial independence from the family because of their need for resources to complete their education or training. This period of continued reliance on the family, termed the **"psychosocial moratorium"** by Erikson, extends into the mid 20s and even the early 30s for some.

> How does timing of pubertal development influence self-concept?

Differences in the timing of pubertal development can significantly influence how adolescents view themselves and are viewed by others beyond the already complex processes that govern general identity formation.

Late-maturing boys are often at a social and athletic disadvantage and may compensate for their small size and physical immaturity by misbehaving. Typically, these so called "late bloomers" channel their time and attention to other constructive activities not requiring a high level of physical competitiveness.

Early-maturing girls have more adipose tissue, are more buoyant, and may be channeled into swimming; late-maturing girls have longer legs, are leaner, and may be directed toward running. Early-maturing girls do well during elementary school but may become self-conscious about their advanced development when they enter junior high school. Overall, they date more but have poorer self-esteem and a lower grade point average.

Affective Development

> How do different "developmental trajectories" manifest themselves during adolescence?

Recent studies of both normal healthy adolescents and those with a variety of chronic illnesses describe three **developmental trajectories: continuous, surgent, and tumultuous.**

Long-term follow-up of youths in each of these categories has shown that no group experiences significantly more psychopathology, and overall adjustment in young adulthood is comparable across groups.

Although most authorities agree that true turmoil is experienced by only one third or fewer teenagers, it is normal to experience **transient disturbances** in self-esteem, anxiety and depression,

Types of Developmental Trajectories

1. Continuous:	No major crisis; high self-esteem; stable environment
2. Surgent:	Prone to depression; less socially active
3. Tumultuous:	Anxious; dependent on peers; less secure self-concept; family problems

and oversensitivity to shame and humiliation. In most instances, these feelings do not reach a clinically significant level but, rather, are situationally determined.

Another key task of adolescent development is learning how to make healthy decisions in the face of strong emotions. Early adolescence is marked by increased emotionality coupled with underdeveloped problem solving and planning skills. As their cognitive coping skills mature, adolescents become better able to resist emotional impulses and make decisions based on longer term goals.

Risk-Taking Behavior

The three leading causes of death among adolescents are **accidents, homicide, and suicide,** collectively termed unintentional and intentional injuries.

First use of **illicit drugs** occurs in some elementary school children but is most common among adolescents. Youth who are rebellious, place a low value on achievement, are alienated from their parents and community, and live in a chaotic environment are most likely to be substance abusers.

Tobacco use remains a major public health problem among adolescents. Approximately 30% of teenage females in the U.S. smoke on a regular basis; the percentage is somewhat lower among males.

The prevalence of **violence** increased dramatically over the last two decades of the 20th century. Active school and community anti-violence programs led to marginal but promising declines just before the turn of the century. However, the percentage of high school students who have carried a gun, knife, or other weapon at least once during the preceding month still exceeds 75% in some urban areas.

Health care providers must be alert to signs of **depression,** especially in accident-prone adolescents, because accidents can represent "masked" **suicide** attempts. Adolescents often have difficulty verbalizing their feelings, allowing depression and suicidal thoughts to go unrecognized.

> When a risk of suicide is present, precautions must be taken to ensure the adolescent's safety, including informing guardians or other responsible adults. Risk of harm to self or others is always an exception to the rule of physician-patient confidentiality.

Gender Identity and Sexual Development

In addition to visible physical changes that occur during puberty, sexual functioning also matures and takes on new meaning. **Menarche** represents the culmination of puberty in the adolescent female and the beginning of the reproductive years for the mature female. Although relative infertility without regular ovulatory cycles is common during the first 3–24 months following menarche, **contraception** is indicated for any sexually active adolescent female. Most hormonal forms of contraception can be used safely beginning immediately after menarche.

Virtually all adolescent boys and many adolescent girls **masturbate.** About 50% of 16-year-old boys and 50% of 17-year-old girls from all social classes have had **sexual intercourse.** About one third of sexually active adolescents become pregnant and 40% of these obtain abortions. **Sexually transmitted diseases,** especially **chlamydial** and **human papillomavirus infections,** are common.

Homosexual fantasies occur among both male and female heterosexual teenagers. Some young adolescents have **exploratory homosexual experiences.** These experiences do not predict future sexual orientation. The percentage of the overall population who identify themselves as exclusively homosexual is difficult to determine but appears to be between 4% and 10%. Although many gay and lesbian adults report having had feelings of marginality or of being different during childhood, **homosexual identity formation** (personally acknowledging, exploring, and accepting) generally occurs during mid-adolescence. The **"coming out"** process (open acknowledgment) typically occurs during late adolescence or young adulthood.

Psychosocial Development

> Why might an adolescent experience problems feeling close to someone?

Psychosocial development during adolescence consists of two stages: **identity vs. role confusion** and **intimacy vs. isolation.**

The search for **identity** is dependent on the capacity to think abstractly so that the adolescent can hypothesize about various identities and compare them against future goals and social norms. Some teenagers are not able to arrive at a consolidated sense of self because of limited opportunity to come to conclusions independently, or because of "tunnel vision" that precludes experimenting with roles.

These individuals often experience **role confusion** as they attempt to individuate from family and to assume more adult roles, but without sufficient personal or career goals.

The unique contribution that friendships make to psychological development is most keenly recognized during adolescence. Learning the responsibilities and nuances of **peer friendships** is a necessary prerequisite to healthy adult friendships. Purely social, rather than athletic or task-oriented activities become increasingly common during this period. This is also a time when adolescents experiment with more **intimate relationships** and social learning becomes based less on peer group influences and more on the influence of an intimate relationship with a partner.

A stable sense of **self** is essential before the young person can merge his own personal needs with that of another and move into the stage of intimacy. **Intimacy,** in this context, is the capacity to commit oneself to the partnership and to fulfill that commitment even if it demands significant self-sacrifice and compromise. **Sexual activity** may or may not be a part of such an intimate relationship. Avoiding intimate relationships because of a fear of loss of ego can lead to self-absorption and **isolation.**

Health Issues

Approximately 20% of presumably healthy 12- to 19-year-olds have previously unrecognized health problems, mostly related to the rapid growth and maturation of puberty. These problems include structural (e.g., idiopathic scoliosis) and functional (e.g., "shin splints") disorders of the skeletal system; failure to achieve puberty at the appropriate time (e.g., pituitary insufficiency); sexually transmitted disease; pregnancy; violence; and substance abuse. Mental health concerns, particularly depression, also become more prevalent during adolescence.

Self-concept is the most important predictor of adherence to a medical regimen. The teenager who has a positive self-image is likely to follow the physician's advice. Other factors that promote adherence include a treatment schedule tailored to the teenager's personal lifestyle (few side effects; simple, easy-to-follow; requires minimal time and effort) and satisfaction (feels fully informed; feels privacy and confidentiality will be respected).

Recommended Reading

Adams G, Berzonsky M. *Blackwell Handbook of Adolescence.* Oxford, UK: Blackwell; 2002.

Craig W. *Childhood Social Development.* Oxford, UK: Blackwell; 2000.

Dahl RE, Spear LP (Eds.). *Adolescent Brain Development: Vulnerabilities and Opportunities.* New York: New York Academy of Sciences; 2004.

Steinberg L. Cognitive and affective development in adolescence. *Trends in Cognitive Sciences* 2005; 9:69–74.

Review Questions

1. Hormonal changes that lead to puberty are
    A. evident as early as age 7 with increases in adrenal steroids
    B. marked by estrogen increases in girls only
    C. measurable after pubic hairs develop
    D. seldom observed during the middle childhood years
    E. unrelated to increases in subcutaneous fat during middle childhood

2. Neurological development during the middle childhood period is characterized by a significant increase in
    A. glial cell proliferation
    B. head circumference
    C. number of dendrites
    D. number of neurons
    E. synaptic connections

3. During middle childhood, most children prefer
    A. any peer who likes the same activities
    B. being with older adults
    C. playing with mixed groups of boys and girls
    D. simple fantasy games
    E. structured games and sports

Key to review questions: p. 393

13 Adult Years

- What is the major task of young adulthood?
- How do relationships with parents change during young adulthood?
- What is the divorce rate of men and women who marry in their teens vs. those who marry in their late 20s?
- What are some of the risks and benefits of becoming a parent?
- How does sexual functioning in middle-aged men and women differ?
- Why do some people have a "mid-life crisis"?
- Why do some empty nests become elastic nests?
- What kinds of organ system changes occur with increasing age?
- What are the common causes of despair in the elderly?

Young Adulthood (20 to 40 Years)

Between the ages of 20 and 30 years, the human body reaches peak strength, flexibility, functioning, and efficiency. The combination of strong musculature, exceptional stamina, high resistance to disease, and rapid repair of tissue damage allows the young adult to develop specialized motor skills and demonstrate maximal athletic and physical prowess.

Cognitive Development

Brain cell development peaks during the 20s. However, **new synaptic pathways** are formed throughout adulthood, permitting the individual to learn new information and skills at virtually any age. Young adults are informed, knowledgeable, and able to make **complex decisions.** They can **organize, plan,** and consider the short- and long-term **consequences** of actions.

   Intellectual functioning continues to evolve throughout adulthood into an advanced phase of problem solving. This level of cognitive functioning is influenced by education, tolerance of diverse viewpoints, and **dialectical thinking** (i.e., re-examination of ideas as a result of critique).

Moral Development

By adulthood, most individuals have developed a **personal standard** of behavior and adhere to **universal ethical principles**, including abiding by a **social contract** and respecting individual rights. When an individual's principles do not conform to existing law, conscience directs behavior.

Gender and Sexuality

The **reproductive system** of both males and females is fully mature by the age of 20. The maximum capacity for reaching orgasm peaks in the late teens for males and occurs during the 30s for females. Sex hormone production is highest in the 20s but sex drive remains high in most persons for several decades, often into the 70s and 80s.

   Observable behaviors and roles are easy for the young adult to evaluate and either incorporate or reject. Intimate behavior, on the other hand, is, by definition, less observable and so less readily modeled. Virtually no discussion about comfort with intimacy is available to the young adult. Thus, **intimacy** is rarely addressed, and many young adults abandon an otherwise promising relationship because of feeling unsure about how to achieve true psychosocial intimacy rather than merely perform intimate acts (e.g., fondling, intercourse).

Consolidation of **sexual identity** and **sexual orientation** occurs during late adolescence and early adulthood. For lesbians and gay males, defining oneself as homosexual internally, and then to other homosexuals, are the first stages of the process of homosexual identity disclosure called "coming out."

Retrospective studies of adult homosexuals have found that gay males typically define themselves as homosexual between ages 19 and 21. Adult lesbians reach self-definition somewhat later, between ages 21 and 23. These milestones have been occurring earlier as a result of improved social acceptance of sexual minorities.

Sexual Relationships

At least 10% of young adults in their 20s and 30s do not marry; this number has been increasing over the past three decades because more women choose to delay marriage to take advantage of educational and career opportunities. **Living together** and sharing sexual activities without being married is common among both heterosexuals and homosexuals. Most of these relationships are short-term and average about 2 years.

Most individuals will marry eventually, but many choose long-term singlehood. **Singlehood** has the advantage of freedom to spend time, money, and other resources according to individual choice; more career opportunities; greater geographic independence; enhanced sense of self-sufficiency; and more psychological autonomy. About 80% of singles report some kind of **coital activity** between the ages of 25 and 50. Sexual activity is equally prevalent among males and females.

Although women in their 50s and 60s are capable of successful **pregnancy**, especially through *in vivo* techniques, most women prefer to bear their children before age 45 when the complication rate begins to increase dramatically. With average life expectancy, bearing children before age 45 also allows women to parent their children into middle adulthood.

Social Development

> **What is the major task of young adulthood?**

Erikson described the major task of young adulthood as **intimacy vs. isolation. Intimacy,** as defined by Erikson, includes the ability to form an interpersonal relationship characterized by commitment, reciprocity, attachment, and interdependency. Because intimacy entails self-disclosure, achieving a truly intimate relationship requires a strong **sense of self** (identity). Intimacy is not limited to sexual or spousal relationships.

Isolation, in contrast to intimacy, includes feeling victimized or exploited by others, experiencing difficulty cooperating with others, and having such a fragile sense of identity that the self-disclosure and analysis required in an intimate relationship are too threatening. Traditionally, women have been able to establish intimate relationships earlier than men, who usually find it easier to engage in intimacy after they develop a secure occupational identity. The increased number of occupational options for women has made this gender difference in timing less pronounced than in the past.

Collegiality with Parents

> **How do relationships with parents change during young adulthood?**

Once a stable and satisfying sense of "self" has developed, young adults begin to discover their parents as complex people. The change to explor-

Intergenerational Relationships

- Young adults are most likely to form stable intergenerational relationships within their family of origin when they adopt a lifestyle similar to, but independent of, their parents, if that choice is an authentic reflection of what the young adult wants to do.
- Conflicted relationships occur when young adults reject parental values and adopt an antagonistic or antithetical lifestyle or they adopt the lifestyle desired by the family of origin but wish they had chosen differently.

ing the interests, feelings, and values of parents is the beginning of a period of mutuality that extends until the individual assumes a caretaking role for the elderly parent. In this initial stage, the young adult tentatively gives support and direction as well as receives it. The response of the parents can range from reluctance to give up their authoritarian role to appreciation for the contemporary perspective their children can provide.

Gender and Career Choices

Today, many women have **occupational goals** that have traditionally been reserved for men. Many men prefer a partner with job aspirations for economic reasons and for the prospect of shared interests. Both men and women who are career oriented are more likely to postpone marriage, delay parenthood, and have fewer children. However, for women, commitment to a career remains problematic. Women are still vulnerable to an employer's concerns about the potential work-related effects of pregnancy, maternity leave, or relocation to accommodate the husband's career and are asked many potentially discriminatory questions about marital status and family situation.

Women who assume the **multiple roles** of wife/ mother, homemaker, and career may find the combination too stressful for their physical and emotional health. On the other hand, the physical and emotional health of women who have no career other than wife and mother also may be in jeopardy. Women who work solely in the home have more depression, acute illnesses, chronic conditions, and health care visits than women who work both inside and outside the home.

Marriage and Parenthood

What is the divorce rate of men and women who marry in their teens vs. those who marry in their late 20s?

Having a satisfying marriage and family life is the goal of about 80% of college students.

Marriage partners typically share similar race, religion, age, social class, level of education and mutual physical attraction. Although the durability of marriage is influenced by many factors, marrying later leads to more stable and satisfying relationships.

Men who marry in their teens have twice the risk of divorce as those who marry in their late 20s.

Women who marry between 14 and 17 have four times the risk of divorce as women who marry in their late 20s.

What are some of the risks and benefits of becoming a parent?

Life changes that challenge the couple who become parents include alterations in their sexual relationship, reduction in personal freedom, increased financial pressure, and concerns about being a good parent. The joys of parenthood stem from the pleasure derived from the child's development, the companionship, bonding, and awareness that the child is an extension of the parent's own self, and the sense that children are the individual's link with immortality. Parenthood often promotes a sense of true adulthood.

Mid-life (40 to 65 Years)

After the growth and development phase peaks in the 20s and 30s, middle age is marked by **declines** in **physical**, **cognitive**, **affective**, and **social functioning**. Many declines are subtle, slowly progressive, and so universally anticipated that the changes are virtually imperceptible until the latter half of middle age.

Loss of neurons and **degeneration of neuronal pathways** result in slower nerve conduction, lengthening reaction times. Unless skills are practiced, they are lost because of active dendritic pruning. Relearn-ing is possible and may require less time and effort if remnants of the neuronal pathways are still functional.

Alzheimer's disease, **Parkinson's** disease, and **Huntington's** disease are specific neurodegenerative disorders. They have known autosomal dominant transmission patterns, although sporadic cases can occur, especially in Parkinson's disease. These diseases typically have onset during late mid-life and early old age. The pathogenesis of neurodegeneration remains unclear. The neuroprotective effects of anti-oxidative therapy are evidenced by delayed deterioration of activities of daily living and cognitive functioning.

Although certain immunologic responses (T cell function, wound healing) and physiologic functions (bladder reflex, hair growth) are diminished, the most significant change with age is the diminished ability of the body to maintain **homeostasis,** particularly during periods of **stress.** When confronted with temperature extremes, emotional strain, or physical injury, middle-aged adults recover less rapidly than younger adults. Many self-regulatory processes are under **neuroendocrine control** suggesting that either neurostimulation, end organ response, or both may be diminished.

Daily caloric requirements decrease with age. Gradual lowering of the **basal metabolic rate** results in reduced energy expenditure. Although it may be typical to be overweight and less physically fit as a result of aging, research has shown that some body changes can be delayed by increased activity and better conditioning. Regular **exercise** slows both calcium loss from bones and the loss of muscle, helps maintain pulmonary functioning, and reduces kyphotic changes in the spine.

Cognitive Development

Cross-sectional studies of traditional IQ test scores show that overall **intelligence** begins to decline at about age 30. However, **"fluid intelligence"** (response speed, memory span), which depends on smooth functioning of the central nervous system, clearly declines beginning in the mid adult years, while **"crystallized intelligence"** (reading comprehension, vocabulary), which depends on education and experience, may continue to increase throughout the adult years.

Affective Development

The middle adult years are characterized by **reflection about life goals,** assessment of personal and professional accomplishments, and critical thinking about the future. Some mid-life adults experience short-term distress over transition but ultimately handle and learn from the crisis. Other adults find that change cripples their decision-making skills, undermines their marriage or partner relationships, or interferes with their ability to be a parent. Good **support systems** enhance coping ability. Other positive factors include higher intelligence, flexible temperament, past successes in other areas of life, and absence of a significant mood disturbance.

Gender and Sexuality

The **menstrual cycle** becomes less regular in the late 30s and 40s and ceases for many women by the early 50s. Factors associated with later **menopause** include child-bearing, early puberty, maternal history, thin habitus, higher SES, northern European ancestry, and Caucasian race. The onset of menopause is associated with a decrease in the size of the reproductive organs and vaginal dryness and atrophy due to decreased **estrogen** production. This process is called the **climacteric.** Despite these changes, reproductive technology enables some postmenopausal women to bear children, suggesting that the pace of the aging process varies among the different organs even within a single system.

Men experience no single event to mark a "male climacteric." The circulating level of **testosterone** does, however, decline with age. Although men remain fertile until late in life, developing an erection requires more time and stimulation, and both the volume of seminal fluid and the force of ejaculation diminish with age.

Sexual Functioning

How does sexual functioning in middle-aged men and women differ?

In general, male potency peaks during the late teens. A decrease in interest and desire may occur at about age 50; a more significant drop in sexual activity occurs after age 70. Women reach peak sexual potency in the mid-30s and experience relatively little loss in capacity thereafter. However, the number of women who remain sexually active and the frequency of these activities decline with age. This decline is highly correlated with the health of the spouse/partner. In contrast, partner health and marital status are poor predictors of sexual activity among older men.

The frequency of sexual intercourse drops to a level of 3–4 times/month among couples married 30 years. Older adults who have access to a regular partner report having intercourse about

2–3 times/month even at the age of 70. There are limited data about the relationship between aging and homosexual activity. Older homosexual men report continued sexual activity and satisfactory relationships. Less is known about the sexual activity of older homosexual women.

Social Development

Why do some people have a "mid-life crisis"

Eric Erikson proposed that the nuclear conflict of the adult years is **generativity vs. stagnation.** Generativity is concerned with guiding and contributing to the next generation. Stagnation refers to lack of productivity or creativity, self-centered behavior, and exploitation of others. Mid-life is typically the time for attaining maximal job/career satisfaction and achievement, especially among men. Prestige and power are at their peak, and many middle-aged adults mentor younger colleagues to achieve a sense of generativity. Jobs requiring heightened sensory capabilities may be subject to age-related performance decrements and provoke early retirement. In contrast, artists and musicians may continue to be creative.

Many factors, such as health, personality, social environment, income, and educational level, affect the feelings and behaviors of the mid-life adult. Marriage, parenthood, career, physical health, and general quality of life may be different from what was expected. Thus, many of the expectations of young adulthood must be reevaluated as time and energy become limited.

Feelings of helplessness and a sense of being "trapped" can lead to a **"mid-life crisis,"** during which individuals reexamine their understanding of themselves and the meaning of life. Many people experience a true **"identity crisis"** similar to that typically associated with adolescence. Extramarital affairs are common during this period of self-discovery, reflecting uncertainty and disappointment about the value of previous commitments, or the need to be reassured about physical attractiveness. If the original marriage/relationship survives, reor-

Predictable mid-life issues include increasing assertiveness and independence among women and increasing emotionality and sensuousness among men.

ganization of roles, redirection of energy, and rejuvenation of sexual activity may result.

Parent-Child Relationships

Why do some empty nests become elastic nests?

The period a married couple spends together from the time the last child leaves home to the time one spouse dies is known as the **"empty nest"** period. This can be a challenging time for both, but particularly for the woman who loses the role of mother. Although there is a sense of loss, there is also relief from the responsibility of daily child rearing, more opportunities to pursue other interests, and increased personal freedom and privacy.

The **"elastic nest"** describes the phenomenon of children leaving the family of origin and then returning **(boomerang effect)** in response to job changes, divorce, or other life changes. This intermittent dependency can be fulfilling to the parents who still feel needed; reassuring to the child who still feels protected; and frustrating to all as they struggle with the challenge of trying to move forward developmentally.

The middle-aged population of the late 20th century has been called the **"sandwich generation."** They are caught between the continuing **needs of their children** on the one side and the new **needs of their aging parents** on the other. Assuming responsibility for providing social, financial, emotional, or physical aid to their parents can be stressful for adult children, who must redefine their relationship with their parents. Such role reversal requires giving up reliance and dependency on the aging parent. How aging parents and their adult children negotiate both the need for assistance and the response each makes depends on competing obligations (e.g., obligations to other family members, work, social networks) and the previous parent-child relationship.

Later Life (65+ Years)

From a health and developmental standpoint, 65 is not old. For example, any man who reached the age of 65 during the late 1990s could expect to live into his early 80s; any woman could expect to live into her mid 80s. Factors that affect longev-

Is there a limit to human life expectancy?

Certain molecular processes appear to regulate the life-span of individual cells and the more complex tissues they comprise. These processes include:
1. the number of individual cell replications;
2. the production of free radical by-products of energy metabolism. These create an intracellular electrical imbalance, which can damage other molecules (including DNA.; and
3. glycosylation (glucose bonding to proteins to form sticky, weblike networks or cross-linkages producing changes such as cataracts and arteriosclerosis).

ity include health and socioeconomic status, with higher levels of income and economic security being associated with longer lifespan. The elderly have become the fastest growing age group; among these, the fastest growing population is the very old age group (> 80). In 2000, the number of Americans 65 or older exceeded the number 25 or younger.

What kinds of organ system changes occur with increasing age?

Changes in biologic functioning due to aging are highly variable. Some elderly exhibit marked declines while others exhibit little or no diminution in organ system functioning. Although most people aged 65 to 80 are not significantly limited by a chronic physical condition, they do have **diminished reserve,** reduced ability to adjust to physical or psychological challenges, and prolonged recovery following injury or disease. Some problems create more widespread dysfunction. **Neurosensory system losses**, such as decreased hearing and vision, are common in the elderly and may cause significant difficulty with eating, following instructions, and ambulation.

Impaired regulation of core body temperature may lead to

- reduced fever response to severe infection
- increased risk for heat stroke during the summer
- increased risk for hypothermia during the winter

While most older individuals have essentially intact immune systems, there is some reduction in T cell function and antibody responses are reduced. These and other changes in host defenses account for increased rates of infection of the urinary, gastrointestinal, and respiratory tracts in older adults. Increased mortality from pneumonia and influenza has been documented.

Reduced cardiac and pulmonary reserve, along with frequent coexisting medical conditions such as arthritis, decrease exercise tolerance contributing to the more sedentary lifestyle typical of many older adults. Most older individuals also have evidence of coronary arteriosclerosis, although this finding is not predictive of any particular functional limitations. Diminished lung elasticity and total capacity decrease respiratory reserve and increase vulnerability to the effects of otherwise minor pulmonary diseases or insults such as smoking.

Kidney function gradually diminishes with age, usually at a rate of about 0.6% per year. This loss of renal function is attributable to both a reduced number of nephrons and a decrease in tubular functioning. Structural and functional changes in the gastrointestinal system include reduced peristalsis and gastric acid secretion and slower emptying times, which contribute to indigestion. Because of slowed metabolic rate and more sedentary lifestyle, obesity is common.

Decreased hepatic drug oxidation rates and renal function lead to **slower drug metabolism** and excretion and, thus, higher blood levels of medications and their active metabolites. Age-related changes in drug pharmacokinetics also include increasing tissue sensitivity, especially in the CNS, resulting in more drug side effects. Given that the standards for the use of most therapeutic agents were determined in younger adults, loading and maintenance doses of medication should usually be reduced for the elderly.

Cognitive Development

Deterioration of mental functioning or **dementia,** is an acquired, chronic impairment in global cognitive functioning that affects comprehension, communication, and daily activities. Fewer than 10% of individuals over 65 have any form of measurable impairment in cognitive functioning.

In dementia, the patient's level of consciousness is usually normal. The onset of cognitive impairment is gradual and may not be noticeable until some consistent threshold of impairment is reached. The typical course is chronic and progressive.

Dementia of the **Alzheimer's** type, which is diagnosable by classic symptoms, signs, course, and autopsy findings, accounts for about half to two thirds of all cases of dementia. A variety of other specific conditions, such as multi-infarct dementia, account for the remaining cases.

Approximately 10–15% of patients with dementia have treatable, potentially reversible disorders such as CNS tumors, subdural hematomas, hydrocephalus, drug toxicity, hypo- or hyperthyroidism, alcoholism, cerebrovascular insults, or depression. Recovery depends on successful treatment of the underlying condition.

Affective Development

Recognition of personal limitations in physical or mental ability, fear of inability to care for oneself, or fear of abandonment can lead to **anxiety.**

> Individuals who developed insecure or mistrusting relationships early in life with their own parents appear most vulnerable to concerns about being taken advantage of by their children.

Anxiety can also arise in association with specific conditions such as depression, dementia, and general medical illnesses. Thus, careful evaluation is critical for identifying potentially reversible causes of anxiety. As is true in other conditions, pharmacologic treatment of anxiety disorders should be cautious because of the increased incidence of medication side effects.

Loss plays a role in many life transitions, which the elderly increasingly experience with the death of spouse and friends. Feelings of loss occur not only in reaction to death but also in reaction to illness. Anger and resentment are typical early reactions to concerns about long-term functioning. Later, preoccupation with diminished health status can lead to depression. The grief process comes to closure as the individual is able to adopt a realistic level of concern regarding the long-term consequences of the condition.

Depression is common in the elderly and may be due to other serious medical conditions, deterio-

ration in functioning, and social losses. Rates of completed **suicide** increase with age in both men and women. In women, the rate plateaus beginning in middle age. In men, it continues to rise slowly through old age.

The prevalence of **alcoholism** in the elderly is estimated to be 10–15%. Approximately one third of elderly alcoholics begin drinking excessively later in life. Those individuals who have a lifelong history of heavy alcohol intake may show evidence of alcoholic dementia.

Gender and Sexuality

The biologic and social differences between men and women result in differences in their level of **sexual activity** during old age. In men, physiologic degeneration of the seminiferous tubules causes decreased semen production and sperm quality. Although orgasm occurs, ejaculation is unlikely with every sexual act and retrograde ejaculation is common. The ability to develop an erection continues in old age, although the degree of tumescence is diminished. The concentration of circulating testosterone varies widely among elderly men, but, overall, serum levels decrease with age. Testosterone levels do not correlate well with impotence when it occurs in elderly men because certain medications (e.g., beta-blocking agents) interfere with erection. Sexual functioning in women is less affected by age than it is in men. Although reproductive function ceases with menopause by the early 50s, this process typically does not affect sexual desire. However, most surveys show that sexual activity is decreased among elderly women. Physiologic changes (e.g., atrophy and drying of vaginal mucosa due to decreased estrogen levels) may play a role, but the decrease in sexual activity appears to be due more to societal than biological influences.

Social Development

> What are the common causes of despair in the elderly?

The psychosocial stage of late life was conceptualized by Erikson as **ego integrity vs. despair.** Ego integrity is maintained when the individual has overall positive feelings of self-worth and accomplishment and is able to view life as a series of personal achievements with challenges and failures put into appropriate perspective. Those who do not view their life positively, are likely to experience despair, isolation, melancholia, and depression.

Isolation is the most significant threat to ego integrity. Stimulus deprivation can result from neurosensory deterioration (e.g., vision or hearing impairments) or from life in an institutional setting where opportunities for tender touch are limited. Elderly who lack a support network of familiar people and objects can lose the will to live.

Physical and neurosensory deterioration lead to reliance on others for normal **activities of daily living.** Many elderly are acutely aware of their loss of independence and ability for self-care. Family decisions about respite or nursing home care for elderly family members should include a professional assessment of level of functioning, ability to perform activities of daily living, and available family and community assistance.

Recommended Reading

Bernstein-Lewis C. *Aging: The Health Care Challenge: An Interdisiplinary Approach to Assessment and Rehabilitative Management of the Elderly.* (3rd ed.). Philadelphia, PA: FA Davis; 1996.

Gill TM, Robison JT, Tinetti ME. Difficulty and dependence: Two components of the disability continuum among community-living older persons. *Annals of Internal Medicine* 1998; 128:96–101.

Thorson J. *Aging in a Changing Society.* (2nd ed.). Philadelphia, PA: Brunner/Mazel; 2000.

Post S. *The Moral Challenge of Alzheimer's Disease.* Baltimore, MD: Johns Hopkins University Press; 2000.

Review Questions

1. Which of the following best describes a typical health-related characteristic among the elderly?
    A. A decrease in completed suicides
    B. A higher than 50% prevalence of dementia
    C. Decreased ability to eat
    D. Diminished physiologic reserve
    E. Increase in pain

2. Among the following, the capability most likely to be spared in a person with dementia is
    A. activities of daily living
    B. communication
    C. comprehension
    D. consciousness
    E. mobility

3. Following are some general statements about old age. Which one is best supported by current evidence?
    A. Decreased independence and isolation are major threats to maintaining ego integrity.
    B. Depression and dementia are inevitable consequences of aging.
    C. Frailty in old age is primarily associated with physical functioning.
    D. Old people typically complain a great deal to their doctors about their health problems.
    E. The physical and mental changes associated with aging follow highly predictable timeline.s

Key to review questions: p. 393

14 Selected Theories of Development

- What are the three basic concepts of psychoanalytic theory?
- How is libidinal energy expressed during various stages of psychosexual development?
- How do Erikson's "ages" compare to Freud's developmental stages?
- According to social learning theory, how does a person "unlearn" maladaptive behaviors?
- What is the relationship between conservation and compensation in cognitive development?
- How do Kohlberg's moral stages relate to Piaget's cognitive stages?

Freud's Theory of Psychosexual Development

What are the three basic concepts of psychoanalytic theory?

Three major concepts of psychoanalytic theory are
1. behavior is motivated by unconscious biological urges, instincts, or drives;
2. behavior is influenced by unconscious memories that are kept from awareness by defense mechanisms; and
3. psychic energy is channeled through three parts of the personality: Id, Ego, and Superego.

The **Id** is the original reservoir for all psychic energy. It expresses drives and impulses based on biologic needs, e.g., food, sleep, and procreation.

The **Ego** serves as the Id's intermediary with the external world. It operates on the reality principle and energizes learning and logical thinking.

The **Superego,** or conscience, assures that Ego actions are socially and morally correct.

Five Stages of Psychosexual Development

How is libidinal energy expressed during various stages of psychosexual development?

Freud proposed five stages of psychosexual development. These stages reflect the developmental sequence of body areas invested with **libidinal energy** (sexual or life force). **Fixation,** or impaired resolution of certain psychological conflicts that arise at the oral, anal, and phallic stages, are presumed to result in specific adult behaviors.

Oral Stage (Birth to 1 Year)
Libidinal energy is concentrated in the mouth, lips, and tongue. It serves the basic need of the infant to take in nutrition. Fixation in the oral stage may manifest itself in adults as excessive smoking, eating, or craving social contact.

Anal Stage (1 to 3 Years)
Libidinal energy is invested in the anal sphincter and bladder. Toilet training demands that urges be inhibited or delayed. Fixation in the anal stage may show itself as excessive orderliness or obstinate, retentive behaviors.

Phallic Stage (3 to 6 Years)
Children become aware of male-female differences and derive pleasure from self-stimulation or masturbation. They develop sexual longing for the parent of the opposite gender and jealousy toward the parent of the same gender **(Oedipal conflict).** Fixation in the phallic stage may manifest as difficulties with sexual relationships.

Latency Stage (6 Years to Puberty)
During this period, sexual strivings are largely suppressed by the Superego. Libidinal energy is chan-

neled into socially acceptable behaviors such as study or sports.

Genital Stage (Puberty through Adulthood)

The onset of this stage coincides with physiologic maturation and reinvestment of libidinal energy in the sex organs. The underlying goal is reproduction through a sexual relationship.

Erikson's Theory of Psychosocial Development

> **How do Erikson's "ages" compare to Freud's developmental stages?**

Erik Erikson agreed with Freud that people are born with biologic drives, but he focused on **society** rather than the family as the setting in which these drives are expressed. Erikson is considered an **ego psychologist** because he emphasized visible, rational, and adaptive aspects of personality.

Erikson's emphasis on relevant, **adaptive behavior** and the **integration of social and cultural factors** into classical psychoanalytic theory highlights the interplay between internal and external reality. Therapy is directed at working through unresolved conflicts, starting at the stage where the person is **"developmentally arrested."** Erikson's psychosocial theory was among the first to formulate personality development as a life-long, sequential process.

Eight "Ages" of Psychosocial Development

For each of the eight developmental stages or "ages of man," Erikson defined the major conflict and its possible resolutions in active, behavioral terms.

Basic Trust vs. Basic Mistrust (Birth to 1 Year)

This age corresponds to the Freudian Oral Stage. The task is to learn to trust a caregiver. If care is not or inconsistently given, infants come to see human relationships as dangerous or unreliable.

Autonomy vs. Shame and Doubt (1 to 3 Years)

This age corresponds to the Freudian Anal Stage. The challenge is to become independent in rudimentary aspects of living: feeding, making choic-

es, keeping and letting go. Failure to pass through this stage successfully will lead to self-doubt.

Initiative vs. Guilt (3 to 6 Years)

This age corresponds to the Freudian Phallic Stage. The need to have mastery over the environment can lead to conflicts with others (e.g., parents) producing guilt. The child must learn to set internal limits and achieve a balance between own and others' desires.

Industry vs. Inferiority (6 to 12 Years)

This age corresponds to the Freudian Latency Stage. Primary challenges are learning to meet school and social demands and acquiring academic and athletic skills. Output is measured and graded, and competition with peers increases. Failure leads to feelings of inequality, inferiority, and worthlessness.

Identity vs. Role Confusion (12 to 20 Years)

This age corresponds to the beginning of the Freudian Genital Stage and marks the transition from childhood to young adulthood. Experiences with role models outside the family (e.g., teachers) broaden the individual's value system. The primary challenge is to establish a sense of self as a physical, sexual, and vocational being. Failure leads to indecision, vacillation, and a sense of purposelessness.

Intimacy vs. Isolation (20 to 40 Years)

In this age, the individual moves from a self-centered focus to affiliation and partnership with others. Love and companionship transcend interpersonal boundaries and permit commitment to another. Lack of friendships and intimate relationships leads to loneliness, emptiness, and isolation.

Generativity vs. Stagnation (40 to 65 Years)

During this age, individuals become teachers of the next generation. They repay society for having nurtured them by sharing their work and creativity and assisting younger people. They develop a sense of responsibility for society. Failure leads to stagnation and boredom.

Ego Integrity vs. Despair (65 to Death)

This age involves acceptance of one's life, with its successes and failures. Reflection leads to an integration of experiences and sense of order and meaning. Without self-acceptance, a person experiences cynicism and hopelessness.

Social Learning Theory

The broad constellation of behaviors that comprise "personality" is presumed to be the result of the individual's social learning history According to **social learning theory,** learning occurs through **observation** and **imitation** of the behavior of others. Learning is a cognitive activity during which internal representations of modeled behavior are constructed. Subsequently, these representations are used to **imitate** (reproduce behaviorally what was observed). Behaviors that are **reinforced** (praised, rewarded, gain attention) are repeated. Both adaptive and maladaptive behaviors are acquired or extinguished through social learning (see Chapter 8, Learning Processes).

> According to social learning theory, how does a person "unlearn" maladaptive behaviors?

Extinction of maladaptive behaviors requires the elimination of the reinforcers of those behaviors and/or pairing those behaviors with noxious consequences; then, by imitating others, learning more adaptive responses. Thus, observing adaptive role models can modify nonfunctional behavior patterns.

In social learning theory, **development** is the result of an ongoing **interaction between the individual and the environment**. Although genetic and biologic factors influence individual predispositions early in life, developmental changes are increasingly influenced by social factors as the individual matures. Critics of social learning theory argue that this view of development is too simplistic and de-emphasizes biologic influences on behavior. Proponents counter that this view of behavior reflects the increasing influence of social factors with age and provides a theoretical framework for societally based clinical interventions.

Piaget's Theory of Cognitive Development

According to Piaget, children are born with two cognitive functions, **organizational ability** and **adaptive ability.** Children construct their understanding of the world by arranging or organizing their experiences into **concepts**, and concepts into more complex structures called **schemas**. In effect, children are theory builders who use concepts and schemas to make sense of the environment, employing two strategies: assimilation and accommodation.

In **assimilation,** experiences are interpreted and acted on within the framework of an existing cognitive schema: "all objects that can be fitted into the mouth provide nutrition." In **accommodation,** schemas are altered to fit disconfirming experiences that cause disequilibrium between cognitive understanding and external reality: "a thumb [put] into the mouth does not, in fact, provide food." As development progresses, schemas are modified further to fit experiences with reality.

Four Major Stages of Cognitive Development

Sensorimotor Stage (Birth to 2 Years)
During the first year of life, cognitive schemas progress from inborn reflexive activity, to repeating interesting acts, to combining acts to solving simple problems. The concept of **object permanence** is established during this stage. That is, objects that have moved out of sight or been concealed are understood to continue to exist and are searched for and found.

> What is the relationship between conservation and compensation in cognitive development?

Preoperational Stage (2 to 7 Years)
During this period, children learn to use language and other symbols. Problem solving is intuitive rather than logical and rational, and analytic thinking is poorly developed. For example, intuitive reasoning common in children this age is illustrated by a child's failure to appreciate the law of **conservation** (recognition that a given property of a substance remains the same despite irrelevant changes such as physical rearrangement). This is illustrated in Piaget's classical conservation experiment in which children in the preoperational stage were not able to appreciate that two identical portions of liquid transferred from identical containers to two differently shaped containers (one taller and thinner than the other) are still equal in volume although unequal in height.

Piaget suggests that inability to conserve is due to the preoperational child's inability to carry out a cognitive function called **compensation** (the ability to consider multiple dimensions of a problem simultaneously and appreciate the interaction between them; in this case, the *in*ability to consider both height and width simultaneously).

Concrete Operational Stage (7 to 12 Years)

In this stage, the child is able to conceptualize the world from an external point of view; thinking becomes dynamic, decentralized, reversible, and relational. Relational thinking is characterized by **transitivity** (mental arrangement of dimensions of objects) and **seriation** (ability to appreciate relationships among objects in a serial order). During the early concrete operational stage, children can only solve a problem if the elements of the problem are physically present **(concrete)**; often they must actually manipulate the elements for full understanding. Later in this stage, they can solve problems of time and space; **conserve** substance, quanity, weight, and volume; and **classify** objects into hierarchical systems, often without any actual experience with the issues or objects, based on past experiences with similar issues or objects.

Formal Operational Stage (12 Through Adulthood)

Formal operational thinking is characterized by the ability to use **abstraction.** Both tangible and intan-

---

Piagetian Stages and Health-Related Behaviors

Piaget's cognitive developmental stages clarify how children and adolescents view illness, illness causation, and death. **Stress** can impair an individual's ability to use higher order cognitive skills, and regressed cognition is common. **Magical thinking** (my wish equals action) or **egocentrism** (my action caused some externally determined and unrelated event), which are common among preschoolers, can occur even in adults who are in crisis. The inability to think futuristically, characteristic of children's thinking prior to late adolescence, hinders their ability to understand the long-term consequences of current actions (e.g., lung cancer as a result of smoking; becoming a parent as a result of sexual intercourse without contraception).

Piaget: Cognitive Development

Age (approximate years)	Stage	Distinguishing characteristics of cognitive function
0 to 2	Sensorimotor	*Preverbal* Reflexive activity leading to purposeful activity Development of object permanence and rudimentary thought
2 to 7	Preoperational	*Prelogical* Inability to deal with several aspects of a problem simultaneously Development of semiotic functioning (use of symbols, representational language)
7 to 12	Concrete operational	*Logical* Problem solving restricted to physically present or real objects and/or imagery Development of logical operations (e.g., classification, conservation)
12 +	Formal operational	*Abstract* Comprehension of purely abstract or symbolic content Development of advanced logical operations (e.g., complex analogy, induction, deduction)

gible problems can be solved through flexible, complex reasoning and **hypothesis formation.** Being able to conceive the ideal forms a backdrop for evaluating specific life circumstances and participating in social action and civil disobedience.

Kohlberg's Theory of Moral Development

Stages of Moral Development

The development of **morality** (i.e., the sense of right and wrong) has been postulated to follow an orderly sequence. Kohlberg proposed three basic levels of morality encompassing six stages of development.

> How do Kohlberg's moral stages relate to Piaget's cognitive stages?

Preconventional morality is characteristic of children in the sensorimotor and preoperational stages of cognitive development. Judgments about right and wrong are based on external consequences (rewards and punishments) and external higher authority (parent). Personal benefit is a highly motivating factor.

Conventional morality is characteristic of children in the concrete operational stage of cognitive functioning. Moral judgments are based on fulfilling the expectations of others and following the rules. Thus, an action is morally good if others say it is and maintaining law and order is essential. In decision making, **intent** is emerging as a more important factor than outcome.

Postconventional morality is characteristic of individuals who are in the formal operational stage of cognitive functioning. **Judgments** are based on personal adherence to principles that are perceived as valid by the individual apart from any external authority or convention.

Laws are judged with regard to their conformity with obligations and contracts and their congruence with basic standards of human rights. Under certain circumstances it may be morally right to disobey a law in the service of broader social principles (**civil disobedience**).

Self-chosen **ethical principles** of justice, reciprocity, respect, and equality inform morality. The moral person who has attained this stage of

Development of Moral Judgment				
Age (approximate years)	Level	Basis of moral judgment	Developmental stage	Characteristics
0 to 2	I. Preconventional (premoral)	Consequences (reward or punishment), Conformity to imposed rules	1. Punishment-obedience	Egocentric, no moral concepts
2 to 6	II. Conventional (moral)	Good and right roles	2. Instrumental-relativistic 3. "Good boy" – "nice girl"	Satisfaction of own needs Desire to please others
6 to 12		Principles, rights, values	4. "Law and order"	Obligation to duty Respect for authority
12 +	III. Postconventional (principled)		5. Social contract legalistic	Relativism of personal values and opinions
			6. Universal-ethical-principled	Conscience dictates action in accord with self-chosen principles

development can transcend his own person and see issues and dilemmas from the perspective of all others involved. This blend of regard for universal justice and compassion and respect for all individuals is considered to lead to optimal moral decision making.

Clinical and Research Considerations

The basic moral developmental milestones elaborated by Kohlberg are useful as markers of individual development. They are also helpful in providing guidelines for effective parenting. That is, successfully rearing children requires understanding what motivates behavior at certain ages so that parental responses to both desirable and undesirable behavior will be appropriate.

Research, including cross-cultural studies, has verified a strong positive correlation between cognitive developmental stage and the sophistication of moral thinking, supporting Kohlberg's contention that the stages are sequential. However, moral development does not progress automatically; **social experience** appears to be essential for the child to advance through subsequent stages.

Questions have been raised about whether moral reasoning predicts moral behavior. In general, the correlation is limited. In addition, the theory has been challenged with regard to its relevance for women. For example, it has been suggested that girls and women faced with solving a moral dilemma are more likely than boys and men (the subjects of Kohlberg's studies) to use **relational thinking** ("how will my actions affect others?") rather than strictly following the rules. The relevance of Kohlberg's theory in non-Western cultures has also been challenged. That is, the emphasis Kohlberg places on **individual moral reasoning**, especially in the post-conventional stages, may not represent the cultural norms present in tribal and hierarchical societies.

Recommended Reading

Bandura A. *Social Learning Theory.* Englewood Cliffs, NJ: Prentice-Hall; 1977.

Crain W. *Theories of Development: Concepts and Applications.* (4th ed.). Upper Saddle River, NJ: Prentice Hall; 2000.

Erickson E. *Childhood and Society.* (2nd ed.). New York: W.W. Norton & Co.; 1963.

Freud S. *New Introductory Lectures in Psychoanalysis.* (2nd ed.). London: Hogarth Press; 1937.

Kohlberg L. *The Meaning and Measurement of Moral Development.* Worcester, MA: Clark University Press; 1980.

Piaget J, Inhelder B. *The Psychology of the Child.* New York: Basic Books; 1969.

Sahler OJZ, Wood BL. Theories and concepts of development as they relate to pediatric practice. In: Hoekelman RA, Adam HM, Nelson NM, Weitzman ML, Wilson NH (Eds.) *Primary Pediatric Care.* (4th ed.). St. Louis, MO: Mosby; 2001, pp. 637–654.

Review Questions

Directions: The items below consist of lettered headings followed by numbered descriptions. For each numbered description choose the one lettered heading to which it is *most* closely associated. Each lettered heading may be used *once, more than once,* or *not at all.*

Match the Piagetian concept with its definition.
A. Accommodation
B. Assimilation
C. Concrete operational thinking
D. Conservation
E. Magical thinking

1. Understanding that a given property of a substance remains the same despite irrelevant changes
2. An object must be physically present for understanding or problem solving
3. Schemas are altered based on experience
4. My wish equals action

Match the Eriksonian age with the descriptor that fits it best.
A Ego integrity vs. despair
B. Generativity vs. stagnation
C. Industry vs. inferiority
D. Initiative vs. guilt
E. Trust vs. mistrust

5. The age of learning that others are consistent and reliable

6. The age of reflection about one's successes and failures in life
7. The age most closely aligned with Freud's oral stage
8. The age of the elementary school child

Match the Kohlberg stage of moral development with the moral action.
A. Good boy – nice girl
B. Instrumental – relativistic
C. Law and order
D. Punishment – obedience
E. Universal – ethical – principled

9. A 5-year-old puts the cookie back in the cookie jar when he hears his mother coming.
10. A 3rd grader does homework in order to watch TV.
11. A college student marches against ethnic discrimination.

Key to review questions: p. 393

Section V

Social and Cultural Determinants

15 Social Behavior and Groups

- What are the five types of socialization?
- What is the difference between status and role?
- How does a reference group differ from a primary or secondary group?
- How does ecology affect a society?
- What is a stereotype?

The individual is the product of biologic, behavioral, cognitive, sociocultural, and environmental influences that interact over the entire lifespan. Although initial interactions primarily involve primitive organism-environment transactions, these interactions evolve to include complex interpersonal and sociocultural phenomena.

Socialization refers to the learning process by which individuals learn to function as cooperative and interdependent members of groups (e.g., peer, work, family, society, culture). Socialization begins at birth and continues throughout the lifespan. During this process, the individual acquires the beliefs, attitudes, and values held by significant others. Developmentally, the individual also acquires a self-identity in the context of social groups.

Beliefs, attitudes, and **values** are the bases for the perceptions, judgments, and ideas that govern the behaviors of group members. This includes the development of health beliefs and behaviors. As socialization proceeds, the individual acquires an understanding and accepts the standards or norms of expected behavior shared by the group. These **norms** are learned through positive reinforcement for adherence and avoidance of reprimand for violation. **Mores** are fixed, morally binding customs that represent the core values and moral attitudes of the group. Violating mores is tantamount to immoral behavior and is accompanied by sanctions from the group.

Social learning is critical to the acquisition of interpersonal and group interaction skills required to survive challenges from the environment (see Chapter 8, Learning Processes). As the individual adopts the group's beliefs and attitudes, these evolve into complex **cognitive structures** within the individual that determine the individual's perceptions of reality as well as behavior (see Chapter 9, Cognition and Emotion).

What are the five types of socialization?

Five Types of Socialization

1. **Primary socialization,** the earliest introduction to group beliefs and expectations during the formative period of an individual's life
2. **Anticipatory socialization,** the learning that prepares individuals for future roles in life
3. **Developmental socialization,** the adaptation of beliefs, attitudes, values, and behaviors learned in primary socialization to new situations
4. **Reverse socialization,** the social learning provided by younger individuals to older individuals
5. **Resocialization,** the learning of new beliefs and attitudes in response to a major destabilizing event in the group

What is the difference between status and role?

Members of societal groups assume positions based on status and roles.

Status refers to the position the individual occupies in the group and is often considered synonymous with prestige. Many factors contribute to status including the family of origin, socioeconomic status, profession, appearance and age. Children born into a family with prestige (the family of the President, a famous athlete or scientist) begin life with a high status. Wealth may determine status. In the U.S., a professor is a respected professional; however, in Asia, a professor is revered.

Role refers to the function the individual is expected to fulfill and is dependent, in part, on the individual's status within the group. Roles vary depending on the nature of the situation. For example, in interacting with her child, an individual will assume the parental role; in interacting with her physician, she will assume the patient role.

Social Groups

A **group** is a collection of people who join together for some common purpose that can be achieved more effectively through collaboration than through individual effort.

Primary groups are small and defined by face-to-face interactions among members. These groups provide basic food, shelter, love, acceptance, and comfort. The family and groups of friends may be included within this category. It is possible that a religious group, such as an Amish community, may be a primary group because of the strong interdependence of members, the strong belief system, and the differences that exist between the Amish and the larger reference group (general U.S. population).

Secondary groups are larger and may involve some members who do not interact directly with all other members. Typically, these groups serve a particular purpose (e.g., church) or a particular interest (e.g., professional or community action group) and provide opportunities for enhancing personal satisfaction, sharing values, or changing society.

How does a reference group differ from a primary or a secondary group?

A **reference group** is any group with which the individual identifies or uses as an anchor point to define values or a standard against which to judge behavior. Individuals may identify with the beliefs of a reference group without belonging to the group (e.g., majority individuals who support and promote the concerns of a minority group). Some groups are identified by their social distance from the reference group. Following the Viet Nam war, many churches sponsored Southeast Asian families so they could begin a new life in the U.S. Many of these churches were in rural communities. Immigrant families were welcomed into the community, but the social distance caused many Southeast Asians to seek cities where immigrant communities were forming.

Under most circumstances, membership in a group does not preclude personal interpretation of group values; for example, a person may identify as "pro-life" and yet favor the death penalty. In some groups, however, personal interpretation is not permitted; in effect, believing wholly as the group believes becomes, itself, a value of the group that must be held in order to be a member.

Primary and secondary groups coalesce to form larger networks usually referred to as **society.** A society is a population that occupies the same territory, is subject to the same political authority, and participates in a common culture. Individual relationship groups are the basic elements of a **social system.** They become organized into an overall pattern of relationships to form the **social structure.** Activities within the social system are governed by certain rules (e.g., marriage, education) that codify and preserve the social structure.

Social Class

Social class is comprised of variables such as occupation, income, education, place of residence, memberships, social interactions, prestige, and self-identified status.

Socioeconomic status may be a useful tool for purposes of research, but in day-to-day interactions,

For research purposes, socioeconomic status (SES) is typically defined in terms of occupation, education, and income as markers for other measures.

such generic labels have limited meaning. Categorization terms are more helpful when specific to a particular issue, such as "disadvantaged" (e.g., lack of opportunity to gain the same economic or educational levels as the general population), "working poor" (e.g., unable to meet basic needs despite having a job), and "undereducated" (not having the same educational opportunities as others).

Ecology and Social Structure

How does ecology affect a society?

Environmental factors such as topography, climate, and food sources comprise the milieu or **ecology** of a society. Ecology influences language structure, perception, memory, coping styles, and social systems. How people earn a living, family structure, hygiene, and clothing are highly influenced by the environment. In turn, these environmental factors are part of the group's social and cultural identity. Just as a person living in Siberia has different needs and cultural affiliations from a person living in Kenya, a person living in rural Minnesota has a lifestyle and psychosocial challenges different from those of a person living in New York City.

Culture

Culture is the collective way of life that has evolved over numerous generations of a group living within a given ecological setting. Culture influences the development of normative beliefs and behaviors of its members. Although culture has constancy, it is not static but, rather, "shifts" in response to contemporary ecological, political, or economic challenges (see Chapter 17, Culture and Ethnicity).

Stereotypes

What is a stereotype?

A **stereotype** is a generalization made by a person or group about the characteristics of another person or group. Stereotypes are usually oversimplifications, but may be based on salient physical or psychological features associated with the group, or on expectations regarding the beliefs or behaviors of the group. Unfortunately, stereotypes are most often negative and racially or culturally based. At one time, the Irish were the target of prejudice and were viewed as primarily alcoholics and untrustworthy.

Individuals who fulfill the expectations associated with a stereotype reinforce it. Typically, however, an individual is assumed to have the characteristics in question (is "stereotyped") prior to any evidence that he or she as an individual does, in fact, have those characteristics. Although stereotypes can be positive, most stereotypic beliefs are negative and arise from uninformed or prejudiced attitudes.

Categorizing people into groups facilitates handling large amounts of information and is useful if it reflects reality, is not overgeneralized and is modified by new information. If new information is not integrated, generalizations become rigid and stereotypes are formed.

Stereotypes focus attention on those characteristics that define the stereotype. Thus, members of racial minorities, regardless of professional success and social position, are at increased risk for stereotyping and discrimination merely because of their physical identity.

Changing Terms for Changing Times

The earliest terms used to denote dark-skinned people of African descent living in the U.S. were "Negro" or "colored." These terms were considered sufficient since virtually all non-Native American dark-skinned people living in the early U.S. were slave-trade immigrants from Western Africa.

Because of racial slurring associated with these terms during the mid 1900s, "Blacks" or "Black Americans" became preferred.

This term, however, did not capture the broad range of skin color among Africans, and the term, "African American," became preferred.

As individuals from the West Indies and Caribbean immigrated to the U.S., many of whom were more brown-skinned than black-skinned, neither Black American nor African American were accurate descriptors. The term, "person of color," was suggested to denote anyone not of Western or Central European Caucasian ancestry.

Stereotyping also defines people by what they are *not*. These exclusionary descriptions create social hierarchies (non-member, non-physician, non-faculty) and imply lower status. Stereotyping influences interpretations of a person's behavior. If a patient who is thought to be demanding makes a request, it is more likely to be interpreted as a demand than if the same request were made in the same way by a person who is not labeled as demanding.

In contrast to stereotyping, an individual's **self-description** as a member of a group is influenced by how he/she wishes to be perceived by others. U.S. citizens of Mexican descent may refer to themselves as Mexican Americans to emphasize their heritage while Asian Americans may prefer to be referred to as Americans of Asian ancestry, accentuating their American citizenship.

Recommended Reading

Blaine D. Social determinants of health: Socioeconomic status, social class, and ethnicity. *American Journal of Public Health* 1995; 85:403–404.

Higgins ET, Kruglanski AW. *Social Psychology.* New York: Guilford Press; 1996.

Stark R. *Sociology.* Belmont, CA: Wadsworth-Thompson Learning; 2001.

Review Questions

1. The learning of new beliefs and attitudes in response to a major destabilizing event in a group is called
   A. anticipatory socialization
   B. developmental socialization
   C. primary socialization
   D. resocialization
   E. reverse socialization

2. Any group with which the individual identifies and uses as an anchor point to define values and standards against which to judge behavior is called a
   A. primary group
   B. reference group
   C. secondary group
   D. social structure
   E. social system

3. Environmental factors such as topography, climate, and food sources define
   A. a culture
   B. a social system
   C. a society
   D. socioeconomic status
   E. the ecology of a society

4. A simplistic generalization made by a person or group about the characteristics of another person or group is called
   A. a more
   B. a role
   C. a stereotype
   D. a value
   E. status

Key to review questions: p. 393

16 Theories of Social Relations

- How does a sociological analysis of behavior differ from a psychological analysis?
- How do implicit theories of life events differ from formal sociological theories?
- How does structural/functionalism theory differ from conflict theory?
- How does symbolic interactionism theory differ from utilitarianism/rational choice theory?

How does a sociological analysis of behavior differ from a psychological analysis?

There are two broad ways to think about **social behavior**. The first highlights the actions and motivations of individuals, and is associated with the field of psychology. The second focuses on the interactions between and among individuals and on collective behavior **(social relations)**, and is associated more with sociology.

The lives of individuals are shaped by the people with whom they interact. In this way, individuals are a product of social groups such as communities or social institutions, cultures and societies of which they are a part. Social relations determine the languages they speak, the religions they practice, the clothing they wear, and the ways in which they see themselves and the world: male/female, black/white, young/old, rich/poor, doctor/patient. Sociologists refer to these orienting phenomena as **social structure.**

Levels of Analysis

The social relations and interactions that make up groups can be viewed from different vantage points – or analytic lenses. One important lens is **level of analysis.** Within the social and behavioral sciences, the smallest unit of analysis is the **dyad.** Other important social entities include **reference groups, communities, society,** and even **countries/nation states.**

Individual vs. Social

Different units of analysis have different properties, which, in turn, influence how we define a problem/issue and what solutions we consider appropriate to apply. For example, when medical students and residents begin training, most will attend an orientation session. Oftentimes, someone from the dean's office or perhaps the Department of Psychiatry will talk to students about the "stresses and strains" of medical training, and how they (or their office/program) have resources for students to help them "cope" with "their" problems. Unfortunately, any invitation to "visit if you have a

One of the earliest examples of a sociological approach to analyzing human behavior was Emile Durkheim's 1897 study of suicide in France. For Durkheim, individual psychological processes, such as mental illness, could not explain suicide satisfactorily. Instead, Durkheim considered suicide to be a "social phenomenon" and concentrated on the role played by factors such as social cohesiveness and social integration. Durkheim hypothesized that individuals who had greater social isolation [anomie] were more likely to commit suicide than those with strong familial and personal bonds. At that time, Durkheim's findings were controversial because people in western society tended to think about suicidal behavior in psychological rather than sociological terms.

problem" or "our door is always open" frames both problems and solutions at the level of the **individual** and his/her **psychological make-up** (e.g., personal stress, low self-esteem, depression). Pushed to the side is any notion that these very same stressors should also be understood or approached at a **social-structural** level, where solutions seek to alter *institutional* policies such as examination and course requirements, patient care responsibilities, and call schedules rather than putting the burden of change only on individuals and their coping or stress management skills. This tendency to define problems and their solution as "belonging" to individuals rather than **social systems** and structures is a core part of medicine's culture. Consequently, trainees learn to define problematic situations such as disease and illness as problems of individuals and not of systems. This, in turn, has direct implications for how they learn to treat disease.

Elements vs. Systems

Our second analytic lens also is grounded in the culture of medicine. Traditionally, medicine has mimicked science by employing the logic and principles of "biological reductionism." Here the scientist/physician takes a complex problem (e.g., the bio-physiologic "nature" of a given disease) and reduces it to the most elemental part deemed responsible for disrupting system equilibrium. Treatment thus becomes a strategy for correcting or compensating for that flawed elemental part, usually via some outside agent (e.g., drug). As knowledge of disease etiology began to accumulate, particularly over the last decade, it became apparent that a strategy of reducing problems to their most elemental levels – be that subcellular or genetic – was not sufficient to understand many disease conditions. This is particularly true for chronic disease, which can manifest itself in different ways, among different people, over time. Thus, a second paradigm began to emerge where the focus is not on "parts" but on **system dynamics** and the constant fluctuating relationships that exist among elements in the system. Here, the focus is not on individual parts of the system but rather the system as a whole, determining the malfunction, breakdown and disequilibrium of interrelationships among the parts, and developing strategies that will return the system to a state of equilibrium (**homeostasis**).

For example, and in addition to their **formal curriculum**, health care students encounter a web of tacit messages throughout training about how best to think about issues of disease etiology and treatment. Within this array of messages, systems – whether that be biologic or sociologic – are marginalized in favor of identifying core parts. As a result, many practitioners are ill-prepared to think of **medicine as a social institution** and physicians as representatives of that institution, and ill-prepared to cope with changes in the organization, financing, and delivery of health care, provide services to communities, and practice "population-based medicine." Because physicians are trained to approach problems in a reductionistic and non-sociological fashion, they often find themselves applying ineffective solutions to problems they really do not understand. This results not only in job dissatisfaction, but also in ineffective patient care.

In addition to appreciating the ways in which different levels of analysis and different types of system thinking influence their understanding and treatment of a medical problem, physicians need to appreciate the distinctions that exist between their own **implicit** theories of the world and the challenges **formal sociological theory** presents to those self-generated "understandings." Sociological explanations may be difficult to apply, especially if they challenge an individual's already formed "implicit" understandings of the world, others, and themselves.

Implicit Theory

> How do implicit theories of life events differ from formal sociological theories?

Each individual develops an informal, implicit understanding of his/her life-space and world learned from, among others, family, community, school, teachers, movies, music, and religion. The importance of this **implicit theory** is its ability to explain why events happen the way they do, thereby enabling individuals, as social actors, to anticipate and control future events, to make sense of, and thus master, the complexities of daily interactions with others. Without these implicit theories, individuals would be forced, each day, to reconstruct social understandings from scratch.

Sociologists refer to an individual's assumption about the world as **implicit theory** and views about others as the **generalized other.** A first-time patient, for example, knows nothing about the particular physician she will be seeing, only about physicians generally. Similarly, the physician knows little about this particular patient. What both parties anticipate (conscious or not) is grounded in their knowledge about patients or physicians in general and, given these previous experiences, both parties will enter this first meeting with closely held expectations about how that interaction will (and should) evolve.

Health care providers should acknowledge the power of implicit theories and understand how they actually construct expectations about social relationships in general and the provider-patient relationship, in particular. Sometimes, different occupational groups (e.g., physicians, nurses, therapists) will hold different definitions of the situation about social relationships and the provider-patient relationship. The functioning of health care teams, clinic units, hospital services, and entire systems are shaped by these expectations. Part of this understanding includes recognizing that individuals do not generate implicit theories in an arbitrary fashion. Notions about what it means to be a "good" patient or "good" health care provider are **shared understandings,** developed through inter-actions and experiences with **socially significant others (reference group members)**. In these ways, implicit theories about relationships are social in nature (see Chapter 17, Culture and Ethnicity).

> When a physician complains to a colleague about a "bad" patient or when a patient tells a neighbor about an "insensitive" provider, each party has some implicit understanding of what the other person means, even if the other person disagrees with that characterization.

Formal Theories of Social Relations

Standing in contrast to implicit theories of social relations are formal theories of interpersonal interactions. There are four major traditions in formal sociological theory. In outlining these theories, their respective applications to today's health care system will illustrate their similarities and differences.

Four Formal Theories of Social Relations

Structural/ functionalism	Systems seek dynamic equilibrium. Change is designed to preserve stability.
Conflict	Systems do not seek equilibrium. Conflict drives change.
Symbolic interactionism	Systems are dependent on micro social interactions. Change is a function of actors making meaning.
Utilitarianism/ rational choice	Systems work best when individuals make informed choices to derive maximum personal benefit.

Structural/Functionalism

Structural/functionalism (SF) emphasizes how **change** in one part of a group or social system has implications for other parts of that group or system. Structural/functionalism arose from an attempt to apply models of biologic functioning to social action. Society is considered analogous to the biologic organism, composed of various parts, each of which contributes to the functioning of the whole, and where all are needed to function in a state of **homeostasis.** Depending on the unit of analysis (e.g., individual, community, state, nation), the object is viewed as composed of interdependent and coordinated parts and, in turn, is itself part of some even larger system of **interdependent and coordinated** parts. Change in one part generates reactive/adaptive change in another (note that the Integrated Sciences Model described in the Introduction is an example). The parallels between SF theory and biological reductionism and its emphasis on homeostasis are not accidental. The parallels were intentional because early SF sociologists attempted to appear "more scientific" by modeling themselves after the dominant scientific paradigm of the time.

As a rule, individuals who apply a structural/functionalism perspective to the analysis of social issues focus more on **outcomes/consequences** (e.g., homeostasis or its absence) than on cause. A pattern of social action is more likely to endure if a given social phenomenon contributes more to achieving system goals than to impeding them. Conversely, if the consequences are considered negative, then that pattern is seen as likely to change. Thus, systems tend toward a pattern of dynamic equilibrium in which change is "met" by the social system in a manner designed to preserve stability and balance.

Today's Health Care System

Evidence of a structural/functionalism approach to health care can be seen in the emergence and failed attempt of "managed care" to control the "skyrocketing" cost of health care. Experts have defined health care to be "out of control" and the prevailing reductionistic approach of the time was to define both problem and solution as a problem of homeostasis and the need for a targeted counter-movement to reestablish a state of equilibrium. The imposition of practice protocols and guidelines (e.g., new standards for the treatment of diabetes), the initiation of new forms of paying for services (e.g., prospective payment), or the formulation of new forms of practice organization such as HMOs (health maintenance organizations), IPOs (independent practice organizations), and PPOs (physician practice organizations) were introduced to rationalize medical practice and to control costs (see Chapter 28, The Health Care System).

Initially, these structural and managerial solutions appeared to be effective as costs stabilized during the mid 1990s. Even so, a number of concerns remain, particularly the large number of people who lack health care insurance (about 47 million) and related problems of access and equity (see Conflict Theory below). Even the initial "victory" of cost controls gained by managed care proved short-lived as costs began a new upward spiral at the end of the 20th century. From a SF perspective, solutions other than strict cost controls must be identified to bring the health care system back into balance.

> How does structural/functionalism theory differ from conflict theory?

Conflict Theory

An example of **conflict theory** is Karl Marx's theory of class struggle in industrialized society. Those who control the means of production exercise social control and dominance. The **unequal distribution of authority** shapes, among other things, patterns of **social class.** Other examples include conflict between the sexes (part of the focus of feminist sociological theory), and between racial, ethnic, political, and religious groups (part of the focus of cultural studies).

Post-structuralism is a more recent version of conflict theory and focuses on the scientific and cultural institutions in society (such as law and medicine) and the power struggles that emerge as a function of the attempts by these institutions to structure daily existence. An example from medicine is **medicalization,** where certain "conditions" (e.g., alcoholism, drug addiction) are considered "diseases" rather than problems of a personal (lack of character/moral fiber), social (e.g., criminal), or religious (e.g., sinful) nature. In contrast to the functionalists, conflict theorists focus more on issues of **inequities** and how the very definition of problems, and the solutions offered, tend to serve the **vested interests** of "a few" (e.g., management and capital) rather than those of "the many" (e.g., workers/employees). A case in point is the fact that, historically, the use of addictive drugs was considered a crime and not a disease ("drug addiction") until drug use moved from the inner cities to the suburbs and began to threaten the social stability and self-identities of the middle and upper classes.

Today's Health Care System

A conflict theorist might focus on how the system of managed care came to be defined as a problem (or not). She also might note that the label is, in fact, a misnomer, since the problem, as originally framed, was that of "runaway" costs as opposed to deficiencies in the quality of services. In turn, she might ask, "Whose interests were being served by this labeling?" Other points of conflict/contention might include efforts by health care corporations to identify their physicians as "providers" and thus group them with other health care workers such as nurses, therapists, or physician assistants/nurse practitioners, or for insurers to pay more for physicians to manage drug regimens rather than to do "talk therapy" with mentally ill patients. Conflict theorists also might study environmental factors such as emergence of patient rights legislation at the state and federal levels and question why legislation to protect patient interests has been so difficult to enact as law. The rise of corporate medicine and the consequent loss of status and influence by physicians are especially relevant to the conflict perspective.

Symbolic Interactionism

Symbolic interactionism, and its related areas of inquiry (pragmatism, phenomenology, and ethnomethodology) begin with three assumptions: (1) people react to the world based on their understandings of it; (2) these understandings come from the interactions people have with others; and (3) people make these understandings on their own by filtering them through their own experiences. Symbolic interactionism gives microsocial relations a more powerful role in the construction of social reality. Not only does society shape the individual, but individuals shape society as well. As such, a symbolic interactionism perspective illustrates how individuals create and use the larger social structures of which they are a part.

Today's Health Care System
Symbolic interactionists tend to focus on the micro-social relations within the larger health care system, specifically the physician/provider relationship, interactions among providers, and the struggles between physicians and the health care systems in which they work. In studying microsystems, the goal is to understand how **social factors** such as the gender, age, and ethnicity of physicians, patients, and other health care workers influence the presentation of symptoms and the response/understanding of health care providers. The symbolic interactionist perspective would be concerned with how styles of interaction and use of language might differ when white male physicians interact with African American female patients, or whether physicians treat African American women the same way they treat Asian American women.

> How does symbolic interactionism theory differ from utilitarianism/rational choice theory?

Utilitarianism/Rational Choice

According to **utilitarianism/rational choice theory**, social behavior is the result of rational actors mutually agreeing to engage in goal-directed behavior via an explicit set of rules regarding **individual interests** and the means of realizing those interests. Human relations and human behavior are influenced by personal desires, objectives, and individual gratification and, therefore, have strong ties to behavioral psychology. Examples of this perspective include **exchange theory** where interaction is based on individuals weighing both past and potential rewards and costs, and **game theory** where individuals are rational actors making decisions based on information about the interactions in which they find themselves. Rational choice theorists assume that the system works best when patients are given access to all information necessary to make rational and, therefore, optimal decisions.

Today's Health Care System
An example of rational choice theory is the promotion of **health savings accounts** to replace work-based health insurance as a principal means of paying for health care services. Calls to establish a health care voucher system, or for individuals to establish their own health care savings accounts presume informed rational choice at the individual level. Rational choice models also are evident in the movement to involve patients more in the management of their own (particularly chronic) disease conditions, and efforts to underwrite the costs of health education systems, particularly for patients who suffer from long-term problems such as diabetes or high blood pressure.

The push to educate patients assumes that there is a direct and positive relationship between the knowledge one possesses about a disease and the practice of **rational (e.g., compliant) health behaviors**. Some rational choice theorists believe that the only way to solve the problem of poor or non-rational health behaviors (e.g., smoking) is to appeal more directly to self-interests. This might mean developing a program of economic incentives to help people stop smoking rather than to spend money "merely" educating people about the dangers of smoking. Taking this example a step further, a rational choice perspective would differentiate between first- and second-hand smoke. Incentives to stop smoking in the former instance (an appeal to self-interest) are different from incentives for decreasing the dangers of second-hand smoke where the primary issue is the health of others rather than the health of the smoker per se.

Thus, strategies that might prove effective in the former case (education) might need to be changed (e.g., direct economic incentives) when the goal is to improve the health of others.

Conclusion

No single theory of social relations can adequately explain the evolving structure and social dynamics that make up "health care." The traditional physician-patient relationship has evolved into a more heterogeneous and more distant provider-customer form of interaction. Complicating this picture are the interactions among other health care providers, and the complex array of factors that attract a significant percentage of the population to alternative or complementary medicine (see Chapter 17, Culture and Ethnicity, and Chapter 29, Complementary and Integrative Medicine). The decision to seek health care, the type of provider seen, the diagnosis rendered, the therapy offered, and the resources ultimately utilized by the patient always have been determined by a complex interplay of social forces and special interests. More of these factors now operate at the organizational and institutional level than in the past. Multiple levels of analysis are required to understand the relationships that underscore the organization and delivery of health care services, as well as determine "health" and "disease."

Recommended Reading

Cockerham W. *Medical Sociology.* (10th ed.). New York: Prentice-Hall; 2006.

Farmer P. *Infections and Inequalities: The Modern Plagues.* Berkeley, CA: University of California Press; 2001.

Lundberg GD. *Severed Trust: Why American Medicine Hasn't Been Fixed.* New York: Basic Books; 2000.

Patel K, Rushefsky ME. *Health Care Politics and Policy in America.* (3rd ed.). Armonk, NY: ME Sharpe, Inc; 2006.

Porter M, Abraham C. *Psychology and Sociology Applied to Medicine.* New York: Churchill Livingstone; 1999.

Review Questions

Directions: The items below consist of lettered headings followed by numbered descriptions. For each numbered description, choose the one lettered heading to which it is *most* closely associated. Each lettered heading may be used *once, more than once,* or *not at all.*

Match each scenario with the Social Relations Theory it exemplifies.
A. Conflict theory
B. Implicit theory
C. Structural/functionalism
D. Symbolic interactionism
E. Utilitarianism/rational choice

1. To gain a broader patient base, a local chiropractor, Dr. Smith, has applied for privileges at Mercy Hospital, the newest hospital in Meta-General's national health care chain. Although Dr. Smith is a long-time, well-respected local practitioner, there is considerable antagonism toward his application from within Meta-General's Board of Directors and the general physician staff. One overriding concern is that acting favorably on this request will allow non-physicians access to a "turf" traditionally controlled by physicians and open the hospital to requests for privileges from other non-physician practitioners. Alternatively, the Chief of Staff is aware of the successful 1990 antitrust suit brought against the AMA by three chiropractors as well as that the AMA's Code of Ethics no longer prohibits physicians from consulting with chiropractors or teaching in schools of chiropractic.

2. To control costs, Good Samaritan Hospital reduced its nursing staff by 20%. Termination was based on seniority and degree status. Initially, the hospital enjoyed considerable savings. However, over the next several months, the number of hospital admissions decreased by almost 30%. A subsequent analysis found that most terminated nurses were admitting nurses, in charge of processing new patients. The efficiency of patient flow decreased and the hospital's financial condition plummeted.

3. A patient is admitted to the neurological ICU with a complete C5 transection. The patient is intubated, placed on a ventilator, and connected to electronic monitors. Every few hours, the staff rolls the patient over to prevent bedsores. Over the ensuing two days, the patient becomes increasingly agitated, distressed, and resists falling asleep. Unable to speak with the patient because of his intubation, the staff calls for a consultant who can read lips. The patient, finally understandable, discloses that the reason the nurses keep turning him is to keep him awake because, "If I fall asleep, I will die." The nursing staff were both surprised and disturbed by this message and reassured the patient that this was not the case. The patient, to everyone's relief, finally falls asleep.

4. Acme Medical Supply Company offers its 30,000 employees several types of insurance coverage, each different with respect to levels of co-pay, access to specialists, and coverage of prescription drugs and mental health services. The rationale is that employees will assess their own needs, maximize their benefits, and choose the desired plan accordingly.

Key to review questions: p. 393

17 Culture and Ethnicity

- What is meant by "cultural humility" and how does it relate to "culturally competent" care?
- What are the four categories of disease causation common to many cultural groups?
- What are the distinctions between "popular," "folk," and "professional" treatments?
- What conditions must be met before a patient can assume the sick role?
- Why are explanatory models important in health care?
- How do sick people decide to seek help from specific healers, or follow specific healing methods?
- What is meant by "culturally appropriate" communication?
- Why is it preferable to use professionally trained interpreters rather than family members?

Culturally Competent Care

What is meant by "cultural humility" and how does it relate to "culturally competent" care?

When physicians provide medical care that is **culturally competent** (similar terms include **culturally sensitive, culturally responsive, or culturally appropriate**) they inquire about, respond to, and respect the diversity of patients' beliefs and desires, regardless of the patient's age, gender, religion, ethnicity, or language. National culturally and linguistically appropriate standards detail specific knowledge, skills, and attitudes necessary for culturally competent care. **Cultural humility** is a life-long attitude and approach to cultural competence. Physicians must be humble about their limited knowledge of patient's beliefs and values, engage in self-reflection so they are aware of their own assumptions and prejudices, and act to redress the imbalance of power inherent in physician-patient relationships. Biomedical physicians tend to focus on the pathological processes of **disease**; patients focus on the psychological experience of **illness;** and the patient's family and community focus on the patient's **sickness** – the social determinants and social ramifications of disease and illness. Culturally competent medical care requires that physicians understand cultural as well as social, and psychological factors that influence how patients maintain health, treat disease, experience illness, and respond to suffering.

Each **core competency** has objectives that prescribe culturally competent care (Table 17.1.). One important skill is the ability to utilize culturally appropriate communication that is both respectful of the individual's beliefs, practices, and background, yet allows the health care practitioner to make precise diagnoses.

Culture influences beliefs about

1. bodily functions;
2. classification of disease;
3. disease causation;
4. treatment options;
5. the meaning of bodily signs and symptoms;
6. medical decision making; and
7. healer/sick person relationships.

Concepts of Bodily Functions

Each ethnic group's ideas about the functioning of the natural, social, and supernatural worlds are germane to their ideas about health, illness, and healing. The **natural realm** includes ideas about the connections between people and the natural environment. The **social realm** includes ideas about how individuals interact with people of different ages, genders, lineages, and ethnic groups. The **supernatural realm** includes beliefs about birth, death, afterlife, and interactions between the spiritual world and the human world.

Classification of Diseases

Since ethnic groups have differing classification systems for diseases, it is difficult to translate disease concepts across cultures. Entities that are recognized by certain ethnic groups and not others are often classified as **folk illnesses** or **culture-**

Mrs. Yolanda Jackson, a 72-year-old African American woman, has high blood. At times, Mrs. Jackson can feel her blood rising up to her head. When she drinks pickle juice and vinegar, she can feel her blood return to normal. Her 28-year-old European American male physician believes she has hypertension and recommends a low salt diet, exercise, and medication. "High blood" is an example of a culture-bound syndrome and "hypertension" is an example of a mainstream biomedical disease. While concepts of folk illnesses and biomedicine may be consistent, complementary, or contradictory, in this case, the two cultural systems are in direct conflict. Mrs. Jackson and her physician should take steps to understand each other, compromise, and implement an approach that works for her, to both relieve her illness and her disease.

Table 17.1. Core competencies and culturally competent care

Expectations for physicians
Patient care
- Communicate effectively and demonstrate caring and respectful behaviors when interacting with patients and their families
- Gather essential and accurate information about their patients
- Make informed decisions about diagnostic and therapeutic interventions based on patient information and preferences
- Develop and carry out patient management plans
- Counsel and educate patients and their families
- Use information technology to support patient care decisions and patient education
- Provide health care services aimed at preventing health problems or maintaining health

Medical knowledge
- Know and apply clinically supportive sciences

Practice-based learning and improvement
- Obtain and use information about their own population of patients and the larger populations from which their patients are drawn

Interpersonal and communication skills
- Create and sustain a therapeutic and ethically sound relationship with patients
- Use effective listening skills and elicit and provide information using effective nonverbal, explanatory, questioning, and writing skills

Professionalism
- Demonstrate respect, compassion, and integrity
- Demonstrate sensitivity and responsiveness to patients' culture, age, gender, and disabilities

Systems-based practice
- Advocate for quality patient care and assist patients in dealing with system complexities

bound syndromes (see Table 17.2.) Such ailments have a defined etiology, course, and treatment, and include expressions of mental or social distress. Some previously considered folk illnesses, such as premenstrual syndrome and chronic fatigue syndrome, are now recognized as biomedical entities.

Theories of Disease Causation

> What are the four categories of disease causation common to many cultural groups?

Every cultural system links sickness to etiological events that provide an explanation for bodily dysfunction and treatments for human suffering. Determining etiology is a complex process that depends on interpretation of the signs and symptoms, responses to therapies, the stature and reputation of the sick person, and historical events that have affected the individual, family, and community. Multiple etiologies may be considered during or even after a single sickness episode. While etiologies differ among ethnic groups, they typical-

ly fall into four categories that are influenced by the cultural group's concepts of the natural, social, and supernatural realms.

1. Individual etiologies include behavioral risk factors for disease (e.g., lifestyle, diet, habits, sexual behaviors) and presume the individual is responsible for the illness.

2. Natural etiologies include germs, environmental factors, humoral factors (hot/cold elements), and the universe (stars, planets, constellations). Because these etiologies are seen as factors beyond human control, the individual has little personal responsibility for causing the illness.

3. Social etiologies arise from social interactions or conflicts (e.g., conflict between friends or family members; jealousy, envy, or hatred; giving someone the "evil eye").

4. Supernatural etiologies reflect the culture's religious beliefs. For example, sinful thoughts or actions may be punished by an angry God; *kharma* forces from previous lives will influence events in this life; not displaying respect for ancestral spirits can cause sickness. Prevention or cure is provided by specific religious prescriptions about what constitutes appropriate behavior or contrition.

Table 17.2. Culture-bound syndromes

Culture-bound syndrome	Ethnic group	Description
Empacho	Mexican, Mexican American	An illness involving intestinal difficulties; believed due to lumps of food blocking the intestines.
Nervios	Latino	"Nerves," a condition affecting both men and women and allowing expression of strong emotions.
Susto	Latino	Illness resulting from a frightening experience; may also refer to illness due to soul loss.
Mal de ojo	Latino, South American, Middle Eastern, North African	A look from an envious person resulting in a variety of illnesses, depending on the cultural group.
Amok	Malaysian, Indonesian	Young men feeling excessive social pressures and role conflict experience a form of hysteria.
Latah	Laotian, Malaysian, Indonesian	Exaggerated responses to startling stimuli; may be related to stress.
High blood	African American	Blood that is too thick or too sweet; having too much blood; blood that is too high in the body.

Mr. Eugene Schmidt, a 65-year-old third-generation German American man, has lung cancer. His physician says it developed because he smoked tobacco for 50 years. His wife thinks God is punishing him, as he turned away from attending church early in their marriage. His daughter admonishes him for not eating the vitamin supplements she bought for him. His son encourages him to sue the ship building industry where he worked during World War II. He, himself, is uncertain, but tells everyone that he has to die sometime, so he might as well continue to enjoy his cigarettes.

Biomedicine emphasizes individual and natural causes, but patients may consider other causes to be equal or more important. Thus, exploration of alternative etiologies based on cultural concepts or differences of opinion will help avoid miscommunication and conflict about appropriate diagnostic or therapeutic approaches.

Types of Treatments

What are the distinctions between "popular," "folk," and "professional" treatments?

Popular or lay treatments are typically applied by the patient, family, or community members. Therapies to relieve symptoms or cure illnesses include herbs, amulets, rituals, and massage. Practices to prevent disease and promote health include wise nutrition, sleep, and exercise; protec-

The Southeast Asian practices of coining and cupping treat illnesses caused by the build up of bad wind, or pressure. The therapies consist of rubbing the skin with a mentholated cream followed by rubbing a silver coin vigorously over the affected area to release the pressure or creating suction with a cup, which relieves the illness. The practices produce linear or circular bruises on the back, chest, or extremities. Unfortunately, sometimes these bruises have been interpreted as marks of physical abuse. Some physicians, ignorant of the therapeutic bases of these practices, have reported family members or community healers to Protective Services with disastrous results.

tive clothing; prayer or maintaining relations with spirits; and cleanliness to avoid spreading contamination.

Folk treatments are applied by sacred or secular healers who have acquired authority through inheritance, apprenticeship, religious position, or divine choice. Their status is affirmed by their reputation for healing, or by revelations. Healers include herbalists, bonesetters, traditional midwives, spiritualists, shaman, and injectionists. Folk healers tend to be holistic, dealing with any individual, natural, social, or supernatural forces that may be related to the sickness.

Professional treatments are applied by health care providers whose authority is recognized by formal education and official licensure or certification. This category of healer includes physicians, nurses, chiropractors, physical therapists, and pharmacists. Complementary-alternative medical practitioners, such as acupuncturists and reflexologists, are in this category. Although their training and licensure vary by field and governmental regulations, they maintain professional relationships, in which payment is exchanged for specialized services.

Interpretation of Bodily Signs and Symptoms

What conditions must be met before a patient can assume the sick role?

Individuals declare themselves "sick" when they interpret their signs or symptoms as abnormal. Socially, family members or healers must concur before the patient can assume the **sick role** and legitimately withdraw from regular work and family responsibilities and receive assistance from

Mr. Garcia Lopez, recently settled in the U.S. from Mexico, was confused. His son was sent home from school with a draining ear, which was a common occurrence in Mexico and not a cause for alarm. But then later, his son was not permitted to stay home from school after he was frightened (*asustado*) from a near-miss car accident, that could have made him vulnerable to many types of illnesses.

others. Different interpretations of bodily signs and symptoms as normal or abnormal will influence this process.

Why are explanatory models important in health care?

The significance patients attach to signs or symptoms of an illness is influenced by individuals' cognitive ideas or **explanatory models (EM)** about the sickness event. Kleinman defines EMs as people's beliefs about a specific illness, including etiology, symptoms, physiological processes, projected course, and appropriate treatments. People's EMs can change over time as symptoms change or as response to treatment occurs. The patient, family members, social network, and health care providers all have their own EMS for the sickness event, which may be congruent, complementary, or contradictory. When physicians understand these diverse EMs, they can respond to patients' needs, expectations, and fears; aim educational messages at patient's uncertainties; and negotiate diagnostic and therapeutic approaches.

A necessary skill in providing culturally competent care is eliciting and listening to patients' and family members' stories of their illness experience, which includes the events, their beliefs about causation, their feelings about their disease, their quest for therapy, and their reactions to biomedical recommendations. Table 17.3. lists questions to elicit their experiences.

Medical Decision Making

How do sick people decide to seek help from specific healers, or follow specific healing methods?

Factors that influence medical decision making include **cultural beliefs, explanatory models, access, cost,** and **perceived efficacy. Ethnic identity** – the extent to which individuals align themselves with a sociocultural group – may influence people to seek healers or professionals from their ethnic background. The degree of **social dissonance** – the distance between the patient and the healer in terms of differences in ethnicity, socio-

Table 17.3. Eliciting the patient's and family's stories

Story
1. Would you please tell me more about yourself?
2. How does this illness fit into or change your life-story?

Illness/problem
3. What health problems or illnesses do you have, for how long, and what kind of care have you sought (conventional medical care, complementary-alternative, traditional)? How has it been helpful? Not helpful?

Impact of the illness on the individual
4. How is this illness affecting your daily life and doing the things that are most important to you?
5. What do you miss most from before you were ill?
6. What do you think will happen in the future?

Impact of illness on the family
7. What changes have occurred in the family since the illness began (daily routines, care, finances)?
8. How well do you feel the family is coping? Is there anything the family wishes they could do differently?

economic class, language, or religion – may become important. The greater the dissonance, the less likely the patient will choose to see the healer or adhere to treatment recommendations.

When people relocate from one geographic area to another, ethnic identity may be modified through the process of **acculturation.** Acculturation is not a unidirectional phenomenon that changes a person's alignment from traditional healing practices to a mainstream healing system. Rather, acculturation is a dynamic, multi-faceted, multi-vectored, and bi-directional process that varies among ethnic groups, individuals, and families. This variation can lead to intra- and inter-familial conflicts regarding appropriate treatments.

Patients can sequentially or simultaneously seek assistance from the three types of treatment systems (lay, folk, and professional sectors). Called the **hierarchy of resort** (first resort, last resort), people often begin with **lay treatments** in the form of self-help or family remedies and then, if lay treatments are insufficient, they seek help from **folk healers** or **professionals**. Such patterns of resort may be sequential or simultaneous. Individual patients may make decisions themselves, or they may look to family members or to social network members to help them choose. A "therapy manager," such as a revered elder, may oversee the help-seeking process.

Mr. Kang Tou Xiong is a 64-year-old Hmong man who had persistent cough and weight loss despite treating himself with Hmong herbal medicines. Alarmed, his wife dragged him to her physician, who thought he had tuberculosis or cancer based on the chest x-ray and CT scan. When neither diagnosis could be proven, the doctor recommended an invasive procedure (bronchoscopy) to obtain sputum. Mr.Xiong discussed his options with his sons, and they then consulted a shaman. The shaman determined that Mr. Xiong's illness was caused by his dead father's ghost wanting him to die and help his father in the afterlife. Mr. Xiong and his family refused the bronchoscopy, as it would render him more vulnerable to his father's ghost, and instead performed a shamanic ceremony that could appease his father's ghost. Most of his family agreed, but one son, who had studied to be a lawyer, thought that his father's and brothers' decisions were outdated and that his father needed to follow the physician's recommendations.

In a society where multiple systems of healing co-exist, patients and their families may use specific healing practices without endorsing the entire healing system. They seek assistance from different healing traditions depending on their interpretation of the situation, the fit between the sickness and the healing approach, the perceived effectiveness of the therapies, and their ethnic identity and degree of acculturation.

Physicians should inquire about what healers have been seen and what treatments patients have already received, as well as whom they will consult to make decisions.

Healer/Sick Person Relationships

Every cultural system has **expectations** about the healer-sick person-family relationship. The social and cultural rules governing this relationship influence the style of **communication**, the **appropriateness** of discussing certain topics, the **social protocol** about sharing or withholding information, and the amount of power or **authority** the healer exerts over the patient and family.

Certain approaches that are preferred by mainstream biomedical physicians may seem rude and antagonistic to patients from various ethnic groups. For example, physicians may attempt to exert control over nature, while patients may prefer to live in harmony with nature. Physicians may value direct and candid communication, while patients may value indirect and polite communication. Physicians may emphasize the importance of the individual and focus on the physical, while patients may emphasize the importance of the group and consider the social and spiritual in addition to the physical. Physicians may look to the future and exalt the young, while patients may look to the past and revere their elders.

To provide effective care for patients from other cultures, physicians must be sensitive to cultural differences between themselves and their patients. Accomplishing this is neither simple nor straightforward. Physicians must be familiar with general information about a cultural group but they cannot assume their patients' beliefs and values based on this general cultural information (i.e., stereotyping). Rather, physicians should use general information about a group to generate

---

Overuse of stereotypes and generalizations can lead to too little care

Mai Nguyen, a 29-year-old refugee from Vietnam, was being seen for a complete physical exam prior to starting a new job. She had numerous somatic complaints. She was hesitant to talk about emotional, familial, or intimate matters and refused a gynecological exam. Her young physician consulted more experienced colleagues who advised accepting her complaints as being consistent with Vietnamese "culture." However, after several encounters with the patient, the physician learned that the patient had escaped from Vietnam in a small overcrowded boat and had undergone significant trauma and sexual abuse while at sea. He came to realize that her complaints were not just "cultural" but were related to posttraumatic stress disorder requiring social and psychiatric interventions.

Overuse of stereotypes and generalizations can lead to too much care

Moshe Kadosh, a 54-year-old recent Jewish immigrant from a small village in Morocco, complained to his doctor about sinus pressure, headache, and dizziness. The physician became alarmed when the patient described discussions with spirits, including hearing the voices of some of his ancestors and long-dead local holy men. He referred Mr. Kadosh to a psychiatrist. After the initial visit, the psychiatrist postulated Mr. Kadosh was schizophrenic and admitted him to the psychiatric ward. Only after working with a psychiatry resident from the same country who interviewed him in his native language, did it become apparent that Mr. Kadosh was not psychotic, but rather exhibiting some of his normal religious practices, as well as expressing some of his distress about his illness and recent move in culturally appropriate ways.

hypotheses about an individual person or family, and then ask those people about their lives and their desires.

Culture of Biomedicine

Like all healing systems, modern **biomedicine** is a cultural system influenced by historical, social, economic, political, religious, and scientific events. It has its own language, vocabulary, and concepts, which can be difficult to translate into lay terms. It also has its own values, and each discipline (e.g., family physicians, surgeons, psychiatrists) are sub-cultural groups with variations on the general biomedical beliefs, values, and behaviors towards health and disease of the profession as a whole. As a sub-culture of Western society, biomedicine has values of the larger society, which specifically fit biomedicine. For example, biomedical providers typically address patients as individuals rather than as people embedded in families; they often focus on diseased bodies as physiological and pathological processes, ignoring social and cultural contexts; they are likely to conceptualize defective body parts as mechanical objects that can be replaced; and they tend to approach natural processes of life and death as periods to be manipulated and controlled.

A new intern begins working up his first patient in the outpatient clinic. The patient is a 32-year-old married woman recently arrived from Africa who complains of diarrhea and lower abdominal pain. The pain has been present for the last several months but has worsened in the past week. The doctor completes his history and physical examination, and orders a broad series of laboratory and imaging tests. He becomes disappointed and frustrated when he is unable to provide a definitive etiology and a patho-anatomical diagnosis. Even worse, the woman's complaints of pain worsen. After several visits, he decides that the woman's pain is "in her head," a conclusion that angers her. After an assessment by his preceptor, it becomes clear that the woman has lactose intolerance, which has been exacerbated by her recent dietary changes, and she is a victim of domestic abuse.

Culturally Appropriate Communication

What is meant by "culturally appropriate" communication?

Communication between the physician and patient is significantly influenced by culture, as reflected in **non-verbal expressions, manner of address,** and **appropriate styles and topics** of

Sombit Suksanakha, a 48-year-old Buddhist monk, felt insulted after his first clinic visit in the U.S. for several reasons. In the waiting room, a female nurse called his name loudly and then indicated for him to come by pointing her fingers upwards which is the way people call animals in Asia, rather than pointing her fingers downward as appropriate to call people. Then she reached out to touch his arm when directing him to the exam room; in Buddhist society a woman may never touch a monk. During history taking, his male physician looked directly in his eyes for a long period of time; he wondered if he were an oddity such that the physician would continue to stare at him. And then, during the physical exam, the physician touched his head without asking permission; in Buddhism, the head is the highest and most sacred part of the body and is treated respectfully.

Victoria Bearclaw, an 82-year-old Native American, feels insulted every time she attends the medical clinic in the city rather than the clinic on the reservation. The doctors and nurses talk quickly; they don't wait even a full second before she can reply, and then they ask her another question as though she's dumb or can't hear. They don't really listen to her concerns, as she tells the full story. Also, they look directly at her as though staring, and they call her by her first name rather than calling her Grandmother in a respectful tone of voice. She always feels as though they don't really care about her and her sufferings.

Mohammed Khan, a 24-year-old Muslim man from Somalia, accompanies his wife to the prenatal clinic to make sure that they treat her well. His has several concerns about the communication at the clinic. His wife doesn't speak English well, so he translates for her. However, one day the clinic had hired a Somali man to interpret, which upset the husband, as either he should translate or a Somali woman should translate. And then the physicians wanted to ask his wife her opinion after he'd given them their answer, as though he was not telling them the truth. The female nurse and doctor repeatedly try to shake his hand, which he has to ignore because, as a Muslim man, he can't touch a woman.

Table 17.4. Working with interpreters

1. Discuss expectations with interpreter before beginning, including first person singular, verbatim translation.
2. Make sure everyone has been introduced.
3. Sit facing the patient, and speak to the patient, not the interpreter.
4. Use lay English terms and simple language structure.
5. Pause intermittently to allow interpretation.
6. Do not assume universal meanings to nonverbal gestures.
7. Periodically check patient's understanding.
8. Do not expect interpreters to resolve conflicts or disagreements or to actively negotiate outcomes.

communication. Nonverbal expressions can have different, even opposite, meanings in different cultures. Appropriateness of style and topic of conversation can vary widely and a physician's insensitivity to such differences can impair the physician-patient relationship. While the cases above help to illustrate these points, physicians must be careful not to apply cultural generalities as stereotypes. Cultural generalities about verbal and non-verbal communication, like all cultural generalities, will not apply to all patients. Physicians must monitor their patients' responses, ask for their input, and seek assistance from bicultural colleagues.

Why is it preferable to use professionally trained interpreters rather than family members?

Although being proficient in a patient's language is optimal, physicians are likely to work through interpreters. **Professionally trained interpreters** should be employed because they provide grammatically correct first-person verbatim translations for physicians and patients, including explanations of medical language in lay terms. Using **family members** as interpreters is less desirable for several reasons. Differences in age and gender may mean that talking about some topics is inappropriate. Differences in acculturation may mean that the family interpreter prefers not to tell the physician what their relative said. Differences in language skills may mean the relative has inadequate knowledge of English medical terminology or medical terms to explain them in their own language. In general, physicians should meet with the interpreter prior to the clinical encounter to clarify guidelines and expectations, ask for "word for word" translations, and listen to the interpreter's insights about relevant cultural practices, meanings, or idioms (see Table 17.4.).

Applying Cultural Competence in Medical Encounters

According to Berlin and Fowkes (see Recommended Reading), being sensitive to culturally relevant information in the clinical encounter requires multiple tasks, which they arranged into the acronym **LEARN**:

1. **LISTEN** with genuine interest to the patient's and family's stories about their illness experiences. Elicit patient's and family's explanatory models. Be aware of whether direct questions are appropriate for obtaining information and gaining understanding.
2. **EXPLAIN** your views, building on the patient's and family's ideas, and address any fears or concerns. Use good patient education tools (e.g., understandable language and pictures), confirm the patient's understanding, and relate the current situation to a past experience.
3. **ACKNOWLEDGE** similarities and differences between the physician's and patient's concepts of bodily functions, disease states, etiologies, projected course, and preferred treatments.
4. **RECOMMEND** a course of action. Explain the treatment and ask permission to proceed. Give options whenever possible. Be prepared for the patient to choose not to proceed.
5. **NEGOTIATE** a plan. Acknowledge and build on a patient's own perspectives about the illness and how it should be treated. Promote active participation and create a sense of partnership. A plan that the patient has helped design is more likely to succeed.

Recommended Readings

Berlin EA, Fowkes WC. A teaching framework for cross-cultural health care application in family practice. *Western Journal of Medicine* 1983; 139:130–134.

Culhane-Pera KA, Vawter DE, Xiong P, Babbitt B, Solberg M (Eds.). *Healing by Heart: Clinical and Ethical Case Stories of Hmong Families and Western Providers*. Nashville, TN: Vanderbilt University Press; 2003.

Ember CR, Ember E (Eds.). *Encyclopedia of Medical Anthropology: Health and Illness in the World's Cultures*. Volumes I and II. Human Relations Area Files. New York: Kluwer Academic/Plenum Publishers; 2004.

Franklin S, Lock M. (Eds.). *Remaking Life and Death: Toward an Anthropology of the Biosciences*. Santa Fe, NM: School of American Research Press; 2006.

Helman CG. *Culture, Health and Illness: An Introduction for Health Professionals*. (4th ed.). Woburn, MA: Butterworth-Heinemann; 2000.

Kleinman A, Eisenberg L, Good B. Culture, illness and care: Clinical lessons from anthropologic and cross-cultural research. *Annals of Internal Medicine* 1978; 88:251–258.

Kukoyi O, Wilbur J, Graber M, House H. Case studies in cultural competence. In Satcher D, Pamies RJ (Eds.). *Multicultural Medicine and Health Disparities*. New York: McGraw Hill; 2006, pp. 389–403.

U.S. Department of Health and Human Services. National Standards on Culturally and Linguistically Appropriate Services (CLAS) in Health Care. Department of Health and Human Services, Office of Minority Health, Federal Register. 2000; 65(247): 80865-80879. Retrieved March 2, 2001 from http://www.omhrc.gov/assets/pdf/checked/executive.pdf

Review Questions

1. Explanatory models (EMs) are concepts which patients, family members, and healers form about a specific sickness. Which of the following statements is true about EMs?
   A. EMs are based primarily upon the pathophysiology of the disorder.
   B. EMs do not change once they are formed.
   C. EMs do not typically address the natural history of the disease.
   D. Eventually, patients, family members, and healers have the same EMs about the sickness.
   E. Greater agreement between people's EMs leads to fewer conflicts.

2. What is the LEARN model?
   A. An acronym for culturally sensitive patient education approaches
   B. An acronym for learning about ethnic groups' cultural beliefs about health, disease, and treatment
   C. An acronym for obtaining patients' cultural beliefs about their illness
   D. An acronym for the sequence of events in a culturally appropriate clinical encounter
   E. A reminder that we must learn from our patients

3. A 4-year-old Cambodian girl has a temperature of 103.5° F and linear bruises on her chest and upper back. Her grandmother brought her to the clinic because of the fever. You do not

have a Cambodian interpreter in the clinic. Among the following, which is the most likely cause of the child's bruises?
A. Child abuse
B. Coagulopathy
C. Coining
D. Mongolian spots
E. Sepsis

4. Which of the following is true about classification of diseases by different ethnic groups?
    A. A standard system of disease classification exists.
    B. All ethnic groups classify disease by physiological systems and etiologies.
    C. All ethnic groups classify disease in similar ways.
    D. Classification systems are static.
    E. Different disease classification systems contribute to miscommunication.

Key to review questions: p. 393

18 Health Care in Minority and Majority Populations

- What are some of the causes of population differences in health care?
- How does access to health care vary among white, Hispanic, and African American populations?
- How are health care and societal problems related among Native Americans?
- How do infant mortality, life expectancy, and cause of death differ among minority and majority populations?
- How do differences in age, income, and education affect health and health care?

Rapid change in the demographics of the U.S. population makes it essential that health care providers understand the effects of cultural factors on health, disease, and health care. Although the population as a whole is growing more slowly than in the past, certain subgroups are growing rapidly. The white majority is becoming both smaller and older relative to the black, Hispanic, Asian, and Native American populations. According to the 2000 census, of the estimated 282 million people in the U.S., 12.9% are African American, 12.5% are Hispanic, 4.5% are Asian/Pacific Islander, and 1.5% are Native American/Alaska Native. In 2000, over one fourth of adults and more than one third of children identified themselves as Hispanic, black, Asian or Pacific Islander, or American Indian or Alaska native.

Projecting to the year 2050, whites will comprise 52% of the U.S. population, blacks 16%, Latinos 22%, and Asians 10%. If present trends continue, by the year 2060, whites will comprise less than half the population.

Population Differences in Health Care

Health statistics for minority and lower socioeconomic populations are worse than those for majority and middle or higher socioeconomic class populations. In 2002, the Secretary for Health and Human Services reported significant improvements in the health of racial and ethnic minorities, but important disparities in health persist among subgroups in the population. All racial and ethnic groups experienced improvements in rates for 10 of 17 health indicators: prenatal care; infant mortality; teen births; death rates for heart disease, homicide, motor vehicle accidents, and work-related injuries; tuberculosis case rates; syphilis case rates; and poor air quality. The total death rate and death rates for stroke, lung cancer, breast cancer and suicide improved for all groups except Native American/Alaska Native. The percentage of children under 18 years of age living in poverty improved for all groups except Asian/Pacific Islanders. The percent of low birthweight infants improved only for black, non-Hispanics.

What are some of the causes of population differences in health care?

Disparities in health status are related to poverty, education level, under-employment and racism. People who are affected by one or more of these factors are more likely to live in environments with increased exposure to disease and limited access to health care.

The giant automakers such as Chrysler, Ford and GM spend more on **health care insurance**

Adjusting for age and sex, Hispanics are most likely to be **uninsured** (32.1%), followed by black non-Hispanics (18.8%) and white non-Hispanics (10.0%). Many uninsured individuals are in seasonal work, part-time employment, or unemployed.

for their workforces than they do on steel for the cars. Other corporate giants schedule their workers as less than full-time employees and do not provide benefits. Department stores, fast-food chains and restaurants, small businesses and convenience stores often do not provide benefits such as health insurance and retirement. Thus, it is easy to see how an individual might hold two or three jobs and not have health insurance, but also have an income too high to qualify for Medicaid or services at a low-income community clinic.

In 2001, 11.7% of Americans were living in **poverty**, up from 11.4% the previous year. One half of black and Hispanic children under the age of 18 and half of the adults over age 65 were living in poverty.

Infant mortality has declined for all groups in the U.S. but remains disproportionately high for black/African American mothers (13.6 deaths per 1000 live births) as compared to all mothers (6.9 deaths per 1000 live births). Infant mortality increases as the mother's level of education decreases.

In 1990, white Americans had a **life expectancy** of seven years longer than black Americans. By 2001, this disparity had been reduced to 5.5 years. Regardless, the death rates for black Americans are 40% higher for stroke, 29% higher for heart disease, 25% higher for cancer, and nearly 800% higher for HIV disease. Much of the progress is due to better access to care, but the disparities continue to exist because of risk factors related to poverty (National Center for Health Statistics, 2003).

How does access to health care vary among white, Hispanic, and African American populations?

Access to care is an important factor in determining health status, especially preventive care and timely treatment of illness and injury. The National Health Interview Study found that 4.4% of white non-Hispanics, 5.9% of Hispanics, and

6.4% of blacks were unable to obtain needed medical care during the year preceding the interview. The same study found that the percent of people whose health was assessed as excellent or very good was lower for Hispanics (61.2%) and blacks (58.6%) than for whites (71.4%). Self perception of one's health is an important indicator of actual health status.

While these statistics are important, the human stories behind them are more important, especially in a nation that spends a larger share of the gross domestic product (GDP), a common economic indicator, on health care than any other industrialized country. In the U.S., $1.4 trillion dollars, or 13.3% of the GDP, is spent on health care annually.

Individuals without health insurance (either public or private) make up about 17% of the population. About 13% of children less than 18 did not have a health care visit during the previous year. Poor children, adults and older adults are more likely to go without medical or dental care. Consequently, almost twice as many poor are hospitalized each year and the average hospital stay is 1.4 days longer. The poor do not have access to regular preventive care, they do not seek care when they are ill, and are less likely to get prescription drugs if they do get care. Thus, their illnesses are often more serious, care is delayed until hospitalization is necessary, and the hospital stay is longer.

African Americans

While most immigrant groups have relocated to the U.S. in search of better political, social, or economic circumstances, most African Americans are descendants of individuals brought to the U.S. as slaves. The rates of **poverty, crime,** and **inadequate education** have been higher among the black population than among the majority population, in part due to state and federal **laws that denied equal access to benefits** until the mid 20th century. Although other immigrant

Overall mortality is almost 3 times higher for black Americans than for white Americans. About one in five black Americans under the age of 65 has no health insurance.

groups have encountered these same problems, most groups have been able to assimilate after one or two generations. In contrast, **discrimination, prejudice,** and **segregation** of African Americans have been more easily imposed and sustained because of skin color differences. Although millions of African Americans have moved up the socioeconomic ladder to create a stable and growing black middle class, African Americans still predominate in the lower socioeconomic classes.

Hispanic Americans/Latinos

A significant proportion of the more than 42 million Hispanic/Latino Americans living in the U.S. in 2005 trace their ancestry to Mexico; the remainder are immigrants from Puerto Rico, Cuba, and Central and South America. About 90% of Hispanic/Latino Americans live in metropolitan areas clustered in neighborhoods where **language** and **customs** are preserved. Many do not seek complete **acculturation** at the expense of relinquishing their culture. In fact, many Hispanic/Latino Americans have actively resisted giving up their language and cultural traditions, and in many parts of Florida, New Mexico, Arizona, Texas, Colorado, and California, the Hispanic/Latino culture is dominant. Bilingual (English-Spanish) signage is used in many government offices and other public accommodations throughout the U.S., although H.R. 3898 declares English as the country's official language and mandates that official governmental and legal business be conducted in English.

Today, there are complex and heated discussions about U.S. policies aimed primarily at people from Mexico who cross the border illegally. On one hand, these are individuals entering the U.S. illegally across the Rio Grande River and other border points. In some cases, they find employment, get public assistance, and their children go to school availing themselves of tax supported programs. On the other hand, many of these individuals were sought as a cheap source of labor in harsh, dangerous and distasteful jobs as field workers, in slaughter houses and meat processing companies, textile mills, and construction. Many of these so-called migrant or seasonal workers stayed in the U.S., realized the American dream of opportunity and joined society as pro-

ductive people. However, technically they remain illegal aliens.

Asian Americans

China and Japan were major sources of indentured laborers for mining during the California gold rush. Nearly 200,000 Chinese laborers were brought to the western U.S. to build railroads. **Anti-Oriental sentiment** grew when, despite completion of the railroads that reduced manpower needs, the rail workers did not return to their home countries. **Anti-Asian legislation** included special taxes levied on aliens and exclusion from gaining citizenship. In 1924, the Immigration Act set quotas on immigration from all countries and prohibited immigration from Asia.

Although some Chinese left the U.S. in response to various discriminatory practices, the majority remained and established self-contained Chinatowns in larger cities. Economically, the Chinese developed a robust tourist industry offering food and commodities and transforming work camp services such as cooking and laundry into lucrative businesses.

The Japanese were hired as field hands and workers for the railroads, canneries, lumber mills, mines, and smelters. Japanese who dreamed of owning a plot of land had to circumvent the **land laws** of the Western states that prevented non-citizens from owning land. Many Japanese purchased land through U.S.-born offspring or by forming partnerships with Caucasians. Japanese were particularly vulnerable to discrimination because they were scattered over the West, did not form an effective sociopolitical group, and were successful in competing with majority farmers.

Anti-Japanese sentiment peaked after the bombing of Pearl Harbor. Approximately 110,000 men, women, and children, both Japanese aliens and Americans of Japanese ancestry, were **interned** in concentration camps. Although released at the end of the war, many Americans of Japanese ancestry lost their farms and businesses while they were held in the camps. The dissolution of the Japanese American community that had been centered along the West Coast forced those leaving the camps into the mainstream as they sought education and opportunity. While Chinese Americans were limited in their assimilation by the development of

Chinatowns, the Japanese were launched into a rapid acculturation process.

By the end of the 20th century, Asians had become the **fastest growing minority** in the U.S. primarily as a result of immigration law reforms enacted in 1965. The 2000 census counted about 1,080,000 Koreans or Korean Americans and 1,125,000 Vietnamese or Vietnamese Americans. Many of the refugees and immigrants were helped to establish themselves by church and community groups. The children of these families, or first generation American born, are well assimilated into American culture. Recent immigrants from Southeast Asia include Cambodians, Hmong, Loatians, Thais, Indonesians, Malaysians, and Myanmars.

Native Americans and Alaska Natives (NA/AN)

Between 1990 and 2006, the Native American Indian and Alaska Native (NA/AN) population increased from 2 million to 3.3 million, although some estimates put this figure at 4.4 million including individuals of mixed race. Most of these individuals are members of over 500 federally recognized tribes with distinctive cultures and histories.

Contrary to popular stereotypes, approximately one fourth of Native Americans and Alaska Natives live on federal reservations. Over half of Native American households own their own home. About 75% of NA/AN over the age of 25 have a high school diploma and 14% have a Bachelors degree. In 2002, receipts from NA/AN businesses reached $26.4 billion. Receipts were highest in retail trade and construction. However, these statistics alone tell only part of the story

> While one fourth of American Indians and Alaska Natives live on reservations, three-fourths are living in rural areas and cities.

The Native American population served by the Indian Health Service comprises 56% of the total population. Thus, 44% of this population group receives health services through other means or not at all. Of particular concern are the urban Native Americans many of whom moved off the reserva-

tions seeking employment. Lack of education and lack of skills have resulted in unemployment.

Approximately 140,000 Native Americans live in Los Angeles County, California, the largest urban population in the U.S. Until the 1950s, most NA/AN lived on or near reservations. Over the years, the federal government ended its recognition of some tribes and withdrew the government's legal obligation to tribe members. The **Bureau of Indian Affairs** encouraged Native Americans to leave the reservations and relocate in urban areas to find economic opportunities. As a result, the urban Native Americans have dispersed rather than remaining in groups or ethnic neighborhoods where they might better be identified and obtain education, health care, and social services.

> How are health care and societal problems related among Native Americans?

Specific Health Issues of Native Americans

The **Indian Health Service** and **Tribal Council Health Care Administrations** provide tribes with outpatient and inpatient services. Tribes have three options for receiving health care: (1) from the Indian Health Service (IHS), (2) contracting with the IHS to have administrative control and funding transferred to tribal governments, or (3) an agreement with the IHS for the tribe to have autonomy in the provision of health care services. The Indian Self-Determination and Education Assistance Act signed in 1975 recognized the government-to-government relationship between the U.S. and the sovereign Tribal nations.

> Some 600 Indian Health Service and Tribal health care facilities are spread over 35 states, most often in rural and isolated areas.

For many Native Americans, IHS or Tribal health care facilities are the only services accessible to them. Unfortunately, much of the needed health care services are not available through IHS or Tribal facilities and must be purchased under contracts with private sector health providers including specialty care, laboratory, imaging and pharmacy.

While the Indian Health Service and Tribal health services are often inadequate and under-funded, they also serve only slightly more than half of the NA/AN population. Of particular concern are the rural poor and urban population groups without access to services.

Among the disparities, the age-adjusted mortality rate for NA/AN is 709.3/100,000 as compared to 869/100,000 for the total U.S. population. The NA/AN population has lower death rates from heart disease, (178.2 vs. 257.6/100,000), stroke (45.0 vs. 60.9/100,000), and cancer (127.8 vs. 199.6/100,000). However, NA/AN have much higher death rates from chronic liver disease and cirrhosis (24.3 vs. 9.5/100,000), diabetes mellitus (41.5 vs. 25.0/100,000), and motor vehicle accidents (27.3 vs. 15.4/100,000). These latter are diseases that reflect a lifestyle of poor nutrition and substance abuse.

Accidents cause almost 40% of all deaths in this population.

Alcoholism continues to pose the most important health problem for the Navajo as well as other tribes. Although the prevalence of alcohol use is lower among Native American adults than other groups, among those who do drink, a larger percentage drink heavily.

> According to the National Institute on Alcohol Abuse and Alcoholism, Native Americans, among all U.S. population groups, have the highest prevalence of alcohol problems and have approximately twice the risk of alcoholism.

Among many Native American groups, alcohol may be a way of coping with problems such as **unemployment, loss of historical tradition,** and **poverty,** which are prevalent on the reservation and in urban ghettos. In addition, Native American youth are more likely to experiment with inhalants, smokeless tobacco, and marijuana than youth in other population groups.

For traditional Native Americans, healing is predominately **spiritual.** In keeping with their belief that harmonious relationships among man, nature, and the supernatural are essential to health, illness is viewed as a major indicator of disharmony. Thus, to create a successful treatment plan, the needs of the body, the mind, and the spirit must be addressed. Healing is sacred and represents the core of the Navajo religion. The aim of healing ceremonies is to remove the cause of the disease and alleviate symptoms.

Health Status and Health Determinants

> How do infant mortality, life expectancy, and cause of death differ among minority and majority populations?

Infant Mortality

Americans today are living longer and are healthier than their parents. The **birth rate** is stable, and the proportion of women receiving **prenatal care** beginning in the first trimester has increased, especially among minority groups and among the poorest in all groups. **Infant mortality** reached a record low of 6.9 deaths per 1,000 live births in 2000, although the infant mortality for African American infants (13.5) remained more than twice the rate for white infants (5.7).

> How do differences in age, income, and education affect health and health care?

Age

More than 35 million people in the U.S. are 65+ years of age. Individuals 85+ years are the fastest growing of all age groups. While health of the older population varies greatly, **rates of illness and disability** increase sharply after age 85.

The "baby boom" generations are reaching the age of 65. With advancing age comes an increase in chronic health problems.

Income

Income is related to most indicators of health status and **access** to health care. Twelve percent of Americans lived with incomes below the poverty threshold in 2001. The proportions of the population below the **poverty threshold** for selected groups were Caucasian, 10%; African American, 23%; and Hispanic American, 23%. About 46% of families comprised of a female head-of-household and school-age children live below the poverty level, making this the single most impoverished population group.

Educational Level

The annual death rate is 570 per 100,000 population for those with less than 12 years of education, 445 for those with 12 years of education, and 250 for those with 13 or more years of education. **Education** as a health factor, per se, is difficult to tease out because it is associated with **socioeconomic status, access to health care,** and **work** and **environmental conditions.**

Life Expectancy

Both **access to care** and **seeking care** remain major barriers to good health. Life expectancy in the U.S. is 74.1 years overall for males and 79.5 years overall for females. However, there are significant racial differences in life expectancy. Among black males, average length of life is 68.2 years and for black females, 74.9 years.

> Life expectancy at birth for white women is five years longer than for black women and the difference in life expectancy for white and black men is seven years. By age 65, the differences for men and women narrow to two years between the two races.

Heart disease and **malignant neoplasms** are the two leading causes of death among Caucasian, black, Hispanic and Asian/Pacific Islander males and females and Native American females. Among Native American males, **unintentional injuries** are second to heart disease and claim more lives than malignancies.

Causes of Death

Firearm deaths have increased for all races with the largest changes occurring among African American males. Since the mid-1980s, mortality from firearms among 15- to 24-year-olds has increased and mortality from **motor vehicle accidents** has decreased.

Deaths from **cancer** have reached a plateau. The estimated cancer death rate for 2002 was 166.2 per 100,000 population. Trend data from the late 1990s suggest that the rate of death from cancer is actually falling. Black males and females have the highest mortality rate from cancer. In large part, decreased cancer survival is associated with being poor and less educated, having less access to care, delaying seeking care, and lower quality treatment as well as higher risks of exposure to occupational and environmental carcinogens.

Conclusion

Examination of health data reveals significant variations in mortality and morbidity based on race, gender, education level, socioeconomic status, and environment. Advantaged groups, as defined by income, education, social class, or race, have better health and lower mortality than disadvantaged groups. The relationship between health and social position suggests hypotheses about the etiology of diseases and strategies and policies to improve the health of the disadvantaged. *As single entities, poverty, lack of education, and race alone do not necessarily predict higher mortality, but combined they have a synergistic negative effect that is profound.*

Recommended Reading

Blane D. Editorial: Social determinants of health: Socioeconomic status, social class and ethnicity. *American Journal of Public Health* 1995; 85:403–404.

Healthy People: Trends in Racial and Ethnic-Specific Rates for the Health Status Indicators: United States, 1990–98. Statistical Note No. 23, 2002–1237. Washington, DC: Public Health Service; 2000.

Health, United States, 2003. Hyattsville, MD: National Center for Health Statistics; 2003.

Proctor PD, Dalakar J. U.S. Census Bureau, Current Population Reports, P 60–219, Poverty in the United States. Washingtion, DC: U.S. Government Printing Office; 2002.

Sorle PD, Backlund E, Keller JB. U.S. mortality by economic, demographic, and social characteristics: The national longitudinal mortality study. *American Journal of Public Health* 1995; 55:949–956.

Winters LI, DeBose HL. *New Faces in a Changing America.* (3rd ed.). Thousand Oaks, CA: Sage Publications; 2002.

Additional Resources

Current population statistics. Available at http://www.census.gov

Review Questions

1. While health status for Americans in general has shown substantial improvement, minorities have typically not enjoyed the same improvements. Among the following, the most likely reason for this disparity is
   A. a combination of factors including risk, access to care, and discrimination
   B. better quality care for the wealthy and minimal health care for the poor
   C. biological inferiority of patients in minority groups
   D. discrimination against all but the wealthy and the insured
   E. poor use of services by minorities who do not avail themselves of health care

2. Among Native American groups, the major cause of death is
   A. accidents
   B. gunshot wounds
   C. homicide
   D. liver disease
   E. suicide

3. Asians were the fastest growing minority in the U.S. at the end of the 20th century because of
   A. census bias due to mixed race children
   B. immigration
   C. low mortality rates
   D. marriage to U.S. servicemen
   E. the highest birthrate

4. Discrimination is most often directed against minority groups
   A. from countries that were once enemies of the United States
   B. from underdeveloped countries
   C. that do not contribute to the economy through gainful employment
   D. that do not speak English
   E. that historically were brought to the U.S. as sources of cheap labor

5. Native Americans and Alaska Natives
   A. are advantaged by the numerous tax supported health and social services programs available to them
   B. are encouraged not to work and to remain on the reservations
   C. are generally responsible for their health care since the majority are not covered by the Indian Health Service
   D. have access to comprehensive health care through a nationwide system of Indian Health Service clinics
   E. rely almost exclusively on their own health care system of healers and ceremonies

Key to review questions: p. 393

19 The Family

- How do family structures differ with regard to boundaries and cohesion?
- What is the value of a genogram in describing families?
- What are the stages of the nuclear family life cycle?
- What is the empty nest syndrome?
- How do respite care and custodial care differ?
- What are five types of post-divorce relationship?

As a new health care professional, you begin your practice with enthusiasm. After a short time, you notice a recurring pattern among your patients: many do not make the changes you have encouraged and come back with, for example, no change in their weight or in their dietary habits. Puzzled, you wonder why changes are not being made. One of these patients brings his wife with him to the next appointment and during the visit you find they have a traditional marriage and she is the person doing the grocery shopping and cooking. You discover, also, that your patient has not told his wife of the dietary and other changes you recommended. His wife is very concerned about her husband and asks you what can be done to improve his health. This gives you the opportunity to discuss some of the behavioral changes he needs to make. At the patient's next visit, you find that he has lost several pounds, is eating better, and taking walks with his wife.

This simple scenario underscores the fact that the family is one of the most important contexts for influencing positive or negative health behaviors. When a basic knowledge of family functioning and dynamics is incorporated into treatment, patient compliance, cooperation, and satisfaction are often enhanced.

The U.S. Census Bureau defines a **family** as two or more persons who live together and are related by blood, marriage, or adoption. By this definition, 81.2% of households in 1970 were family households as compared to about 70% currently. It should be noted that social scientists often expand this definition of family to include those who live together for other support (i.e., emotional, financial).

The traditional **nuclear family** is the basic unit of husband, wife and child(ren). The **extended family** includes other relatives such as grandparents, aunts, and uncles. The **family of origin** is the family into which a person was born. There are variations and differences among families culturally and otherwise, so sensitivity to the **diversity** of family life is vital.

The number of **married couples with children** in the home declined from 40.3% of all households in 1970 to 23.3% in the early 21st century in response to such factors as older age at first marriage, postponement of childbearing, births to persons not married and high rates of separation and divorce. The number of **single parents** rose from less than 3.5 million in 1970 to 12 million currently. About 80% of single-parent households are maintained by mothers.

Family Structure

How do family structures differ with regard to boundaries and cohesion?

Family structure refers to the way the family is organized. **Boundaries** define who is a member and who is not and the degree to which a family interacts with others. The permeability of family boundaries range along a continuum from diffuse to closed. **Diffuse** boundaries allow individuals to come and go at will, with little to distinguish between those who are family members and those who are not. Thus, family members, especially children, in such families may not have the protection and security they need. **Open** boundaries allow for a healthy exchange of information and interaction with those outside the family. **Closed** boundaries make entering and exiting the family more difficult and can lead to social isolation of the family. Healthy families have predominately open boundaries, but the flexibility of boundaries can change according to the immediate needs of the family. Boundaries also reflect the nature of individuals within the family and the "space" between members.

Emotional closeness or bonding among family members is termed **cohesion.** It varies from **disengagement** (closed boundaries between individuals and low emotional reactivity) to **enmeshment** (diffuse boundaries between individuals and high emotional reactivity). When members of a family are disengaged, there are strict interpersonal boundaries and little sharing of emotion or sensitivity to the feelings or events affecting others. When members of a family are enmeshed, there are fewer interpersonal boundaries, little private action or thought, and emotional processes resonate quickly throughout the whole family.

Family Functioning

Roles define the functions a person fulfills in a group; **tasks** define the responsibilities associated with a role. In the traditional family, roles and tasks are gender specific. In such families, women function in the role of caretaker, while men function in the role of protector-provider. The clearer definition of roles in past generations resulted in more role stability and predictability, but less flexibility, especially for females. In current society, role flexibility is required to accommodate the socioeconomic needs of the changing family, resulting in more symmetric and less gender-specific role allocations.

Family Communication

Communication among family members can be **functional** (direct, and clear) or **dysfunctional** (indirect and confused). Communication occurs at verbal as well as nonverbal levels. The actual words of **verbal** communication are modified by **prosody** (i.e., tone, volume, pitch of the voice) and **nonverbal behavior** (gestures, facial expressions, touches). Healthy families demonstrate congruent verbal and nonverbal communication, express emotion and caring, and share feelings and thoughts.

The Genogram as a Diagnostic Tool

> What is the value of a genogram in describing families?

Genograms (see Figure 19.1.) are a type of family tree used to diagram life events, illnesses, and interpersonal relationships to enhance understanding of family structure, health, and functioning. The genogram not only records the family history of illnesses but also ethnic, religious, and relationship histories as well as the incidence and pattern of occurrence of certain problems (e.g., substance abuse, marital conflict).

Types of Families

Traditional Family

Traditional families are composed of two parents with one or more biologic or adopted children. Contemporary traditional families have fewer differences in gender role assignments, less patriarchy, more equality among members, and fewer children than traditional families of the past. Dual careers require that the nuclear family share its usual childrearing functions with extended family or day care centers, schools, and the workplace. The range of functions for which the family has primary responsibility has narrowed in recent decades.

Figure 19.1. Selected examples of genogram symbols

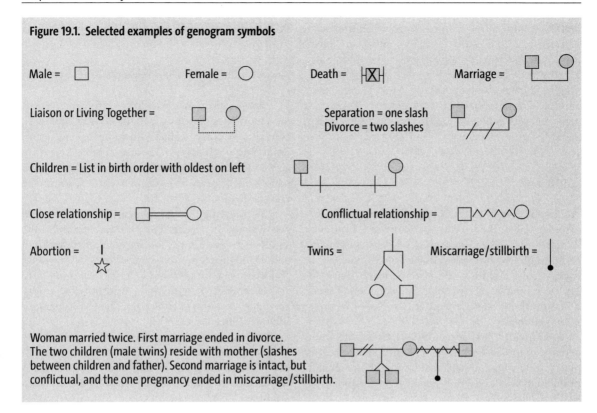

Male =

Female =

Death =

Marriage =

Liaison or Living Together =

Separation = one slash
Divorce = two slashes

Children = List in birth order with oldest on left

Close relationship =

Conflictual relationship =

Abortion =

Twins =

Miscarriage/stillbirth =

Woman married twice. First marriage ended in divorce. The two children (male twins) reside with mother (slashes between children and father). Second marriage is intact, but conflictual, and the one pregnancy ended in miscarriage/stillbirth.

Childless

Couples may wish to have children but experience infertility. Infertility can lead to personally invasive physiologic evaluations and expensive treatments with no guarantee of success. Treatments that diminish the spontaneity of sexual relations by making them mechanical and technical acts can lead to marital dissatisfaction.

For couples who do not wish to have children, improved contraception, sterilization, and abortion have made childlessness an option. However, couples who choose not to have children face certain social pressures especially from extended family members who may misunderstand their choice.

Single-Parent

Most **single-parent families** are the result of unmarried teenage or adult pregnancy, separation, divorce, or spousal death. A small but growing number of single-parent families are the result of adoption. The majority of single parents are females who hold lower paying jobs and who must balance work and family responsibilities with little social or financial support. As a result, many single-parent families are impoverished and have a higher percentage of children with academic and behavioral difficulties. When income is similar, there are fewer differences between children in two-parent and single-parent families.

Divorced/Remarried/Blended

Most divorced persons remarry. Incorporating children from a previous marriage into a new family structure results in a **"blended family."** Varying loyalties to the divorced biologic parents, anger about the dissolution of the previous family, blame directed at some or all of the involved adults, and guilt about personal responsibility for causing the divorce can produce pervasive confusion and conflict. In addition, if the newly formed couple has biological children between them, the complexity of the pattern of relationships and loyalties is increased.

Some blended families adjust well. In others, **stepparents** may be rejected by children who see the stepparent as intruding on their relationship with their biologic parent. In these situations, biologic parents typically are caught in the middle of a battle between their new spouse and their children by their previous marriage. Most parents and children are unprepared for the degree of reorganization and adaptation required for adjustment to the new family structure.

Same-Sex

Although currently denied formal marriage by law in most states, the number of **same-sex families** is increasing. These families confront a number of homophobic stressors. For example, society's focus on the couple's sexuality typically detracts from considering their social, financial, and emotional needs, which are similar to those of heterosexual couples.

Historically, lesbian and gay individuals who become divorced from a heterosexual spouse were rarely given custody of children if their sexual orientation was known. It has also been more difficult for same-sex couples to adopt, but societal and legal views are gradually changing. Some gay or lesbian couples have children from previous heterosexual relationships or through donor insemination or surrogate childbearing. In general, children in gay and lesbian families have not been found to have more behavioral problems than children of heterosexual parents. They do not seem to experience negative effects due simply to the parents' sexual orientation nor are they more likely to be gay or lesbian themselves.

Communal

Communal families subscribe to common ownership of property, performance of tasks, and upbringing of children. Families living in communes have similar values and beliefs and the larger group exercises many of the functions traditionally assigned to the nuclear family. Some of the oldest, most successful and best-researched modern communes are found in Israel. Beyond the notion of commitment to the ideals, goals, and lifestyle dictated by what is perceived as a supportive group, communes and their members vary. Each must be understood in the context of the particular lifestyle and family structure involved.

Nuclear Family Life Cycle

What are the stages of the nuclear family life cycle?

The phases of the nuclear family life cycle reflect the entering and exiting of family members as in marriage, divorce, cohabitation, birth, and death. Some life cycle events are predictable based on age and sociocultural expectations. Other events vary with lifestyle and the particular form of the nuclear family.

The most traditional nuclear family life cycle consists of six stages: (1) between families: the single young adult; (2) joining: the newly married couple; (3) incorporating: the family with young children; (4) letting go/holding on: the family with adolescents; (5) launching children: the empty nest; and (6) withstanding time: the family in later life (see Table 19.1.).

Transitions between life cycle stages require adaptation to new ways of functioning (e.g., changing the marital relationship to accommodate a child; accepting the independence of a child who graduates from school). When a family system is not flexible enough to adapt to change, it may become dysfunctional. Life cycle transitions, like any change, place stress on the family system. However, families that have anticipated the changes that will be required and that have identified useful coping strategies are most likely to maintain good individual and family health.

Between Families: Single Young Adults

This lifecycle phase involves the young adult establishing independence and autonomy, moving out of the parental household, separating from parents, establishing new relationships, increasing responsibility for financial management, and assuming responsibility for place of residence and health care.

Joining: Newly Married Couples

The median age at first marriage in the U.S. has increased over the past three decades (females 20.8 to 26 and males 23.2 to 27). The selection of a partner is influenced by geographic, socioeconomic, religious, and age factors as well as love.

Table 19.1. Stages of the family life cycle

Family life cycle stage	Emotional process of transition: Key principles	Changes required for evolution
Between families: Single young adults	Accepting emotional and financial responsibility for self	a. Differentiation of self in relation to family of origin b. Development of intimate peer relationships c. Establishment of vocation and financial independence
Joining: Newly married couples	Commitment to new system	a. Formation of marital system b. Realignment of relationships with extended family and friends to include spouse
Incorporating: Families with young children	Accepting new members into the system	a. Adjusting marital system to accommodate children b. Sharing childrearing, financial, and household tasks c. Realignment of relationships with extended family to include parenting and grandparenting roles
Letting go/holding on: Families with adolescents	Increasing flexibility of family boundaries to permit children's independence and grandparents' dependence	a. Shifting of parent/child relationships to permit adolescents to move into and out of the system b. Refocus on midlife marital and vocation issues c. Beginning shift toward caring for older generation
Launching children: Empty-nest couples	Accepting exits from and entries into the family system	a. Renegotiation of marital system as a dyad b. Development of adult-to-adult relationships between grown children and their parents c. Realignment of relationships to include in-laws and grandchildren d. Dealing with disabilities and death of parents (grandparents)
Withstanding time: Couples in later life	Accepting shifting generational roles	a. Maintaining own and/or couple functioning and interests in face of physiological decline b. Support for more central role of middle generation c. Adjusting to loss of spouse, siblings, and peers and preparation for death

Adapted from: Carter B, McGoldrick M (Eds.). *Expanded Family Life Cycle: The Individual, Family, and Social Perspectives.* 3rd ed. Boston, MA: Allyn and Bacon; 1999.

Homogamy is the term given to the selection of marriage partners who have similar social characteristics. However, differences **(heterogamy)** also can be attractive. Homogamy tends to be secure and comfortable; heterogamy tends to be unpredictable and exciting. **Closed boundaries** around the partners enable them to establish their own identity as a couple and a new family system, but can create tension with in-laws who see the new partner as a threat to their relationship with their offspring.

The glossing over of conflicts or difficulties common in the early stages of a relationship is called **romantic idealization** or the "utopia syndrome." Because each partner comes with his or her own family of origin experiences, ideas about how a marriage and family should function, and expectations about rules and roles, the new couple has the task of integrating the expectations they each bring from their respective families. Family planning also involves negotiation between the spouses regarding contraception and child bearing.

Incorporating: Families with Young Children

With the arrival of children, the partners must adjust to meeting the child's needs, the resultant disruption in family routines, and decreased time alone. Differences in child rearing practices, thresholds for exhaustion and privacy, and balancing demands for time and attention required by the children must be negotiated. As children grow and develop they interact with larger systems, such as peer groups and schools. On the one hand, these experiences bring new ideas and energy into the family. On the other hand, these experiences lead the child to challenge the family's belief system and routines. This process gains momentum with the approach of adolescence.

Letting Go/Holding On: Families with Adolescents

The major issue of adolescence is **autonomy.** If the family has allowed the child to gain gradually increasing autonomy with increasing age and maturity, the family system will adjust more easily to the adolescent's demands for independence and separation. If, instead, the family system has been authoritarian, rigid, and enmeshed, it is more difficult to make this life cycle transition. Thus, parents and adolescents who **avoid extreme positions** and **negotiate compromises** make the most successful transitions. These families usually establish only a few basic ground rules that are not overly restrictive, but that do provide adequate structure and safety.

Many of the concerns that teenagers present to their physicians relate to **self-image** (e.g., puber-

tal development, height, weight, skin problems). Because of their sense of personal invulnerability, they may be unresponsive to preventive counseling about **risk-taking** behaviors. As a result, adolescents often engage in dangerous behaviors. **Motor vehicle accidents** are the leading cause of death and **substance abuse, pregnancy, sexually transmitted diseases, violence** against others, and **suicide** are major problems that must be addressed despite the typical adolescent's reluctance to do so.

Launching Children: Empty-Nest Couples

What is the empty nest syndrome?

This stage of the family life cycle is the period between the time the children exit and retirement. While many couples derive satisfaction and relief from knowing that the phase of rearing dependent children is past, others become so child focused that the continuing development of the couple relationship is neglected, producing a feeling of uselessness (**"empty nest"**). Not all families launch their children during young adulthood and some launch the same child several times (**"elastic nest"**). Because of educational, financial, career, or marital considerations, adult children may return to their parents' home repeatedly. This phenomenon of returning home (**"boomerang effect"**) is a prime example of why the family life cycle is best viewed as a flexible series of stages and transitions, some of which are extended or repeated.

As parents enter middle age, they become aware of **health problems** in peers and begin their own **physical changes** (e.g., increased weight, decreased metabolic rate), motivating many to initiate better health practices. Age-related bodily changes occurring at this stage typically signal decline. Coping with these reminders of mortality stress psychologic well-being and marital adjustment. Struggles with **personal identity** or the integrity of the marriage can produce a **mid-life crisis.**

This is the period when most couples experience the loss of their own parents and assume the roles of matriarch/patriarch of the family for the younger generations. The addition of grandchildren may bring the generations closer together as the new parents come to appreciate the contributions their parents made to their own care and upbringing. Grandparents can enjoy their grandchildren without the demands of parenthood, but must be prepared to respect and support their adult children as parents.

Withstanding Time: Couples in Later Life

Adjustments during this period of life include retirement and shifting generational roles. **Physical and intellectual decline, custodial care, loss,** and **bereavement** become major issues. For some, the later stage of life is a rewarding time of enjoying accomplishments and finding satisfaction in the freedom to pursue new interests. For others, the transitions and adjustments are overwhelmingly negative.

Retirement requires significant adjustment if the couple has difficulty tolerating the amount of time they now have together or if the partners disagree about how to divide their time between outside interests and each other. Those who have derived their **identity** from their vocation miss the satisfaction of their job or become isolated if their social network and status depended on work contacts. Retirement can strain **financial resources.** Income is typically reduced just at the time assisted living and medical expenses increase.

The most significant loss experienced during this stage is the **death of the spouse.** The narrowed social circle produced by retirement results in more time and activity with the spouse, who may be the primary person giving purpose and meaning to life. When a death occurs, the extended family must realign and adjust to new relationships. If death was preceded by a chronic illness, burnout among caregivers may complicate the adjustment process, limiting support for the grieving spouse.

How do respite care and custodial care differ?

Many persons remain active and functional into old age but physical and intellectual decline eventually concern both the individual and the family. Some individuals can be cared for with periodic **respite care.** Other patients require **custodial care,** such as that provided in an **assisted living facility** or **nursing home.** This transition can be emotionally traumatic and cognitively disorienting because of loss of familiar objects and activities.

Assessing the attitudes of each family member about custodial care, the family's emotional and logistical resources without placement, the financial resources for placement, and timing of the placement is vital. Options such as home health nursing care, bringing a full-time caretaker into the home, and accessing community services also should be explored. Some individuals move to another geographic area to be near their adult children. Changes should be undertaken cautiously since losing years of friendships and routines and trying to establish new relationships and habits may not be tolerated well.

Special Issues of Contemporary Families

Occupation and Career

Two-career families must balance child rearing, household chores, and careers. However, women generally retain the major responsibility for running the home even if they have other employment. Despite the added stress of multiple responsibilities, however, women who work outside the home report enhanced self-esteem. In contrast to past generations, most persons today change jobs several times during their lifetime. If job or **career obligations** typically take precedence over family life, this uneven allegiance can produce tension in both marital and parental relationships. Due to the ready-made network provided by the workplace, the family member who accepts a job transfer may have less difficulty with the change than the other family members.

More than 50% of mothers with children less than 1 year of age are employed outside the home. Comparisons between children raised by **"stay-at-home" mothers** and children placed in home or **agency child care** reveal that the effect of early child care on infant development is influenced by many factors such as group size, child-to-caretaker ratio, and consistency of the child care provider.

"Latchkey children" are youngsters less than 13 years old who care for themselves at home while their parents work. Although parents may be concerned about leaving their children at home alone, many have few alternatives. Lack of appropriate supervision increases risk of behavioral problems.

Geographic Mobility

The high degree of **geographic mobility** in U.S. society results in separation from extended family that might otherwise be available to provide support and nurturance. **Job relocations** can be especially difficult for the spouse and children who, unlike the person being transferred, do not have the positive status reinforcement of a promotion or other career advancement. Indeed, they are likely to lose the status they have achieved in their own workplace, school, or community.

Divorce

It is estimated that almost 50% of all U.S. marriages will end in **divorce**. The family life cycle of divorc-

ing families has different phases (see Table 19.2.). As a result of family instability and parenting disruption, children, preteens and adolescents whose parents have divorced are at increased risk for depression and conduct problems. Increased risk does not imply all children of divorced couples will experience these difficulties. The majority adjust well. The impact of the divorce depends upon the ability and manner in which parents dissolve the marriage, continue to parent, and restructure the family. Usually older children adjust better because they have a better understanding of what is occurring.

Litigation in court is the most common approach to divorce settlements in general, and to child custody, in particular. It is typically costly, time consuming, and adversarial.

Divorce mediators function as a neutral party to negotiate divorce settlements. The goal is to find

Table 19.2. Phases of the family life cycle for divorcing families

Phase		Emotional process of transition: Prerequisite attitude	Developmental issues
Divorcing	Decision to divorce	Accepting the relationship must end	Accepting personal responsibility for the failure of the marriage
	Planning the breakup of the system	Supporting viable arrangements for all parts of the system	a. Working cooperatively on Problems of custody, visitation, and finances b. Dealing with extended family about the divorce
	Separation	Co-parenting cooperatively Beginning dissolution of attachment to spouse	a. Mourning loss of intact family b. Restructuring marital and parent-child relationships c. Realignment of relationships with own and spouse's extended family
	Divorce	Overcoming hurt, anger, and guilt	a. Mourning loss of intact family, giving up fantasies of reunion
Post-divorce	Single parent (custodial household or primary residence)	Maintaining cooperative co-parenting	a. Making flexible visitation arrangements with ex-spouse and family b. Rebuilding own social, financial, and emotional resources
	Single parent (noncustodial)	Maintaining cooperative co-parenting Fulfilling financial responsibilities Maintaining parental contact and supporting custodial parent's relationship with children	a. Finding solutions to problems of visitation and distance parenting b. Maintaining financial responsibilities to ex-spouse and children c. Rebuilding own social, financial, and emotional network

Adapted from: Carter B, McGoldrick M (Eds.). *Expanded Family Life Cycle: The Individual, Family, and Social Perspectives.* 3rd ed. Boston, MA: Allyn and Bacon; 1999.

a mutually acceptable solution to division of assets and authority. Successful mediation results in less intense conflict and fewer legal battles, but is contingent on both partners' willingness to negotiate without intimidation. The resulting agreement is usually reviewed by the attorney and financial consultant representing each party.

Legal custody can be sole (i.e., one parent has the legal right to make decisions regarding the child) or joint (i.e., both parents have the legal right to share in decisions regarding the child). **Physical custody** can be either sole or joint. In sole physical custody, the child lives with one parent and the other parent may have visitation rights as determined by the court or the parents. In joint custody, the amount of time the child spends at each home is negotiated and is not necessarily equally divided between the households.

Reduced standard of living is a major problem for the children of divorced parents. In some instances, true financial hardship arises from the need to maintain two households. Nonpayment of child support is also a problem. Recently enacted laws permit delinquent payers to be pursued for enforced compliance. Unresolved conflict between the former spouses is a primary motivation for nonpayment. Withholding child support is used to punish the former spouse, without regard for how nonpayment affects the child. From the children's perspective, financial support can be perceived as a measure of how much the non-custodial parent loves and cares for them.

Adjustment to divorce includes vacillation between relief and depression. Unless patients are aware that this emotional turmoil is normal, they may feel they are becoming mentally ill. Rapid movement into another relationship provides escape from emotional pain. Such transitional or **"rebound"** relationships are usually short term, but act as conduits to the next phase of relationship building.

Surrogate Mothering

"Surrogate mothering" refers to bearing a child for someone else, usually in return for a fee. Reasons for choosing a surrogate mother include infertility, repeated miscarriages, hysterectomy, or other health conditions. Whenever possible, the couple **("commissioning couple")** supply both the sperm and the egg, which, when fertilized *in vitro*, is implanted in the surrogate mother's uterus **("gestational carrier surrogate")**. This procedure circumvents the issue of whose child the woman is carrying because all genetic material is

Post-Divorce Relationships

Perfect Pals: Disappointment about the failed marriage does not impair positive elements of the relationship. Share decision making. Spend holidays together and maintain relations with extended families. Many feel they are better parents divorced than married.

Cooperative Colleagues: Work together around concerns of children and family, but are not close friends. Able to manage conflicts and separate spousal from parental issues.

Angry Associates: Like cooperative colleagues but not able to compartmentalize anger. Most likely to end up being tense, hostile, or in open conflict.

Fiery Foes: Intensely angry and litigious years after the divorce. Unable to recall anything good about the marriage. Cling to very old wrongs. Still attached, but quick to deny it.

Dissolved Duos: After the divorce, have no further contact.

(Adapted from: Ahrons CR. Divorce: Not the end, but a change in a relationship. *The Brown University Family Therapy Letter.* Providence, RI: Manisses Communication Group, Inc; Copyright 1990. Used by permission.)

What are five types of post-divorce relationship?

Although highly educated women are the least likely to do so, most divorced persons remarry within a few years. Some persons experience feelings of loss when their former spouse marries because they must confront retained fantasies about reconciling the marriage.

derived from the couple. In some situations, the sperm or egg may be provided by an anonymous donor bank. Potential confusion regarding parental rights, still debated in the court system, makes the surrogate mother the least desirable egg donor.

Moral, ethical, and legal issues raised by surrogate mothering include arguments that it is a form of human exploitation, particularly of the poor. That is, although "renting" a woman's uterus places her at risk for pregnancy- and delivery-associated complications, some women might be willing or feel obliged to take this risk in return for the financial gain. Others argue that it is a positive technologic advance that can lessen the emotional pain of infertility by providing a means to having a biologic child.

Home-Based Care

Recent trends in early discharge from the hospital or other health care facilities have led to the growth of **home health agencies.** Agency personnel assist and instruct family members with their caretaking responsibilities including home dialysis, home chemotherapy, and ventilator management. The burden on the family is mitigated by the benefit the patient and family derive from being in the home setting. The patient may recover more function more quickly than in an institutional setting, and the family may experience a heightened sense of accomplishment. Parents of children, in particular, may feel in better control of the care and comfort their child receives. Even with good resources and the ability to give adequate care, however, caregiver burnout is common.

Recommended Reading

Benokraitis N. *Marriages and Families: Changes, Choices, and Constraints.* (4th ed.). Englewood, NJ: Prentice Hall; 2001.

Crane D. *Handbook of Families and Health.* Thousand Oaks, CA: Sage; 2006.

Gottman M, Declaire D. *The Relationship Cure: A Five-Step Guide for Building Better Connections with Family, Friends, and Lovers.* New York: Crown Publishing; 2001.

McBride J. *Family Behavioral Issues in Health and Illness.* New York: Haworth Press; 2006.

Powers P, Orto A. *Families Living with Chronic Illness and Disability: Interventions, Challenges, and Opportunities.* New York: Springer Publishing; 2004.

Review Questions

1. A family does not provide protection or structure for its children from outside influences. What kind of boundaries is this family most likely to have?
    A. Closed boundaries
    B. Diffuse boundaries
    C. Open boundaries
    D. Rigid boundaries
    E. Tight boundaries

2. Which of the following is considered a primary indicator of transition in the family life cycle?
    A. Birthdays
    B. Celebrations
    C. Closeness and distance
    D. Entering and exiting
    E. Rituals

3. The couple who seek a surrogate mother in order to have a child is called the
    A. biological couple
    B. commissioning couple
    C. embarking couple
    D. enabling couple
    E. gestational couple

4. Which descriptor of the family indicates emotional processes flow quickly through the family system?
    A. Alliance patterns
    B. Circular causality
    C. Disengagement
    D. Enmeshment
    E. Strong individual boundaries

5. Currently, what is the average age at first marriage for males in the U.S.?
    A. 23
    B. 24
    C. 25
    D. 26
    E. 27

Key to review questions: p. 393

Section VI

Societal and Behavioral
Health Challenges

20 Obesity

- How is obesity defined?
- To what degree is obesity genetic?
- How does stress influence obesity?
- What behavioral factors contribute to obesity?
- What is the "behavioral approach" to treating obesity?

How is obesity defined?

Obesity is defined as excessive accumulated fat in the body. In most clinical settings, measurement of body fat is difficult. **Body mass index (BMI)** is a surrogate measure to estimate adiposity. It is calculated from height (m) and weight (kg) measurements. BMI does not directly measure body fat, therefore clinical assessment of body composition (e.g., muscular habitus) is important.

$$BMI = \frac{weight\ (kg)}{height\ squared\ (m^2)}$$

Adults

Among adults, **obesity** is defined as a BMI = 30 or higher. Overweight is defined as a BMI between 25 and 29. Extreme obesity is defined as a BMI ≥ 40 or higher.

Children and Adolescents

Due to the stigma associated with the term "obesity," childhood obesity is termed "overweight." Specifically, childhood overweight is defined as a BMI ≥ the 95% on gender- and age-specific BMI growth charts. A second category of "at-risk-for overweight" describes youth with a BMI between the 85th and 95th percentiles. Youth at-risk-for overweight warrant further assessment to prevent obesity.

Other methods used to estimate body fat and body fat distribution include skinfold thickness and waist circumference. For adult men, a waist circumference > 40 inches and for adult women a waist circumference > 35 inches is associated with

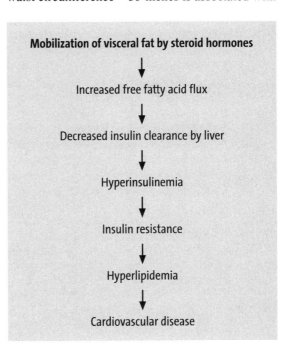

Mobilization of visceral fat by steroid hormones

↓

Increased free fatty acid flux

↓

Decreased insulin clearance by liver

↓

Hyperinsulinemia

↓

Insulin resistance

↓

Hyperlipidemia

↓

Cardiovascular disease

increased risk of metabolic diseases associated with obesity. Individuals with central body obesity, specifically abdominal adiposity, are at significantly greater risk for cardiovascular disease and type II diabetes mellitus than those with lower body adiposity. The increased risk for morbidity and mortality of obese persons is primarily due to increases in **visceral fat deposition** that triggers metabolic changes that, in turn, mediate many of the complications of obesity.

Obesity Trends

In the U.S., about one third of all adults and nearly 20% of children and adolescents are overweight. While obesity occurs in all ethnic and socioeconomic groups and both genders, health disparities exist. Overweight contributes to over 300,000 deaths each year making it second only to smoking as a source of mortality. Medical complications of obesity include diabetes mellitus, hypertension, heart failure, dyslipidemia, hepatosteatosis (fatty liver), osteoarthritis, cholesterol gallstones, sleep apnea, and respiratory insufficiency.

Childhood onset is associated with greater genetic predisposition, adipose tissue hyperplasia, and more severe overweight. Key predictors of obesity during adulthood include obesity during childhood, especially later adolescence, and obese parents.

Regulatory Determinants

To what degree is obesity genetic?

Genetics

Obesity and overweight are the results of consuming more energy (calories) than an individual expends. For approximately every 3,500 kcal consumed in excess of energy expended, one pound will be gained. However, some individuals are more vulnerable to overweight than others due to complex interactions between genetic and environmental factors. Adoption, twin, and twins-reared-apart studies have shown that **heritability**

accounts for about 33% of an individual's BMI. **Genetic factors** appear to be especially important in determining regional distribution of fat (including the size of the visceral fat store) rather than total body fat, per se.

Body Fat

Adipose cellularity is defined as hypertrophic (an increase in the size of cells), hyperplastic (an increase in the number of cells), or both. Average-weight adults have about 25 billion fat cells; **weight gain is associated with increased size (hypertrophy), rather than increased number (hyperplasia) of fat cells.** Individuals who have been overweight from childhood, however, have both hypertrophy and hyperplasia, and may have as many as 150 billion fat cells. Weight loss results in smaller cells but not a decrease in number, which helps explain the elevated body weight (fat) set point of hyperplastic obese patients.

Stress and Hormones

How does stress influence obesity?

Stress-induced neuroendocrine responses are important mechanisms in increasing appetite and the quest for **"comfort food."** In response to stress, the hypothalamus triggers the sympathetic nervous system and releases corticotropin releasing hormone (CRH), initiating an emergent stress response and short-term (minutes) suppression of appetite.

However, CRH, in turn, stimulates release of adrenocorticotrophic hormone (ACTH), which initiates a cascade of events culminating in adrenal release of glucocorticosteroids. Glucocorticosteroids subsequently stimulate appetite over a longer period of time (hours).

In cases of stress-related eating (**"emotional eating"**) and obesity, the act of eating may provide comfort rather than the food consumed. This lack of discrimination between eating out of true hunger and eating out of frustration, anger, or depression may help explain why satiety and satisfaction are less easily achieved in the latter instance. Because eating does relieve these negative emotions, the individual continues to eat and, over time, gains weight. Ironically, becoming obese often adds further to negative feelings and a vicious cycle ensues.

Satiety

The physiological gastrointestinal signals and hormonal mechanisms leading to satiety are intricate. There are several hormones involved with satiety and two are highlighted here. **Leptin** is a satiety hormone produced from adipocytes. Leptin resistance may lead to hyperphagia, obesity, insulin resistance, and hyperinsulinemia. **Cholecystokinin** is released when the stomach expands with a meal and contributes to satiety. When individuals eat rapidly, they are able to consume a significant volume of food – and calories – before these mechanisms and hormones are able to signal satiety.

What behavioral factors contribute to obesity?

Two behavioral factors are particularly important influences on obesity: **diet and lifestyle.** The increase in the fat content of the typical U.S. diet from 32% in 1910 to 43% in 1985 mirrored the increase in the prevalence of obesity over the same time period. Dietary fat promotes obesity since it has greater caloric density (9 kcal/g) than either carbohydrate or protein (each, 4 kcal/g); it is converted into body fat 25% more efficiently than is either carbohydrate or protein; and intake is not internally regulated (i.e., the amount of fat eaten at one meal does not influence fat intake at the next meal). However, another important contributor to the continuing fattening of the U.S. population has been the erroneous belief that "low fat means low calorie." In fact, **many low- or nonfat foods have a high carbohydrate content making them as calorie-dense as "regular" foods.**

The decrease in **physical activity** associated with labor saving devices, and sedentary work and leisure activities has paralleled the increase in obesity, although the correlation is not perfect. For example, it has been found that **exercise** can prevent the development of obesity if the genetic tendency to overweight is weak, and can mitigate, but not prevent, obesity if the tendency to overweight is strong.

Treatment

What is the "behavioral approach" to treating obesity?

The younger the age at onset and the longer the duration of the obesity, the poorer the prognosis for successful weight management. Recent expert recommendations have focused on the idea of weight maintenance or slowing the rate of excessive weight gain, rather than weight loss, during childhood. Weight loss, however, is the goal in children who have complications from obesity or whose BMI is > 95th percentile for height and age. Weight loss is also the typical goal in adults who are overweight.

Methods of treatment include **self-care; nonclinical** or **commercial programs** (Weight Watchers, Jenny Craig); and **clinical programs** that provide professional medical, nutritional, and psychological care. Clinical programs include pharmacotherapy, very-low-calorie diets, and behavior therapy. Individuals for whom conservative treatment is ineffective and who are at significant risk for serious complications, may require surgical interventions such as jejunoileal bypass, gastric restriction (e.g., "stapling"), or gastric bypass. Long-term weight management is poor with any technique, including surgery, unless the individual is committed to making lifestyle changes that insure that caloric intake does not exceed expenditure.

A major problem in the treatment of obesity is the prevalence of **fad or quick-fix diets** that do not provide nutritionally balanced intake sufficient for long-term healthy eating. Adherence to these diet plans can result in **rapid weight loss,** but this loss is usually due to shifts in water balance rather than reduction in body fat.

When real body weight loss does occur, it involves a loss of lean body mass (muscle) as well as fat. Unfortunately, when weight is regained, in the absence of muscle-building activity, most of it is stored as fat because this is the quickest way for the body to process extra energy (calorie) intake. Ultimately, "see-saw" weight changes result not only in obesity but also in poorer overall health. The **behavioral changes** needed to be successful require an "all things in moderation" approach to nutrition, and a commitment to **balancing caloric intake and energy expenditure**.

Reinforcement of small steps, as in any behavioral modification program, is critical. Obese individuals are frequently less responsive than others to gastrointestinal cues of fullness, and more responsive to external stimuli such as the sight of food. Thus, stimulus control is an important element in retraining eating behavior.

Stimulus control strategies include eating small forkfuls, chewing fully, and swallowing before taking the next bite; laying down the fork or spoon between bites; refusing second helpings; eating only at set times each day, spaced throughout the waking period; eating only in the presence of other people; drinking 8 ounces of water before any meal or snack; not shopping for food when hungry; buying only from a predetermined list; and buying lower-fat products that are not high in processed sugar.

Esteem-building self-help groups can be useful in assisting patients to accept their tendency to be overweight, remain active and functional, and resist "lose weight – regain more weight" dieting cycles. The philosophy espoused by such groups is that it is better to maintain a weight in the mildly to moderately obese range than to experience large swings in body weight that ultimately produce profound obesity associated with replacement of lean body mass with fat.

Recommended Reading

America Dietetic Association (ADA). Position of the American Dietetic Association: Individual-, family-, school-, and community-based interventions for pediatric overweight. *Journal of the American Dietetic Association* 2006; 106:925–945.

Dallman MF, Pecoraro N, Akana SF et al. Chronic stress and obesity: A new view of "comfort food." *Proceedings of the National Academy of Sciences of the U.S.A.* 2003; 100:11696–11701.

Dietz WH. Health consequences of obesity in youth: Childhood predictors of adult disease. *Pediatrics* 1998; 101:518–525.

Fairburn CG, Brownell KD. *Eating Disorders and Obesity.* (2nd ed.). New York: Guilford Press; 2001.

Wadden TA, Stunkard AJ. *Handbook of Obesity Treatment.* New York: Guilford Press; 2002.

Review Questions

1. A 16-year-old girl weighs 80 kg and is 150 cm tall. Her body mass index (BMI) is closest to
   A. 25
   B. 30
   C. 35
   D. 40
   E. 45

2. Which of the following combinations of sensitivity to satiety cues and responsiveness to environmental stimuli is most characteristic of obese compared to normal weight people?

	Sensitivity to Satiety Cues	Responsiveness to Environmental Stimuli
A.	Same	+
B.	+	–
C.	–	+
D.	–	Same
E.	Same	Same

3. Fad diets often produce rapid weight loss. This change in weight is primarily due to shifts in body
   A. adipose tissue
   B. glycogen stores
   C. muscle mass
   D. salt
   E. water

Key to review questions: p. 393

21 Substance Abuse

- Which drugs are most likely to be abused?
- What are other dangerous health behaviors associated with substance abuse?
- What factors contribute to substance abuse?
- What physical and psychological factors contribute to drug dependence?
- What are three types of treatment programs and how do they work?
- What is a "network intervention" approach?
- What is a "harm reduction" program?

Substance intoxication is a reversible syndrome that develops after recent ingestion of a drug. It is accompanied by maladaptive behavior or psychological changes due to the effect of the substance on the central nervous system. **Substance abuse** is a maladaptive pattern of substance use that disrupts or impairs functioning at work, school, home, and leisure, and may cause or precipitate physical and psychological harm and persistent legal, social, and interpersonal problems. **Substance dependence** reflects the need to rely upon a substance, which is expressed as a pattern of behavioral, physiologic, and cognitive symptoms and signs, usually indicated by tolerance, withdrawal, and significant distress. The state of **tolerance** is signaled either by the need for increased amounts of the substance to achieve the desired effect, or by the diminished effect attained with the use of the same amount of the substance. Substance **withdrawal** is the syndrome of specific physical and psychological signs and symptoms that occurs when a person stops using a substance that has been used heavily or for a long time. Withdrawal causes impairment in physical, psychological, social, and occupational functioning which typically can be reversed if the drug is used again.

Persons who abuse or depend on substances are locked into a disordered pattern of behavior that compels them to cyclically repeat the destructive pattern. The pattern itself prevents them from exercising the sound judgment that would give them the option to resist. This leaves such persons vulnerable to many risk behaviors. Among these, the best-studied is sharing needles, which is associated with drug use by injection. In "shooting galleries," drug users can engage in communal drug injecting and needle sharing. Because any cleansing or discarding of needles and syringes between uses is rare, such practices result in frequent micro blood transfusions and attendant disease transmission. The risk is multiplied by the fact that drug users who inject heroin alone or in combination with cocaine shoot up, on average, three to five times a day, and users of IV cocaine may inject every 15 minutes to maintain a high.

Which drugs are most likely to be abused?

Alcohol is the most common psychoactive drug used worldwide. Sixty-five percent of American adults admit to drinking alcohol and 11% admit drinking, on average, 1 oz. of alcohol daily. Fifteen percent of the U.S. health care dollar is used to treat alcohol-related disorders, and alcohol-related deaths rank third behind heart disease and cancer.

What are other dangerous health behaviors associated with substance abuse?

Intravenous drug use is an important vehicle for the acquisition and transmission of **infectious dis-**

Psychoactive Substances Most Likely to Be Used in Maladaptive Patterns

- Alcohol
- Opioids (opium, morphine, meperidine, methadone, pentazocine)
- Sympathomimetics (amphetamine, cocaine)
- CNS depressants (barbiturates, methaqualone, meprobamate, benzodiazepines)
- Inhalants (nitrous oxide)
- Hallucinogens (LSD, mescaline)
- PCP
- Volatile hydrocarbons (petroleum derivatives)
- Belladonna alkaloids (atropine, scopolamine)
- Cannabis, nicotine, caffeine
- Designer/"Club" drugs (MDMA, ketamine, GHB)

---

eases (e.g., hepatitis B and C, HIV/AIDS), and ranks immediately behind **unsafe sex practices** as the most common risky behavior in which individuals who have HIV/AIDS engage. More than 45,000 cases of AIDS in the U.S. have been attributed to IV drug use. Although the rate of infection among IV drug users nationwide stabilized at approximately 30% in the late 1990s, the rate of HIV infection among injecting drug users in New York City has been estimated to be 50%.

Sustained and chronic **alcohol abuse** can have damaging effects upon various organ systems of the body. **Hepatic impairment** or damage may be evidenced by fatty liver, hepatitis or cirrhosis. **Cardiovascular impairment** may be evidenced by arrhythmias or cardiomyopathy. **Neurological damage** most frequently associated with chronic alcoholism includes Korsakoff dementia and neuropathy. Alcohol induced **immune system suppression** can result in increased risk of infections and some cancers. The teratogenic effect of alcohol impacts **reproductive system** functions and may contribute to anovulatory cycles and early menopause in women and testicular atrophy in men. Alcohol ingestion by pregnant women increases the risk of **fetal alcohol syndrome** in their offspring

Trends

Use of **crack/cocaine** appears to be decreasing, especially in the northeastern U.S. Use of **mari-**

juana, in contrast, has increased in most areas primarily because of resurgence among adolescents. The rate of use of substances, such as **inhalants** and **LSD**, is also increasing among adolescents, and even preadolescents.

The use of **heroin**, which is considered to be a more benign drug than crack/cocaine, is increasing. Greater purity of the heroin available on the street makes the high obtained by inhalation similar to that obtained by injection. Inhalation is especially appealing to female users. The purer forms of both heroin and crack are often sprinkled on marijuana and smoked. This combination frequently serves as an adolescent's introduction to the harder drugs of abuse.

Substance Use and Family Systems

What factors contribute to substance abuse?

Although imitation of peers is a potent factor in drug use, children and adolescents often first consider experimentation with drugs as a way of **coping with tension** in the family. Adolescents sometimes use drugs to attract their **parents' attention**; that is, the negative attention and punishments imposed are viewed as preferable to being ignored. Conversely, drug use by an acting-out adolescent may be tacitly encouraged by the family as a means of avoiding focusing on major underlying problems that threaten the integrity of the family.

Patterns of Substance Use

- Experimental (may abate, intensify, or turn into the other types)
- Social-recreational (may remain as such, intensify, or become compulsive)
- Circumstantial-situational (opportunistic, may intensify, or become compulsive)
- Intensified (may be an added quality of the other patterns)
- Compulsive (maladaptive)

Note: While all patterns of drug abuse can become maladaptive (impair functioning), compulsive patterns are always maladaptive.

Parental use of alcohol or other drugs may be perceived by children as condoning drug use or as hypocritical if they prohibit and punish behaviors they themselves exhibit. Alcohol use, which is pervasive in all segments of society, poses an especially difficult challenge for adolescents who may view drinking alcohol as just another aspect of identity formation and a milestone to adulthood.

Family problems associated with substance abuse include marital discord, neglect, job loss, and frequent relocations that result in disrupted peer relationships and social instability. Children of substance abusers may be stigmatized in school and the community. Dealing with these stresses can lead to substance abuse among those who adopt the behavior they see modeled by their parents. Even if this behavior is understood to be both intellectually and emotionally maladaptive, the children may not be aware of resources to break the behavior cycle or may not be in a position to access these resources without parental assistance.

Ending Dependence

> What physical and psychological factors contribute to drug dependence?

The **brain reward circuits** include dopaminergic neurons located in the ventral tegmentum that project to the nucleus accumbens via the medial forebrain bundle. The nucleus accumbens sends projections to the cortex and other centers. The brain reward circuit is initiated by stimulation or disinhibition of **dopaminergic neurons** in the ventral tegmentum. The terminal projections of these neurons release dopamine in the nucleus accumbens, resulting in a rewarding experience. Positive reinforcement of addictive substances stimulates the brain reward mechanism and negative reinforcement occurs when the physical and psychological withdrawal is relieved by the same or similar substances.

Based on this physiologic explanation of addiction, there are three **principles for developing treatment plans:**

1. Adverse physical symptoms must be minimal (i.e., few people knowingly put themselves in a position where discomfort and pain are likely);

> **Repeated exposure to a drug can produce enduring changes in the signaling properties of neurons in three systems:**
>
> - Physical control systems, which mediate autonomic and other somatic functions leading to physiologic dependence;
> - Motivational control systems, which oversee motivated behavior; and
> - Associative memory systems, which produce powerful cue-dependent drug cravings.
>
> All three systems are active in perpetuating dependence. However, the physical control system is the most significant, although not necessarily essential to producing addiction.

2. The motivation for giving up the substance must be greater than the motivation for continuing use; and
3. Places, activities, and other situations that are strongly associated with using the substance (e.g., smoking while drinking a cocktail or coffee) must be avoided.

The Role of the Motivational System in Substance Abuse

Most drugs of abuse act on neural mechanisms that mediate incentive behavior in response to positive emotions. Alcohol, marijuana, heroin, co-caine, and other dependency-inducing substances activate mesolimbic dopamine-containing neurons and associated opioid receptors in the brain. This system is hypothesized to be a common final pathway for reward and the regulation of motivation. Drugs of abuse create a pleasurable signal in the brain that reinforces continuing drug use. This leads to further drug-seeking behavior, which displaces other, more adaptive, behaviors. Treatment cannot begin until the patient takes at least some initial steps toward recovery by entering into a therapeutic relationship with a counselor or a program. Although recidivism is high among recovering addicts, it approaches 100% among those who are involuntarily enrolled in treatment.

Substance Abuse Treatment Programs

What are three types of treatment programs and how do they work?

Supportive care during withdrawal depends on the type of drug used and where the patient is within the withdrawal cycle. Patients who are experiencing a bad trip from LSD may need only a quiet space and a warm reassuring person to talk them down. In contrast, a patient who is withdrawing from alcohol may require hospitalization, hydration, and sedation to avoid a life-threatening crisis.

With the exception of hallucinogens, marijuana, and caffeine, most drugs have significant **withdrawal symptoms** requiring prompt recognition and treatment. Although there are no major physiological effects associated with withdrawal from cocaine, there are serious emotional and psychological consequences, including risk for suicide.

Types of Treatment Approaches

1. Detoxification (acute; 5–21 days)
2. Rehabilitation (short-term; 28 days)
3. Residential (long-term; 6–24 months)

Detoxification units are usually available in hospitals or other medical care settings to treat the acute physical effects of withdrawal from opiate, alcohol, and sedative hypnotic dependence. Average length of stay ranges from 5 days for alcohol detoxification to 21 days for benzodiazepine detoxification. Opiate detoxification typically requires 14 days. In general, detoxification programs are designed to prevent potentially life-threatening withdrawal syndromes. Affected patients are usually given a substance for which they have a cross-tolerance, administered in tapered doses over a defined number of days as prescribed by protocol. Most detox programs are staffed by physicians, nurses, social workers, rehabilitation and occupational counselors, and certified alcoholism and substance abuse counselors. They also provide **12-step programs** and **relapse prevention groups.**

After detoxification, many patients enter a **short-term rehabilitation program** for up to 28 days. Short-term units offer a full schedule of structured activities to divert attention away from wanting or needing drugs. Typical activities include support groups; spirituality, relaxation and meditation groups; acupuncture; health education; HIV counseling; individual supportive or insight-oriented counseling; rehabilitation/vocational services; and activities of daily living groups (personal grooming, housekeeping, recreational/gym activities). These activities attempt to motivate the patient to continue in recovery and prevent a relapse.

Some patients enter a **residential therapeutic community** for 6 months to 2 years of intense therapy with limited contact with the outside environment. Successful treatment requires commitment and adherence to the strict rules imposed on residents. Many addicts enroll only under court order as an alternative to incarceration. The goal is to produce change in the personality structure and belief system of the individual. Residents who are poorly motivated or who enter the program only to satisfy others may be unable to tolerate the continuous scrutiny or engage in the self-reflection characteristic of such programs.

Like most substance abuse programs, therapeutic communities rely heavily on recovering addicts to provide counseling and to serve as role models. Therapeutic community programs are also designed to provide residents with job training, education, and an improved emotional state. The overall goal is to enable the resident to maintain lifelong sobriety and abstinence from drugs.

Network Intervention Approaches

What is a "network intervention" approach?

Network intervention engages the addicted patient, family and friends to provide support, encouragement, and monitoring. In this technique, the therapist recruits the assistance of significant others to provide accurate assessment of progress in recovery (e.g., quantity and pattern of use). Involving the social network also reinforces the message that the patient has not been abandoned and that others are invested in the program and its success. Network intervention is a philosophy of care and can occur in any treatment setting (residential, non-residential; short- or long-term).

Smoking Cessation Programs

Smoking cessation programs follow the same tenets as programs designed to treat other drug addictions. The emphasis is on recovery and relapse prevention. Symptoms from nicotine withdrawal are similar to those from other drugs. Many smoking cessation programs use transdermal nicotine patches and nicotine gum as replacement therapy in addition to social support and motivational counseling. Psychoeducational sessions are designed to counter media messages about smoking. Many programs are located in schools and directed toward children and adolescents. Since peer pressure and curiosity are the most common reasons young people begin smoking, prevention is the key to anti-smoking programs in this age group.

Harm Reduction Strategies

What is a "harm reduction" program?

Harm reduction programs attempt to minimize the consequences of illicit drug use in persons who have little on no motivation to change their behavior. The most desirable outcome is stopping drug use. However, if the individual wants to continue use, then stopping drugs by injection becomes the goal. If injection is desired, then not sharing injection equipment is the goal. If sharing will continue, using a decontaminating agent between users is the goal. In harm reduction, any positive steps are reinforced. Demanding an all-or-nothing commitment prohibits outreach to persons who fall into transition categories in their movement toward change. By encouraging and reinforcing smaller steps, it is hoped that the ultimate goal, stopping usage, will eventually be realized (see Chapter 37, Changing Risk Behavior).

Needle exchange programs (NEP) are an example of a harm reduction method, although use remains controversial. At an NEP, addicts are given a supply of sterile needles in return for dirty used needles. At some NEPs, bleach kits are distributed for cleaning needles between injections. Condoms

may be distributed. These programs often operate out of mobile centers that travel to high drug use areas on a regular schedule. These centers also provide medical care, program referrals, and food in an attempt to engage their clients.

Recovery readiness programs are similar to harm reduction programs. Program goals include outreach to users who are not responsive to overtures from drug treatment programs.

Methadone Maintenance Programs

Methadone is a synthetic narcotic that has pharmacologic effects similar to those of heroin and morphine although it inhibits the euphoric effects of narcotic agents. It has a similar addictive liability but has a 24- to 36-hour half-life, permitting once-a-day dosing. In contrast, heroin is typically used every 3–4 hours or more often throughout the day. Methadone given in sufficient doses not only blocks the euphoria-producing effects of heroin, it also stops heroin craving.

Methadone maintenance programs provide lifelong daily doses of methadone to heroin addicts at a regular time and place. The intent of these programs is to reduce the need for addicts to participate in criminal acts to fund their addiction and to reduce physiologic effects associated with withdrawal. Success is defined as reduction or cessation of heroin use, cessation of criminal activity, and appropriate productive functioning in the community. Methadone maintenance programs provide a safe place for patients to come to on a daily basis and be reinforced for their steps towards recovery.

Misconceptions about methadone include the belief that methadone is absorbed into bones and teeth causing pain and weakness, and that it is more addictive than heroin. These concerns are unfounded. Methadone is the least expensive drug treatment available for those persons who cannot be drug free.

Acupuncture in the Treatment of Addictive Behaviors

Auricular acupuncture, needle insertion limited to defined anti-addiction points on the ear and lobe, is gaining popularity as a therapy for such addictions as alcoholism, smoking, and obesity. In Oregon, no methadone treatment programs, for example, are available for alcoholics. Instead, addicts receive regular periodic auricular acupuncture treatments. In some cases, small pellets or seeds are implanted in the lobe for up to two weeks and patients are instructed to press the point several times a day to stimulate the flow of Qi to reduce cravings. Anecdotal and small cases series reports have described good success rates that are comparable to pharmacologic and cognitive-behavioral treatments. Few randomized controlled trials exist. Unfortunately, the recidivism rates for all treatment approaches remain relatively high.

Recommended Reading

American Psychiatric Association Practice Guideline for the Treatment of Patients with Substance Use Disorders. *American Journal of Psychiatry* 2006; 163(Suppl.):8.

Bachman JG, O'Malley PM, Schulenberg JE, et al. *The Decline of Substance Abuse in Young Adulthood*. Mahwah, NJ: Erlbaum; 2002.

Graham AW, Schultz TK, Mayo-Smith M, Ries R (Eds.). *Principles of Addiction Medicine*. (3rd ed.). Chevy Chase, MD: American Society of Addiction Medicine; 2003.

Sadock BJ, Alcott Sadock V. Substance-Related Disorders. In: *Synopsis of Psychiatry. Behavioral Sciences/Clinical Psychiatry*. (9th ed.). Philadelphia, PA: Lippincott Williams & Wilkins; 2003; pp. 380–470.

Tucker JA, Donovan DM, Marlatt GA. *Changing Addictive Behavior*. New York: Guilford Press; 2000.

Review Questions

1. Among the following, which condition must be met in order for substance abuse treatment to be successful?
   A. The counselor must be available at all times of crisis.
   B. The family must insist on therapy.
   C. The individual must be voluntarily enrolled.
   D. The pain associated with abuse must be greater than the pleasure.
   E. The threat of legal action must be substantial.

2. The recommended definition of substance abuse is use that it
   A. disrupts activities of daily living
   B. is associated with criminal activity
   C. is limited to injectable substances
   D. produces withdrawal symptoms when stopped
   E. requires long-term residential treatment

3. The basic goal of harm reduction programs is
   A. development of supportive peer and family networks
   B. improved education about the negative effects of drugs
   C. minimization of the consequences of drug use
   D. provision of assistance to recovering addicts
   E. substitution of a less addictive drug

4. A 62-year-old male is admitted to the hospital for an elective knee replacement. Three days after surgery he complains to the surgical resident that he has been seeing a cat under his bed and has been feeling scared and anxious. On physical exam he is tremulous, his pulse is rapid and his blood pressure is elevated. When the resident returns with the attending physician, the patient is having a seizure. What is the most likely cause of his problems?
   A. Alcohol intoxication
   B. Alcohol withdrawal
   C. Amphetamine intoxication
   D. Cocaine withdrawal
   E. Heroin intoxication

5. A 35-year-old lethargic male with slurred speech is brought to the emergency room after being found in the street. He is inattentive and unable to give a good history due to memory difficulties. On physical examination, he is noted to have constricted pupils. What is the most likely diagnosis?
   A. Alcohol intoxication
   B. Alcohol withdrawal
   C. Amphetamine intoxication

D. Cocaine intoxication

E. Heroine intoxication

6. A 55-year-old female has been taking benzo-diazepines in therapeutic doses prescribed by her primary care physician, for many years. She decides to stop taking the medication. After three days without medication, she calls her doctor. Which of the following symptoms she is most likely to report?

   A. Decreased sensory sensitivity

   B. Increased appetite

   C. Rhinorrhea

   D. Tremors

   E. Yawning

7. A 40-year-old male patient tells his doctor that he has been abusing cocaine. Which of the following symptoms is most likely to be seen as a result of cocaine withdrawal?

   A. Dysphoric mood

   B. Flushed face

   C. Hypertension

   D. Tachycardia

   E. Tremors

Key to review questions: p. 393

22 Interpersonal Violence

- What are four major forms of abuse?
- What children are at risk for abuse?
- What are the clinical signs of partner abuse?
- What is the Trauma Syndrome?
- What are the characteristics of the typical perpetrator?
- What external factors contribute to violence?

What are four major forms of abuse?

A **violent act** is defined as any act of physical aggression or coercion toward a person against their will, without their consent. This definition includes psychological as well as physical **abuse** and emphasizes the issues of real or perceived **power and control.**

There are four major forms of abuse:

1. **Physical abuse** should be considered in any case of unexplained injury, as evidenced by bruises, welts, burns, lacerations, abrasions, fractures, bites (human or animal), or incidents of slapping, punching, kicking, choking, assault with a weapon, or tying down or otherwise restraining.
2. **Psychological/emotional abuse** is defined as controlling behavior where the perpetrator exercises power over another person or violates the person's rights and freedom through fear, degradation, threats of harm, extreme jealousy and possessiveness, deprivation, intimidation, or humiliation.
3. **Sexual abuse** includes acts of exposure, sexual exploitation (including childhood prostitution), and forced, coerced or any other unwanted sexual contact.
4. **Social/environmental abuse** is defined as behaviors that control a victim's activities including social contacts with other people, access to transportation, or withholding financial or other sources of support as a method of control.

In a violent relationship, abusive incidents are repetitive and often escalate over time.

Types of Abusive Relationships

Stranger-to-stranger violence includes acts of workplace violence, random violence, and institutional acts of violence, (sexism, sexual harassment, ageism, and racism). Many episodes of **rape and assault** occur between parties who know each other, as in date or acquaintance rape. Contrary to popular beliefs, stranger-to-stranger violence is among the least common forms of violence in the U.S. Nonetheless, stranger assault and violence rates in the U.S. are among the highest in the world. Although stranger assault carries a lower risk of repetition and escalation than intra-family assault, physical and psychological effects can be greater. Many victims become emotionally disabled by the apparently senseless and unpredictable quality of the violence and withdraw from what they perceive as an unsafe world.

Family violence includes spouse/partner abuse, child abuse, child sexual abuse/ incest, sibling abuse, marital rape, and elder abuse. Family or **"domestic" violence** is characterized by a continuing relationship between the victim and the perpetrator. There is a high risk of repeated or increasingly violent encounters because of common living quarters and ongoing contact that provide easy access to a vulnerable victim. **Power dynamics** in the family render the victim dependent, fearful, and ambivalent about leaving the relationship or seeking and accepting help. Because many episodes of family violence occur in private, they are often undetected and unreported.

Child Maltreatment and Abuse

What children are at risk for abuse?

Child maltreatment includes both **physical** and **psychological abuse** and **neglect** of children. It was the first type of domestic violence to be legally defined, legislated against, and designated as a violent act. It **must be reported** to the appropri-

---

Child Risk Factors for Abuse

- Difficult/unwanted pregnancy
- Traumatic delivery
- "Difficult" child
- Colic
- Hyperactivity
- Congenital abnormalities
- Chronic illness
- Physical disabilities
- Inadequate parental bonding or attachment

Clinical Signs Suggestive of Child Abuse

- Multiple injuries of different stages of healing
- Fractures caused by pulling, twisting, shaking
- Rib fractures in the absence of accidental trauma
- Multiple skull fractures suggesting repeated blows to the head
- Cerebral edema and retinal hemorrhages suggesting violent shaking
- Burns to the hands, buttocks, feet, and legs
- Scalding of the feet, lower legs, or in a stocking/glove pattern suggesting immersion in hot water
- Grip marks on the thighs, bite marks on the breast or buttocks, perineal lacerations or scars, bruising of the genitalia or anus suggesting sexual abuse
- Any unexplained injury

---

ate authorities (police, Child Protective Services) whenever suspected by individuals serving in health or educational capacities (physician, nurse, social worker, teacher).

Child maltreatment refers to any act of omission or commission that endangers or impairs the child's emotional or physical heath and development. Typically, however, it is the intentional, nonaccidental use of force by an adult caretaker aimed at injuring the child that is reported to authorities. In cases of Shaken Baby Syndrome, the caretaker is as likely to be a poorly skilled boyfriend or babysitter as a parent. Estimates vary from 60,000 to over 3 million affected children annually.

Children are especially vulnerable to **emotional abuse** because of their physical and emotional dependence and inability to protect themselves. Emotional abuse, although more difficult to identify and quantify than physical abuse, may be more profoundly damaging.

Definitions of **neglect** (inadequate food, shelter, clothing, and supervision) vary by state and may be mitigated by circumstances including intentionality, ignorance, poverty, and mental illness of the adult caretaker.

Discipline vs. Abuse

Determining when **parental discipline** is severe enough to be considered child abuse is complicated by sociocultural factors. That is, disciplinary practices vary among ethnic groups and over time. Severe physical punishment was acceptable discipline to many parents in the U.S. until the 1950s. Current standards of childcare, however, require the parent or guardian to meet the child's basic needs for shelter, nutrition, safety, and hygiene. These standards also require the parent or guardian to refrain from physical acts that may result in welts, bruises, or other enduring physical marks on the child. In cases where such injury is inflicted, the **health care professional** is obligated, by law, not only to provide care for the immediate injury, but also to intervene to protect the child from further abuse.

Child protective authorities must be notified in all cases of suspected child abuse so that a comprehensive investigation and assessment of future risk to the child can be performed.

Sexual abuse refers to sexual acts perpetrated on children by adults or on any individual below the age of consent by another individual who is at least 4 years older. **Incest** refers to acts perpetrated specifically by a family member on a child. It is estimated that each year more than 250,000 children are subjected to various acts of incestuous contact.

Sibling abuse refers to a violent act perpetrated by full siblings, half siblings, and adopted siblings. It is the most common form of family violence, and is estimated to involve more than 29 million children each year.

Partner Abuse

Partner abuse includes marital, non-marital, and same-sex adult partners. Although psychological and verbal abuse are the most common kind of abuse in partner relationships, this abuse also includes physical and sexual maltreatment, as well as property damage. Child abuse and pet abuse may also occur concomitantly.

Although the majority of partner/spouse abuse reported in the U.S. is perpetrated by the male partner, a significant number of women are also verbally and physically aggressive in domestic settings. This is particularly true in cases of child and elder abuse in which women are abusive at rates equal to or greater than men.

Men and women perpetrate violent acts differently. Up to 90% of severe partner/spouse injuries are perpetrated by men. Many of the assaultive acts and criminal homicides committed by women appear to occur in response to aggression and threats by the male partner. Conversely, men often have difficulty asking for help when they are victims.

Partner/Spouse Abuse

- Occurs in > 1 in 4 households
- The most likely place for homicide to occur is in the home
- ~ 30% of adult women are beaten at least once in their lifetime by the man with whom they are living
- ~ 12% of women are beaten repeatedly

Marital Rape/Date Rape

Marital rape definitions vary by state depending on whether, and to what extent, intention to have sexual relations is implicit in longer-term consenting adult relationships. **Date rape,** a sexual act perpetrated on an individual in short-term, non-committed relationships without consent, is also subject to interpretation of intent. Approximately 15% of married women in the U.S. have been raped by their husbands. Specific statistics are difficult to obtain because of differing medical and legal definitions of what constitutes abuse and differing definitions of "partner." In some instances, abuse is applied mutually, further complicating the definitions of victim and perpetrator.

What are the clinical signs of partner abuse?

Signs of Partner Abuse

- Multiple bruises, cuts, blackened eyes
- Defensive trauma to the hands, wrists, arms
- Cerebral concussion
- Strained or torn ligaments
- Fractures
- Blunt injuries to the chest or abdomen
- Loss of hearing or vision
- Burns or bites
- Knife or gun shot wounds
- Vaginal, perianal, and cervical tears and lacerations
- Miscarriage, placental hemorrhage, fetal fractures, rupture of the uterus, and premature labor

Many victims may mask interpersonal violence injuries as "accidents" or justify being hurt by blaming themselves. Attempting to avoid further threats and violence, some women restrict their activities and become less assertive. They accept apologies by their partner hoping the situation will improve. They are reluctant to report battering because of financial dependency, or fear that the perpetrator will punish them or their children. Consequently, repeated injury is likely. It is essential to examine the patient's entire **medical history** for indications of previous abuse and to document findings and suspicions in those cases in which the patient's diagnosis cannot be made. Domestic violence cases can initially present as stress, anxiety, and depressive disorders and be characterized by over-utilization of medical services through vague, recurring complaints

Ending the relationship does not necessarily end the violence. Up to 40% of women without a current relationship are at risk of violence by a past partner as a result of persistent threatening behavior or stalking.

Elder Abuse

Elder abuse statistics generally involve adults > 60 years. There are approximately 500,000 to 1 million victims of elder abuse each year. Thus, it occurs less frequently than partner/spouse abuse but may be as common as child abuse. The National Center on Elder Abuse estimates that more than two thirds of elder abuse perpetrators are spouses, children, or other relatives. Thus, although some abuse of the elderly occurs in institutional settings, the majority of abuse takes place in the home.

Evidence of **physical assault** is often not visible to the casual observer and may become apparent only when assisting with bathing or performing a physical examination. Physical abuse must be differentiated from accidental falls and mishaps resulting from infirmity. Physical abuse is often coupled with **neglect** and occurs in the context of caregiving challenges (e.g., dementia, handicaps, self-care limitations) that the family member is poorly prepared to handle.

As in the case of child abuse, the elderly may be unable to report maltreatment because they are **dependent** on the perpetrator. Wrongdoing may be denied by the victimized elder and attempts made to cover for the offending family member. Self-dis-

Types of Elder Abuse (% of substantiated cases)*	
Neglect	50%
Emotional/psychological abuse	35%
Financial exploitation	30%
Physical abuse	25%
Abandonment	4%

* > 1 type of abuse may be present concurrently

paraging comments made by the victim regarding being old or of no value, communicating a sense of resignation, or acceptance of low self-worth may be signs of emotional abuse.

> Clinical signs of elder abuse include multiple bruises or fractures at different sites and of different ages; genital and urinary tract infections; bleeding; malnutrition; excessive or inadequate medication; and poor hygiene.

Violence-Related Trauma Syndrome

What is the Trauma Syndrome?

The psychological effects of violence closely parallel those experienced by victims of other traumatic events. **Psychophysiologic distress** is characterized by pervasive fear and anxiety and accompanied by sleep deprivation, early morning awakening, and recurrent nightmares. **Loss of resiliency, inability to concentrate,** and **emotional instability** are common. **Somatic complaints** may result from actual physical injuries, but more often are related to **stress. Suspiciousness, anger** and **rage** can evolve into morbid hatred of the perpetrator. **Grief, depression,** and **suicidal ideation,** especially following multiple traumatic events, can occur. **Avoidance, denial, emotional numbing** or blocking, and, in some cases, **detachment** or **psychogenic amnesia,** may also occur.

Cognitive Signs

Cognitive and mental distress is indicated by viewing the world as unsafe, insane and devoid of meaning; viewing oneself as damaged; guilt and self-blaming; a sense of personal powerlessness and limited hope for the future **(learned helplessness);** and acceptance of the inevitability of violence and abuse. **Disturbances in interpersonal relationships** include pathologic detachment and dependency on the perpetrator after family violence; loss of emotional connection with loved ones after stranger assault; inability to trust or be intimate; emotional instability; avoidance of opportunities for new or more satisfying relationships; difficulty setting limits or establishing boundaries with others; and repetition of previous patterns of interaction.

Posttraumatic Stress Disorder (PTSD)

Although the diagnosis of **PTSD** was initially given to survivors of natural disasters or war, the disorder is prevalent among individuals who experience interpersonal violence. Victims of violence experience a range of symptoms, but not all develop PTSD. The most common traumatic event listed for PTSD in the DSM-IV is "a serious threat to one's life or physical integrity; [or] a serious threat or harm to one's children" (see Chapter 41, Anxiety Disorders).

Assessment of Potential for Victimization

A. **Define abuse/violence**
B. **Assess associated behavioral characteristics** including depression, sadness, rationalization of behavior, protection of the perpetrator, and the use of drugs or alcohol to mask pain, hurt, embarrassment, and guilt.
C. **Assess stages of the cycle of violence, if present**
   Stage 1. The tension building phase includes verbal accusations, threats, and throwing objects as tension escalates.
   Stage 2. The incident of violence itself, which can be either physical or psychological battering.
   Stage 3. The contrition phase, is characterized by apologies, gift giving, and promises the behavior will never occur again. Some perpetrators enter treatment at this stage, but typically only briefly. If the victim believes the abuser, the relationship continues until the cycle occurs again. The cycle will repeat itself indefinitely unless timely and consistent clinical intervention is provided.
D. **Clinical assessment protocol** includes identifying the victim and providing confirming **psychological testing** by an experienced clinical psychologist and **corroboration** (from medical, employment, shelter, social agency, criminal justice, school, church, or military records) for court hearings, education and prevention.

Common Features of PTSD

– Intrusive memories or flashbacks of the original trauma
– Nightmares
– Heightened arousal such as exaggerated startle response
– Hypervigilance to potential danger
– Numbness
– Disturbances in interpersonal relationships (mistrust, inability to become intimate)
– Fear, anger, depression
– Sexual dysfunction

Risk factors for developing PTSD include repeated severe psychological or emotional abuse, having experienced both physical and sexual assault, and a perception of life threat or sense of helplessness. Approximately 35% of women in domestic violence shelters suffer from PTSD but often present with less fully developed symptom clusters in the form of Battered Woman's Syndrome.

Perpetrators of Interpersonal Violence

What are the characteristics of the typical perpetrator?

Characteristics of perpetrators of domestic violence include exposure to family violence during childhood, drug or alcohol abuse, rigid assumptions about gender roles, denigration of women, exaggerated need to control, jealousy or paranoia, low self-esteem or depression, difficulty verbally communicating feelings, anger, hostility, and aggressiveness.

Perpetrators of violence are found in every socioeconomic, educational, racial, ethnic, religious and political group and are of all ages and both genders.

Typically, **perpetrators of child abuse** have a history of violent treatment or neglect by their parents during their childhood, which then serves as their model for parenting behavior. As a result, there may be impaired bonding to the child, deficits in child rearing skills, or developmentally inappropriate expectations for the child's behavior. Stressors, such as socioeconomic pressure, lack of adequate family support, spousal discord, and conflicts over childcare responsibilities, are common in abusing families.

Societal and Situational Factors

> What external factors contribute to violence?

Violence is sanctioned and modeled in sports, the military, law enforcement, in certain situations as self-protective acts by regular citizens, and in the media. Violence is often precipitated by social and environmental events such as **interpersonal conflicts** with intimate family members, by **territorial disputes** between strangers, and by **domineering/ unjust authority figures.** It also involves psychological factors such as acceptance of aggression as a means of resolving conflict, unrealistic expectations regarding certain types of relationships, prejudicial sentiments toward groups of people, and learned responses to stress and challenge. Recent job loss and relationship loss (due to separation or divorce), or being denied access to children can be major events and risk factors.

Influence of Drugs and Alcohol

Drug and alcohol intoxication increases the risk of violence. The severity of an assault is correlated with the use of alcohol or drugs by the perpetrator or the victim. In some instances, individuals with no history of violence but who are taking benzodiazepines can become violent, especially following the ingestion of alcohol. Careful history regarding current prescribed and non-prescribed drugs can help detect potential chemical interactions and diagnose atypical reactions to medication. Abuse of illicit drugs such as cocaine, LSD, amphetamines, and phencyclidine hydrochloride (PCP) heightens the risk of violence by increasing arousal, irritability, and the possibility of inducing psychosis or paranoia.

Central Nervous System

Damage to the **hypothalamus** or **frontal and temporal lobes** of the brain increases the likelihood of assaultive behavior. The individual who has such brain damage may have limited ability to assess degree of threat, or to manage frustration or anger. Rarely, a seizure disorder (e.g., temporal lobe or complex partial seizures) can elicit violence, but this type of behavior is usually diffuse, disorganized, and stereotyped. The number of people who perpetrate violent acts due to neurologic impairment may be limited but this etiology should be considered as it represents a potentially treatable cause of aggressive behavior.

Psychiatric Conditions

Violent behavior is not specific to individuals with psychiatric conditions. With the exception of intermittent explosive disorder, which includes violent behavior by definition, many diagnostic categories list aggressive behavior as one of many possible manifestations of **affective instability and impaired impulse control.** Thus, psychopathology is best viewed as a **vulnerability factor** that makes anger and assaultive behavior more likely, rather than as a causal factor. That is, the presence of a psychiatric illness is neither necessary nor sufficient for violence and victimization to occur.

Violence as a Crime

The types of violence discussed above are crimes in most states. Some types, such as spouse and child abuse, are considered crimes in all states. Although they are crimes, current professional policy dictates attention by both the criminal-justice and health care systems. Health care providers must become familiar with reporting laws in the particular jurisdiction in which they practice to insure compliance with these laws. The Joint Commission on Accreditation of Hospitals requires the identification of abuse in clinical settings and the implementation of hospital polices that mandate protocols for identification, assessment, and diagnosis. Health care providers must be able to recognize cases of violence, assess the risk for further harm, and make reasonable efforts to protect the patient, family members, and potential victims from physical and emotional harm. Excepting cases involving threats to life, serious bodily injury or harm, or use of a weapon, most states do not require mandatory reporting of spouse abuse. Such decisions are usually best made in collaboration with the victim in order to preserve trust and to avoid inadvertently exposing him or her to increased risk.

Intervention

The Center for Disease Control and Prevention has adopted the RADAR system to encourage health providers to intervene in case of interpersonal violence. This acronym stands for the following steps in practice:

R – Routinely screen for violence- and abuse-related injury and symptoms during the course of customary care.

A – Ask questions directly in a nonjudgmental manner.

D – Document findings in the chart, preferably using body maps and photos for evidentiary purposes.

A – Assess the patient's immediate safety and develop a safety plan.

R – Review and refer patient to in-house and community-based resources

---

The following 4-question screening instrument (HITS) has been validated for both female and male patients to assist in the evaluation process.

How often does your domestic partner (or anyone else):
1. hurt you physically?
2. insult you?
3. threaten you with harm?
4. scream or curse at you?

Education and Prevention

Tertiary prevention of violence and abuse requires crisis programs with trained professionals, shelters, emergency response communication,

and clinical protocols to manage presenting problems. **Secondary prevention** requires education, particularly among health care professionals, and effective public service campaigns. **Primary prevention** involves eradicating sexism, power imbalances, racism, ageism, and elitism and increasing individual responsibility for promoting zero tolerance for violence.

Recommended Reading

Arias I, Corso P. Average cost per person victimized by an intimate partner of the opposite gender: A comparison of men and women. *Violence and Victims* 2005; 20:379–391.

Barnett O, Miller-Perrin CL, Perrin RD. *Family Violence Across the Lifespan*. Thousand Oaks, CA: Sage Publications; 2005.

Campbell J, Jones AS, Dienemann J. Intimate partner violence and physical health consequences. *Archives of Internal Medicine* 2002; 162:1156–1163.

Maiuro RD. Intermittent explosive disorder. In DL Dunner (Ed.). *Current Psychiatric Therapy*. (Revised ed.). Philadelphia, PA: W.B. Saunders; 1996.

Shakil A, Smith D, Sinacore JM, Krepcho M. Validation of the HITS domestic violence screening tool with males. *Family Medicine* 2005; 3:193–198.

Thompson RS, Rivara FP, Thompson DC, Barlow WE, Sugg NK, Maiuro RD. Identification and management of domestic violence: A randomized trial. *American Journal of Preventive Medicine* 2000; 19:253–262.

Review Questions

1. Which of the following is the best estimate of how many children are subjected to various acts of incestuous contact annually?
    A. 25,000
    B. 100,000
    C. 250,000
    D. 500,000
    E. 1,000,000

2. The most common form of family violence, involving more than 29 million individuals each year, is
    A. child sexual abuse

B. elder abuse
C. marital rape
D. sibling abuse
E. spouse/partner abuse

3. The percentage of married women in the U.S. who have been raped by their husband is closest to
A. 5%
B. 15%
C. 25%
D. 35%
E. 45%

4. Male partners perpetrate approximately what percentage of violent acts in partner abuse?
A. 10%
B. 25%
C. 50%
D. 75%
E. 90%

Key to review questions: p. 393

23 Poverty and Homelessness

- How is poverty defined?
- What proportion of various subgroups live at or below the poverty level?
- What are the consequences of poverty?
- What poverty-related factors contribute to homelessness?
- What health problems are prevalent among the homeless?
- How are the effects of homelessness passed on to future generations?

How is poverty defined?

Poverty is defined as the lack of resources necessary to maintain a minimally adequate standard of living but, lacking a definition of adequate standard of living, poverty in the U.S. has come to be defined in reference to the national average income.

The official poverty population statistic reported each year by the U.S. Census Bureau is called the **poverty threshold**. It is based on a matrix of measures that include family size and whether or not the person is elderly. Since families of three or more spend about one third of their income on food, poverty level is set at three times the cost of food. For two-person families and persons living alone, this calculation is adjusted. Poverty threshold figures are updated every year to reflect changes in the **Consumer Price Index**.

Poverty guidelines are simplified versions of the poverty thresholds that are used for administrative purposes. The guidelines also vary by family size but, unlike the poverty threshold, which provides for no geographic variability, there is one set of guidelines for the 48 contiguous states and the District of Columbia and one set each for Alaska and Hawaii.

The administrative function of the guidelines is to determine an individual's eligibility for a number of federal programs such as the Low-Income Home Energy Assistance Program, Community Food and Nutrition Program, AIDS Drug Assistance Program, Community Health Centers, Family Planning Services, Food Stamps, Nutrition Program for Women, Infants and Children (WIC), National School Lunch Program, School Breakfast Program, Weatherization Assistance for Low-Income Persons, Migrant and Seasonal Farmworkers Program, and Legal Services for the Poor.

In 2000, 11.3% of Americans lived in poverty, and the percentage has increased each year

2006 HHS Poverty Guidelines

Person(s) in Household	48 States & DC	Alaska	Hawaii
1	$9,800	$12,250	$11,270
2	$13,200	$16,500	$15,180
3	$16,600	$20,750	$19,090
4	$20,000	$25,000	$23,000
5	$23,400	$29,250	$26,910
6	$26,800	$33,500	$30,820
7	$30,200	$37,750	$34,730
8	$33,600	$42,000	$38,640
Add /person	$3,400	$4,250	$3,910

From the *Federal Register,* Vol. 71, No. 15, January 24, 2006, pp. 3848–3849 since. In 2004, 12.7% of Americans lived in poverty. Poverty varies by time, situation and group. Layoffs in businesses and industry may create a poverty situation for an individual or family that had not previously experienced poverty. The layoff may be temporary or companies may close their doors. Natural disasters such as hurricanes, tornadoes, floods, droughts or severe winters may create long- or short-term poverty. Health plays a significant role in creating poverty situations. Illness or injury may prevent a person from working or result in loss of a job, uninsured or under-insured health care, high drug costs or long-term or nursing home care. No one is immune to poverty.

What proportion of various subgroups live at or below the poverty level?

The **standard of living** and the **distribution of wealth** in the U.S. shows variation by subgroups of the population. While poverty cannot be generalized to a subgroup, there are disturbing patterns of association with **racism, discrimination, under-education** and **under-employment**.

Poverty shows striking variations by racial and ethic groups. Twice the number of blacks and Hispanics/Latinos live in poverty when compared to whites and Asians in the U.S. population.

Poverty is highest among families headed by single women, particularly black or Hispanic/Latino. In 2004, 28.4% of the households headed

Numbers of Poor Over Time		
Year	**Millions**	**%***
1960	40	22
1978	24	12
1995	36.4	14
2001	32.9	12
* rounded		

by single women were poor. If the head of household was black or Hispanic/Latino, almost 40% were poor. In comparison, 13.5% of male head of household and 5.5% of couple households were poor (University of Michigan National Poverty Center).

Thus, living at or below the poverty level is correlated with being African American, living in a single-parent household, and having less than an eighth-grade education. Children, elderly, minorities, recent immigrants, less educated, working poor, and unemployed are also vulnerable to becoming a member of this group.

Consequences of Poverty

What are the consequences of poverty?

Resources such as **financial assets, shelter,** and **social support** allow humans not only to survive, but also to have a positive sense of self. Over time, people have become genetically programmed to exist in an **average expectable environment.** This is the environment in which the infant is equipped to cope at birth and in which the person is capable of thriving throughout development.

Poverty denies people the resources and resilience to cope successfully or even survive. Poor children typically receive inadequate nutrition for the development of a healthy body. Maternal malnutrition can result in poor fetal growth and development including impaired brain growth. Hungry children cannot learn at school. Such sequelae are good predictors of impaired adjustment to life and lowered resiliency to stress.

Poor children are likely to receive less **social and intellectual stimulation.** Impoverished fami-

Percentage of People Living in Poverty (2001)	
By ethnic group	**%**
General population	11.7
Caucasians	9.9
African Americans	22.7
Hispanics/Latinos	21.4
Asians/Pacific Islanders	10.2
By age	
< 18 years	16.3
> 65 years	10.1
By geographic location	
New Mexico (highest %)	17.7
California (lowest %)	0.7

lies are usually overwhelmed by the practical necessities of meeting basic needs for food and shelter. Parents may consider age-appropriate play and stimulation for the child a low priority. This can result in **impaired neurobehavioral development, poor skill acquisition,** and **increased risk for academic failure,** frustration, and anger. Typically, poor children are educated in crowded schools with limited resources that provide little more than custodial care. Many students have learning or developmental disabilities that are inadequately identified and seldom remediated. When they leave school, many poor children have **few occupational skills** and become trapped in **low-paying jobs** with no expectation of advancement, or they remain jobless.

Other vulnerable groups include the rural poor, immigrants, and the elderly. Largely forgotten, the **rural poor** scratch out a meager living on small farms, perhaps selling produce in open markets. Others hunt and fish and do odd jobs when available. These people are being squeezed out by agribusiness, disappearing wildlife areas, and the demand for natural resources. **Immigrants** seeking the American dream usually must begin with low-paying jobs. **Elderly** who worked hard to own their homes and live in old, often ethnic neighborhoods that are surrounded by more expensive houses may find their property taxes have risen above what they can pay on a fixed income.

Homelessness

What poverty-related factors contribute to homelessness?

It is estimated that on any given night, 700,000–800,000 people are homeless. In the U.S., 2.5–3.5 million people will experience homelessness during the year. About half of the people who have the experience of being homeless are single adults and about half are part of a family group. Typically, about two thirds of the homeless are single adults and one third are families. Most single adults move in and out of being homeless, many entering a shelter for a month or less. About one tenth of homeless adults live within a system of shelters, hospitals, and jails. Little is known about the estimated 1.5 million children and youth who expe-

rience at least one night of homelessness during a year (National Alliance to End Homelessness, 2006).

During the latter decades of the 20th century, the **deinstitutionalization** movement in psychiatry added patients with chronic mental illness, and the drug epidemic contributed addicts to the homeless group. During the **recessions of the 1980s,** and around the turn of the century, the number of people unable to pay rent increased. Those unable to live with family or friends became homeless. **Gentrification** dislodged urban poor from their homes. Abused wives, runaway children, and single- and two-parent poor families also joined the group.

As noted above, about 30% of all homeless persons live as part of a homeless family. Although some homeless live in cars, subways, or tunnels, the majority live on the street. Most homeless people use free community resources such as food samples in stores, soup kitchens, and public facilities for their daily needs. Some hold part-time jobs, recycle bottles and cans, or receive financial assistance or charity. Many openly appeal to others on the street – begging or panhandling – as their only source of money.

> The average homeless person in the U.S. is in their thirties. About 2 million persons (10%) are < 18 years old and about 1 million (5%) are > 65. Currently, more than 20% are women. Half of the homeless are Caucasian, 38% African American, 9% Hispanic/Latino, and 3% Native American/Alaska Native. Proportionately, minorities are overrepresented.

People often move in and out of homelessness in episodic fashion. The **literally homeless** use public shelters or creative alternatives (e.g., offices, public buildings, abandoned buildings, cardboard boxes) to spend the night, while the **paired homeless** are temporarily living with others. More than 26 million people, or about 15% of the U.S. population, have been homeless by one definition or the other at some point in their lives. Almost 6.5% of the population has been literally homeless for their lifetime. The initial episode of literal homelessness ranges from one day to more than a year but typically lasts about three months.

Most families that experience homelessness have a housing crisis such as inability to pay rent or mortgage payments, eviction for other reasons, or disasters such as fire, flood, hurricane or tornado. Many of the homeless experience psychosocial dysfunction in their lives such as alcoholism or other drug addiction, mental health problems or family disruption such as divorce or separation, or domestic violence.

Illness Among the Homeless

What health problems are prevalent among the homeless?

The **life expectancy** of a homeless person is about 20 years shorter than the average for race and gender. **Upper respiratory infections** are considered epidemic in this population and account for 33% of visits to health care facilities. **Trauma** accounts for 25% of visits and skin disorders 19%. About 2% of the population is **malnourished** and almost 30% have at least one chronic condition such as hypertension; arthritis; musculoskeletal problems; dental problems; gastrointestinal conditions; peripheral vascular disease; neurologic problems; ophthalmologic, genitourinary, or otologic conditions; or chronic obstructive pulmonary disease.

The prevalence of **communicable disease** is 20% among the homeless. Prevalence rates of specific conditions include AIDS, 230/100,000; HIV seropositivity, 170/100,000; tuberculosis, 968/100,000, and sexually transmitted diseases, 29,000/100,000. Other medical problems follow patterns similar to those of the general population, although in most instances at higher rates. Almost 40% of the homeless use alcohol; 13% use other drugs. It is estimated that up to 50% of the homeless have mental health-related problems; often there is a dual diagnosis of **mental illness and substance abuse.** These data must be interpreted in terms of what constitutes mental illness among the poor and homeless. Given the life stresses (e.g., loss of significant others, material possessions,

Some released prisoners commit crimes as a way to re-enter the prison system, which they prefer to homelessness

self-esteem), certain responses are predictable. Alcohol or drug abuse may represent attempts at adaptation (i.e., an expedient way to escape from physical or emotional pain).

Anxiety and **affective disorders** are the most prevalent mental disorders in the general population. In contrast, chronic major mental illness is more frequent among the homeless. **Schizophrenia** is 38 times more prevalent among the homeless than among the general population; antisocial personality, 22 times; affective disorders, 6 times; and dementia, 5 times. **Developmental disorders** are three times more prevalent among homeless children than among the general population of children, and up to half of homeless children between 3 and 5 years of age need psychiatric intervention. Among homeless adolescents, the prevalence of depression approaches 80%, especially among selected populations such as runaways and throwaways.

How are the effects of homelessness passed on to future generations?

Many homeless grow up in institutions or move from family to family to residential settings, lacking any stable family life. Adults tend to foster their own values and recreate for their children the environment they experienced themselves during childhood. Limited family nurturance and social opportunities result in psychosocially disadvantaged individuals who often choose or fall into marginal or antisocial lifestyles in the belief these are their only options. This cycle becomes perpetuated over generations unless real and realistic alternatives are made available.

Recommended Reading

Guendelman S, Wyn R, Tsai YW. Children of working poor families in California: The three effects of insurance status on access and utilization of primary health care. *Journal of Health & Social Policy* 2002; 14:1–20.

Heuveline P, Guillot M, Gwatkin DR. The uneven tides of the health transition. *Social Science of Medicine* 2002; 55:313–322.

Lee S. Putting a face on poverty. *Bioethics Forum* 2001; 17: 39–42.

Pheley AM, Holben DH, Graham AS, Simpson C. Food security and perceptions of health status: A preliminary study in rural Appalachia. *Journal of Rural Health* 2002; 18:447–454.

Rank MR, Hirschl TA. Welfare use as a life course event: Toward a new understanding of the U.S. safety net. *Social Work* 2002; 47:237–248.

Review Questions

1. The basis for determining poverty levels is
    A. clothing costs
    B. food costs
    C. housing costs
    D. percentage of median income
    E. percentage of the population

2. Children in poor families are likely to receive less social and intellectual stimulation because
    A. impoverished families are overwhelmed with anger and frustration
    B. impoverished families' immediate priority is food and shelter
    C. the children have impaired neurobehavioral development
    D. the parents are poorly educated and have few interests
    E. the parents lack the adaptive skills and creativity to train children

3. The life expectancy of a homeless person, compared to a non-homeless person, is
    A. 20 years shorter
    B. 5 years shorter
    C. about the same
    D. 5 years longer
    E. 20 years longer

4. The most frequent health problems of the homeless are related to
    A. AIDS and HIV seropositivity
    B. homicide and suicide
    C. hypertension and peripheral vascular disease
    D. substance abuse and mental illness
    E. sexually transmitted disease and tuberculosis

5. The prevalence of homelessness is highest among
    A. blended families
    B. couple relationships
    C. married couples with children
    D. single adults
    E. teenagers

6. Poverty is highest among
    A. immigrant families
    B. married couples with children
    C. single adults
    D. single mothers with children
    E. unmarried couples with children

Key to review questions: p. 393

24 Suicide

- What are the suicide rates among various ethnic groups in the U.S.?
- What are the risk factors for suicide?
- What are the suicide risk factors for patients with medical/surgical disorders?
- What life experiences are risk factors for suicide?
- How do you assess suicide risk?

What are the suicide rates among various ethnic groups in the U.S.?

Suicidal behavior ranges from **completed suicide,** to **suicide attempts**, to **gestures** or **"pseudosuicide"**, to suicidal ideation. More Americans die from suicide than homicide annually. The age-adjusted suicide rate for the U.S. in 2001 was 10.7 per 100,000 population and is currently the third leading cause of death in youth aged 15–24, and the eleventh leading cause of death overall. Suicide rates are lowest in winter, and highest in spring. Among the elderly, particularly white males, suicide rates in the U.S. have been increasing since 1974 and are among the highest in the world. The overall rate of suicide among youth has declined since 1992, due, in part, to increased diagnosis of depression and use of antidepressant medication, especially in Caucasians. Suicide rates are highest among Native American youths. Women are likely to *attempt* suicide by a ratio of 3:1 while men are four times more likely to *die* from suicide than women. Men are more likely to complete suicide because they choose more lethal means (e.g., firearms versus drug overdoses), and are less likely to communicate their suicidal intentions. Ready availability of firearms in the home is associated with an increased rate of successful suicide. Men, especially those who are elderly or chronically ill, may engage in **"passive suicide"** (e.g., starving, noncompliance with medical regimens), although suicidal intent in such cases may be difficult to determine.

Differences in Suicide Rates Among Various Population Groups

- African American women have the lowest rates of suicide (2.0/100,000) in the U.S. at all ages.
- Puerto Rican males and females living on the U.S. mainland have suicide rates that are three times higher than their peers living in Puerto Rico.
- 90% of Puerto Ricans residing in the U.S. who commit suicide were born in Puerto Rico.
- Mexican men and women living in the U.S. have increased suicide rates when compared to men and women living in Mexico.
- Suicide rates are higher in the western states and Florida, and lower in eastern and Midwestern states.

Homicide-Suicide

In homicide-suicide an individual (typically a white male) commits a homicide (usually against a white female sexual partner) and then, within 24 hours, commits suicide. Rates of homicide-suicide in several regions of Florida are more than double the national estimates and are increasing in the 55 and older age group. In west central Florida, the group most likely to experience homicide-suicide is composed of white married couples in their seventies; half of the victims have failing health and half of the perpetrators have evidence of major depres-

Homicide-suicide events often involve an older depressed caregiver of a patient who has a chronic illness. Because Americans are living longer, there is an increased likelihood that a given individual will develop a chronic illness that is perceived as "manageable at home" by the medical community, but is, in fact, an unmanageable burden to the caregiver. Older men appear to be at particular risk of not coping successfully. "Caregiver stress" contributes to the high rates of homicide-suicide in this geriatric group.

sion or alcohol abuse. In southeast Florida, the group most likely to commit homicide-suicide is composed of Hispanic (primarily Cuban) perpetrators in their late 60s and homicide victims in their 40s. A history of verbal discord between perpetrator and victim is reported in over 50% of cases.

Although 20% of the perpetrators were known to be depressed at the time of suicide, less than 2% had antidepressants in their serum at the time of death. This suggests that although depressed, depression was not recognized, they did not seek medical attention, they were not adequately treated, or the perpetrator did not comply with treatment.

Risk Factors

What are the risk factors for suicide?

Risk Factors for Suicide

- Previous suicide attempt
- Psychiatric disorder, especially depression
- Substance use disorder
- Family history of suicide
- Childhood abuse or neglect
- Hopelessness
- Impulsivity or aggression
- Barriers to mental health treatment
- Losses (relationships, work, social, financial, physical, cognitive)
- Easy access to lethal methods
- Unwillingness to seek treatment
- Isolation from others
- Cultural/religious beliefs

Social support (from relatives, friends, employers, coworkers, faith-based groups) is a significant protective factor in enabling individuals to successfully **cope with stress**, and safeguard against suicide. Adults are less likely to consider suicide when they are active members of a **religious, social,** or **community support** network. Being married is less protective for elderly males than for younger persons due to concerns about saddling family members with financial burdens and costs of medical care.

Psychiatric Disorders

More than 90% of individuals who complete suicide evidence a **diagnosable psychiatric condition** at the time of death. **Major mood disorders** account for up to 90% of cases of suicide. Patients with major depression who have suffered a **personal crisis** describe an **emotional pain** that feels worse than any physical pain they have ever experienced. If they feel hopeless about recovery, suicide may be seen as an option to end their pain. **Panic disorder** and **other anxiety disorders** are risk factors for suicide when they are **comorbid** with a primary mood disorder. The distribution of psychiatric illness associated with suicide varies with age. Suicide at a younger age is associated with **primary psychotic disorders** such as schizophrenia and schizoaffective disease. Suicide at an older age is associated most commonly with major depression.

Most people who commit suicide saw their primary care physician in the 60-day period prior to their death and 40% saw their physician within one week of the suicide. Between 25% and 50% of people who complete suicide have attempted to do so in the past. Screening for depression and suicidal ideation in primary care is an effective strategy to identify patients at risk for suicide.

Substance Abuse

Substance abuse is implicated in up to 55% of suicides. About 2.5% of alcoholics die by suicide and there is a temporal relationship between the suicide and the onset of late complications of **chronic alcoholism** including cirrhosis. Alcoholic patients who also use cocaine are at added risk.

Medical and Surgical Disorders

What are the suicide risk factors for patients with medical/surgical disorders?

Hospitalization

Medical patients exhibiting suicidal ideation are more likely than those without suicidal ideation to have had a **medical hospitalization** within the previous year; the risk of suicide is especially high during the period immediately following discharge. Although not as significant as a psychiatric illness, an active or **chronic medical illness** is an important risk factor for attempting suicide. Individuals 55–59 years of age are at particular risk for committing suicide as a direct result of a physical problem

Human Immunodeficiency Virus

Patients infected with **human immune deficiency virus (HIV)** are most vulnerable immediately following diagnosis and at times of disease exacerbation. There is also a group of individuals at increased risk for suicide because they believe they are infected with the virus despite negative laboratory results. They usually have a diagnosable psychiatric illness (e.g., major depression, somatic delusions, hypochondriasis, phobia). Because they actively seek medical attention in the primary care setting, appropriate diagnosis and management is essential.

Alzheimer's Dementia

Patients with Alzheimer's dementia are at risk of suicide if they have:
– a college degree or higher education
– worked as a professional
– insight into memory deficits and the nature of the illness
– participated in experimental drug protocols but with poor results
– access to firearms
– decreased brain serotonin levels
– awareness of the caregiver's burden and stress

– a family that is unable to cope with the demands of providing care

Cancer

Cancer patients are at increased risk during the first few months after diagnosis even if remission has been induced, particularly when associated with depressive or anxiety symptoms or pain. Cancer patients, especially elderly men, may become depressed and suicidal when presented with threats to their physical integrity and independence. The treatments for cancer may pose such a threat and raise doubts about sexuality (e.g., prostatectomy, mastectomy)

Indicators of Suicidality in Cancer Patients

– Withdrawal from social contacts
– Depression
– Verbalization of suicidal thoughts
– Previous suicide attempt

Like patients who believe they have HIV disease despite negative test results, patients who believe they have cancer despite normal findings are more likely to have a psychiatric illness.

Chronic Medical Disorders

Occasional thoughts of death are common among the terminally ill but those thoughts are usually transient. In general, a patient confronting any **chronic medical disorder** involving (1) unremitting pain; (2) depression; (3) loss of independence; (4) intolerable physical limitations; and (5) loss of control over his/her life is at increased risk for suicide.

Organ Transplantation

Although many transplant patients have situational depression or anxiety as a result of their prolonged illness and treatment side effects, major depression and suicide are not normal reactions to transplantation. However, individuals are at risk for suicide just prior to and several months after receiving an organ transplant of any type. Contributing factors include high-dose corticosteroid therapy for immunosuppression that can induce a mood disorder, medication side effects that cause disfiguring bodily changes (e.g., cushingoid appearance, alopecia), and complications of the transplantation process (e.g., organ rejection, opportunistic infections, protracted hospital stays, financial stresses, inability to work). **Noncompliance** with immunosuppressive therapy is among the methods used for suicide. Thus, as transplant patients are monitored for possible graft-versus-host disease, organ rejection, and infection, they must be monitored for depression and risk of suicide.

Theories of Suicide

What life experiences are risk factors for suicide?

While a high association with psychiatric disorder suggests biologic predisposition, life experiences and ineffective coping abilities also play an important role in determining suicidal behavior. Early critical life experiences include loss of parents through death, divorce or abandonment, physical and sexual abuse, suicidal behavior in relatives and friends, and life in dysfunctional families. High levels of stress are experienced in the year leading up to the suicidal act, and are especially intensified during the preceding week. Type of

stress depends on the life stage. Younger individuals are more susceptible to interpersonal stressors while older individuals evidence a broader range of stressors (work, finances, illness, family).

Emile Durkheim argued that suicide is an indicator of the degree to which the individual feels alienated from society.

Assessment of Suicide Risk

How do you assess for suicide risk?

Factors to Consider in Assessment of Suicidality

1. Past personal history of suicidal behavior
2. Family history of suicidal behavior
3. Evidence of impulsive aggression
4. Hopelessness disproportionate to the situation
5. Current level of ideation. To determine current ideation, the physician must ask the patient directly about death wishes, thoughts of suicide, whether the patient has a plan, and if the chosen method is available
6. Potential for lethality, the likelihood that the patient will be rescued
7. Availability and reliability of the patient's support system

Biologic Theories

Chronic stress-induced elevated levels of **glucocorticoids** in the blood stream have been associated with major depression and completed suicide. These sustained elevated levels of glucocorticoids have a catabolic effect upon the **hippocampus,** the brain structure that plays a primary role in adaptive problem solving based upon learning from past experience. The result is a degradation of hippocampus volume and the failure of the individual to cope with and adapt to stressful conditions (e.g., learned helplessness).

Suicide victims have been found to have decreased concentrations of **serotonin** in the brainstem, particularly in the raphe nuclei. Inhibition of the serotonin system can provoke aggressive

Durkheim's Four "Types" of Suicide

1. Egoistic	Performed by persons who exhibit excessive individualism or who have no meaningful social interactions and, thus, are isolated from the group
2. Anomic	Performed by persons who have not experienced societal regulations and suddenly feel subject to intolerable limits
3. Altruistic	Performed by persons with excessive integration who sacrifice themselves for the greater good of society
4. Fatalistic	Performed by persons who feel regulated to such extremes that they have no hopes or dreams and all opportunities for improvement seem blocked

behavior in animals and poor impulse control in humans. In fact, lower levels of the serotonin metabolite, **5-HIAA,** have been found in the cerebrospinal fluid (CSF) of murderers as well as in the CSF of both patients who attempted and have completed suicide, independent of their underlying psychiatric diagnosis. Whether the decreased levels of seratonin are also attributible to high levels of glucocorticoids is not clear. However, the findings suggest that increased suicidal risk is associated with a cascade of neuroendocrine events set into motion by chronic, unremitting stressful events with which the individual is unable to cope effectively.

Preventive Intervention

Given the association between reduced serotonergic activity and suicidal behavior, at-risk patients may benefit from **selective serotonin reuptake inhibitors (SSRI).** Such agents are preferable to tricyclic antidepressants which have greater suicide potential themselves because of their overdose lethality. Children and adolescents may experience an increase in suicidal ideations, particularly early in treatment, or following a dosage change in the antidepressant. They, their parents and caregivers should be warned about this potential side effect and informed to immediately contact their treating physician. Patients with a history of schizophrenia or schizoaffective disorder and suicidal behavior are likely to benefit from the use of clozapine, which received FDA approval for this indication in 2002. White blood cell counts must be monitored (initially, weekly) due to the potential incidence of agranulocytosis.

A patient with a sense of hopelessness who has a clear plan, with a lethal available method, and who lives with someone who is away or at work for most of the day, may require **psychiatric hospitalization.** Patients at high risk who are treated as outpatients may require frequent, even daily, visits. Prescriptions for antidepressant medications should be written so that the total amount dispensed is not lethal regardless of the agent prescribed.

Patients who are experiencing severe chronic stress require **focused interventions.** "What is so bad in your life that this seems to be the only solution?" will help to focus the "problem" and identify options other than suicide for its resolution. A woman going through divorce may benefit from psychotherapy about the impact of the divorce and how to cope with it; an elderly widower with no children available to help him may benefit from referral to a senior day treatment program for a socialization and activity program; a teenage boy who is using drugs may benefit from a peer support group. A patient might also respond to encouragement to become involved with a faith-based group if he or she has an attachment with a religious group.

Recently, the use of collaborative care models that include "depression case managers" have demonstrated improved rates of depression remission in elderly patients with suicidal ideations. Importantly, suicidal thinking also responded to this intervention.

Suicide Survivors

Should a patient commit suicide, care must be provided to surviving **family members.** In their distress, families have many reactions, including anger at the patient and at the medical establishment, disbelief, sadness, and guilt. Some relatives develop depressive disorders that require treatment. If an attempt is unsuccessful, the same family issues that led to the attempt are likely to re-emerge if not addressed. It is in the patient's best interests to explore these issues privately and then in conjunction with involved family members.

Recommended Reading

Bruce ML, Ten Have TR, Reynolds CF, et al. Reducing suicidal ideation and depressive symptoms in depressed older primary care patients: A randomized controlled trial. *JAMA* 2004; 291:1081–1091.

Centers for Disease Control and Prevention, National Center for Injury Prevention and Control (producer). Web-based Injury Statistics Query and Reporting System (WISQARS) [Online]. (2004). Available at: http://www.cdc.gov/ncipc/wisqars/default.htm

Cohen D, Llorente M, Eisdorfer C. Homicide-suicide in older persons. *American Journal of Psychiatry* 1998; 155:390–396.

Institute of Medicine. *Reducing Suicide: A National Imperative.* Washington DC: National Academies Press; 2002.

LeDoux J. *Synaptic Self.* New York: Viking Press; 2002.

Mann JJ. The neurobiology of suicide. *Nature Medicine* 1998; 4:25–30.

U.S. Department of Health & Human Services. *The Surgeon General's Call to Action to Prevent Suicide (1999).* Available at: http//www.surgeongeneral.gov/library/calls.htm

Review Questions

1. The risk of suicide among Alzheimer's patients is increased if the patient is
    A. a former factory worker
    B. a high school dropout
    C. female
    D. insightful about prognosis
    E. unaware of having the disease

2. Dysregulation of serotonin turnover has been suggested as a cause of violent behavior. Support for this theory is provided by which of the following findings in the CSF of people who attempt or complete suicide?
    A. Decreased beta-endorphin
    B. Decreased 5-HIAA
    C. Decreased norepinephrine
    D. Increased epinephrine
    E. Increased histamine

3. The class of drugs preferred for the treatment of adult patients at risk of suicide is
    A. antiepileptics
    B. barbiturates
    C. benzodiazepines
    D. selective serotonin reuptake inhibitors
    E. tricyclic antidepressants

4. The population group in the U.S. with the lowest rate of suicide is
    A. adolescent males
    B. African American females
    C. alcoholic females
    D. elderly widowers
    E. recently divorced females

Key to review questions: p. 393

25 Geriatric Health and Successful Aging

- What are some of the physiologic changes of aging?
- What are two common mental health problems of aging?
- What substances are elders most likely to use?
- How does chronic illness affect sexual functioning?
- What living arrangement options exist for the elderly?

The world is experiencing an unprecedented increase in the aging population. China alone will have an estimated 270 million people over the age of 60 within the next 20 years. Census data reveal that the greatest advances in aging will be seen among people of color and in underdeveloped regions of the world. As a result of this growth in the aging population, health care professionals must be informed about the health care issues and disorders associated with the aging process.

> What are some of the physiologic changes of aging?

The Aging Process

Aging results in variable physiological changes resulting in gradual loss of functional abilities. Changes in the **fat/muscle ratio** lead to decreased flexibility, motor strength, and endurance and affect the ability to metabolize medications. **Losses in all sensory system** functioning increase with age. Decreased sensitivity to touch and to pain, hearing loss especially in high frequencies (presbycusis), diminished visual acuity (presbyopia), and greater sensitivity to light, are common. Impaired visual acuity and mobility impact an individual's ability to shop and cook, and lead to falls, fear of falling, and greater immobility. Changes in taste occur as a result of illness,

smoking, pollution, or medications. Dentures can make chewing food difficult, and loss of appetite can occur. Undetected, these changes can lead to malnutrition, decreased strength, functional disabilities, and mood disorders.

Sleep disturbances and changes in sleeping patterns are common in older adults. Insomnia and daytime naps disrupt normal circadian rhythm. This age group uses the highest percentage of sedative-hypnotic drugs, even though long-term usage of these medications can exacerbate insomnia. Caregiving responsibilities, chronic illness, mood disorders, caffeine, nicotine, and sedative-hypnotic drug and alcohol use all contribute to sleep disturbances.

> Most individuals experience the onset of **chronic illness** during the fifth and sixth decades of life. Women, in particular, are at risk for hypertension, arthritis, diabetes, and osteoporosis. Heart disease, cancer, and stroke are the leading causes of death but pneumonia, influenza, and chronic obstructive pulmonary disease are also significant causes of death among older people.

The prevalence of **Alzheimer's Disease** is 1% among 65 to 74 year olds, but increases to 25% in people ≥ 85. Currently, about 4 million people suffer from Alzheimer's Disease (AD) and the projections for the future are staggering. With the advent of aging baby boomers, it is expected that more than 14 million people will be diagnosed with AD by the year 2030. This means one in 45 persons will develop AD. While the probability of developing this disease is a function of advancing age and heredity, factors that mitigate the onset and severity of AD include education and diet, topics that need to be raised in middle adulthood.

Individuals with a **thinner margin of health** (e.g., genetic predisposition to certain diseases) and lower income experience higher rates of disability due to greater exposure to risk factors and limited access to health care. Individuals who rely upon governmental insurance programs that pay only a fraction of health care costs receive less than optimal care. Members of minority groups receive fewer diagnostic tests and surgical procedures, thus subjecting them to greater risks of disability and premature death.

Diagnostic Assessment of Cognitive Functioning

Comprehensive assessment is required to differentiate between dementia, substance-related disorders, delirium, and "masked depression." Co-morbid dementia and depression is a common finding and treating for depression during the early and middle stages of dementia can aid in clarifying the diagnostic picture.

The **Mini-Mental Status Exam** (MMSE) is among the most commonly used diagnostic tools for assessing cognitive decline. The **Cornell Scale for Depression in Dementia** has been validated for use with older individuals with and without dementia. Both the **Geriatric Depression Scale (GDS)** and the **Center for Epidemiological Studies Depression (CES-D) Scale** have proven to be reliable tools in assessing depression in older adults. The CES-D also has been validated with Spanish-speaking samples and has been studied with Native American/Alaska Native populations. However, there may be significant limitations in the use of these instruments in minority populations due to language ability, translation issues, educational levels, cultural concepts, and culturally appropriate expressions of mental health disorders. It is important to recognize how these factors may influence the results of testing and to develop alternative strategies for assessment. Clinicians should always familiarize themselves with the cul-

tural variations in expression of symptoms characteristic of the ethnic group populations they serve (see Chapter 17, Culture and Ethnicity).

> What are two common mental health problems of aging?

Psychiatric Disorders

Wrinkles, graying or loss of hair, and decreased height are signs of normative aging and, although not life threatening, can result in loss of self-esteem. Declining physical and adaptive abilities make older adults more vulnerable to depression and other mental disorders. Many elderly patients take multiple medications for chronic conditions; side-effects can contribute to depressive symptoms. Individuals who have suffered myocardial infarctions, stroke, and hip fractures, or chronic illnesses such as arthritis and diabetes are especially at risk for depression.

> A suggested new classification of depression associated with aging, "**vascular depression**," is defined by the onset of depression at age 60 or older, the presence of hypertension or a history of transient ischemic attacks, or a history of surgery for vascular disease. It is associated with decreased depressive symptoms, psychomotor retardation, and cognitive dysfunction (lack of insight, inability to plan, impaired naming ability).

Stressors associated with aging can exacerbate lifelong behavioral or mental health problems. Some elderly experience increased stress in family relationships if they become the primary caregiver for grandchildren, or are affected by the successes/failures of children or grandchildren. Assimilation and acculturation stresses are common for foreign-born seniors who experience communication difficulties with grandchildren, whom they believe have abandoned traditional values, including respect for elders.

The experience of real or perceived **losses** (physical abilities, social status, family relationships, friendship networks, income, pets) heightens vulnerability, and can result in isolation, withdrawal from normal activities, and feelings of loneliness. The loss of role and status associated with retirement often contributes to a lowered sense of self-esteem and personal competence. Bereavement is complicated by practical necessities such as decisions to keep/sell one's home, or distribute assets. If the deceased spouse was the primary caregiver, relocation can precipitate other losses (e.g., the neighborhood, support networks, sense of safety, transportation, health care, familiar stores and restaurants).

> The U.S. Department of Health and Human Services (USDHHS) estimates that 20% of older adults will experience some type of mental disorder not associated with normal aging. The USDHHS projects that the prevalence of mental health problems in the elderly will double during the next 25 years, including significant increases in mood disorders, dementia, substance abuse, and schizophrenia.

Depression is one of the most common mental disorders in later life, especially among women. Bereavement and accumulative loss, and alcohol and medication abuse contribute to the prevalence of depression among older adults. **Masked depression** occurs when an individual or family member attributes symptoms of depression (e.g., memory problems) to the onset of dementia.

Anxiety is under-diagnosed in the elderly due to overlapping symptoms with depression as well as some physical disorders and the tendency of practitioners to assume the symptoms are associated with the "normal" worries of aging. The underlying basis for somatic expressions of anxiety, such as somatoform disorders and hypochondriasis, can go unrecognized and be attributed to the aging adult's physical health status. However, approximately 10% of older adults, mostly women, appear to have some type of anxiety disorder. Older patients with both major depression and generalized anxiety have a worse prognosis than individuals who have either diagnosis alone. Patients with co-morbid disorders are more likely to have chronic and functional impairments, higher utilization of health care services, and increased suicide risk. Aging individuals develop social phobias more frequently than younger people. This is related to self-consciousness about appearance, health conditions, and social fears (e.g., worrying about becoming incontinent in a social situation).

Posttraumatic stress disorder (PTSD) is sometimes seen in older adults, especially among those who have immigrated to the U.S. from war-torn regions. The immigrant population exhibits criteria meeting psychiatric diagnoses at more than three times the rate of the general population. Older individuals who have witnessed or experienced torture, physical trauma, or sexual trauma as a result of civil wars and political uprisings often present with multiple somatic complaints or culture-bound syndromes (see Chapter 17, Culture and Ethnicity).

High **suicide** rates exist for both older women and men. Individuals at risk are women, Caucasian males > 85 years old, and those with limited social supports, lower socioeconomic levels, and significant medical disability. High suicide rates are also found among older Chinese women, older Japanese men, Native Americans, and Alaska Natives. Suicide is generally associated with depression related to poor health.

> In assessing suicide risk in the elderly, caregivers should be sensitive to behavioral changes such as a disregard for personal hygiene, or actions such as giving away prized possessions. Verbal expressions of suicidal thought such as "You won't have me around much longer" or "I won't burden you much longer" should be taken seriously and an assessment of suicide lethality conducted.

Rational suicide and **physician-assisted suicide** are likely to gain more attention as aging populations increase. Physician-assisted suicide appears to be particularly attractive for some older adults who reflect upon their desires for dignity, a desire to die with integrity and without pain, a need to preserve some elements of financial security for the remaining spouse, and a desire to avoid becoming incapacitated.

Elder abuse includes **physical, emotional, psychological and financial abuse** as well as **self-neglect** or **neglect by caregivers**. Forms of self-neglect include failure to take medications, cluttering/hoarding, pet collecting, and poor hygiene. Fiscal or financial abuse is an area of growing concern as strangers prey on elders via internet scams, solicitations for home repairs, and collections for charitable donations. However, family and friends have also contributed to the rise in financial abuse cases. Agencies working with victims of elder abuse are forming FAST (**financial abuse specialist teams**) to assess and intervene in these cases.

What substances are elders most likely to use?

Substance Abuse

Older people drink less **alcohol** than the general population since the physiological changes of aging require less alcohol to achieve intoxication. The prevalence of alcoholism among older adults in the general community appears to be about 5–10%, but the rate of alcoholism among individuals in hospitals, nursing homes, and other health care settings ranges from 15–58%. Some studies state that as many as 88% of nursing home residents have alcohol-related problems. Two thirds of older "early onset" drinkers (those who developed problem drinking behaviors before age 40) are men. Women are more likely to be "late onset" drinkers, whose drinking seems related to life stress events.

Nicotine is the most frequently used substance among the current age cohort of seniors with approximately 15% of older adults smoking. This is followed by alcohol problems and prescription drug misuse. The present generation of seniors rarely uses illicit drugs. However, it is anticipated that the use of marijuana, heroin, and cocaine will continue to rise among older adults as the next generation ages. The belief that illicit drug use will decrease in older populations due to premature death, incarceration, or a switch to "legitimate" drugs such as prescription medications or alcohol is proving to be inaccurate.

The National Household Surveys on Drug Abuse (NHSDA) and the National Survey on Drug Use and Health (NSDUH) predict that illicit drug use will increase significantly as baby boomers age due to the greater lifetime use of drugs among that generation.

Older adults consume approximately one third of all **prescription drugs** and nearly two thirds of all **over-the-counter** (OTC) medications. It is not unusual for an older person to take seven or more prescription medications along with OTC medications and herbal products. The consumption of alcohol along with these medications can potentiate the effects of the medications; in other instances, it can diminish their effectiveness. Individuals who use alcohol and are depressed may be at increased risk of suicide.

Diagnosis of substance-related disorders is complicated by age-related changes in the patterns of substance use and the symptoms identified among older adults. As a result, older adults do not fit well into the DSM-IV diagnostic categories for substance abuse or substance dependence. Ideally, all adults should be screened for substance use disorders. The presence of severe cognitive impairment can complicate the assessment process.

Treatment should be encouraged if problem drinking or drug misuse is detected. Age-specific group therapy is recommended as a part of an overall approach. Harm reduction techniques are generally successful with older alcoholics.

Psychiatric Treatments

Few clinicians would agree with Freud who stated that older patients were not appropriate candidates for therapy because they do not have enough life left to complete the process; yet, many clinicians are reluctant to treat what they regard as a difficult and challenging population. Reimbursement issues for practitioners and a lack of appropriate training and experience are concerns contributing to the limited number of therapists treating older adults.

Patient sensitivity to the stigma of mental disorder, the belief in resolving personal problems within the home/family, and limited accessibility (transportation, location of services, mobility) contribute to the low utilization of mental health services by older adults. Individuals in rural environments have limited access to qualified therapists, while aged individuals from other cultural backgrounds are less likely to utilize psychotherapeutic resources if they lack confidence in the value of therapy.

Older adults are appropriate candidates for therapeutic interventions such as short-term, problem-focused individual counseling, cognitive-behavioral therapy (CBT), dialectical behavior therapy (DBT), group therapy, self-help groups, support groups, reminiscence groups, life review groups, book clubs and reading groups, couples' counseling, and family therapy. **Life Review Therapy** is especially beneficial to older patients since the primary goal is to facilitate the integration of past and present experiences through structured reminiscence, constructive reappraisal of the past, and recollection of previously used successful coping mechanisms. Life review therapy can include both individual and group activities such as writing a life history, sharing photo albums, or listening to music.

> Psychotropic medications can be beneficial in the treatment of depression and anxiety in older patients if applied judiciously. In general, older patients are more physically sensitive to medication side effects and, therefore, require adjustment of standard dosages. The indiscriminate overmedication of elderly patients is of increasing concern to geriatric specialists.

Medications in combination with psychotherapy, when administered by an experienced clinician, may produce results equal to or better than treatment regimes relying on medications or psychotherapy alone. Electroconvulsive therapy (ECT) is generally only considered in older adults who have unremitting depression, or who have multiple medical conditions that require multiple medications.

Non-Traditional Treatments

Community mental health centers located in ethnic communities often offer **culturally sensitive treatments** that may not be offered in the general therapeutic community (e.g., a community mental health center in Chinatown that offers acupuncture as a treatment for depression). Other alternative therapies include music, art, dance and drama therapy. More recently, the health and mental health benefits of exercise (walking, Tai Chi, Qi Gong, longevity stick), touch and aroma therapy are being studied. Many of these therapies embrace cultural values and forms of expression familiar to elders from varying backgrounds.

The therapeutic value of **companion animals** has been demonstrated in both the medical and behavioral science literature. Studies have demonstrated decreases in blood pressure and agitation among Alzheimer's patients when animals are present. However, not all individuals or all animals should be included in a pet-facilitated therapy program. Organizations such as the Delta Society (which certifies a variety of animals other than dogs), Therapy Dogs International, Paws for Life, and Bright and Beautiful Therapy Dogs offer comprehensive testing of animals before they are approved as "therapets."

Sexuality and Sexual Health

Physiological changes in the sexual response cycle of aging women include decreased estrogen level, reduced elasticity and muscle tone, atrophy of the uterus, and loss of vulvar tissue. Vaginal lubrication is decreased, which may result in dyspareunia and bleeding. Changes in the intensity of orgasm and painful spasms during orgasm may occur. Aging women may need more direct manual stimulation to become aroused. Men may require more direct genital and mental stimulation, experience increased time to achieve an erection, and have decreased tumescence during penetration, decreased volume of ejaculate, and increased refractory time.

Chronic illness, disability, medications, mobility, psychosocial issues and ageistic beliefs can impact the sexual functioning of older adults. It is important to discuss sexual functioning in an open and sensitive manner, including the sexual orientation of the patient, although there has been little research on the sexual needs and health care concerns of aging gay, lesbian, bisexual, and transgender persons.

> How does chronic illness affect sexual functioning?

Sexuality and Chronic Disease

Individuals who have had heart attacks, strokes or chronic illnesses such as diabetes, COPD and arthritis can maintain healthy and satisfying sexual lives. However, many of the medications used to treat these conditions can contribute to sexual dysfunction, e.g., selective serotonin reuptake inhibitors (SSRIs), used to treat mood disorders, have a significant negative sexual side effect. Older adults, who are counseled about adapting their sexual activities and are open to suggestions about timing and positional changes, can maintain satisfying sexual lives. Organizations (e.g., the Arthritis Foundation) often have information on disorder-specific sexual issues.

Sexual Expression in Dependent Living Facilities

Fears of liability (e.g., falls, other health consequences) along with biases of family, staff, and health care personnel, contribute to restraints on privacy and sexual expression in nursing home environments. Barriers to sexual expression in dependent living situations include unavailability of a partner, physical and cognitive decline, inability to control the environment, lack of privacy and body image concerns. Some nursing homes may consider appropriate sexual behavior to be acceptable as long as the individual understands what he/she is doing and respects the rights of others.

Sexuality and Dementia

Elderly residents with Alzheimer's disease can participate/initiate sexual activity as long as certain criteria are met. Behavior should be consistent with lifelong sexual behaviors. Patients should also be cognitively able to engage in sexual activities, and be able to recognize the partner. However, patients and partners may experience conflict about continuing the sexual relationship. For example, role changes may take place in that the previously passive partner now becomes the initiator of sexual behavior. The clinician should explore the sexual wishes and needs of the patient and partner and ascertain whether a sexual relationship is mutually beneficial. The provider must be alert to the possibility of abuse should one of the partners no longer consent to engage in sexual activities.

HIV/AIDS

The current cohort of seniors has been neglected with regard to prevention of sexually transmitted diseases. They have not been adequately informed as to safe sexual practices with the result that there has been a steady rise in the diagnosis of HIV and other sexually transmitted diseases in the > 60 age group. Up to 10% of all new cases of AIDS are among people over the age of 50. Diagnosis of AIDS is complicated by early symptoms (fatigue, confusion, loss of appetite) that are common in other age-related illnesses. AIDS stigma among the elderly contributes to their underutilization of health and mental health services.

Successful Aging

The term **successful aging** is used frequently by the baby boomer generation and is synonymous with U.S. cultural norms that emphasize the importance of maintaining independent functioning, continued physical mobility, and a sense of well-being. The reality is that many individuals may not be able to age well due to poverty, education, economics, losses, and lack of access to care. Individuals who are frail may need another set of standards to be deemed to be "aging well."

Retirement and Volunteerism

Many baby boomers plan to continue working after they reach the traditional **retirement** age of 65. Some will alternate between periods of working and leisure time, while others will embark on second careers. The reasons for continuing to work include not only financial concerns but also a desire to maintain the mental stimulation and challenges associated with working. Currently, baby boomers have the highest rates of **volunteer** participation and volunteer for longer hours than any age group except the current older generation. Agencies as diverse and demanding as the Peace Corps are seeing an increase in volunteer applications from seniors.

What living arrangement options exist for the elderly?

Long-Term Care: Conservative Care or Creative Options

Advances in medical treatment and the advent of managed care have complicated access to health care for seniors. A recent AARP survey indicated that 70% of its members believed that **long-term care insurance** was a good thing yet only 17% had purchased any form of coverage, due in part to the high cost.

The continuum of care that is **long-term care** includes home and community-based services along a spectrum of specialized health, rehabilitative, and residential care. These services focus on the biopsychosocial, spiritual, residential, rehabilitative, and supportive needs of individuals and their families. Traditionally, long-term care referred to a range of medical and social services designed to help people with disabilities or chronic health care needs. Contrary to the belief of many elders, long-term care services are not synonymous with nursing homes; they may be delivered in a person's home, in the community (senior centers, mental health facilities, cultural clubs, churches, schools), or in residential care facilities (assisted living or nursing homes). A variety of factors determine the types of services needed, including income, type of housing/safety/ease of access, health status (including self-rated health), age/frailty, and availability of community resources.

Changes in public policies granting greater access to affordable community services are needed to alleviate the burden of long-term care borne by family caregivers. Governmental agencies (e.g., Veterans Health Administration, the Bureau of Indian Affairs, and Indian Health Services) will be called upon to develop new approaches to service delivery to meet the burgeoning aging population. The **National Family Caregiver Support Program** (NFCSP) was established in 2000 to support education, information, support groups, and some limited services such as respite care to local communities (e.g., support to grandparents who are raising grandchildren).

Long-term care services in the home and the community provide many older adults with their first experience with aging-related services at a senior center where they attend exercise classes, participate in congregate meal programs, or select from a wide variety of other activities.

Home health care services provide a wide-range of health-related services in the client's home including skilled nursing care, psychiatric nursing, physical therapy, occupational therapy, speech therapy, home health aides, and social work services.

In-home supportive services may be considered a part of home health care and include help with meal preparation, shopping, light housekeeping, money management, personal hygiene, laundry and chore services.

Adult day care/adult day health programs provide functionally impaired adults with daytime community-based programs in a protective setting. Therapeutic interventions can be adapted to focus on the behavioral and mood-related problems associated with psychiatric disorders, Alzheimer's disease, and other health maintenance issues.

Senior Centers

Senior centers offer an opportunity for older adults to engage in social activities, exercise, nutrition programs, and a variety of other educational activities. Senior centers in multi-ethnic communities provide a nutritional ethnic meal program and activities that are culturally acceptable (e.g., exercise classes using a "longevity stick" in a Vietnamese community or Tai Chi classes in a Chinese community).

Respite Care

Short-term home care for the patient may be extremely helpful to **stressed caregivers**. **Respite care** allows caregivers to take some time off to regain perspective on what they are doing. Respite care services that acknowledge cultural significance and provide volunteers or trained staff who speak the language of the patient are most likely to be used. Respite care has been identified as the service that would be most helpful in relieving the stress of Native American/Alaska Native families. Home and community-based long-term care services such as alternative housing and board and care as well as rehabilitation and extended care facilities are also needed in Native American/ Alaska Native communities.

The Range of Long-Term Care Services

Long-term care options for individuals no longer able to live at home include **congregate housing** (including Section 8 rent-subsidized housing), **assisted living**, **board and care**, **intermediate care**, and **extended care** facilities. Residents in extended care facilities are subject to pre-admission screening and annual reviews under the Omnibus

Budget Reconciliation Act (OBRA) of 1987. OBRA closely regulates the quality of care in these facilities, including the use of psychotropic and other medications. This oversight is especially important since as many as 88% of nursing home residents exhibit symptoms of mental health problems.

The transition from living independently to life in an extended care facility is fraught with emotion for both the elder and the family. It amplifies the elder's fears of being abandoned and may trigger feelings of loss, anger, helplessness and despair in the elder who is now viewed as old, sick, and frail. The older adult must now confront mortality, the reality of declining health, and realization that this may be the final move. Family reactions (guilt, anger, resentment) may contribute to the distress the older person feels upon admission to an extended care facility.

Hospice Care

Hospice care is based on the philosophy that death is a natural event and should be treated as a normal phase of life. It recognizes that through the provision of palliative care and pain management, individuals can be spared the pain of terminal illness and accorded **death with dignity**. Creative approaches to pain control such as acupuncture, massage, and exercise may be used. A key facet of hospice care is providing these services in a comfortable home-like setting where care is focused not only on the needs of the dying person, but also on the needs of family members. A multidisciplinary team of physicians, nurses, social workers, therapists, and pastors provide hospice services that include assistance with funeral and burial preparations and help with the disposal of personal items. Ongoing bereavement counseling after the death of the family member is also an integral part of hospice care (see Chapter 30, Palliative Care).

Special Populations

Gay, Lesbian, Bisexual, and Transgender Elders

There are an estimated three million older gays and lesbians in the U.S. This number is expect-

ed to double by 2030. Despite their numbers, this has been a largely invisible group and little research has been devoted to aging in this population. Many of today's older gays and lesbians grew up when being homosexual was illegal and often considered immoral or sinful. Discrimination and stigma have resulted in marginalization from the health care and mental health sectors and disenfranchisement from aging organizations, housing, employment, and long-term care facilities (see Chapter 27, Health Care Issues Facing Gay, Lesbian, Bisexual, and Transgender Individuals).

Future Outlook for Older Minorities

Extended care facilities have been underutilized by minority populations due largely to cultural concerns (traditions of family care, lack of ethnic meals, few bilingual staff, inattention to cultural traditions), social isolation and access issues. **Medicare and Medicaid** are the primary payers for nursing home services, yet many minority families may not qualify for these programs. The Indian Health Service has never provided nursing home care although the Bureau of Indian Affairs has been charged with providing nursing home care. The first Native American/Alaska Native nursing home was founded in 1969. Today, there are fewer than 20 such facilities on tribal lands/reservations with extended care facilities located at great distances from reservations. This has prompted tribal groups to contemplate building their own facilities using money acquired from tourism or gaming. While advancements are being made, the status of older minority members is not likely to improve significantly in the immediate future. In fact, the factors that determine quality of life (education, employment, income, health care) are not likely to vary much among any of the minority populations now approaching retirement age.

Recommended Reading

Atchley RC. *Social Forces and Aging*. (9th ed.). Belmont, CA: Wadsworth; 2000.

Birren JE, Shaie KW (Eds.). *Handbook of the Psychology of Aging*. (5th ed.). New York: Elsevier; 2006.

Gillick MR. The *Denial of Aging: Perpetual Youth, Eternal Life, and Other Dangerous Fantasies*. Boston, MA: Harvard University Press; 2006.

Hooyman NR, Kiyak HA. *Social Gerontology: A multidisciplinary perspective*. Boston, MA: Pearson; 2005.

Kempler D. *Neurocognitve Disorders in Aging*. Thousand Oaks, CA: Sage; 2005.

Review Questions

1. Which of the following characteristics describe a late onset alcoholic?
   A. Drinking began early in life, health problems related to drinking, male gender
   B. Drinking began early in life, no changes in drinking patterns with age, lack of family support
   C. Normal patterns of drinking through early years, pattern changes related to loss, female gender
   D. Periodic drinking throughout life, increasing drinking with age, limited family support

2. Which of the following therapies is most effective in treating mood disorders in older adults?
   A. Combined drug and short-term psychotherapy
   B. Drug therapy
   C. Electroconvulsive therapy
   D. Problem-solving psychotherapy

Key to review questions: p. 393

26 Human Sexuality and Sexual Disorders

- What are the phases of the sexual response cycle?
- What are some barriers to taking a sexual history?
- What are the five main categories of sexual disturbance?
- What is the most common sexual complaint patients discuss with their physician?

Sexual Response Cycle

What are the phases of the sexual response cycle?

The **sexual response cycle** includes an initial **desire phase,** followed by an **arousal phase,** an **orgasmic phase,** and, finally, a **resolution phase.**

During the **desire phase,** the **arousal phase** is induced by visual, tactile, auditory, gustatory, or olfactory stimulation or by mental imagery or fantasy. Physical response includes erection in the male and vaginal lubrication in the female. Nipples become erect in both genders, and the clitoris and testicles become engorged. Respiratory rate increases up to 60 breaths per minute, and heart rate up to 180 beats per minute. Blood pressure may rise 40–80 mm Hg systolic and 20–50 mm Hg diastolic. Increased muscle tone is demonstrated by flexion of toes and fingers, and facial grimacing. Peripheral vasodilation results in a flushed appearance and sweating.

In the male, arteriolar dilation causes engorgement of the erectile body and obstruction of venous outflow. The amount of engorgement is limited by the fascial sheath, which causes rigidity. Other events include scrotal engorgement, retraction of the testicles, and secretion of pre-ejaculatory fluid by the Cowper's glands. In the female, vasoconstriction elevates the uterus, and increases the depth of the vagina. The upper two thirds of the vagina expands, and the lower third becomes engorged and narrowed.

The **orgasmic phase** is a brief physiologic response involving involuntary motor activity. Ejaculation occurs in the male, as muscular contractions of the prostate, urethra, and perineum create pressure, propelling seminal fluid through the urethral opening. Up to 15 vaginal and perineal muscular contractions occur in the female.

The **resolution phase** is the period during which physiologic parameters gradually return to normal. In the male, orgasm is impossible until after completion of the **refractory period,** which lasts from minutes to hours depending on a variety of factors, including age. Females are capable of multiple successive orgasms.

The Sexual History

Sexuality issues depend on age and life situation. Consultation regarding sexual functioning varies depending on whether the patient requires only reassurance that a particular behavior is "normal," basic information about how to resolve a particular problem (e.g., adequate foreplay and lubrication to resolve pain on intromission), specific treatment suggestions for more complex problems (e.g., sensate focus therapy as a treatment for disorders of arousal), or more intensive psychotherapy or specific surgical interventions for more serious difficulties.

What are some barriers to taking a sexual history?

Barriers to Taking a Sexual History

Physicians should ask about sexual functioning as they review all aspects of physical or psychological functioning. **Value conflicts** may preclude physicians discussing certain topics, such as termination of pregnancy. In such instances, it is the physician's responsibility to refer the patient to another professional who can discuss all the options the patient may wish to explore. The interview should be seen as an opportunity to educate the patient about appropriate terminology for sexual anatomy and physiology. Thus, a combination of common and medical terms may be necessary. The physician's primary goal is to obtain enough information to determine whether the patient's problem is within his/her expertise or requires referral.

Timing of History Taking

The appropriate time to take the sexual history is when sexual content may be the presenting complaint (painful intercourse), part of the medical history (e.g., poor penile erection due to antihypertensive medication), the social history (e.g., with whom a patient lives may reveal sexual orientation), or the family history (e.g., divorce due to sexual abuse). Review of systems, particularly genitourinary or gynecologic problems provides an opportunity to ask about sexual functioning. The physical examination and laboratory findings may reveal trauma, infection, or sexually transmitted disease.

Defining the Problem

Open-ended questions allow patients to describe the problem in their own words. Useful information includes date and context of onset, frequency and duration, situations in which the problem occurs, patient beliefs about the cause of the problem, what the patient has done to alleviate it, and the patient's expectations about resolving it. Questions should be **nonjudgmental** and **unbiased** about sexual orientation, lifestyle, or behavior. For example, rather than assuming that a patient is heterosexual, the physician should ask, "Are you married, partnered, or single?"

Age and Situation-Specific Sexuality Issues

Childhood and Adolescence

Screening Questions

1. How many kids that you know are sexually active?
2. What kinds of protection do kids usually use?
3. What questions do you have about sexual activity?

Adolescent sexual behavior often includes masturbation and various forms of noncoital stimulation with partners of the same or opposite gender. Adolescents today engage in intercourse at an earlier age than their parents. By age 15, a majority of African American males and more than a quarter of African American females and Caucasian males and females have had coitus. By age 18, most adolescents have had sexual experience that included coitus.

Thirty-five percent of adolescents do not use contraceptives during their first sexual experience. Although 20% of all pregnancies occur during the first two months of sexual activity, most teens postpone using contraception for at least six months. Surveys have shown that adolescents know little about either the risks of not using contraceptives or the types of contraceptives that are available. Reasons for not using contraceptives also include cost, religious beliefs, reduced penile sensation, refusal to accept responsibility for obtaining contraceptives, and limited discussion by health care professionals.

Many adolescents avoid medical consultation for fear of parental disapproval or rejection making it essential to provide the teen with a confidential relationship that promotes requesting information, expressing concerns, and seeking treatment. While some states require parental permission, many states allow treatment of minors for possible sexually transmitted diseases without parental permission.

Contraception

Essential information for determining method of contraception includes (a) type and frequency of intercourse (a woman having infrequent inter-

Screening Questions

1. Do you have any current need for contraception?
2. If you do, what methods are you using?

course may prefer a barrier to a continuous method); (b) number and type of partners (a woman with several partners is better protected using condoms and spermicide with oral contraceptives, than oral contraceptives alone); (c) health history of the partner (the female partner of a man with genital herpes should use condoms rather than a diaphragm); (d) timing of a future desired pregnancy (a barrier method may be preferred to a long-term method such as injectable progesterone); (e) number of previous pregnancies (an IUD or relatively permanent contraception such as tubal ligation may be appropriate in a parous female in a mutually monogamous relationship); (f) degree of discomfort with touching one's body (oral contraceptives may be preferred to a diaphragm); and (g) concurrent medical conditions (oral contraceptives may be contraindicated). Finally, ambivalence about contraconception in either partner may decrease compliance with any method.

Pregnancy

Screening Questions

1. How has pregnancy affected your sex life?
2. Do you have any questions about having sex after you deliver your baby?
3. How do you think nursing your baby will affect having sex?
4. How will being a parent affect your sex life?

During early pregnancy, fatigue, nausea, or **breast tenderness** may interfere with sexual desire. However, absence of concern about contraception may increase interest in sex. In the second trimester, bothersome symptoms decrease, but issues of **body image** often arise. Some women feel unattractive, others feel more sexual. Some men are concerned about "hurting the baby" and avoid intercourse. Late in pregnancy, various conditions may require abstaining from vaginal intercourse.

However, in most cases, other forms of sexual intimacy (e.g., mutual masturbation, oral sex) are possible.

The discomfort of the healing perineum after **episiotomy** can interfere with resumption of sexual activity after childbirth. **Sleep deprivation** caused by an infant who awakens during the night can decrease libido.

Some women find **breastfeeding** to be sexually stimulating; others feel ambivalent about their partner touching or stimulating their lactating breasts. Marital strain can occur when a husband feels replaced by an infant, who receives much of the mother's attention. Conflict can arise over the distribution of infant-related chores or financial pressures of an expanded family.

Chronic Illness

Screening Questions

1. How have your medical problems affected your sexual activity?
2. How have your medications affected your sexual functioning?

Regardless of physical disability, people still have sexual needs. A patient may need information about comfortable lovemaking positions if physical limitations interfere with positioning. Information about reproductive options such as electroejaculation is important for men with spinal cord injury. **Medical problems** such as diabetes can interfere with vascular competency causing erectile dysfunction. Patients may be embarrassed about appliances such as catheters, ostomies, or artificial limbs, or about surgical scars. A postmastectomy patient's body image and relationship with her partner help determine whether reconstruction or a prosthesis should be considered.

A comprehensive **drug history,** including all prescription drugs, over-the-counter medications, supplements, herbal preparations, alcohol, and "recreational" drugs is essential to the evaluation of sexual dysfunction. Antihypertensive drugs frequently cause erectile dysfunction and although alcohol, sedatives, and narcotic analgesics may reduce inhibitions, they also may interfere with normal physiologic functioning.

Aging

> **Screening Questions**
>
> 1. How has your sexual activity changed over the past few years?
> 2. What factors make it difficult for you to be intimate with your partner?

Although sexual desire does not necessarily diminish with age, physiologic function does change. The postmenopausal woman who is not taking **hormone replacement therapy** experiences decreased vaginal lubrication, mucosal thinning, and diminished vaginal expansion and vasocongestion. Older men require longer to achieve full penile erection and, if interrupted, may not gain full tumescence. Ejaculation is less intense and forceful.

Women typically cease to reproduce at **menopause**, but men have been reported to reproduce into their nineties. Medical conditions and medications can interfere with sexual functioning at any age, but these problems become more prevalent with increasing age. Common issues for older persons include a fear of embarrassment or family disapproval, and lack of privacy in congregate living facilities or in homes of family members who do not recognize the elderly patient's need for intimacy.

Social and Cultural Expectations

> **Screening Questions**
>
> 1. Are there religious rules or customs that influence your sexual behavior?
> 2. Do you believe your sexual behavior is different from other people your age?

Every culture has **norms** regarding sexual behavior. Sex may be acceptable only for procreation or only after a postmenstrual ritual cleansing bath. Extramarital sex or polygamy may/may not be acceptable. Some **religions** prohibit contraception unless the life of the mother is at risk. In some cultures, unwed mothers are common and accepted, while in other cultures they are ostracized.

Infertility

> **Screening Questions**
>
> 1. Have you been successful getting pregnant when you wanted to?
> 2. If not, what have you done to increase your chances of becoming pregnant?

Difficulty getting pregnant can cause conflict and concern. Monitoring, scheduling intercourse, taking medications, and undergoing testing can be stressful. Respecting concerns, informing, counseling, and minimizing blame and guilt are essential components of managing infertility.

Termination of Pregnancy

> **Screening Questions**
>
> 1. Was this pregnancy planned?
> 2. What are your plans for continuing or terminating this pregnancy?

Unplanned pregnancy is most common at the extremes of a woman's reproductive life. While political, religious, and ethical controversy surrounds this issue, providing information to the patient about alternatives is essential, even if that means referral to another provider. Current options include the **"morning after pill,"** which is a high dose of oral contraceptives taken within 72 hours after sexual intercourse; mifepristone (RU 486), an abortifacient; methotrexate and misoprosol, to induce spontaneous abortion; and vacuum aspiration. **Adoption** as an alternative should be offered as well. Familiarity with community resources and separating personal bias from the care of the patient are essential to good care.

Safer Sex and Sexually Transmitted Diseases (STD)

Common STDs that can usually be cured with antibiotics include gonorrhea, syphilis, and chlamydia. Viruses that cause STDs include human immunodeficiency virus, human papillomavirus, cytomegalovirus, and herpesvirus. Some strains of human papillomavirus have been associated with cervical cancer. Other sexually transmitted conditions such as trichomonas, molluscum contagiosum, pubic lice, scabies, and monilial vaginitis are bothersome, but rarely cause serious long-term problems. Bacterial vaginosis, frequently caused by *Gardnerella, Haemophilus, or group B streptococcus,* has been implicated in premature labor and small-for-gestational-age infants. Thus, women of childbearing age should be screened.

Less common STDs include lymphogranuloma venereum, granuloma inguinale, and chancroid. Rectal intercourse or anal contact can transmit enteric organisms such as *Shigella, Giardia*, and hepatitis A, B, and possibly C. Hepatitis B and human papilloma virus can be prevented by immunization.

Prevention of STD requires trust, honesty, and communication between patient and partner. Consistent use of effective protection is imperative. Condoms, although not perfect, provide the best mechanical protection when used in conjunction with an appropriate lubricant or spermicide. Latex gloves, finger cots, or condoms can be used for manual stimulation. Dental dams (plastic sheets used by dentists to isolate a tooth during a procedure) can be used during oral sex. In cases of latex allergy, non-latex skins can be applied either over or under other coverings depending on which partner is allergic.

Least risky sexual behaviors include gentle kissing, mutual masturbation, fellatio with a condom, and non-shared sex toys. **More risky** behaviors include oral sex on a male (fellatio) without a condom and without ejaculation; oral sex on a female (cunnilingus) without using a dental dam; and vaginal or anal intercourse using a condom

and spermicide and withdrawing prior to ejaculation. The **most risky** behaviors include anal or vaginal intercourse without a condom with or without ejaculation and fellatio without a condom and with ejaculation.

Correct techniques for using a **condom** should be taught and common reasons for not using condoms should be discussed. Role play of typical situations in which a patient may find him or herself confronted by a partner who does not want to use a condom is an effective teaching tool, particularly for adolescents.

Sexual Dysfunction

The sexual disorders encompass five main categories of **sexual disturbance**: sexual response dysfunction (desire, arousal, or orgasm); sexual pain; gender identity disturbances; paraphilia; and disorders due to a medical condition. Table 26.1. offers information on definitions and estimated frequency of sexual disorders.

Sexual disorders in any phase of the sexual response cycle may involve problems with cognition (ideas, fantasies), behavior (object choices), or biology (physiology of the sexual response). Disturbance in any of these domains can lead to generalized or situational sexual dysfunction. Sexual disorder entails sociocultural stigma, shame, and threats to relationships or social status. As a consequence, the study of sexual disorders is difficult and many individuals receive no treatment, even though treatments are available.

Disorders of Desire

Table 26.1. Sexual and gender identity disorders: Definitions and estimated frequency

Disorder	Estimated frequency	Definition
Sexual desire disorders Hypoactive desire disorder	20% of adult population	Reduced desire for sexual contact or total aversion to sexual activity
Sexual aversion disorder	Unknown	
Sexual arousal disorders Female sexual arousal disorder	33% married females	Inability to attain or maintain sexual arousal sufficient to initiate or complete sexual acts
Male erectile disorder	2–4% < 35 years old 75% > 80 years old	
Orgasmic disorders Female orgasmic disorder	5% adult females	Excessive orgasmic delay, absence of orgasmic response, or premature orgasm
Male orgasmic disorder	4% adult males	
Premature ejaculation	30% adult males	
Sexual pain disorders Dyspareunia	Unknown	Pain in sexual organs during sexual activity that interferes with or prevents sexual activity
Vaginismus	Unknown	
Paraphilia Exhibitionism Fetishism Frotteurism Pedophilia Masochism/sadism Transvestic fetishism Voyeurism	Unknown	Deviant arousal patterns and object choices
Gender identity disorders	Unknown	Discomfort with or nonacceptance of primary sexual identification and desire to change sexual identification to the opposite gender
Sexual dysfunction due to medical conditions	Common	Variable sexual dysfunction resulting from identified medical conditions or treatment

Source: Sadock VA. Normal Sexuality and Sexual Dysfunction. In Sadock BJ, Sadock VA (Eds.). *Kaplan and Sadock's Comprehensive Textbook of Psychiatry.* (7th ed.). Philadelphia, PA: Lippincott Williams and Wilkins; 2000.

Disorders of sexual desire, arousal, and **orgasmic function** affect men and women differently because of gender differences in sexual arousal patterns and sexual organ functions.

What is the most common sexual complaint patients discuss with their physician?

Decreased libido is the most common sexual complaint patients discuss with their physician. A level of sexual desire that causes either difficulty in a relationship or concern on the part of the patient is defined as a **disorder of desire.** Frequently, the concern is precipitated by a change in the patient's "normal" level of sex drive.

Decreased libido may be person-specific (a particular partner) or global. Decreased libido is relative and depends on the patient's definition, or a discrepancy between partners' expectations of frequency or activity (e.g., she desires intercourse once a week while her partner desires it daily).

The most common **causes of decreased libido** are anger or dissatisfaction with a relationship. Other etiologies include underlying medical or psychiatric problems that interfere with sexual functioning, use of medications, substance abuse, stressors (e.g., difficulties at work), and normal differences in desire. Sudden onset of a change in desire that is unrelated to a specific stress (e.g., extramarital affair, childbirth, financial crisis) suggests an underlying medical or psychiatric problem.

Disorders of Arousal

The term "erectile dysfunction" is preferred to the term "impotence." **Erectile dysfunction** is the consistent inability to attain and maintain a penile erection sufficient to permit satisfactory intercourse. Up to 30% of men with erectile dysfunction have no identifiable organic basis for the problem. Differentiation of **psychogenically** based erectile dysfunction from **organically** based erectile dysfunction is critical to appropriate treatment.

Screening Questions

1. Do you have problems with lubrication/discomfort during intercourse? Are there people, places, sex acts that help you feel more aroused or comfortable?
2. In what situations do you have problems getting/maintaining an erection? Are there people, places, or sex acts that help you get or maintain an erection?

History and physical examination should identify medications (e.g., antihypertensive or antidepressant agents) or medical conditions (e.g., diabetes) that might cause dysfunction. Vascular studies can uncover arterial or venous outflow problems. Oral medications that increase blood flow provide effective treatment in many cases. Surgical intervention may be necessary in more severe cases. Phosphodiesterase inhibitors such as sidenafil are usually effective. Endocrinologic evaluation may

also be appropriate to determine if drug therapies such as administration of testosterone, alpha adrenergic receptor antagonists, penile self-injections, or use of urethral suppositories containing a vasodilator would be helpful. Vacuum pumps that provide negative pressure to obtain an erection that is maintained by an elastic band at the base of the penis, and various malleable or rigid penile implants are other options.

It is important to determine if an erection is obtained at any time, and if it is, with which partner. The presence of spontaneous erections support a nonorganic etiology. Nonorganically based, or combined, erectile dysfunction in the male and disorders of arousal in the female often benefit from **sensate focus therapy.** This therapy includes having couples engage in progressive, sensual touching exercises with focus on the patient's sexual sensations. **Performance anxiety** is removed by initially excluding intercourse from the exercises.

Disorders of Orgasm

Screening Questions

1. Do you have any problems coming to orgasm/ejaculating when you want to?
2. If so, in what situations does this occur?
3. In what situations does this not occur?

"Rapid ejaculation," previously termed "premature ejaculation," is defined as ejaculation without sufficient voluntary influence over timing. For some men, ejaculation may be considered rapid if it occurs within the first 2 minutes of vaginal intercourse; for others, it may be defined as ejaculation before 10 or more minutes of vaginal intercourse. Treatments include the "stop and start" technique (repeated cycles of withdrawal of stimulation before ejaculation becomes inevitable) and the "squeeze" technique (application of pressure below the coronal ridge or at the base of the penis for 5–10 seconds until the urge to ejaculate ceases). Both methods involve helping the patient develop control over the timing of ejaculation.

Men generally find vaginal intercourse an effective method of stimulation. Intercourse, however, is not the most effective means of stimulation for the female because the vagina is less sensitive to stimulation than the clitoris, which retracts under its hood during intercourse. Thus, direct stimulation of the clitoris usually provides more effective arousal of the female than does intercourse. Therapy for women who cannot achieve orgasm includes learning direct methods of clitoral stimulation such as masturbation, either by the patient or the partner; oral sexual stimulation; or use of appliances such as vibrators.

Psychologic issues contributing to disorders of arousal include conflicts between an individual's own level of sexual interest as compared with perceived "norms"of arousal and enjoyment (e.g., "nice girls don't have sex for orgasm," or "it's a wife's duty to have intercourse"). Sometimes couples describe a change in their ability to "let go" when their role changes from date to spouse or from partner to parent. Sensate focus exercises may have the benefit of increasing the frequency of orgasm since less emphasis is placed on achieving it.

Dyspareunia

The **sexual pain disorders,** such as vaginismus or dyspareunia, affect women primarily. Onset may follow sexual trauma or gynecological surgery, and often has both physical and psychological origins.

Screening Questions

1. Do you have difficulty or discomfort during intercourse?
2. How long have you had this problem?
3. Have you always had this problem with all your partners?

Discomfort during intercourse, **dyspareunia,** can occur at all times or only in certain situations or with certain partners. The discomfort due to inadequate foreplay, which can cause pain on intromission because of insufficient lubrication, must be differentiated from pain on deep penetration, or overt **vaginismus** (the inability to allow any object into the vagina due to involuntary muscular contractions).

Pain on intromission may be due to vaginal infection, irritation, anatomic abnormalities, changes resulting from irradiation, inelasticity

(e.g., in scleroderma or due to insufficient estrogen), or trauma. Pelvic examination and vaginal cultures or smears should be performed to aid diagnosis. Pain on deep penetration can be caused by infection or other conditions such as endometriosis. True vaginismus, or involuntary spasm of the perineal muscles, can be treated with vaginal accommodators; the size is increased gradually to allow relaxation of the spasm to a point where intercourse is possible. **Sexual trauma** must be ruled out as an etiologic factor in any case of dyspareunia, but especially in suspected vaginismus.

Sexual Orientation

Although evidence of sexual orientation may be first noted during childhood, it generally becomes apparent with the onset of active sexual behavior in adolescence and early adulthood.

Homosexuality and Bisexuality

Screening Questions

1. Have your partners been male, female, or both?
2. Are you married, partnered, or single?
3. Is there a significant person in your life?

Most individuals develop a behavioral preference for the same or opposite sex partners during adolescence. While neuroscience and genetic research suggest a possible role for genes and neurobiological factors in determining sexual orientation and gender/sexual role behaviors, it is not clear what causes a person to have a particular sexual orientation

More than 40% of males will have at least one homosexual experience leading to orgasm in their lifetime, but only about 10% of men practice homosexuality at any given time, and about 4% are exclusively homosexual for longer than 10 years. Homosexuality is thought to be less prevalent in women than in men, but prevalence depends on definition; that is, women are less genitally focused than men, and definitions related to number of homosexually induced orgasms may not accurately reflect a person's perception of his or her own sexual orientation. Although 10% to 13% of women have had sexual experiences with other women, only 3% of all women describe themselves as lesbian. Note that different studies arrive at different conclusions regarding these percentages. The Centers for Disease Control and Prevention has initiated a broad-based study.

Persons who identify themselves as being **bisexual** are sexually involved or attracted to members of both sexes. Although only a few people describe themselves as bisexual, many members of both genders have had sexual experiences with members of the same and the opposite sex in their lifetime.

Gender Dysphoria

> **Screening Questions**
>
> 1. Have you ever felt that you were born into the body of the wrong gender?
> 2. How often do you wish you were the opposite gender?

Transsexualism

Transsexuals feel an incongruity between their anatomic gender and their gender identity often describing their problem as being "trapped in the wrong body." For some individuals, this realization occurs during childhood; for others, it occurs during adolescence or later. Transsexuals can have any sexual orientation. However, all transsexuals, by definition, desire to have or have had gender-changing procedures or surgery to acquire a physical appearance consistent with their gender identity.

Before sex reassignment surgery, the affected individual must undergo extensive psychological evaluation to exclude mental disorders and must meet with a therapist individually or in a group for at least 6 months to ensure that **gender dysphoria** is the correct diagnosis. During the next step, hormone therapy (e.g., estrogen for males, testosterone for females) is administered. The male-to-female patient develops breasts, and the female-to-male patient develops facial hair, clitoral enlargement, deepened voice, altered distribution of body weight, and, sometimes, male-pattern baldness.

Some patients undergo genital-altering surgery. Before any procedures are performed, however, transsexuals must live for a period of time as their desired gender in all aspects of their life.

Sex reassignment surgery for male-to-female transsexuals includes construction of an artificial vagina for intercourse and insertion of breast implants if further breast enlargement is desired. Sex reassignment surgery for female-to-male transsexuals is more complicated. The surgery required to fashion a penis is extensive and expensive, and a penile prosthesis must still be used to have a sexually functional penis. Therefore, some female-to-male transsexuals choose to have breast reduction only.

Sex change is complicated also by legal factors. Documents such as a driver's license and birth certificate must be changed to reflect the new gender.

Varieties of Sexual Behavior

Paraphilias

> **Screening Questions**
>
> 1. What activities or objects do you use or think about to become sexually aroused?
> 2. How often do you use or think about them?
> 3. Do you get sexually aroused without them?

The essential feature of **paraphilia** is the need for a specific behavior to induce sexual excitement. How much this behavior interferes with normal daily functioning must be determined. Distinguishing between behavior and fantasy is critical to making this diagnosis. Many individuals who have any thoughts or fantasies involving unusual settings, different partners, or bondage are concerned about being "abnormal" or "perverted." In addition to differentiating between action and thought, it is also essential to distinguish between occasional behaviors, such as blindfolding a consenting partner, and behavior that is repetitive and necessary for sexual arousal. Consenting versus non-consenting by the partner is obviously critical.

There are many forms of paraphilia. **Transvestitism** is persistent cross-dressing, usually by a heterosexual male, for the purpose of sexual excitement. **Fetishism** is the repetitive or exclusive use of inanimate objects (e.g., articles of clothing such as undergarments) for sexual excitement. **Sadomasochism** is the infliction, on oneself or a consenting or non-consenting partner, of physical or psychological suffering in order to achieve sexual excitement.

Hypersexuality

Screening Questions

1. How often does your need for sexual activity interfere with your daily activities?
2. How does the frequency/type of your sexual activity distress you/your partner?

While no criteria have been established for "excessive sexual activity," hypersexuality has been described by some authorities as an addiction to sexual activity that temporarily alleviates anxiety, loneliness, and depression. According to some authorities, when the need or compulsion to have sexual experiences reaches a degree or frequency that interferes with normal activities and relationships, the condition should be viewed as a compulsion similar to drug addiction or other substance abuse. Hypersexual individuals often develop feelings of unworthiness and shame, which begin at an early age and continue into adulthood. Hypersexuality can present within the context of a committed relationship, as extramarital activity (i.e., outside the primary relationship), or as a primary mode of sexual relations.

Prostitution

Screening Question

1. Have you ever had sex for money, drugs, or other payment?

Prostitution may be defined as the exchange of sex with another person for the explicit purpose of receiving immediate payment in money or valu-

ables. Female prostitution for heterosexual activity is more prevalent than male prostitution, which is usually homosexual. Prostitution is complicated by the risks of sexually transmitted disease, assault or injury by customers, exploitation by pimps or other agents of organized crime, involvement of minors, and arrest for illegal activity. Some countries, and some counties in Nevada, regulate prostitution to minimize these risks. Customers seek out prostitutes for a variety of reasons including unavailability of a partner, desire for specific sexual behaviors not available in their other relationships, or a wish to have a sexual encounter without investment of time or emotion.

Sexual Exploitation

Screening Questions

1. Have you ever had sexual contact against your wishes?
2. Have there been times when you were uncomfortable with the type of touching or sexual attitude someone had toward you?

Rape

Rape is a legal term, not a medical term. Rape usually is defined as penile penetration of the vagina without mutual consent or with a person who is less than a certain age **(statutory rape).** Although rape is often thought of as a sexual act, it is primarily an expression of violence or power. The perpetrator may be a stranger, an acquaintance, a date, a spouse, or a lover. Both men and women can be victims.

In some states, a marital relationship exempts a person from being accused of rape, although it does not exempt them from being convicted of other forms of physical assault. It is typically more difficult to "prove" a rape took place if the persons were dating, if there is no evidence of a physical struggle such as bruises or lacerations, or if the assault occurred without evidence of ejaculation.

Rape centers are specialized facilities that care for victims to ensure appropriate evaluation for forensic purposes and to provide counseling and support. Psychological assessment of the victim and the perpetrator should always be included as part of the evaluation.

Incest

It is estimated that one in four girls and one in five boys experience sexual abuse. Most perpetrators are persons known to the victim. **Incest** between siblings or child relatives is more common but less often reported than incest perpetrated by an adult relative. In some families, only one child of many may be victimized; in other families, many children may be abused. Although most sexually abused children are between 8 and 12 years of age, younger children, including infants, have been assaulted. Some children experience incest as a onetime event; others may experience it on an ongoing, even daily, basis for years.

Long-term **sequelae of incest** among victims include difficulty establishing intimate relationships, sexual dysfunction during adulthood, and an increased number of genitourinary complaints in later life. **Dissociation** is a common coping mechanism used by children while they are being assaulted. As a result, some victims never have conscious memories of the events; others remember them years later either spontaneously or during the course of psychotherapy. Incest survivors who require psychotherapy should be referred to professionals with particular expertise.

Sexual Harassment

The legal definition of **sexual harassment** in the workplace includes sexual advances or other sexual conduct that interferes with the employee's working environment, performance, or conditions of employment. A study of federal employees found that 44% of women and 19% of men had felt sexually harassed at work during the preceding 24 months. Although regulations exist to prevent and eliminate sexual harassment in the workplace, it often is subtle and difficult to prove. Most cases involve male perpetrators and female victims, although successful suits have been brought by men against women. Recent court cases have broadened the definition of sexual harassment to include unwanted sexual contact between members of the same sex.

Sexual Abuse in Intimate Relationships

Screening Questions

1. Have you ever been forced to have sex by your partner when you didn't want to?
2. Have you ever been hurt by your partner during lovemaking?
3. Is your partner excessively jealous?

Individuals in a relationship can be sexually abused by their partner. Women who experience physical violence in their relationship often experience being forced to have sex against their wishes. In fact, before age 15, a majority of first intercourse experiences among females are reported to be non-voluntary. Women in such situations may be at risk if they leave the relationship precipitously. Although reported much less commonly, men can have similar experiences and are also at risk. Couples in a violent relationship should not be referred for conjoint counseling. The victim may not disclose information at all or the batterer may retaliate physically or emotionally if the victim does disclose. Referring the victim and the perpetrator individually to counseling services is imperative.

Sex in Professional Relationships

Screening Question

1. Have you ever been spoken to or touched by your physician in any way that made you feel sexually uncomfortable?

While feeling sexual attraction to a patient can occur, acting on it is not ethical. Because patients are physically and emotionally vulnerable, professional guidelines have been set regarding sexual contact with current or former patients. How long an interval is appropriate between termination of the professional relationship and subsequent contact is a subject of ethical and legal debate. In general, it is deemed unethical to have a sexual relationship with a current patient. Sexual relationships with former patients are considered unethical at least until an extended period of time has lapsed. In some situations, such as severe mental illness or retardation, it may never be considered ethical (see Chapter 32, Ethical and Legal Issues in Patient Care).

Recommended Reading

Leiblum SR. *Principles and Practice of Sex Therapy.* (4th ed.). New York: Guilford Press; 2006.

Sadock VA. Normal Sexuality and Sexual Dysfunction. In BJ Sadock, VA Sadock (Eds.). *Kaplan and Sadock's Comprehensive Textbook of Psychiatry.* (7th ed.). Philadelphia, PA: Lippincott Williams and Wilkins; 2000.

Strong B, De Vault C, Sayad BW. *Core Concepts in Human Sexuality.* London: Mayfield; 1996.

Review Questions

1. During sexual intercourse the male experiences orgasm. Repeat orgasm is impossible until after completion of which of the following?
   A. Arousal
   B. Initial desire
   C. Orgasmic phase
   D. Refractory period
   E. Resolution

2. Which of the following sexual disorders is common in the course of another medical disorder?
   A. Arousal disorder
   B. Gender identity disorder
   C. Paraphilia
   D. Premature ejaculation
   E. Vaginismus

3. Which of the following is a common sexual consequence of aging?
   A. Exhibitionism
   B. Female orgasmic disorder
   C. Frotteurism
   D. Male erectile disorder
   E. Voyeurism

4. Pedophilia is an example of which of the following sexual disorders?
   A. Gender identity disorder
   B. Obsessive-compulsive disorder
   C. Paraphilia
   D. Sexual arousal disorder
   E. Sexual desire disorder

Key to review questions: p. 393

27 Health Care Issues Facing Gay, Lesbian, Bisexual, and Transgender Individuals

- What is the difference between sexual orientation, sexual behavior, and sexual identity?
- Why are there limited research data on the health care problems of GLBT individuals?
- What are the major areas of GLBT health care concerns?
- What are the potential risk factors for cancer among GLBT individuals?
- What are the rates of anxiety and depression among GLBT individuals?
- What are the guidelines for providing informed care for GLBT individuals?

People who are members of sexual minorities (gay, lesbian, bisexual or transgender [GLBT]) face the same health care problems as the population in general. However, some GLBT individuals have additional, unique health concerns that derive from the consequences of the societal discrimination that they face because of their sexual minority status. These health issues may be the direct result of the discrimination (lack of access or poor clinical care, hate crimes) or result indirectly from the psychological stress associated with being GLBT (realistic fears about coming out, societal messages about the immorality of same-sex sexual activity). The competent, ethical provision of physical and mental health care services to GLBT patients requires that all providers have a basic understanding of these unique stressors as well as their health consequences.

Empirical data indicate that many GLBT individuals have had negative experiences with health care providers in the past. Thus, it is critical that current providers give appropriate medical care in a professional and respectful manner.

What is the difference between sexual orientation, sexual behavior, and sexual identity?

Sexual orientation is the most widely accepted term for referring to the way in which an individual defines his or her sexual identity. Examples of sexual orientation are "opposite sex" or "het-

erosexual" and "same sex" or "lesbian," "gay," or "bisexual." (Note that transgender individuals may have a sexual orientation that is same sex or opposite sex. **Gender identity** and **sexual orientation** are independent constructs.) Sexual orientation is typically viewed more favorably than terms such as "sexual preference" or "lifestyle," which are seen as invalidating or trivializing an individual's sexual identity. It is also important to note that sexual identity and sexual behavior are not synonymous. A man may engage in same-sex sexual behaviors but not identify as gay, for example, or may self-identify as gay without engaging in same-sex sexual behaviors.

Historically, **homosexuality** had been included in the roster of mental illnesses reflecting prevailing beliefs and attitudes on the part of society and the health care establishment. However, in 1973, the American Psychiatric Association removed homosexuality from the *Diagnostic and Statistical Manual of Mental Disorders* (DSM), and the other major mental health associations soon followed suit. A vast literature supports the fact that there is no difference in any number of indicators of mental, emotional, or psychological adjustment between nonclinical samples of heterosexual and GLBT individuals.

Despite the general reduction in **cultural prejudice** against GLBT individuals over the past 30 years, prejudice still persists in numerous social arenas. GLBT individuals who have internalized negative attitudes about their sexual orientation from their families or religious or other cultural groups may seek to change their sexual orientation through psychotherapy or other means. Such therapies have no credibility among mainstream mental health organizations, given their astounding lack of success and potential to actually harm individuals seeking their services.

In order to be respectful of patients who may be GLBT, providers should assess behavior and identity separately and use appropriately inclusive language when questioning patients. For example, it would be heterosexist (assuming heterosexuality universally) to say to every female patient, "Do you have a boyfriend?" and inclusive to ask, "Are you in a significant relationship?" Also, when a patient reports sexual activity, one could ask, "Were your partners men, women, or both?" in order to identify people who engage in same-sex sexual behavior but who do not necessarily identify as GLBT.

Why are there limited research data on the health care problems of GLBT individuals?

Research on GLBT populations, as hidden minority groups, is limited regarding prevalence. This is true for estimates of the size of the GLBT population overall as well as of relevant health and mental health factors. Because of the relatively small number of GLBT people, and the **societal stigma** attached to identifying as such, the data yielded by population-based studies must be viewed as an under-representation of the true figure. The most widely accepted prevalence figures for GLBT individuals range from 1.4% to 4.6% among women and 2.8% to 15.8% among men. Also, it is somewhat misleading to group together all GLBT individuals or, for example, to assume homogeneity within the "L" or "G" categories. It is more accurate to speak about GLBT communities since there is substantial diversity in cultural background, ethnic or racial identity, age, education, income, place of residence, and many other characteristics.

One additional area of diversity, for patients who do identify as GLBT, is the degree to which sexual orientation is central to identity. This is an important area for providers to note. Many GLBT individuals have other identity labels which, they feel, are more definitive, such as being Latino, being a mother, or being Christian. Some young GLBT people may eschew identity labels altogether. To the extent that it is relevant to patient care,

providers are encouraged to ask GLBT patients about their identity and its importance and not make assumptions.

What are the major areas of GLBT health care concerns?

The political climate of the early 21st century put a chill on funding for GLBT research. Nevertheless, except for HIV/AIDS, data suggest that GLBT individuals do not generally experience any health-related concerns, including alcoholism and drug abuse, at rates different from heterosexuals. For GLBT individuals, good health, fewer illnesses, and positive health behaviors have been shown to be associated with affirmative self-esteem.

A review of the literature to date has yielded six particular areas on which health care providers may want to focus their efforts. These areas comprise (1) physical fitness and cardiovascular health, (2) sexual risk behaviors (HIV and other sexually transmitted diseases), (3) alcohol and substance use (including tobacco dependence), (4) interpersonal violence, (5) cancer, and (6) mental health issues, including depression and suicidality.

Physical Fitness and Cardiovascular Health

Emerging areas of interest among public health researchers are the health behaviors of GLBT individuals related to **physical fitness,** including **diet, exercise,** and overweight or **obesity.** Compared to heterosexual men, sexual minority men appear to have higher rates of body image problems and disordered eating including purging behavior and binge eating episodes, in addition to clinically diagnosable eating disorders. Important consequences of such eating behaviors include blood pressure changes, osteoporosis, dehydration and electrolyte imbalance, muscle loss, and tooth decay. Currently, there is no universal support for any one specific mechanism, e.g., the hypothesis that sexual minority men identify more with the female gender and, thus, have taken on a stereotypical female quest for thinness.

In contrast, sexual minority women tend to report more satisfaction with their body image than heterosexual women. However, sexual minority women report less exercise than heterosexual women and are more likely to be overweight or obese. The consequences of the weight problems experienced by sexual minority women include increased risk of hypertension, heart disease, and diabetes. There is speculation that the specific cultural norms within lesbian groups (e.g., eschewing the drive for thinness) may contribute to a lack of motivation to avoid being overweight.

Importantly, **heart disease** is the most frequent cause of death among women and, thus, risk factors should be monitored closely as there are no data describing differential risks for lesbian versus heterosexual women. Indeed, it may be especially important to consider cardiovascular health (including hypertension) among sexual minority women, given the higher rates of overweight, smoking, and elevated stress levels due to their sexual minority status. Given the higher rates of smoking, alcohol, and substance use, sexual minority men may also be at increased risk of heart problems. Furthermore, because heart problems are highly prevalent among African Americans, African American GLBT patients may be at particularly high risk.

Sexual Risk Behaviors

Since the initial clinical presentation of **HIV/ AIDS** in 1981, it is estimated that up to 42 million people have been infected in the world, with more than 1 million of those infections occurring in the U.S. More than half of those people are thought to be men who acquired the virus through sex with other men (MSM) irrespective of their sexual identity. Early in the epidemic, most affected men were white. However, the demographics of the U.S. epidemic have shifted and, beginning in 1998, the majority of people living with HIV/AIDS are black and Latino MSM. Recent data also indicate that many HIV-positive MSM of color do not identify as gay or bisexual. This is a crucial point, as most HIV prevention programs have erroneously lumped together behavior and identity; that is, they have targeted men who identify as gay or bisexual by recruiting people for programs in predominantly gay neighborhoods or bars. This recruitment strategy has

made it difficult to generalize findings to non-gay identified MSM.

The advent of **combination therapy** (protease inhibitors mixed with anti-retrovirals) has made it possible for HIV/AIDS to be a condition with which many can live productive, satisfying lives. Nevertheless, HIV continues to spread among gay men of all generations, albeit not at rates previously noted. A number of factors seem to play a role: some, especially younger, gay men view HIV as a manageable condition, or one that is associated with another "older" generation. Furthermore, some gay men abandon safe sexual practices because substance abuse impairs judgment, or simply because of an unwillingness to relinquish the pleasure associated with unprotected anal intercourse, the primary high-risk sexual behavior within this group.

HIV prevention programs have, in aggregate, shifted the trend in sexual behavior toward the use of barrier protection for gay or bisexual men. Prevention programs that have achieved greater success use targeted interventions that focus directly on the behaviors of safer sex and are designed to be "culturally appropriate," that is, tailored to the unique barriers and strengths of a given subgroup. Several psychosocial factors that influence sexual risk-taking are self-esteem, social support, mood prior to sexual encounter, overall optimism or fatalism, age, education, and alcohol or drug use. The majority of patients do not discuss sexual activity with physicians, which is a missed opportunity for education and intervention.

Besides HIV, MSM are also at risk of acquiring other STDs, including urethritis, proctitis, pharyngitis, prostatitis, hepatitis A and B, syphilis, gonorrhea, chlamydia, herpes, and HPV/anal and genital warts. Rates of some STDs are higher among MSM than among men who only engage in sex with women. Increasing rates of HIV infection parallel the rising rates of unprotected sex and other STDS. There are no data showing that women who have sex with women have any higher rates of STDs; indeed, the opposite appears to be true. However, while sexual minority women are at lower risk for acquiring HIV, the risk is not zero. HIV could be spread through even occasional unprotected sex with a male partner (for behaviorally bisexual women) or through sharing sex toys. Providers should routinely take a sexual history as well as screen for STDs in all sexually active patients.

Alcohol and Substance Use

Much of the early research on **alcohol use** found GLBT individuals reporting significantly higher rates of problem drinking. However, these studies relied on sampling methods that may have artificially inflated prevalence estimates (recruiting participants at bars or gay pride events). More recent data seem to refute these early reports by finding no significant differences in rates of problem drinking (gay men, lesbians) or frequency of bargoing behavior (lesbians) compared to same gender, heterosexual counterparts. A few studies have found higher rates of heavy drinking or abstinence from alcohol among gay men, potentially related to the individual's past alcoholism or in response to a family history of alcoholism.

Research to date on substance use other than alcohol indicates higher rates of **smoking** among sexual minority men and women. Tobacco use is a leading cause of death among the general population, and up to 50% of both sexual minority men and women are more likely to smoke. Lesbians are the only demographic subgroup whose rate of smoking actually increases with age. Rates of **marijuana and cocaine use** are also higher in lesbians compared to heterosexual women. Compared to heterosexual men, gay men have higher rates of use of inhalents (e.g., amyl or butyl nitrite, also called "poppers," and usually used during sex), hallucinogens, and illicit drugs overall. Gay men and lesbians in the 18-to 25-year-old age range report higher rates of substance use compared to older age cohorts and to their heterosexual peers.

Health researchers have often focused their attention on the **recreational drugs** that gay men use at a nightclub or dance party, because drug use is correlated with unprotected sex. These drugs include ketamine ("Special K") and MDMA ("ecstasy") and, more recently, crystal methamphetamine ("meth" or "Tina"). Gay men in particular may abuse crystal methamphetamine at high rates, especially in urban areas. Crystal methamphetamine increases the drive for sex over a period of many hours while simultaneously delaying orgasm. This combination is currently being investigated due to initial reports that it increases HIV transmission and decreases the effectiveness of anti-HIV medication. While gay men appear more likely to use more drugs, there is no evidence that gay men possess higher levels of drug addiction or dependence at threshold diagnostic levels.

Interpersonal Violence

The psychological and physical health consequences of **interpersonal violence** are well documented, and include psychological distress and mental disorders (depression, PTSD), acute health problems (fractures, lacerations) and chronic health problems (lower back pain, fibromyalgia). Rates of traumatic victimization appear higher among sexual minority individuals both during childhood (psychological, physical, and sexual abuse), and during adulthood (psychological or physical coerced sexual experiences, rape).

Providers should always screen for partner violence. The literature regarding violence perpetrated by a romantic partner suggests that the rates of abuse and battering may be comparable in male-male, female-female, and male-female couples. The interpersonal violence literature speaks clearly to the discomfort and fear that patients have about disclosing abuse. However, in same-sex relationships, there is also another barrier to reporting (i.e., sexual minority women tend not to perceive their female partners as abusive and sexual minority men tend not to perceive themselves as victims).

Cancer

What are the potential risk factors for cancer among GLBT individuals?

Like all women, sexual minority women should be screened routinely for both **breast and colon cancer**. Like all men, sexual minority men should receive routine screening for **prostate, testicular, colon, and anal cancer.** In general, GLBT individuals are no more likely to develop cancer than heterosexual individuals. In some cases, however, the health behaviors of the individual patient may lead to an increased likelihood of developing cancer based on general cancer risks like smoking or alcohol consumption. Another potential problem may be a lack of preventive health care, since delayed detection and diagnosis are associated with negative outcomes. Another factor may be fear and distrust of health care providers based on previous negative experiences. For example, research has demonstrated that lesbians access gynecologic care less frequently than heterosexual women. Another barrier to routine screenings may be rooted in provider attitudes, such as feeling an implicit or explicit discomfort about working with sexual minority patients around topics like sex and reproduction.

One type of cancer for which sexual minority individuals, especially men, do have an increased risk is anal cancer possibly because of higher rates of HPV. Anal cancer can be detected through a pap smear-like test performed rectally. Some providers may not be familiar with the high prevalence or appropriate diagnostic procedures.

Mental Health Issues

> What are the rates of anxiety and depression among GLBT individuals?

Typically, major, large-scale studies of the prevalence of mental disorders in the general population have not included sexual orientation as a demographic variable. Most of the remaining work that has been done has looked at sexual orientation within populations with specific disorders or has used symptom scales that may be correlated with mental disorders at a diagnostic/criterion level. With these caveats, rates of mood and anxiety problems among GLBT individuals appear to be higher than among heterosexuals. This is not surprising given the social stigmatization of GLBT identity and the prejudice and even violence that many sexual minority individuals routinely face.

Rates of **anxiety and depression** among GLBTs are especially high if they are not "out" about their sexual orientation or if they lack social support. The situation is likely compounded for younger GLBTs, who may lack role models and fear abandonment from their family of origin, and for GLBTs of color, who face the additional stress of managing another stigmatized identity. The result is higher rates of health and mental health care utilization and, in some subgroups, higher rates of suicidal and self-harm behaviors. Screening for mental health problems, suicidal or self-harm behaviors, and psychosocial stressors should be a part of routine health care for GLBT individuals.

Transgender Patients

The term **transgender** refers to a variety of identities and behaviors indicative of gender expression that is at variance with an individual's anatomically assigned gender. Unlike the same-sex attraction experienced by gay and lesbian individuals, transgender refers to a crisis of gender identity, the experience of being male or female. The term includes **transvestites**, for instance, who are individuals that derive pleasure, sometimes erotic, from **cross-dressing** (wearing attire of the opposite gender). Such behaviors may be episodic or regular; typically they are chronic and are usually experienced by heterosexually-identified persons. In and of themselves, transvestic behaviors do not pose unique health-related concerns. In addition, this category includes **intersex** individuals, whose anatomically assigned gender at birth is ambiguous. Such individuals may or may not claim a primary male or female identity in adult life.

True transgenderism, or **transsexualism**, is characterized by a chronic and persistent sense of having been "born in the wrong body." This means that the individual likely exhibited gender astereotypical play interests in youth; feels most comfortable when attired in the manner of the opposite gender; and seeks to evolve toward a stable life and presentation as the opposite gender. Transgender individuals may be either "M to F" (genetic males seeking gender reassignment as females) or "F to M" (genetic females seeking reassignment as males). Most, but not all, transgender individuals have as their goal eventual sex reassignment through surgery. Prior to this, a series of medical and social prerequisites must be met (see Chapter 26, Human Sexuality and Sexual Disorders).

The transgender individual seeking **sex reassignment** must be under the care of a psychologist or psychotherapist in advance of initiating any changes in hormonal state or physiognomy. The first medical step for transgender individuals is usually hormone therapy, initiated after a 6- to 12-month period of psychological counseling. In the case of M to F trans individuals, the person may seek removal of body hair through electrolysis or laser treatments; facial feminization surgery; and a number of other procedures prior to seeking Sex Reassignment Surgery (SRS). According to the International Standards for Gender Change, the person should be living full time in the role of his/her desired gender for a period of one year prior to being eligible for the surgery. This usually includes living and working in role, as well as coming out to family and friends. The process can be challenging, but the determination with which most transgender individuals approach it is testament to the deeply felt nature of the syndrome. The actual medical and psychological management of transgender cases usually requires specialized competence and training.

Tips for Providers: Working with GLBT Patients

What are the guidelines for providing informed care for GLBT individuals?

Providers interested in more in-depth discussion of research findings related to GLBT health issues are directed to the Columbia University-Gay and Lesbian Medical Association's "White Paper" on GLBT health issues, which was also published as a review article by Dean and colleagues (see Recommended Readings). Those interested in more details about how to work with GLBT patients should consult the Gay and Lesbian Medical Association's *Guidelines for Care of Lesbian, Gay, Bisexual, and Transgender Patients.* The following suggestions will help providers screen for problems and better understand their patients who may have certain vulnerabilities because of their sexual orientation:

- Always take a thorough sexual history regardless of the partner/marital status of the patient. For example, ask a heterosexually married man if he only has sex with his wife and if he only has sex with women. Patients who identify as heterosexual may occasionally engage in same-sex sexual behavior (increasingly referred to in the public health literature as being "on the down low").
- Ask about the patient's understanding regarding safe sex practices and how successfully he or she follows his or her own boundaries of safety. Are there circumstances (certain place, certain partner, when feeling sad, when using drugs) under which he or she is more likely to engage in unsafe sexual practices? Referral to a mental health professional or community clinic

focusing on healthy sexual behaviors may be warranted.
- Sexually active patients should be screened for sexually transmitted diseases and encouraged to receive appropriate vaccinations (e.g., Hepatitis A and B, papilloma virus).
- Be aware that GLBT individuals may be more vulnerable for certain psychological problems such as depression and anxiety disorders, including panic. GLBT adolescents may have higher rates of suicidal ideation than heterosexual adolescents. It is also important to understand the protective factors available to the patient. Inadequate social support has been shown to be related to higher suicidality in GLBT adolescents and good social support to serve as a protective factor. Ask the following:
  • Who knows about your sexual orientation/gender identity?
  • What has their reaction been?
  • Do you have people in your life that you trust and with whom you can share concerns?
  • Whom do you consider to be family? Are they biological relatives or a network of friends with whom you share a particular bond?
  • What substances (alcohol, tobacco, other drugs) do you use?
  • How do you resolve conflicts with your romantic partner? Do arguments or fights ever become violent?

Be aware that many GLBT individuals have good reason not to trust the medical establishment. GLBT individuals have often been viewed as mentally disordered, and may currently be treated as sexually out-of-control. Transgender patients are often treated with intolerance or labeled as having a mental disorder. The GLBT patients' reluctance to be forthcoming with personal information may not be a sign of lack of cooperation, but due to legitimate fears based on personal history or to accurate inferences based on anti-GLBT attitudes from society at large.

Recommended Readings

Dean L, Meyer IH, Robinson K, et al. Lesbian, gay, bisexual, and transgender health: Findings and concerns. *Journal of the Gay and Lesbian Medical Association*; 2000: 4:101–151.

Gay and Lesbian Medical Association. *Guidelines for Care of Lesbian, Gay, Bisexual, and Transgender Patients*. San Francisco, CA: 2006.

Meyer IH, Northridge ME (Eds.). *The Health of Sexual Minorities: Public Health Perspectives on Lesbian, Gay, Bisexual and Transgender Populations*. New York: Springer; 2007.

Review Questions

1. Of the following, HIV/AIDS is most prevalent among
    A. black and latino lesbians
    B. black and latino men having sex with men
    C. black and latino transgendered people
    D. white lesbians
    E. white men having sex with men

2. Sexual minority men are at risk for which of the following conditions?
    A. Anal cancer
    B. Drug abuse
    C. Eating disorders
    D. Suicidal death
    E. All of the above

3. Among the following, the major reason why GLBT people receive less-than-optimal preventive health care is
    A. appropriate care requires specialized training
    B. gays and lesbians hide their sexual orientation
    C. insurance does not cover atypical sexually transmitted diseases
    D. practitioners are uncomfortable talking about sex practices
    E. typical surveillance/screening tests are inadequate

Key to review questions: p. 393

Section VII

The Health Care System, Policy, and Economics

28 The Health Care System

- What forces drove the development of our current health care system?
- What are the levels of health care delivery?
- What are the categories of health care services?
- What are the main administrative units in a hospital and their functions?
- What are the three primary methods of ensuring competency of health care providers?
- How do fee-for-service and capitation differ?
- What are the various third-party payment systems for covering medical costs?
- What are the primary mechanisms of cost control in managed care?
- What are the various HMO organizational structures for providing managed care?
- What recent landmark studies and reports called for improving health care systems?

Evolution of Health Care Delivery

What forces drove the development of our current health care system?

There are four distinct periods in the evolution of the health care system.

1. **Institutionalization** of health care began in the mid-1800s with the opening of the first large hospitals in New York City (Bellevue Hospital), Boston (Massachusetts General Hospital), and Baltimore (Johns Hopkins Hospital). Prior to that time, health care consisted of a loose collection of individual services provided by variably trained healthprofessionals who functioned independently. As medical education became better standardized at the beginning of the 20th century in response to the *Flexner Report,* additional large teaching hospitals were established to provide a visible focus for the organization of health services.

2. The second period was the advent of the **scientific method** in medicine in the late 1800s and early 1900s. More effective medical treatments and surgical practices were based on scientific discoveries and advances.

Especially innovative was the **germ theory of disease,** which emphasized the existence of specific causative pathogens for which, ultimately, corresponding specific curative agents could be developed. Improvements in medical education, licensing requirements, and the effectiveness and availability of care led to hospitals becoming the centers of health care delivery. At the same time, advances in public health practices and immunizations dramatically reduced the incidence of communicable diseases.

3. The third period, the **social and organizational restructuring** of health care, followed the Great Depression and World War II. During the Great Depression, the economic vulnerability of both the hospitals that provided health services and the population that needed health services led to the formation of **private insurance plans** (e.g., Blue Cross and Blue Shield) and commercial indemnity plans.

   Collective financing of health care resulted when World War II changed society's view of responsibility for health care. Veterans became **entitled** to receive medical benefits provided by the federal government at little or no cost. In addition to acclimating people to government-subsidized health programs, the war encouraged the expansion of private insurance, since insurance benefits were excluded from wage and salary freezes imposed during the war. These insurance plans enabled members to pool individual contributions to achieve the group objective of financial protection and security.

WWII also resulted in an increased **concentration of power in the federal government** as the best talent and resources were assembled to care for the wounded and advance health care. This resulted in a massive research effort that led to the development of numerous antibiotics and new surgical techniques for trauma and burns. As scientific knowledge and technology proliferated, specialized skills and services increased the interdependence of health workers in the health care system.

During this same time period, chronic conditions such as cardiovascular disease and cancer became the biggest health problems in the U.S. These conditions are also the most difficult to prevent and most expensive to treat. Consequently, health care expenditures increased dramatically.

Two government programs were created to help meet the rising cost of individual health care for those who could least afford it: **Medicare,** a government-sponsored health insurance plan for the elderly and disabled; and **Medicaid,** a federal and state partnership health insurance program for certain categories of the poor. The creation of Medicare, especially, had two far-reaching implications: (1) it established the need to ensure equity; and (2) it significantly increased the role of the federal government in the planning, financing, and monitoring of health services.

4. Health care has entered a fourth period characterized by limited resources, restricted growth, and **restructured financing and delivery.** In 2005, the annual expenditure for health care services in the U.S. was approximately $1.9 trillion and accounted for about 16% of the Gross Domestic Product. This expenditure is expected to increase by about 7% per year and reach $3.6 trillion in 2014. In an effort to control costs, attention has been focused on value received for resources expended. Consequently, hospitals and hospital systems are operated as big businesses and are often one of the largest employers in their communities.

The health care system continues to evolve to address new challenges faced by our society. These newest developments include emergency preparedness, syndromic surveillance, and identification of critical access hospitals.

Periods in the Evolution of the Health Care System

1. Institutionalization
2. Scientific method
3. Social and organizational restructuring
4. Restructured financing and delivery

Levels of Health Care Delivery

What are the levels of health care delivery?

Primary care consists of preventive, diagnostic, and treatment services most of the people need most of the time for common, uncomplicated conditions. The primary care provider serves as the coordinator of services, patient advocate, and a common point of entry into the health care system. Primary care providers address approximately **85% of health problems.**

Secondary health care services are more complicated than primary care services but still available routinely, especially in ambulatory or short-term hospital settings. The secondary care sector of the health care system accounts for about **12% of health problems.**

Tertiary health care services are highly technical, sophisticated medical services usually available only in large, specialized medical centers. Tertiary care consumes much of the resources spent

Components of Primary Care

1. Primary prevention:	Reducing risks by eliminating agents that cause disease/accidents
2. Preventive health care:	Detecting and preventing diseases
3. Primary health care:	Initial diagnosis, treatment of common problems, planning specialized services

on professional health care despite the fact that it is needed for only about **3% of health problems.**

Coordination of Health Care Delivery

Continuity of care refers to managing all the health care that will be needed by a patient over time. Continuity **within a single episode** of care arises when a single clinical episode involves several interactions with the patient (e.g., suturing a wound and later removing the sutures). Continuity **between episodes** of care involves multiple encounters over time with the same patient. New health problems may or may not be related to previous problems (e.g., one month the patient has a sprained ankle, and the next month a urinary tract infection). Continuity of care **over time** is a long-term, extended physician-patient relationship, especially important for individuals with chronic diseases, such as diabetes or coronary artery disease.

Integration of health care services insures that ...

1. level, type, and amount of resources are appropriate to patient needs;
2. services change in response to the patient's condition;
3. services are coordinated among providers and sites; and
4. a comprehensive record includes clinical, financial, and utilization information over time.

Categories of Health Care Services

What are the categories of health care services?

Home-Based Care

Home-based care maximizes functional independence of the patient. This category includes assisted living with support (e.g., shopping, housekeep-

ing), behavioral health services (e.g., counseling, socialization), and physical health services (e.g., nursing care, medication monitoring). Other living arrangements within this continuum include **continuing care retirement communities, congregate care facilities,** and **adult family homes.**

Home health services can be long- or short-term and are directed at homebound individuals whose nursing, therapeutic, and support needs can be met outside an institution, but who cannot easily travel to receive these services.

Community-Based Care

Community-based care includes a range of readily accessible services.

Ambulatory care services are provided in facilities such as outpatient clinics, professional offices, adult day care centers, and day hospitals. **Ambulatory surgery centers** contain the equipment and personnel to provide one-day surgical care for patients with no medical contraindications. **Urgent care clinics (convenience clinics)** are similar to office-based practices, except that the focus is on treating an acute episode of illness. Typically, these clinics exist in areas not served by an emergency department and are accessible during extended hours such as evenings and weekends.

Institution-Based Care

Institution-based care includes a range of services provided in an inpatient or residential setting.

Acute inpatient care is provided through admission to a hospital or medical center for childbirth and treatment of a major or potentially life-threatening physical or mental health problem. The goal is to restore functioning to a level where services can be provided in a less resource-intensive environment.

Extended inpatient care is long-term physical or mental health care that requires support services that cannot be provided in the home. Extended care facilities are provided on certain hospital wards, in nursing homes, and in state-administered mental hospitals. Residential drug treatment facilities are also included in this category.

Emergency departments provide emergency, acute, and trauma care. Although not intended to do so, emergency departments often provide primary care to the poor and the uninsured.

Long-term care is designed to meet the health, social, and custodial needs of individuals who do not have the physical or mental capacity to care for themselves. These facilities, also known as **nursing homes,** have inpatient beds and an organized professional staff that provides continuous clinical, psychosocial, rehabilitative, and custodial services. They are categorized according to the level of care provided: skilled nursing, intermediate care, and residential care.

Mental health hospitals provide care for patients who have psychiatric illness or organic brain disease. Some nursing homes have assumed the long-term custodial care once provided in mental health hospitals.

Health Promotion/Disease Prevention

Wellness programs include health education, health screening, and programs focusing on specific primary prevention components. The major function of wellness programs is to reduce the risk factors for poor health, such as smoking, lack of exercise and poor eating habits, which will lead to better functioning, less disease, and reduced cost of health care. **Outreach programs** take medical and social support services to consumer-oriented locations, such as malls and senior centers. Types of outreach include home health services, satellite clinics, school-based care, care in the workplace, and mobile care facilities. Providing transportation to a source of care is another form of outreach.

Forms of Health Care Practices

In **solo practice,** the practitioner provides all aspects of care and fosters long-term continuity. The weaknesses of the solo practitioner model are limited resources and reliance on a single practitioner.

A **group practice** consists of physicians formally organized to provide medical care. Equipment, clinical facilities, records, and personnel are shared. In general, hospital-based and sur-

gical specialty physicians are more likely to belong to **single-specialty groups,** whereas primary care providers (e.g., general internists, family practitioners) are more likely to belong to **multispecialty groups.** The aggregation of multiple specialties in a single location can improve coordination of services, encourage peer interactions, and enhance physical access to care. Other advantages to physicians include centralized administrative functions, flexible work scheduling, and shared coverage after hours.

Disadvantages of group practice include less individual freedom and independence. The aggregation of providers in a single location may reduce the geographic dispersion of services, making access more difficult for patients who live at a distance.

Many hospitals have **institution-based practices** to provide both primary and specialty care. These departments and clinics increase the time-use of technologic and ancillary services housed in the hospital and build patient loyalty to the facility. **Hospitalists** are physician specialists who provide care only to hospitalized patients. They serve as an extension of the community-based physicians who admitted the patients.

Hospitals

Hospitals may be allopathic (M.D. physicians) or osteopathic (D.O. physicians). They can be free-standing or independent; part of a system, chain, or affiliation; community based or specialty; managed by contract; a subsidiary; or a holding company.

> **What are the main administrative units in a hospital and their functions?**

The administrative responsibility for a hospital lies with three groups:
1. **board of directors**
2. **hospital administration**
3. **medical staff**

The **board of directors** is ultimately responsible for all administrative and medical activities that occur in the hospital. It adopts policies to guide the operations of the facility. It delegates responsibility for operational management of day-to-day activities to an administrator whom the board selects and supervises. It appoints practitioners to the medical staff, approves the self-governing structure of the medical staff, and delegates responsibility to the medical staff for providing high quality care.

Hospital administration is responsible for implementing board policies and managing the day-to-day operations of the hospital effectively. The administration ensures the financial viability of the organization, acquires and maintains safe, efficient equipment and facilities, hires and supervises trained personnel, and coordinates the activities of the various departments. The administration also ensures that the hospital meets accreditation and licensing standards.

The **medical staff** is the professional group to which the governing board delegates responsibility for providing patient care. In most instances, members of the medical staff are not employees of the hospital but rather function as a self-governing unit, which develops a set of bylaws (subject to approval by the board) to regulate the form, functions, and responsibilities of the medical staff. The medical staff is responsible for establishing the qualifications for appointment and clinical privileges, the standards of care to be met, the rules and regulations for providing care, and the process by which performance of members of the medical staff will be reviewed.

Categories of Appointment to the Medical Staff

- *Active:* full clinical privileges commensurate with training, education, and competence
- *Associate:* being considered for active status once certain conditions have been met
- *Adjunct or courtesy:* eligible for active status but admit few patients to the hospital
- *Consulting:* practice primarily in other hospitals/private offices but provide expertise as needed
- *Honorary:* contribute to the organization (e.g., teaching), but not active. Recognized on the basis of older age/notable contribution
- *Provisional:* eligibility criteria for active status are not yet met
- *House:* residents (house officers) employed by the hospital who function under senior medical staff supervision

---

Competency of Providers

What are the three primary methods of ensuring competency of health care providers?

Licensing is the process by which an authority (e.g., the state) grants legal permission to engage in an activity, practice, or occupation. A license is granted on the basis of meeting certain education or examination requirements. The goal of licensure is to ensure minimum competency among professionals. It also restricts the number of people working in that profession. Licenses can be restricted or revoked for incompetence, criminal behavior, or moral turpitude. It is unlawful for an individual to perform or practice these professions without a license. Most health professions require licensure to practice.

Certification is the process by which individuals are recognized for their adherence to certain standards. The authority granting certification is usually not a government entity and does not possess the legal power to prohibit non-certified individuals from practicing the profession. Unlike licensing, which is designed to protect the public through establishing minimum competencies, certification is intended to assist the public in identifying providers who have achieved certain levels of training and experience. An example would be a Board Certified Family Physician, meaning that the physician completed a residency program in Family Medicine and successfully passed an examination administered by the American Board of Family Medicine. Most specialty boards in medicine require their members to recertify every 5–10 years, in order to assure ongoing competency over their practice lifetime.

Accreditation recognizes an organization, program, or group as complying with stated criteria and standards. Medical accrediting agencies include the **Liaison Committee for Medical Education (LCME)**, which accredits medical schools; the **Accreditation Council for Graduate Medical Education (ACGME)**, which accredits medical residency programs; the **Joint Commission on Accreditation of Health Care Organizations (JCAHCO),** which accredits hospitals, nursing homes, community mental health centers, and home care organizations; and the **National Committee on Quality Assurance (NCQA)**, which accredits health plans.

Public Health

Public health is concerned with the health of populations rather than individual patients and focuses mainly on primary prevention. It is organized into federal, state, and local levels. Intergovernmental relationships are complex and may overlap.

The **federal government** finances certain services and regulates the programs providing these services. It also provides programs at the national level that would not be possible at the state level, such as a system to monitor disease outbreaks and standard data reporting mechanisms.

The **state** supervises statewide data collection processes, sets and enforces state policies and standards and provides technical support to local agencies.

The **local public health agency** (county or municipal) provides six functions to geographically specified populations or individuals.

Six Functions of Local Health Departments

1. Recording, interpreting, and publishing vital statistics (e.g., data on births, deaths, and reportable diseases)
2. Controlling communicable diseases
3. Ensuring sanitation
4. Providing laboratory services to determine the presence of communicable disease agents
5. Preserving maternal and child health, especially the health of school-age children
6. Promoting a healthy lifestyle, especially through health education

Payment For Health Care Services

How do fee-for-service and capitation differ?

The organization of health care delivery is based as much on the payment mechanisms available as on the demands of medical practice. At present, there are two basic methods by which health care delivery is financed: fee-for-service and capitation.

Fee-for-service payment is made to the provider after the service is delivered. Charges are typically set at the practitioner's discretion. Payment is made directly to the practitioner by the patient,

often with the assistance of a third-party payer such as an insurance company or the government. Since practitioners are paid for procedures performed, the incentive for the provider is to increase the amount of service with the result that the patient may receive more medical care than is needed.

Capitation pays the provider a set fee per group member on a periodic basis (e.g., monthly), and the provider is responsible for all costs associated with meeting the medical care needs of that member. Since the practitioner is paid a fixed amount per person enrolled in the practice, the financial incentive is to minimize the amount of service without increasing the need for services at a later time. Thus, patients may not receive all of the services they need.

Under **full capitation**, the primary physician is at financial risk for all medical services (e.g., primary, specialist, behavioral, and hospital care) required by a member of the panel. Under **limited capitation**, each type of provider (primary, specialist, behavioral, hospital) is at risk only for the component of service that he or she provides. Full capitation encourages the management of all care by placing the greatest financial risk on the practitioner. Limited capitation encourages fragmentation and episodic care, by limiting the risk of the individual provider.

Third-Party Payers

What are the various third-party payment systems for covering medical costs?

Since the cost of health care exceeds the ability of most individuals to pay on their own, third-party payments, either as indemnity insurance from private carriers or entitlements from government, provide the financial assistance necessary to cover the cost of health care. In recent years, employer groups have begun to play a major role in shaping the packages and determining the providers that they will make available to their employees.

Indemnity Insurance

Although insurance contracts differ, most contracts require the individual to pay a **premium,** usually monthly. Some employers will pay part of the health insurance premium as a benefit to the employee. By paying the premium, the individual purchases the insurance company's assistance in paying for health care services. Typically, the individual is responsible for paying a **deductible** and a **co-payment.**

A deductible is a preset, threshold amount that the individual patient must pay before insurance coverage begins. This may be an **annual deductible** (the patient pays the first $X on a yearly basis) or a **per occurrence deductible** (the patient pays the first $X each time health care charges are incurred). In general, the amount of the deductible is inversely related to the monthly premium (e.g., lower deductible = higher premium).

After the deductible is satisfied, the remainder of the charges is split (20%-80%; 30%-70%) between the patient and the insurance company according to contract. The portion paid by the patient is the co-payment.

Most insurance contracts limit the maximum amount the insurance company will pay, either during a calendar year or over the lifetime of the policy. Insurance contracts may also exclude certain types of service (e.g., dental care) to which they will contribute. Insurance contracts may also exclude coverage for medical conditions that existed before the contract was put into place.

The **benefit** of indemnity insurance is **flexibility**. Most insurance contracts will pay any reasonable provider for the delivery of any health care service deemed medically necessary. Thus, the patient has wide choice regarding the physicians, hospitals, or other health care providers from whom they receive care. The **drawback** of indemnity insurance is the **cost** of the premium and the **financial risk** to the patient inherent in the co-payment provisions.

Entitlement Programs

Entitlement programs are government-administered plans that contribute to the payment of health care for patients who meet certain defined criteria.

Medicare

Medicare is a federal program that provides health insurance for the elderly, disabled persons, and children of disabled persons. Medicare is funded by a special payroll tax and is administered by the **Health Care Finance Authority (HCFA).**

Currently, Medicare is composed of four parts: **Part A** covers hospital costs, **Part B** covers physician services, **Part C** replaces Parts A and B through private insurance and allows for supplemental programs, and **Part D** is for prescription drug benefits not covered under Part C. The *proposed* **Part E,** Medicare Extra, would provide a comprehensive benefit option eliminating the need for "Medigap" insurance (see below) or private drug plans.

Part A is provided automatically for all those who are eligible. Qualified persons who wish to be covered by Part B pay a modest premium. Medicare generally functions like standard indemnity insurance. That is, it provides a set fee-for-service and patients are required to pay the remaining charges.

Medicare Part A covers some elements of care but not others. For example, Medicare covers: hospital care, laboratory testing, medical supplies, prescription drugs that must be administered by others (e.g., intravenously), ambulatory surgery, speech, physical and occupational therapy, rehabilitation, kidney dialysis, ambulance transport, and pneumococcal and hepatitis B vaccinations.

Medicare Part A does not cover: routine physical examinations, evaluations for hearing aids or glasses, most immunizations, routine foot care, custodial care, self-administered medications, or nursing home care.

Medicare has limitations on calendar year and lifetime payments for any individual. Because of this, many people purchase so-called **"Medigap" insurance** from private carriers to ensure a lifetime of medical care coverage.

Four Common Entitlement Programs

- Medicare
- Medicaid
- Veterans Administration Health System
- State Children's Health Insurance Programs (SCHIP)

Medicare Eligibility

- Elderly: > 65 years, or
- Disabled: unable to work > 1 year for medical or psychiatric reasons

Medicaid

Medicaid is a jointly financed federal and state program under Title XIX of the Social Security Act. Medicaid covers all medical services, including prescription medications and nursing home care. Because those who qualify are poor, the program has no deductibles and no required co-payments.

Although Medicaid pays for all medical care services, the level of payment is far below that charged by most health care providers. Some providers decline to accept Medicaid patients. However, Medicaid was never intended to fully compensate health care providers but rather to provide a small incentive for *pro bono* care to those in need.

The **eligibility criteria** for Medicaid are determined separately by each state that administers the program. A person can qualify for Medicaid in one state but not in another. Furthermore, eligibility rules vary from year to year within a given state as the state seeks to balance its fiscal priorities.

Medicaid Eligibility

Low-income persons receiving public assistance (eligibility varies by state)

Veterans Administration Health System

The **Veterans Administration (VA) Health System** was established by an act of Congress in 1930 and funded by federal tax dollars to ensure adequate health care for veterans of the U.S. Armed Services. All honorably discharged veterans, their spouses, and their dependent children are eligible to receive care in VA facilities. The VA system is a fully integrated health care delivery system offering a wide range of health care services including dental and psychiatric care at locations distributed across the country. In a fiscal year, the VA system provides treatment through more than 800,000 inpatient admissions and over 30 million outpatient visits.

State Children's Health Insurance Program (SCHIP)

The Balanced Budget Act of 1997 established **SCHIP** as Title XXI of the Social Security Act. Although SCHIP does not create universal coverage for all children, it does offer expanded insurance coverage to a large portion of uninsured children. The program provides more than $40 billion in federal grants to states over a 10-year period to pro-

vide health insurance coverage to children through 18 years of age who are uninsured and ineligible for Medicaid. States must, however, contribute a defined share of funds to obtain federal matching funds. The legislation gives flexibility to states in designing and implementing their programs.

Under SCHIP, states are able to select from among three approaches to providing health insurance coverage to children: 1) expand Medicaid; 2) create or expand a non-Medicaid children's health insurance program; or 3) combine both options. Most states have created a non-Medicaid SCHIP program for at least some of their SCHIP-eligible children. Whichever approach a state chooses, it receives an enhanced federal matching rate above the Medicaid rate.

Managed Care Systems

Managed care plans are designed to control costs while still providing quality medical care. To achieve this goal, restrictions in medical practice and reductions in physician autonomy have been instituted.

What are the primary mechanisms of cost control in managed care?

Initially, managed care functioned as a traditional insurer and assumed the financial risk for health services provided to subscribers. Controls were imposed on providers and enrollees to curtail use of resources through three primary mechanisms:

1. **Utilization review** – auditing medical services provided to ensure appropriateness for the medical condition being treated
2. **Prior authorization** – requiring the provider to obtain the consent of the payer before proceeding with treatment
3. **Second opinion** – concurrence of another health care professional that the recommended treatment is appropriate

Recently, managed care has moved to a **provider-based model** in which providers assume the financial risk and responsibility for managing the care of a population of patients. In the provider-based model, internal controls for managing costs and quality are used to minimize risk. These internal controls include:

1. **Peer review** – the provider's medical decisions are evaluated by other persons in the same profession.
2. **Clinical guidelines** – formalized decision trees.
3. **Protocols** – well-defined, standardized clinical processes targeted to specific procedures or courses of action.

Most Common Forms of Managed Care

- Health maintenance organization (HMO)
- Preferred provider organization (PPO)
- Physician-hospital organization (PHO)

Health Maintenance Organizations (HMOs)

What are the various HMO organizational structures for providing managed care?

An **HMO,** is a prepaid group practice in which providers agree to provide all needed medical care in exchange for a set monthly premium that is paid directly to the health care provider organization. Thus, the HMO serves as both insurer and provider and is thereby able to reduce costs and charge lower premiums.

There are four types of HMOs: staff, group, network and independent practice association (IPA). These four subtypes are differentiated based on (1) how the physicians are paid; (2) who owns the facilities in which the physicians practice; and (3) how important the HMO patients are to the physicians' practice. The most popular are the group and IPA models.

Staff, Group, and Network HMOs

In the **staff model HMO,** the providers are salaried employees of the HMO, which handles the business while the providers care for the patients.

In the **group model HMO,** separate multi-specialty medical groups, rather than individuals, contract with the HMO to provide services exclusively to members in facilities owned by the HMO.

In the **network model HMO,** an HMO contracts with physicians who may also provide independent fee-for-service care or contract with other HMOs.

Independent Practice Association (IPA)

In the **independent practice association (IPA),** the HMO contracts with multiple practices comprised of either solo practitioners or small groups and pays them either by capitating for a set number of patient care visits, or by negotiating a fee-for-service rate. The IPA is decentralized, and providers are geographically dispersed.

Preferred Provider Organizations (PPOs)

PPOs contract with an insurance company, or directly with employers, to purchase services from a select group of providers. The PPO uses incentives rather than controls to change the behavior of consumers. If the consumer receives medical services from a provider participating on the preferred panel, typical incentives include reduced rates for co-payments (i.e., the portion of the fee paid by the consumer) and waiver of the deductible amount. Providers gain access to patients who have signed on to the plan by agreeing to accept discounted fee-for-service payments or negotiated fees. Reduced fees for the providers are compensated for by increased volume.

Physician-Hospital Organizations (PHOs)

PHOs are a joint venture between a hospital and a group of providers, usually the medical staff of the hospital. The organizations join to create an entity that can function as a coordinated unit. Physicians join individually or as a group. Although the PHO incorporates physicians into a single organizational structure, it may not necessarily create greater integration of services. PHOs are attractive because physicians retain autonomy in decision making. However, the PHO can influence provider behavior.

Other Health Care Models

Managed indemnity plans are usually sponsored by traditional insurance companies. They do not transfer financial risk to the provider but impose utilization controls such as preadmission certification, second opinions, prior authorization, and case management.

Exclusive provider organizations (EPO) are usually initiated by employer groups to control costs through utilization management and preferred premium rates. The EPO combines features of an HMO with those of a PPO. Consumers are restricted to receiving care from a selected set of providers. The premium rates are negotiated based on the specific experience of the employees of the group. This allows employers to pay lower health premiums while the health care providers focus on caring for a defined population with a known medical risk history. Thus, costs can be predicted more accurately and better controlled.

Point-of-service (POS) plans allow the enrollee to select the coverage of an HMO, PPO, or indemnity plan each time a service is used. When a medical service is needed, the member selects indemnity coverage, which allows the member to choose any provider but requires a substantial out-of-pocket payment at the time of service. Alternatively, the member can select a provider on a restricted PPO panel and receive an out-of-pocket discount, or elect to use HMO providers and incur little or no out-of-pocket expense.

Health System Improvement

> What recent landmark studies and reports called for improving health care systems?

The landscape of American health care changed irrevocably in 1999 with the Institute of Medicine's publication, *"To Err is Human: Building a Safer Healthcare System"* and it's companion report, *"Crossing the Quality Chasm: A New Healthcare System for the 21st Century,"* in 2001. These seminal publications compellingly publicized the large gap between current health care quality and what should be achievable, especially for patients with chronic medical conditions. Data on the size of the gap needing attention soon followed in McGlynn's major study of quality of care in the U.S., which showed that only 55% of patients received the type of care required by quality indicators for 30 acute and chronic conditions. The IOM "Chasm Report" called for fundamental changes in the health care delivery system, including the creation of better methods for disseminating and applying knowledge to practice, and fostering the use of informa-

> **Recommendations for New Care Model from the Institute of Medicine**
>
> 1. Redesign of care processes based on best practices
> 2. Use of information technologies to improve access to clinical information and support clinical decision making
> 3. Knowledge and skills management
> 4. Development of effective teams
> 5. Coordination of care across patient conditions, services, and settings over time
> 6. Incorporation of performance and outcome measurements for improvement and accountability

tion technology in clinical care. They identified six component aims for quality: safety, timeliness, effectiveness, efficiency, equity and patient centeredness.

The IOM reports and the supporting studies initiated perhaps the greatest paradigm shift in health care in modern times. Most important among the major changes is the assertion that health care is not delivered by an individual but by a system. This has increased emphasis on continuously improving the processes and outcomes of care through the work of interdisciplinary teams of health care professionals. National organizations, such as the not-for-profit Institute for Healthcare Improvement in Cambridge, Massachusetts, have led this shift toward evidence-based improvement through national efforts like the **Campaign to Save 100,000 Lives** initiated in 2004.

The Health Care Team

The increased complexity and specialization of medicine have decreased the independence of the individual provider and enhanced the need for a team approach involving medical, nursing, psychological, and other allied health professionals, as well as administrators. To function effectively in the ever-changing health care system, a health care team must address four core functions: adaptation, goal attainment, integration, and maintaining group values.

Adaptation is the capacity to change in response to challenges or opportunities in the environment.

Goal attainment is the capacity to organize and work together to achieve a desired outcome, setting aside personal agendas.

Integration is the mechanism for maintaining open internal communication, fostering cohesion, and achieving the group's external goals. The more unified the goals and efforts of the members of the team, the more integrated the team.

Maintaining group values promotes consensus and provides a common referent for identifying differences within the group. When team members share ideas, experiences, expectations, and values, they communicate and perform effectively. These shared assumptions may be unspoken or even subconscious.

Recommended Reading

Kongstvedt PR. *The Managed Health Care Handbook.* (4th ed.). Boston, MA: Jones and Bartlett; 2001.

McGlynn EA, Asch SM, Adams J, et al.: The quality of health care delivered to adults in the United States. *New England Journal of Medicine* 2003; 348: 2635–2645.

Shi L, Singh DA. *Delivering Health Care in America: A Systems Approach.* (3rd ed.). Boston, MA: Jones and Bartlett; 2004.

Sultz HA, Young KM. *Health Care USA: Understanding Its Organization and Delivery.* (5th ed.). Boston, MA: Jones and Bartlett; 2006.

The Institute of Medicine. To Err is Human: Building a Safer Healthcare System. Released on November 1, 1999. Available at http://www.iom.edu/CMS/8089/5575.aspx

The Institute of Medicine. Crossing the Quality Chasm: A New Health System for the 21st Century. Released on March 1, 2001. Available at http://www.iom.edu/CMS/8089/5432.aspx

Review Questions

1. The primary care sector of the U.S. health system provides adequate care for approximately what percent of the population?
    A. 85%
    B. 50%
    C. 35%
    D. 12%
    E. 3%

2. Continuity between sources of care involves
    A. long-term, expanded patient-professional relationships
    B. managing all services needed by the patient
    C. multiple interactions with a patient for a single clinical episode
    D. multiple interactions with a patient for medically unrelated encounters
    E. transfer of responsibility for care from one provider to another

3. The most restrictive mechanism for defining the scope of practice of health professionals is
    A. accreditation
    B. certification
    C. licensing
    D. prior authorization
    E. privileging

4. The ability to influence the activities of a team to achieve a goal defines
    A. authority
    B. control
    C. leadership
    D. legitimacy
    E. power

Key to review questions: p. 393

29 Complementary and Integrative Medicine

- How do complementary medicine and conventional medicine differ?
- Why is the popularity of complementary medicine increasing?
- How is complementary medicine classified?
- Which complementary medicine practices are licensed in the U.S.?
- What distinguishes behavioral science-based treatments from complementary medicine treatments?
- Why do some proponents of complementary medicine reject accepted scientific standards for research?
- What is integrative medicine?

How do complementary medicine and conventional medicine differ?

Conventional medical practice in the U. S. is based on the biomedical model that had its origins in the 1911 *Flexner Report* recommending more scientifically-based training and practice. **Complementary medicine** refers to models, practices, and procedures that are generally regarded as lying outside the domain of contemporary biomedicine. Yet, complementary medical treatments are currently used by over 50% of the population in the U.S. and by an estimated 80% of the population worldwide. Moreover, the vast majority of users of complementary medicine combine such practices with biomedical therapies.

Why is the popularity of complementary medicine increasing?

Increased interest in complementary medicine has been attributed to a variety of factors including the high cost, invasive nature, and noxious side effects of many conventional treatments, greater interest in prevention, and the more user friendly, palliative nature of complementary care practices. In 1993, Eisenberg, et al published a landmark study in the *New England Journal of Medicine* reviewing the demographics, utilization of treatments and consumer goods, motivation for use, and financial expenditures for complementary medicine and found that usage was significant. By 1997, an estimated $47.5 billion was being spent annually on complementary medicine, and this number has continued to grow steadily.

Most medical schools now include some aspect of complementary medicine in their curricula. A few schools offer specialized fellowship training and continuing medical education offerings are common. Currently, it is estimated that at least 35,000 physicians integrate complementary medical treatments in their practices and that by 2010, 17% of health care providers will be from the complementary medicine professions. Although few M.D. physicians are trained to deliver complementary care, many are asked by patients for information or referral, especially in situations where biomedical therapies have not been successful or where patients are interested in non-pharmacologic or non-surgical approaches to treatment.

National Center for Complementary and Alternative Medicine

In the mid 1990s, the National Institutes of Health (NIH) established the Office of Complementary and Alternative Medicine (OCAM) with a budget of $2 million to support research on various complementary medicine treatment approaches. In 1999, the office was upgraded to and renamed the National Center for Complementary and Alternative Medicine (NCCAM) with a budget of $110 million.

In March, 2000, the White House Commission on Complementary and Alternative Medicine Policy was established to review this body of medical care and develop administrative and legislative proposals aimed at creating safe and effective complementary medicine opportunities for the public. Specifically, the Commission is accountable for: (1) establishing standards that are equal for both conventional and complementary medicine; (2) education and training of health care practitoners and consumers regarding high quality research in complementary medicine; and (3) proposing insurance coverage policies.

Types of Complementary Medicine

How is complementary medicine classified?

Initially, the NIH defined complementary and alternative medicine as "health care practices not taught in conventional western medical schools." However, the NIH has subsequently developed a more descriptive and useful taxonomy with five classifications of complementary medicine practices identified by the CAM Advisory Board in 2001–2002 (see Table 29.1.).

Modalities of Complementary Medicine

Complementary medicine includes traditional medical theories and practices such as the Ayurvedic, Chinese, Greek, and Arabic systems formulated over the past 2500+ years (see Chapter 1, Evolving Models of Health Care), Native American, homeopathic, chiropractic and naturopathic healing systems, as well as more limited practices that have specific therapeutic goals and are adjuncts to a larger system of care (e.g., creative arts therapy, acupuncture, therapeutic touch). Many complementary therapies share several basic holistic assumptions, such as (1) individuals possess a life force and seek balance among physical, spiritual, emotional, social, mental, and environmental factors through diet, family, lifestyle, spirituality and culture; (2) illness is a complex manifestation of imbalance within the person's life experience; and (3) restoring and maintaining balance between mind, body and spirit induces wellness. In attempting to achieve wellness, the holistic practitioner assists patients in creating and maintaining their own well-being by providing education, encouraging personal responsibility, and enhancing innate strengths to maximize healing potential.

Which complementary medicine practices are licensed in the U.S.?

Currently, four complementary medicine practices are licensed professions in the U.S.: chiropractic, acupuncture, naturopathy, and massage. As a

Table 29.1. Classifications of complementary medicine with examples

Alternative medical systems	Mind-body interventions	Biologically based therapies	Manipulative/ body-based methods	Energy therapies
– Homeopathy – Naturopathy – Ayurveda – Traditional Chinese medicine	– Meditation – Prayer – Mental healing – Creative outlets (art, music, dance)	– Dietary supplements – Botanical medicine	– Chiropractic – Osteopathy – Massage	– Biofield therapies (Qi gong, Reiki, Therapeutic touch) – Bioelectromagnetics (electromagnetic fields)

Licensed Complementary Medicine Professions

1. Chiropractic
2. Acupuncture
3. Naturopathy
4. Massage

---

professional in one of these areas, a practitioner must graduate from an accredited school recognized by the Department of Education and pass a standardized national examination. In addition to these four professions, there are a variety of complementary treatment approaches that are provided by practitioners who have successfully completed a certification process. A few examples of specific complementary medicine practices are reviewed below.

Homeopathy

Homeopathy was founded by Samuel Hahnemann in late 18th century Germany. By the end of the 19th century, 25% of physicians in the U.S. were trained in homeopathy. With the advent of biomedicine, that number has declined to less than 5% today. Homeopathy in some form is widely practiced throughout Europe, North and South America, India and Australia. In Britain, 42% of general practitioners refer patients to homeopaths, and in the Netherlands, 38% of general practitioners use homeopathy in their practices. India relies on homeopathy as well as Ayurveda for much of its primary care and has over 100 homeopathic medical schools.

Two Major Tenets of Homeopathy

1. Like cures like.
2. Small well-shaken doses are more efficacious than standard pharmacologic doses.

A fundamental tenet of homeopathy is that **"like cures like."** The concept, originally derived from Greek or Hippocratic medicine, maintains that a morbific agent that generates symptoms similar to those of the disease can help cure this same disease. For example, digitalis, initially derived

from the dried leaf of *Digitalis purpurea* (purple foxglove), causes tachycardia in a healthy person. However, in an individual with certain tachycardias, especially supraventricular tachycardia, it slows the heart rate.

A second tenet of homeopathy is that **small doses** of the morbific agent are more effective than standard pharmacologic doses and that those solutions that are shaken more vigorously during the dilution process exhibit more potent effects. Homeopathic remedies are derived from herbs, minerals, and animal products so diluted in solution that minimal or even no measurable amount of the original substance remains in the medicine to be administered. It is presumed that the solution has a **"signature energy waveform"** based on its molecular structure that is then amplified by the absorption of kinetic energy via shaking and stored by the water/alcohol solvent.

Thus, homeopathic remedies are purported to act on an **"energetic"** rather than biochemical level and to achieve their healing effects by interacting with the electromagnetic field of the body. It is argued that homeopathic treatments help to regulate complex biologic processes such as the immune system by **"attuning"** these systems to the disease condition, regulating their function, and **"expelling the energy system of the pathogen."** This principle is based on the law of physics that two like charges cannot occupy the same space at the same time.

It is claimed that nuclear magnetic resonance, Raman laser spectroscopy, and infrared spectrophotometric analysis studies conducted in Europe and the U.S. indicate that homeopathic remedies have energy properties different from pure solvent, even though they are chemically identical. While preliminary, these research results are thought to show that there may be a demonstrable mechanism within diluted solutions to account for homeopathic effects.

Efficacy

Because homeopathy's claims appear contrary to the principles of modern scientific medicine, research on the efficacy of homeopathic treatments has been controversial. Homeopathic practitioners assert that, since effective treatment requires precise symptom matching, or individualization of treatment, accepted methods of scientific investigation (i.e., randomized clinical trials of standardized treatments on non-homogeneous patient samples) are not necessarily appropriate for homeopathy. However, despite this disclaimer, there does appear to be supporting scientific evidence for the efficacy of some homeopathic treatments of certain disorders. For example, a meta-analysis of scientifically valid studies of homeopathic treatments by Dutch researchers, published by the *British Medical Journal* in 1991, reported that 15 out of 22 well-controlled studies showed positive results. While these findings attest to the effectiveness of some treatments, they have not clarified the mechanisms of action nor do they necessarily substantiate homeopathic explanations.

It has been argued that homeopathic efficacy may be due in part to placebo response. Although the doctor-patient relationship and other aspects of the placebo response may be present and are a legitimate treatment modality, a 1997 meta-analysis of 89 randomized, double-blind, placebo controlled studies reported in *Lancet* indicated that the placebo response did not entirely account for homeopathic efficacy. It is anticipated that continued research under the aegis of the National Center for Complementary and Alternative Medicine will begin to distinguish among specific homeopathic treatment approaches, define their efficacy in the treatment of specific disorders, and clarify the mechanism of action.

Acupuncture

Acupuncture is a component of **traditional Chinese medicine** (classically consisting of herbal therapy, dietary therapy, qigong exercise therapeutics, tuina massage, and acupuncture/moxibustion). Treatment involves the insertion of fine needles (typically 0.25 mm in diameter) into defined acupuncture points at specific anatomic locations. These points are located on 14 main **meridians** (energy pathways) which may run parallel to but are distinct from the circulatory and nervous systems. There are 361 primary points corresponding to differing organ systems and functions of the body.

Acupressure is a variant of acupuncture. In this case, pressure, rather than skin puncture, at the primary points is used to obtain effect

The goal of acupuncture is to promote the smooth flow of energy, or **Qi** (pronounced "chee"), throughout the body to restore balance and good

health. Needles placed in the appropriate acupuncture points are presumed to facilitate energy flow along the meridians. In certain cases, **electroacupuncture,** the application of a weak electric current to an inserted needle to strengthen the degree of stimulation, is used. Most regimens of acupuncture consist of 4–6 treatments followed by booster treatments every 1–6 months for preventive maintenance.

> The mechanism of action of acupuncture in pain management appears to be enhancement of specific neurotransmitter activity within the CNS, particularly through increased circulatory release of endorphins and enkephalins, opioid-like hormones that have analgesic and anxiolytic properties.

Training and Licensure

In 2001, acupuncture was licensed in 41 states with 8 additional states investigating licensure. Licensing requirements for acupuncturists are set by individual states, but typically include graduation from an accredited school (three to four-year master's level programs) and passing a national standardized exam. The Accreditation Commission for Acupuncture and Oriental Medicine (ACAOM) is recognized by the Department of Education. The number of acupuncturists in the U.S. nearly doubled from 1992 to 1998 growing from 5,525 to 10,512. In 2006, there were 56 acupuncture schools in the U.S. Approximately 30% of acupuncturists also hold M.D. degrees.

Efficacy

In November 1997, the NIH convened an expert, multidisciplinary panel to determine the effectiveness of acupuncture as medical treatment. The panel determined that acupuncture is an effective treatment for nausea associated with chemotherapy, pregnancy, post-operative recovery, and motion sickness; analgesia for dental pain, headaches, menstrual cramps, fibromyalgia, osteoarthritis, and low back pain; and anesthesia for certain surgical procedures. The NIH Consensus Conference on Acupuncture Report states "an important value of acupuncture is that the incidence of adverse effects is substantially lower than many of the drugs and other accepted medical procedures used for the same conditions."

Chiropractic

Chiropractic examines the relationship between the structure and function of the spine, and how it affects the nervous system and body functioning. Loss of structural integrity, termed **subluxation,** can result in loss of normal physiology or function. The goal of chiropractic therapy is the correction of subluxation with resulting restoration of function. This goal is accomplished primarily through the use of joint manipulation **(adjustment).**

Adjustment involves a high velocity, low amplitude maneuver to restore normal joint alignment and mobility. The site of adjustment is determined by symptoms, clinical examination (e.g., palpation), or diagnostic assessment (e.g., thermographic patterns).

> The biological basis for the structural and physiological effects of chiropractic is poorly understood. Known responses to manipulation include elevation of serum beta-endorphin levels, increased joint mobility, enhanced neutrophil activity, and attenuation of spinal electromyographic activity.

Training and Licensure

Chiropractic is licensed in all states, but there is significant variation in the scope of practice. Some states allow only spinal manipulation (adjustment), and restrict the use of clinical examination procedures. Other states permit chiropractors to perform certain laboratory procedures (e.g., venipuncture), practice acupuncture, give nutritional advice, and dispense supplements.

Chiropractic training requires four years. All schools currently have at least a two-year undergraduate requirement that includes prescribed hours in the sciences and humanities. A bachelor's degree is becoming an increasingly common requirement for admission. There are 16 chiropractic colleges in the U.S. accredited by the Council on Chiropractic Education (CCE), the accrediting agency recognized by the Department of Education. Thirteen colleges are also accredited by regional accrediting agencies for secondary and post-secondary colleges. Following the completion of educational requirements, the chiropractor must pass state and national examinations to become

licensed. Graduate level studies that lead to specialty certification include sports chiropractic, rehabilitation, chiropractic sciences, orthopedics, neurology, and nutrition.

Efficacy

Most conditions treated by chiropractors involve low back complaints. Non-low back complaints are usually musculoskeletal conditions involving neck pain, mid-back pain, arm or leg pain, and headache. Non-musculoskeletal complaints such

> Based on reviews of published research findings, spinal manipulation has been shown to be of short-term benefit in the alleviation of acute low back pain, neck pain, and headaches.

as asthma, otitis media, and gastrointestinal distress account for less than 3% of all patient visits to chiropractors. **Uncomplicated low back pain** is the most widely researched condition commonly treated by manipulation.

The Agency for Health Care Policy and Research has recommended spinal manipulation in its published guideline on the management of acute low back pain. A five-year pilot program, initiated by Congress in 1995 to assess the effectiveness of chiropractic care in the military, concluded that patients with neuromuscular complaints had: (1) better outcomes with chiropractic care, (2) increased satisfaction with medical care, (3) less lost duty time, (4) and reduced hospitalization time and costs. The National Center for Complementary and Alternative Medicine and the National Institute of Arthritis and Musculoskeletal and Skin Diseases have funded the first federally funded Center for Chiropractic Research.

Contraindications

Contraindications for chiropractic care include conditions caused by serious underlying disease (cancer and cardiac disease), unfavorable response to manipulation, fractures, ligament injury, inflammatory arthritis, ankylosing spondylitis, bone disease, osteoporosis, infection, disc prolapse, and bleeding disorders.

Complications

The most serious complication of cervical manipulation is vertebrobasilar artery injury resulting in a cerebrovascular accident (CVA). The incidence of developing a CVA after cervical manipulation is estimated at between 1 in 500,000 to 1 in 2 million manipulations. Lumbar manipulation carries a lower risk for serious complication. The incidence of developing cauda equina syndrome after manipulation is estimated to be 1 in several million manipulations.

Naturopathy

While **naturopathy** had its origins in the natural healing movements of the 18th and 19th centuries, its establishment in the U.S. is associated with the work of Benedict Lust. Dr. Lust, an immigrant from Germany, came to the U.S. in the 1890s, completed his own medical training (studied allopathic, chiropractic, osteopathic, and homeopathic medicine), and established the first school of naturopathic medicine in New York City. About the same time, Dr. James Foster established a school of naturopathic medicine in Idaho. These two individuals subsequently collaborated in establishing the new profession of naturopathy which drew on an array of natural healing interventions derived from traditional Chinese, Ayurvedic, and Greek medicine, Native American healing systems, and modern scientific principles and technology.

By the 1920s, these were approximately 20 colleges of naturopathy in the U.S. and licensure in most states. As a result of the increasing influence

Six Basic Principles of Modern Naturopathy

1. Nature has the power to heal and it is the physician's role to enhance the self-healing process.
2. Treat the whole person so that every aspect of a patient's natural defenses and function is brought into harmonious balance.
3. "First, do no harm" reflects the Hippocratic creed that the physician should utilize methods and substances that are non-toxic and non-invasive.
4. Identify and treat the cause, in contrast to suppressing symptoms.
5. Prevention is an important aspect of cure that the physician should promote.
6. Doctors should be teachers and educate the patient about his/her personal responsibility to maintain health.

Naturopathic Modalities

1. Clinical nutrition and the therapeutic use of diet, including drug-nutrient interactions;
2. Physical medicine procedures such as hydrotherapy, exercise, massage, manipulation, immobilization, braces, splints, ultrasound, diathermy, heat therapy, electrical stimulation, and balneology;
3. Homeopathic treatments that simulate the body's own natural forces;
4. Botanical medicine including the use of herbs and other natural substances and compounds to maximize desirable effects and minimize undesirable side effects, including drug-herb interactions;
5. Natural childbirth;
6. Traditional Chinese medicine including the use of Chinese herbs and acupuncture;
7. Ayurvedic medicine;
8. Mind-body techniques that emphasize the facilitative and supportive effects of counseling, psychotherapy, behavioral medicine, hypnosis, stress management, and biofeedback; and
9. Minor surgery, such as superficial wound repair, removal of foreign masses, minor hemorrhoid surgery, circumcision, and setting fractures.

of biomedicine, however, naturopathy declined in popularity until the 1970s when it experienced a resurgence due, in part, to the high costs of biomedicine and changes in health care financing. Currently there are four recognized colleges/universities of naturopathic training in the U.S.

Drawing on effective treatments from a wide range of healing approaches, naturopathy has been shown to be an effective **complement to biomedicine** in disease prevention, the treatment of acute illnesses, and supportive treatment of chronic and degenerative conditions. Naturopathic physicians recognize that conventional medicine is excellent in addressing more complex medical crises such as acute trauma, childbirth emergencies, fractures, corrective surgery, and acute life threatening illnesses. Recognition of their relative strengths and limitations has led to increasing collaboration between biomedical and naturopathic physicians.

Training and Licensure
As of May 2006, naturopathic physicians were licensed as primary health care providers in 14 states, the District of Columbia, two U.S. territo-

ries (Puerto Rico and the Virgin Islands), and are recognized in five Canadian provinces. Legislation for licensure is pending in New York, North Carolina, and several other U.S. states.

All states and provinces with licensure laws require at least four years of study at a college or university recognized by the state examining board. The Council on Naturopathic Medical Education is recognized by the U.S. Department of Education. Naturopathic physicians receive training in anatomy, cell biology, physiology, pathology, neuroscience, histology, genetics, biochemistry, pharmacology, clinical and physical diagnosis, laboratory diagnosis, biostatistics, and epidemiology. To qualify for licensure, the applicant must pass the naturopathic licensing examination (NPLEX). Post-graduate medical education is available and there are several specialty societies, including the Oncology Academy of Naturopathic Physicians.

Efficacy

Naturopathy appears to be increasingly integrated into conventional medicine due to cost effectiveness and the relatively less distressing nature of its natural treatment alternatives. It has received increasing respect from the American health care consumer, government bodies, and the biomedical community. There is positive evidence for the effectiveness of some of the common naturopathic interventions. However, because of its wide-ranging nature (i.e., drawn from a large number of healing systems), it cannot be assumed that this provides conclusive evidence of the efficacy of all naturopathic or associated complementary healing systems. Well designed and controlled research is required to determine the efficacy of specific techniques for specific disorders.

Creative Arts Therapies

The National Coalition of Arts Therapies Associations (NCATA) lists six member associations representing the disciplines of art therapy, dance/movement therapy, drama therapy, music therapy, psychodrama, and poetry therapy. These therapies share the use of the arts, creative processes, and therapeutic relationships to effect change and promote healing in physical, emotional, cognitive, and social functioning.

The four professions of art therapy, dance/movement therapy, drama therapy, and music ther-

apy educate and clinically train skilled artists to become therapists, using their respective art forms. While there is some common history and shared principles of practice deriving from the human experience and expression of art in general, these professions are separate and distinct disciplines, each with its own professional association, educational and clinical training standards, credentials, standards of practice, and code of ethics.

Art Therapy

Art therapy, the use of art media, images, the creative art process and patient responses to the created products has two primary approaches to treatment. The first is an **"art as therapy"** approach where process rather than product transforms and changes behavior in patients. The second is adjunctive where psychotherapy is supplemented with art materials and artistic activities to **release symbolic speech** and generate nonverbal and verbal communication.

Dance Therapy

Dance therapy, the **psychotherapeutic use of movement,** assumes that dance communicates, that dance and movement qualities relate to culture, personality, mental status, and the relationship to self and others, and that dance permits many levels of kinesthetic expression (e.g., sensorimotor, iconic, symbolic, abstract). **Movement empathy** (the kinesthetic analogue of reflection, paraphrase, and verbal empathy) generates and supports the therapeutic alliance between the dance/movement therapist and the patient.

Drama Therapy

Drama therapy, the systematic and intentional use of drama/theater processes, is based on psychodynamic and cognitive-behavioral therapy approaches, and theories derived from theatre, creative drama, and play. Individual counseling and group dynamic strategies are applied in the context of drama therapy.

Music Therapy

Music therapy, the prescribed use of music to effect positive changes, combines music modalities with humanistic, psychodynamic, behavioral, and biomedical approaches to help patients attain therapeutic goals. Appropriately designed music therapy interventions allow the patient to derive therapeutic benefit from the structure of music, the rhythm, and the social interaction attending it. Of particular importance is the effect of rhythm, which can serve to relax, energize, and stimulate.

Therapeutic Touch

Therapeutic touch is based on the principles of several ancient healing practices that postulate that persons are open energy systems that interact with the environment. The human energy system is believed to be composed of three parts: the energy field or **aura,** composed of seven layers; the seven related energy centers or **chakras;** and the energy tracts or **meridians.** Practitioners use the hands to direct human energies toward healing and assist patients to self-heal by restoring harmony and balance in the human energy system.

It is assumed that a person's health and quality of life are affected by the health and quality of the energy system, and that the environment as well as thoughts, emotions, actions, and intents influence the energy system. It is further assumed that potential illness appears in the energy field before it manifests on the physical structural level. A therapeutic touch treatment is composed of four stages: centering, assessment, rebalancing or repatterning, and stopping. Therapeutic touch practitioners "assess the energy field" through kinesthetic, visual, auditory, or intuitive clues about patterns of energy. After determining a patient's treatment needs, a practitioner is thought to act as a conduit to access and transfer universal energy to the patient's energy system.

Efficacy

Therapeutic touch is used largely by nurses, massage therapists, chiropractors, and osteopathic physicians in the treatment of conditions such as pain, anxiety and stress, depression, chronic fatigue, and side effects of cancer treatments. A few randomized, controlled studies to date have shown therapeutic touch to be effective in the treatment of mood disturbances (tension, anxiety, confusion), to affect associated biochemical indicators, and to increase pain tolerance and vigor in experimental versus control groups.

A study examining the effects of therapeutic touch on pain and anxiety levels of 99 burn victims showed a reduction in pain and anxiety for the experimental group. Blood drawn on days 1 and 6 for lymphocyte subset analysis showed a decrease in total CD8+ lymphocyte concentrations for the experimental group. The control group,

which received sham therapeutic touch treatment, did not demonstrate changes.

However, not all studies report significant or positive results. Currently, it appears that the most reliable effects of touch are rapid relaxation response, pain reduction, facilitation of the healing process, and reduction of psychosomatic symptoms.

Complementary Medicine and the Behavioral Sciences

What distinguishes behavioral science-based treatments from complementary medicine treatments?

In his book, *The Best Alternative Medicine,* Pelletier states: "Of all the CAM interventions, mind body medicine is supported by the greatest body of scientific evidence for the greatest number of conditions for the largest number of people. It has also gained the widest acceptance within the conventional medical system" (p. 59). He then traces the evolution of **"mind body"** medicine from its origins, the revolt against the reductionism of biomedicine, through the shifts in focus from infectious diseases to lifestyle and public health-based disorders, to the increasing recognition of the interplay of environmental, psychological, social and lifestyle factors. What Pelletier is describing is, in fact, the emergence of the **"biopsychosocial" model**, although he does not use that term. Since its inception, the biopsychosocial model has gained increasing acceptance, largely through the supporting empirical evidence accumulated via research on the role of the behavioral sciences in medicine. These research efforts have given rise to the emerging fields of behavioral medicine, health psychology, and psychoneuroimmunology, all of which have focused on identifying the mechanisms of biobehavioral interaction.

Empirically-based treatment modalities developed out of these research efforts include relaxation, meditation, hypnosis, imagery and visualization, cognitive-behavioral therapies, and biofeedback. All are forms of treatment based on research into the role of behavioral and cognitive factors in the etiology of select medical disorders. As Pelletier points out, they are now widely accepted within the conventional biomedical system so, by definition, they can not be subsumed under the "complementary medicine" rubric.

Complementary Therapies and the Scientific Method

Why do some proponents of complementary medicine reject accepted scientific standards for research?

Many proponents of complementary medicine argue that accepted standards of scientific investigation are not appropriate for evaluating CAM methods and treatments. The argument is based on two assumptions.

(1) The first assumption is that CAM treatments are individualized and therefore cannot be fairly assessed by large sample randomized controlled trials. The argument is not unique to CAM adherents as biomedical researchers in general realize that large-scale studies do not enable the clinician to make predictions about individual case responses, especially those requiring individualized treatment. At the same time, biomedical researchers believe that the efficacy of any treatment approach must first begin with demonstrated effectiveness within population samples.

(2) The second assumption is that CAM approaches are based on explanations fundamentally different from those of conventional biomedical approaches and, therefore, should not be judged on the same biomedical criteria. This argument infers that the "theoretical" causal explanations of CAM are not biological, cognitive, behavioral, sociocultural, or environmental in nature, but rather attributed to phenomena that lie outside the realm of generally accepted scientific explanations for human functioning, disease, and disorder. Not all adherents of CAM agree with this position. Naturopathic physicians, for example, recognize and undergo stringent training in the biomedical and behavioral sciences.

In growing numbers, proponents of CAM are offering research evidence from controlled studies demonstrating the efficacy of certain CAM treatments for certain disorders. However, in both CAM and biomedicine, simple treatment outcome studies (treatment versus no treatment, or treat-

ment A versus treatment B) do not necessarily confirm hypotheses about the cause of the underlying malady. More sophisticated designs are required to address such issues.

Thus, while there is evidence that certain CAM treatments can be effective in the treatment of selected disorders and can serve palliative and supplementary roles with biomedical approaches, continued research into the efficacy of specific treatments for specific disorders and their mechanisms of effect is required. In 2005–2006, NCCAM funding for CAM research was approximately $122 million or 0.5% of the total NIH budget. Additional research funding from the NIH will play a key role in increasing understanding about how each CAM modality is best used and for which conditions.

In 2005, the Institute of Medicine report on complementary and alternative medicine in the U.S. stated that health care should be both comprehensive and evidence based with biomedicine and CAM following the same research principles but recognizing that new research methods need to be developed to test some therapies in *both* conventional and complementary medicine.

The "N of 1" design, for example, that can accommodate individualized approaches to providing and evaluating specific treatments is becoming more widely accepted in the literature.

Integrative Medicine

What is integrative medicine?

As complementary medicine modalities have become more mainstream and the efficacy of many practices have begun to do be demonstrated scientifically, physicians may incorporate one or more modalities into a patient's overall health care plan. For example, a patient with chronic back pain may not only be prescribed an analgesic, to take every 8 hours, but also be prescribed to have a massage weekly and to use music therapy regularly to release some of the negative emotions that have developed in association with activity limitations.

In this scenario, the physician works with the patient to identify and explore complementary medicine practices to augment what biomedicine can provide to the patient. In integrative medicine, communication among all of the practitioners working with the patient is vital to insure that treatments will complement each other to the fullest degree possible.

Recommended Reading

Eisenberg DM, Davis RB, Ettner SL, et al. Trends in alternative medicine use in the United States, 1990–1997. *JAMA* 1998; 280:1569–1575.

Faass N. *Integrating Complementary Medicine into Health Systems.* Gaithersburg, MD: Aspen; 2001.

Micozzi M. *Fundamentals of Complementary and Alternative Medicine.* New York: Churchill-Livingstone; 1996.

Novey DW. *Clinicians' Complete Reference to Complementary and Alternative Medicine.* St. Louis, MO: Mosby; 2000.

Pelletier KR. *The Best Alternative Medicine.* New York: Fireside; 2000.

Robson T (Ed.). *Introduction to Complementary Medicine.* London: Allen & Unwin; 2004.

Zollman C, Vickers A. What is complementary medicine? *British Medical Journal* 1999; 319:693–696.

Review Questions

1. As of 2002, four CAM therapies were licensed in the U.S. Which one of the following was in that group?
    A. Dance therapy
    B. Homeopathy
    C. Music therapy
    D. Naturopathy
    E. Therapeutic touch

Directions: The items below consist of lettered headings followed by numbered descriptions. For each numbered description choose the *one* lettered heading to which it is *most* closely associated. Each lettered heading may be used *once, more than once,* or *not at all.*

Match the CAM modality with its principal therapeutic intent.
A . Acupuncture
B. Chiropractic
C. Homeopathy
D. Naturopathy
E. Therapeutic touch

    2. Using like to cure like
    3. Adjustment of subluxation
    4. Facilitating the flow of Qi
    5. Balancing human energy fields

Various government agencies have determined that certain CAM modalities may be useful in the management of specific disorders. Match the modality with the condition for which it appears to be efficacious.
A. Acupuncture
B. Creative arts therapy
C. Homeopathy
D. Naturopathy
E. Therapeutic touch

    6. Anesthesia for surgery
    7. Low back pain
    8. Hyperemesis gravidorum

Key to review questions: p. 393

30 Palliative Care

- What are palliative care and hospice care?
- When is palliative care appropriate?
- What are the four main end-of-life trajectories?
- What are common events during the dying process?
- What is complicated grief?

What are palliative care and hospice care?

The role of **palliative care** is to provide relief of physical symptoms and suffering (psychological, spiritual, and social) that patients may experience. Unlike hospice (reserved for patients in the last months of life and focused on comfort), palliative care can be initiated at any point in the illness and given in tandem with disease-directed treatment. Basic palliative care skills should be a part of the clinical armamentarium of all clinicians who care for seriously ill patients; more complex illnesses or refractory symptoms may require the involvement of palliative care specialists.

Inpatient palliative care consultation services work with the attending physician and treatment team to address symptom management, prognosis, goals of care, and end-of-life issues. Some hospitals have designated inpatient units for patients receiving primarily palliative care. **Outpatient clinics** provide access to palliative care consultation for patients not admitted to the hospital, and offer follow-up care for those who need ongoing treatment and support. **Home visit programs** provide palliative care physicians and nurses who evaluate and follow patients in their own homes. This is often the best option for those who cannot physically tolerate being transported to and from an outpatient clinic. Ideally, the **palliative care team** is interdisciplinary and, at a minimum, includes physicians, nurses, social workers, psychologists, and chaplains who provide coordinated multi-faceted care.

Hospice

If cure is not possible, or treatment becomes too burdensome, palliative care may become the sole focus of therapy. In such cases, the patient may be a candidate for **hospice,** a Medicare-funded program designed to provide palliative care for terminally ill patients. To qualify, a patient must have an expected survival of less than six months, and forego curative therapies. For many patients, **home hospice** is their first choice. However, since home hospice provides only a few hours daily of patient care, many well-intentioned families are unable to shoulder the burden of caregiving. For such patients, hospice houses and hospice care at nursing homes are alternatives. **Hospice houses** are staffed by trained volunteers and provide a home-like environment. Patients who elect **nurs-**

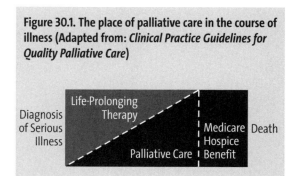

Figure 30.1. The place of palliative care in the course of illness (Adapted from: *Clinical Practice Guidelines for Quality Palliative Care*)

ing home hospice care receive custodial care, as well as extra aide service daily covered by the hospice benefit. **Acute hospice units**, freestanding or within a hospital, provide intense nursing care and physician oversight for patients with recalcitrant symptoms or who are imminently dying.

Clinical Application – Part I

Joseph Amato is a 71-year-old man with idiopathic pulmonary fibrosis. Prior to his diagnosis 4 years ago, he was an avid golfer but increasing shortness of breath has limited his recreation to monthly fly-fishing outings with his granddaughter. Mr. Amato has been on corticosteroids and immunosuppressant therapy with only marginal benefit. He understands he has "some sort of lung disease" and is glad it's not emphysema which his brother succumbed to 2 years ago. At that time he remarked to his wife, "When my time comes, just let me go." Mr. Amato goes to his pulmonologist for routine follow-up. After a hurried exam, the physician reports that "nothing's really changed" since the last visit and gives a relieved Mr. Amato medication refills. Mr. Amato has significant shortness of breath but believes that nothing can be done about it. On his way to check out, Mr. Amato notices a pamphlet about hospice care, but because he thinks hospice is "where you go to die," he does not take one.

When is palliative care appropriate?

Palliative care providers can offer family and patient support, guidance in medical decision making, and assistance in clarifying goals of care. They can facilitate communication between patients, families, and medical staff, which is critical when a patient is seeing multiple subspecialists. "Triggers" for urgent **palliative care consults** include imminent death, increasing patient suffering in the face of a poor prognosis, or decreasing response to aggressive treatment.

The Patient Interview

In preparing for a patient interview, information is gathered from all involved medical teams regarding the disease process, treatment options, and prognosis. Making note of areas the teams agree on, and determining what information has already been shared with the patient, limits miscommunication and enables the provider to synthesize information with the patient and family.

After introductions are made, an **explanation of palliative care** should follow. Usually a straightforward description will suffice, such as *"We help relieve pain and other uncomfortable symptoms, and we also help patients and families with difficult decision making."* The patient and family should be asked to tell their story about how the illness is affecting them, their perception of events and what they mean, and their expectations for the future. The treatment team should **clarify misunderstandings**, and try to reconcile the patient's understanding with the information gathered by the team. At the end of the interview, the discussion should be summarized, options described, and a follow-up meeting arranged.

Delivering Bad News

One of a physician's most daunting tasks is delivering bad news, such as when a serious illness is first diagnosed, or with each decline in the patient's condition. Before meeting with the patient, facts about the patient's illness, prognosis and treatment options must be reviewed to ensure accurate discussion. The meeting should be held in a quiet, private setting and everyone the patient desires should be present. If the patient's health status impairs understanding, the health care proxy or other surrogate should be present.

The first step is to assess what the patient and family understand about whatever area is to be discussed (test results, treatment, prognosis). Helpful statements to prepare them for hearing the news include *"The test results didn't turn out as well as we'd hoped,"* or *"I'm afraid I have some news that may be hard for you to hear."* **Give information in small chunks**, to avoid overwhelming the patient or family with details. **Allow time for the patient's response**; be prepared for grief, anger, denial, anxiety, or acceptance. No matter what response the news elicits, **acknowledge and legitimize emotions**: *"You look angry. This must seem so unfair."* **Allow for questions.** Repeat key points and assess for understanding. Provide detailed information if requested. Before concluding the meeting, determine if the patient is at risk for self-harm. Ensure a safe ride home, as patients can be too distracted to drive safely. Offer to call relatives or friends to provide support. Establish a clear follow-up plan, such as another visit or a phone call the next day. If any appointments for subspecialists, tests, or procedures are needed, offer to arrange them. Finally, reassure the patient that you will continue to work with him or her no matter what the course of the disease.

Clinical Application – Part II

Two months later, Mr. Amato is hospitalized with pneumonia. He still requires supplemental oxygen and desaturates with minimal exertion after 2 weeks of treatment. During a conversation with his primary care physician, who has known him for almost 20 years, Mr. Amato talks about his plans to attend his granddaughter's college graduation in 6 months. Not wanting his patient to lose hope, his physician keeps silent about the low likelihood of Mr. Amato's surviving until that event. After the visit, the physician requests a palliative care consult to assist in clarifying prognosis and treatment options.

Dr. Keats, a physician on the palliative care service, sees Mr. Amato and asks that his wife and his three children stay in the room during the visit. Dr. Keats begins by asking Mr. Amato to tell his version of the events that landed him in the hospital. Early on, it becomes clear that Mr. Amato does not know the nature of his illness or his prognosis. When he asks for more information, he is told what his disease is called and how it affects the lungs. Mr. Amato says he has never heard the term idiopathic pulmonary fibrosis and that he thought his illness was "not that serious." "I'm afraid it can be serious for many patients," Dr. Keats replies. Mr. Amato indicates that he wants to hear more and is given a "typical" scenario of worsening dyspnea and fatigue. After a period of silence, Mr. Amato asks, "Will this kill me?" "Eventually, yes. I wish I could tell you differently," is Dr. Keats' response.

Mr. Amato seems stunned. The patient, physician, and family sit quietly for several seconds. Clearly not ready to absorb further information, Mr. Amato asks for time alone with his family. Dr. Keats and the patient and family agree to talk again that afternoon. Dr. Keats tells Mr. Amato how to reach him in the interim, should he have questions.

Giving Prognosis

In general, physicians tend to be overly optimistic in giving prognoses, probably motivated by a desire to preserve or maximize patient "hope." However, patients and families generally value a **balance of realism and compassion**. A realistic understanding of the disease course and timeline can aid patients in prioritizing family visits, vacations, financial issues, spiritual/religious needs, or guardianship arrangements. Before giving a prognosis, it is critical to determine the likely course of the patient's disease, including the average length of survival. Certain illnesses, such as cancer, congestive heart failure, and dementia, have distinct trajectories and uncertainties that can lead to better understanding of the prognosis. Some patients, upon hearing their initial diagnosis, may ask "How much time do I have?" Others may want little or no information. Ask the patient if information is desired before providing it. If a timeline is requested, give averages and allow for outliers in both directions. Note the possibility for longer survival than average, which allows for hope, but also shorter survival, which encourages preparation. "Let's hope for the best but prepare for the worst."

Clinical Application – Part III

At his return visit, Dr. Keats explains to Mr. Amato that some patients want estimates of how much time they have left. Mr. Amato doesn't want much detail, but does want to know his chances of surviving until his granddaughter's graduation in 6 months. Dr. Keats explains, "Although I hope you make it to the graduation, I wouldn't be surprised if you died before then. In a disease like yours, the odds of living 6 months are 50/50. You might live considerably longer than 6 months, but it could also be shorter if you get another pneumonia or some other complication."

What are the four main end-of-life trajectories?

Disease Trajectories

The four main end-of-life trajectories are: (1) sudden death, (2) terminal illness, (3) organ failure, and (4) frailty (see Figure 30.2.). Palliative care is appropriate in three of these trajectories. The first is one that many cancers follow: a relatively rapid predictable decline over weeks to months. This trajectory best fits the hospice option since, once the decline begins, death is likely within 6 months. The second trajectory, sudden decline with intervening periods of relative stability, is more characteristic of organ failure, such as congestive heart failure or pulmonary fibrosis. For these patients, one cannot reliably predict if the prognosis is 1 day or 6 months. Exacerbations tend to come suddenly, and the patient either recovers or dies, or potentially becomes dependent on mechanical ventilation. The third trajectory, gradual progressive decline resulting in an often lengthy period of frailty, is characteristic of Alzheimer's dementia. Here the prognosis can be years, depending on how aggressively illnesses and complications

are treated. It is critical that patients and families understand which trajectory applies to their illness, and use that information in decision making.

Do-Not-Resuscitate Orders

Responsible care for seriously ill patients requires a candid discussion of **Do-Not-Resuscitate (DNR)** and **Do-Not-Intubate (DNI)** orders. Unfortunately, misconceptions about the effectiveness of **cardiopulmonary resuscitation (CPR)** have been fueled by media depictions of miraculous, highly successful interventions. In fact, less than 5% of cardiac arrest victims survive to hospital discharge. Of those who do survive, many have neurological impairments and are not able to live independently. In the setting of

Figure 30.2. End-of-life trajectories (Adapted from: Lunney JR, Lynn J, Foley DJ, et al. Patterns of functional decline at the end of life. *JAMA* 2003; 289:2387–2392)

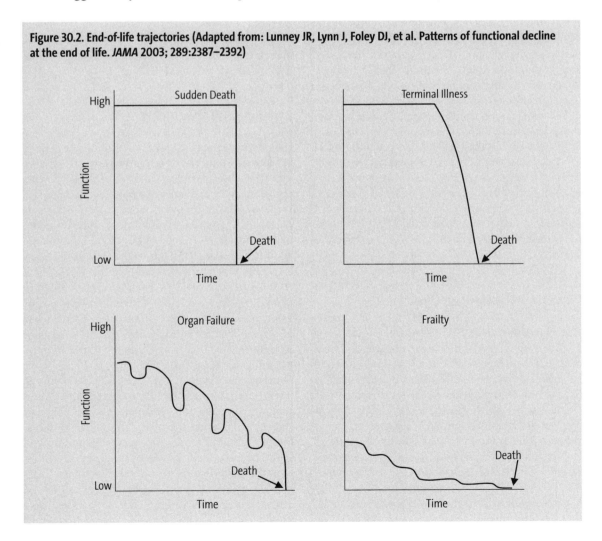

Clinical Application – Part IV

Mr. Amato is ready for discharge. He has decided to continue disease-driven treatment so he can have his "best shot" at seeing his granddaughter graduate. In the hospital, Dr. Keats began treatment with low-dose around-the-clock opioids to help relieve Mr. Amato's dyspnea, and arranges to see him in the outpatient palliative care clinic. He and Mr. Amato will re-evaluate his treatment plans as his health status and goals evolve. Prior to discharge, Mr. Amato agrees to a DNR order since he understands such efforts would likely be futile. He considers a trial period of intubation, then decides against it after his physicians explain that the most likely outcome would be lifelong mechanical ventilation.

Clinical Application – Part V

Mr. Amato returns to the hospital several times over the next few months because of respiratory insufficiency. He and Dr. Keats continue to talk about the benefits and burdens of treatment. Mr. Amato holds firm to his goal of seeing his granddaughter graduate. Dr. Keats lets him know he supports this decision, and works aggressively to reduce his dyspnea with opioids, searching for reversible elements of the underlying disease. Mr. Amato's appetite has been poor. The hospital nutritionist notes Mr. Amato's weight has declined sharply over the past 8 weeks and recommends placement of a feeding tube. Dr. Keats discusses the risks and benefits of a feeding tube with Mr. Amato. Mr. Amato decides against tube placement at this time.

severe chronic illness, CPR is even less effective. If the patient survives the initial event, the underlying disease process still progresses. Similarly, patients with chronic illness who are intubated and on a ventilator have difficulty being weaned. When discussing **resuscitation status,** physicians should inform the patient if CPR is likely to result in unacceptable outcomes. The patient should also understand that a decision to withhold CPR or intubation does not preclude other more efficacious aggressive medical interventions. "Given your desire to live as long as possible, but not to lose your independence, I suggest we try all potentially effective treatments, but I also recommend that you avoid CPR. It is a harsh treatment and unlikely to work in your circumstance."

Presenting the Hospice Option

Broaching the option of hospice care is often a "bad news" discussion. Since a hospice patient must have a prognosis of less than 6 months and be willing to forgo disease-directed treatment, the patient must confront the prospect of impending death. The physician should emphasize that choosing hospice is not "giving up." The goal of care is being shifted from unrealistic curative treatments that may add to a patient's suffering, to making the patient comfortable. This means aggressive symptom control, and giving patients the opportunity to gain emotional, spiritual, existential, and social closure. The physician promises to not abandon

the patient simply because disease-driven treatment is discontinued; instead, the patient-physician partnership is maintained, and sometimes even strengthened, until the end of life.

Experimental Treatments

Academic centers and other institutions occasionally provide **experimental therapy** as part of clinical trials. For patients unlikely to do well with conventional treatments, such opportunities offer the possibility of remission or even cure. However, potential downsides to experimental therapy must be carefully considered. First, what is the **toxicity of the treatment**? Many patients will not want to pursue treatments that have severe side effects if the benefit is small or unknown. Second, **time** is precious for seriously ill patients who may not want to spend it in medical settings. Third, what **outcome** does the therapy offer? If the treatment extends survival by a few months, those months may not be worthwhile if quality of life is poor. On the other hand, if side effects, time commitment, and possible benefits are acceptable, then pursing experimental treatment can be compelling. Experimental therapy or palliative disease-directed treatment may be important to patients who have invested the majority of their hope in the possible efficacy of medical treatments. Such patients prefer to "go down swinging" and would see stopping disease-directed treatment as "giving up." Patients need realistic information about the potential benefits and burdens of treatments available, and what their physician recommends. Those who hope for the best should be prepared in the event the treatment does not work, and make back-up plans accordingly.

Clinical Application – Part VI

Mr. Amato's son, while searching the Internet, finds several clinical trials for patients with pulmonary fibrosis. After he reviews the information with Dr. Keats, it becomes apparent that Mr. Amato is not a good candidate because he has late-stage disease and the side effects of the experimental therapy are beyond his tolerance.

The Family Meeting

Family meetings should be conducted in a quiet conference room, or the patient's room if he/she is too ill to be moved. Ensure everyone required is present, especially the health care proxy if the patient is unable to make his or her own decisions, and other figures of authority (chaplain, matriarch, patriarch, primary care doctor) whose input would be valued by the rest of the family.

Encourage all to contribute their perspective of the present situation and develop a collective understanding of the illness and its prognosis. If the patient is unable to make personal medical decisions, surrogates should be encouraged to think in terms of *what the patient would want* rather than what they want for the patient. This can be challenging if the patient never expressed any wishes regarding end-of-life care. Sometimes a patient's wishes have to be inferred from prior health decisions or personal values. If a patient declined invasive procedures in the past, it is likely that he or she would not want them now. Sometimes patient preferences clash with those of the proxy or family. It is important to remind decision makers to make decisions as they imagine the patient would (using **"substituted judgment"**), and not decide based on their own wishes. If the practitioner believes that certain choices are best for the patient, given what is known of his/her clinical circumstances and values, the proxy and family should be so informed. Often a physician's recommendation is welcome and can ease the

Clinical Application – Part VII

During Mr. Amato's last admission, hypoxia renders him drowsy and unable to participate in medical decisions. The palliative care team meets with his family and primary care physician, whose opinion the family trusts. Dr. Keats explains that the frequent hospitalizations, delirium, and hypoxia are all indicators of approaching death despite aggressive treatment. Mrs. Amato, who is her husband's health care proxy, and their children review Mr. Amato's goals. Attending his granddaughter's graduation is no longer possible. Recalling his statements at the time of his brother's death, Mrs. Amato is sure her husband would "just want to be made comfortable." His primary care physician recommends hospice, a recommendation echoed by the palliative care team. Once reassured that Mr. Amato will receive diligent care, the family chooses a home hospice program.

uncertainty and guilt that can accompany end-of-life decisions.

Pain Management

A basic approach to pain management has been outlined by the World Health Organization (see Figure 30.3.).

Pain is rated on a scale of 0–10, with 0 being no pain and 10 the worst pain imaginable. **Mild pain** (1–3) can be treated with non-opioid medications, e.g., acetaminophen and nonsteroidal anti-inflammatory drugs (NSAIDs). **Moderate pain** (4–7) is treated with opioid and non-opioid regimens, often using medications that combine the two classes. **Severe pain** (8–10) is best managed with strong opioids. Adjuvant modalities, drugs not usually used for analgesia but that have benefit for specific types of pain, can be used at any level of discomfort. An alert patient with mild or intermittent pain often can be treated with **p.r.n. (as-needed) analgesics**. However, patients with severe or constant pain require a combination of **scheduled pain medication** as well as p.r.n. dosing. Providers may hesitate to schedule opioid medications fearing respiratory depression. However, since sleepiness almost always precedes respiratory depression, the next scheduled dose can be withheld if lethargy

Figure 30.3. Pain management

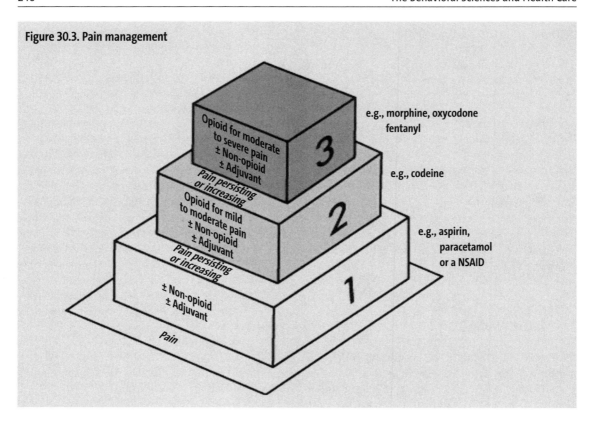

e.g., morphine, oxycodone
fentanyl

e.g., codeine

e.g., aspirin,
paracetamol
or a NSAID

develops and the following doses adjusted accordingly.

Exaggerated fear of using opioids often stems from a misunderstanding of tolerance, dependence, addiction, and pseudoaddiction. **Tolerance** means that increasing doses of opioids may be required over time to achieve the same analgesic effect; fortunately, opioid tolerance is usually limited. **Physical dependence** is an expected result of chronic opioid use and means the body has adapted to opioid use. In the dependent patient, abruptly decreasing the opiod dose can result in a withdrawal syndrome. Both tolerance and dependence can be managed by dose titration or switching to a different opioid.

Addiction is characterized by impaired control over drug use, craving, erratic behaviors, and continued use over time despite harm. True addiction is infrequent in palliative care in the absence of pre-existing substance abuse problems, and should not be a reason to avoid opioid use. **Pseudoaddiction** appears similar to addiction, but is, in fact, a result of inadequate pain relief. The behavior disappears when the patient's pain is properly treated. Tolerance, dependence and pseudoaddiction can be managed by careful dose adjustments.

Clinical Application – Part VIII

Dr. Keats receives a call from the home hospice aide the day after Mr. Amato is discharged. The aide reports that the patient is complaining of severe pain in his lower back. Also, Mr. Amato has anxiety due to feeling short of breath. After examining Mr. Amato at home, Dr. Keats suspects compression fractures and increases the opioid dose. Although the opioids may reduce any anxiety Mr. Amato experiences as a result of dyspnea, Dr. Keats also prescribes a benzodiazepine "as needed" as a back-up medication.

Finding the right regimen of pain medications can be a complex task. Chronically ill or dying patients often require dose titration and adjuvant therapies. Converting from one opioid to another is frequently necessary to minimize side effects or for ease of dosing. Calculating the **equianalgesic dose** of a strong opioid with a variable, dose-dependent half-life such as methadone, requires considerable expertise. Enlisting the aid of palliative care or other pain management specialists is advisable in such cases.

Special Issues in Terminal Care

Balancing Aggressive Management and Alertness

If a dying patient experiences increasing pain, **strong opioids** in increasing doses may be necessary, although such treatment may be accompanied by **decreased mental status**. Since some patients prefer to be as alert as possible, even if it means they may experience more discomfort, it is important to ascertain the patient's preferences. The patient and family should be reassured that, should suffering become severe, the team will seek solutions that keep the patient in charge of pain relief.

Artificial Nutrition and Hydration

In many cultures, preparing and serving food is an expression of caring. Witholding food can seem unforgivable, even though many dying patients experience anorexia. Providing the family information while empathizing with their concerns can help with decisions regarding **feeding tubes and intravenous fluids**. First, feeding through a gastric tube has not been shown to prolong the life of most patients, except those with select cancers (e.g., oropharyngeal or esophageal). Second, tube feeding and intravenous fluids can increase the discomfort of actively dying patients as they lose the ability to mobilize fluids and handle respiratory secretions, resulting in significant generalized edema and respiratory distress. Third, delirious patients often pull at intravenous lines and feeding tubes, necessitating the use of restraints. Finally, it is the taste and texture of food and the social engagement at mealtime that makes eating enjoyable; artificial feeding offers none of these benefits.

Patients and families should be reminded that not eating or drinking much toward the end of life is a **natural process**, and does not appear to result in suffering. People who have voluntarily fasted have reported that, as long as their mouth was kept moist, the experience was not unpleasant. Some describe an almost euphoric state after a few days without food. Furthermore, dying patients who do not receive tube feeds or intravenous fluids can still take small amounts of whatever food or beverage they desire. The mouth of a patient who is unable to eat or drink at all can be kept clean and moist with diligent mouth care.

Clinical Application – Part IX

According to his daughter, Mr. Amato will no longer take any food or drink and "looks like a skeleton." She is concerned that he is suffering from thirst and hunger, and asks if tube feeds can be started. Dr. Keats reassures her that her father is likely not experiencing any discomfort as a result of not eating or drinking. He also explains that starting tube feeds would actually cause discomfort through fluid overload, resulting in edema and worsening shortness of breath. The daughter feels more at ease after these reassurances. She increases the use of moist mouth swabs and puts balm on her father's lips, which becomes one of the ways she expresses her love for him.

Delirium and Agitation

Under usual medical circumstances, **delirium** leads to an extensive metabolic and anatomic work-up. Toward the end of life, however, delirium can be a natural phase in the dying process, and is usually handled more symptomatically. This does not mean that it is not treated aggressively; delirium and agitation can be extremely distressing for both patient and family. In many cases, symptoms can be handled with **antipsychotics or benzodiazepines.** Environmental modifications, such as a quiet atmosphere with limited interruptions and the regular presence of caring family and staff, can also decrease agitation. The removal of any equipment such as intravenous lines, urinary catheters (if patient is able to void), telemetry, and nasogastic tubes can help calm the patient. Physical restraints should rarely be used in terminal care and, if needed, should be transitioned to continuous family presence with chemical restraints as necessary. On rare occasions, delirium is intractable and requires **palliative sedation.** The administration of high-dose sedatives relieves extreme suffering by intentionally reducing the patient's level of consciousness and is used as a last resort once conventional management has failed. Before implementation, informed consent is obtained from the patient (if capable) or the proxy. The patient, proxy, family, and medical staff should develop a clear plan that includes the reasons and endpoints for sedation. The patient is sedated until restlessness and agitation cease, and then is maintained at that level of sedation. Frequent reassessment is needed to ensure the level of sedation is adequate to relieve distress. Support should be provided to the family throughout the process. Palliative sedation should only be utilized under the guidance of a palliative care specialist.

Clinical Application – Part X

After a week of home hospice, it becomes evident that everybody is exhausted. Mr. Amato has become increasingly agitated despite medication, attempting to strike his caregivers and occasionally injuring himself. He also appears to be "seeing things" in his room that frighten him. Dr. Keats adds an antipsychotic medication, and gives direction for regular around-the-clock dosing as needed. He asks the family to call with a progress report in 24–48 hours.

Requests for Physician-Assisted Death

Well-meaning and humane individuals are divided on the ethics of **physician-assisted death**. Requests for such assistance often result from intolerable symptoms or fear of further (physi-

---

Clinical Application – Part XI

Mrs. Amato asks the hospice nurse, "Can't we just end it all? I can't stand to see him like this." Dr. Keats speaks at length with Mrs. Amato and learns that she is most bothered by her husband's extreme agitation, which has not responded to increasing doses of antipsychotics and anxiolytics. The family decide that Mr. Amato's needs can no longer be met at home despite all the efforts. Mr. Amato is admitted to an inpatient acute hospice unit. Although the family is relieved, they feel guilty that they were unable to let him die at home. The hospice team reassures them that they have made the most loving decision in bringing him to the inpatient unit where he could be made the most comfortable. In the acute hospice unit, his antipsychotic regimen is adjusted so that he is calmer, but also more sedated. All agree that this is acceptable.

---

cal, emotional, spiritual, or psychological) suffering. The patient's request should be explored and possible underlying delirium, depression, or anxiety evaluated. Usually, a patient's suffering can be addressed within the bounds of standard palliative care. However, the patient should be informed that, if suffering becomes intolerable, palliative sedation or voluntary cessation of eating and drinking are legal options; some patients find comfort in knowing they have some control over the manner and timing of their death.

What to Expect During the Dying Process

What are common events during the dying process?

Because most people have not witnessed a death, they are anxious and uncertain as it approaches. Preparing the family can alleviate their concern. Generally, a dying patient will become more somnolent, and may develop congested breathing because of secretions. Breathing patterns can become irregular and resemble gasping respirations. The family may interpret this as suffering and should be reassured that such signs are usually more distressing for onlookers than for the patient.

Grief and Bereavement

Grief is the emotional response that results from loss. A dying patient experiences several losses in addition to death itself, such as loss of employment, family, self-image, and independence. During **anticipatory grief,** or grief that occurs prior to death, some patients review their life while the family adjusts to the idea of a future without their loved one. There is opportunity to ask for and give forgiveness, or to express thanks and love. Some have described this as a time of personal growth.

What is complicated grief?

In **uncomplicated grief**, the survivors gradually move toward accepting the loss. Their sense of self is intact, life retains meaning, and relationships with others are resumed. In comparison, **complicated grief** is characterized by a sense of purposelessness, disbelief, and emotional detachment. Emotions such as unrelenting loneliness, anger, and bitterness become prominent. The bereaved may experience intrusive thoughts of the deceased. While complicated and uncomplicated grief can both demonstrate these features, in complicated grief the symptoms last longer and cause a high degree of impairment. **Risk factors** for complicated grief include unexpected or traumatic death, a history of mental illness, family dysfunction, low self-esteem, prior dependency on the deceased, and isolation.

Bereavement is the state of loss that occurs after death. Bereavement is a health risk, and can result in increased and sometimes improper use of medical services. Most palliative care teams and all Medicare-certified hospice programs include bereavement specialists who monitor families for complicated grief and use preventive measures, such as counseling, for survivors at risk. Expressions of condolence from the medical team (sending a card, making a phone call, attending the funeral) can be powerful gestures much appreciated by the bereaved.

Although current medical therapies can be life saving, they can also prolong the suffering of chronically ill or dying patients. Palliative care provides symptom control and assists patients in choosing the medical interventions that best help them achieve their personal goals of care.

Recommended Readings

Kinzbrunner B, Weinreb N, Policzer J. *20 Common Problems in End-of-Life Care.* New York: McGraw-Hill; 2002.

Institute of Medicine. *Approaching Death: Improving Care at the End of Life.* Washington, DC: National Academies Press; 1998.

Lunney JR, Lynn J, Foley DJ, et al. Patterns of functional decline at the end of life. *JAMA* 2003; 289:2387–2392.

Morrison RS, Meier DE. Clinical Practice: Palliative Care. *New England Journal of Medicine* 2004; 351:1148–1149.

National Consensus Project for Quality Palliative Care. *Clinical Practice Guidelines for Quality Palliative Care.* 2004. Available at http://www.nationalconsensusproject.org

Quill TE. Initiating end of life discussions with severely ill patients: Addressing the elephant in the room. *JAMA* 2000; 284:2502–2507.

Quill TE, Lo B, Brock DW. Palliative options of last resort: A comparison of voluntarily stopping eating and drinking, terminal sedation, physician-assisted suicide, and voluntary active euthanasia. *JAMA* 1997; 278:2099–2104.

Review Questions

1. A patient with cancer has bone metastases and 8–10/10 pain. According to the WHO, the best pain management is likely to result from the administration of
   A. adjuvant modalities
   B. non-opioid medications
   C. opioid and non-opioid regimens
   D. strong opioids and adjuvant modalities

2. Which of the following people is MOST likely to experience complicated grief?
   A. 58-year-old woman whose husband dies peacefully at home after a 2-year battle against cancer
   B. 62-year-old mother of two young adults who participates in a bereavement support group
   C. 75-year-old man whose 99-year-old mother dies in a nursing home

D. 86-year-old childless man whose wife of 62 years dies suddenly of a stroke

E. 90-year-old woman who has moderate Alzheimer's disease whose 30-year-old grandson dies of muscular dystrophy

Key to review questions: p. 393

31 Competencies in Medical Education

- How has the competency movement reshaped graduate medical education?
- What are the six core competencies identified by the Accreditation Council for Graduate Medical Education?
- How has the competency movement begun to change undergraduate medical education?
- How are competencies best assessed?

Introduction

Medical education is changing. One of the principle social forces driving this change is of the so-called "**competency movement**," which seeks to develop behaviorally defined professional standards for health care practices. Presently, efforts to embed competencies within medical education programs are most evident in graduate (residency) education. The Accreditation Council for Graduate Medical Education (ACGME) has identified six core competencies (see Table 31.1.) that must be mastered before a trainee is certified to have completed training. Although no specific competencies have been identified for undergraduate medical education, individual schools, anticipating a time when all levels of medical education will operate under a standard competency banner, have begun to restructure their educational offerings using the ACGME's core competencies.

How has the competency movement reshaped graduate medical education?

The issue of competencies is significant because it represents a break with previous models of medical education and its accreditation. In the past, training programs were developed around issues of structure and process (e.g., the number of course hours or types of patients seen) rather than what was produced (e.g., the ability of graduates to deliver good medical care). Although seemingly small, this shift from structure and process to out-comes and quality represents a profound change within a social institution long associated with the phrase "reform without change."

Today, residency programs are being required to demonstrate that graduates are, indeed, competent to practice medicine and to document how the learning environments offered do, in fact, contribute to resident mastery of key competency areas. This is the reality of GME now and it will become the reality for undergraduate and continuing medical education tomorrow.

Socio-Historical Background

Traditionally, allopathic medicine has framed issues of practitioner quality/competence as an internal professional matter. To this end, organized medicine has argued that its work was complex, that it involved fundamental uncertainties, and that the practice of medicine was built upon an esoteric knowledge base and therefore its work could not – and should not – be judged by outsiders. In short, medicine insisted that **professional autonomy** (as well as **professional dominance** over the non-physician work force) be a condition of medical work. In return, medicine promised to apply the principles of science to health care, and that its members would place patient welfare ahead of their own personal well-being. Compliance would be "guaranteed" by the willingness of physicians to operate as fiduciaries by giving highest priority to patient welfare, operating a conscientious system of **peer**

review, and gearing the educational system to produce competent practitioners. Unfortunately, too often, **provider competency** and the **quality of services** delivered were imputed rather than critically assessed and verified. Physicians delivered good medical care, it was argued, because they had been trained to do so, because all physicians were certified as having completed that training, and because all physicians possessed a personal ethic of public service. Deviations from this ethic of excellence were internally defined as rare with exceptions attributed to chance (bad luck), to patients (uncooperative, noncompliant, ignorant), or as opportunities to learn. The possibility that errors might flow from an ill designed or dysfunctional health care system would have to wait until the rise of the patient safety movement in the 1990s.

Prior to the competency movement, medical school accreditation tended to focus on the **structure and process** of the educational edifice emphasizing measures such as *where* students trained (e.g., characteristics of schools and related clinical settings) and *what* happened to them at those facilities/sites (e.g., the type and ordering of courses and clinical experiences, the number of course credits, patients seen). **Direct assessment** of trainees and their ability to deliver quality medical services was infrequent, at best. Most often, the competency of students was based either on **qualities of training sites** or on the **type of cognitive testing** (knowledge-based) conducted by the National Board of Medical Examiners. The only other form of quality control was the rate at which trainees failed to complete their training. Early in the 20th century, as many as one third of students failed to satisfactorily complete their training. By the 1970s, however, this number had dropped to less than 2%. In short, being accepted into medical school had become a *de facto* license to practice medicine.

An Earlier Paradigm Shift

The current move to assess competencies within medical training and clinical practice represents a break with this tradition, something characterized as a "paradigm shift." The old system stressed **curriculum** and was focused on what teachers taught, and sometimes on how well they taught it. This system also stressed the **basic science** roots of medical practice, the legacy of an earlier paradigm shift that took place in 1910 when **Abraham Flexner** described the shocking conditions (haphazard clinical apprenticeships buttressed by little or no basic science training) he found when he visited medical schools in the U.S. and Canada. Major changes ensued, but the lack of subsequent meaningful reforms have left our *current* system of medical training more reflective of the conditions and problems encountered by Flexner a century ago than the problems and conditions facing medicine today. Of note, Flexner's call to reinforce the basic sciences and to close deficient schools effectively ended medical education for women and African Americans in this country, resulting in a still chronic undersupply of minority physicians and, until recently, also of women physicians.

What was not an issue for Flexner, given the types of problems he encountered, was the considerable gulf that can exist between teaching and learning, i.e., between curricular content and what students learn, and between the acquisition of knowledge and its application. While there were some attempts within the American labor force in the 1930s to link job performance and functional abilities, the history of competencies in the U.S. usually is dated to the 1970s and the work of social psychologist David McClelland. Reform efforts took place largely outside medicine in fields such as physical therapy, pharmacy, and nursing, and were short lived. An appreciable competency movement in U.S. allopathic medicine did not begin until the 1990s, with the release of two reports by the Institute of Medicine (*To Err is Human* and *Crossing the Quality Chasm*), and with the work and sponsorship of two organizations, the Accreditation Council for Graduate Medical Education (ACGME) and the American Board of Medical Specialties (ABMS).

The ACGME and Competencies

What are the six core competencies identified by the Accreditation Council for Graduate Medical Education?

The major change agent responsible for the shift from a focus on structure and process to outcomes and competencies in the U.S. is the Accreditation Council for Graduate Medical Education (ACGME),

Table 31.1. Six ACGME core competencies

1. Patient care

2. Medical knowledge

3. Professionalism

4. Systems-based practice

5. Practice-based learning and improvement

6. Interpersonal and communication skills

which accredits nearly 8,000 U.S.-based residency programs. In the early 1990s, the ACGME undertook an internal assessment regarding the feasibility of moving to a **competency-based accreditation process.** As part of this effort, the ACGME identified six core competencies and put in place a

Although it is unwieldy to detail each competency, it is helpful to take one competency, patient care, for example, and explore how the ACGME has conceptualized and defined what is, after all, a core element of physicians' work.

The ACGME defines patient care as: "compassionate, appropriate, and effective (care) for the treatment of health problems and the promotion of health." In turn, the ACGME specifies a list of general competencies for this care.

- Communicate effectively and demonstrate caring and respectful behaviors when interacting with patients and their families.
- Gather essential and accurate information about their patients.
- Make informed decisions about diagnostic and therapeutic interventions based on patient information and preferences, up-to-date scientific evidence, and clinical judgment.
- Develop and carry out patient management plans.
- Counsel and educate patients and their families.
- Use information technology to support patient care decisions and patient education.
- Perform competently all medical and invasive procedures considered essential for the area of practice.
- Provide health care services aimed at preventing health problems or maintaining health.
- Work with health care professionals, including those from other disciplines, to provide patient-focused care.

structure for evaluating residency programs based on these competencies.

Currently, the ACGME has created definitions and suggested assessment practices for each competency. The ACGME is also working with residency programs to identify "best practices" in competency definition and assessment, as well as the broader issue of quality of care linkages.

Ultimately, the ACGME seeks to develop **common language** for competencies and **common metrics for assessments** that will span the educational continuum, from undergraduate, through graduate, and on to continuing medical education. Furthermore, the ACGME seeks to use accreditation as a lever for change as it moves to develop formal alliances among professional organizations. Ultimately, the ACGME seeks to shift the current profession-centered oversight process to one that is **patient centered.**

The focus on competency at the GME level represents only one part of the medical education system. One area thus conspicuously absent from the competency movement is undergraduate medical education.

Competencies and Undergraduate Medical Education

How has the competency movement begun to change undergraduate medical education?

While the organization responsible for undergraduate medical education, the AAMC, does call for the assessment of competencies (See "Medical Education Database, Section II – Educational Program, ED-1-A"), the AAMC also prefers the language of "objectives" and "outcomes" to that of "competencies." Moreover, the AAMC does not specify any particular competencies. Instead, it refers member schools to the ACGME core competencies, the CanMEDS 2000 (Canadian) competency standards (see below), and the AAMC's own MSOP Report, which identifies altruism, knowledge, skills and dutifulness as key "attributes"/ "objectives." Nor has the AAMC formally announced any future plans to employ an accreditation process grounded in the principles and practices of competencies.

Specialty Certification

In contrast to the current situation between the ACGME and the AAMC, formal linkages exist between the ACGME and the American Board of Medical Specialties (ABMS), a professional organization representing 23 medical specialties. This partnership has resulted in a flurry of competency-focused activities with specialty areas (e.g., surgery, primary care), and individual specialty groups (e.g., neuropathology) tailoring their specialty-specific educational activities and certification standards to the ACGME's competencies.

Continuing Medical Education

To date, Continuing Medical Education (CME) lacks a substantive competency profile. Links between the ACGME and the Accreditation Council for Continuing Medical Education (ACCME) are nascent. Furthermore, when compared to the relatively structured practices of undergraduate and GME accreditation, CME is highly variable. Because physicians are required (by state licensing boards and specialty organizations) to accumulate a certain number of CME hours over a defined period of time (e.g., the State of Minnesota requires 75 hours for all state licensed physicians over a three-year period; the American Board of Family Medicine requires that its diplomats accumulate 300 hours over six years), CME has become a major "profit center." CME hours are offered by a large number of educational entities including medical schools, community hospitals, and a host of private companies and corporations, all formed and configured with little reference to competencies.

To summarize, there are a variety of social and medical organizational forces driving the competency movement today. Some are **external and regulatory** (e.g., payers who require that physicians providing "covered" services have and maintain certain credentials) while others are more **internal and professional** (e.g., the ACGME competencies, CME hours). The growth of the federal government as a major purchaser of health care, along with the growing technological ability of payers to access and process data on physician practice patterns, has facilitated the growth of a competency-based regulatory system. Institute of Medicine studies on patient safety and quality

of care also have played an important role in the development of a competency consciousness within medicine. In fact, all three of the major social revolutions occurring within organized medicine today, **evidence-based medicine, professionalism,** and the **patient safety movement,** can be subsumed under "quality of care," and, thus, have both explicit and implicit links to the competency movement.

Assessment

How are competencies best assessed?

This question is critically important because it speaks to the underlying epistemology of medical education. This includes the purpose (both functionally and in terms of the social contract between society and medicine) and the expectations we have of students (in terms of knowledge, skills, attitudes and values) at different points in their training. Even when there is agreement on the *how* (e.g., portfolios), there remains substantial disagreement on criterion "thresholds," or the points at which one differentiates between attainment or non-attainment of a given competency. Set the bar too low and attainment begins to resemble the current system where virtually everyone admitted to medical school becomes a physician; set it too high and nobody proves worthy.

Identifying specific tools to measure authentic competencies is a moving target. First, any such selection is heavily dependent upon what is to be evaluated and, second, the tools themselves are constantly undergoing revisions. Nevertheless, the ACGME "toolbox" available online is a reasonable starting place.

Gradations of Competency

Because education is based on **progress toward proficiency,** competencies must be conceptualized and assessed in terms of some gradient. For example, first-year medical students may be capable of meeting a basic competency threshold in "Interpersonal and Communication Skills" (one of the six ACGME competencies), but not yet so for "Patient Care" competencies (another ACGME core competency). Alternatively, third-year students should perform at a more advanced level on Interpersonal and Communication Skills, while also satisfying some basic level competencies in Patient Care.

> Several models of scaling have been utilized in framing competencies. One popular model, developed by Hubert and Stuart Dreyfus, employs five gradations (novice, beginner, competent, proficient, and expert) where novice forms the base and expert the apex of a triangle. Another model is George E. Miller's four stages: (1) Knowledge ("knows"), (2) Competence ("knows how"), (3) Performance ("shows how"), and (4) Action ("does"). In both examples, a student's ability to manifest a given competency is linked to increasingly more complex patients or health care problems.

Conclusions

The move to assess competencies is part of a more general movement within Western medicine to establish *quality* (e.g., quality of providers, quality of services, quality of education) as a pre-eminent value across the various domains of health care. These efforts are having a considerable impact on organizational structure and pedagogical practices. For the first time in nearly a century, medical education is being transformed from an emphasis on **what teachers teach** to an emphasis on **what students learn,** and from a **physician-centered** to a **patient-centered** assessment system. In the end, the promises of genuine quality in patient services, a reenergized professionalism within provider ranks, a real social contract between society and medicine, and increased trust between patient and provider bode quite well for the future of medicine as a social institution.

Recommended Readings

Batalden P, Leach D, Swing S, et al. General competencies and accreditation in graduate medical education: An antidote to overspecification in the education of medical specialists. *Health Affairs* 2002; 21:103–111.

Carraccio C, Wolfsthal SD, Englander R, et al. Shifting paradigms: From Flexner to competencies. *Academic Medicine* 2002; 77:361–367.

Flexner A. *Medical Education in the United States and Canada.* Boston, MA: Merrymont Press; 1910.

Halpern R, Lee MY, Boulter PR, et al. A synthesis of nine major reports on physicians' competencies for the emerging practice environment. *Academic Medicine* 2001; 76:606–615.

Review Questions

1. As of 2006, the Accreditation Council for Graduate Medical Education (ACGME) competencies have been formally adopted by which of the following organizations?
   A. Accreditation Council for Continuing Medical Education (ACCME)
   B. American Board of Medical Specialties (ABMS).
   C. American Medical Association (AMA)
   D. Association of American Medical Colleges (AAMC)
   E. Royal College of Physicians and Surgeons of Canada (CanMEDS)

2. The competency movement is best related to
   A. health care insurance reform
   B. reform of Medicare and Medicaid
   C. the move to conjointly train different health professions
   D. the redistribution of work traditionally limited to physicians
   E. the quality of care movement

3. Which of the following is not an ACGME (Accreditation Council for Graduate Medical Education) core competency?
   A. Health advocacy
   B. Medical knowledge
   C. Patient care
   D. Professionalism
   E. Systems-based practice

Key to review questions: p. 393

32 Ethical and Legal Issues in Patient Care

- What is informed consent?
- What are legitimate exceptions to patient confidentiality?
- Under what conditions do minors have authority to make their own decisions regarding health care?
- What is the difference between a vegetative state and brain death?
- What are two types of advance directives and how do they differ?
- What is the difference between "do not resuscitate" and "comfort care" orders?
- What are the arguments for and against physician-assisted suicide?
- What is the principle of clinical equipoise?

Traditional medical ethics emphasized two principles, beneficence and nonmaleficence. **Beneficence** requires that the physician provide for the patient's best interest, balancing potential benefits and risks to the patient. **Nonmaleficence** (in the original Greek Hippocratic version, "at least do no harm") requires the physician to avoid heroic efforts if they inflict unnecessary suffering or give the patient unrealistic hope. Instead, the physician should focus on comfort care and relief of suffering.

These two principles left the primary decision-making responsibility to the physician, which some physicians interpreted as license for unquestioned authority in making all decisions regarding a patient's medical care. However, during the patient rights movement in the 1970s, these rights came to be seen as a part of civil rights. The issue of who has proper authority to make decisions about medical care gained prominence just as the number of treatment options was rapidly expanding. Thus, with more at stake in medical decisions, a third important ethical principle evolved – patient autonomy.

What is informed consent?

Patient autonomy requires that patients be given complete information about their diagno-sis, prognosis, and treatment options, in terms they can understand, and affirms their right to make their own decisions about their lives (see Chapter 16, Theories of Social Relations). The legal doctrine that supports this principle is **informed consent.** Under the informed consent doctrine, patients can *refuse* treatment suggestions as well as consent to them. Informed consent entitles the patient to a fully informed decision. It is not intended to defend the physician legally should there be an unexpected and undesired outcome.

> The doctrine of informed consent has its historical roots in a decision by the great American jurist Benjamin Cardozo. In 1914 in the Schloendorf decision, he said: "Every human being of adult years and sound mind has a right to determine what shall be done with his own body."

The term "informed consent" was coined in the 1957 *Salgo* decision, which said "a physician ... subjects himself to liability if he withholds any facts which are necessary to form the basis of an intelligent consent by the patient."

What patients require to make an intelligent decision is still debated. Some state laws tend to support more disclosure than others, letting patients have more input into that issue than professional societies. (This dispute is often referred to as "the reasonable person standard" versus "the professional standard of practice.") All in all, the best advice is to err on the side of greater disclosure. Such informational support as brochures, preprinted duplicate consent forms, and videos can be helpful tools to achieve the goal of an informed patient.

These three principles of medical ethics are accepted as *prima facie* (i.e., assumed to have face validity), and are independent (i.e., can yield recommendations that potentially conflict with other principles). They are meant to serve as guidelines to help clarify ethics issues. They have been influential in the codes of ethics written by the American Medical Association, the American College of Physicians, and by most specialty groups.

Justice and Social Activism

The fourth principle of medical ethics is the newest and most controversial: **Justice**. It can be interpreted as meaning that a medical professional should find some way to reduce the inherent injustice of society, whether by fighting for some form of universal health care, increasing the number of people who are insured, by volunteering one day a month at a clinic, or by playing some other leadership role whose goal is to help vulnerable groups in society (e.g., the homeless, prisoners, victims of violence, mentally ill, and developmentally disabled). Justice can also be interpreted to mean fighting against overuse and waste of resources, especially if it is with the intent of using them more wisely to help those who would not otherwise get treated fairly (as opposed to cost savings to increase profits or income). Lastly, there has been an enormous increase in international medical research in the past decade, raising interesting questions of what standards to use when working with people from other cultures. This too can be seen as a challenge for Justice: Should we adhere to our own standards of informed consent, for example, or follow the (lower) standards of the country of origin, presuming that any benefit they gain from us is more than they would have otherwise enjoyed?

Malpractice, Negligence, and Good Samaritans

The laws that concern physician practice and conduct are often state laws. Some laws are legislated; others are case laws based on precedents established by court decisions.

Malpractice is, in legal terms, a civil claim, not a criminal offense. The standard of evidence in the courtroom is lower (preponderance of the evidence rather than beyond a reasonable doubt), the jury smaller (usually six rather than twelve), and the penalty less severe (a financial award to the plaintiff, rather than a prison sentence for the guilty party).

Civil law is primarily intended to compensate a victim for being wronged, not to punish the wrong-doer. To be found guilty of malpractice, a physician must not only have harmed a patient, but it must be shown that the doctor should have known better. That is, it must be proven that the physician was **negligent** in knowledge or performance and failed to meet the accepted standard. This can include not explaining the known risks and side effects of a treatment or procedure, i.e., a failure to meet the standard of informed consent.

Laws in many states grant immunity from malpractice when a physician encounters a medical emergency such as a vehicular accident (**Good Samaritan Law**). In fact, there is no real difference between states with and without these laws. The risk of being sued is minuscule, and the risk of being found at fault is easily defensible by the claim that the physician acted in good faith.

The Role of Confidentiality

> What are legitimate exceptions to patient confidentiality?

The physician must never reveal information about a given patient without explicit permission except to other members of the health care team or a professional to whom the patient is being referred. There are, however, **legitimate exceptions** to the physician's responsibility to keep patient information confidential. All are related to the potential for **danger to the patient or others** in the future. If a patient admits to planning to kill someone, it must be reported to the proper authority. In a famous case from California, *Tarasoff*, a psychologist and psychiatrist were found negligent because they reported a psychotic student with homicidal intent to the University's security force but did not follow up with the police. This can be used as guidance in other states, depending upon the other state's already existing legislation and case law.

Suspected **child or elder abuse** and neglect must be reported to the appropriate social service agency. **Sexually transmitted diseases** should be reported to the Department of Health, which can then locate and inform sexual contacts anonymously if the patient chooses not to do so personally. In each of these examples, the patient's confidentiality is compromised to protect someone else from a known and immanent danger, but exceptions should be kept to the minimum to preserve all patients' willingness to confide in their physicians.

Decision-Making Capacity

> Capacity requires that a patient understand the nature of the illness, the treatment options available, and the consequence of the decision.

Capacity is presumed to be present in all adults; and any clinician can determine a given patient's capacity. Psychiatric illness does not necessarily rule out capacity to make medical decisions; and psychiatric consultation is not necessary to determine capacity.

The physician should obtain **informed consent** from the patient before doing any procedure or prescribing any medication. It is not necessary that a written form be signed. Such forms were developed as a reminder for physicians of which topics should be discussed with the patient and to provide documentation that the discussion took place. The only **exceptions** to the general rule of informed consent are if the patient is clearly **incapacitated** (e.g., unconscious) or there is a **life-threatening emergency** of such urgency that there is no time for explanation before taking action. As soon as the patient regains capacity or the immediate danger passes, the patient should be informed about what has been done and included in discussions about further treatments. Any treatment that

has been started can be stopped. This option for the patient to forgo the treatment later is the basis for the ethical and legal justification for unilateral decision making by the physician when the situation demands such action. When there is a difference of opinion between the physician and patient, respect for the patient's preference should be an overriding concern.

Legitimate concerns have been expressed in some quarters that this view of patient autonomy and informed consent reflects values of our dominant Western culture, and is not respectful of most developing world cultures from Asia, Africa, and the Middle East. While a valid point, the conclusions to be drawn must be carefully chosen. Many people who left those countries to be in the U.S. sought out freedom, and would not want our medical culture to presume otherwise.

> With regard to the principles of patient autonomy and informed consent, the best counsel is to talk to each patient individually in order to determine if they want the information you offer, and if they wish to be the decision maker in control of their own fate. If they refuse (sometimes called deferred consent) then they should be asked who they wish to be their surrogate. Fully document this information in the patient's chart.

Minors and Capacity

> Under what conditions do minors have authority to make their own decisions regarding health care?

Parents of minors have the authority to make decisions about medical treatment for their children, but this authority is not absolute. Children develop capacity as they mature. Teenagers, in particular, can be determined to have capacity by their clinician, using the same criteria as for adults. This process, known as the **mature minor doctrine,** provides a way for minors to participate fully in decisions about their medical treatment. In most states, statutes known as the **emancipated minor doctrine** also empower minors to make their own medical decisions if they are married, live independently of their parents, have children of their own, or are in the military.

The Role of Religious Beliefs

Religious beliefs are valid reasons for adults to refuse treatment; the two most common are Jehovah's Witnesses' refusal to accept blood transfusions, and Christian Scientists' refusal of some medical treatment. Whereas adults are assumed to be capable of making their own decisions based on faith, minors are not held to the same standard regardless of their parents' wishes.

> "Parents have the right to make martyrs of themselves, but not of their children."   Benjamin Cardozo

Thus, if reasonable treatment of a minor is refused by parents, solely on the basis of the parents' religious beliefs, a **court can authorize** such treatment. Infants and children are considered members of the human community first, and cannot be presumed to understand and accept religious beliefs (and refuse reasonable treatment on religious grounds) until they also understand the alternatives and consequences.

Adolescents may be in need of much direction, and the input of the physician can be as important as that of the parents. This means that when a teenager disagrees with his or her parents, the physician cannot simply side with the parents. The teen patient should have a confidential doctor-patient relationship, and have significant moral standing as the person who will suffer the consequences of any decision.

Efforts at persuasion that arise from sincere concern are commendable, but must never become coercive. While the physician urges the patient to consider the issue with an open mind, the physician must be prepared to accept the patient's decision *not* to accept treatment with an open mind.

Even if the patient is 17 instead of 18, the **standard of capacity** remains the same: the ability to understand the alternatives and appreciate the consequences of her choice. A teenager who meets that standard can be determined to be a mature minor by the clinician, and her choice can be respected on that basis. Only individuals who **lack capacity** due to their developmental age should have their parents make decisions on their behalf. For cases in a gray area, including most elementary school-age children, the minor should be included in the informational and decision-making process and, at least, give **assent** to the outcome.

Psychiatric Illness and Capacity

Capacity is frequently questioned in individuals who have been given a psychiatric diagnosis or who have suffered brain injury. Unless it is clear that a condition is affecting the patient's judgment with regard to weighing options, all adults are presumed to have capacity, including those who have mental or physical illness

> If patients can participate in a conversation with family or caregivers about their illness, treatment choices, and the consequences of their choice, they are demonstrating capacity. If the reasons behind their decisions are understandable, these decisions should be accepted even if they are not those that most people would make.

Conversations to collect ethically relevant information about the personal history and values of the patient, what is most meaningful in life, what constitutes the moral of his or her life story, and what goals are being sought will enable the physician to use reflection and judgment to resolve ethical dilemmas about capacity. When a person's decision is consistent with past decisions, it is generally a violation of the integrity of that person's life history for the decision to be denied.

Clinical Application

An 18-year-old woman who is a Jehovah's Witness presents with aplastic anemia. Her physician must decide whether to override her refusal of treatment (a bone marrow transplant). The importance of the decision must be made clear to her, over a series of outpatient clinic appointments. That is, she should be made aware that she would not only die as a result of refusing the transplant, but also loose all the things she may wish for herself in the future, including (perhaps) marriage and children of her own.

Neurological Illness and Capacity

The capacity of patients who have neurologic disease, such as dementia, is virtually always questioned. In fact, however, early dementia can coexist with capacity. Patients with a mild but progressive neurologic illness are the *sine qua non* of individuals for whom **advance directives** would be appropriate. Commonly, the most likely course of the disease can be predicted, enabling patients to complete clinically useful advance directives. Because such discussions are uncomfortable, they are frequently deferred (by both clinicians and family members) until too late for the patient to exercise his or her right to self-determination.

> Most patients want to address end-of-life issues, but wait for the doctor to raise the subject.

Unconsciousness

> What is the difference between a vegetative state and brain death?

Coma, vegetative state, and brain death are three distinct types of unconsciousness. **Coma** is an unconscious sleep-like state lasting from hours to weeks and, in some rare instances, months and years. Patients in coma may die, regain consciousness, or emerge into a **vegetative state** in which there is no conscious activity but there is a continuation of vegetative or involuntary functioning (e.g., breathing without assistance, eye movements, and some reflexes). There can be improvement from a vegetative state, but the longer the state continues the less likely it is that improvement will occur. The vegetative state is considered **"persistent"** after 1–3 months of unconsciousness (depending upon the cause); it is considered **"permanent"** after 6–12 months. After 1 month, the chance of significant or meaningful improvement is small. However, patients can live for decades with little more support than full nursing care and a feeding tube. The issue to be determined is whether the patient would have wanted that conclusion to his or her life.

Brain death is a lack of brainstem as well as cortical functioning. There is no breathing, eye movement, or reflexive activity and no chance of regaining consciousness. The diagnosis can be made clinically or by electroencephalography that reveals no electrical activity in a 30-minute tracking obtained in the absence of hypothermia and central nervous system intoxication from drugs or any other substances. The physiologic functions of brain dead patients can be maintained for weeks or even months with the use of ventilators, vasopressors, and other supportive therapies. The consensus among ethicists is that families do not have the authority to request continued treatment for patients who are brain dead. Usually a day or two for family to travel to see the patient is provided, although there is disagreement about whether this brings comfort or closure.

Some sects of ultra-orthodox Jews assert that their beliefs demand that treatment continue despite a diagnosis of brain death. New York and New Jersey have recognized the need to "reasonably accommodate" these beliefs without defining that phrase further.

Maximizing Patient Self-Determination

The physician should always talk openly and directly with patients. If the patient understands the situation and the treatment options and can make a choice, that choice must be respected. The physician's duty to the family is to counsel the family about the **primacy of the patient's wishes** so that if a conflict arises, no family member can usurp the patient's right to choose. If the patient has some understanding but it is compromised, undeveloped, wavering, or uncertain, the physician must seek to achieve a **collaborative partnership.** In these situations, patients often require more advice from the physician, but the goal of the partnership is to maximize the patient's input into decisions about care. Initiation or withdrawal of some treatments that will enhance, even temporarily, the patient's decision-making capacity may also be justified in this situation.

All patients should be encouraged to complete a **living will** and **health care proxy** to name a surrogate decision maker (see below). All patients should also be asked under what conditions, if any, they would want possible future treatments to be discontinued. Answers should be recorded in the patient's chart and living will. Patients unable to discuss these potentially frightening existential issues can at least be encouraged to select the surrogate they would most trust to make these decisions for them.

Ideally, the **surrogate** chosen by the patient understands the task to be restricted to choosing as the patient would have chosen if the patient were capable of decision making. Input from family and friends may be solicited, but should be carefully limited (e.g., used to shed light on what the patient would want). The physician must serve as both educator and collaborator: although the surrogate's understanding is uncompromised, the physician's goal is to determine, together with the surrogate, **what the patient would have wanted in this situation**, not what the surrogate wants. That is, the physician must ask the surrogate what the patient would say if he or she could suddenly sit up and speak, but knew that returning to his or her current state was inevitable. The source of justification in this situation is respect for the patient's values and preferences, although they are being determined indirectly.

If the patient was never capable of decision making (e.g., is a newborn or is severely mentally handicapped), then the focus of the physician's partnership with the family or guardian is to determine what is in the best interests of the patient.

Factors to Consider in Making a "Best Interests Decision" for a Patient

Interests exist only where there can be an awareness of a benefit; thus, if a patient cannot experience the benefit from a procedure, then it has none.
If a patient can experience pain or discomfort from either a procedure or the continued existence it would produce, then it is a burden and should not be done, unless balanced by equal or greater benefits gained from continued life.
Primum non nocere or "at least do no harm" means the physician must maximize quality, and not just length of life, and prohibits lengthening the process of dying. The objective benefits and burdens measure of the patient's best interest is only justified where there is the lack of both direct and indirect evidence of the patient's values and preferences.

Advance Directives, End-of-Life Decisions, and Futility

What are two types of advance directives and how do they differ?

Physicians who are hesitant to deliver bad news, frequently rationalize withholding such information as a way to avoid harming a patient who would be psychologically devastated by the truth. In fact, no empirical research has ever supported this claim. Currently, the only acceptable exceptions are patients who requested that they not be told, or that someone else be told instead, or patients who are members of groups known to fear the supernatural effects of spoken bad news (e.g., the Navajo). For most patients, delivering bad news honestly gives them a **sense of control** through active participation in health care decisions.

Advance directives are the best method for individuals to ensure that their health care wishes are carried out. There are two major types of advance directive: **proxy** (legally known as a durable power of attorney for health care decision making) and **living will.** In the proxy type, the patient names a surrogate who will make decisions if the patient loses capacity. The surrogate should be someone who knows the patient's wishes well and who can advocate for them effectively even in difficult emotional situations.

In completing a **living will,** the patient makes statements about treatments he or she would or would not want under specified circumstances.

It is usually advisable to complete both types of advance directives; living wills are often too vague for doctors to feel comfortable interpreting, but they can help the surrogate make decisions desired by the patient and avoid feeling guilt as a result. With either kind of advance directive, the physician should offer to discuss with the patient any likely future scenarios (e.g., ventilator support, dialysis) and their side effects. The patient can then discuss these issues with the surrogate or leave written instructions.

What is the difference between "do not resuscitate" and "comfort care" orders?

Some authorities have interpreted patient self-determination to mean that even **futile treatments** must be offered to patients and provided if requested. In general, however, this is not true: futile treatments should not be offered, and any request for them should be patiently and sympathetically denied, with a clear explanation. Compassion does not require compliance but, rather, concern and guidance. However, **futility** is difficult to define. Some physicians use "futile" in a value-free physiologic or biologic sense (i.e., a treatment that cannot maintain or extend life); others intend a more value-laden or biographic sense (a treatment that cannot offer a quality of life acceptable to the patient or that will not contribute positively to the patient's life story).

When further treatment is *biologically* futile, a **"do not resuscitate" (DNR)** order should be recommended and meticulous attention paid to pain control, palliative care, and avoidance of unnecessary tests and procedures. In contrast, when further treatment is *biographically* futile, the patient must determine the values inherent in an acceptable quality of life and caregivers respect those choices. **Quality of life** is a key ethical concept, as long as the focus of authority in deciding it is the patient rather than the physician or society. What is acceptable to one person is sometimes a demeaning loss of dignity and independence for another, and vice versa.

When family, rather than the patient, demands treatment, the ethical problem is the same, although the situation is emotionally more complex. Such demands are best understood as expressions of love in a context of despair and denial. Patience and compromise may be appropriate temporary measures, with firm time limits ("We can continue this for two days and see if she improves"). The question to be put to the family is whether "doing everything" is what the patient would want.

Do not resuscitate (DNR) and **comfort care** are two closely related but distinct concepts. A **DNR** order simply states that, should a cardiopul-

DNR orders can be rescinded by the patient at any time, and any patient, no matter how healthy, may choose not to be resuscitated. DNR orders, however, cannot rightfully be rescinded (or "lifted") by the physician unilaterally; for the physician to do so imposes an unwanted aggressive intervention on the patient.

monary arrest occur, resuscitation efforts (commonly, cardiopulmonary resuscitation, cardioversion, intubation) will not be performed. The patient could nevertheless still consent to individual components of resuscitation (e.g., intubation is acceptable if it is likely to be only a temporary measure).

DNR has no bearing on the treatment plan; it only specifies treatment to be withheld in the event of an actual arrest at some future time. A DNR is thus best thought of as another type of advance directive, but one which requires a physician's order.

Finally, patients should understand the process of **advanced cardiac life support** (ACLS), including intubation, cardioversion, and ventilation, as well as the alternatives before their consent for either a DNR order or for full resuscitation can be considered to be informed and, hence, valid. The chance of a successful outcome as defined by the patient is also important information and should be included in the consent process. If successful outcome is taken to mean survival of the hospitalization to discharge, the probability is surprisingly small, ranging from 0% to 15%, depending on the patient's underlying condition (i.e., 85–100% of "resuscitated" patients don't survive to discharge). For this reason DNR orders are increasingly being called **Do Not Attempt Resuscitation** or **DNAR** orders.

Patients often do not realize they will probably die, and they will certainly wake up in an ICU uncomfortable and unable to talk if they survive. A significant percentage of survivors will also suffer brain damage or depression, and fully half say they would not want to be "coded" again. All this should be included in the informed consent process.

Comfort care implies a general withdrawal of curative or life-prolonging care in favor of making the patient's comfort the primary goal of any treatment offered. Comfort care includes aggressive pain management based on balancing the patient's desires to be free of pain yet to be alert to people and events. Inconveniences such as monitoring vital signs and phlebotomy are eliminated. Typically, diagnostic efforts are also abandoned unless an intercurrent condition that is easily treatable but causing undue discomfort is suspected. All of these are elements of good **hospice care.**

Palliative care shares many of these goals, but is more typically done as a referral in an acute setting, in which more aggressive interventions may still be pursued.

Medicine cannot prevent death, but it can make death less frightening by giving patients some control over its manner and timing. Any treatment that can be started can be stopped. For example, withdrawal of ventilatory and nutritional support is now accepted as ethically and legally proper, given clear understanding that withdrawal represents the patient's wishes. Often discontinuing a medical treatment will hasten a painless death.

Death and Dying

A painless and dignified death is an important value to most people in the U.S. Patients have the right to refuse life-sustaining treatments. A physician may prescribe a treatment for palliation of suffering and that treatment may have the unintended consequence of shortening a patient's life. For example, a terminally ill cancer patient with multiple bone metastases and severe pain may require such high doses of narcotics to manage the pain that the medication eventually suppresses the respiratory drive. Under such circumstances, the use of such high doses of medication can be justified by the rule of **"double effect."**

The most common obstacles to death are continuation of life-sustaining treatments, administration of antibiotics, and insertion of feeding tubes. Some authorities argue that physician-assisted suicide would never be necessary if withdrawing of feeding tubes or refusal of food by mouth by

patients capable of eating was always considered an appropriate option.

What are the arguments for and against physician-assisted suicide?

Withdrawal of life-sustaining treatment must be distinguished from physician-assisted suicide (PAS) and euthanasia. **Physician-assisted suicide** can be defined as a physician *dispensing* a drug to a patient with capacity who has requested the prescription for the sole purpose of self-administering the medication to cause death. PAS is, in turn, distinguished from **voluntary euthanasia,** in which the physician *administers* the lethal drug *with* the patient's consent and cooperation. **Involuntary euthanasia** is physician *administration* of a lethal drug *without* the patient's consent or cooperation.

Neither PAS nor any form of euthanasia is sanctioned by medical governing bodies. However, organizations such as the American College of Physicians and some political groups (including voters in the state of Oregon) have recognized the existence of medical situations where such action "needs to be explored in depth." In 1997, the Supreme Court ruled that assisted suicide is not a Constitutional right, but did allow states to legalize it.

In an article about PAS in the *New England Journal of Medicine* in 1989, 10 of the 12 authors "believe that it is not immoral for a physician to assist in the rational suicide of a terminally ill person." For those who defend assisted suicide as a reasonable means to achieve a pain-free death actively (through the self-administration of medication that will cause death) instead of passively (through withdrawal of life-sustaining measures), certain safeguards to prevent abuse are generally insisted on: The patient must request assisted suicide without outside pressure, must make the request on more than one occasion over a sustained period of time, and not be suffering from any mental illness that impedes judgment. Furthermore, assisted suicide should be contemplated, if ever, only when all other avenues to relieve suffering have been tried and failed.

It has been argued that, in sanctioning PAS, the definition of who would be allowed to commit suicide could be expanded without justification. Physician-assisted voluntary euthanasia has been officially tolerated for some time in The

Studies have found that terminally ill patients typically do not experience either pain or suffering when artificial nutrition is discontinued. Proper comfort care usually also requires discontinuing hydration at the same time, to prevent fluid overload, aspiration pneumonia, and other problems.

A gradual process of malnutrition and dehydration, leading to an increase in endogenous endorphins, loss of consciousness, and a quiet death over the course of one or two weeks, is an accurate description of this situation. This is probably the best description of the type of "natural death" that occurred in times past, before modern medicine.

Netherlands for patients who are terminally ill, and some observers have claimed that patients with chronic illnesses or mental illnesses were also being "euthanized." In Oregon, which legalized PAS in 1997, there are no indications of abuse after almost 10 years of experience.

Arguments In Favor of PAS

1. Mentally competent individuals have the right to self-determination, even regarding the timing of their death, and they should be able to do so legally with the aid of their physician; and
2. a physician is acting humanely by helping otherwise terminally ill persons die before they experience extreme physical pain, limitation, or loss of personal dignity; and
3. it enables more patients to die at home rather than in the hospital or a hospice, the preference of the overwhelming majority of persons.

Arguments Opposing PAS

1. It violates many religious prohibitions, the Hippocratic Oath, and, in most states, legal statues; and
2. patients may be coerced into PAS for financial or other self-serving reasons by families or institutions; and
3. distinction between "mentally competent" or "rational" suicidal thoughts and depression in people with terminal illness is unclear.

Personal and Professional Relationships

It is incumbent on the physician to always maintain professionalism in the physician-patient relationship and to be unambiguous in choice of word and tone of voice. The patient deserves to be able to have faith in the physician's expertise and truthfulness, and to have confidentiality and independence respected. Only the patient should reveal confidences and vulnerability, and then only with the purpose of allowing the physician to act in the patient's best interest; that is, the physician-patient relationship is a partnership with the interest of only one partner in mind. This is sometimes called a **fiduciary relationship.**

> The physician-patient relationship is not a relationship among equals, even when the patient is also a physician.

A **personal** or **sexual relationship** between unequal partners could easily seem unfair in retrospect. In fact, some studies have shown that the emotional influence of some physicians over their patients remains powerful for years after terminating the physician-patient relationship. This has led some states to consider sexual activity with a patient a criminal act up to two years after the professional relationship has terminated. Thus, not even termination and transfer to another physician suffices to justify beginning a personal relationship with a former patient.

Academic and Financial Conflicts of Interest

> What is the principle of clinical equipoise?

> The first basic principle of the Nuremberg Code (1948) begins with the statement: "The voluntary consent of the human subject is absolutely essential."

For an academic physician, the pressure to perform and publish research can be so great that the patient's best interests become secondary to career interests. Patients have the right, being fully informed, to participate in clinical trials that have little hope of helping them, but their motives must be altruistic (to help future patients). The fear of death and the instinct for self-preservation are so strong that this type of self-deception has a name, **the therapeutic misconception.** It is incumbent on the researcher to ensure that the patient understands that agreement to participate is beyond the call of duty and not based on false hope. Patients enrolling in a study must also be told they can withdraw at any time.

In some instances, the protocol under investigation has a likelihood of benefit, and is being compared to a known beneficial treatment in a double-blind trial. In this situation, the physician's clinical obligations to the patient are balanced with the chance to improve patient care in the future. If the information gathered indicates that the protocol is either significantly better or more dangerous than the established regimen or procedure, then it is the obligation of the principal investigator to end the trial. But this should be done only after the evidence has scientific credibility beyond mere anecdotal reports.

> Clinical investigators must meet the standard of clinical equipoise, waiting until sufficient data are collected to draw a sound conclusion, but no longer than necessary because of the risk to patients.

Accepting **gifts** from pharmaceutical or medical supply companies must be balanced against the compromise to objective judgment that such gifts are meant to create. Most larger gifts (e.g., vacations) are now illegal. Smaller gifts (e.g., pens, note pads) probably damage the physician's image more than his or her objectivity. Gifts of intermediate value such as free lunches or dinners with a sponsored educational talk or bonuses for enrolling patients into studies or giving new drug prescriptions are legal, but the evidence supports that these change prescribing habits in ways that are not always justified scientifically. This is a violation of the principle of **beneficence** and the **fiduciary duty,** which are the essence of professionalism.

Medication samples, if used to help patients who would have difficulty purchasing needed drugs, can be defended by the principle of **justice**. However, if the patient is saddled with a more expensive medication when a generic would have sufficed, justice would suggest providing samples of generics instead. Use of samples by the physician's family or friends clearly cannot be justified since the cost of medication is increased to everyone by the provision of "free" samples.

Interest in a facility (laboratory, radiology clinic) to which a physician refers patients should be revealed to the patient (e.g., printed on a consent form, consultation request, prescription pad). The facilities must offer services that meet standards of care and charge reasonable fees.

The Role of Medical Students and Residents

Honesty is an important character trait and essential to establishing patient trust. Medical students should not be evasive and use euphemisms like "doctor in training," which invites confusion with residents. Patients appreciate honesty and concern for their well-being while understanding the need to learn. Of all the members of the team, the medical student is often the person who has time to talk with the patient; and, in some cases, talking is the most valuable service the system has to offer.

Recommended Reading

ACP Ethics Committee. Ethics Manual. (5th ed.). *Annals of Internal Medicine* 2005; 142:560–582.

Barsky AE, Gould JW. *Clinicians in Court: A Guide to Subpeonas, Depositions, Testifying and Everything Else You Need to Know.* New York: Guilford Press; 2002.

Beauchamp TL, Childress JF. *Principles of Biomedical Ethics.* (5th ed.). New York: Oxford University Press; 2001.

Chochinov HM, Wilson KG, Enns M, et al. Desire for death in the terminally ill. *American Journal of Psychiatry* 1995; 152:1185–1191.

Eighth Annual Report on Oregon's Death with Dignity Act. March 9, 2006. Oregon Department of Human Services. Available at: http://egov.oregon.gov/DHS/ph/pas/ar-index.shtml

Lo B. *Resolving Ethical Dilemmas – A Guide For Clinicians.* (3rd ed.). Philadelphia, PA: Lippincott Williams & Wilkins; 2005.

Review Questions

1. Informed consent, as a legal doctrine, is based on which of the following principles of biomedical ethics?
   A. Autonomy
   B. Beneficence
   C. Fiduciary
   D. Justice
   E. Nonmaleficence

2. Which of the following groups of patients are
    presumed to lack capacity, but may be deter-
    mined to have capacity by a clinician?
    A. Dementia patients
    B. Manic-depressive patients
    C. Minor patients
    D. Schizophrenic patients
    E. The elderly

3. The best tool for capacity assessment is
    A. a comprehensive neuropsychological eval-
        uation
    B. a discussion with the patient about her ill-
        ness and treatment goals
    C. the Folstein mini-mental status exam with
        a score of 20 or less
    D. functional Magnetic Resonance Imaging
        (fMRI)
    E. the Stanford-Binet Test of Intelligence
        with an IQ of 80 or less

4. DNR orders are
    A. an order for comfort care only
    B. a type of advance directive
    C. revocable by any physician
    D. revocable by the patient's hospital attend-
        ing
    E. revocable by the patient's primary care
        doctor

5. Which is the best recommendation for most
    patients who express a desire for comfort care
    and "a natural death"?
    A. Continue artificial hydration and aggres-
        sive symptom management while discon-
        tinuing artificial nutrition and other life-
        sustaining treatment
    B. Continue artificial nutrition and aggressive
        symptom management while discontinu-
        ing artificial hydration and other life-sus-
        taining treatment
    C. Continue artificial nutrition and hydra-
        tion and aggressive symptom management
        while discontinuing other life-sustaining
        treatment
    D. Discontinue artificial nutrition and hydra-
        tion and other life-sustaining treatment
        while continuing aggressive symptom
        management
    E. Discontinue all interventions

Key to review questions: p. 393

Section VIII
The Physician-Patient Interaction

33 Health Literacy

- How is literacy measured and reported?
- How are literacy and health linked?
- What is health literacy?
- How is health literacy measured?
- What promotes health literacy?

What is Literacy?

Literacy is best understood as a reflection of an individual's grasp or appreciation of the social, religious, economic and cultural context in which he or she lives. Literacy describes the ability to negotiate society in all its contexts, as the need arises. During the 19th century, the definition of literacy evolved from the ability to make your mark, usually with an 'X', to the ability to recite prose, usually scripture. Just 100 years ago, although books were readily available, the ability to sign one's name was the commonly accepted measure of literacy. With the rise in compulsory public education in the 20th century, literacy became equated with educational achievement. The army required soldiers to have a 5th grade education while the Census Bureau established a 6th grade educa-

tion as the standard for literacy in civilian life. By the middle of the 20th century, the Department of Education had come to recognize that number of years of education does not necessarily reflect literacy skills and changed the standard to an 8th grade *reading* level. However, experts argued that equating adult literacy to a school grade level is uninformative and misleading. For example, in accordance with the bell curve of normalcy, in any given 7th grade class, there will be students reading at the 2nd grade level and others reading at the high school graduate level. Nevertheless, current medical literature continues to report literacy as a school grade level equivalent.

The 1991 National Literacy Act established the concept of **functional literacy**. In this broader view, adult literacy level is determined not by skill level but by what those skills enable a person to *do*. An individual's functional literacy level varies

---

How understandable are informed consent documents?

Below are three versions of the opening statement of a consent form with the Flesch Reading Ease (FRE) score of each. A score of 90 is easy reading.

You are being asked to participate in this research study on hypercholesterolemia and hypertension because you have a family history of early stroke before the age of 55.	FRE: 14.4
We are asking you to take part in this research study on high cholesterol and high blood pressure because you have a family history of early stroke before the age of 55.	FRE: 46.6
We are doing a research study. We ask you to join because a family member died before age 55 from a stroke. We will look at your cholesterol and blood pressure.	FRE: 63.9

Literacy today means the ability to:

- read, write and speak in English
- compute and solve problems
- function on the job and in society
- achieve one's goals
- develop one's knowledge and potential

(U.S. Congress 1991 National Literacy Act)

with circumstance and social context. For example, a man may function at a high level in familiar surroundings at home and on the job. He does not need to read a map or a bus schedule because he boards the bus at the same time and place each day. He does not need to read street signs because he knows what they say; they serve as landmarks. Since he learned his job through demonstration and practice, he did not need to read an operators' manual. This man is functionally literate in his usual environment. However, in unfamiliar contexts, such as the health care environment, the same man's functional literacy may plummet. For example, he may encounter difficulty finding the institution and the specific clinic, to filling out forms, or understanding and adhering to treatment. In this context, he is said to have **low functional health literacy**. In the same way, a person with high functional health literacy may have low computer literacy.

The current definition of literacy in the U.S. specifies proficiency in *English*. This reflects the fact that, regardless of a person's intelligence and literacy skills in other languages, with limited English proficiency, he or she has low functional literacy (i.e., low access to the opportunities and benefits of the U.S. information economy).

Measuring Literacy

How is literacy measured and reported?

The 1992 **National Adult Literacy Survey (NALS)** was designed to assess adult functional literacy. In an effort to move away from reporting literacy as a school grade level equivalent, NALS used a scale of 1–5 for prose literacy (comprehension of text), document literacy (capacity to use forms, maps, charts) and quantitative literacy (using numbers) in a nationally representative sample of 26,000 adults over age 16. The results of this research showed that 48% of the U.S. population scored at a Literacy Level of 1 or 2. That is, they could read short simple text to locate a single piece of information, enter personal information on a form, or perform simple calculations with numbers provided. Most professionals scored at Level 3; they could make low level inferences, integrate information from lengthy text, and generate a response based on easily identifiable information. Less than 5% of adults scored at Level 5 indicating ability to search for information in dense text, make high level inferences, use specialized knowledge, and use background knowledge to determine quantities and appropriate numerical operations. In the medical literature, these findings have been extrapolated to estimate that 90 million Americans lack sufficient literacy skills to use the health care system.

Skills Needed to Use the U.S. Health Care System

- Conceptual knowledge
- Speaking
- Listening
- Writing
- Reading
- Numeracy

(Institute of Medicine 2004)

Attempts to develop an alternative to the grade level definition of literacy gained little acceptance as most reports, including those in medical journals, translated the NALS Literacy Levels back to grade level equivalents. The 2003 **National Assessment of Adult Literacy (NAAL)** introduced the current method of reporting literacy in four levels from Below Basic to Proficient. **Below Basic** indicates the lowest levels of performance such as signing a form or adding the amounts on a bank deposit slip. **Basic** means a person can perform simple everyday tasks such as comparing the ticket price of two sporting events or understanding a pamphlet that describes how a person is selected for jury duty. **Intermediate** means that a person can do moderately challenging tasks such as calculating the cost of an order from an office supply catalog or identifying a specific location on a map. A person

NAAL Level	Capacity	% U.S. Adults
Below Basic	Very simple, concrete tasks	14%
Basic	Simple everyday tasks	29%
Intermediate	Moderately challenging tasks	44%
Proficient	Complex tasks	13%*

* Significant drop from 1992

Proficient in English can perform complex activities such as comparing viewpoints in two editorials or interpreting a table about blood pressure and physical activity. NAAL found Americans' literacy levels to be essentially unchanged in the 10 years since the NALS except for a statistically significant drop in the percentage of adults proficient enough to complete complex literacy tasks. Therefore, health care providers should be prepared to engage and treat patients with limited literacy skills, limited English proficiency, and limited contact with health care environments.

Health and Literacy

How are health and literacy linked?

Research in several countries has repeatedly documented the negative effect of limited literacy on virtually all aspects of health including overall levels of morbidity and mortality, accidents, and a wide range of diseases including diabetes, cardiovascular disease, and rheumatoid arthritis. Disease, violent death, and hospital utilization by children are highest in communities with limited literacy levels.

Literacy influences health both directly and indirectly. Persons with low literacy find it difficult to access, understand and use health information and services. Those with less than proficient literacy encounter difficulties at every level of the health care system, especially in completing forms, understanding informed consent, and interacting with health care providers. They may have trouble seeking timely appropriate intervention, administering medication, following treatment regimens, and engaging in self-care.

Not only is literacy a major determinant of health, it is also closely associated with other socioeconomic conditions that indirectly influence health, such as income, social status, employment opportunities, social support, and early childhood development. People with limited literacy are relegated to low-paying jobs and so are likely to live in poverty with limited food supplies, poor quality housing in unsafe neighborhoods, low quality schools, high stress, low self-esteem, and social isolation. Thus, they are likely to have poorer health, higher rates of injury, more chronic disease and earlier death. Parents with low literacy skills and low functional literacy face significant barriers to fostering healthy development and school readiness in their children.

What is health literacy?

Health literacy is a type of functional literacy. Like computer literacy, it develops with need, opportunity and experience. While much attention has been given to "patients who can't read", and the difficulties of working with them and the extra costs they incur, such patients are the exception. The majority of Americans can read to some degree, but nearly everyone has low **functional health literacy**; that is, they lack background knowledge, medical vocabulary, and experience in the health care system. For example, few people have need or opportunity to learn about diabetes until they experience it. However, once that diagnosis is made their health literacy or, more specifically, "diabetes literacy" begins to develop. Until a person needs certain medical services and utilizes the health care system, he or she will lack the background knowledge and vocabulary to navigate the system efficiently. With experience, however, their health care literacy improves and they

Health literacy is:

"... the degree to which individuals have the capacity to obtain, process and understand basic health information needed to make appropriate health decisions."
Ratzan & Parker,
Institute of Medicine
American Medical Association

"... the ability to function in the health arena."
Ian Bennett, MD

progress toward higher levels of functioning in the context of that system.

Health Literacy Research

How is health literacy measured?

Health literacy research in the last decade has focused on the individual patient's ability to read in a health care setting. Researchers have adapted reading and comprehension tests from the field of education to identify patients with low health literacy so that providers can tailor communications to increase understanding and compliance. The **Rapid Estimate of Adult Literacy in Medicine (REALM),** a word recognition test, and the **Test of Functional Health Literacy in Adults (TOFHLA)** are the tests of reading and comprehension commonly used. The latter can be administered in English and in Spanish. While these tests have established a necessary foundation for understanding health literacy, they have been shown to be useful only for research purposes since they are stressful, embarrassing for patients, and time consuming for providers. The two tests are closely correlated and not measures of functional health literacy, *per se*, but rather measures of reading ability.

In an effort to assess functional health literacy, researchers developed the **Health Activity Literacy Scale (HALS)** using the results of 191 health-related literacy tasks from NALS. HALS-based findings indicate that large percentages of vulnerable populations in the U.S. do not have adequate skills to meet many of the health care-related demands they are likely to encounter. Only 18% of adults scored in the Proficient range and would be expected to function well in the health care system. Adults with low functional health literacy are generally those who have not completed high school or obtained a GED. They tend to have

HALS – Health Activity Literacy Scale 2004

Below Basic Health Literacy	19%
Basic	27%
Intermediate	36%
Proficient	18%

health-related restrictions on their ability to attend school or work, and are members of minority population groups or have immigrated to the U.S. relatively recently. They are likely to live in poverty, and less likely to read for fun, use a library or vote. Television is their primary information source. Thus, low health literacy may exacerbate existing disparities in health care access and outcomes.

A significant body of research supports an association between people's ability to read printed health information and a variety of health outcomes. Still, the impact of the mismatch between the average health literacy skills of U.S. adults and the sophisticated demands of the U.S. health system has not been fully assessed. Additional research is needed to expand understanding of health literacy beyond the current focus on reading skill. The role of social support and channels for promoting health literacy outside the health care system needs to be explored. Instruments for measuring the *function* in functional health literacy, particularly longitudinal studies to document individual's progress over time, also need to be developed.

What promotes health literacy?

To date most efforts to improve health literacy have focused on health care providers enhancing information delivery. The source of most health care communication problems is the mismatch between providers and patients in logic, language and experience. While physicians may interact daily with medical institutions and health care technology, for many patients, major illness or injury marks their first encounter with an institution of any kind. Even with native-born patients proficient in English, culture and language can be barriers to efficient, effective care. Federal and state law, Medicare and Medicaid regulations, and accreditation standards place responsibility for patient understanding squarely with the physician. Psychiatrist and anthropologist Arthur Kleinman developed a set of interview questions to elicit a patient's experience and perception of a condition and its treatment. Practitioners can use these questions to close gaps between a patient's logic, language and experience and their own.

Over 300 studies make clear that most written health information exceeds patients' literacy skills.

See from the patient's view

- What do you call the problem?
- What do you think has caused the problem?
- Why do you think it started when it did?
- What do you think the sickness does?
- How severe is the sickness? Will it have a short or long course?
- What kind of treatment do you think the patient should receive?
- What are the most important results you hope to receive from treatment?

Adapted from: Arthur Kleinman as quoted in Fadiman A, *The Spirit Catches You and You Fall Down. A Hmong Child, Her American Doctors and the Collision of Two Cultures.* New York: The Noonday Press/Farrar Straus & Giroux; 1997, pp. 260–261.

Numerous guidelines have been published to increase the readability of health education materials, including the FONBAYS method for simplifying the readability of text and survey questions (see p. 275).

"... give it to them briefly so that they will read it, clearly so they will appreciate it, picturesquely so they will remember it, and above all accurately so they will be guided by its light."

Joseph Pulitzer

Improved information delivery alone is not likely to mitigate the relationship between low literacy and poor outcomes. Investigating whether and how literacy skills and functional health literacy affect self-efficacy, self-care, trust and satisfaction may lead to effective strategies. Social support from family, friends or social services providers may buffer the negative impacts of low health literacy by enabling a person to understand information, enter and navigate the health system and adhere to treatment regimens. Collaboration between health care organizations and literacy enhancing community services, such as adult basic education and English language learning classes, may also prove beneficial.

To facilitate health literacy,
- become aware of the culture of medicine and of your institution

- become aware of your patients' culture
- use the patient's language. Say 'walk' instead of 'ambulate'
- be aware of the pictures your words create in the patient's mind. Be especially aware of common words used as medical terms (e.g., stool, screen, cap)
- ask the patient to "teach back" to confirm understanding
- focus on behavior. Talk about what the patient needs to do, not the facts about the condition. Limit discussion to the "critical minimum" information the patient needs now to cope and recover
- say the most important thing three times. Adults learn by repetition
- select or prepare written information that is easy to read and understand
- ask patients to read aloud the most important part of treatment instructions, since reading aloud facilitates learning
- refer patients with less than a high school education who do not read for fun to literacy enhancing services
- encourage formal education
- encourage reading for fun, especially reading aloud (e.g., reading to children)
- never assume a given patient understands your instructions or printed information

Recommended Reading

Calderón JL, Beltran R. Pitfalls in Health Communication: Health Policy, Institutions, Structure and Process of healthcare. *Medscape General Medicine* 2004; 6(1) Available at: http://www.medscape.com/view-article/466016_5

Chall JS. The beginning years. In: BL Zakaluk, SJ Samuels (Eds.). *Readability, Its Past, Present and Future.* Newark, DE: International Reading Association; 1988, pp. 2–13.

Fadiman A, *The Spirit Catches You and You Fall Down. A Hmong Child, Her American Doctors and the Collision of Two Cultures.* New York: The Noonday Press/Farrar Straus & Giroux; 1997, pp. 260–261.

Lee S-YD, Arozullah AM, Young IC. Health literacy, social support and health: A research agenda. *Social Science & Medicine* 2004; 58:1309–1321.

Smith SA. Patient education and literacy. In: JB Labus, A Lauber. *Patient Education and Preventive*

Medicine. Philadelphia, PA: WB Saunders; 2001, pp. 266–290.

Recommended Resources

Maximus. *The Health Literacy Style Manual*. Available at: http:coveringkidsandfamilies.org/resources/docs/stylemanual.pdf

Nielson-Bohlman L, Panzer AM, Hamlin B, et al. (Eds.). *Health Literacy: A Prescription to End Confusion*. Prepublication Copy. Institute of Medicine. Washington, DC: National Academies Press; 2004. Available for free download at www.nap.edu

Institute of Education Sciences, National Center for Health Statistics. *National Assessment of Adult Literacy (NAAL). A First Look at the Literacy of America's Adults in the 21st Century*. Jessup, MD: U.S. Department of Education. Available at http://nces.ed.gov/NAAL/PDF/2006470.pdf

Bennett IM, Robbins S, Haecker T. Screening for Low Literacy Among Adult Caregivers of Pediatric Patients. *Family Medicine* 2003; 35:585–590.

Doak C, Doak L, Root J. *Teaching Patients with Low Literacy Skills*. (2nd ed.). Philadelphia, PA: JB Lippincott; 1996.

Review Questions

1. A true statement about health literacy in the U.S. is:
    A. The term "Limited English Proficiency" is reserved for people who do not speak English.
    B. An eighth grade education ensures adequate literacy skills to negotiate health care delivery systems.
    C. The readability of health documents exceeds the reading skills of most patients.
    D. The level of functional literacy tends to be the same in all contexts.

2. A 40-year-old obese African American woman with elementary school education and low socioeconomic status, diabetes and hypertension took public transportation for her 7-year-old daughter's routine pediatric check-up. The child is up-to-date in her immunizations but is slightly overweight. The girl is doing well in school.

    Among the following, this woman has demonstrated that she is health literate about her
    A. daughter's care
    B. diabetes
    C. hypertension
    D. weight management

Key to review questions: p. 393

Readability Enhancement Using the FONBAYS Method
Adapted from Calderon JL, Smith S, Baker R. 'FONBAYS': A simple method for enhancing readability of patient informa-tion. *Annals of Behavioral Science and Medical Education* 2007 (in press).

1. **Identify compound sentences**
    - A compound sentence has multiple clauses; more than one thought.
    - A clause is a complete simple sentence; only one thought.
    - A clause has one subject, predicate, and object.

2. **Identify and separate compound sentences into clause elements**
    - A clause element is an incomplete simple sentence.
    - Separating clause elements is done at the words *for, or, nor, because, and, yet, so* (FONBAYS).
    - Also separate sentences at colons and semicolons.

3. **Identify and reduce compound clause elements**
    - Compound clauses have more than one subject, object.
    - Separate subjects or objects.

4. **Eliminate or convert free modifiers into clause elements**
    - These are elements that are not part of the basic sentence structure.
    - They may be omitted without changing the meaning of the sentence.
    - They may be converted into an independent clause.
    - They are separated from the rest of the sentence by a comma or commas.
      Example: Born to wealthy parents, he was able to pursue his career without financial worries.

5. **Remove elements in parentheses**
    - These are elements that are not part of the basic sentence structure.
    - They may be omitted without changing the meaning of the sentence.
    - They may be converted into an independent clause.

6. **Write an independent clause using each clause element**
    - Make a simple complete sentence.
    - This may require repeating some sentence elements.
    - Repetition is good for enhancing comprehension.

7. **Identify clauses that may fit under one sub-heading**

8. **List similar clauses under one sub-heading**
    - I.e., Benefits to Society
    - Bullet independent clauses under sub-headings.

9. **Convert bullet into a vision friendly font**
    Use 12 to 14 Font Bookman Old Style; or
    Use 12 to 14 Century Gothic.
    Arial, Tahoma and Verdanda are also readable fonts. Avoid Times New Roman.

These instructions have a Flesh-Kincaid Formula reading grade level of 6.7.

This project was supported by the National Center for Research Resources, Research Centers in Minority Institutions (G12-RR03026 and U54 RR019234), UCLA/DREW Project EXPORT, National Institutes of Health, National Center on Minority Health & Health Disparities, (P20-MD00148), the National Institutes of Health, UCLA/Drew EXCEED Program Grant (P01 HS10858), the Agency for Healthcare Research and Quality Minority Research Infrastructure Support Program M-RISP (1R24-HS014022-01A1) and the Centers for Medicare and Medicaid Services (1H0CMS300041).

34 The Physician-Patient Relationship

- What are the responsibilities and rights of physicians?
- What are the responsibilities and rights of patients?
- What is "informed consent"?
- What is the difference between transference and countertransference?
- What are patients' two main fears?
- What influences patients' adherence to treatment recommendations?
- What is the leading cause of physician impairment?

The **Hippocratic Oath** required the physician to be responsible for the patient's well-being, but did not require the physician to inform the patient or follow the patient's wishes. In fact, the physician could deceive the patient if the deception was intended to offer hope. By the end of the 18th century, Benjamin Rush, a physician and signer of the Declaration of Independence, was urging physicians to share information with patients while John Gregory, of the University of Edinburgh, proposed that patients be more responsible for their own health education and that physicians aid their efforts.

Today, the physician-patient relationship is presumed to be based on a **mutual exchange of information** and **collaborative decision making.** The patient's right to determine his or her care is a pervasive element of the implicit contract that exists between physician and patient. It is critical that the patient's values and preferences be discussed and incorporated into the treatment plan and that the physician and patient also share responsibility for managing medical problems and concerns. While the dominant culture of the U.S. emphasizes patient autonomy, active involvement, and independent functioning, patients from more family-oriented cultures may find this type of physician-patient relationship offensive or discourteous. Instead, in these cultures the family is viewed as the agent of decision making, although negotiating treatment is still a major element of determining care. Hence, the physician should be especially sensitive to these

cultural differences and the effect they will have on patient expectations and practices (see Chapter 17, Culture and Ethnicity).

Responsibilities and Rights of Physicians

What are the responsibilities and rights of physicians?

The physician has a **responsibility to inform** the patient, to the best of her/his ability, regarding the nature of the disorder, probable course if untreated, and available and recommended treatments. The physician also has an obligation to **elicit and listen** to the patient's concerns, **address** them objectively and sensitively, and **respect** the patient's decisions even though the physician may disagree with them. Above all, the physician has a responsibility to use her/his authority always in the best interest of the patient and must avoid the abuse of this authority that may result from personal conflicts of interest.

Refusal to Perform Certain Procedures

The physician may refuse to perform any act that conflicts with personal moral or ethical principles (e.g., performing an abortion or withdrawing life support). However, the physician has the responsibility to **respect the patient's wishes** and make a referral to another physician who is likely to be more comfortable and responsive to the patient's wishes.

Recommending Appropriate Treatments

Although treatment costs must be considered in medical decisions, the most important principle is that patients receive **appropriate care.** For example, a 60-year-old, otherwise healthy patient who has suspected pneumonia expects and should receive appropriate diagnostic studies and medication. Among terminally ill patients, whose feelings regarding prolongation of life vary, however, the same situation may raise complex ethical dilemmas that require balancing expectations for cure against the realities of quality of life.

Rights and Responsibilities of Patients

What are the responsibilities and rights of patients?

In 1972, the American Hospital Association developed the **Patient's Bill of Rights**. Patients obtained the right to receive complete information, the right to refuse treatment (unless the patient is incompetent or the decision poses a threat to the community), and the right to know about a hospital's possible financial conflicts of interest. **Informed consent** is the patient's right to know all treatment

Informed Consent

The Patient Self-Determination Act requires health care institutions to advise patients that:
1. they have the right to refuse or accept medical care
2. they have the right to execute an advance directive concerning their care or to designate a person (proxy) to make decisions for them if they are unable to do so

options and to decide which care is appropriate for him or her. To empower the patient to make a rational decision, the physician must provide information and full, accurate, and understandable explanations. Until the late 1970s, decisions regarding life-sustaining treatment were considered the domain of physicians. Respect for patient participation in such decisions led to the passage of the **Patient Self-Determination Act** in 1991.

What is "informed consent"?

Informed consent is **an open communication process between the patient and physician** that results in the patient approving a medical intervention or course of action. For example, under most circumstances, care can be withdrawn at a patient's request. However, it is illegal in most states for a health care worker to actively hasten death even at the patient's explicit request (e.g., physician-assisted suicide). Parents are empowered to make legal decisions for their children, but over the past 30 years there has been a movement to allow children to participate more actively in medical decision-making. In the case of experimental protocols, children as young as 7 years of age are mandated by some institutions to give **informed assent** prior to being accepted as a participant and their parents must give **informed consent.** Adolescents may make their own decisions regarding sexual matters (e.g., contraception, STD treatment, abortion) although some states require parental notification or involvement (see Chapter 32, Ethical and Legal Issues in Patient Care).

Factors Influencing the Physician-Patient Relationship

A cornerstone of medical practice is the physician's ability to communicate caring and concern to the patient.

Accurate empathy is the ability to understand the patient's illness experiences from the patient's perspective, to communicate this understanding to the patient, and to have this understanding confirmed by the patient. Patients list kindness, understanding, interest, and encouragement as primary expectations they have of their physicians. They

> Hippocrates emphasized the importance of relationship by admonishing the physician to: bear in mind his manner of sitting, reserve, arrangement of dress, decisive utterance, brevity of speech, composure, bedside manners, care, replies to objections, calm self-control ... his manner must be serious and humane, without stooping to be jocular or failing to be just; he must avoid excessive austerity; he must always be in control of himself.

want their physical, interpersonal, and emotional needs met in a mutually understood, courteous, warm, and personal manner that permits them to feel they are partners with the physician.

Sympathy is different from empathy. Whereas empathy is *understanding* the patient's experience, sympathy is *feeling and experiencing* the emotions expressed by the patient. This distinction is important because it is not necessary to experience the patient's feelings to be helpful. In fact, over-identification with the patient can lead to ineffective communication or complicate the relationship.

What is the difference between transference and countertransference?

The broadest definition of **transference** is bringing the beliefs, expectations, and perceptions from previous relationships into a current life experience. Transference may become particularly evident in long-term therapeutic relationships. For example, a physician is providing care to a patient with insulin-dependent diabetes who has not complied well with dietary restrictions. The patient grew up in a household with a harsh, critical parent. If the physician attempts to counsel the patient about proper dietary habits and expresses these recommendations in a firm fashion, the patient may become angry and feel belittled because the physician has not appreciated the patient's efforts to control her diet. In this instance, the patient is reacting as if the physician were a parent (transference).

Countertransference is an inappropriate reaction the physician has to a patient. If the physician perceives the patient as a "nice little old lady" who is just like a favorite aunt, the physician may find it difficult to ask her questions that seem intrusive (e.g., about how frequently she voids or if she

has urinary incontinence). Effective medical care involves being objectively vigilant and aware that the patient *and* physician bring past emotional experiences to each encounter.

Understanding Patient Fears

What are patients' two main fears?

A patient typically has two main fears: **losing bodily integrity** and **becoming dependent.** The degree to which these fears affect the patient depends on the patient's age and stage of development, personality, and life experiences. Young athletes are usually able to tolerate injury and pain, yet they have little tolerance for discomfort or inconvenience if an illness limits their activities or makes them dependent on others. In contrast, older persons with a chronic illness may accept limited independence, being more concerned about maintaining basic functioning essential for sedentary activities and maintaining their own home.

Acceptance of Dependency Is Influenced by Life Stage

1. Young children are used to being dependent on others, but may be highly fearful because they do not understand illness.
2. Adolescents struggle to establish their identity and may find any threat to independence difficult to accept.
3. Adults may find it difficult to tolerate absence from work or isolation from friends, especially if they define themselves in terms of their work or friendships.
4. Elderly adults may experience illness as a signal that their healthy life is jeopardized and there may be no hope of recovery.

Ensuring Treatment Plan Success

The success of any intervention depends on the physician and patient reaching agreement about the nature of the problem and its proper treatment (see **explanatory model** in Chapter 17, Culture and Ethnicity).

The patient's explanation of the illness influences beliefs about causation and determines what assistance he or she will seek and accept. Therefore every effort should be made to accurately explain the nature of the illness, its etiology and its treatment in terms that are in keeping with the patient's explanatory model, culture, and treatment expectations.

> **What influences patients' adherence to treatment recommendations?**

> **Adherence to treatment will depend on the patient's belief that:**
>
> 1. the illness warrants treatment
> 2. the treatment is effective
> 3. cost of treatment is reasonable given the benefits
> 4. treatment is feasible

It is rare for patients to follow treatment recommendations rigorously. In fact, the adherence rate for prescribed medications is about 50% even in the treatment of acute illness. Furthermore, the proportion of patients completing treatment decreases as the duration of treatment increases. Thus, higher dose but shorter course treatments are now used for a wide variety of infections.

Patient **adherence** to therapy recommendations often depends on: (1) the complexity of the regimen; (2) the persistence of symptoms; and (3) the frequency and quality of contact with the physician.

The Impaired Physician

> **What is the leading cause of physician impairment?**

The demands of the increasingly complex health care sector, together with the sustained stressors of trying to balance professional, personal and familial obligations, take their toll on practicing physicians. At least one third of physicians will experience a period of **impairment** during their career. Physicians who are impaired have a diminished capacity to fulfill professional and personal responsibilities. Impairment has typically been associated with dependence on **drugs or alcohol** and **psychiatric illness,** but impairment can also stem from **behavioral addictions** such as compulsive gambling; **medical conditions** such as dementia, stroke, or HIV-related disease; depression; and the **normal aging** process. Denial and ambivalence on the part of the physician, the family, and the community often accompany impairment.

Alcoholism or other chemical dependence is the cause of physician impairment in up to 85% of cases. It is estimated that 17,000 practicing physicians have substance abuse problems, and 6–8% of physicians will develop drug abuse problems during their career. It is also estimated that about 100 deaths (the equivalent of one medical school class) occur annually among practicing physicians as the result of alcohol or drug abuse.

Although **depression** is the most common emotional disturbance among physicians, they experience major depression and suicide at a rate that is only slightly higher than that of the general population. Female physicians have a higher incidence of depression and suicide than their male counterparts; their rate of suicide is two-fold higher than the general population.

> **Signs of Physician Impairment**
>
> 1. Behavioral disruptions at work
> 2. Chaos at home
> 3. Deteriorating job performance
> 4. Frequent moves or job changes
> 5. Legal involvements (e.g., DUIs, self-prescribing)

Most types of impairment can be treated successfully. A survey of physicians impaired by alcohol abuse, drug abuse, psychiatric illness, or physical illness found that 75% had been in recovery for an average of 88 months. The recovery rate for similarly impaired persons in the general population is about 50%. One factor that may contribute to the better prognosis for recovery among physicians compared to non-physicians is that they have a greater incentive to return to their medical practice for financial and psychological rewards. Each state typically has a mechanism, usually through the state medical society, to assist the impaired physician and provide education.

Recommended Reading

Carillo JE, Green AR, Betancourt JR. Cross-cultural primary care: A patient-based approach. *Archives of Internal Medicine* 1999; 130:829–834.

Leape LL, Fromson JA. Problem doctors: Is there a system-level approach? *Annals of Internal Medicine* 2006; 144:107–115.

Levinson W, Roter DL, Mullooly JP, et al. Physician-patient communication. *JAMA* 1997; 277:553–559.

Osterberg L, Blaschke T. Drug therapy: Adherence to medication. *New England Journal of Medicine* 2005; 353:487–497.

Rosser RR, Kasperski J. The benefits of a trusting physician-patient relationship. *Journal of Family Practice* 2001; 50:329–330.

Roter DL, Stewart M, Putnam SM, et al. Communication patterns of primary care physicians. *JAMA* 1997; 277:350–356.

Review Questions

1. The concept of patient self-determination developed largely
   A. as a result of the writings of Benjamin Rush
   B. as an integral part of the Hippocratic Oath
   C. from the concepts in Percival's treatise, *Medical Ethics*
   D. from the tenets of Traditional Chinese Medicine
   E. in response to life-prolonging medical technology

2. Dr. Johnson was approaching retirement and, at the age of 67 years, had provided care for patients in a rural town in South Dakota for almost 35 years. Although felt by patients to be "a bit old fashioned" he was respected as a capable and caring physician who had always been available to meet his patients' needs. His preferred role in relationships with patients was a paternalistic one, a role encouraged during his medical school education. A characteristic of paternalistic physician roles is
   A. deferring decision-making authority to the patient's family
   B. mutual exchange of information between physician and patient
   C. patient passivity during encounters with a physician
   D. physician respect for patient autonomy
   E. sharing of medical decision making between physician and patient

3. Among the following, which choice is an example of transference in career decision making?
   A. Choosing a career in biomedical research after winning many science awards
   B. Choosing a health care career after a significant childhood illness
   C. Choosing a helping profession because of a family history of alcoholism
   D. Choosing medicine based on a physician role model outside the family
   E. Choosing to be a physician after being raised in a physician's family

4. Which of the following best describes the basic requirement of informed consent?
   A. The patient must have a designated proxy to make decisions if the patient becomes incompetent.
   B. The patient must have all necessary information before agreeing to medical treatment.
   C. The patient's family must be advised before medical procedures are undertaken.
   D. The patient's primary care physician must be informed before a subspecialist performs a procedure.
   E. The physician must be well-informed before consenting to perform a procedure.

5. The presence of empathy is crucial in the development of the physician-patient relationship. The core element in the establishment of empathy focuses on
   A. avoiding excessive emotional detachment
   B. mastering active or reflective listening
   C. modeling how to remain in calm self-control
   D. providing reassurance about a positive outcome
   E. using exclusively open-ended questioning

Key to review questions: p. 393

35

The Medical Encounter

- What is rapport?
- What are the guidelines for protecting confidentiality?
- What should be observed in the patient's initial evaluation?
- What kinds of questions should be avoided?
- What are eight data gathering techniques?
- What are six potential impediments to communication?

Setting, time constraints, and purpose determine the structure of each physician-patient medical encounter. In an emergency or triage situation, the interview is limited to essential information sufficient to initiate care. In contrast, in a new-patient office visit, data collection is more thorough and comprehensive, requiring sufficient time to accomplish the goals of the visit. Whatever the circumstance, every patient encounter should be documented in writing to facilitate communication and consistency of care.

Introductions

The interviewer should always introduce him/herself even if wearing a name tag. The patient should be addressed using a formal title (i.e., Mr., Mrs., Ms.) and the patient's last name unless the patient is a child or has asked to be addressed in another way. Many clinicians shake hands with the patient and anyone accompanying the patient. However, care should be taken to respect differences in social practices and expectations if the patient is from another culture.

Developing Rapport

What is rapport?

Rapport is a state of mutual confidence and respect between two people. Because the physician is perceived as being in a position of authority, developing rapport is essential to ensuring that a mutually respectful relationship will be established. The development of trust comes when patients believe the physician understands and respects their concerns. A patient's perception that the physician is interested and respectful promotes rapport.

Sensitivity to Emotions

Responding appropriately to an expression of emotion by the patient can be reassuring and facilitate the interview. It is important for the physician to be comfortable with emotion in order to allow the patient to be comfortable expressing it. When a patient cries, showing respect and caring merely by waiting or offering a tissue can be comforting even if nothing is said. With an angry or hostile patient, acknowledging the anger, remaining calm and listening reflectively, and encouraging the patient to discuss it are likely to diffuse the situation. Above all, the physician should avoid taking the patient's display of anger as personal.

Cultural Appropriateness

Every patient has a set of culturally based health beliefs, illness behaviors, and explanatory models for what is normal or abnormal. Understanding and respecting the patient's cultural context increases the likelihood the patient will participate fully in developing and adhering to an effective treatment plan (see Chapter 17, Culture and Ethnicity).

Establishing Limits of Confidentiality

Except in situations where the physician is concerned that the patient will harm him- or herself or someone else, or in situations that involve mandatory reporting (child abuse, communicable diseases), nothing the patient tells the physician may be shared with others without the patient's expressed consent. The physician-patient relationship carries an obligation on the part of the physician that patient information be discussed only with individuals who are involved in the patient's care, or with members of a teaching group in a controlled environment away from areas where the discussion could be overheard.

All physicians must now be aware of the **Health Insurance Portability and Accountability Act of 1996 (HIPAA).** This act took effect in 2003 and provides new standards to protect patients' written and electronic medical records and other health information that is provided to health plans, physicians, hospitals, and other health care providers. These new standards give patients access to their medical records and more control over how their personal health information is used and disclosed.

What are the guidelines for protecting confidentiality?

Guidelines for Protecting Confidentiality

- Conduct the interview in private.
- Tell patients with whom and under what circumstances information will be shared.
- Teach or consult about patients in private.
- Override confidentiality when safety of the patient or others is a concern.

Attentive Listening

Attentive listening communicates interest, concern, and understanding about what the patient is saying and feeling. The physician's interest enhances the patient's impression of professional competence. This perception of competence, in turn, facilitates trust and prompts the patient to be more open and candid.

To promote attentive listening:

1. the setting should be comfortable
2. the physician should face the patient with an erect but relaxed posture
3. eye contact should be frequent or culturally appropriate (see Chapter 17, Culture and Ethnicity)
4. the physician should use gestures and facial expressions that are congruent with what is being said, and speak in a pleasant voice
5. the physician should address the topic the patient has introduced and encourage the flow of information by using occasional verbal facilitative words and phrases

Observation

What should be observed in the patient's initial evaluation?

Careful observation is an important part of a patient's evaluation and should begin the moment the physician first sees the patient. How is the patient groomed? Is the patient relaxed? Impatient? Frightened? When the patient is accompanied by others, their interaction can provide important information on interpersonal or family relationships. Initial hypotheses begin to form as the physician notes apparent age, gender, race, dress, affect, and whether the patient appears healthy, ill, or in distress.

Touching

Touching between the physician and the patient in the interim between shaking hands during introductions and the laying on of hands during the physical examination may or may not be appropriate. For example, although touching can be interpreted as empathetic by some patients, others can construe it as intrusive or seductive. Backing away, stiffening, or becoming silent are clues that a patient prefers not to be touched. Most experienced physicians use measured, appropriate physical contact to reassure patients and enhance rapport unless the patient signals that this is unwelcome.

Conducting the Interview

Interviewers usually begin with open-ended questions, follow with more focused questions, and end with closed-ended questions to confirm data. **Open-ended questions** ("How have you been getting along?" "How can I help you?") help to define the areas of concern and allow the patient to discuss topics he or she wishes to address. Although it may seem paradoxical, open-ended questions elicit the maximum amount of information in the minimum amount of time because they impose few values or expectations, involve the patient in the interview and problem-solving processes, and allow the patient to reveal information about matters that the interviewer may not think to ask.

Focused questions narrow the area to be discussed but still give the patient some latitude in answering. Questions to **focus exploration of a topic** include... "What is your understanding of your situation?" or "How do you think this happened?" Questions to help **clarify certain points** are "What do you mean when you say ...?" or "What are some examples of ...?"

Closed-ended questions prompt more specific responses and are appropriate for clarifying details

or facilitating decision making in triage or emergency situations. Closed-ended questions are also useful for controlling or directing the interview. Questions that elicit **specific information** are "Where does it hurt?" or "What did you eat today?"

What kinds of questions should be avoided?

Questions to be *avoided* include **compound questions,** which are several questions asked together (e.g., "Tell me what happens when you have chest pain, like is it when you're walking up stairs or exercising, or does it come after you've eaten something or maybe when you're feeling anxious?") and **leading questions,** which prompt the patient to give a specific response ("You haven't been drinking alcohol again, have you?").

Ending the Clinical Encounter

Before ending the clinical encounter the physician should **review** the relevant clinical information, the diagnosis and explanation of the patient's problem, and the mutually agreed upon step-by-step plan for treatment, ending with the scheduled next appointment.

Every clinical encounter should end with:

1. a review of the information gathered by the physician
2. an explanation of the problem
3. if medically appropriate, reassurance about the patient's concerns.
4. an agreement on the next steps to be taken
5. the next scheduled appointment time

What are eight data gathering techniques?

Open-ended questions can quickly elicit:

1. common triggering events that lead the patient to seek help
2. attributions or explanatory models for the patient's symptoms
3. the patient's expectations about what can or should be done
4. the patient's major concern or most pressing or potentially serious problems

Some Successful Data Gathering Techniques

1. Nonverbal techniques, such as head-nodding and verbal cues ("Tell me more about that") prompt the patient to expand and report what he or she feels is most important

2. Checking – Review or repetition to ensure accuracy of the data being recorded ("You think this started last Thursday?")

3. Clarification – Asking the patient to clarify either by restating or by giving examples. The physician can paraphrase what the patient has said in fewer words without changing the meaning ("So, your headaches occur both day and night but are the absolute worst when you wake up, is that correct?")

4. Interruption – Breaking the flow if the patient is rambling. Acknowledge the importance the patient attaches to the information being given, then provide a transition to another topic ("Mrs. Jones, your son's school problems are certainly taking a lot of your time and energy, but how about you? How's that arm healing?")

5. Transition – A statement that links what the patient has been saying with a change in direction ("What you've been talking about reminds me to ask you....")

6. Reflection – Paraphrasing what the patient has said, demonstrating that the physician has been listening ("You've told me a lot of things. Let's see if I've understood them all.")

7. Information sharing – Interpreting and explaining the problem. Information sharing can be used to clarify goals and establish shared expectations for outcomes. Written information is suggested. However, the physician should determine whether the patient can read the language and at the level in which the material is written.

8. Giving directions – Explanations of various tasks and responsibility for completing them should be clear, realistic, and checked to ensure understand-

Impediments to Communication

What are six potential impediments to communication?

Sensory Impairment

Communication is likely to be inhibited to some degree by impaired hearing, sight, or verbal expression. **Hearing-impaired individuals** may need to use sign language, require a signer to translate, or be able to read the lips of a physician who speaks clearly and slowly. For patients with hearing impairment who are literate, the interview may be facilitated by the use of written material, such as questionnaires. The **blind** patient's need for verbal explanation and description exceeds that of all other patients. The patient who is mute may be able to sign and, therefore, may require a translator. When any patient has an impairment, the physician must inquire about the extent to which physical or cognitive assistance will be required to adhere to the therapeutic plan and if that assistance will be available.

Language Differences

Virtually every physician will need to communicate with a patient through a **translator** or an **interpreter** at some time. Because of differences in language structure, literal translations may not be possible or accurate. Therefore, efforts should be made to ensure that the patient's complaints and condition are clearly communicated. An interpreter, in contrast to a translator, brings his or her own cultural and ethnic background values, knowledge, and belief system to the exchange. In effect, **the role of the interpreter triangulates the encounter**. For example, if the patient is angry, but the interpreter feels that displaying anger is inappropriate, the physician will not be told and the patient's answers will be softened or references to anger, blame, or guilt removed. If the translator or interpreter is a child or family member of the patient, issues such as confidentiality become especially important.

The time needed for an interview involving a translator or interpreter is usually twice as long as one solely between the physician and the patient. The physician should acknowledge to the patient that there may be difficulty in arriving at a diagnosis and management plan as a result of the language difference but that they will work together to overcome these problems.

Cognitive Differences

Cognitive differences include the disparity between how the patient and the physician **conceptualize experiences,** and how they understand and explain the world, including the disease and its treatment. The burden is on the physician to inform the patient in a way the patient can understand. Cognitive differences are most obviously influenced by environment, culture, life experiences, and age (see Chapter 9, Cognition and Emotion, and Chapter 17, Culture and Ethnicity).

Age Effects

Since age is associated with increased experience, younger physicians are sometimes challenged for being too young and may need great patience to win the patient's confidence. Seeing themselves as children or even grandchildren, younger physicians sometimes have difficulty advising older patients.

Psychosocial Factors

Psychosocial stresses and psychiatric disorders may pose an impediment to the interview. Psychosis, paranoia and some personality disorders may stop the physician from being able to form a therapeutic relationship with the patient. Also, patients with various types of dementia, especially in the early stages, may confabulate or provide unreliable or inaccurate medical information. In these cases, having family members involved in the interview to confirm information can be valuable. In trauma situations, such as rape or domestic violence, the physician must be aware of the need for privacy and support. The patient should be given clear guidance concerning the process of the physical examination and other data collection. In such cases, the patient should not be left alone in the exam room.

Gender Effects

Male physicians offer the same number of **explanations** to men and women patients but explanations to women are given in less technical language. Female patients are more likely to ask questions and receive more **information**. The male physician is likely to be more empathic toward women patients.

Male and female physicians have different **communication styles.** Female physicians are less likely to interrupt patients. Although male and female physicians do not appear to ask different questions of men and women patients, patients are more likely to initiate discussion of both medical and psychosocial issues with female physicians than they are with male physicians. Men patients are more likely to bring up personal habits with female physicians.

Recommended Reading

Kaplan HI, Sadock BJ. *Synopsis of Psychiatry.* (8th ed.). Baltimore, MD: Lippincott, Williams & Wilkins; 1998, pp. 240–274.

Makoul G. Essential elements of communication in medical encounters: The Kalamazoo Consensus Statement. *Academic Medicine* 2001; 76:390–393.

Platt FW, Gordon GH. *Field Guide to the Difficult Patient Interview.* (2nd ed.). Philadelphia, PA: Lippincott, Williams & Wilkins; 2004.

Robinson G. Effective doctor-patient communication: Building bridges and bridging barriers. *Canadian Journal of Neurological Sciences* 2002; 29:S30–32.

Review Questions

1. Which one of the following statements is consistent with the guidelines for protecting confidentiality?
    A. Conduct interviews in a setting where privacy can be maintained.
    B. Hallway discussions are preferable to talking in front of an anxious patient.
    C. Keeping confidentiality overrides any other agreement between patient and physician.
    D. Only family members should have the opportunity to review files without patient consent.
    E. The patient should be protected from knowing who has access to his/her medical record.

2. Which of the following is an open-ended question?
    A. Are you sexually active?
    B. Do you have any questions?
    C. How can I help you this morning?
    D. Where is the pain?
    E. You don't smoke, do you?

3. "Now that you have told me about your head-
    aches, I would like to ask you some questions
    about your job situation" is an example of
    a(n)
    A. check
    B. clarification
    C. interruption
    D. reflection
    E. transition

4. Of the questions below, which one would you
    use to begin a clinical encounter?
    A. "Do you get the pain when you eat or when
        you walk?"
    B. "Just give me the short list of your prob-
        lems."
    C. "What brings you in to see me today?"
    D. "Where does it hurt?"
    E. "You haven't been drinking, have you?"

5. Only a few clinical encounters should end with
    a(n)
    A. agreement on the next steps
    B. explanation of the problem
    C. follow-up plan
    D. medication prescription
    E. review of the patient's information

Key to review questions: p. 393

36 The Clinical Decision-Making Process

- What are the six steps in the clinical decision-making process?
- What is included in the comprehensive medical history?
- What is the Mental Status Examination?
- What four intervention strategies are key to developing an optimal treatment plan?
- What are eight sources of error in clinical decision making?

The fundamental process in clinical decision making is **systematic, step-wise problem solving.** The problem faced by the clinician is how to reduce the discrepancy between how the patient feels (ill) and how the patient wishes to feel (healthy). The solutions to this problem become apparent during the clinical decision-making process.

What are the six steps in the clinical decision-making process?

The physician's part in the clinical decision-making process often begins before the patient enters the office. It is set in motion through a self-made appointment or a professional referral seeking answers to questions about the patient's condition. These questions determine the parameters of the physician's role in dealing with the patient, and the decisions the physician will be asked to make. **Referral questions** provide the basis for defining the initial problem. At this stage, the physician develops a set of hypotheses that determine what information will be required and how it will be obtained. If, for example, the patient is a hyperactive child being seen because a teacher has expressed concern to the parent, the physician may seek assessment of school performance, gather data about behavior at home, and meet with the child's parents and teachers in addition to examining the child in the office. A patient referred for marital problems may need to be interviewed with her spouse. A patient who complains of chest pain may require laboratory studies to evaluate for a possible myocardial infarction.

The Six Steps of the Clinical Decision-Making Process

1. **Defining the problem** – clarifying the specific nature of the problem, including an appreciation of the patient's cognitive context (i.e., beliefs, assumptions, expectations).
2. **Defining outcome goals** – defining the desired resolution of the problem in attainable terms.
3. **Generating alternative solutions** – possible alternative solutions to resolve the problem.
4. **Selecting the best solution** – conducting a "cost-benefit" analysis based on the merits of each alternative solution (probable consequences; good vs. adverse effects; approximation to desired outcome), developing a strategic plan for the implementation of each solution (how much will it "cost" in time, money, energy), and then choosing the solution not only most likely to produce health but also most likely to be followed.
5. **Implementing the solution** – carrying out the plan.
6. **Evaluating the outcome** – determining if the goal was achieved and the problem solved. If not, reformulating the plan to reach a desirable end. Sometimes, as in chronic illness, the patient must redefine "health" to reach an accessible end point.

Defining the Problem

Defining the patient's problem requires two kinds of data, which are collected during the initial medical encounter: **subjective data,** such as the description and chronology of symptoms; and **objective data,** such as observations made by the examiner during the interview and physical examination.

The History

What is included in the comprehensive medical history?

A comprehensive medical history includes:

1. *Identifying data:* name, age, gender, occupation, and a brief statement of the major presenting problem in one or two sentences.
2. *Reliability* of the source of data: patient, family member, chart records, letter of referral.
3. *Chief complaint:* the reason for seeking care in the patient's exact words.
4. *History of the present illness:* a narrative account of each current problem including its beginning, course, diagnosis, management, family incidence, and risk factors. What is the patient's explanation for the problem and how has it affected his/her life? ("I salt my food too much." "Diabetes runs in my family.") Each symptom should be described in multiple dimensions: timing or chronology, quality or character, quantity or severity, location, setting in which it occurs, aggravating and alleviating symptoms, and associated manifestations.
5. *Past medical history:* medical, surgical, obstetrical, and psychiatric problems that are not currently active, including injuries and hospitalizations.
6. *Current health status and habits:* information regarding prescription, conventional over-the-counter, and herbal or supplemental medications, allergies, habits (including use of all kinds of tobacco, alcohol, "recreational drugs"), environmental exposures, travel, diet, immunizations, exercise, and health maintenance and prevention.
7. *Family history:* a narrative and genogram of the family, including details about as many generations as possible, with dates of birth and death, causes of death, and illnesses. Specific inquiry should be made

about the occurrence of any diseases that are similar to that presented by the patient or any disease known to be a risk factor for the patient's probable disorder (e.g., breast cancer in the mother of a woman with a lump in her breast).

8. *Social history:* a biographical sketch of the patient's birthplace, parents, education, places of residence, work, marital status and relationships, children, leisure activities, hobbies, satisfactions, and stresses.
9. *Review of systems:* a standard set of questions about common symptoms associated with each organ system that help to disclose any disease not yet discussed. Any data about a significant problem should be included as an additional problem in the present illness. The review of systems is usually the last part of the interview, although some physicians integrate it into the physical examination.

Mental Status Examination

What is the Mental Status Examination?

The **Mental Status Examination (MSE)** bridges the history and the physical examination. It begins with observation at the beginning of the encounter, continues with assessment throughout the interview, and concludes with a more formal evaluation of the cognitive status of the patient. The formal evaluation of mental status includes assessment of level of consciousness; attention; memory (short- and long-term); orientation to time, place and person; thought processes; thought content, insight and judgment; affect; mood; language; vocabulary; fund of knowledge; and ability to abstract, calculate, and copy (see Chapter 38, Introduction to Psychopathology).

The Physical Examination

The physical examination elicits **signs** (observable objective data) indicative of disease. Signs primarily confirm hypotheses that have been generated during the interview process. The physical examination, like the history, may be complete or focused. When a patient has **symptoms** (subjective complaints) that are limited to a specific region or organ system, the examiner may decide to limit the examination to that area. The risk is that a significant finding will be undetected (e.g., a heart murmur in a child with acute rheumatic fever but who presents complaining only of a limp). Physical alterations can occur over the natural course of a disease, and can be detected by **observation, palpation, percussion,** or **auscultation.**

Generally, a complete physical examination is conducted by region, starting with the head and neck and concluding with the extremities. The recording of the findings should begin with a descriptive general statement followed by a listing of the vital signs. The remainder of the data should be recorded under the following categories: skin, head, eyes, ears, nose, mouth and pharynx, neck, lymph nodes, thorax and lungs, cardiovascular system, breasts, abdomen, genitalia, rectum, peripheral vascular system, musculoskeletal system, and neurological system.

Laboratory Investigation

Under most circumstances, any necessary laboratory studies are ordered after data from the history and physical examination have been collected and an initial **differential diagnosis** (list of diagnostic possibilities with their relative probabilities) has been generated. Diagnostic laboratory studies are likely to be most helpful when the probability of a particular disease is in the intermediate range, although some diagnostic tests are obtained to confirm a highly likely diagnosis. Tests should be ordered based on **predictive value** (likelihood of providing diagnostic help) as well as **cost benefit.** It is poor medical practice to order tests automatically or to order an entire panel of tests merely because they can be processed simultaneously.

Defining the Problem

The **problem list** serves as an organizing point for clinical problem solving. The list is a compilation of all the symptoms, signs, problems, and issues (e.g., family incidence of breast cancer) of concern. As the list is developed, symptoms and signs may cluster under a single diagnosis, hypotheses become better defined, and certain problems may be eliminated as new data are acquired.

Clinical Application – Part I

A 41-year-old female engineer who has had increasingly severe migraine headaches for which no physiologic basis can be determined is referred to the Behavioral Medicine Clinic by a neurologist. History and physical examination reveal no past or current medical problems aside from the migraine headaches. Further questioning reveals that the patient experiences headaches most frequently in the mid-morning hours, Monday through Friday, and occasionally in the evenings. Personal and social history reveals the patient is married to another engineer, a "Type A workaholic." They both leave for work at 6 AM and return home at 6 PM, at which time the patient prepares dinner. After dinner, they prepare construction materials for two cabins they are building on weekends. The patient reports no personal time, no recreational activities, and feeling pressured to work as hard as her husband. Her job as a middle manager in a large firm requires her to manage contract negotiations between the company and government agencies. Her office is in a large manufacturing plant, with continuous exposure to production noises (e.g., metal saws, riveting), dust, and debris. The initial referral hypothesis, that her headache problem may be stress-related, is supported by: (1) she is working in a physically stressful work environment; (2) she is working in a psychologically stressful work environment; (3) her home environment is stressful; and (4) she has no private/personal time or recreation.

Tentative hypotheses generated by the referral question are tested and refined in light of the information obtained from history taking and physical examination. These, in turn, are subjected to verification through the selection of appropriate tests. The physician should be knowledgeable about the validity and reliability of each potential test to ensure that the selected test measures what needs to be measured, and does so in a consistent, accurate, reproducible, and conceptually meaningful way. (See Epidemiology and Biostatistics, Appendix A)

Defining Outcome Goals

Initial diagnostic impressions or hypotheses based on referral questions, history, and examination may rule out some diagnoses but raise questions about others. Further data gathering will produce a limited set of problems and diagnoses. At this point, the physician and patient must carefully weigh realistic and attainable **outcome goals** – what is the patient's desired health condition at the conclusion of successful treatment? Once these goals have been negotiated and agreed to, the physician and patient, again in collaboration, generate alternative solutions to these problems in the form of various treatment modalities.

> ### Clinical Application – Part II
>
> Outcome goals for the patient's defined problems were discussed and agreed to as follows: (1) reduce work environment stress; (2) reduce work-related psychological stress; (3) reduce stress at home; and (4) increase personal/private time and recreation.

Generating Alternative Treatment Solutions

> What four intervention strategies are key to developing an optimal treatment plan?

Given the symptom complaints and diagnosis, what solutions or **intervention strategies** can the patient use to remediate the problems and achieve the outcome goals? Here, the decision-making process focuses on how to (1) modify behavior or

> ### Clinical Application – Part III
>
> The physician and patient together decided on the following solutions for each of the patient's outcome goals: (1) develop a scenario for requesting enclosed sound-and-dust-proof office space; (2) develop a scenario for requesting staff support to cope with government contracts; (3) meet with the patient and her husband to discuss reducing stress at home by limiting the number of evenings devoted to cabin preparation work, and planning one "no work" weekend a month for getting away together; and (4) assist the patient in arranging to attend aerobics class after work two nights a week, and allowing sufficient time for a relaxing bath before bedtime.

cognitions, (2) alter biologic functioning, (3) facilitate changes in the environment, and (4) tap social resources. This stage of the decision-making process is critical to eventual treatment outcome. The physician's training and experience, command of a wide repertoire of treatment alternatives, intellect, capacity for deductive reasoning, and pragmatic creativity are brought to bear on helping the patient find cost-effective solutions to the various problems inherent in her situation.

Selecting the Best Solution

In developing the treatment plan, the physician must review the defined problems with the patient and determine with her not only the **best methods** for resolving these problems but also the order of **priority** in which various problems should be addressed. Thus, the decision process involves deciding what to do and in what sequence.

> ### Clinical Application – Part IV
>
> The patient decided the home situation was the most critical. Hence, she made the implementation of solutions 3 and 4 top priority. She further decided that because solutions 1 and 2 would require time to develop, prepare, and rehearse, she would give some thought to how to approach her supervisor and plan to do so in about a month.

Implementing the Solution

The treatment plan, thus formulated, is ready to be implemented. The various steps should unfold in

> ### Clinical Application – Part V
>
> The patient's husband initially failed to see the link between his own behavior and his wife's medical condition. Once aware, however, he became alarmed, concerned, and highly cooperative. He was supportive of her having more personal recreation time and opportunities for relaxation. Both goals 3 and 4 were implemented immediately.

logical sequence (i.e., each step setting the stage for the next step). The strategy is to have the treatment course build to a final resolution of the patient's problem.

Evaluating the Outcome

The decision about whether treatment has been successful and the outcome goal achieved will be determined by the selection and assessment of appropriate **outcome criteria.** Optimally, outcome criteria should be observable and quantifiable (e.g., symptom reduction, measurable changes in biologic function, behavior, or cognition). However, qualitative assessments are also legitimate (e.g., assessing changes in quality of life or the perceived intensity of pain). Successful outcome, including the resolution of the original problems and the termination of treatment, are the final goals. However, if assessment reveals that treatment has not been fully successful, the treatment plan must be modified by selecting alternative solutions or changing the strategy. The revised solutions are then implemented and the outcome assessed. This **"back to the drawing board"** process continues until the treatment goals are attained.

Clinical Application – Part VI

Both goals 3 and 4 were achieved for the patient who went to her aerobics class two days a week and took a relaxing bath before bedtime each evening. The couple rediscovered their love of walking and bicycling on their monthly weekend holiday. The patient's husband was also helpful in formulating strategies and scenarios for requesting changes in his wife's work situation. Her requests for changes (solutions 1 and 2) were responded to favorably by the company, resulting in a more quiet office, and a part-time assistant to help with contract negotiations. The intensity and frequency of the patient's headaches began to decrease almost immediately, and within 8 weeks after the initial referral she was experiencing only occasional minor headaches.

Sources of Error in Clinical Decision Making

What are eight sources of error in clinical decision making?

Sources of Error in the Clinical Decision-Making Process

1. **The physician's theoretical and personal biases:** physicians interpret medical information in accordance with personal and theoretical orientations that can distort clinical data. The traditional biomedical model biases physicians' judgments toward (1) reduction of clinical phenomena to anatomic structure and biologic function; and (2) mind-body dualism, which draws a distinction between the physical and the nonphysical, the observable and the subjective, the material and the spiritual, and the "medical" and the "psychiatric." Thinking, emotions, attitudes, values, and sociocultural influences should not be viewed as distinct from "medical" phenomena such as tissue trauma, organ malfunction, biochemical reactions, and neurotransmission.

2. **Diagnosis by formula:** trying to fit patients into preconceived categories.

3. **Optimism/pessimism:** the physician's desire to seek the best for the patient may result in explaining problems and their treatment too optimistically. Conversely, fearing litigation, physicians may over emphasize the worst case scenario.

4. **Too many hypotheses:** only a limited number of hypotheses can be adequately examined simultaneously. Thus, the physician should systematically rule out the most improbable hypotheses as soon as possible.

5. **Oversimplification:** the physician may assume that all the patient requires is a simple explanation and treatment plan, when, in fact, the patient's concerns are more complex, emotionally based, and resistant to intervention.

6. **Reorganizing the abnormal:** the physician should avoid making personal judgments about the "normal limits" of test values, the behaviors or beliefs of patients from different sociocultural backgrounds, or patients with an unusual genetic history.

7. **Physician-patient interactions:** dislike, distrust, and disdain can breed distortion and defective deci-

sions. Patients who question the physician are sometimes labeled as "crocks," or uneducated. Such attitudes and labels do not promote objective clinical judgment.

8. **Mistaking correlation for causation:** clinical phenomena are rarely straightforward, linear, cause-and-effect processes. Instead, patients live within complex interactive systems.

Participatory Decision Making

Patients who participate in the decisions regarding their care are more likely to adhere to the treatment plan. Successful **participatory decision making** requires that the patient be fully informed about the clinical findings (i.e., the nature of their condition), the treatment options available, and the efficacy and risks associated with each option.

Methods for clearly communicating clinical evidence to the patient include the following:

1. present options for how the patient may participate in the decision-making process;
2. present options for how clinical detail is presented to the patient;
3. state information regarding clinical procedures in terms of absolute risk since relative risk-reduction statements may be confusing and misleading;
4. carefully weigh the order in which information is presented;
5. carefully present the time frame of treatment outcome; and
6. in presenting outcome rates, use proportions rather than percentages, especially with less educated or older patients.

Effective participatory decision making inevitably depends upon the physician's interpretation and presentation of the effectiveness of available treatments. How the information is interpreted will be influenced by:

1. patient knowledge, fears, and prioritized treatment goals. It is imperative that the physician be familiar with the patient's level of knowledge, concerns, and treatment goals, and be prepared to inform and advise the patient where necessary
2. physician knowledge, resources, biases. The physician should insure that his/her knowledge

base is up to date, resources are indeed available, and that personal biases are openly discussed and fairly presented

3. external resources, accessibility to facilities, limitations in time and practice. The physician should insure in advance that external resources and facilities are available, and that practice constraints and demands will not impede patient care.

Recommended Reading

Aberegg SK, Terry PB. Medical decision-making and healthcare disparities: The physician's role. *Journal of Laboratory and Clinical Medicine* 2004; 144: 11–17.

Epstein RM, Alper BS, Quill TE. Communicating evidence for participatory decision making. *JAMA* 2004; 291:2359–2366.

Ghosh AK. On the challenges of using evidence-based information: The role of clinical uncertainty. *Journal of Laboratory and Clinical Medicine* 2004; 144:60–64.

Jongsma AL, Peterson LM. *The Complete Adult Psychotherapy Treatment Planner.* (2nd ed.). New York: John Wiley & Sons; 1999.

Nezu CM, Nezu AM. Clinical decision making in everyday practice: The science in the art. *Cognitive and Behavioral Practice* 1995; 2:5–25.

Review Questions

1. Which of the following pieces of information belongs in the social history?
   A. The patient had his appendix removed.
   B. The patient is allergic to penicillin.
   C. The patient takes calcium supplements.
   D. The patient is a high school teacher.
   E. The patient's mother had breast cancer.

2. Which of these steps comes first in the clinical decision-making process?
   A. Acting on the proposed solution
   B. Defining outcome goals
   C. Defining the problem
   D. Evaluating the outcome
   E. Selecting the best solution

3. An assessment of the patient's attention, memory, orientation, and judgment is part of the
    A. examination of the head
    B. mental status examination
    C. past medical history
    D. review of systems
    E. social history

4. The differential diagnosis is a list of
    A. all the patient's active and inactive medical problems
    B. diagnostic possibilities and their probabilities
    C. diagnostic tests to be ordered
    D. reasons the patient is being seen at this visit
    E. symptoms that have been present for at least one month

5. Encouraging patients to participate in the clinical decision-making process
    A. complicates and impedes the treatment course
    B. decreases patient confidence in physician competence
    C. increases patient adherence to treatment regimens
    D. increases the risk of poor outcomes and litigation
    E. raises ethical issues with regard to clinical responsibility

Key to review questions: p. 393

37 Changing Risk Behavior

- Why is changing patient behavior an effective treatment strategy?
- Why is giving information and advice not always an effective treatment strategy?
- What is a patient's "decision balance"?
- What is the "stages of change" model?
- What are the five key principles of motivational interviewing?
- Why is self-efficacy essential to motivating behavioral change?

Why is changing patient behavior an effective treatment strategy?

The empirical evidence linking patient behavior to almost 50% of the causes of preventable death is now well established (see Table 37.1.). Therefore, changing patient behavior from high risk health threatening behavior to health promoting behavior has become the most important and effective intervention strategy in health care.

Table 37.1. Deaths by cause in 2000 ▲

Tobacco	435,000	(18.1%)
Poor diet & physical inactivity	400,000	(16.6%)
Alcohol consumption	85,000	(3.5%)
Microbial agents	75,000	(3.1%)
Toxic agents	55,000	(2.3%)
Motor vehicle	43,000	(1.8%)
Firearms	29,000	(1.2%)
Sexual behavior	20,000	(0.8%)
Illicit drug use	17,000	(0.7%)
Total	1,159,000	(48.2%)

▲Adapted from: Mokdad AH, Marks JS, Stroup, DF, et al. Actual causes of death in the United States, 2000. *JAMA* 2004; 291:1238-1245.

Why is giving information and advice not always an effective treatment strategy?

In attempting to change patient risk behaviors, practitioners often invoke evidence-based treatments but encounter wide discrepancies between the realities of clinical practice (time constraints; expertise) and optimal research-based outcomes. Clinical research typically quantifies the impact of behavioral interventions on populations (what proportion of the population can be expected to benefit from a standard intervention applied to all patients?) but does not provide guidance on how to individualize treatments for each patient. As a result, given practice and experiential constraints, practitioners typically rely on their traditional "teaching" role by simply giving information and advice to patients who must then pursue the interventions on their own. However, this approach is effective only with that minority of patients who are open to and ready to change their behavior. The vast majority of patients will receive the physician's rational recommendation for treatment but may not be ready for or open to change.

"I should change but …" is a universal human response. Failed New Year's resolutions (e.g., quit smoking) are a good example of such unfulfilled "good intentions." The short-term rewards (reinforcement) of unhealthy habits (e.g., smoking to relax) too often outweigh the long-term and distant benefits of behavior change (e.g., avoiding preventable diseases and living longer). Thus, in order to successfully initiate behavior change, the physician must adopt a motivational role and assist the patient in:

1. becoming aware of, and changing distorted perceptions (minimizing risks and maximizing benefits of risk behaviors);
2. understanding and lowering resistance to change, enhancing motivation, reducing reinforcers for risk behaviors; and
3. recognizing and addressing discrepancies in values (e.g., valuing health but not changing risk behaviors).

Changing Professional Role

In the motivational role, the practitioner helps patients become the researcher and initiator of their own behavior change, with the practitioner as a collaborator or co-investigator in the change process. Practitioners help patients decide for themselves if they want to change their perceptions and values about behavior change. Instead of conducting a question and answer, information-giving interview, they engage patients in dialogues to assist them in defining their ambivalence about change, considering the barriers, weighing the pros and cons, and developing individualized interventions that meet the patient's changing needs over time.

What is a patient's "decision balance"?

Clinical Application – Part I

Mrs. S., a 45-year-old woman, went to her family physician, Dr. M., for a follow-up to her HIV test. Two years ago, she remarried after being divorced for many years. She had recently moved back to her home town after her husband broke his parole and was returned to jail. Mr. and Mrs. S. had regularly attended an HIV clinic because Mr. S. was HIV positive. Even though Mrs. S. knew how to put a condom on her husband, he did not want to wear one. Fortunately, she remained HIV negative even without practicing safe sex. The doctor at the HIV clinic had advised Mrs. S. to have an HIV test done every three months. Dr. M. ordered the HIV test and asked her if she would be willing to fill out a decision balance in order to better understand why she did not want to use condoms. She agreed.

Assessing resistance and motivation
When Dr. M. reentered the room, he read what Mrs. S. had written and pointed to the left-hand column. He asked her to use a scale from 0 to 10 (0 = not important and 10 = very important) to rate her reasons for not using condoms. Mrs. S. gave a resistance score of 9. Dr. M. then asked to rate her reasons for using them. She gave a motivation score of 4.

Assessing thoughts and feelings about change
Dr. M. asked her whether her scores were based on her feelings or her thoughts. Mrs. S. stated that her scores

Mrs. S's Decision Balance About Condom Use*

Reasons not to use condoms	Reasons to use condoms
1. Benefits of not using condoms – Not make him feel he is failing at being sexually competent – He feels secure that I'll stay with him	**2. Concerns about not using condoms** – Don't want HIV – Don't want my family hurt – Maybe people will think he doesn't care to protect me
3. Concerns about using condoms – He will have erection problems and it will make him sad – He will wish he were with his ex-girlfriend (who is HIV positive) so he won't have to use them	**4. Benefits of using condoms** – Won't get HIV so won't upset family – Won't get sick myself so I can take care of him when he gets sicker – Will feel that he cares enough about me and will not allow me to get sick
Resistance score = 9 Feeling score = 9 Thinking score = 6	Motivation score = 4 Feeling score = 4 Thinking score = 8

were based on her feelings. In other words, she was an "emotional decision maker" on the issue of condom use; her scores represented how she felt about change, rather than what she thought about it. Dr. M. then asked her to rate her overall reasons to stay the same versus her reasons to change based on what she thought. Mrs. S. gave a score of 6 for her cognitive resistance and a score of 8 for her cognitive motivation. This process helped her to better understand how much her heart ruled her head in making decisions. Emotionally, she felt that she should stay the same, but rationally she thought she should protect herself.

Understanding her emotions and values
Looking over her decision balance again, Dr. M. reflected back to Mrs. S. that she must really love her husband. Mrs. S. smiled in total agreement and expressed devotion to her husband, stating that she wanted to care for him when he gets terminally ill. Dr. M. asked her how she valued her relationship with her husband in comparison to herself and the relationship with her own family. Mrs. S. loved her husband so much that she was willing to sacrifice her life for him, but admitted to having mixed feelings when thinking about her children.

Differing Perspectives on Risk/Benefits

Understanding the patient's beliefs and perceptions in contrast to the physician's perspective is to successfully address the barriers to the patient's behaviour change. Typically, the patient maximizes the benefits of the risk behavior and minimizes its risk while the practitioner will tend to minimize the benefits of the risk behavior and maximize its risk (see Figures 37.1. and 37.2.). Figure 37.3.

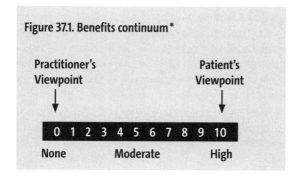

Figure 37.1. Benefits continuum*

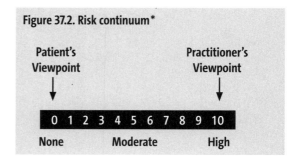

Figure 37.2. Risk continuum*

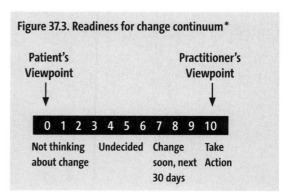

Figure 37.3. Readiness for change continuum*

illustrates the mismatch between practitioner and patient and how the discrepency can serve as a barrier to behavioral change on the part of the patient.

What is the "stages of change" model?

Stages of Change Model

Patients are thought to progress through **five stages** in preparing to make a behavioral change: precontemplation, contemplation, preparation, action and maintenance. A patient's **decision balance** provides a way to understand the pros (motivation) and cons (resistance) that affect patients' readiness to change as they move through the change process. Patients perceive or assess the pros and cons differently at each stage of change.

In the **precontemplation stage**, the cons outweigh the pros. Some precontemplators may be largely unaware of the risks (heart disease) of a particular behavior (smoking) or may minimize the pros for change and maximize the cons against change. Other precontemplators, such as some die-hard smokers, are fully aware of the risks but totally disregard them.

Stages of Change Model

- **Precontemplation:** has no intention of changing within the next six months
- **Contemplation:** intends to make change within the next six months
- **Preparation:** intends to change within the next 30 days
- **Action:** has changed for <6 months
- **Maintenance:** has changed for >6 months

The pros and cons equalize in the **contemplation stage**. Patients become ambivalent because their reasons to change (pros) and their reasons to stay the same (cons) are equally compelling. While they are concerned about their health, chronic contemplators may think about changing a lifestyle behavior for many years before taking action. In the **preparation stage**, patients perceive the reasons to change (pros) as outweighing the reasons to stay the same (cons). They will set a date to change in the near future (within a month or so).

In the **action stage**, patients do something to achieve their goal. These goals may range from making short-term, incremental changes (lose 4–6 pounds in one month) to adopting long term, ideal recommendations (reduce to ideal body weight in one year). Patients move into the **maintenance stage** when they have achieved their goal for six months or more. A *lapse* at this stage is a temporary setback, such as smoking a couple of cigarettes over a few days, whereas a *relapse* is complete reversion to a previous pattern of behavior, such as smoking a pack of cigarettes daily. When patients relapse, they need to restart the process of change.

Clinical Application – Part II

The **stages of change model** is a useful, cognitive framework for understanding the differences in the intentions between the practitioner and patient. Mrs. S was cognitively in favor of change and emotionally against it. The practitioner did not fall into the trap of getting ahead of the patient, in terms of readiness to change. He did not follow her cognitive inclination but responded to the emotional factors that were holding Mrs. S from protecting herself. However, a shortcoming of this model is that it does not explicitly address the barriers to change and the patient's resulting ambivalence.

Motivational Interviewing

What are the five key principles of motivational interviewing?

Miller and Rollnick developed an intervention strategy called **motivational interviewing** to help patients work through their ambivalence about behaviour change. Motivation is not regarded as an individual trait that is difficult to change but as a state that is changeable, a product of the patient-practitioner interaction and therefore influenced by the practitioner's interviewing style. Practitioner confrontation can increase patient resistance whereas an empathic, non-confrontational stance can help to reduce patient resistance. Practitioners use five basic strategies for enhancing the patient's motivation and commitment to change:

1. Expressing empathy through listening rather than telling
2. Identifying the discrepancy between where the patient is now (i.e., risk behavior) and where he or she wants to be
3. Avoiding argumentation (i.e, trying to convince patients by force of argument)
4. Rolling with resistance rather than challenging patient resistance head-on

Table 37.2. Strategies for motivation enhancement

A. Build motivation for change
1. Ask open-ended questions
2. Listen reflectively
3. Affirm the patient
4. Summarize
5. Present personal feedback
6. Handle resistance
7. Reframe statement
8. Elicit self-motivational statements

B. Strengthen commitment to change
1. Recognize readiness for change
2. Discuss a plan
3. Communicate free choice
4. Discuss consequences of action/inaction
5. Give information and advice
6. Deal with resistance
7. Make a plan

5. Supporting self-efficacy, instilling hope and encouraging patients' belief that they can change

Motivational interviewing is divided into two major phases: **building motivation to change** and **strengthening commitment to change** (see Table 37.2.). Practitioners can use motivational enhancement strategies to help resistant and ambivalent patients become more receptive to the possibility of change and then deploy strategies to strengthen their commitment to change. After patients have changed, practitioners use relapse prevention strategies to help maintain change.

Clinical Application – Part III

The practitioner adopted a nonconfrontational stance in his interaction with Mrs. S. He empathized with her decision-making process, even though he did not agree with her decision. Rather than confronting her, he "rolled" with her resistance and began to explore her ambivalence about change, based on how she *felt* about not using condoms and what she *thought* about using them.

Understanding Self-Efficacy and Outcome Expectancies

Why is self-efficacy essential to motivating behavioral change?

Self-efficacy is a person's expression of confidence that he or she is capable of achieving a behavioral goal. For patients with low self-efficacy, practitioners will have to explicitly boost their confidence and ability to change

Outcome expectancy is distinct from self-efficacy in that it reflects the individual's belief that a given behavior (e.g., a low-calorie diabetic diet and physical exercise) will produce a particular outcome (e.g., normal glucose levels and weight reduction for diabetics). Patients may have high self-efficacy about sticking to a low-calorie diabetic diet and exercise program but doubt that these lifestyle changes will produce the desired change (40-pound weight loss and normalized blood glucose levels). Therefore, even with high self-effica-

---

Clinical Appliation – Part IV

Self-efficacy is an important predictor of behavior change. Mrs. S. knew how to use condoms. She believed that condoms would protect her from getting HIV from her husband. Her reasons for not using condoms reflect her insecurity and low self-efficacy as manifested by fear of losing her husband if she uses them.

---

cy, a patient with a low outcome expectancy may not bother making lifestyle changes.

Understanding Motives

Patients have a blend of motives that can vary in response to differing circumstances. The theory of self-determination describes four categories of motives:

- *Indifferent motives – "I don't care if I live or die."* Indifference may be due to factors such as: stress, depression, environmental and social barriers.
- *External (controlled) motives – "I'm only changing because my family wants me to."* A patient may only comply because he does not want to upset his wife or doctor. Relapse may occur when external reinforcement is absent or insufficient to maintain the behavior desired by others.
- *Introjected (controlled) motives – "I ought to quit smoking."* Individuals act out of a sense that they should change their behavior. Outwardly, they appear to have autonomous motives (see below), but inside they feel conflicted because of ambivalence. They initiate and maintain change by internally prompting themselves. Relapse may occur in the absence of such internal reinforcement.
- *Integrated (autonomous) motives – "I love to exercise. It makes me feel great."* With autonomous motives, individuals experience a true sense of volition about their behavioral choice. The initiation and maintenance of behavior change is self-regulated and driven by the patient's values and freely chosen motives, as opposed to being influenced by others.

Patients' motives are more likely to change for autonomous reasons than for controlled reasons. If practitioners act in autonomy-supportive ways ("It's up to you whether you change, but I can help you improve your health if you like."), patients are more likely to develop autonomous motives for change. Conversely, if practitioners act in controlling ways, they are more likely to stifle patients' sense of autonomy and generate indifference or resistance. Paternalism ("I'm the expert so you should follow my advice") can make patients feel pressured and resentful and resistant to change.

Clinical Application – Part V

Mrs. S. was not indifferent about the prospects of getting HIV. She did not want to get AIDS. She did not use condoms because her husband did not want her to. She felt conflicted because she knew that her children would disapprove of what she was doing. She did not tell her children about this situation. Mrs. S. lacked self-esteem and she valued others (particularly her husband) far more than she did herself. Her decision was influenced much more by her husband's value system than her value of her health. Her external motives were more powerful than her introjected and integrated motives.

Managing Competing Priorities

Competing priorities can reduce the time and energy patients can put into the change process. Life circumstances and challenges can make it difficult for patients to change their risk behaviors. A psychosocial assessment can help practitioners

---

Clinical Application – Part VI

Mrs. S. came from an abusive family. She suffered from chronic low self-esteem. As an adult, she became an alcoholic and raised her children with her first husband. She divorced, recovered from her alcoholism without formal treatment and remarried. Mrs. S. has felt overwhelmed most of her life and had chronic anxiety and recurrent bouts of depression. She cares for her husband and is willing to help him until his death from AIDS. She has little time and energy left to address her needs.

---

understand the challenges that some patients face in managing their health issues. A willingness to assist the patient in addressing competing life stresses is essential.

Using Motivational Principles

In facilitating behavior change, practitioners should use the motivational principles outlined in Table 37.3. These principles enable the practitioner to engage patients in change dialogues that

---

Table 37.3. Motivational principles*

A. **Support and respect autonomy**
- Invite participation
- Gain consent
- Be nonjudgmental
- Offer choice

B. **Understand patients' perspective**
- Develop empathic relationships
- Clarify roles and responsibilities
- Clarify patients' issues about change
- Work at a pace sensitive to patients' needs
- Understand patients' perceptions, motives and values

C. **Adopt a positive, non-directive stance**
- Focus on strengths rather than weaknesses
- Focus on health rather than pathology
- Focus on solutions rather than problems
- Provide constructive feedback
- Help patients believe in healthy outcomes
- Encourage patients to do emotional work

D. **Elicit patients' problem-solving skills**
- Enhance patients' confidence and ability
- Increase supports and reduce barriers
- Negotiate reasonable goals for change
- Develop plans to prevent relapses
- Use "failures" as learning opportunities

E. **Maintain long-term engagement**
- Maintain a learning partnership
- Monitor resistance and motivation
- Negotiate frequency of follow-up
- Adjust goals to changing circumstances

can guide development of individualized interventions. Practitioners should use a blend of patient-centered learning methods that accommodate individual preferences.

Recommended Readings

Miller W, Rollnick S, Conforti K. *Motivational Interviewing: Preparing People for Change.* (2nd ed.). New York: Guilford Press; 2002.

World Health Organization. Noncommunicable Diseases and Mental Health. In: *Innovative Care for Chronic Conditions: Building Blocks for Action.* Geneva: World Health Organization; 2002.

Rollnick S, Mason P, Butler C. *Health Behavior Change: A Guide for Practitioners.* London: Churchill Livingston; 2002.

World Health Organization. *Preventing Chronic Diseases: A Vital Investment.* Geneva: World Health Organization; 2005.

Additional Resources

Botelho R. *Motivate Healthy Habits: Stepping Stones to Lasting Change.* Rochester, NY: MHH Publications; 2003.

Botelho R. *Motivational Practice: Promoting Healthy Habits and Self Care for Chronic Diseases.* (2nd ed.). Rochester, NY: MHH Publications; 2004.

www.motivatehealthyhabits.com for more information about these books and an online video demonstration.

Review Questions

Directions: The items below consist of lettered headings followed by numbered descriptions. For each numbered description choose the *one* lettered heading to which it is *most* closely associated. Each lettered heading may be used *once, more than once,* or *not at all*.

Match the scenario with the stage of change
A. Precontemplation
B. Contemplation
C. Action
D. Maintenance
E. Relapse

1. A 43-year-old man who smokes a pack of cigarettes per day tells you that his 80-year-old father has smoked for almost 65 years.
2. A 28-year-old woman who was arrested for DWI has not had a drink in more than a year.
3. A 35-year-old man checks himself into a day detoxification program.
4. A 47-year-old woman who weighs 275 lbs has lost 10 lbs in the past 2 months.

Key to review questions: p. 393

---

* Reproduced with permission. Rick_Botelho@urmc.rochester.edu

Learning Exercise Using a Decision Balance

Draw a copy of the decision balance (below). Allow up to 15 minutes for an interview.
- Identify a smoker who does not want to quit smoking but is willing to share with practitioners why he/she wants to smoke. Do not provide any quit-smoking information and/or advice.
- Interview the patient by asking these four questions and record the patient's responses.

Reasons to smoke	Reasons to quit
1. What are the benefits of smoking?	2. What concerns do you have about smoking?
3. What concerns would you have about quitting?	4. What are the benefits of quitting?
Overall score for reasons to smoke = Feeling score = Thinking score =	**Overall score for reasons to quit =** Feeling score = Thinking score =

Assessing Patient's Resistance and Motivation to Change

"The left column of your decision balance represents your reasons to smoke. The right column represents your reasons to quit. On a scale of 0–10, 0 meaning none and 10 meaning very high, what score would you give for your reasons to smoke? [Let the patient respond.] And what score would you give for your reasons to quit?
- Are your resistance and motivation scores based on what you think, or how you feel about change? Or a combination of both?
- What score would you give for your reasons to smoke, based what you think and how you feel?
- What score would you give for your reasons to quit, based what you think and how you feel?
    Some patients take time to understand the differences between what they think and how they feel about change." [Give the decision balance back to the patient to reflect more about his/her health decisions.]

Section IX

Psychopathology

38 Introduction to Psychopathology

- How does the behavioral system relate to other organ systems?
- What are the five axes of the multiaxial diagnostic system?
- What are the five categories of etiological factors in psychopathology?
- Which histories are required to make an accurate diagnosis?
- What are the components of the Mental Status Examination?
- What are three indications for psychological testing in clinical evaluation?

How does the behavioral system relate to other organ systems?

The study of pathology in medicine is organized according to **organ systems** (e.g., cardiovascular system, gastrointestinal system), defined by anatomical structure and physiological function. The behavioral system has neither an identifiable anatomic structure nor a single physiological function. Rather, it integrates all organ systems and the **complex interaction** among **biological**, **behavioral**, **cognitive**, **sociocultural**, and **environmental variables** that promote the healthy functioning of the organism. Breakdown in this complex interaction or any of the variables contributes to the development of psychopathology.

Because of the complexity of this interaction, the etiology of most psychiatric conditions is still not clearly understood. The various psychiatric disorders are defined as **syndromes** or clinically recognizable patterns of physical, emotional, cognitive, perceptual, or behavioral **symptoms** and **signs** with an identifiable history and response to treatment. Syndromes are named according to their defining features (e.g., major depression,

The American Psychiatric Association *Diagnostic and Statistical Manual of Mental Disorders (DSM)* defines the various psychiatric disorders and gives diagnostic criteria for each.

social phobia) and classified into groups according to their similarities (e.g., mood disorders, anxiety disorders).

Multiaxial Diagnostic System

The (DSM) and the *International Statistical Classification of Diseases and Related Health Problems (ICD)* contain compatible classifications of psychiatric disease. The former is now in its fourth edition, or DSM-IV, which underwent a text revision and now is called DSM-IV-TR. ICD, now in its 10th edition, ICD-10, is the official **World Health Organization** compendium of psychiatric and other medical disease. Most countries use ICD-10 alone for the classification of all disease. The United States and Japan are among the few countries that use compatible or modified classifications for psychiatric disorders. DSM-IV-TR is the official U.S. classification of psychiatric disorders, developed by the American Psychiatric Association, based upon input from practicing clinicians who contributed their direct observations of psychiatric disorders. These clinical findings helped to define the essential components of key criteria for each disorder. Criteria include signs, symptoms, their order of appearance, and duration of the disorder, and guide the diagnostic process. To qualify as diagnostic criteria for a specific psychiatric disorder, signs and symptoms must be sufficiently intense, appear in sufficient numbers, often in a given order, and have specified duration. Thus, diagnosing a psychiatric disorder depends on gathering clinical information and matching it to specifically stated criteria for that disorder. Diagnoses such as schizophrenia, anxiety disorder, mood disorder, and somatization disorder have more predictive value than do diagnoses such as personality disorder or adjustment disorder. The DSM Task Force maintains the status of the manual by periodically revising its content in response to new knowledge.

What are the five axes of the multiaxial diagnostic system?

DSM-IV-TR uses a multidimensional or **multiaxial** diagnostic system.

    Axis I: Clinical disorders. Axis I codes for all psychiatric disorders, except personality disorders and mental retardation, and for conditions that do not meet diagnostic criteria for a mental disorder but that are the focus of clinical attention (e.g., relational problems, abuse and neglect, bereavement).

    Axis II: Codes for personality disorders and mental retardation but can also be used to record maladaptive personality features (e.g., dependent traits).

    Axis III: General medical conditions that lie outside the psychiatric section of ICD (e.g., hyperthyroidism). While they merit a separate but equally weighted dimension to encourage a comprehensive clinical assessment, Axis III conditions may be intimately related to those coded on Axis I (e.g., Axis I: Anxiety Disorder Due to Hyperthyroidism; Axis III: Hyperthyroidism).

    Axis IV: Psychosocial and environmental problems that may affect a patient's diagnosis or care (e.g., homelessness).

    Axis V: Coded on the Global Assessment of Functioning (GAF), a scale that discriminates from 1 (minimum) to 100 (maximum), the individual level of psychosocial, occupational, and academic functioning. For example, 1: serious suicidal act with clear expectation of death; 100: superior functioning.

Etiology

What are the five categories of etiological factors in psychopathology?

Psychopathology is the scientific study of mental disorders, and the factors that influence their onset, course, and treatment. While current theories focus on the role of genetic predisposition and neuroendocrine vulnerability, the Integrated Sciences Model emphasizes the complex interaction among five categories of etiological factors.

Five Categories of Etiologic Factors in Psychopathology

1. Biological
2. Behavioral
3. Cognitive
4. Sociocultural
5. Environmental

Biological Factors

Neuroanatomy, neurochemistry, and the endocrine and immune systems all appear to have roles in mental disorders. Yet there is no well-established evidence of a single discrete neuropathological locus to account for the signs and symptoms found in, for example, schizophrenia, mood disorders, or antisocial personality. Although current best evidence points to disturbances in modulation of neural circuits and **neurotransmitters** in many mental disorders (e.g., dopaminergic system in schizophrenia, norepinephrine and serotonin systems in depression), these remain incomplete explanations. It is established that the **neuroendocrine** and **immune systems** play important roles in determining and mediating the individual's response to stress. That is, evidence has been accumulating that predictable perturbations in endocrine and immune function are associated with mental illness.

    Genetic studies have shown that mental disorders, like many other medical conditions, result *in part* from genetic predisposition. For Huntington's disease, for example, chromosomal studies can identify individuals at risk. However, the answer to, "What is being inherited?" may lie in a molecule, like a malfunctioning enzyme critical to a neurotransmitter system. Yet, candidate genes remain elusive for the majority of mental disorders even those for which inheritance and familial risk have been established (see Chapter 5, Predisposition).

Behavioral Factors

Learned behavioral responses are essential to successful adaptation to the environment and survival. Genetic programming and neuroendocrine factors enable the organism to learn and benefit from interactions with the environment, and to modify coping strategies and create innovative solutions to life challenges. Assessing the effect of maladaptive learning on behavior is critical, e.g., parenting behavior that promotes psychopathology in offspring (see Chapter 7, Stress, Adaptation, and Illness).

Cognitive Factors

How humans sort, interpret and assign meaning to their experience is another factor that influences the onset, course, and treatment of psychiatric disorders. **Cognition,** like behavior, is learned and can be adaptive or maladaptive. Sigmund Freud's psychodynamic theory was one of the first attempts to explain the cognitive process of symptom production. Freud also demonstrated that even cognition occurring outside of awareness influences feeling, thinking, perception, and behavior. Maladaptive cognition may be corrected through **cognitive behavioral therapy,** which has become an important treatment for depression and anxiety disorders. In this form of therapy, patients are taught to recognize inaccurate concepts, beliefs, attitudes, and values that bias their view of themselves, others, and their life experience and to make changes in thinking styles that contribute to psychiatric symptoms (see Chapter 9, Cognition and Emotion).

Sociocultural Factors

Through social learning or **socialization,** individuals in social systems acquire **values** and **norms:** they learn what to think, how to behave, and what is expected of them. When an individual steps outside societal norms (e.g., when socialization fails), **social control** is exercised, both externally (social pressure) and internally (guilt). Thus, as

do biological, behavioral, and cognitive dimensions, the sociocultural dimension contains a balancing mechanism that maintains **sociocultural homeostasis. Deviance** results when individuals do not respond to these processes and remain outside the limits of normally sanctioned standards (see Section V, The Individual and Social Groups).

Environmental Factors

Environmental determinants of psychopathology range from **toxic substances** to complex **ecological factors** that influence the sociocultural milieu, language, cognitive structures, and adaptive experiences of the individual. For example, the language structure, and cognitive, behavioral, and sociocultural systems of Native Alaskans, compared with sub-Saharan tribespeople or urban Europeans, are clearly related to the ecological systems in which they have evolved. Deviance is similarly distinct as it is defined according to its links to the ecological setting. Survival is dependent on adaptation to all etiological factors, and includes the maintenance of **ecological homeostasis.** Thus, psychopathology derives from faulty adaptation to the challenges of survival.

The Psychiatric Evaluation

The **psychiatric evaluation** relies on the systematic gathering of data from the patient, interviews with family members and other collateral sources (e.g., school, medical, military, and legal records and sources), physical, neurological, and mental status examinations, and ancillary tests. Findings from history, mental status, and physical examination will determine the extent and type of ancillary testing (including laboratory, neuroimaging, and psychological tests) required to establish the diagnosis.

Clear documentation is essential for maintaining a current, accurate database and for communicating information about the patient to other health care providers. Although the approach is basically similar to evaluating any illness, the following sections provide a specific framework for gathering, organizing, and documenting data for the psychiatric evaluation.

History Taking

Which histories are required to make an accurate diagnosis?

The History of the Present Illness

It is essential to characterize the **onset, location, duration, intensity,** and **ameliorating** and **aggravating factors** of any clinical finding. Because psychiatric patients may not be fully aware of their symptoms, it is important to obtain information from someone close to the patient who can provide an objective view of the patient's life story. Understanding the **temporal sequence** and **environmental context** of symptom development can be particularly important in psychiatric diagnosis. Consider these two examples: A patient presents with major depression prior to developing delusions and hallucinations. The sequence makes major depression with psychotic features a more likely diagnosis than schizophrenia. Another patient presents with signs and symptoms suggesting major depression, but in the context of the death of a spouse within the last month. This makes bereavement a more likely diagnosis than major depressive disorder. **Context** also helps answer the question: "Why now?" Psychiatric disorders often occur or recur in the face of stressors.

The Patient's "Other" Histories

Taking a careful **general medical history** reduces the risk of missing a physical or substance use disorder when the patient presents with psychiatric signs and symptoms. In the general medical history, one includes previous illnesses, current health status, substance use, use of prescribed, over-the-counter, and herbal medicines, and the review of systems.

Family history aids in diagnosis and treatment because psychiatric conditions often show a pattern of familial aggregation and may respond to medication in similar fashion. A family history of certain behaviors (e.g., poor impulse control, suicidal behavior) may reveal risk factors for certain conditions (e.g., violence and suicide, respectively). Familial relationship can also give

clues to triggers of relapse. For example, in families of schizophrenics, high levels of expressed emotions or in-your-face expressions of negative emotions, especially anger, tend to induce relapse.

The **social and developmental histories** provide information about the family's sociocultural context and the patient's functioning, daily patterns of behavior, social networks, and personality characteristics that existed prior to the illness. This aids in recognizing personality disorders and developmental impairments and in understanding the patient's resources.

It is also necessary to gain an accurate perspective on the following aspects of the patient's personal history: academic performance, working patterns and relationships, religious practices and affiliations, legal troubles, and military service.

Mental Status Examination

What are the components of the Mental Status Examination?

The **Mental Status Examination (MSE)** evaluates the patient's appearance, motor activity, mood and affect, speech and language, thought form and content, perception, capacity for insight and judgment, and cognitive functioning. Although the MSE is reported as a distinct section of the psychiatric evaluation, assessment of the patient's mental state actually begins during the initial contact with the patient.

Appearance

Observations of the patient's general demeanor and attitude, state of health, grooming and dress are included. Clinical examples include the exhausted demeanor and poor grooming of a severely depressed patient, and the odd, eccentric dress of the patient with schizophrenia.

Individuals and cultures vary widely in their baseline level of **motor activity;** it is important to know the patient's baseline to prevent over diagnosing. Observations include activity level, eye contact, gait, abnormal movements (e.g., tremors, tics, dyskinesias, choreoathetoid movements), and use of body language. Clinical examples include the

Mental Status Examination Format

Appearance	Attitude toward the examiner, grooming, appropriateness of dress
Motor behavior	Level of activity, gait, eye contact, body language, abnormal movements
Mood	Patient's subjective emotional state
Affect	Observations of patient's emotional state: range and modulation, consistency with speech, thought and mood.
Speech & language	Rate, prosody, modulation of tone and volume, articulation, spontaneity
Thought content	Amount of thought, themes, abnormal content (e.g., delusions, obsessions, preoccupations, overvalued ideas)
Thought form	Rate of thinking process, flow of ideas, organization of thought
Perception	Nature and quality of perceptual disturbances that occur in any of the five senses
Insight/judgment	Nature and quality of insight and judgment
Cognitive functioning	Level of consciousness, attention, memory, language functions, calculation, praxis, typically using a standardized instrument (Folstein Mini Mental State Examination)
Risk assessment	Ideation, motivation, intention, and planning of suicidal or violent behavior

restlessness and agitation of patients with delirium or mania, and the retarded motor behavior of those with severe depression or dementia.

Mood is a *sustained subjective emotional state as reported by the patient,* such as happiness, sadness, worry, anger, or indifference. **Affect** is more immediate and transitory than mood; it is an *observed emotional state,* typically noted in facial expression. Mood and affect should be consistent with each other and with the content of the patient's thought.

Speech and Language

Speech characteristics to be assessed include amount, rate, tone, volume, fluency, articulation, and spontaneity. Clinical examples include the slow, monotonic answers and lack of spontaneity seen in major depression, contrasted with the loud, rapid, difficult-to-interrupt speech of mania.

Thought Form and Content

Normal thought flows directly from one idea to the next and communicates ideas clearly. Disorders of the linear flow of thought, or thought form, are common in mania, schizophrenia, and dementia and may be present in other mental disorders.

Disorders of thought form include **tangentiality, circumstantiality,** and **derailment** ("loose associations"). Observers will experience the speech or writing of a patient with a disorder in thought form as difficult to follow or frankly impossible to understand. Typically, the patient is unaware of the degree to which communication is failing and disregards feedback about it. Mild forms of disorganized thought are found in normal people, but do not seriously affect communication.

Thought content disorders range from transient preoccupation to intractable delusions. Examples of abnormal thought content include rumination (constant preoccupation with recurrent thoughts as seen in depression and anxiety), obsession (unwanted and distressing concerns, ideas, images, or impulses that repeatedly invade the conscious awareness), phobias (unrealistic, excessive, and persistent fears), and delusions (unshakable false beliefs that persist despite obvious evidence to the contrary and are foreign to the individual's sociocultural or religious background).

Perception

Perceptual disturbances can occur in any of the five sensory modalities. Two major types of perceptual disturbances are illusions and hallucinations. **Illusions** are perceptions that are misinterpreted (e.g., a person feels a tree branch brush his or her arm and thinks it is another person). **Hallucinations** are sensory experiences that occur without external stimulation (e.g., hearing voices when no one else is present).

Executive Functions

Insight is subjective awareness and understanding. **Judgment** is the capacity to organize and manipulate information to make appropriate decisions or display appropriate behavior. Lack of insight is associated with poor judgment. In contrast, the presence of insight does not ensure application of good judgment. Many psychiatric conditions impair both insight and judgment.

Cognitive Functioning

The most often used cognitive function screening tool is the **Folstein Mini Mental State Examination (MMSE).** The MMSE assesses cognition beginning with the **level of consciousness**, or sensorium, followed by, in hierarchical order, the ability to sustain attention and concentration, language, memory, abstraction, calculation, praxis, and other higher functions. Disturbances at lower levels of functioning frequently impair performance at higher levels, even though the higher functions, per se, may be intact (e.g., a person who is delirious may have difficulty naming objects but may not necessarily have aphasia). Psychologists use psychological test batteries to assess cognitive function in more detail (see Table 38.1.).

Risk Assessment

Risk of harm to or by the patient (e.g., **suicide or violence)** should be assessed as part of every complete psychiatric evaluation. Certain conditions such as major depression, psychosis, and intoxication are particularly associated with high-risk behavior. Assessment involves direct questioning about **feelings, attitudes, ideas, motives, plans,** and **intentions** to harm oneself or others. It is also essential to ascertain the **means** and **opportunity** the patient has available and the extent of **planning** (time, place) that the patient has already done. Because past behavior is the best predictor

of future behavior, impulse control and past suicidal or violent behavior must be explored. A **family history** of poor impulse control, suicide, or violence increases the patient's risk of carrying out a violent act (see Chapter 22, Interpersonal Violence, and Chapter 24, Suicide).

Physical and Neurological Examinations

Neurological, endocrine, and toxic-metabolic states (including drug intoxication) are the most frequent conditions that mimic psychiatric disorders.

Laboratory and Other Studies

Laboratory and other special studies are used to substantiate the most likely diagnosis and rule out differential diagnoses. Tests may also uncover conditions that can influence decisions about pharmacological treatment (e.g., renal impairment will contraindicate the use of lithium).

Neuroimaging and **electroencephalography (EEG)** are among the special studies sometimes indicated in psychiatric assessments (see Methods for Evaluating Brain-Behavior Associations in Chapter 3, Brain Structures and Their Functions). Sleep studies, functional neuroimaging (PET, SPECT and fMRI), special body fluid and tissue analyses, and genetic studies are occasionally indicated.

Magnetic resonance imaging (MRI) is the imaging study of choice for most psychiatric evaluations because it is well suited to discovering small masses, vascular abnormalities, and inflammatory or demyelinating processes that may be causing psychiatric-like symptoms.

Psychological Testing

Various psychological tests (see Table 38.1.) measure different aspects of psychological function including emotions, cognition, behaviors, and personality characteristics. Tests are designed to insure that they measure what they purport to measure **(validity)** and that they do so consistently **(reliabil-**

Table 38.1. Psychological tests

Test	General description	Common uses
Intelligence or ability tests – Wechsler Scales (WAIS-III, WISC-III) – Stanford Binet-IV – Kaufman Scales (K-ABC)	A set of standardized tasks tapping a range of cognitive abilities believed to represent "intelligence." Intelligence scales yield an overall intelligence quotient (IQ), as well as component index scores representing major cognitive domains (e.g., verbal, visual, quantitative, sequential reasoning). IQ or index scores are ratios reflecting an individual's performance on an intelligence test compared with others of a similar age. An IQ score of 100 places an individual at the 50th percentile compared with the general population of age peers; the standard deviation is 15.	– Diagnosis and classification of mental retardation and other developmental cognitive disorders – Determination of general cognitive ability to guide treatment planning and disposition – Academic placement and vocational planning – Assessment of cognitive dysfunction due to acquired brain damage/disease (as part of larger neuropsychological battery)
Achievement tests – Wide Range Achievement Test – Woodcock Johnson – Wechsler Individual Achievement Test	Tests of academically based skills and knowledge, e.g., reading, spelling, mathematics, written expression. Scores are typically reported as grade levels and age percentiles.	– Diagnosis of learning disability – Academic placement and vocational planning
Neuropsychological tests – Halstead Reitan Battery – Wechsler Memory Scales – Boston Naming Test – Rey Complex Figure Test – Dementia Rating Scale – Verbal Learning Tests	Standardized tests of memory, language, attention, concentration, spatial abilities, sensory/motor integrity, and frontal-executive functions. Tests may be administered as a fixed battery or tailored to the individual patient and assessment purpose. Scores are typically reported as age percentiles, index scores (similar to IQ scores, with 100 as average and a standard deviation of 15), or impairment index.	– Assessment of cognitive dysfunction due to acquired brain damage or disease for diagnostic, treatment/rehabilitation, or disposition planning – Assessment of developmental cognitive disorders for academic and vocational planning
Objective tests of personality and psychopathology – MMPI-2 – MCMI-II – Beck Depression Inventory – Beck Anxiety Inventory – State-Trait Anxiety – Symptom Checklist-90-R	Objective tests assess emotional states, attitudes, behavioral traits/tendencies, interpersonal relations, motivation, and the presence/severity of psychopathology through a standardized set of questions and response options (e.g., questionnaires with true-false or structured ratings). Self-report tests are subject to response bias (e.g., social desirability, symptom exaggeration, defensiveness). MMPI-2 and MCMI-II include validity scales to determine these test-taking attitudes.	– Assessment of personality structure and presence or severity of psychopathology – Screening for psychopathology (e.g., mood or anxiety disorders) – Assessment of malingering or symptom exaggeration
Projective tests of personality and psychopathology – Rorschach Test – Thematic Apperception Test – Projective Drawings – Sentence Completion	Projective tests use ambiguous, unstructured test stimuli to assess unconscious motives and feelings or response tendencies. This method is based on the *projective hypothesis*, which says that when an individual is forced to impose meaning on an ambiguous stimulus, the response will be the projection or reflection of his or her perceptual style, feelings, thoughts, attitudes, desires, experiences, problem-solving skills, and needs. Subjectivity in interpretation often limits the reliability and validity of projective tests, although many are widely used to develop hypotheses for further exploration using other assessment methods.	– Diagnosis of psychopathology – Assessment of emotional needs, reality testing, thought organization, and attitudes regarding interpersonal relationships

ity). Each test has operating characteristics **(psychometric properties)** defined by features such as specificity, sensitivity and standard measurements of error. Formal psychological tests should be performed and interpreted by licensed psychologists who are familiar with the proper tests to answer specific clinical questions and who are trained in test administration and interpretation.

What are three indications for psychological testing in clinical evaluation?

There are three main indications for psychological testing in clinical psychiatric evaluation.

The first indication is to define/refine a **diagnosis** in cases with ambiguous symptoms. For example, a patient may present with a history of poor school and social performance and findings including odd speech, affect, behavior, and preoccupation with religious ideas that may be delusional in nature. A psychologist may be asked to conduct testing to determine this patient's **level of intellectual functioning** to aid in defining whether findings are more consistent with a diagnosis of mental retardation/developmental disability, personality disorder, or psychosis.

The second indication is to define a **baseline** or compare new testing to a previous assessment. For example, to determine if there has been a measurable impact on cognitive abilities, a psychologist may be asked to conduct neuropsychological testing subsequent to a traumatic head injury and to compare the results to previous testing done in academic settings. In a program of rehabilitation undertaken for this patient, a psychologist may perform testing at set intervals to help determine progress in meeting goals.

The third indication, use of psychological tests as **screening** tools, relies on those psychological tests that are useful for determining whether a given patient is likely to have a particular mental disorder. The psychologist can use this information to determine the need of additional evaluation to define a diagnosis. Examples of tests used to screen for mental disorders include **personality inventories** (e.g., the Minnesota Multiphasic Personality Inventory, MMPI) and symptom checklists (e.g., Beck Depression Inventory, Symptom Checklist-90 – Revised). Screening tools have been modified for use in primary care settings (e.g., Prime-MD).

Recommended Reading

American Psychiatric Association. *Diagnostic and Statistical Manual of Mental Disorders.* (4th ed.). Text Revision. Washington, DC: American Psychiatric Association; 2001.

Gabbard GO. Mind and brain in psychiatric treatment. *Bulletin of the Menninger Clinic* 1998; 58:427–446.

Kandel ER. A new intellectual framework for psychiatry. *American Journal of Psychiatry* 1998; 155:457–469.

Kandel ER. Biology and the future of psychoanalysis: A new intellectual framework for psychiatry revisited. *American Journal of Psychiatry* 1999; 156:505–524.

Zuckerman M. *Vulnerability to Psychopathology.* Washington, DC: American Psychological Association; 1999.

Review Questions

Directions: The items below consist of lettered headings followed by numbered descriptions. For each numbered description choose the one lettered heading to which it is *most* closely associated. Each lettered heading may be used *once, more than once,* or *not at all.*

Match each example to the type of etiological factor that it best represents.
A. Behavioral
B. Biological
C. Cognitive
D. Environmental
E. Sociocutural

1. A 25-year-old man achieved remission from use of smoked cocaine two months ago. He has been struggling with craving sensations each time he drives through his neighborhood and passes the house where he used to purchase cocaine. He worries that he will relapse.

2. The dopamine hypothesis for schizophrenia is based on observations that drugs or processes that elevate dopamine levels in the brain can cause psychotic symptoms, while medications that block dopamine from interacting with dopamine receptors in the brain treat psychosis.

3. Mild to moderate major depressive episodes can be effectively treated by psychotherapy techniques that address inaccurate/negative beliefs, schemas, attitudes, distortions and automatic thoughts.

4. A 50-year-old Japanese immigrant is being treated for major depression. She gratefully accepts a prescription for antidepressant medicaion. Failing to achieve remission after two months of a therapeutic dose, the clinician discovers from her daughter that the patient is not taking the medication. At each follow-up visit she has convincingly claimed compliance with the treatment.

5. Twin studies demonstrate only a 50% concordance in the diagnosis of schizophrenia among pairs of identical twins.

6. The Folstein Mini Mental Status Examination screens for which of the following conditions?
   A. Cognitive dysfunction
   B. Mood disorders
   C. Movement disorders
   D. Personality disorders
   E. Psychotic symptoms

7. Among the following, the neuroimaging study that is most sensitive in the evaluation of patients with psychiatric complaints is
   A. computerized axial tomography
   B. magnetic resonance imaging
   C. positron emission tomography
   D. single photon emission computed tomography
   E. ventriculography

Key to review questions: p. 393

39 Eating Disorders

- Who is at risk for an eating disorder?
- What are the primary characteristics of anorexia nervosa and bulimia nervosa?
- How do the clinical features of anorexia and bulimia differ?
- How are eating disorders treated?
- Do patients with an eating disorder get better?

Clinical Application

Kristen, an 18-year-old college freshman, is brought to the student health service by her roommate after Kristen fainted on the way to the bathroom. Friends accompanying them report that Kristen spends at least 3 hours in the gym exercising each day. On examination, she appears mildly depressed and anxious. She reports that she has felt stressed due to being away from home and to an imminent break-up with her boyfriend. She reports eating one meal per day at noon consisting of salad, crackers, and diet coke. She admits to self-induced vomiting 2–3 times per day. Her height is 5 ft 9 in and her weight is 114 lb. She has had a 20-lb weight loss since her pre-college physical examination 4 months ago. Laboratory findings reveal low serum potassium and elevated serum bicarbonate levels.

Anorexia nervosa (AN) and bulimia nervosa (BN) constitute two major categories of eating disorders; a third category is eating disorder not otherwise specified (ED NOS), constituting disorders that do not fully meet criteria for AN or BN (e.g., binge eating disorder). The primary manifestations of AN and BN are abnormal eating behavior and impaired perception and experience of body weight and shape. Specific diagnoses are defined by the pattern of eating behavior that is most prevalent: restriction of intake, binging or purging (see Table 39.1.).

Table 39.1. Diagnostic indicators of eating disorders

Anorexia nervosa
- Refusal to achieve or maintain a healthy body weight
- Body weight < 85% of expected
- Intense fear of becoming fat
- Disturbance in perception of body weight/shape
- Amenorrhea for 3 consecutive cycles

Bulimia nervosa
- Recurring episodes of binge eating
- Recurring compensatory behaviors: vomiting, laxative/diuretic abuse
- Binge eating and compensatory behaviors occur ≥ 2 times/week for 3 months
- Inappropriate influence of body weight/shape on self-concept and self-esteem

From: *Diagnostic and Statistical Manual of Mental Disorders*, (4th ed.), pp. 544–545, 549–550, 1994. Washington, DC: American Psychiatric Association. Adapted with permission.

Who is at risk for an eating disorder?

Eating disorders currently affect up to 3% of young women. These disorders typically appear during adolescence and young adulthood; onset beyond the fourth decade is rare. In the United States, eating disorders appear to be about as common in young Hispanic and Native American women as in Caucasian women, and less common in African American and Asian women. Eating disorders are common across socioeconomic classes in Westernized societies and have increased in non-Western societies exposed to Western culture and modernization. Part of this increase may relate to a change in women's roles and the belief that weight loss and body reshaping guarantee social and economic advancement.

Estimates of the **male-female prevalence ratio** for eating disorders range from 1:6 to 1:10, and ED NOS and BN are more common in males than AN. Among men, gay males are at increased risk due to the cultural emphasis on thinness and appearance. Other groups at risk include athletes, models, and dancers regardless of gender. Male body builders are also at risk and can develop muscle dysmorphia or "reverse AN" in their desire to increase muscle and "get bigger." Dieting is an eating behavior that represents an especially significant risk factor in the development of disordered eating behavior. The causal relationship between dieting and eating disorders is unclear but may involve internalization of a "thin ideal", the experience of negative social comparison, family or peer pressure to be thin, or peer teasing, which can create body dissatisfaction leading to dieting.

While the specific **etiology of eating disorders** is unclear, biologic, behavioral, cognitive, environmental and sociocultural risk factors are all contributory. Family aggregation, twin, and linkage and association studies suggest some genetic risk. Heritability estimates for AN range from 48% to 76% and for BN range from 54% to 85%, but these heritability estimates are developmentally related. Genetic vulnerability may be activated in girls at early and mid-stage puberty due to neuroendocrine changes. Speculations about what is inheritable include eating regulatory mechanisms, temperament and character styles, and biologic predispositions such as ovarian hormone activity, and those mediated by serotonin systems in the brain that help regulate hunger, satiety, and mood. The dysregulation of serotonin systems appears to be involved in the development and maintenance of eating disorders. Recent studies also suggest that, in AN, there may be a dysfunction in the cortico-striatal-insular neural network, wherein the insula fails in its role as a connection and regulator between cortical and sub-cortical structures most relevant in AN.

Maturational issues (e.g., leaving home; physical, sexual, and emotional changes) precipitate eating disorders in individuals who are vulnerable. Position in the family, internal and external performance expectations, level of self-esteem, personality style, and previous relationship disruptions/losses are contributing psychosocial factors. Young women are more prone to develop eating disorders than men because they are confronted with multiple, ambiguous, and contradictory role expectations and a different set of societal values for behavior and appearance. Eating disorders are **diseases of disconnection** in which a biogenetically vulnerable individual has difficulty staying connected to and developing an authentic sense of self within relationships with others. This struggle is intensified with the effects of starvation, binging or purging, and a culture that emphasize thinness, appearance, and performance.

> What are the primary characteristics of anorexia nervosa and bulimia nervosa?

Anorexia Nervosa

Patients who have AN typically present at a younger age (by age 18) and have severe weight loss complicated by the manifestations of starvation (see Table 39.2.). Those with AN-restricting type (AN-R) use natural measures (e.g., severe restriction of intake, excessive exercise) to maintain or lose weight. However, a sub-group of patients with AN (like Kristen in the clinical vignette) have binge-purge type (AN-B/P) and also engage in binge eating and/or purging (e.g., self-induced vomiting; abuse of laxatives, diuretics, enemas or ipecac). The majority of patients with AN may experience hunger but can ignore it. They perceive their restricted eating and weight maintenance behavior as sources of status and accomplishment, rather than as problems. Starvation is reinforcing as it numbs underlying anxiety, and purging leads to endorphin release and decreased tension states.

Individuals with AN-R tend to present with a constricted affect and emotionally restricted personality style leaving them socially withdrawn, isolated, and sexually inactive. Perfectionism and negative affect have also characterized this group.

Table 39.2. Eating disorders: Common physical findings and causes

System	Findings	Causes
Fluid and electrolyte balance	Weakness; fatigue; constipation; depressed mood; bloating; peripheral edema; alkalosis; dehydration	Vomiting and laxative and diuretic abuse resulting in decreased potassium, chloride, and sodium; malnutrition
Endocrine	Amenorrhea; menstrual irregularities	Decreased fat stores; hormonal changes (LH, FSH)
Musculoskeletal	Osteoporosis; osteopenia; fractures; decreased muscle mass	Decreased estrogen; increased cortisol levels; alterations in parathyroid hormone; starvation
Metabolic	Hypothermia; hypoglycemia; increased β-hydroxy-butyric acid and fatty acids	Hypothalamic disturbance; decreased T_3; starvation
Cardiovascular	Bradycardia; hypotension; cardiomyopathy; arrhythmias; sudden death	Starvation; decreased T_3; ipecac abuse; starvation; electrolyte disturbances due to vomiting, diuretic/laxative abuse, or ipecac abuse
Renal	Renal calculi; increased BUN; tubular damage	Chronic dehydration; decreased potassium
Gastrointestinal	Constipation; stomach bloating; abdominal pain; parotid gland hypertrophy; esophagitis; esophageal rupture; dental enamel erosion	Starvation; laxative abuse; delayed gastric emptying; high carbohydrate intake; fluid and electrolyte changes; vomiting
Dermatological	Hair loss; brittle hair and nails; lanugo (soft downy hair); dry skin; cold extremities; yellowish discoloration; skin changes over dorsum of hand (knuckle calluses)	Starvation; dehydration; carotene pigmentation; abrasions due to mechanical induction of vomiting
Neurological	EEG abnormalities; weakness; enlargement of cerebral ventricles	Fluid and electrolyte disturbances; starvation; fluid and cortisol disturbances
Hematologic	Anemia; leukopenia; thrombocytopenia	Starvation

Those with AN-B/P can present as described above or can present with an impulsive or emotionally dysregulated personality style, similar to a subgroup of individuals with BN.

Bulimia Nervosa

Patients who have BN commonly present at an older age (in their late teens and 20s) and have little, if any, weight loss. Individuals with BN feel hunger and resist it for a period of time until starvation amplifies their urge to binge. Individuals with BN compensate for their binge eating with fasting or excessive exercise (BN-Nonpurging type) or more commonly, with purging (BN-purging type). Those with BN-purging type have significant physiologic complications as a result of their use of artificial means to purge. They may present with a high functioning personality style sometimes combined with perfectionism and negative affectivity. Alternatively, those with BN may present with an impulsive or emotionally dysregulated personality style that commonly includes negative affectivity, and may include self-loathing, sensitivity to rejection, and fears of abandonment. Individuals with BN are more socially and sexually active than patients with AN. A significant proportion have preexisting personality difficulties, disturbed interpersonal relationships, a history of trauma, or problems of impulse control and substance abuse. Many BN patients have evidence of anxiety or depression. Patients with BN are uncomfortable with their eating behaviors and are more likely than patients with AN to seek help.

> How do the clinical features of anorexia and bulimia differ?

Differential Features

By DSM-IV criteria, patients with AN have a body weight less than 85% of the norm for their height. Patients with BN may be normal weight, slightly underweight, or overweight.

Findings on physical examination of the patient with AN include emaciation, skin and hair changes (e.g., alopecia, lanugo hair), delayed development of secondary sex characteristics, dry or ulcerated mucous membranes, cardiomegaly or heart failure, hypotension, bradycardia, and hypothermia. These features are signs of the **downregulation of the sympathetic nervous system** necessary for survival during periods of food restriction or excessive exercise, since sympathetic tone is a major determinant of thermogenesis and metabolic rate. Patients with AN-R may have normal lab values due to the body's accommodation to chronic starvation. However, those with AN at very low weights are at risk of serious electrolyte and cardiac problems during the process of nutritional rehabilitation (i.e., refeeding syndrome) when the body moves from a catabolic to an anabolic state.

The patient with BN may have normal findings on examination. In particular, those with normal-weight BN do not show the profound **hypercortisolism** associated with AN or other starvation states, since eating is protective against severe malnutrition. However, patients with BN and with AN who excessively purge can experience major **electrolyte imbalances** and fatal sequelae such as sudden death from cardiac arrhythmia and car-

diomyopathy. Also, patients with AN or BN who induce vomiting may have discolored and decayed teeth from exposure to stomach acid, or calluses over the knuckles of the hand used to stimulate the posterior pharynx to induce vomiting.

Symptoms reported by patients who have an eating disorder include abdominal complaints (nausea, diarrhea, bloating) and nonspecific systemic complaints (chills, myalgias, sore throat, fatigue, weakness). **Amenorrhea** of at least 3 or more months' duration is one of the DSM-IV criteria for diagnosis of AN. Patients who have BN may or may not have menstrual irregularities.

Evaluations to exclude medical and psychiatric conditions that present with significant weight loss, starvation syndromes, or pathological eating behavior are critical to accurate diagnosis. Many medical conditions, including metabolic, endocrine, neurological and gastrointestinal disorders and cancers, may present with severe malnutrition or binge eating. However, intense fear of fat/weight gain and abnormalities in the self-perception and experience of body weight and shape, are typically not associated findings.

> How are eating disorders treated?

Treatment

The treatment of eating disorders requires a **multidisciplinary, biopsychosocial** approach informed by the patient's personality style. In general, medications have not been shown to be effective in the treatment of AN, although appetite-stimulators (e.g., cyproheptadine) or anxiolytics (e.g., lorazepam) taken before meals, may be helpful for some patients with AN. Recent studies suggest the use of olanzapine with chronic, low-weight AN, as it can stimulate appetite and weight gain and help with agitation, pre-meal anxiety and distorted beliefs regarding eating and body image. Medications that will decrease appetite, promote weight loss, prolong the QT interval or promote hypotension should not be prescribed for AN patients.

Antidepressants are helpful in treating BN. Selective serotonin reuptake inhibitors can be used as first-line medication as they have less adverse cardiac effects compared to tricyclics. MAO inhibitors decrease binging and purging but should be

"Rule of Thumb" for Determining Appropriate Weight	
Women	100 lb for first 5 feet 5 lb for each additional inch
Men	106 lb for first 5 feet 6 lb for each additional inch

used as a last resort due to their associated dietary restrictions. Topiramate has also been used effectively to decrease binge eating in BN and binge eating disorder, but it can also decrease weight. The use of bupropion should be avoided, as it can decrease the seizure threshold in purging BN patients who are already medically compromised.

Research suggests that medications should be started if binge eating and purging have not been responsive to six sessions of cognitive-behavioral therapy, or initiated at the start of treatment if there is serious comorbid mood disturbance. Medication should be continued for at least 6–9 months and taken at times during the day when there is decreased risk of vomiting. The mainstay of biologic treatment for eating disorders, however, is good nutrition with normalization of eating behaviors and restoration of weight. Dangerously emaciated patients require admission to the hospital to monitor refeeding; less affected patients may require only dietary counseling, psychoeducation, and support. Dietitians are essential members of an effective treatment team.

There have been few randomized controlled trials (RCT's) regarding treatment of AN. Findings from these RCT's, as well as recommendations from the British National Institute for Clinical Excellence (NICE) and the American Psychiatric Association (APA) encourage **family therapy** or counseling for effective treatment of **adolescents** (e.g., Maudsley approach), a **multidisciplinary approach** including nutritional rehabilitation and supportive psychosocial interventions, and treatment in the outpatient setting whenever possible by a therapist who specializes in eating disorders. Clinicians in everyday practice often use an approach of combined **psychosocial interventions** for AN including educational, cognitive, behavioral, psychodynamic, interpersonal, and family therapy approaches. These efforts are targeted toward providing accurate information, restructuring cognitions, developing a new alliance with one's body,

improving coping and problem-solving abilities, identifying and mediating conflict, and helping the individual change and grow within relationships with others. Setting attainable treatment goals is critical, especially for patients who have chronic AN. For them, achieving a low but safe weight, rather than an average weight, is considered a successful outcome. The **physiologic goal** is to restore normal hormonal function as manifested by regular menstrual cycles. Since hormone replacement therapy (HRT) has not been shown to be as effective in restoring bone density in patients with AN compared to those without AN, first-line therapy for bone health is nutritional rehabilitation. HRT also sends a message that weight gain can be avoided and symptomatic treatment can alleviate or prevent problems.

In contrast to RCT's of treatment for AN, there have been a number of RCT's of treatment for BN. Findings from these RCT's, as well as recommendations from the British National Institute for Clinical Excellence (NICE) and the American Psychiatric Association (APA) encourage individual **cognitive-behavioral therapy** as a first line intervention. **Interpersonal therapy** is a second choice because effects equal to those associated with CBT take longer to achieve. Medication and self-help programs are beneficial adjunctive treatments.

While binge eating is often used to regulate emotions and cope with stress in a way similar to substance abuse, this functional similarity does not make binge eating an addictive disorder. The treatment of BN advocates flexible and healthy eating without a focus on dieting or rigid abstention from particular foods.

Do patients with an eating disorder get better?

Prognosis

The prognosis for eating disorders is variable and depends on body mass index, self-esteem, personality disturbance, presence of vomiting, and premorbid family relationships. From 8% to 62% of patients with AN develop bulimic symptoms. Overall, the effectiveness of treatment for eating disorders ranges from 40% to 80%. About 5% of AN patients develop fatal complications. AN and BN are associated with increased physical and psychiatric comorbidity, decreased quality of life, and in the case of AN, increased mortality. AN is the most fatal psychiatric illness with a mortality rate of 5% per decade. For those between the ages of 15 and 25, the death rate (often due to suicide or starvation-related complications) is 12 times higher for women with anorexia nervosa compared to women in the general population. Given the fact that AN is characterized by denial of illness and high mortality, and BN is associated with shame and secrecy, patients and families should be engaged in treatment as early as possible. Attention to the patient's stage of change and the use of motivational interviewing is essential. Treatment should be delivered with an emphasis on developing mutually empathic and empowering relationships with patients and families in order to engage and keep them in treatment.

Recommended Readings

American Psychiatric Association. *Practice Guideline for the Treatment of Patients with Eating Disorders* (3nd ed.). Arlington, VA: American Psychiatric Association; 2006, pp. 257–332.

Andersen, AE. (Ed.). Eating Disorders. *Psychiatric Clinics of North America* 2001:24(2).

Brownell KD, Fairburn CG. (Eds.). *Eating disorders and obesity* (2nd ed.). New York: Guilford Press; 2002

Wonderlich S, Mitchell JE., de Zwaan M, Steiger H. *Annual Review of Eating Disorders* (Part 2). Oxford, UK: Radcliffe Publishing; 2006.

Tantillo M. (2006). A relational approach to eating disorders multifamily therapy group: Moving from difference and disconnection to mutual connection. *Families, Systems, & Health* 2006; 24:82–102.

Review Questions

1. A true statement about the epidemiology of eating disorders in the U.S. is:
   A. Eating disorders are about as common in African American women as in Caucasian women.
   B. Male to female incidence is about 1 to 3.
   C. The occurrence of eating disorders is limited to Western cultures.

D. They occur most often in Caucasian females of higher socioeconomic status.

2. Which one of the following sets of clinical findings is most likely in a patient with an eating disorder?
   A. Brittle hair, amenorrhea, bradycardia, and dry skin
   B. Hypertension, increased muscle mass, fever, and dental enamel erosion
   C. Menorrhagia, abdominal pain, tachypnea, and warm extremities
   D. Tachycardia, night sweats, hyperglycemia, and bloating

3. Which of the following abnormalities must be considered in a patient who has a history of ipecac abuse?
   A. Cardiomegaly
   B. Hypoglycemia
   C. Hypothermia
   D. Renal calculi

4. Laboratory studies of a patient with an eating disorder are most likely to reveal
   A. fluid and electrolyte abnormalities
   B. increased LH and FSH
   C. increased T3
   D. leukocytosis

5. In treating an adolescent with AN who weighs 80% of average body weight for height and age, which of the following is likely to be most helpful initially?
   A. Dietary counseling and follow-up with the primary care physician
   B. Nutritional rehabilitation combined with family therapy
   C. Nutritional rehabilitation combined with individual psychotherapy
   D. Small doses of lorazepam before meals

6. In treating an individual with BN, which of the following is considered the best initial treatment?
   A. Antidepressant medication
   B. Individual cognitive-behavioral therapy
   C. Refeeding and dietary guidance
   D. Psychodynamic group psychotherapy

Key to review questions: p. 393

40 Adjustment Disorders and Somatoform Disorders

- What are common precipitating stressors for adjustment disorders?
- What are three factors that contribute to the development of adjustment disorders?
- What are the six subtypes of adjustment disorder?
- What should be the focus of psychotherapy for adjustment disorders?
- What is somatization?
- What is hypochondriasis?
- How is body dysmorphic disorder defined?
- What is psychogenic pain disorder?
- What is Munchausen syndrome by proxy?

Adjustment Disorders

Clinical Application

Janice W. complains of fatigue, a 5-pound weight loss, and mood swings. She is a 38-year-old mother of three whose husband was transferred to his company's corporate headquarters 3 months ago, prompting the family to move to another state, far from the small community where they had lived for more than 15 years. Janice's husband is working long hours establishing his office and meeting with other executives. The children started their new school and after-school activities six weeks ago.

Janice was initially excited about the move and furnishing her new house. Now she often awakens during the night, feels tired "all the time," has lost her appetite, feels "down and blue," and cries almost every day. Neighbors invite her to social events but she refuses the invitations saying she has "lots to do." She spends most days home alone

What are common precipitating stressors for adjustment disorders?

Adjustment disorders are **short-term** emotional or behavioral reactions to **stressful life events**.

Symptoms usually appear within 3 months of the onset of the precipitating stressor and are severe enough to warrant clinical attention. Stressors that precipitate an adjustment disorder vary with the person's developmental phase and personality. Examples of **common stressors** for adolescents include school problems, parental divorce, parental rejection, and parental substance abuse. For adults, marital difficulties, divorce, work and financial problems are among the most prominent precipitating stressors.

What are three factors that contribute to the development of adjustment disorders?

Three factors contribute to the development of adjustment disorders: the precipitating stressor; the context and meaning of the stressor; and predisposing vulnerabilities due to past life experiences.

Clinical Features

To warrant a diagnosis of adjustment disorder, a person must show a **level of distress** that exceeds what would be expected. Further, the distress causes significant **impairment** in social, vocational, or academic functioning. Finally, the symptoms are not the result of bereavement or manifestations of another psychiatric disorder. When the stressor is resolved, adjustment disorders typically remit within 3–6 months. Adolescents may require a longer time. If the stressor continues, the adjustment disorder may become chronic (i.e., lasts > 6 months). The specification **acute** or **chronic** should be incorporated into the diagnosis.

Adjustment disorders are among the psychiatric diagnoses most commonly made in patients hospitalized for medical and surgical reasons. Although diagnosed most frequently among adolescents, adjustment disorders may occur at any age. Women are affected about twice as often as men. Single women are at greatest risk.

What are the six subtypes of adjustment disorder?

The six subtypes of adjustment disorder are classified according to the most predominant symptoms. Some patients who initially receive a diagnosis of adjustment disorder subsequently are found to have a mood disorder or a substance-related disorder.

Six Subtypes of Adjustment Disorder

Adjustment disorder with:
1. depressed mood
2. anxiety
3. mixed anxiety and depressed mood
4. disturbance of conduct
5. mixed disturbance of emotions and conduct
6. unspecified symptoms

Treatment

What should be the focus of psychotherapy for adjustment disorders?

Treatment of adjustment disorders consists primarily of **psychotherapy** focused on identifying and understanding the nature and impact of the **stressor** and developing effective ways of **coping** that permit the individual to function normally. After therapy, some patients become emotionally stronger than they were prior to developing the adjust-

ment disorder. If the symptoms are persistent and incapacitating, short-term treatment with anti-anxiety or antidepressant medication, depending on the target symptoms, may be beneficial.

Somatoform Disorders

What is somatization?

Somatization is characterized by two complementary conditions: a) **physical complaints** without demonstrable physical findings; and b) the presence of **psychosocial factors** sufficient to initiate,

Clinical Application

Ellen, a 25-year-old graduate student, tells her doctor she was well until one week ago when she awoke with such severe pain in her legs and hips that she was unable to walk. She took a combination of ibuprofen and acetaminophen, every four hours, a regimen that had worked for headaches in the past and that allowed her to move around her apartment when absolutely necessary. Otherwise, she has remained in bed with curtains drawn and lights off because she feels best when she lies perfectly still. She denied any physical trauma, infection, or other illness. The evening before the pain began, she had participated in a jazz competition in which she had played her own arrangement of "Walkin' in the Rain." She was very disappointed with having placed last, but now states, "It doesn't really bother me any more."

As she is taken to the examination room, she stands with difficulty and walks only a few feet with an unsteady hesitant gait before asking to lie down. The physical examination reveals normal pulses and reflexes, good skin color and hydration, and no evidence of joint swelling or deformity. Testing of passive range of motion is severely compromised as Ellen resists and complains of unbearable pain in all joints. However, she does not complain – and her joints show normal passive range of motion – when the doctor explains he must move her legs in preparation for performing other maneuvers (e.g., lifting her leg to test the patellar reflex).

Which somatoform disorder does this patient have?

maintain, or worsen the physical complaints. That is, there is symptom formation and the physical complaints are the symptoms. Effective evaluation of a suspected somatoform disorder requires attention to both the physical complaints and the psychosocial factors. The patient should be assured that the clinician regards the symptoms as real and causing distress, that their cause will be investigated, and that the symptoms will be eradicated or controlled.

Sufficient diagnostic studies should be performed to reassure both the physician and the patient that there is no underlying pathophysiologic state that requires immediate biomedical or surgical treatment. Attention should be given to ruling out conditions identified by the patient as especially worrisome (e.g., heart disease, cancer). Somatic concerns should be reevaluated at every subsequent encounter to be certain that no pathophysiologic process is evolving. Regularly scheduled appointments should be instituted regardless of fluctuations in symptoms; frequent (e.g., weekly) appointments may be necessary initially.

The patient should keep a **symptom diary** (type of symptom, severity, precipitants, actions taken and their efficacy) that is carefully reviewed at every encounter. **Positive reinforcement** for effective **self-management** helps promote other attempts at self-care and enhances the patient's sense of control over the symptoms. Joint problem solving around additional strategies when treatments are ineffective helps the patient become an active partner in symptom management.

Specific treatments directed at the symptom (e.g., range of motion exercises for a patient with joint pain) provide a physiologic basis for "giving up" the symptom and improving functionality. This approach is more socially acceptable to patients than the notion that "it's all in your head."

At the same time that somatic concerns are addressed, it is essential to also explore sources of **stress** and other psychosocial symptom-perpetuating factors. It can be especially useful to recommend appropriate articles or books to patients. Not infrequently, patients will present with entrenched symptoms not amenable to primary care interventions, or will have personality disorders, addictive potential, self-destructive behavior, or deep-seated emotional problems. They should be referred for concurrent mental health consultation and treatment.

Somatization Disorder

Somatization disorder is a type of somatoform disorder characterized by multiple diffuse somatic symptoms involving a variety of organ systems. The disorder is recurrent, more common among persons from the lower socioeconomic sectors of the population, and begins before age 30. Women are affected 20 times more often than men. The estimated lifetime prevalence for somatization disorder in the general population is 0.4%.

Criteria for diagnosis include pain reported in four or more sites in the body, at least one gastrointestinal complaint, at least one symptom involving the reproductive organs or sexual functioning, and neurologic symptoms or defects that do not correspond to nerve pathways.

Somatization disorder is the fourth most frequently encountered diagnosis in ambulatory primary care medicine. It affects 10% to 20% of female first-degree relatives of women with the disorder. Male first-degree relatives of women with the disorder are at increased risk for antisocial personality disorder and substance use disorders.

Somatoform Disorders

Disorder	Characteristics
Somatization disorder	Multiple, diffuse somatic symptoms
Conversion disorder	Sensory or motor deficits not explainable physiologically
Hypochondriasis	Preoccupation with fear of serious disease
Body dysmorphic disorder	Imagined or grossly exaggerated body defect or disagreeable feature
Psychogenic pain disorder	Pain initiated, exacerbated, or maintained by voluntary simulation of symptoms due to psychological factors
Factitious disorders (e.g., Munchausen syndrome) Malingering disorder	Feigning of symptoms for personal gain or advantage

Adoption studies have shown that **familial** and **environmental stress** factors contribute to risk of somatization disorder. Affected persons often have anxious or depressed mood and comorbid substance use disorders, panic attacks, and sociopathy. A history of suicide attempts and occupational, marital, or interpersonal difficulties is common.

Patients who have somatization disorder should have a psychiatric consultation even when they resist. The psychiatrist will confirm the diagnosis, treat any comorbid psychiatric conditions, and provide crisis intervention. Continuous clinical management to "control" rather than "cure" the patient's symptoms should be the focus of treatment.

Conversion Disorder

Persons with **conversion disorder** show sensory or motor function deficits that cannot be explained physiologically. Conversion disorder is often mono-symptomatic (e.g., paralysis of a particular voluntary muscle group, pseudo-blindness), but impaired occupational and interpersonal functioning is common. Manifestations of the disorder are not under voluntary control and are precipitated or worsened by exposure to **stressors**. An **underlying conflict** appears to produce the functional impairment. That is, the symptom is an attempted, but maladaptive, resolution of the conflict.

Conversion disorder is **comorbid** with somatization disorder, antisocial personality disorder, and alcohol and other substance use disorders. It can occur at any time from early childhood to old age. In males, conversion disorder is often associated with their vocation. Although conversion disorder can be found in people across the educational spectrum, its prevalence is highest in psychologically unsophisticated lower socioeconomic and rural populations. Among uneducated individuals, conversion symptoms only crudely resemble physical conditions. In more highly educated individuals, the symptoms more closely resemble a physical condition. It is estimated that about 20% of hospitalized medical patients for whom a psychiatric consultation is requested have conversion disorder.

Patients who have conversion disorder are susceptible to suggestion, which can be used to produce symptom relief. Short-term psychotherapy with a strong **supportive** component that suggests relief is imminent may produce good initial results. Sustained improvement requires a focus on **stress management** and enhancing adaptive **coping** mechanisms. A short-term hospitalization may be useful. Most cases resolve quickly, but some become chronic and resistant to treatment. Cognitive-behavioral therapy that addresses specific patient needs can be beneficial in persistent cases.

Hypochondriasis

What is hypochondriasis?

Hypochondriasis is excessive preoccupation with and fear of serious disease accompanied by misinterpretation of bodily functions and sensations as manifestations of the feared disease. The diagnosis requires that symptoms be present for at least 6 months, and that no evidence exists of psychosis or body dysmorphic disorder (see below). Severe emotional distress and interpersonal and occupational dysfunction accompany the symptoms. Reassurance and explanation produce only partial temporary relief from the disabling preoccupation and fear, and are not, in themselves, therapeutic.

The prevalence of hypochondriasis is unknown. Onset is in the middle to older years and men and women are equally affected. Low socioeconomic status, prior serious physical illness, and certain parental disease-promoting attitudes appear to be predisposing factors.

Hypochondriasis is best managed by primary care physicians with psychiatric consultations as needed. Regular appointments should be scheduled in advance and not dictated by symptomatology. Associated depression or anxiety requires treatment.

Body Dysmorphic Disorder

How is body dysmorphic disorder defined?

Persons with **body dysmorphic disorder** are preoccupied with an imagined or grossly exaggerated defect or disagreeable bodily feature, which results in emotional distress and interpersonal and occupational impairment. To fit the diagnosis, signs and symptoms must not be features of an existing primary psychiatric disorder such as an eating disorder (e.g., anorexia nervosa) or psychosis.

Affected persons feel ugly. They believe their perceived "defects" (blemishes, facial features) compromise their whole being and are noticed by others. Concerns about the face are most common. The onset of body dysmorphic disorder is most common during adolescence and young adulthood and the disorder typically persists for many years. However, transient adolescent distress over rapid body changes should not be diagnosed as body dysmorphic disorder.

Patients persistently seek help from primary care physicians, dermatologists, and plastic surgeons. Although sometimes resisted, psychiatric consultation is important to diagnose and treat the more tenacious or puzzling cases and any associated depression or anxiety.

Combined psychotherapy and pharmacotherapy constitute the best management. Effective medications in the treatment of body dysmorphic disorder include tricyclic antidepressants (TCAs), especially those that affect the serotonin system; selective serotonin reuptake inhibitors (SSRIs); monoamine oxidase inhibitors (MAOIs); and pimozide. Agents in the first three categories are primarily antidepressants; pimozide is an antipsychotic drug that suppresses body preoccupations.

Psychogenic Pain Disorder

What is psychogenic pain disorder?

In **psychogenic pain disorder:** 1) the patient presents with pain of such severity that it causes distress and impairs interpersonal and occupational functioning; 2) **psychologic factors** are instrumental in the onset, severity, or maintenance of the pain; and 3) a general medical condition may coexist, but it is not the primary cause of the pain.

Psychogenic pain, which is as "real" as pain from any other origin, occurs in up to 40% of persons whose main complaint is pain. Psychogenic pain is familial, twice as common in women as in men, and typically begins during or after the fourth decade, although it can occur in childhood. A family history of alcoholism, depression, or anxiety is common.

Biofeedback, transcutaneous electrical nerve stimulation (TENS), nerve block, and **cognitive-** **behavior therapy** can be used in conjunction with simple analgesia to manage the disorder. Tricyclic antidepressants are useful both for controlling associated symptoms of anxiety or depression and for their own pain-relieving properties.

Factitious Disorders

Factitious disorders and malingering (see below) are distinct disorders that share common features, such as **somatization** and **voluntary control** over clinical manifestations.

Patients who have a **factitious disorder** (sometimes known as **Munchausen syndrome**) voluntarily simulate or produce signs and symptoms of a disease. The person's only intention is to assume the patient role; that is, there is no evidence of personal gain as an incentive for simulating disease. Patients with this disorder seek to deceive physicians into diagnosing medical conditions that merit medical intervention to obtain attention from those who provide their medical and surgical care. They seek and submit to diagnostic and treatment procedures, and relinquish control of their bodies to physicians. The average age of onset of factitious disorder is 30 years but ranges from adolescence to old age. The typical patient is a young, intelligent, educated upper-middle-class, socially conforming woman who is familiar with the medical field. Less frequently, the patient is male, of low socioeconomic status, chronically socially maladaptive, a pathologic liar, and a wanderer.

Treatment requires collaboration between the primary care physician and a psychiatrist. Although the psychiatrist ultimately makes the diagnosis, the primary care physician must confront the patient, if needed, in a nonpunitive fashion and provide noninvasive care, while discouraging invasive procedures. The family should be involved in providing pertinent historic details and setting limits on illness behavior. The psychiatric consultant should diagnose and treat associated anxiety, depression, or other comorbid psychiatric disorders. The history of a patient who has a factitious disorder often includes a traumatic childhood and evidence of developmental failures.

Factitious disorders should be considered in the evaluation of both psychologic and physical conditions.

What is Munchausen syndrome by proxy?

Cases have been reported of **factitious disorder (Munchausen syndrome) by proxy,** in which caregivers induce illness in someone under their care, often a child. All other diagnostic criteria for the disorder are the same as for factitious disorder. The caregiver virtually always meets criteria for the diagnosis of a personality disorder.

Malingering

Malingering is the feigning or gross exaggeration of physical or mental signs, symptoms, or illness motivated by personal gain or advantage. Malingering may present together with other mental disorders such as somatoform and personality disorders, especially antisocial personality disorder. Because bona fide physical and psychologic disorders may actually be present in the malingerer and because some malingerers may have partly unconscious motivations for their behavior, the physician should adopt an exploratory, nonjudgmental attitude.

Recommended Reading

DeGucht V, Fischler B. Somatization: A critical review of conceptual and methodological issues. *Psychosomatics* 2002; 43:1–9.

Richard K, Gask L. Treatment of patients with somatized mental disorder: Effects of reattribution training on outcomes under the direct control of the family doctor. *Psychosomatics* 2002; 43:394–399.

Sharpe M, Carson A. "Unexplained" somatic symptoms, functional syndromes, and somatization: Do we need a paradigm shift? *Annals of Internal Medicine* 2001; 134:926–930.

Review Questions

Directions: The items below consist of lettered headings followed by numbered descriptions. For each numbered description choose the *one* lettered heading to which it is *most* closely associated. Each lettered heading may be used *once, more than once,* or *not at all.*

Match the clinical scenario to the most likely diagnosis.

  A. Body dysmorphic disorder
  B. Conversion disorder
  C. Hypochondriasis
  D. Pain disorder
  E. Somatization disorder

1. A 15-year-old girl was the victim of a rape experience. Three days later, she developed scanning speech, hemianesthesia, and paralysis of both legs and complained of stomach pain and headache.

2. A 28-year-old woman has consulted several plastic surgeons for surgical correction of what she perceives as asymmetry in the horizontal relationship of her eyes. She insists this requires correction.

3. A 40-year-old woman complaints of abdominal bloating and loose stools. History reveals three normal GI studies. She also reports headaches, ear pain, paresthesias in the legs and feet, and chronic temporomandibular joint pain. She has a long history of menstrual irregularity and anorgasmia. Five years ago she had sudden onset of bilateral leg paralysis that resolved with physical therapy after two weeks.

4. A 50-year-old man was injured in a manufacturing accident and developed chronic leg and back pain. There are no radiological findings to suggest any structural disease in his spinal column or cord, yet he has been unable to stop taking narcotic pain relievers or return to work.

5. A 55-year-old woman is making her third visit to her primary care physician concerned that symptoms, including palpitations associated with hyperventilation, are signs of a heart attack. Several acute ECG tracings in the office and emergency room have been normal. Three months ago, she was convinced that episodes of gas and abdominal bloating were signs of cancer, and insisted on a colonoscopy to rule this out.

Key to review questions: p. 393

41 Anxiety Disorders

- What are the components of anxiety?
- What factors contribute to the development and maintenance of anxiety?
- What are the clinical features of the major anxiety disorders?
- What are the three characteristic symptoms of PTSD?
- What are the elements of cognitive-behavioral therapy for anxiety?

Neuroendocrine arousal is a basic component of the human **stress response** to all forms of challenge. A moderate amount of arousal alerts the individual, promotes planning for the future, and the weighing of both positive and negative outcomes for a given situation. However, when the arousal is over-amplified, either biologically, situationally or cognitively, the symptoms of the response themselves can become a source of anticipatory dread and intense negative affect that can impair functioning. Thus, **anxiety** is severe apprehension about being unable to predict or control possible future negative events and one's response to them. Anxiety differs from fear, which is an immediate alarm reaction to impending danger (the "fight or flight" response).

The cognitive component also consists of heightened sensitivity to the **biological** component, or the physical sensations of arousal such as tachycardia, tachypnea, tremor, increased muscular tone, dizziness, and tightness in the chest associated with the neuroendocrine stress response. In some patients, concern that the sensations indicate a heart attack or other feared physical event increases the symptoms further.

The **behavioral** component consists of avoiding cue situations in attempts to avoid triggering anxiety. Because the behavior provides momentary relief, it is reinforced and strengthened. Thus, an individual with anxiety maintains a state of apprehension characterized by hypervigilance for danger, chronic physiologic arousal, and behavioral avoidance of any anxiety provoking cues.

Components of the Anxiety Response

What are the components of anxiety?

The **cognitive** component consists of thoughts, attributions, beliefs, and images. Persons with anxiety disorders characteristically expect negative events and catastrophic outcomes with which, they believe, they will be unable to cope. Fearful of their thoughts, patients frequently engage in cognitive avoidance or covert neutralizing thoughts.

Etiology

What factors contribute to the development and maintenance of anxiety?

The development and maintenance of anxiety involves four factors: (1) **genetic transmission** of neuroendocrine sensitivity involving the GABA-benzodiazepine, noradrenergic, serotonergic, and dopaminergic systems; (2) **cognitive factors** resulting from early conditioning experiences such as perceived helplessness in certain situations; (3)

Table 41.1. Anxiety disorders and their foci

Diagnosis	Focus of anxiety
Panic disorder (+/- agoraphobia)	Fear of internal physical sensations (future panic attacks), going crazy, or losing control
Agoraphobia (without panic disorder)	Fear of inability to cope with stress situations leading to inability to leave a familiar environment without sufficient perceived support
Generalized anxiety disorder	Anxiety about life situations (e.g., finances, health, employment) accompanied by physiological symptoms
Social phobia	Fear of negative evaluation, embarrassment by others
Specific phobia	Fear of a specific situation or stimulus out of proportion to the actual risk incurred (e.g., heights, driving, storms, animals, blood)
Obsessive-compulsive disorder	Repetitive thoughts, images, behaviors that are difficult to control (obsessions) leading to behaviors (compulsions) designed to minimized the anxiety
Posttraumatic stress disorder	Fear of the recurrence of a traumatic event accompanied by feelings of intense horror and helplessness

learned avoidance behaviors; and (4) **environmental, sociocultural,** and **interpersonal stressors** (e.g., childhood abuse, illness, divorce) that activate an individual's stress response.

Clinical Features

> What are the clinical features of the major anxiety disorders?

To be assigned a diagnosis, there must be evidence of clinically significant distress or impairment in social, occupational, or other important areas of functioning. Although symptoms may be shared among all anxiety disorders, the focus of the anxiety differs across diagnoses (see Table 41.1.). Table 41.2. presents a summary of current epidemiologic and onset data and the expected course for each disorder.

Physical Disorders Presenting as Anxiety

All patients presenting with an anxiety disorder should have a careful history and physical examination performed. Common medical causes for anxiety include hyperthyroidism, substance intoxication or withdrawal, and temporal lobe epilepsy.

Panic

Panic is an extreme and intense form of anticipatory anxiety. **Panic attack** is the abrupt intense experience of fear accompanied by an intense worry about losing control, not being able to cope or function and having this witnessed by others. Panic attacks may be **cued** or **situationally bound.** If an individual has not identified what cue triggers a panic attack, attacks will seem to occur randomly. Because the individual does not know when to expect an attack, dread of future panic attacks increases. Some panic attacks may be **situationally predisposed** to occur, i.e., an individual feels more likely to experience panic in certain stimulus cue situations, such as those in which the individual would find escape to be difficult (e.g., a

> **Clinical Application**
>
> A 32-year-old woman has only been able to leave her house when accompanied by her mother. If her mother is with her, she can go anywhere; if not, she experiences significant anxiety when she even thinks of leaving the house. She will awaken from sleep with episodes of marked anxiety including the thought that she is losing her mind, palpitations, the sensation that she cannot breathe, and the fear that she is having a heart attack. Each episode lasts about 20 minutes.

crowded mall, on a limited access highway, or in an airplane).

Panic disorder is diagnosed if the patient (1) experiences recurrent panic attacks, (2) extended over at least 1 month, and (3) followed by persistent concern about having additional attacks, worry about the implications or consequences of the attacks (e.g., having a stroke, losing control, "going crazy"), or a significant change in behavior related to the attacks. To meet the criteria for panic disorder, panic attacks cannot be due to the physiologic effects of a substance (e.g., drugs, medication) or to a general medical condition (e.g., temporal lobe epilepsy, hyperthyroidism) or result from a specific phobia.

Diagnostic Criteria for a Panic Attack

Discrete period of intense fear or discomfort during which as least four of the following symptoms develop abruptly and reach a peak within 10 minutes:
1. Palpitations, pounding heart
2. Sweating
3. Trembling, shaking
4. Dyspnea, feeling smothered
5. Choking sensation
6. Chest pain, tightness
7. Nausea, abdominal distress
8. Dizziness, fainting
9. Paresthesias
10. Chills, hot flashes
11. Fear of dying
12. Fear of going crazy
13. Derealization, depersonalization

Generalized Anxiety Disorder

Clinical Application

A 52-year-old man has always been a worrier. He consistently anticipates the worst possible outcome to almost any situation. His worries keep him up at night and he has begun to drink excessively every evening in order to sleep. His wife sends him in for treatment because of this and because of his increasing irritability.

Generalized anxiety disorder (GAD) is characterized by excessive anxiety and worry (apprehension) most days about a variety of events or activities for at least 6 months. To meet the criteria for diagnosis, the patient must manifest at least three of the following symptoms:
– Restlessness or feeling on edge
– Fatigue
– Poor concentration
– Irritability
– Muscle tension
– Sleep disturbance

Persons with GAD worry excessively about everyday life issues. They also typically worry continuously without being able to focus their attention on pleasant activities or distractions.

Phobia

Clinical Application

A 36-year-old social worker has to make an oral presentation every week at a meeting of her Department. She dreads these presentations and is quite certain that everyone is staring at her as she blushes and stammers. She realizes intellectually that she is presenting well, but finds this task more and more difficult.

Social phobia is a persistent fear of social or performance situations in which the person is exposed to possible scrutiny by others. The individual recognizes the fear as excessive and either avoids social situations or endures them with distress.

Clinical Application

A 28-year-old attorney is eager to become pregnant but has been unsuccessful. Her obstetrician would like her to undergo a fertility work-up, but she will not do so since she knows that this will involve blood work and injections. She experiences intense anxiety as she thinks about the needles that would be involved.

Specific phobia is an excessive fear of a specific object or situation. Exposure to the feared

Table 41.2. Epidemiology, onset, course and comorbidities of major anxiety disorders

Disorder	Epidemiology	Onset	Course	Common Comorbidity
Panic disorder	1–3% community; 3–8% primary care patients Female: male 2:1	Early teens through age 40	Chronic in 20% Relapsing remitting in others	Agoraphobia, depression, mitral valve prolapse, substance abuse
Generalized anxiety disorder	5% lifetime prevalence Female: male 2:1	Mid-teens to mid-20s	Chronic, recurrent course; duration 6–10 years	Depression, panic disorder, substance abuse
Social phobia	3% lifetime prevalence Female: male 3:2	Bimodal peaks at 5 years and early adolescence	Chronic, unremitting disorders in some	
Specific phobia	11% lifetime prevalence Sex differences vary with subtype	Blood: 9 years Situational: 2–7 years and early 20s Animals: 7 years	With avoidance, course may be chronic	
Posttraumatic stress disorder	1–2.5% lifetime prevalence 5–6% lifetime prevalence for men and 10–14% lifetime prevalence for women	Any age	Course depends on the traumatic event, premorbid functioning, social support, access to treatment, socialcultural factors	
Obsessive-compulsive disorder	2–3% prevalence male = female	20s–30s Childhood onset is a bad prognostic sign	Typically chronic and lifelong	Depression, Tourette syndrome

situation produces an anxiety response that interferes with the individual's ability to carry on normal activities. Although fears of various objects or situations are common especially at certain developmental stages (e.g., fear of dogs in preschool-aged children), specific phobias can be distinguished from subclinical fears on three dimensions:

- the phobic response is **out of proportion** to the degree of actual threat (e.g., instead of standing still or gently swatting, a person with bee phobia may scream, run, or flail at the bee);
- the phobic response **persists or escalates** overtime; and
- the phobic response **interferes with functioning** beyond a moment of mild apprehension.

Obsessive-Compulsive Disorder

Clinical Application

A 52-year-old man spends two hours getting ready for bed each night. He has to check several times to make sure that each window and door is locked and that all electrical appliances are unplugged. He knows intellectually that safety in his home is not an issue but he will experience intense anxiety as he thinks about not checking the windows, doors, and appliances. His anxiety gets better each time he checks, but will reappear very quickly. There are nights when he cannot get to bed at all, spending the entire night circling around his house.

Obsessive-compulsive disorder (OCD) may involve obsessions, compulsions, or, most typically, both.

Obsessions are recurrent and persistent thoughts, impulses, or images that are experienced as intrusive and inappropriate and cause marked distress. Attempts to suppress, neutralize, or ignore the obsessions are unsuccessful.

Compulsions are repetitive behaviors or mental acts that the person feels driven to perform in order to prevent some feared event from occurring. To meet the criteria for the diagnosis of OCD, symptoms must occur for more than 1 hour per day and significantly interfere with routine functioning.

Posttraumatic Stress Disorder

Clinical Application

A 56-year-old man has always worked as a truck driver hauling cement blocks. His truck has an arm that lifts up to load and unload the blocks. One day, while driving at 60 miles per hour, the arm unfurls and hits an overhead bridge causing significant damage to both the bridge and the truck. The driver is not hurt physically, but starts to regularly re-experience the accident. Being around other trucks causes marked anxiety. He is unable to drive due to this fear. He is hypervigilant and loud noises startle him greatly. He ends up losing his job and can no longer support his family.

What are the three characteristic symptoms of PTSD?

Posttraumatic stress disorder (PTSD) occurs in individuals who have experienced or been confronted with an event or events that they perceive as representing an actual or threatened death or serious injury. The response at the time of the traumatic event must involve intense feelings of fear, helplessness, or horror. The disorder is characterized by three symptom clusters that must be present for at least 1 month.

1. **Re-experiencing the event** involves intrusive recollections of the event in the form of nightmares, flashback episodes, and intense psychological distress when exposed to inter-

nal or external cues that recall the traumatic event.
2. **Avoidance symptoms** involve efforts to avoid images, thoughts, or feelings associated with the trauma; activities, situations, or people that provoke recollection of the trauma; selective amnesia for certain aspects of the traumatic event; loss of interest in usual activities; feelings of detachment from others; restricted range of affect; and a sense of a foreshortened future (i.e., early death).
3. **Persistent symptoms of increased arousal** include sleep disturbance, irritability, or outbursts of anger; impaired concentration; hypervigilance; and exaggerated startle response.

Diagnosis requires impairment in functioning associated with the illness.

Treatment

Effective treatment includes cognitive-behavioral therapy and anti-anxiety medications. Specific subtypes of behavioral therapy are indicated for specific disorders.

Cognitive-Behavioral Therapy

What are the elements of cognitive-behavioral therapy for anxiety?

Cognitive-behavioral therapy targets learned avoidant behaviors and associated cognitive beliefs through psychoeducation, cognitive restructuring, somatic management skills, and exposure to the feared stimuli.

Psychoeducation is the presentation of information about the nature of the patient's anxiety or panic and the physiologic basis of these reactions from a protective, evolutionary perspective.

In **cognitive restructuring,** patients are taught to examine their beliefs about their inability to cope with stress and counter these cognitions with realistic, coping thoughts.

Specific **somatic management** skills, such as deep breathing and muscle relaxation, are taught to assist the individual to tolerate and manage the symptoms of anxiety or panic.

Exposure methods involve repeated, graduated exposure to the feared stimuli or situations that allow the patient to increasingly tolerate the stress response and manage the anxiety.

Pharmacotherapy

Pharmacotherapy for anxiety disorders involves two classes of medications: antidepressants and benzodiazepines.

Specific Treatment of Anxiety Disorders

Panic Disorder

Antidepressants can be quite helpful in preventing panic attacks; they have limited utility in terms of anticipatory anxiety which is often the more crippling component of the illness. **Benzodiazepines** are often helpful, but discontinuation syndromes can mimic panic symptoms. Since patients with panic disorder are hypervigilant about bodily sensations, considerable support and education is necessary to ensure treatment adherence. Symptoms often return with discontinuation of benzodiazepines, so they should be regarded as second-line medications. Because cognitive therapy centers on teaching patients to manage their anxiety, ablating symptoms with benzodiazapines is often counter-productive. Patients with agoraphobia are most effectively treated with graduated exposure or imaginal or *in vivo* **desensitization** Medications are best reserved for patients who are unwilling or unable to access CBT.

Obsessive-Compulsive Disorder

Medications that inhibit reuptake of serotonin (SSRI's, clomipramine) are helpful. Onset of action is delayed, taking up to 10 weeks, far longer than the onset of the anti-depressant effect. Behavioral work centers around exposure and response prevention. Patients develop a hierarchy of their fears and with the use of therapist modeling and homework are encouraged to expose themselves to their feared stimuli. Repeated exposure desensitizes the patient to the feared object or activity. **Exposure** and **response prevention** behavioral therapy reinforces pharmacotherapy and vice versa.

Generalized Anxiety Disorder

While benzodiazepines work acutely, questions about the development of tolerance and difficulty with discontinuation, combined with frequent comorbidity with depression, have led to increasing use of **antidepressants** as first-line pharmacotherapy. Benzodiazepines do, however, have a more rapid onset of action and may be used initially. There is strong evidence for the efficacy of **CBT** and for applied relaxation training.

Post-Traumatic Stress Disorder

The most important element of treatment is to give the patient a sense of safety and support. Psychoeducation is vital with symptoms identified as biological and cognitive responses to stress and not character flaws. Support groups of patients with similar issues can often be quite helpful. Pharmacotherapy centers on the use of antidepressants.

Social Anxiety Disorder

The data are strongest for the use of SSRI's or monoamine oxidase inhibitors. For those who are able to anticipate episodes (lecturers, musicians) and who find that manifestations of autonomic overload (e.g., tremor, palpitations, tachypnea) precipitate an episode, **beta blockers** can be beneficial. **Exposure** *in vivo* is the most helpful and lasting intervention. This is the principle behind such groups as Toastmatsters.

Specific Phobias

Graduated exposure therapy combined with education regarding the nature of the stress response is recommended.

Recommended Reading

Beck AT. The current state of cognitive therapy. *Archives of General Psychiatry* 2005; 62:953–959.

Fricchione G. Generalized anxiety disorder. *New England Journal of Medicine* 2004; 351:675–682.

Jenike MA. Obsessive-compulsive disorder. *New England Journal of Medicine* 2004; 350:259–265.

Katon WA. Panic disorder. *New England Journal of Medicine* 2006; 354:2360–2367, 2006.

McLean PD, Woody SR. *Anxiety Disorders in Adults.* Oxford, UK: Oxford University Press; 2001.

Raj BA, Sheehan DV. Social anxiety disorder. *Medical Clinics of North America* 2001; 85:711–733.

Yehuda R. Post-traumatic stress disorder. *New England Journal of Medicine* 2002; 346:108–114.

D. Psychodynamic

E. Supportive

Key to review questions: p. 393

Review Questions

Directions: The items below consist of lettered headings followed by numbered descriptions. For each numbered description choose the *one* lettered heading to which it is *most* closely associated. Each lettered heading may be used *once, more than once,* or *not at all.*

Match the description to the disorder that it best represents.

A. Agoraphobia

B. Obsessive-compulsive disorder

C. Panic disorder

D. Posttraumatic stress disorder

E. Social phobia

1. Recurrent intrusive thoughts or images that typically result in anxiety-neutralizing behavioral or mental rituals

2. Fear of internal sensations and situations resulting in anticipatory anxiety and avoidance

3. Fear of being in a situation where anxiety may occur and escape is impossible

4. Fear of recurrence of a situation in which one feels trapped, helpless, or horrified

5. Fear of negative evaluation and embarrassment when one is or could be the focus of attention

6. Which of the following medication classes is indicated for the treatment of anxiety disorders?
   A. Anticholinergic
   B. Antidepressant
   C. Antiepileptic
   D. Antihistamine
   E. Antipsychotic

7. Which of the following psychotherapies is most effective for anxiety disorders?
   A. Cognitive-behavioral
   B. Interpersonal
   C. Marital

42 Major Mood Disorders

- What are the major mood disorders?
- What are the common signs and symptoms of mood disorders?
- How are mood disorders diagnosed?
- What causes mood disorders?
- What medical conditions most commonly mimic a mood disorder?
- What are the evidence-based treatments for mood disorders?
- What are the roles of patient and family education and peer support?

What are the major mood disorders?

There are three primary groups of mood disorders recognized in the Diagnostic and Statistical Manual of Mental Disorders (DSM). The disorders differ by the nature and quality of the primary mood change (depression or mania/hypomania) and by the nature, quality and duration of symptoms.

1. **Depressive disorders** (Major Depressive Disorder, Dysthymic Disorder, and Depressive Disorder NOS [not otherwise specified]);
2. **Bipolar disorders** (Bipolar I Disorder, Bipolar II Disorder, Cyclothymic Disorder, and Bipolar Disorder NOS); and
3. **Other mood disorders** (Mood Disorder Due to a General Medical Condition, Substance-Induced Mood Disorder and Mood Disorder NOS).

What are the common signs and symptoms of mood disorders?

Pathological mood change in depressive disorders involves intense, unremitting sadness or a loss of interest or pleasure in usual activities (anhedonia). Irritable mood change can substitute for depressive mood change or anhedonia in children. In bipolar disorders, the mood change involves elevated, expansive, or irritable mood.

Mood disorders include signs and symptoms involving four domains:

1. Pathological mood change
2. Neurovegetative features
3. Cognitive features
4. Psychomotor features

Neurovegetative features refer to normal "housekeeping" functions of the body including sleep and appetite regulation, weight maintenance, sexual function, and energy level. In depressive disorders, sleep, appetite and weight are typically reduced, but may be increased. Energy is typically reduced and sexual function is often impaired. In bipolar disorders, sleep is usually reduced, energy is elevated and the individual may feel highly sexualized.

Cognitive features of depressive disorders generally include slowed mentation, memory impairments, and a bias toward negative thinking about oneself and the future. Hopelessness, helplessness, thoughts of worthlessness and guilt, indecisiveness and thoughts of death or suicide are common. In bipolar disorders, thought, and its products like speech, are increased in rate and production. The individual is often unrealistically positive and full of expansive ideas.

Psychomotor change in depressive mood disorders typically involves slowing and loss of usual animation, but can include agitation and restlessness in some cases, especially in elders. In bipolar disorder, psychomotor activity is generally increased and the patient may appear to have boundless energy and excessive activity.

How are mood disorders diagnosed?

The mood disorders are diagnosed by the nature of the prominent mood change and differentiated by the nature, quality and duration of signs and symptoms.

Clinical Application

A 25-year-old woman presents reporting a 4-month history of persistent fatigue and depressed mood. She has no zest for life, thinks she is ineffective at work and wants to break up with her fiancé as she feels unworthy of his love. She has been unable to sleep past 4 AM and has lost 10 lbs. An episode like this resulted in a leave of absence in her junior year of college. Her mother has a history of highly recurrent depression.

Depressive Mood Disorders

To make the diagnosis of **major depressive disorder (MDD)** five symptoms/signs must be present for at least two weeks. One of these symptoms/signs must be persistent depressed mood change or anhedonia plus four other associated symptoms involving neurovegetative, cognitive and/or psychomotor change.

SIGECAPS is a useful mnemonic to remember the cardinal symptoms of major depression:
S (sleep),
I (interest, pleasure),
G (guilt),
E (energy),
C (concentration, attention, memory),
A (appetites for food, sex),
P (psychomotor change),
S (suicidal thinking, behavior).

The sleep disturbance of MDD involves middle and terminal insomnia (early morning awak-

ening). Depressed patients may also complain of various physical symptoms including constipation and pain. Complaints of fatigue, pain and sexual dysfunction are commonly the first mentioned to primary care providers.

MDD has several **subtypes** that are important to recognize because subtypes may affect treatment decisions. For example, milder severity MDD may respond equally well to psychotherapy or antidepressant medication whereas MDD with melancholic features is less likely to respond to psychotherapy alone; highly recurrent MDD requires antidepressant maintenance to prevent recurrence; and MDD with atypical features is more likely to respond to MAOI (monoamine oxidase inhibitor) or SSRI (selective serotonin reuptake inhibitor) antidepressants. See Table 42.1. for additional information about substypes/variants.

Dysthymic disorder has the same general features as MDD although symptoms are more prominent than signs and generally fewer in number. The diagnosis requires at least 2 years of continuous symptoms. Superimposed episodes of major depression **(double depression)** can complicate the course of dysthymic disorder. While referred to as a less severe depressive disorder, dysthymic disorder still may cause significant functional disability. Treatment with selected antidepressants and depression-specific cognitive-behavioral or interpersonal psychotherapies can be effective.

Depressive disorder not otherwise specified (NOS) is a disorder that does not meet criteria for other named disorders that have depressive symptoms, such as MDD, Dysthymic Disorder, and Adjustment Disorder with depressed mood.

Clinical Application

A 17-year-old boy is brought by his parents who report that for the last 6 weeks he has slept less than two hours a night, is convinced that he has developed a new operating system for computers that will supplant Microsoft and has been making international calls in the middle of the night to sell his idea. He is irritable and threatened his father. In the interview, he laughs constantly, cannot sit for long, is hard to interrupt, and shouts loudly at his parents.

Table 42.1. Variants of major depressive disorder: Features and clinical implications

MDD subtype/variant	Distinguishing features	Clinical implications
Atypical	Reactive mood Hypersomnia Hyperphagia Heavy immobilizing feelings in limbs ("leaden paralysis") Long-standing pattern of interpersonal rejection sensitivity	MAOI type antidepressants are the most effective for this subtype. SSRI type antidepressants are second line, but much easier to use. Atypical features are common in bipolar and seasonal depression.
Psychotic	Delusions or hallucinations that are typically congruent with mood	Requires combination of antidepressant and antipsychotic medication or ECT. Highly recurrent course. High risk of suicide and violence.
Melancholic	Prominent anhedonia, unreactive mood, and high number of neurovegetative symptoms	Unlikely to respond to psychotherapy alone. Clinical features predict response to antidepressants or ECT.
Seasonal	Consistent pattern of seasonal recurrence and remission; typically a fall-winter depression and spring summer remission pattern	Light therapy has 70% response rate if pattern is seasonal. Many types of antidepressants (e.g., SSRIs, SNRIs, DNRIs, NaSSAs) are effective.
Catatonic	Psychomotor changes include slowing (that may proceed to stupor) or excessive activity (that may proceed to dangerous overactivity); resistance to movement, posturing, ("waxy flexibility"), echolalia or echopraxia (mimicking speech or movements)	Requires antidepressants or ECT; antipsychotics may be needed. Observe general nutrition and fluid support needs closely.
Postpartum onset	Appears within 1 month postpartum by DSM-IV-TR criteria though some experts suggest that onset within the first year postpartum should qualify. Postpartum depression occurs following at least 10% of live births	Postpartum depression has a high risk of future recurrence at next delivery. Distinguish from postpartum blues (mild, self limited mood change occurring in up to 50–70% of deliveries) or postpartum psychosis (which is an emergency that occurs in 0.1–0.2% of deliveries). Desire to breastfeed will affect treatment selection.

Bipolar Mood Disorders

Bipolar I disorder is the classic syndrome previously referred to as manic-depressive illness/disorder. The defining characteristic is the manic episode involving an irritable, elevated or expansive mood that persists for 4 days or more unless adequately treated. The classic **manic episode** builds over several days or weeks to a crescendo of dramatic activity that often requires hospitalization. Mood becomes increasingly elated or irritable. Energized and inspired with creativity, patients are driven to pleasurable activity, racing thoughts, pressured speech, and diminished need for sleep. Thoughts may become disorganized as a result of **flight of ideas** (moving rapidly from one

Comparing and Contrasting the Symptoms of Major Depression and Bipolar Disorder

Dimension	Major depressive episode	Bipolar disorder, manic episode
Mood	Profound sadness and/or ahendonia Irritability in children	Elation, expansiveness Irritability
Neurovegetative features	Insomnia (or hypersominia in atypical variant) Early morning awakening Appetite and weight loss (or hyperphagia and weight gain in atypical variant) Decreased motivation and interest Decreased sexual interest and activity Fatigue	Decreased need for sleep Loss of appetite, too busy to eat Increased sexual interest and activity Boundless energy
Psychomotor features	Slowed movements Diminished expressiveness Slowed/latent speech responses	Excessive activity Restlessness Increased speed and amount of speech
Cognitive features	Slowing of mental function Difficulty concentrating Helplessness Hopelessness Memory deficits Indecisiveness Decreased interest Decreased pleasure Negativistic thought distortions Thoughts of death or suicide	Increased speed and amount of thought Inattention Distractibility Excessive self-confidence Inflated self-esteem Impulsive and excessive pleasure seeking
Mood congruent psychotic features	Delusions of guilt, sin, illness, poverty, nihilism	Delusions of grandiosity, influence eroticism, special powers

idea to another), **tangentiality** (getting off point and never returning to the original subject), and **circumstantiality** (including extraneous information in long, circuitous responses to questions but eventually getting back to the original subject). Social judgment decays as inflated self-confidence convinces the patient that normal rules of social behavior do not apply. Impulsive pleasure seeking, with financial and sexual indiscretions, is common. Some patients go on to develop psychotic symptoms before adequate treatment can be initiated. The patient with Bipolar I disorder has episodes of mania alternating with episodes of major depression. Typically, there are more depressive than manic episodes, and the bulk of the disability and risk for suicide is due to the depressive episodes.

Bipolar II disorder is manifested by major depression and hypomania (mild form of mania

that does not result in psychosis or hospitalization); if a true manic episode has occurred, the diagnosis is Bipolar I. This condition is sometimes hard to differentiate from other "moody" conditions like borderline personality disorder and is easily over diagnosed if DSM criteria are not followed.

Cyclothymic disorder is a less severe variant of bipolar mood disorder. Patients with this condition have a cyclic pattern of mood changes with many depressed and hypomanic cycles that do not reach the level of severity, duration per episode, number of symptoms or impairment to qualify for a Bipolar I or II diagnosis. Diagnosis requires a minimum of 2 years of continuous symptoms. Some patients with cyclothymia progress to full manic, mixed or depressive episodes of mood change. Treatments with mood stabilizing medications and psychotherapies have been variably successful.

Bipolar Disorder NOS refers to a disorder with bipolar features that does not meet criteria for other bipolar disorders.

Other Mood Disorders

Mood Disorder due to a General Medical Condition (GMC) is a mood change presenting in the course of a medical disorder where the findings are due to the direct physiological consequences of the medical condition and the syndrome is not better explained by a primary mood disorder.

Substance-Induced Mood Disorder can present with depressed or manic-like mood change depending on the substance and phase of use: acute intoxication, chronic use, withdrawal. Substances may include drugs of abuse, toxins or prescribed medications. The mood change must be the direct result of the substance, not simply a substance exacerbating a primary mood disorder.

Mood Disorder NOS is a disorder of pathological mood change difficult to categorize as any other specific mood disorder including Depressive or Bipolar Disorder NOS.

> The lifetime prevalence of MDD is about 12% for men and 25% for women; the lifetime prevalence for bipolar disorder is about 1% for both men and women. Up to 10% of persons seeking primary medical care could be diagnosed with MDD.

Mood disorders typically have their **onset in late adolescence or early adulthood**. Onset in childhood usually predicts a highly recurrent and often difficult course and onset in older life suggests organic causes. The length of time between mood episodes varies between individuals. MDD and bipolar disorder tend to be recurrent conditions and each episode predicts higher likelihood of a future recurrence. After a first episode of MDD, 50% will have a recurrence within 2 years; after a third episode, the rate of recurrence is 90%. Most patients with bipolar disorder experience more depressive episodes than manic or hypomanic episodes over the course of the illness. The interval between cycles may shorten over time, sometimes resulting in rapid cycling (four or more mood episodes per year). After an index episode of bipolar disorder the risk of recurrence rises from 50% at

> In 2001, the World Health Organization (WHO) reported that MDD and bipolar disorder ranked 4th and 9th, respectively, as the leading causes of disability worldwide.

one year to 90% by year three if mood stabilizing treatment is not continued.

The **goals of treatment** are to achieve and sustain remission of symptoms, otherwise the patient is at high risk of enduring disability, future recurrence and other negative outcomes including completed suicide. Unfortunately, even after achieving remission, 30–40% of patients with bipolar disorder do not regain their previous capacity to work.

Rates of completed **suicide** in MDD and bipolar disorder range between 3% and 15%. Suicide is more frequent early in the course of these disorders and early in the evolution of episodes. In bipolar disorder, suicidal behavior is usually seen in the depressive phase. All patients with mood disorders should be screened for suicide risk at evaluation and reassessed frequently in the acute phase of treatment.

The most common co-occurring psychiatric disorders affecting individuals with mood disorders are anxiety, personality and substance use disorders.

Psychosis is a serious complication of MDD and bipolar disorder. Delusions or hallucinations are usually congruent with mood (e.g., grandiose delusions in mania, voices telling the person he is worthless in depression). Because psychosis does not track neatly with severity, all patients with MDD should be screened; at least 10–15% of more severely ill patients have psychotic features. Failure to recognize psychosis in patients with MDD will result in lack of response to antidepressants alone. Patients with psychotic symptoms have higher risk for dangerous behaviors and are more likely to require hospitalization.

> What causes mood disorders?

> Genetic, neurobiological and stress-related factors determine who will develop a major mood disorder and when it will occur.

Compared to the general population, a person having a first-degree relative with MDD has about twice the risk of developing MDD. A person with a first-degree relative with bipolar disorder has 5–10 times greater risk than the general population of developing bipolar disorder.

Sleep regulation appears to be an important factor in the development and maintenance of mood disorders, especially in bipolar disorder. Disturbances in the nature and quality of sleep are among the biological markers of mood disorders, but it is unclear whether sleep disturbance is a cause or by-product of the mood disorder.

Dysregulation of the **catecholamine** (norepinephrenine and dopamine) and **indolamine** (serotonin) systems and their projections in the brainstem, midbrain, limbic system, hypothalamus, and frontal lobes appears to be involved in development of mood disorders. Disturbances in the neuroendocrine systems involving hypothalamic regulation, most importantly thyroid and corticosteroid hormones, are also apparently important in the neurobiology of mood disorders. One theory is that chronic **stress-induced** elevated levels of **corticosteroids** have a catabolic effect upon the **hippocampus**, impairing the ability of the individual to learn from experience and adapt to new stressful situations. These repeated failures to adapt are manifested as stereotypic maladaptive responses, learned helplessness and associated depressed mood.

The role of **life stressors** in MDD appears to be most important in early episodes; as the disorder becomes more recurrent, episodes appear to arise independent of stress induction. In bipolar disorder, the role of stressors is such an important concern that specific therapies for individuals and families have been developed to reduce the occurrence and impact of life stress and develop healthy social rhythms.

What medical conditions most commonly mimic a mood disorder?

The symptoms and signs of mood disorders are largely non-specific, so there are many medical or neurological illnesses that can mimic a mood disorder. An exhaustive list of conditions that cause mood symptoms is beyond the scope of this chapter. However, examples include endocrine disorders, CNS disease, malignancies, anemia, chronic infections (syphilis, HIV, TB), autoimmune disorders

> A comprehensive evaluation of a patient presenting with a mood disorder should include a careful medical and neurological history and examination followed by studies that are indicated by this review. Common routine testing includes a complete blood count, metabolic profile, chemical dependency screen, and thyroid testing.

(SLE), and substance use/abuse. Even among individuals who are severely or terminally medically ill, certain findings like severe anhedonia, decreased talkativeness, disinterest in family, expressions of worthlessness, guilt or suicidal thinking are uncommon and suggest the presence of MDD.

What are the evidence-based treatments for mood disorders?

Evidence-based treatments for mood disorders include **somatic treatments** such as antidepressants, mood stabilizers, ECT, and light therapy, as well as individual, group and family psychotherapies. **Cognitive-behavioral therapies in combination with pharmacotherapies** have been shown to be especially effective. Some newer technologies are showing promise including vagal nerve stimulation, now FDA-approved for treatment of refractory depression. Transcranial magnetic stimulation and deep brain stimulation are still in investigational stages.

Treatment for a mood disorder may take up to several weeks to have therapeutic effects. Patients and their doctors should be mindful of this so that treatments are not changed too rapidly, leading to discouragement. Combined pharmacological and psychotherapeutic treatments are most effective in achieving and maintaining remission.

Phases of Mood Disorder Treatment

Mood disorder treatment is organized into three phases: acute, continuation and maintenance.

The goal of **acute phase** treatment is remission; it comprises the time from diagnosis to remission. Frequent follow-up (weekly/biweekly) is indicated during this phase.

By most definitions, **continuation phase** treatment extends from remission to recovery of function. The goal of continuation phase treatment is relapse prevention and recovery. Medication monitoring visits are typically tapered to monthly during this phase, although psychotherapy sessions may be more frequent as indicated.

The goal of **maintenance phase** treatment is prevention of future recurrences. Maintenance phase antidepressant or combined treatment with psychotherapy is indicated for some patients with MDD who have had two episodes and all patients with three episodes. Maintenance mood stabilizer and psychotherapy treatment is indicated for all patients with bipolar disorder. Visits typically range from monthly (if psychotherapy is involved) to every 3–6 months for medication management.

Measurement-Based Care

It is important to identify all symptoms and track treatment response in mood disorders to improve the quality of care. This is best accomplished with a rating scale. Several scales including the Patient Health Questionnaire (PHQ-9), Quick Inventory for Depressive Symptomatology (QIDS) and Beck Depression Inventory (BDI) are available for MDD, and mood charts, such as the Young Mania Rating Scale and the Mood Disorder Questionnaire, are useful tools in bipolar disorder.

Treatment of Major Depressive Disorder

In **mild to moderate** severity MDD, depression specific psychotherapies (cognitive-behavioral, interpersonal, brief dynamic, problem-solving) and antidepressant medications appear to be equally effective. More **severe** episodes, those with melancholic features, and highly recurrent MDD will require antidepressant treatment. **Psychotic depression** must be treated with a combination of antidepressant and antipsychotic medication or ECT. Seasonal depression may respond to light therapy even if suicidal ideation is present.

There are over 25 antidepressants available on the market, many available as generics, organized into seven classes reviewed in Table 42.2. Each class is defined by its pharmacological **mechanism of action**(s) that affect the availability of catecholamine and indolamine neurotransmitters (norepinephrine, dopamine and serotonin) at the synapse.

These actions include blocking of reuptake pumps, pre- and post-synaptic receptor antagonism or agonism and blocking monoamine oxidase enzymes that break down neurotransmitters. All antidepressants require 2–4 weeks to determine effectiveness at a given dose. Patients remitting on antidepressants should continue the medication at the same dose for at least 6 months before considering discontinuation. Some patients may require a year's continuation while others may require long-term maintenance.

Many antidepressants have a **discontinuation syndrome** (flu-like syndrome sometimes associated with dizziness, imbalance and shock-like symptoms in the limbs) that is not dangerous, but indicates **slow tapering** when discontinuation is considered.

Selection of the antidepressant is made by considering safety, tolerability, efficacy, cost and simplicity of use, personal choices, and in some cases, family history.

Safety issues include risks related to age, underlying medical disorders (e.g., epilepsy, cardiac conditions), possible drug-food-herbal interactions, pregnancy, lactation and suicide potential. A thorough list of all the patient's prescribed and over-the-counter medications (including supplement products) and careful review of drug interactions involving the CYP-450 hepatic microenzymes and protein binding should be completed before selecting an antidepressant. Some antidepressants have unique safety issues that include hypo- or hypertension, cardiac arrhythmia, seizure provocation, or hepatic toxicity and should be understood and considered as selection is made. Table 42.2. includes some common safety issues of the classes of antidepressants.

Recently, concerns about a possible association between antidepressant exposure and suicidal ideation or behavior in children and adolescents have emerged. While studies and experts disagree on these issues, all newer antidepressants are now labeled with a warning about this concern. It is wise to inform all patients about suicide risk and the possibility of provoking anxiety or agitation during initiation of an antidepressant. These problems are among the reasons to see patients frequently after treatment is begun.

Tolerability (side effects) of antidepressants can be predicted by the pharmacological properties of the drug. Each class of antidepressants has typical side effects and individual antidepres-

Table 42.2. Antidepressant medications: Classes, common and serious side effects

Class/example medications	Common side effects	Serious side effects	Special concerns
Tricyclic (TCA) Desipramine Nortriptyline	Blurred vision Dry mouth Orthostatic hypotension Sedation Sexual function Weight gain	Cardiac conduction defects Seizure provocation Worsen glaucoma/urinary retention Drug-drug interactions	Very dangerous in overdose Elders and youths more sensitive to side effects
Selective serotonin reuptake inhibitor (SSRI) Citalopram Escitalopram Fluoxetine Paroxetine Sertraline	Nausea Diarrhea Sedation or insomnia Sexual function Headache Weight gain in long term	Drug-drug interactions for some Agitation ? Increase in suicidal ideation or behaviour in youth	Withdrawal syndrome (exception fluoxetine due to long half-life)
Serotonin and norepinephrine reuptake inhibitor (SNRI) Venlafaxine Duloxetine	Similar to SSRI profile	BP should be monitored; may cause sustained elevation. Hepatic toxicity (duloxetine)	Withdrawal syndrome
Dopamine and norepinephrine reuptake inhibitor (DNRI) Buproprion	Insomnia Anxiety Agitation	Seizure risk escalates at doses above maximum recommended doses and if excessive single doses are taken Psychosis in elders and those with risk factors like schizophrenia	Seizure risk in OD Contraindicated in eating disorders
Serotonin antagonist and reuptake inhibitor (SARI) Nefazodone Trazodone	Sedation	Hypotension for trazodone at higher doses Hepatic toxicity and drug-drug interactions for nefazodone Priapism	
Norepinephrine and specific serotonin antidepressant (NaSSA) Mitazapine	Sedation Weight gain		Sedation and/or weight gain lead to discontinuation in about 10% of exposures
Monamine oxidase inhibitor (MAOI) Phenelzine Selegiline transdermal Tranylcypromine	Sedation or insomnia Weight gain Orthostatic hypotension	Dangerous hypertension with tyramine ingestion and drug-drug interactions require dietary restrictions and careful patient education	Selegiline transdermal does not require dietary restrictions at low doses (6 mg)

sants have certain unique side effects (see Table 42.2.). Any antidepressant is likely to have some side effects during the initiation period. Most are dose related and usually abate within the first two weeks of treatment.

Efficacy refers to the types of depression for which an antidepressant has demonstrated effectiveness, and the comorbid conditions that it may target. For example, bupropion may treat both MDD and tobacco dependence and an SSRI may treat both MDD and an anxiety disorder.

Cost to the patient is determined by insurance coverage (or lack thereof). This is no small matter, as many patients need to stay on their medication for long periods or a lifetime. Many patients will not discuss cost unless asked. Cost is a major determinate of adherence.

Simplicity of use refers to issues such as need for titration, medical monitoring needs, dietary or other restrictions and complexity of dosing schedule that affect short- and long-term compliance.

Treatment of Bipolar Disorders

The mainstays of treatment for bipolar disorders are mood-stabilizing medications. A "perfect" mood stabilizer would treat both depressive and manic/hypomanic episodes in their acute phase and prevent recurrence of each phase. The only drug that has demonstrated this capacity is lithium.

Lithium and three other **mood stabilizers**, valproic acid (VPA), carbamazepine and lamotrigine, have the largest established evidence-base for efficacy. VPA and carbamazepine have demonstrated more efficacy for manic/hypomanic phase symptoms than for the depressive phase. Lamotrigine is indicated as an add-on treatment that has been most effective in treating/preventing recurrence of depressive phase episodes.

Atypical antipsychotics, such as aripiprazole olanzapine, risperidone, quetiapine, and ziprasidone, have demonstrated efficacy in acute manic and mixed episodes. Olanzapine has demonstrated efficacy in delaying recurrence and in the treatment of depressive phase episodes. Antidepressants may be necessary in the treatment or prevention of depressive episodes, but exposure should usually be time-limited to prevent provocation of hypomanic or manic episodes or progression to rapid cycling.

General Principles of Mood Stabilizer Use

Drug interactions are common and should be considered whenever prescription or co-prescription is considered. Lithium, VPA and carbamazepine are each known teratogens in the first trimester of pregnancy; patient education regarding pregnancy prevention and pre-treatment pregnancy testing is indicated. All blood level monitoring should be done at trough (12 hours post dose).

Lithium can cause hypothyroidism (typically reversible) and worsening of cystic acne and psoriasis (relative contraindications). Many patients have polyuria/polydypsia during initiation; few will develop diabetes insipidus. Whether lithium injures the kidney outside of repeated episodes of toxicity remains unclear. Routine monitoring of lithium levels, BUN, creatinine and TSH are indicated. The therapeutic blood level for acute and maintenance treatment is usually maintained between 0.8 mg/ml and 1.0 mg/ml. The therapeutic index between effective and toxic levels is low; levels of about 1.4 mg/ml will generally create toxicity symptoms; levels above 2.0 mg/ml can be dangerous. Drugs that reduce renal clearance or upset sodium balance will increase the risk of toxicity. Dose adjustments and/or level monitoring will be indicated with non-steroidal anti-inflammatory drugs, COX-2 inhibitors, ACE inhibitors and sodium wasting diuretics as examples. Maintaining good hydration status and sodium balance is important. Rapid cessation of lithium has been associated with much higher rates of recurrence than very gradual tapering.

Valproic Acid (VPA) can suppress the bone marrow, typically affecting white and platelet cell lines. Rare cases of hepatic toxicity and hemorrhagic pancreatitis have been reported. A possible association with polycystic ovarian syndrome has been reported. Routine monitoring of complete blood counts, hepatic profile and VPA levels are indicated. Therapeutic blood levels have not been definitively established in bipolar disorder, but evidence suggests that it is best to maintain the level in the range of 50–100 mcg/ml.

Carbamazepine is a tricyclic molecule and can produce side effects typical of tricyclic antidepressants including prolongation of the QT and QRS intervals. Like VPA, it can affect the bone marrow and liver, and also can produce hypothyroidism, hyponatremia (SIADH) and folate deficiency. Rashes are common and a reason for immediate discontinuation. Routine monitoring of complete blood counts, hepatic profile, TSH and blood levels are indicated. Therapeutic blood levels have not been definitively established in bipolar disorder, but evidence suggests that it is best to maintain the level in the range of 4–12 mcg/ml.

Lamotrigine has been associated with a dangerous skin rash that can progress to Stevens-Johnson Syndrome or Toxic Epidermal Necrolysis. The risk of rash is significantly reduced by obeying rules to titrate the dose depending on whether VPA or other enzyme inducing antiepileptic drugs are co-prescribed. Package inserts should routinely be consulted when starting lamotrigine or adding or removing a drug to the regimen.

Psychotherapies that have been shown to be especially efficacious in the treatment of mood disorders include interpersonal psychotherapy (IPT), cognitive-behavioral therapies (CBT), and hybrid combinations of IPT, CBT and brief psychodynamic therapies designed to target the disorder-specific pathologies of mood disorders. One such development, **Cognitive Behavioral Analysis System of Psychotherapy**, in combination with pharmacotherapy, has been shown to be especially effective in the treatment of chronic depression.

Key educational issues in mood disorders include:

- Education about the nature and course of the mood disorder and the nature and rationale for treatment
- Dispelling myths and stigma
- Reviewing the harmful consequences of substance use
- Emphasizing the importance of maintaining healthy sleep-wake cycles and sleep hygiene
- Offering clear information about the importance of aggressive treatment to achieve remission and the importance of continuation/maintenance treatments as required
- Aiding the patient and family in talking about the disorder, developing symptom management techniques, reducing unnecessary stress, and improving social support
- Preventing missed medication doses
- Improving early identification of symptoms/signs of recurrence
- Developing a crisis plan to respond to new or increased suicidal ideation

---

What are the roles of patient and family education and peer support?

Patient and family education can be critical to compliance and outcome. Peer support through organizations like the Depressive and Bipolar Support Alliance (www.dbsa.org) are helpful to many patients and a good resource for educational materials.

It is important that patients, families and their doctors accept the reality that most mood disorders are highly recurrent and affected patients are rarely "cured."

The best outcomes are achieved when comprehensive treatment plans address the medical and psychosocial dimensions of mood disorders, incorporating multidimensional and interdisciplinary treatments that promote wellness, prevent recurrence and optimize function.

Recommended Reading

American Psychiatric Association. Practice Guideline for the Treatment of Patients with Major Depressive Disorder. *American Journal of Psychiatry* 2000; 157(4 Suppl.):1–45. (also available at: www.psych.org)

American Psychiatric Association. Practice Guideline for the Treatment of Patients with Bipolar Disorder (revision). *American Journal of Psychiatry* 2002;159 (4 Suppl.):1–50. (also available at: www.psych.org)

Dubovsky SL, Dubovsky AN (Eds.). *Concise Guide to Mood Disorders*. Washington, DC: American Psychiatric Press; 2002.

McCullough JP. Cognitive behavioral analysis system of psychotherapy. In: JC Norcross, MR Goldfried (Eds.). *Handbook of Psychotherapy Integration*. (2nd ed.). London: Oxford University Press; 2005.

Weissman, MM. *Treatment of Depression: Bridging the 21st Century*. Washington, DC: American Psychiatric Press; 2001.

Review Questions

1. SIGECAPS is a mnemonic for
   A. common side effects of antidepressants

   B. drug interactions

   C. factors in antidepressant medication selection

   D. suicide risk factors

   E. typical symptoms of major depression

2. Mania is a criterion for diagnosis of which of the following disorders?

   A. Bipolar I disorder

   B. Bipolar II disorder

   C. Cyclothymic disorder

   D. Dysthymic disorder

   E. Major depression with psychotic features

3. Continuation phase antidepressant treatment in major depressive disorder (MDD) is required in which of the following cases

   A. all patients who remit with medication

   B. MDD with early life onset

   C. MDD with highly recurrent course

   D. MDD with melancholic features

   E. MDD with psychotic features

4. Maintenance treatment (continuing antidepressant medication for years) should be considered in

   A. female patients

   B. patients that attempted suicide

   C. patients with a history of post-partum depression

   D. patients with psychotic features

   E. patients with three or more episodes

5. Which of the following medications has proven effective in treating acute mania and acute major depression and prevention of manic and depressive phase recurrence in bipolar disorder?

   A. Carbamazepine

   B. Fluoxetine

   C. Lamotrigine

   D. Lithium

   E. Valproic acid

Key to review questions: p. 393

43 Dissociative Disorders and Cognitive Disorders

- What is the difference between normal and pathologic dissociation?
- What is the hypothesized cause of dissociation?
- What is the difference between amnesia, fugue, and dissociative identity disorder?
- What history is usually associated with dissociative identity disorder?
- What is depersonalization disorder?
- What are common treatments for dissociative disorders?
- What are the manifestations of cognitive impairment?
- What are the three major types of cognitive disorder?
- How are cognitive disorders evaluated and treated?

Dissociative Disorders

What is the difference between normal and pathologic dissociation?

Dissociation is a disorder in which the usual integration of memory, consciousness, and personal identity is disrupted. **Memory loss** is characteristic except in depersonalization disorder. Dissociative phenomena exist on a continuum from normal to pathologic. An example of everyday **normal dissociation** is an episode of such intense absorption in a book or movie that the person becomes completely unaware of events occurring in the environment. In **pathologic dissociation,** more profound dissociative phenomena interfere with psychological, social, and work functioning.

What is the hypothesized cause of dissociation?

Pathologic dissociation is thought to represent the person's attempt to cope with overwhelming or **traumatic stress** through partial consciousness, as in depersonalization disorder, or through frank amnesia for specific events or personal identity, as in dissociative amnesia or dissociative fugue.

Predisposing factors include a history of severe family dysfunction and poor premorbid emotional, social, or occupational functioning.

Clinical Application

A 32-year-old woman, Susan, seeks treatment for chronic depression, anxiety, and thoughts of suicide. She describes a period of childhood sexual and physical abuse and an incident of rape during adulthood. She complains of "spacing out" for minutes to hours with amnesia for that time. When she emerges from these episodes, she is in uncharacteristic situations (e.g., walking unfamiliar streets far from home) or finds herself wearing an article of clothing, in a style different from her own, that she does not recall purchasing. She reports hearing angry voices inside her head. During one session, she became quiet and closed her eyes. When she spoke, she introduced herself as Kim. Her speech was different from Susan's usual timid speech. Kim said she knows everything about Susan, but that Susan knows nothing about her. She mocks Susan's timidity and is irritable and aggressive, especially when discussing fears. Minutes later, Susan returns, has no memory of Kim, but is aware of a time gap during the session.

Dissociative Amnesia

> What is the difference between amnesia, fugue, and dissociative identity disorder?

Dissociative amnesia is characterized by an inability to remember important **personal events**, especially those that are **stressful** or traumatic. This memory impairment may present suddenly and dramatically in response to an event, such as a natural disaster.

More often, dissociative amnesia presents as noticeable gaps in an individual's retrospective reporting of personal history. Although the amnesia usually is confined to a particular event, it can be generalized to an individual's entire life. Similarly, the memory impairment typically is selective for only parts of events, but amnesia for entire events can occur.

Diagnosis requires that the individual experience significant distress (e.g., depression or anxiety) or have impairments in functioning as a result of the disorder. Episodes may last minutes or persist for years.

Dissociative Fugue

Dissociative fugue is sudden, unexpected departure from usual activities accompanied by amnesia for parts of the personal history. In some cases, people have assumed entirely new personal identities. More often, individuals in fugue states recall some aspects of personal identity or history. As with dissociative amnesias, fugues may follow extreme stress or traumatic events.

Individuals in fugue states may be in no apparent distress or have significant emotional upset associated with their personal confusion. They may travel for hours or months over short or long distances. The disorder is rare. Women are estimated to be affected three times more often than men.

Dissociative Identity Disorder

Dissociative identity disorder, previously referred to as **multiple personality disorder,** is a controversial diagnosis. Experts dispute whether it is truly a dissociative disorder or whether it is a sociocultural phenomenon that is produced for primary gain (to gain comfort, support, and patient role) or produced iatrogenically through suggestion. Diagnostically, it is distinguished from the other dissociative disorders by the presence of two or more **personality states** that recurrently "take charge" of an individual's behavior; significantly impaired memory is typical. Separate personality states occur because the affected individual is unable to contain emotions and memories in a single, integrated experience of self. These **personality states,** sometimes known as **alters,** have distinct emotions and expressive styles. Personality states may claim their own personal histories, identities, and names. The scope of memories, as well as knowledge of other alters, is variable among the personality states.

> What history is usually associated with dissociative identity disorder?

Diagnosis is difficult with this disorder. As with dissociative amnesia, it is associated with a **history of trauma,** especially severe sexual or physical abuse during childhood. The disorder may appear during childhood, but the diagnosis is most often made during adulthood. Symptoms and functional impairments wax and wane over time. More frequent switching among personality states occurs during periods of increased life stress.

Depersonalization Disorder

> What is depersonalization disorder?

Depersonalization disorder is manifested as the experience of being *emotionally detached from and observing one's own thinking or actions.*

Because this phenomenon is common, the diagnosis of depersonalization disorder is only made when symptoms are sufficiently frequent or intense to cause distress. Affected individuals

> Depersonalization disorder is unique among the dissociative disorders because it does not include frank amnesia for personal history or identity. What is missing, or "forgotten," is the individual's experience of meaningful reality.

experience themselves as machine-like and surrounding events as devoid of personal meaning or impact.

Like the other dissociative disorders, depersonalization is considered a response to extreme **stress** or trauma. The course can be chronic, although symptoms vary with the degree of stress.

Differential Diagnosis

Before the diagnosis of a **dissociative disorder** can be made, alternative explanations for the presenting symptoms, such as organic mental disorders (processes directly or indirectly affecting the CNS such as seizure disorders, stroke, tumor, head injuries, metabolic disorders) or memory impairments due to use of prescribed medications or illicit substances must be excluded. Common differential diagnoses for the dissociative disorders include posttraumatic stress disorder, personality disorder, anxiety disorder and malingering. Dissociative phenomena are also seen in psychotic states.

Treatment

What are common treatments for dissociative disorders?

Psychotherapy is useful in treating active symptoms and in assisting with recovery following a dissociative experience. Patients in the midst of an amnestic or depersonalization episode require supportive psychotherapy focused on reassurance and gentle exploration of events that might be causing the dissociative impairment.

Hypnosis must be used cautiously because dissociative patients are suggestible. Psychotherapy directed at mastering the stress or trauma which triggered the dissociative symptoms should be provided to minimize the possibility of relapse. Some patients diagnosed with dissociative identity disorder are eventually able to achieve integration of the personality states into a coherent, single whole.

Medications that target dissociative symptoms, per se, may have limited effectiveness. However, alleviation of associated symptoms (e.g., depression, anxiety) may, in turn, alleviate some of the dissociative pathology.

Cognitive Disorders

What are the manifestations of cognitive impairment?

Cognitive impairment is the hallmark feature of **cognitive disorders,** and is manifested as disturbances in level of consciousness, attention, memory, orientation, intellectual capacity, language, judgment and the ability to perform skilled tasks. The diagnosis is made when the disturbance is severe enough to impair social or occupational functioning.

Cognitive disorders account for about 10% of the psychiatric disorders encountered in general medical and surgical populations and include: delirium, dementia, amnesia, and cognitive disorders with psychosis. Men and women are affected equally; the prevalence is highest in the very young and the very old. The disorders may result from structural or neurochemical brain dysfunction that may be caused by various medical or neurological disorders, toxins, heavy metal poisoning, brain injury or complications of aging.

Diagnosis

What are the three major types of cognitive disorder?

Delirium manifests as global cognitive impairment, fluctuation in the level of consciousness, and disturbance in the sleep-wake cycle. It has an acute onset, typically lasts briefly, and is generally reversible. Aggressive work-up should be undertaken to determine the etiology; treatment depends on the underlying cause. If psychosis or severe behavioral disturbance complicates the course, antipsychotics are sometimes used symptomatically.

Dementia is a generalized loss of intellectual abilities, including memory, judgment, and abstract thought. Personality changes are an associated feature. Dementia typically has an insidious onset and a protracted and deteriorating course. Level of consciousness is not affected unless there is a superimposed delirium. Named dementias include Alzheimer's, Pick's, and vascular. Reversible causes include metabolic disorders, nutritional deficiencies, hypothyroidism, and CNS infection. The work-up should include testing for reversible causes. Environmental manipulations that improve orientation/reorientation help the patient considerably. Stocking the patient's room with familiar objects and a clock, calendar, radio and television are helpful to maintain orientation. Treatment with cognitive enhancers is variably helpful to many patients with irreversible dementias; as the dementia progresses they become less effective.

Amnestic disorders are characterized by the inability to form new memories **(antegrade amnesia)** or recall past events **(retrograde amnesia).** The memory loss can be global, circumscribed, or selective. Onset frequently occurs after a physically or emotionally traumatic event. Duration is variable, but can be lifelong. Other cognitive functions are preserved.

How are cognitive disorders evaluated and treated?

The **Mini-Mental Status Examination (MMSE)** is a common, sensitive screening tool to determine the presence and severity of a cognitive impairment. It requires 5 to 10 minutes to administer and score. The MMSE probes orientation, attention, concentration, short-term memory, language functions and constructional skills. Findings will guide further **neuropsychological testing** that can tease out the nature and extent of the cognitive impairment. Various medical and neurological disorders can produce cognitive impairment. Careful **history** and complete **physical examination** will guide testing that may include **neuroimaging, lumbar puncture, electroencephalography** and testing for autoimmune, endocrine, infectious, and metabolic disorders along with malignancy and toxins.

The first rule of management is to identify and treat any underlying reversible disorder. If the underlying condition is not reversible, management should be directed toward minimizing, controlling, or relieving distressing symptoms while providing a supportive and comfortable environment. Psychosis and behavioral disturbances can complicate the course and symptomatic treatments may include antipsychotics, although there is an increased risk of morbidity and mortality when antipsychotics are used in dementias. For those patients with irreversible processes, measures must be taken to maximize the patient's quality of life, despite the presence of the illness.

Recommended Reading

Folstein MF, Folstein DE, McHugh PR. "Mini-mental state": A practical guide for grading the cognitive state of patients for the clinician. *Journal of Psychiatric Research* 1975; 12:189–198.

Bremner JD, Marmar CR. *Trauma, Memory, and Dissociation.* Washington, DC: American Psychiatric Press; 1998.

Goldman LS, Wise TN, Brody DS (Eds.). *Psychiatry for Primary Care Physicians.* (2nd ed.). Chicago, IL: American Medical Association; 2004.

American Psychiatric Association. Practice Guideline for the Treatment of Patients with Alzheimer's Disease and Other Dementias of Late Life. *American Journal of Psychiatry* 1997; 154(5 Suppl.):1–39 (Available at: www.psych.org).

American Psychiatric Association. Practice Guideline for the Treatment of Patients with Delirium. *American Journal of Psychiatry* 1999; 156(5 Suppl.):1–20. (Available at www.psych.org).

Review Questions

1. Dissociative amnesia is characterized by which of the following?
   A. Emotional detachment
   B. Inability to remember stressful/traumatic events
   C. Sudden unexpected changes in behavior
   D. Presence of two or more personalities
   E. Surrounding events are devoid of meaning

2. It is hypothesized that all dissociative disorders are a response to which of the following?
   A. Cognitive confusion
   B. Competing demands of personality states
   C. Extreme stress or trauma
   D. Loss of identity
   E. Loss of memory

3. Cognitive disorders account for approximately what percentage of psychiatric disorders encountered in general medical populations?
   A. < 1%
   B. 2%
   C. 10%
   D. 25%
   E. 33%

4. A general loss of intellectual ability, including impaired memory, judgment, and abstract thought, is characteristic of which of the following conditions?
   A. Amnestic disorders
   B. Antegrade amnesia
   C. Delirium
   D. Dementia
   E. Retrograde amnesia

Key to review questions: p. 393

44 Schizophrenia and Other Psychotic Disorders

- What are the characteristic features of schizophrenia and other psychotic disorders?
- What etiologic factors most likely contribute to schizophrenia?
- What are the three phases of schizophrenia?
- What are the specific symptoms most commonly observed in schizophrenia?
- What are the common thought disorders found in schizophrenia?
- What are the subtypes of schizophrenia?
- What are four psychotic disorders other than schizophrenia?

What are the characteristic features of schizophrenia and other psychotic disorders?

Psychotic disorders are characterized by **delusions and/or hallucinations,** and varying degrees of **disorganized thought, speech, behavior,** and **social impairment** that affect the patient's ability to meet the ordinary demands of life. Psychotic disorders are differentiated from one another by the quality and quantity of the clinical findings manifested by the patient, by the impact of the disorder on personality and social functioning, and by etiology if known.

Schizophrenia

Schizophrenia is the most common psychotic disorder affecting about 1–2% of the population. Both genders are equally affected. It is a pervasive disorder that affects many areas of psychological functioning, may change personality, and typically leads to some deterioration in motivation, and ability to work, occupy oneself, and relate to other people. Schizophrenia is usually a chronic condition with periods of remission and exacerbation. Worldwide, management of schizophrenia accounts for more inpatient treatment days per year than any other medical illness.

Clinical Application

Previously fastidious and outgoing, a 20-year-old college sophomore now rarely comes out of his room, is unkempt, is preoccupied with the meaning of life, mumbles to himself, and is expressionless except for bursts of inappropriate speech. His speech is sparse but talks about his "vision quest" to find "the inner soul of the patrician monarchy." He becomes hostile when questioned and accuses the interviewer of attempting to "steal my mind to insert your sins." Physical examination and screening laboratory studies reveal no obvious medical problems and urine drug screen is negative.

What etiologic factors most likely contribute to schizophrenia?

The cause of schizophrenia is not known, although several hypothesized etiologic factors are under investigation including the roles of dopamine, serotonin, gamma-aminobutyric acid (GABA), and glutamate. The **"dopamine hypothesis"** is based on findings that increased activity of the neurotransmitter dopamine is associated with schizophrenia and other psychotic states such as amphetamine-induced psychosis. This hypothesis is considered only a partial explanation, given the complex interplay of neurotransmitters in brain function and malfunction.

Anatomical and **functional** brain imaging studies suggest that **abnormalities** of frontal, prefrontal, temporal and subcortical areas of the brain are all likely involved in the development of the illness. Metabolic hypofunction of the frontal lobes and ventricular enlargement are findings associated with the diagnosis and clinical findings.

Genetic risk has been established, but is not a complete explanation. The concordance among monozygotic twins is only 50% indicating that the presence of factors other than genes are necessary to develop the illness. **Family history** often includes other examples of individuals with schizophrenia. Thus, the illness most likely results from a **convergence** of genetic and acquired neurobiological and psychological vulnerabilities, and precipitating psychosocial stresses.

Clinical Features

What are the three phases of schizophrenia?

Schizophrenia typically presents in late adolescence or early adulthood; rarely beyond the fourth decade. It typically proceeds through three distinct phases: **prodromal**, **active** and **residual** (see Table 44.1.). Most patients experience some enduring symptoms in the residual phase of the illness and

Table 44.1. Phases of schizophrenia

Phase	Features
Prodromal	Gradual change in behavior that may appear as personality or mood change (aloofness, preoccupation, moodiness, oddities of thought or behavior) lasting weeks to months before the active phase begins.
Active	Classic findings of delusions, hallucinations, disorganized thinking and behavior. May include agitation, sleeplessness, and dangerous behaviors.
Residual	Continuing oddities of thinking and behavior, often with prominent "negative" symptoms. Delusions or hallucinations are typically absent.

recurrence of active phase symptoms is common. The diagnosis of **schizophrenia** requires meeting two **criteria:**

1. an active phase with prominent psychotic symptoms lasting more than 1 week, unless symptoms are interrupted by effective treatment; and

2. a total duration of symptoms, regardless of phase, of at least 6 months.

Symptoms

What are the specific symptoms most commonly observed in schizophrenia?

Delusions are false beliefs that are not changed by reason or evidence that controvert them. In schizophrenia, these erroneous beliefs are often bizarre, incongruent with mood, and tend to guide how the individual interprets reality and behavioral responses. Examples include beliefs that one's body, mind or soul has been mysteriously changed, beliefs that supernatural or alien forces are influencing events, inserting or removing ones' thoughts, or causing one's thoughts to be broadcast without speaking them. Some delusions are less bizarre and involve themes of persecution, grandiosity, jealousy, illness, guilt, religious conviction, or sin.

Auditory hallucinations are most common, although any of the five perceptual senses may be involved. The hallucinations are typically more complex and bizarre than those of other psychoses. Auditory hallucinations may be experienced as conversations between several different voices that speak together about the individual, comment on thoughts, or command the person to behave in a way that is uncomfortable and uncharacteristic for him or her. Other odd perceptual experiences include perceptions that someone or something is controlling the thoughts (thought insertion, withdrawal, manipulation), emotions and behaviors of the patient.

What are the common thought disorders found in schizophrenia?

Thought disorder (see Table 44.2.) is characterized by the absence of linear and logical connections between ideas. Communication in speech

Table 44.2. Selected named thought disorders

Thought disorder	Description
Derailment (loose associations)	Random connection between ideas leading to loss of meaning
Tangential	Responses to questions are only partially or remotely connected to the topic
Circumstantial	Excessively circuitous speech that eventually results in a response to the question
Neologism	Creation of words with unique meaning only understood by the individual
Blocking	Loosing track of the goal of speech and not being able to return to the topic
Word Salad	Complete disregard for conventions of word usage or grammar leading to incoherence
Clanging	The sounds of words, instead of the meanings or conventions of speech, determine the flow of speech

Table 44.3. Key features of schizophrenia subtypes

Subtype	Key features
Paranoid	A central delusional theme predominates without prominent disorganization of thinking or behavior
Catatonic	Prominent psychomotor changes including stupor, excessive excitement, posturing, mechanical speech
Disorganized	Disorganized thinking and behavior are prominent; multiple delusions are often poorly formed into frag-mentary themes
Undifferentiated	Insufficient differentiation of symptoms to classify
Residual	Marked incapacity related to negative symptoms, social and emotional disabilities without prominent delusions or hallucinations

and/or writing is also disorganized and may become incomprehensible. The classic thought disorder of schizophrenia is characterized by **loose associations (derailment)** where ideas are strung together in a random, convoluted manner such that the listener cannot understand or make sense of the patient's conversation.

Affective and social symptoms such as flattening of affect, apathy, indifference, and social withdrawal account for much of the enduring disability associated with schizophrenia. These **"negative" symptoms** may have a different neurobiological origin from "positive" symptoms (e.g., hallucinations, delusions).

Subtypes

> What are the subtypes of schizophrenia?

There are five **subtypes** of schizophrenia defined by criteria in DSM-IV: (1) **paranoid,** (2) **catatonic,** (3) **disorganized,** (4) **undifferentiated,** and (5) **residual** (see Table 44.3.). The overall prognosis is best for patients with the paranoid subtype and worst for patients with the disorganized subtype.

Differential Diagnosis

Evaluation should exclude any physical cause for the symptoms and signs of a psychotic illness before a primary psychiatric diagnosis is made. The common differential diagnoses that should be systematically considered include delirium and dementia, anatomic brain lesions, seizure disorder, CNS infection, and drug and alcohol use or withdrawal. Acute mania and psychotic depression can present with features similar to schizophrenia.

Treatment

Antipsychotic medications are especially effective in treating the active phase of the illness including ameliorating or eliminating delusions, hallucinations, and gross disorganization of thought and behavior. Typical (first generation) and atypical (second generation) are the two classes of antipsychotics; each is effective in reducing or remitting positive symptoms. **Typical antipsychotics** (haloperidol, thorazine, and many others) tend to cause undesirable motor/muscular extrapyramidal side effects and tardive dyskinesia with prolonged exposure. Depending on the drug chosen, **atypical antipsychotics** (aripiprazole, clozapine, olanzapine, risperidone, quetiapine, zisprasidone) limit or eliminate the motor/muscular side effects, but carry risks for weight gain and impairment of glucose and lipid metabolism. Clozapine and olanzapine appear to be the highest risk medications for these metabolic side effects. For a time, research reports suggested that atypical antipsychotics were more effective against the negative symptoms and cognitive impairments of schizophrenia, but later research has shed considerable doubt on the effectiveness of these medications on these symptoms. Other medications, like antidepressants and mood stabilizers, and electroconvulsive therapy sometimes have roles in treatment. Because of the pervasive impact of the illness on the individual and family and because antipsychotic medications are not completely effective in the treatment of affective, cognitive and social symptoms, *combinations* of pharmacotherapy with individual, group, family, and rehabilitation therapy are critical to recovery, relapse prevention, and limiting chronic disability.

Prognosis

The course of schizophrenia is variable. Prior to the development of effective antipsychotic agents, multiple recurrences, unremitting psychotic states, and gradual deterioration of mental and social abilities leading to institutionalization were common.

Today the acute phase of the illness can almost always be remitted within a few days or weeks of treatment initiation, but the disorder is highly recurrent unless the patient accepts maintenance treatment with antipsychotic medications. The prognosis is better for recovery, supported or independent community living, and employment than it once was. Common complications of schizophrenia include major depression, suicide, chemical dependency, chronically poor social functioning, unemployment, and homelessness.

> What are four psychotic disorders other than schizophrenia?

Schizophreniform Disorder

Schizophreniform disorder is differentiated from schizophrenia by recovery after a shorter period of psychosis than the 6 months required to diagnose schizophrenia. The prognosis for full recovery is better than in schizophrenia. A family history of schizophrenia, although more common than in the general population, is not as common as in the pedigree of patients with schizophrenia.

Schizoaffective Disorder

Schizoaffective disorder is distinguished by the co-occurrence of either major depression or mania with psychotic symptoms characteristic of schizophrenia, and the continuation of psychotic symptoms in periods when the mood symptoms are absent for more than 2 weeks. This diagnosis has been controversial and may represent a variant of mood disorder with psychotic features or schizophrenia. Acute treatment typically includes an antidepressant or mood stabilizer combined with an antipsychotic. Antipsychotic maintenance is required as in schizophrenia, and often antidepressant or mood stabilizer maintenance as well. The psychosocial treatments are the same as those offered in schizophrenia.

Delusional Disorders

Delusional disorders present with a single non-bizarre delusion of a persecutory, jealous, grandiose type as an isolated finding. Organization of thought, personality, and social functioning remain relatively unaffected. Onset is typically later in life than schizophrenia, schizoaffective disorder, or schizophreniform disorder. Antipsychotics and serotonin-specific antidepressants (SSRI) have been used alone and in combination with variable success.

Brief Psychotic Disorder

Brief psychotic disorder is a transient psychosis that presents suddenly, usually after a highly **stressful life event,** remits rapidly with minimum intervention, and does not typically develop a pattern of recurrence. Treatment is symptomatic, generally including a brief course of antipsychotic medication.

Recommended Reading

Freedman R. Schizophrenia. *New England Journal of Medicine* 2003; 349:1738–1749.

Miyamoto S, Lamantia AS, Duncan GE, et al. Recent advances in the neurobiology of schizophrenia. *Molecular Interventions* 2003: 3:27–39.

American Psychiatric Association. *Practice Guideline for the Treatment of Patients with Schizophrenia.* (2nd ed.). Arlington, VA: American Psychiatric Association; 2004. (Available at: www.psych.org)

Sheehan S. *Is There No Place on Earth for Me?* New York: Random House; 1982.

Review Questions

1. A 35-year-old man presents with bizarre delusions, auditory hallucinations, disorganized thinking, insomnia and agitation. These changes in personality and behavior began nearly a year ago when he lost his job. He became obviously ill in the last month, but resisted evaluation until he assaulted his wife. Neurological examination, screening laboratory tests, urine drug screen, and substance use history are negative. The most likely diagnosis is
   A. bipolar disorder, manic phase, with psychotic features
   B. brief psychotic disorder
   C. major depression with psychotic features
   D. schizophrenia
   E. schizophreniform disorder

2. Which of the following symptoms of psychosis would be most responsive to treatment with antipsychotic medication?
   A. Delusions
   B. Depressed mood
   C. Negative symptoms
   D. Social withdrawal
   E. Thought disorder

3. The prevalence of schizophrenia in the U.S. is closest to
   A. 0.1%
   B. 1%
   C. 5%
   D. 10%
   E. 15%

4. In the last 6 months, a 50-year-old woman has become convinced that relatives are swindling her out of her savings. She insisted her bank manager investigate but he found no evidence to support her contention. A comprehensive medical work-up shows no evidence of medical or neurological disease, dementia, or substance use disorder. On examination, there is no evidence of thought disorder. She continues to work. Relationships with people other than family are intact. The most likely diagnosis is
   A. brief psychotic disorder
   B. delusional disorder
   C. major depression with psychotic features
   D. schizophrenia
   E. schizophreniform disorder

5. A 45-year-old man presents with intense delusional thinking and signs of major depressive disorder. The family reports that he began describing delusional ideas about 3 weeks before his mood changed. Two years ago he had a similar episode. After the major depression remitted, he continued to express delusions for 2 months before these also remitted. The most likely diagnosis is
   A. delusional disorder
   B. major depression with psychotic features
   C. schizoaffective disorder
   D. schizophrenia
   E. schizophreniform disorder

6. Which group of symptoms is most consistent with the prodromal phase of schizophrenia?
   A. Agitation, insomnia, negative thinking

B. Delusions, hallucinations, disorganized behavior
C. Disorganized thinking, hallucinations, loss of appetite
D. Odd behaviors, aloofness, preoccupation
E. Posturing, mechanical speech, agitation

Key to review questions: p. 393

45 Personality Disorders and Impulse Control Disorders

- What are the Cluster A, B, and C personality disorders?
- What causes personality disorders?
- Why are personality disorders difficult to treat?
- What are the effective treatments for personality disorders?
- What are the six impulse control disorders?
- What predisposing/precipitating conditions are associated with intermittent explosive disorder?
- What maintains kleptomania?
- Which treatments are effective for trichotillomania?

Clinical Application

Jean, a 34-year-old single woman, lives alone in the family home. She wanted to become a physician like her father, did well academically, but was not accepted to medical school. She was told her lack of involvement in extracurricular activities weakened her application. Jean was puzzled, feeling her dedication to laboratory research was more important than playing sports. After several years of unsuccessfully applying to medical school, Jean decided to remain at home. Her parents are deceased. She is unemployed, embittered, and living off her trust fund. She dotes on her three cats. Friends have stopped reaching out to Jean, who refuses all social invitations. She now dresses in clothing that belonged to her mother, and speaks to others only when necessary (e.g., shopping or having her car serviced).

Personality is the aggregate of an individual's characteristic patterns of thinking, feeling, and behaving which develop early and remain stable over time. Individuals who have a well functioning personality can cope with and master the environment, have a sense of themselves as persons in the world, learn from experience, and have a reasonable array of behavioral options. Individuals who have a disordered personality have a set of maladaptive traits that are resistant to change and that

impair attempts to cope with day-to-day life. To meet DSM-IV diagnostic criteria for a **personality disorder,** the maladaptive traits must be rigidly fixed, apparent in a variety of settings, cause subjective distress, and lead to significant impairment in either social or occupational functioning.

Clinical Application

Philip, a 46-year-old married father of twins, is seeking psychotherapy to "save my marriage." During the first session, he flooded the interview with the derivations of his sons' names and the weather conditions on his wedding day. He has been married for 20 years, his sons are in college, and his wife has given him an ultimatum to change his behavior or she will leave him. He works 6 days a week as a tax attorney, refuses to take vacations, and "worries about everything." He often argues with his wife about her care of the house and the car. He gives her exact directions for parking her car in the driveway so that the prevailing winds will not blow sap from the neighbor's tree onto the hood and mar the finish. Also, he dampens and irons his paper money so that it will lie flat in his wallet. His recent demand that his wife iron her money as well led to her ultimatum.

Personality disorders appear on Axis II of the DSM diagnostic schema. A patient may have both an Axis I and an Axis II disorder concurrently. Careful history taking in the adult patient will generally allow the clinician to resolve whether personality psychopathology predated the acute phase of an Axis I condition. During the acute phase of an Axis I condition, personality psychopathology should not be diagnosed unless a reliable and consistent history of personality function can be gathered. An example of the challenges in differentiating Axis I disorders and personality disorders is the maladaptive behavior of patients with active chemical dependency. An adult man with alcoholism may exhibit patterns of thinking and behavior that would otherwise appear much like the conduct of an antisocial character. If one were not aware that this same patient had no history of conduct disorder in youth, and no adult antisocial behavior until the onset of his alcoholic drinking, an inaccurate diagnosis of antisocial personality disorder would be assigned when the behavior problems were actually a feature of the man's active alcoholism.

History taking to develop a profile of personality functioning requires the clinician to understand how the person typically thinks, feels and behaves in a variety of interpersonal relationships (how does this person relate to family, peers, friends, neighbors, coworkers, lovers, spouses?), educational and occupational roles (has this person achieved as much as native intellectual capacities would predict and is he/she capable of attaining and sustaining employment, working effectively with others, pursuing goals, delaying gratification?), intimate relationships (how does he/she seek out, maintain and regulate romantic/sexual relationships or tolerate being alone or rejected?), recreational pursuits (are diversions satisfying?) and parenting roles (can he/she care for others?). This complex understanding of personality generally requires interviewing, observing and experiencing the patient over several encounters. Diagnostic conclusions should not be offered until the clinician is comfortable that a reliable set of observations will support the diagnosis of personality disorder.

Personality Disorders

What are the Cluster A, B, and C personality disorders?

The personality disorders are grouped into three clusters on Axis II.

Cluster A

Cluster A is composed of persons who are prone to odd ideas and behaviors and feel alienated from or disinterested in others. There are three types.
1. **Paranoid** individuals view others in the world as out to trick, cheat, or demean them. They respond with proactive behavior that is aimed at letting others know that they are aware of these devious motivations and that no one can take advantage of them.
2. **Schizoid** individuals are aloof loners who disdain interpersonal encounters. The inability to achieve genuine intimacy with others is a hallmark of the disorder.
3. **Schizotypal** individuals have markedly eccentric cognition that is typically manifested in odd speech or behavior, and they may believe they have special powers. Their odd beliefs fall short of full-blown delusion. Their mild paranoid tendencies and general eccentricity are obvious enough to others, however, to result in social isolation. Although this disorder is considered a part of the **"schizophrenic spectrum,"** deterioration to frank schizophrenia is rare. When these individuals are stressed, they may appear psychotic.

Cluster B

Cluster B includes four disorders. The behavior manifested by persons diagnosed with these disorders is dramatic or flamboyant. Unlike patients in Cluster A, patients in Cluster B are very involved (or over involved) with others.
1. **Antisocial** individuals typically exploit others. The behavior that comprises the disorder extends beyond simple criminality to encompass an attitude of far-ranging irresponsibility including dishonesty; difficulty holding a job and maintaining relationships; and, in general, not adhering to society's standards. A common associated feature is substance abuse.
2. **Borderline** personality patients have major difficulties sustaining stable relationships. At the core of the difficulty is rapidly shifting affect,

anger and the fear of abandonment; much of the borderline patient's behavior is aimed at pulling others closer or pushing them away. Substance abuse, mood disorder, and recurrent suicidal behavior complicate the treatment of such patients.

3. **Histrionic** personality disorder is characterized by excessive emotionality, which interferes with interpersonal relationships. Pleasing appearance, creativity, and charm are initially attractive features that are ultimately used for demanding manipulation of others.

4. The individual with **narcissistic** personality disorder is grandiose, self-important, and generally disdainful of others. Much is asked of friends. Typically others are first idealized and then devalued when the patient's excessive demands cannot be met. When the patient's inflated self-image is wounded by rejection or other challenges, these individuals become overwhelmed by anxiety and dysphoria. Typically, the dysphoria is short lived and the sense of self-importance is restored.

Cluster C

Cluster C is comprised of three disorders. Excessive anxiety and ineffective coping strategies to deal with it are the core features of this cluster.

1. **Avoidant** persons would like to have intimate relationships but are extremely fearful of rejection. They are typically anxious, self-doubting, and have low self-esteem. Fear of failure and social embarrassment impairs social and occupational functioning.

2. **Dependent** persons rely on others to make decisions for them. Fear of loss of emotional support impels dependent individuals to remain in a destructive relationship rather than risk being on their own.

3. **Obsessive-compulsive personality disorder** is a condition which is distinct from obsessive-compulsive anxiety disorder. Affected individuals are perfectionistic, orderly, driven by logic rather than emotion, and inflexible. Others view them as cold, stubborn, constricted, stingy, and demanding of their own way.

What causes personality disorders?

Epidemiological studies suggest that certain types of personality psychopathology have familial patterns of transmission especially schizotypal, borderline, and antisocial personality disorders. Certain personality traits are heritable, (e.g., anxious apprenhension in the face of novel stimuli), and certain traits are correlated with genetically mediated neurobiological function (e.g., the relationship between the trait of impulsivity and the expression of the serotonin transporter gene). Thus, genetic-environmental interactions may explain why certain individuals with trait vulnerabilities will develop maladaptive coping in response to certain types of environmental stress. Particular stressors appear to be important mediators of personality development; among these are early parental loss, parental neglect and traumatic events, especially persistent physical or sexual abuse.

Why are personality disorders difficult to treat?

Effective treatment of personality disordered patients is difficult because not only are the distinctive maladaptive traits manifested by these individuals resistant to change but also patients lack insight. Many personality disordered patients use primitive defense mechanisms, for example projection, that results in the patient seeing problems as having an origin outside oneself. Many patients do not present for treatment unless influenced to do so by others including a court order.

Types of Personality Disorder

	Traits	Disorder
Cluster A:	Odd ideas and behaviors Alienated Disinterested in others	Paranoid Schizoid Schizotypal
Cluster B:	Dramatic, flamboyant Overinvolved with Others Inflated self-image	Antisocial Borderline Histrionic Narcissistic
Cluster C:	Excessive anxiety Ineffective coping	Avoidant Dependent Obsessive- compulsive

Co-occurring diagnoses of other psychiatric disorders (especially substance use and mood disorders) are very common. When the personality disordered patient is injured by an acute psychiatric disorder or medical problem, already limited coping strategies are easily overwhelmed and intensification of the disordered personality features may occur. Treatment of comorbidities such as substance use and mood disorders is critical to best outcomes, but the clinician must also know that the presence of a comorbid personality disorder generally reduces the expected rate of response to treatments for co-occurring Axis I conditions.

What are the effective treatments for personality disorders?

In general, the treatment of choice for personality disorders is **psychotherapy** including supportive, psychodynamic, interpersonal, and cognitive-behavioral treatments. **Dialectical behavioral therapy** has been shown to be especially effective with borderline personality disorder. Peer groups that offer both support and confrontation can be particularly useful for patients who can tolerate them.

Psychopharmacological treatments are available but these should always be offered as adjunctive to psychosocial treatments. The best studied are medication treatments for borderline personality disorder; which antidepressants, mood stabilizers and low dose antipsychotics have demonstrated efficacy. Cluster A disorders may respond to antipsychotics and some Cluster C patients respond to antidepressants, especially those that improve serotonergic function.

While personality disorders are clearly resistant to change there is reason to be optimistic about treatment outcome. For example, borderline patients in long-term follow-up actually can stabilize and improve function over time.

Impulse Control Disorders Not Elsewhere Classified

What are the six impulse control disorders?

Clinical Application

Margaret is the 38-year-old wife of an insurance company executive. She is stopped by a security guard at the exit door of a large department store. In the security office, she is found to have an inexpensive bracelet and pair of earrings in her handbag. Both items still have price tags attached, and she has no receipts. She offers to return the earrings and bracelet. However, this is the third such incident within the past 2 months and the security officer informs Margaret that the police must be called. She pleads that her sister be called instead. The sister arrives and takes Margaret, who is sobbing uncontrollably, home.

The diagnostic category, **impulse control disorders** not elsewhere classified, is composed of six disorders:

- intermittent explosive disorder
- kleptomania
- pyromania
- pathological gambling
- trichotillomania
- impulse, temptation, or drive to act in a manner that is harmful to themselves or to others

Affected persons report that, on occasion, they consciously resist the impulse and on other occasions plan the act. Prior to committing the impulsive act, they feel increased tension or arousal; after they act, they feel pleasure or release (thus reinforcing the impulse and the resultant behavior). Afterward, they usually feel regret and guilt.

Intermittent Explosive Disorder

Affected patients have circumscribed episodes of loss of control of anger, assault of others, or destruction of property. The aggressive display is disproportionate to the triggering stress events. These "attacks" or "spells," as patients often call them, remit spontaneously, and are usually followed by deep regret. No aggressiveness or impulsivity is typically evidenced between episodes. The disorder may begin at any age, but onset is most common during the second and third decade; severity decreases during middle age. Men are affected more than women. First-degree relatives of affected persons are at increased risk for the disorder.

What predisposing/precipitating conditions are associated with intermittent explosive disorder?

Persons who have impulse disorders tend to be hyperactive and accident-prone. There may be aura-like experiences, hypersensitivity to photic and auditory stimulation, and postictal-like sensorium changes such as partial memory loss. The EEG may show nonspecific abnormalities. All of these characteristics suggest that cortical dysfunction may have a role in these syndromes. Therefore, it is not surprising to find that **predisposing factors** during childhood include perinatal trauma, head trauma, encephalitis, and hyperactivity. However, a disruptive psychosocial environment (e.g., exposure to alcoholism, child abuse and neglect, promiscuity, and threats to the life of the child) is considered a more important **precipitating factor.**

The diagnosis of intermittent explosive disorder requires multiple episodes of loss of control and the exclusion of a psychotic disorder, attention-deficit/hyperactivity disorder, conduct disorder, substance intoxication, personality change due to a general medical condition, and antisocial or borderline personality disorder.

The most effective treatment is a combination of psychotherapy and pharmacologic interventions. Many pharmacologic agents (e.g., anticonvulsants, antipsychotics, propranolol, and lithium) have been used with mixed results. Selective serotonin reuptake inhibitors (e.g., fluoxetine, paroxetine, sertraline) have produced the best results.

Kleptomania

Persons with **kleptomania** cannot resist the impulse to steal things they do not need. Stolen objects are returned, given away, or hidden. Tension mounts before the act; relief of tension is experienced immediately after the act and serves to **reinforce** future similar behavior. Guilt, anxiety, and remorse usually follow later. For affected persons, the act of stealing is an end in itself. The objects they steal are items they could easily purchase. Although they do not plan, they avoid situations in which the danger of being caught is obvious. Despite this, they usually get caught multiple times, causing humiliation.

Women have kleptomania more often than men. The frequency of stealing episodes can range from less than once per month to more than 100 times per month. Although the disorder waxes and wanes, it tends to be chronic and recurs during periods of stress.

What maintains kleptomania?

Brain disease, mental retardation, faulty monoamine metabolism, cortical atrophy, lateral ventricular enlargement, and focal neurological signs have been associated with kleptomania. However, **reinforcement** through tension reduction appears to be significant in the maintenance, if not the onset, of the disorder.

Kleptomania should not be diagnosed if steal-

Fewer than 5% of shoplifters have kleptomania.

ing is a symptom of another disorder (e.g., conduct disorder, mania, or antisocial personality).

Psychotherapy is an effective treatment for persons who experience sufficient guilt and anxiety, if these feelings motivate the patient to change. Behavior modification can be effective even when motivation is low. The use of selective serotonin reuptake inhibitors is effective in some cases.

Pyromania

Repetitive, deliberate fire setting that relieves tension or produces arousal, and attraction to fires and fire-fighting equipment characterize **pyromania.** Persons who have pyromania usually make elaborate preparations prior to setting a fire. This disorder often begins in childhood and its consequences become more destructive over time. It is more common in men than in women and is frequently associated with mental retardation, alcoholism, or delinquency traits such as truancy or cruelty to animals.

Pyromania should not be diagnosed if there is another motivation for fire setting (e.g., socio-political beliefs, personal gain, or vengeance) or if the fire setting is a symptom of a major psychiatric disorder (e.g., a response to schizophrenic hallucination).

Legal problems are a compelling force for seeking help, but often only incarceration controls the behavior of adults. Children are likely to respond to intensive, non-punitive behavioral therapy. Due to its potentially devastating consequences, pyromania must be treated as soon as it is diagnosed. An affected child will generally make a full recovery.

Pathological Gambling

Pathological gambling includes preoccupation with gambling; increasing stakes to achieve excitement; gambling to escape problems and to recoup losses; lying to hide the magnitude of the problem; supporting gambling through illegal but usually nonviolent means (e.g., embezzlement and fraud); and relying on others to pay gambling debts.

> Pathological gambling is estimated to affect up to 3% of the adult population in the U.S. It is more prevalent among men than women. Among men, the disorder typically begins during adolescence; among women, it begins during middle age. Sons of affected fathers and daughters of affected mothers are at risk for the disorder. Affected women are likely to be married to alcoholic, generally absent men.

Pathological gambling is often comorbid with mood and anxiety disorder. **Predisposing factors** include childhood attention deficit disorder, loss or absence of a parent before age 15, inappropriately harsh or lax parental discipline, parental modeling and exposure to gambling during childhood or adolescence, lack of family emphasis on financial planning, or excessive emphasis on material goods.

Impaired metabolism of catecholamines (especially norepinephrine) has been associated with the development of pathological gambling. The reinforcing effects of self-stimulation and tension reduction (relief) serve to maintain and increase the behavior.

The most effective treatment is the 12-step peer group support offered by **Gamblers Anonymous (GA).**

Trichotillomania

Persons with **trichotillomania** regularly pull out their hair, producing noticeable hair loss. **Hair pull-**

ing episodes are preceded by mounting tension and followed by relief of tension thus contributing to the reinforcement of the behavior. Although any area of the body may be involved, the scalp is the most common site of hair pulling.

Examination of an affected area reveals normal hairs, broken strands, and bald spots without evidence of skin disease. Biopsy shows characteristic histopathological changes of the hair follicle **(trichomalacia),** which helps differentiate trichotillomania from other types of alopecia. Associated signs include evidence of self-mutilation (e.g., scratches, superficial cuts), nail biting, and head banging.

Trichotillomania usually begins during childhood or adolescence but may begin later in life; the potential to become chronic increases with advancing age at onset. Remission and relapse are common. Trichotillomania is more common in women than in men. It is comorbid with obsessive-compulsive disorder, borderline personality disorder, and depression. **Etiology is not known** although separation anxiety, strained mother-child relationships, loss in childhood, depression, and self-stimulation have been suggested.

> Which treatments are effective for trichotillomania?

The disorder is difficult to treat. However, hypnosis, insight-oriented psychotherapy, behavior therapy (e.g., biofeedback), general dermatologic treatment (e.g., topical corticosteroids and oral hydroxyzine), selective serotonin reuptake inhibitors and other antidepressants, anxiolytics, antipsychotics, and pimozide have each been reported to have some efficacy

Recommended Reading

Costa Jr. PT, Widiger TA. *Personality Disorders and the Five Factor Model of Personality.* (2nd ed.). Washington, DC: American Psychological Association; 2002.

Gunderson JG. *Borderline Personality Disorder: A Clinical Guide*. Washington, DC: American Psychiatric Press; 2001.

Gabbard GO. Mind, brain, and personality disorders. *American Journal of Psychiatry* 2005; 162:648–655.

Hollander E, Stein DJ. (Eds.). *Clinical Handbook of Impulse-Control Disorders*. Washington, DC: American Psychiatric Press; 2006.

Review Questions

Directions: The items below consist of lettered headings followed by numbered descriptions. For each numbered description choose the *one* lettered heading to which it is *most* closely associated. Each lettered heading may be used *once, more than once,* or *not at all.*

Match the case scenario with the personality disorder type it describes.
A. Antisocial
B. Borderline
C. Histrionic
D. Obsessive-Compulsive
E. Paranoid

1. L.J. is a 42-year-old woman brought to the Emergency Department following her third suicide attempt. She has been divorced twice. Her current husband of 6 months describes her as excessively demanding, angry, reckless, and an alcoholic who seems very fearful that he, too, will "abandon" her.

2. R.S. is a 27-year-old graduate teaching assistant who was recently placed on administrative leave after breaking into a professor's office to read his TA evaluations. He accused the professor of substituting the evaluations of another graduate student, who was being investigated for theft, as a way of ruining R.S.'s career.

3. M.F. is a 19-year-old waitress who seeks help because she cannot take orders quickly because the writing looks too messy on her note pad. She always starts at the right back corner of a table to take orders and gets frustrated when the manager tells her to start with the oldest-appearing woman regardless of seating. At the end of the day she requests her share of the tips in check form to avoid handling paper money or coins.

4. Which one of the following is the primary treatment method for patients with a personality disorder?
    A. Electroconvulsive therapy
    B. Inpatient psychiatric hospitalization
    C. Occupational therapy
    D. Pharmacotherapy
    E. Psychotherapy

Key to review questions: p. 393

46 Disorders of Infancy, Childhood, and Adolescence

- How is mental retardation classified?
- What is the definition of a learning disorder?
- How are expressive and receptive language disorders related?
- What are some examples of pervasive developmental disorder?
- When does oppositional defiant disorder become conduct disorder?
- What is a tic?
- How should enuresis be treated?

The disorders of infancy, coming as they do so early in the individual's developmental course, reflect the greater influence of genetic and biological predisposition. With advancing age (e.g., childhood and adolescence), we see the increasing influence of environmental, familial, and experiential factors (behavior, cognition, culture, learning).

The disorders reviewed in the early part of this chapter represent those that are suspected of having their origin in largely genetic predisposition or biological dysfunction. The disorders toward the end of the chapter represent problems that appear to be increasingly influenced by psychosocial factors. Keep in mind that these are not exclusive etiological categories but rather a developmental continuum that reflects changes in the relative influence of etiological factors.

The psychiatric assessment of children and adolescents attempts to ascertain normal functioning and the prevalence, persistence, and severity of dysfunction in areas that include emotions, cognition, thriving, intellect, academics, play, social performance, speech/language, behavior, motor activity, and adaptability. Special attention is paid to growth, development, maturation, age-appropriate interviewing, family context, and supplemental sources of information.

Developmental disorders are characterized by limitations in one or more areas of functioning, such as academic, communication, social, motor, and intellectual funtioning. The limitations are apparent in infancy or childhood as delays in the acquisition of expected developmental milestones, and developmental deficits or gaps become more noticeable.

Mental Retardation (MR)

Clinical Application

William is a 13-year-old male who lives with his mother. She can no longer control his outbursts as he has entered puberty and has become physically larger and stronger. She struggles with whether to send him to a residential treatment center far away. Her pregnancy with him was normal, but as an infant, he did not smile or babble, and had marked delays in his speech. He then began to bang his head and flap his hands, sometimes injuring himself. He does not play with other children, and wants to do the same things repeatedly. In school, he becomes aggressive when a new teacher is present, or when there is a change in his class schedule. His IQ has been measured to be 45.

How is mental retardation classified?

Mental retardation (MR) is characterized by intellectual functioning below an intelligence quotient (IQ) of 70; impaired adaptive functioning in two of the following areas: communication, social skills, self-direction, health and safety, academics, leisure, work, home-living, use of community resources; and onset before 18 years of age. MR may be difficult to diagnose in children <5 years of age since test results are less reliable in younger children, and difficulties often do not manifest until the school years. The degree of MR is defined by the number of standard deviations (1 SD = 15 IQ points) below the mean (100) at which the child scores (see Table 46.1.).

MR should be suspected when a child has delayed developmental milestones, especially in language skills.

MR is associated with the pervasive developmental disorders (see below), Down's Syndrome (DS), fragile X syndrome (FXS), cerebral palsy, and intoxication by environmental agents such as lead. Around 95% of DS cases are caused by trisomy of chromosome 21; 4% by fusion of chromosome 21 with chromosome 13, 14, or 15; and 1% by mosaicism. This latter form is often less severe.

FXS is an X-linked dominant disorder. It is the most common inherited neurodevelopmental disorder, and is twice as common in males (prevalence: 1:4,000 births) as in females. In this disorder, the CGG nucleotide sequence is exaggeratedly repeated in the FMR1 gene, located on the long arm of the X chromosome, which reduces production of the protein FMRP. This reduction produces abnormal brain development with cognitive, emotional, behavioral, and neurological impairments. The wide range of impairment in children with FXS

may be explained by mosaicism, the presence of both normal and abnormal cells in the same individual. Although the distinguishing features of the disorder (long face, prominent jaw and forehead, large ears, and large testicles in males) become most apparent around puberty, they are not reliable as a basis for the diagnosis.

In many cases, the cause of MR remains unknown. Potential causes include maternal abuse of alcohol and other substances during pregnancy; metabolic disruption involving mother and/or fetus (e.g., congenital hypothyroidism); trauma; and CNS infections such as toxoplasmosis and rubella. MR is often diagnosed in conjunction with pervasive developmental disorders like autism, and neurological disorders like epilepsy.

About 85% of persons with MR fall in the mild/educable range. Although no intervention will significantly alter IQ, most mentally retarded persons can find suitable vocations and function to maximal capacity with proper behavioral management, social support, and education.

What is the definition of a learning disorder?

Learning Disorders (LD)

The diagnosis of LD is based on scores on standardized tests of reading, written expression, or mathematics that are ≥ 2 years below age, schooling, and intellectual ability levels.

Table 46.1. Functional capacity by approximate IQ

115–85	Average	Mean IQ = 100; SD = ±15; normal functioning
85–70	Below average	1–2 SD below 100; borderline intellectual functioning
70–55	Mild MR	Can develop delayed language and social skills; good motor development; academic achievement < 6th grade by late adolescence; can be self-supporting
55–40	Moderate MR	Can talk or sign; fair motor development; some self-help skills; academic achievement < 2nd grade; may find employment in sheltered setting
40–25	Severe MR	Can profit from systematic habit training; can use words or gestures but few expressive skills, needs supportive living
< 24	Profound MR	Minimal functional capacity in sensorimotor areas; indicates wants/needs with sounds or body movements, needs support for basic functions

Reading Disorder

Commonly called **dyslexia, reading disorder** is manifested by impaired reading (slow, inaccurate reading; reversal of letters; poor word recognition, reading comprehension, or spelling) in the absence of MR or sensory deficits. The additional diagnoses of expressive, receptive, or mixed language disorder, or disorder of written expression may be warranted.

Reading disorder is often apparent by 6 years of age, although recognition may be delayed in children of above average intelligence. About 5–10% of school-aged children are estimated to have reading disorder, with boys affected more often than girls. Although the prevalence of reading disorder in families of affected individuals is increased, a genetic link has not been confirmed.

Intervention, including remedial education, management of any emotional problems, and parent counseling, should begin by third grade. Otherwise, reading is likely to remain impaired, with consequent low self-esteem and poor school attendance.

Mathematics Disorder

Mathematics disorder is characterized by gross deficiencies in four arithmetic-related skill areas that are not explained by poor education or neurological, sensory, or cognitive impairments: 1) **linguistic skills** (understanding of mathematical terms and conversion of verbal instructions into mathematical symbols); 2) **perceptual skills** (recognition of symbols and ordering of number clusters); 3) **performance skills** (carrying out and appropriately sequencing the four basic arithmetic operations); and 4) **attention skills** (exact copying of figures and performance of operations designated by symbols).

Diagnosis is usually made during or after the second grade. Almost 5% of school-aged children of average intelligence are affected.

Remedial education is the treatment of choice. Children who are undiagnosed or inadequately treated will continue to perform poorly, and may develop poor self-esteem, depression, anger, frustration, disruptive behavior disorders, or school refusal.

Disorder of Written Expression

Diagnosis of **disorder of written expression** is often made after the third grade and is character-

ized by poor spelling, frequent gross grammatical and punctuation errors, and poor handwriting. The disorder appears to be familial and affects between 3% and 10% of school-aged children. Boys are affected more than girls. The etiology is unknown although dysfunction in cerebral information-processing areas is suspected because it often accompanies expressive and mixed receptive/expressive language disorders and reading disorders.

Communication Disorders

How are expressive and receptive language disorders related?

Expressive Language Disorder (ELD)

Characteristics of **expressive language disorder** are limited vocabulary, inability to produce complex sentences, inability to use correct tenses, and impaired word recollection. The diagnosis is confirmed by expressive language test scores that fall significantly below receptive language scores.

ELD affects 3–10% of school-aged children; boys are affected two to three times as frequently as girls.

While the **etiology is unknown**, the disorder is more prevalent in families that have a history of communication disorders. ELD is usually a developmental disorder, but it may also result from a neurological insult (e.g., trauma, seizure disorder).

About 50% of affected children recover spontaneously. Severely affected children will have mild to moderate language impairment, if the ELD is untreated. Speech and language therapy is essential. Psychotherapy and parental counseling may be warranted by associated symptoms such as low self-esteem, frustration, performance anxiety, and depression.

Mixed Receptive/Expressive Language Disorder (R/ELD)

Because **receptive language disorder** impairs development of expressive language, the DSM-IV classification combines these two disorders. Mixed R/ELD is usually developmental but may be learned. The criteria for diagnosis of R/ELD include: disrupted academic achievement and social communication, receptive and expressive language test scores significantly below expectations for age and developmental stage, and language scores significantly below performance scores on standardized IQ tests, without evidence of pervasive developmental disorder or functional impairment not due to MR, neurologic disorder, or sensory defect.

> For both ELD and R/ELD, audiologic evaluation is essential to rule out hearing impairment, the most common sensory defect contributing to poor language development.

Mild R/ELD may not be identified until adolescence and produce minimal long-term language impairment. Etiology is unknown. However, children with R/ELD respond more to environmental sounds than to speech sounds, suggesting auditory discrimination difficulties. Ambidexterity and left-handedness are increased among affected individuals.

Phonologic (Articulation) Disorder

Phonologic disorder is characterized by speech sounds that are incorrectly produced, omitted, or substituted for appropriate sounds. Phonologic disorder, also known as **articulation disorder**, is reminiscent of immature speech. Diagnosis is made in the absence of anatomic-structural, physiologic, neurologic, or sensory (e.g., auditory) abnormalities.

The disorder occurs in 5% of children overall, although it may be present in up to 10% of children less than 8 years of age. Boys are affected more frequently than girls and first-degree relatives are at increased risk.

Although **etiology is unknown**, phonologic disorder is probably caused by **maturational delays** in the brain processes underlying speech. Phonologic disorder is correlated with large family size and lower socioeconomic status, suggesting insufficient stimulation of speech development as an etiologic factor. Spontaneous remission is common before age 8, but rare thereafter. **Speech therapy** provides the most successful treatment. Parental counseling and education are helpful adjuncts.

Stuttering

Stuttering is speech that lacks fluency and temporal patterning, resulting in repetition and prolongation of sounds and syllables. The deficits must exceed any disturbance produced by a speech-motor, neurologic, or sensory impairment. Stutterers develop anticipatory anxiety and try to avoid situations in which they expect they will stutter. Many develop tics, eye blinking, or trembling of the lips and jaw in anticipation of speaking.

The **etiology is unknown** but is probably multifactoral, with a **significant learning component.** Spontaneous remission occurs in up to 80% of cases. Children who do not recover entirely may experience months of remission but relapse at times of stress. Treatments focusing on stuttering as a learned behavior and on restructuring speech fluency are most successful. Children and adolescents recover better than adults.

Developmental Coordination or Motor Skills Disorder

Children with **developmental coordination disorder** experience delayed developmental milestones (sitting, crawling, standing, walking), clumsiness, accident proneness, and poor fine motor skills (tossing a ball, fitting puzzle pieces together). The disorder may interfere with academic progress and trigger emotional and behavioral disorders.

Standardized evaluations matching a child's age with skill level help establish the diagnosis. Boys are affected two to four times as frequently as girls. No definite etiology has been discovered. Risk factors include hypoxia at birth, prematurity, low birth weight, and perinatal malnutrition.

The most effective treatment includes physical therapy (for gross motor skills), occupational therapy (for fine motor skills), perceptual motor training, neurophysiological exercise techniques, and modified physical education.

Pervasive Developmental Disorders

Pervasive developmental disorders are characterized by disrupted acquisition of behavioral milestones, language, and social skills during childhood, with repetitive behaviors.

What are some examples of pervasive developmental disorder?

Autistic Disorder

Autistic disorder (autism) typically appears before age 3 and is characterized by:
1. seriously impaired social interactions (e.g., lack of eye contact, adequate peer relationships, and social/emotional reciprocity);
2. major communication deficits (e.g., delay or lack of verbal skills; repetitive, stereotyped and idiosyncratic language; absence of spontaneous symbolic play); and
3. repetitive, stereotyped, and idiosyncratic behaviors, interests, and activities (e.g., exclusive dedication to a particular interest; rigid adherence to routines that lack functional purpose; motor mannerisms such as hand flapping or head banging).

Autism occurs in 2–5 children per 10,000, although recent studies suggest an increase to 9/10,000. Boys are affected up to five times as often as girls, but girls are more likely to have a family history of serious cognitive impairment, and their symptoms are more severe. About 75% of autistic children have some degree of mental retardation.

Associated Findings Suggestive of Possible Etiologies for Autism

- Prenatal and perinatal complications
- Minor congenital anomalies, abnormal dermatoglyphics, and ambidexterity
- Higher concordance rates among monozygotic compared with dizygotic twins
- Fifty times greater risk among siblings
- Autistic-like behavior in persons with temporal lobe lesions or severe tuberous sclerosis
- Decreased numbers of Purkinje cells in the cerebellum
- Grand-mal seizures, EEG abnormalities, and ventricular enlargement
- Diminished response to infection and pain

The prognosis is variable. Autistic children with IQ >70 and reasonable language skills by age 5 years have the best prognosis. A few autistic children who have high IQ improve to the point of no longer meeting criteria for the disorder, even though they retain some of its manifestations. Up to 2% of affected children become fully independent and 5% to 20% become semi-independent. However, more than 70% will require substantial family or institutional care as adults.

Treatment includes educational and behavioral techniques that encourage normal social interactions, discourage bizarre behaviors, and improve interpersonal communication, such as applied behavioral analysis (ABA). Autistic children function best in structured settings. Psychopharmacologic agents are useful for autistic youths who exhibit severe perseverations, impulsivity, aggression and self-injurious behavior.

Asperger's Disorder

This diagnosis presents as a less severe type of autism, without extensive cognitive and language disturbances. Children who have Asperberger's disorder typically have abnormal communication, with stilted and monotonous speech. They often have trouble developing social relationships, are awkward in reciprocal interactions, and lack emotional sharing. They have difficulty with transitions and are especially sensitive to changing routines.

Asperger's disorder is much more common than autism, occurring in 2–4 children per 1,000. Boys are affected more often than girls.

Affected children often become very shy adults who are uncomfortable in social interactions and may exhibit thinking oddities; careers in areas with limited human contact are commonly chosen. High IQ and high-level social skills predict a good prognosis. Management techniques are similar to those used to treat autistic disorder.

Rett's Disorder

In **Rett's disorder,** one of the known causes of retardation, development may be normal for the first several months after birth. Development then begins to decelerate between 5 and 8 months of age. Loss of hand skills appears between 5 and 30 months, and is replaced by repetitive wringing of the hands and fingers in front of the mouth and other stereotypic behavior. Other manifestations include loss of social engagement, poorly coordinated gait and trunk movements, and impaired development of receptive and expressive language.

Rett's disorder is found only in girls and has a prevalence of 6–7 per 100,000 females. It has been found to be 100% concordant in monozygotic twins. A mutation in the X-chromosome methyl-CpG binding protein 2 (MeCP2) gene has been established as the basis for the disorder. The protein is essential for neuronal maturation.

Treatment is symptomatic. Physical therapy can help ease discomfort from muscular maladaptation and behavioral techniques can be useful in controlling self-injurious behavior.

Childhood Disintegrative Disorder

Childhood disintegrative disorder is characterized by the deterioration of social, cognitive, and language functions after at least two years of normal development. The onset may be abrupt or, more often, insidious over several months. The child loses those skills usually acquired before the age of 10 years (e.g., expressive and receptive language, bladder control, and ability for social interaction). Diagnostic features include impaired social interaction and communication skills, stereotypical behavior, and seizures. The disorder is believed to be more common in boys and its prevalence is estimated at 1 per 100,000.

Pervasive Developmental Disorder, NOS

Children with **PDD NOS** do not fit exactly into the above four categories. These children most often have some characteristics of autism or Asperger's disorder with an average or above average IQ, some social interactions but limited friendships, and mild disturbances of the social communication aspects of language (prosody or voice modulation, use of gestures). However, the PDD NOS designation can also include more severely disturbed children who do not meet criteria for the any of the main types. The term **autism spectrum disorders** has also been used to describe the broad range of pathology seen in PDD.

Attention-Deficit and Disruptive Behavior Disorders

Attention-deficit/hyperactivity disorder (ADHD, formerly known as ADD) is characterized by attentional problems and motor/verbal overactivity. Children may have predominantly attention problems or both attention and motoric problems. Boys are more likely to have the combined type; girls are more likely to have the inattentive type.

ADHD affects about 10–15% of children. Up to two thirds continue to have significant symptoms into adulthood. Children with ADHD are at risk for dropping out of school, substance abuse, motor vehicle accidents, higher rates of emergency room visits, and difficulty sustaining employment.

Characteristics of ADHD

- Impulsivity
- Easy distractability / inattention
- Difficulty following directions
- Fidgeting and being disruptive
- Trouble taking turns and sharing
- Difficulty completing tasks without supervision

The etiology of ADHD is unclear. Frontal lobe dysfunction, dysfunction of the reticular activating system, and deficiency of noradrenergic neurotransmitters have all been suggested. Genetic vulnerability is supported by the findings that children with ADHD are likely to have parents or other relatives who have ADHD, and parents with ADHD are likely to have children with ADHD, even if the children are reared apart from the parents (e.g., adoption). Indeed, the heritability of ADHD is as high as 1%. The vulnerability is increased by environmental factors, such as intrauterine exposure to tobacco smoke or cocaine. Treatment includes tutoring, behavioral incentive programs, consistent limit setting, and structured settings and times for schoolwork and chores. Most children respond well to stimulant drugs. Parental support and education should be provided by the clinician. Additional assistance is available through national support groups such as CHADD (Children with Attention-Deficit Disorder).

Oppositional Defiant Disorder

Oppositional defiant disorder (ODD) is persistent (> 6 months) negativistic and defiant behavior in a child who is at least 3 years old. Symptoms include frequent loss of temper, defiance, irritability, spitefulness, and vindictiveness. ODD should be considered when these symptoms impair functioning and are not due to a mood disorder or psychosis. Approximately 10–20% of children have oppositional defiant disorder; ADHD and LD are common comorbidities.

Etiologies include inconsistent caretaking, poor limit setting, neglect, abuse, and other family dysfunction. Assessment includes a careful history from the parents or caregivers that focuses on their methods of discipline and conflicts within the family. Treatment includes parenting education and treatment of comorbid disorders.

> When does oppositional defiant disorder become conduct disorder?

Conduct Disorder

Conduct disorder (CD) is more severe and socially destructive than **ODD**. Onset may be during childhood or adolescence. Symptoms include aggression or cruelty toward people or animals, bullying, using weapons, vandalism, fire-setting, deceitfulness, forgery, and rule violations. Approximately 6% of children have some degree of conduct disorder; boys are affected four times as frequently as girls.

CD is virtually always comorbid with ADHD or LD. Children with CD are also at risk for substance abuse, homelessness, prostitution, incarceration, suicide, and homicide. If symptoms persist beyond 18 years of age, the adolescent is rediagnosed as having antisocial personality disorder. The diagnosis of **antisocial personality disorder** is dependent on a history of conduct disorder, but only about 50% of adolescents who have CD develop antisocial personality disorder. Others become less symptomatic or die as a result of homicide, suicide, or other violent events.

The **etiology of CD is not clear,** but certain family characteristics are typical. The father is likely to be alcoholic and have a history of violence and incarceration. The child may have been abused, grossly neglected, or harshly or inadequately disciplined, and have no consistent role models for moral behavior. Biologic markers for development of conduct disorder in boys include low serum levels of dopamine β-hydroxylase and muted galvanic skin responses to noxious stimuli.

Treatment includes management of comorbid disorders (e.g., ADHD), which, unfortunately, is best achieved using highly abusable and salable agents. Affected children respond best to immediate and concrete reward. Intensive short-term inpatient behavioral modification may be transiently effective. Placement in a long-term treatment facility is beneficial in some cases.

> What is a tic?

Tic Disorders

Tics are recurrent sudden, rapid, nonrhythmic stereotypical movements or vocalizations.

Tourette's Disorder

Tourette's disorder has its onset before 18 years of age and consists of multiple motor tics and at least one vocal tic. Tics occur numerous times a day for at least one year, impair functioning, and are not caused by a medical disorder.

Tourette's disorder occurs in 2% of the population; males are affected three times more often than females. Motor tics are usually evident by age 7 years. Vocal tics appear by age 11. **Coprolalia,** the use of socially inappropriate words or phrases, occurs in a small minority of affected persons. Patients report that they have some control over their tics, which they describe as "compelling" ("things would just not feel right") rather than totally involuntary. Tourette's disorder appears to have a **genetic component** and exists on a continuum with chronic motor tics and vocal tic disorder. It is an autosomal disorder transmitted in a **bilinear mode** (i.e., between recessive and dominant).

The etiology is unclear. Dysfunction of the dopamine system may be involved. The endogenous opiate system is involved in cases of comorbidity with obsessive-compulsive disorder and the adrenergic system appears to be involved in cases that respond to clonidine, an alpha-adrenergic agonist. The basal ganglia, the site of certain movement disorders (e.g., Huntington's disorder), may be involved. A poststreptococcal autoimmune reaction is another possible etiologic factor.

Pharmacotherapy is the most effective form of treatment. Behavior therapy is of some benefit, especially if focused on reducing reactivity to stress.

Chronic Motor or Vocal Tic Disorder

Chronic motor or vocal tic disorder is manifested by motor or vocal tics but not both. Onset is before age 18. Prevalence is estimated at 1–2%. School-aged children are at highest risk. Children who have onset of motor or vocal tics between the ages of 6 and 8 years are likely to become symptom free an average of four years after onset. Patients with facial tics have a better prognosis than those with tics involving larger muscle groups.

Treatment depends on severity and degree of academic, social, and emotional impairment. Behavioral techniques and pharmacotherapy can be effective. Supportive psychotherapy is helpful in the management of secondary emotional problems, difficulties coping with peer reactions, and low self-esteem.

Transient Tic Disorder

Transient tic disorder consists of one or more vocal or motor tics, or both that begin before 18 years of age, occur many times a day for at least 1 month, but last no longer than 12 months. Up to 25% of school-aged children have a history of tics that tend to intensify or reappear in times of stress.

Tics with a **psychogenic origin** may remit spontaneously; those with a **biologic origin** tend to be familial. Patients with tics that progress to a chronic motor or vocal tic disorder are thought to have a mixed organic and psychogenic condition.

If symptoms are mild and there is little or no functional impairment, no treatment is needed and parents should be counseled to ignore the problem. If the problem does not remit, or if the person shows decline in social, emotional, or academic functioning, behavioral treatment should be considered.

Stereotypic Movement Disorder

Stereotypic movement disorder is manifested by repetitive stereotypical movements, without apparent functional purpose that impair age-appropriate activities and may cause injury to the child. Examples include: self-biting, self-hitting, head banging, handshaking, and picking at skin. These behaviors must be present for at least 1 month and not explained by drug effects or medical conditions, compulsions, or developmental disorders. The disorder is more common in boys. Up to 20% of mentally retarded children are affected.

The course is variable. Prognosis is correlated with the frequency and intensity of self-injurious behavior. Control often requires the use of physical restraints. Pharmacotherapy and behavioral treatment (e.g., reinforcement and behavioral shaping) are the most effective strategies available and should focus on the specific behavior to be controlled.

Feeding and Eating Disorders

Pica

Individuals with **pica** eat nonnutritive material (e.g., clay) that is inappropriate to their developmental level and alien to their culture. Boys and girls are equally affected. Prevalence is up to 30% in children less than 6 years of age, and less than 10% in older children. About 25% of institutionalized mentally retarded children and adolescents have pica. Spontaneous remission is common unless MR is present. Pica in pregnant women resolves after delivery.

Etiology is unknown. Parental neglect and cravings caused by dietary deficiencies (e.g., iron and zinc deficiency leading to eating clay) may be contributing factors. Treatment includes behavioral, environmental, psychological, and family interventions.

Rumination Disorder

Rumination refers to repeatedly regurgitating and rechewing food for at least 1 month with sufficient severity to merit clinical attention, usually because of failure to thrive, in a person who previously had normal eating patterns. The disorder typically starts after the third month of life. Affected infants appear to derive pleasure from the behavior. Thus, treatment includes parenting education and behavioral modification.

Elimination Disorders

Encopresis

By the age of 4 years, more than 95% of children in Western cultures have acquired bowel control. By the age of 5 years, 99% have acquired bowel control.

Encopresis is repeated, intentional, or involuntary passage of feces in inappropriate places. Diagnostic criteria include: at least one episode per month for 3 months, developmental age of at least 4 years, and no substance or medical condition accounts for the behavior.

The **etiology** of encopresis is **multifactorial**. Contributing factors include power struggles over toilet training and inefficient/ineffective sphincter tone. Most encopretic children do not have a psychiatric disorder associated with the encopresis. For many, the disorder is **behavioral**. In contrast, persons who can control their bowel but **voluntarily** deposit feces in inappropriate places should be suspected of having a primary psychiatric disorder.

Developmental and maturational difficulties such as distractibility, poor frustration tolerance, and poor motor coordination are common in affected children. After bowel control has been firmly established, regressive reactions to a loss or other life stressors may precipitate encopresis.

Many encopretic children develop **psychogenic megacolon**. This condition arises when painful defecation or voluntary withholding leads to fecal impaction, which, in turn, produces colonic enlargement. Loss of colonic tone reduces sensitivity to pressure that signals the need to defecate. In many cases, encopresis remits spontaneously and rarely persists beyond adolescence.

Nonpunitive parental involvement is essential for a favorable outcome. Reward-based behavioral techniques, psychotherapy, and family therapy are indicated.

Enuresis

Enuresis is repeated involuntary or intentional urination into clothes or the bed by an individual who is at least 5 years old developmentally. The behavior must occur at least twice weekly for 3 consecutive months or be accompanied by emotional distress or functional impairment. The behavior cannot be explained as the direct effect of a substance or a physical dysfunction. Failure to acquire bladder control at the appropriate age and loss of bladder control after it is acquired are both defined as enuresis.

Although there appears to be some **genetic** predisposition, **psychosocial factors** (e.g., family toilet training practices, family distress) are also etiologic. Enuresis is unrelated to sleep stages.

How should enuresis be treated?

Many cases remit spontaneously. In other cases, restricting liquids close to bedtime, encouraging urination at bedtime, waking the child up to urinate, and having the child be responsible for cleaning soiled sheets are useful. Operant reward systems are also useful. Classical conditioning using a device that detects urine dampness and triggers an alarm that wakes the child are therapeutic mainstays. Supportive and family therapy can promote constructive coping with the enuresis. Pharmacotherapy with synthetic vasopressin may be necessary but, most often, symptoms recur when the medication is discontinued unless the behavior, itself, has changed.

Other Disorders of Infancy, Childhood, and Adolescence

Separation Anxiety Disorder (SAD)

Separation anxiety disorder (SAD) is the most common anxiety disorder in children. It occurs with equal frequency in boys and girls. Usual onset is at about 7 years of age. Prevalence is estimated at 4% of school-aged children and 1% of adolescents.

The **etiology of SAD is multifactoral**. Psychosocial factors include abnormally intense but otherwise developmentally appropriate fears (e.g., fear of

Diagnostic Criteria for Separation Anxiety Disorder

At least three of the following behaviors must be displayed when separation is occurring or anticipated:
- Recurrent distress
- Persistent worry about losing the attachment figure
- Persistent fear of separation from the attachment figure
- Reluctance or refusal to go to school
- Reluctance or refusal to go to sleep
- Nightmares about separation
- Physical complaints (e.g., headache, stomach ache)

losing the mother, fear of bodily harm) and heightened response to environmental stressors. The principal learning factor is **parental modeling.**

Treatment includes psychotherapy, family education, and family therapy. Pharmacotherapy with anxiolytics can be useful in refractory cases. The presence of school refusal requires prompt intervention with the child, family, and school. The goal is to return the child to school immediately, at least part time. Time spent in school is then gradually increased to full attendance.

Selective Mutism (SM)

Selective mutism is consistent refusal to speak in certain social situations where speech is expected, when the child is known to speak in other situations and to have age-appropriate language skills. The difficulty must be present for at least 1 month and interfere with academic and social functioning. The diagnosis should be reserved for children whose symptoms are not explained by a communication disorder, a developmental disorder, or a psychotic disorder. SM usually remits within weeks, but may persist for years. Children who do not improve by 10 years of age have a worse prognosis. Up to one third of children with selective mutism develop other psychiatric disorders, especially another anxiety disorder.

The prevalence is estimated at less than 1 per 1,000 children and affects girls more frequently than boys. Up to 90% of children with SM have a history of social phobia. Early psychologic trauma is a risk factor.

Treatment includes individual cognitive-behavioral psychotherapy for the child, counseling and

supportive therapy for the parents, family interventions, and pharmacotherapy.

Reactive Attachment Disorder

Reactive attachment disorder (RAD) occurs before 5 years of age. The etiology is associated with moderately to grossly **apathetic caregiving**. Affected children demonstrate markedly inappropriate social relatedness that is not fully explained by developmental delay or PDD. The child may fail to thrive physically and have delayed motor and psychosocial milestones. There are two types of reactive attachment disorder.

Inhibited type: consistent failure to initiate or respond to social interactions in a developmentally appropriate fashion, and

Disinhibited type: unselective, undifferentiated, and uninhibited social relatedness.

Reactive attachment disorder is more common among children from lower socioeconomic groups. Family disorganization, single-parenting, psychosocial deprivation, and poverty appear to increase vulnerability.

Children with RAD may eventually behave normally. However, depending on the severity and duration of pathologic caregiving, manifestations can progress to inanition and death.

Treatment includes hospitalization to protect the child if there is risk of abuse, if the pathologic caregiving is extreme, or if the child is malnourished. The therapeutic goal is normalization of the child-caregiver relationship. Management includes support services (e.g., child care, improved housing, financial assistance); decreasing social isolation of the family; comprehensive medical and psychiatric care; parent counseling and education, especially parenting skills training; and close, supportive follow-up. Long-term placement of the child may be indicated.

Recommended Reading

Cheng K, Myers KM. *Child and Adolescent Psychiatry: The Essentials.* Philadelphia, PA: Lippincott Williams and Wilkins; 2005.

Lewis M. (Ed.) *Child and Adolescent Psychiatry: A Comprehensive Textbook.* (3rd ed.). Philadelphia, PA: Lippincott Williams and Wilkins; 2002.

Review Questions

1. Sara is 9 years old. She was apparently normal at birth, the fourth and last child within a caring, intact family. At age 2 months, Sara suffered atypical seizures followed by crying spells. Neurologic consultation revealed nonspecific static encephalopathy. Sara's development has been slow. She has never been capable of understandable speech and cannot meet her basic needs. Her mother bathes, dresses, and feeds her, although Sara can eat finger foods independently. She has been unable to learn and the primary goal of schooling has been basic socialization. Among the following, the most likely diagnosis is
   A. attention-deficit/hyperactivity disorder
   B. learning disorder
   C. mental retardation
   D. reactive detachment disorder
   E. Rett's syndrome

2. Mario is 8 years old. At age 18 months, he underwent a dramatic change in behavior. He became isolated, appeared not to enjoy playing with adults, and ignored other children. He played with toys in an unusual fashion, as though he did not understand their purpose. He flapped his hands frequently and had severe temper tantrums if his routine was changed. His speech consisted of a few words repeated from games and television. Over time, he became emotionally unresponsive to his parents and other family members. He has never developed good peer or adult relationships. Among the following, the most likely diagnosis is
   A. attention-deficit/hyperactivity disorder
   B. autistic disorder
   C. learning disorder not otherwise specified
   D. pervasive developmental disorder not otherwise specified
   E. reactive attachment disorder

3. Ralik is a 10-year-old boy who is the class clown, always joking and talking to his peers when the teacher is trying to instruct and during tests. He has been suspended for refusing to follow the teacher's directions and trying to hit the principal. He scored over 2 years behind his age level on reading tests. Ralik failed 4th grade and is repeating it since his parents refused summer school; he rarely wants to go to school. He was in the ER recently for the third time since he was hit by a car when he ran into the street without looking. His father drinks heavily and is punitive. His mother cannot keep a job and is very lax with limit setting. Ralik ignores his mother and does whatever he wants until his father gets home. He has been experimenting with cigarettes and alcohol that he finds in the house. The most likely diagnoses are
   A. Asperger's disorder and learning disorder, NOS
   B. attention-deficit/hyperactivity disorder, oppositional defiant disorder, and reading disorder
   C. childhood disintegration disorder and separation anxiety disorder
   D. conduct disorder and developmental coordination disorder
   E. Tourette's disorder and enuresis

4. For years, 14-year-old Johnny has shown a pattern of cruelty to animals and aggression toward his siblings and peers. This pattern has intensified over the past year and now includes lying, running away from home, and stealing. Yesterday, he was caught vandalizing and setting a small fire in a neighbor's house. This symptom constellation is most suggestive of
   A. attention-deficit/hyperactivity disorder
   B. autistic disorder
   C. conduct disorder
   D. mental retardation
   E. oppositional-defiant disorder

Key to review questions: p. 393

47 Principles of Psychopharmacology

- What are the key principles that guide psychopharmacologic intervention?
- Why is it important to establish a meaningful set of differential diagnoses?
- How important is the cost of a medication?
- Why is it important to understand pharmacodynamic and pharmacokinetic principles?
- What are the major classes of psychotropic medications?

Chlorpromazine, the first psychotropic agent to have significant public impact, was discovered in 1955. Even though the U.S. population has almost doubled in the past 50 years, the current psychiatric inpatient population is a tenth of what it was then. While this is not exclusively a product of pharmacotherapy, antipsychotics and other pscyhotropics have been major contributors to the decline in hospitalization rates. These gains for patients have not occurred without a price. We are now increasingly aware of such complications as **tardive dyskinesia** and the development of the **metabolic syndrome** associated with the use of these medications. Antidepressants have made a major difference in many patients' lives, yet they are often accompanied by significant impairment in sexual activity. How, then, are we (both patients and their treatment providers) to decide on when the use of these medications is appropriate?

Tracking how a patient presented initially and whether therapeutic interventions are improving the patient's status or not is criticial. Many psychiatric rating scales have been developed to document the patient's progress. The **Hamilton Depression Rating Scale**, for example, is useful in monitoring effectiveness of antidepressants; the **Positive and Negative Symptom Scale** is a helpful way to document the impact of antipsychotics. A helpful Internet-based compendium of rating scales is listed at the end of this chapter.

Why is it important to establish a meaningful set of differential diagnoses?

Establish a meaningful set of differential diagnoses.

A patient can present exactly the same symptomatic findings from ingesting cocaine, experiencing schizophrenia, or having meningitis. Hypothyroidism can mimic the signs and symptoms associated with depression. It is therefore essential to take a complete history and to evaluate the probabilities of different diagnostic options.

What are the key principles that guide psychopharmacologic intervention?

Key Principles

Document the signs and symptoms that are amenable to pharmacotherapy and are useful indicators of the patient's overall clinical state.

Obtain a detailed drug history.

A patient's previous response to medication is always the best predictor of subsequent treatment.

Clinical Application

A 34-year-old nurse presents with a four-week history of crippling anxiety. She describes episodes of palpitations, tremor, fear of "going crazy", and dyspnea. She has become fearful of going out of the house. The onset of her symptoms was three weeks postpartum. Her pregnancy was very much desired. She has not been able to return to work. Physical examination reveals tremor and hyperreflexia. Laboratory results are consistent with hyperthyroidism. She has developed postpartum thyroiditis. Reasonable diagnostic considerations would have included postpartum depression and anxiety about separation from her infant. The treatment of each is significantly different

In any but emergency situations, do not commence pharmacotherapy until you have completed the above steps.

This will require the ability to resist internal pressure, and pressure from patients and their families to do "something". Doing "something" without a well-thought-out rationale often leads to mistreatment.

Whenever possible avoid changing more than one variable at a time.

This is a difficult goal to fully realize. Circumstances change in patients' lives beyond their taking medications and these changes often have impact on their illness. It is usually possible, however, to manipulate one pharmacologic variable at a time. To do otherwise leaves open the possibility of considerable confusion as to which change in medication was responsible for the (desirable or undesirable) change in the patient's condition.

Within a class of drugs, you must prescribe on the basis of side effects; few convincing data exist to suggest a difference in efficacy between members of a given class.

With the possible exception of clozapine having greater efficacy than other antipsychotics, there is little to suggest differences between one member

of a class of psychotropics and any other. However, side effects do differ significantly. Physician and patient must discuss side effects fully before deciding which medication to attempt. The patient should also be encouraged to report more-severe-than-expected or unexpected side effects promptly.

Psychotropics treat symptoms, not diseases.

Antipsychotics are effective for treating hallucinations and delusions; they are far less helpful in treating negative symptoms associated with schizophrenia. Antidepressants have proven beneficial for symptoms associated with obsessive-compulsive disorder and anxiety disorders as well as for depression. Being familiar with the specific signs and symptoms that individual medications target allows the practitioner to provide options if a given medication is ineffective or has intolerable side effects.

Pharmacotherapy is no more effective than treatment adherence.

The best medication regimen will not be effective if the patient is unwilling or unable to take the medication. Working with the patient in a collegial fashion is vital. The physician should be an objective expert about the medications prescribed; patients should be encouraged to be objective experts about themselves. Doctor and patient are, therefore, mutually dependent. The quality of the doctor-patient relationship is the single strongest predictor of patient adherence with medications.

How important is the cost of a medication?

Consider costs when prescribing.

Antipsychotics can cost as little as pennies a day or as much as $30 a day. We must think about the financial impact of the medications we prescribe. We must know whether a patient can afford a given prescription. There are clearly times when the higher cost is justified, but money must be part of the calculation. Whenever possible, prescribe generically. Generic drugs are significantly cheaper and, in general, equally efficacious.

If the patient is a working parent with multiple home and office responsibilities, a once-a-day brand-name medication may be essential to compliance.

In contrast, if the patient is on a fixed income, a twice-a-day generic may be critical to affording to obtain the drugs.

Decisions on medications should be evidence based.

For too long physicians have been dependent on industry sponsored clinical trials and on drug sales representatives for information. Better sources of data are available and should be utilized. The Cochrane Registry of Clinical Trials (referenced at the end of this chapter) is an excellent source of well-researched information. Micromedex (also referenced) is another good source of impartial information about medications. The recent development of practical clinical trials is beginning to yield information on responses to medication experienced by the kinds of patients seen by most clinicians as opposed to those who enter drug company sponsored trials.

Why is it important to understand pharmacodynamic and pharmacokinetic principles?

Clinical Application

A 36-year-old carpenter presents with chronic depression. He has seen three previous psychiatrists and has been treated with desipramine, imipramine, and paroxetine. He was unable to tolerate any of the medications, even at minimal doses. He stopped seeking treatment three years ago, convinced that it would do him no good and accepting a previous therapist's explanation that his reaction to medications must be psychogenic in origin. He returned to treatment only because of mounting desperation. A rechallenge with desipramine revealed a therapeutic blood level at 10 milligrams per day, a dose far below that which would ordinarily be utilized. It became apparent that he was one of the 5–10% of Caucasians who are poor metabolizers at the level of the 2D6 cytochrome P450 isozyme.

Understand basic pharmacodynamic and pharmacokinetic principles.

Understanding basic pharmacodynamics and pharmacokinetics is critical when prescribing for pediatric or elderly patients and the medically compromised. Each of these population groups has the potential to metabolize and excrete drugs differently from the well young and middle-aged adult population. The medically compromised of any age have the added challenge of taking other medications that may interact with (inhibit or enhance) any additional medication being considered. Although most interactions fall into the nuisance category, some are fatal. An excellent web site for drug interactions is listed at the end of this chapter.

Good pharmacotherapy should reinforce good psychotherapy and vice versa.

This is true for many reasons. A profoundly depressed patient, mired in hopelessness, will find it difficult to engender sufficient energy or hope to invest in psychotherapy. Effective antidepressants can provide enough of a "kickstart" to enable the patient to take advantage of cognitive therapy. Similarly, taking medication often has considerable psychological meaning. If this is not understood, the chances of adherence with medication decrease.

What are the major classes of psychotropic medications?

Classes of Psychotropics

Antidepressants
Antipsychotics
Mood stabilizers
Sedatives/hypnotics
Stimulants

Recommended Reading

Belmaker RH. Medical Progress: Bipolar Disorder. *New England Journal of Medicine* 2004; 351:476–486.

Freedman R. The choice of antipsychotic drugs for schizophrenia. *New England Journal of Medicine* 2005; 353:1286–1288.

Insel TR. Beyond efficacy: the STAR*D trial. *American Journal of Psychiatry* 2006; 163:5–7.

Recommended Internet Resources

Medical information in general: Medline, accessible through PubMed at http://www.ncbi.nlm.nih.gov/entrez/query.fcgi?db=PubMed

Information about medications: Micromedex, available at http://www.micromedex.com/solutions/academics/

Drug interactions: http://medicine.iupui.edu/flockhart/

Scales to assess psychopathology and impact of treatment: http://www.medal.org/visitor/

Evidence-based assessment of clinical trials: http://www3.interscience.wiley.com/ cgi-bin/mrwhome/106568753/HOME?CRETRY= 1&SRETRY=0

Review Questions

Directions: The items below consist of lettered headings followed by numbered descriptions. For each numbered description choose the *one* lettered heading to which it is most closely associated. Each lettered heading may be used *once, more than once, or not at all.*

Match the clinical scenario to the most applicable principle of psychopharmacology.

A. Change one variable at a time
B. Document progress
C. Establish the differential diagnosis
D. Psychotropics treat symptoms not disease

1. A 22-year-old man with schizophrenia begins hallucinating shortly after stopping his medication.
2. A 55-year-old woman has the same score on the Hamilton Depression Rating Scale 3 months after starting an antidepressant as she did before treatment.
3. A teenaged patient is on an antidepressant and an anxiolytic. She would like to wean off medication.

Key to review questions: p. 393

Appendices

Appendix A: Epidemiology

Epidemiology is "the study of the distribution and determinants of health related states in a defined population." The tools of epidemiology are ratios or rates. In their simplest form, ratios are the number of people with a condition, divided by the number of persons in the population who are "at risk" for having that condition. **Risk** means a person is vulnerable to a condition. It does not mean that the person will get the disease, only that it is a possibility

> Ten senior high school girls were diagnosed with dysfunctional menstrual bleeding during the last school year. The school had 275 senior girls. The ratio 10/275 defines how many of the individuals at risk actually have the condition. The numerator (N), 10, is the number of diagnosed cases, and denominator (D), 275, is the number of females at risk. This ratio, N/D or 10/275, defines what proportion of the at-risk community has the condition.

Most risk estimates use a **standardized denominator.** This is done by multiplying the ratio by a constant, usually 100,000, yielding a rate per 100,000 of the persons at risk (N/D x 100,000). The ratio of students who have dysfunctional menstrual bleeding over all students at risk, 10/275 or 0.036, now becomes 10/275 x 100,000 or 3,636 per 100,000. Thus, among a group of 100,000 high school senior girls, about 3,636 are likely to have dysfunctional menstrual bleeding. This estimate for the entire U.S. is limited by how closely the female high school senior population at the local city high school resembles the population of high school females in the U.S. We would expect this number to be representative if the distribution of local high school senior girls was ethnically, racially, and socioeconomically similar to the U.S. population.

Incidence and Prevalence

The two most widely used types of rates are called incidence and prevalence. **Incidence** is the number of new cases in a given time period divided by the number of persons at risk to *catch* the disease. **Prevalence** is the total number of cases that exist in a given period, whether the cases are new or old and divided by the number of persons at risk to *have* the disease. **Period prevalence** is the number of cases of a disease divided by the population at risk over a given *span of time.* **Point prevalence** is the number of cases of a disease divided by the population at risk at a given *moment in time.*

Incidence gives the rate at which people *acquire* a disease, while prevalence is the total number of people who *have* the disease or condition. Thus, incidence is a good index for tracking the course of acute conditions such as influenza while prevalence is more suited to tracking chronic conditions such as hypertension.

The relationship between incidence and prevalence is shown by the formula: **Prevalence = Incidence × Duration,** where duration is the length of time that someone has the disease **(see Figure A.1.).** As either incidence or duration rises, prevalence rises. Conversely, a decline in either incidence or duration reduces prevalence.

Screening Tests

Screening is designed to identify who has a disease and who does not. In developing screening criteria, a sample of the target population is measured on a key dimension. Scores on this dimension are used to classify people as having the disease or not, according to predefined criteria. People who meet the criteria are considered to have the dis-

> To detect hypertension in the population at large, a researcher might take the blood pressure of a sample of people. People with a systolic blood pressure higher than 130 mm Hg might be defined as hypertensive, while those who have a systolic blood pressure lower than this cut-off score would be considered to be in the normal range.

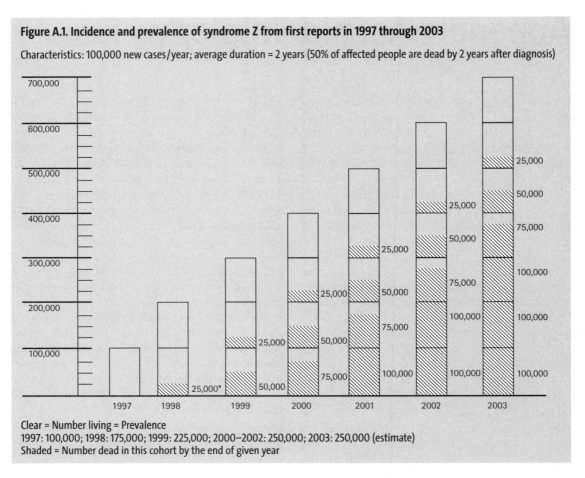

Figure A.1. Incidence and prevalence of syndrome Z from first reports in 1997 through 2003

Characteristics: 100,000 new cases/year; average duration = 2 years (50% of affected people are dead by 2 years after diagnosis)

Clear = Number living = Prevalence
1997: 100,000; 1998: 175,000; 1999: 225,000; 2000–2002: 250,000; 2003: 250,000 (estimate)
Shaded = Number dead in this cohort by the end of given year

ease, while those who do not are assumed to not have the disease.

A key consideration in constructing a screening test is that the measure must be as **accurate** as possible. The best test would detect all of the people with the disease and correctly exclude the healthy people. A screening test should also be **less expensive and easier to administer** than a definitive evaluation. The results of a screening test, when compared with the "gold standard" evaluation can be displayed as a simple 2 × 2 table **(see Figure A.2.)**. This figure contains all the logical possibilities for matching screening classifications with the "gold standard" diagnosis. Optimally, there is agreement between the results of the screening test and the gold standard as to who has disease (true positives) and who is disease free (true negatives). Persons classified by the screening test as diseased who are really disease free are called false positives; they are positive on the screening test, but are false (not confirmed) on the gold standard. Persons classified by the screening test as disease free who really have

disease are called false negatives; they are negative on the screening test, but are false in that according to the gold standard they have the disease.

Five characteristics are used to determine the quality of a screening test. **Sensitivity** concerns the detection of disease: out of all the persons with disease in the population, what proportion were identified correctly? **Specificity** targets the healthy people: out of all the healthy people in the population, what proportion was labeled correctly? If the disease for which the screening is being done is some type of virulent, contagious disease, a screening test with high sensitivity would be preferred. If, in contrast, the disease requires painful, expensive medical treatment, a highly specific test would be preferred. Sensitivity and specificity are properties of the screening test itself and are unaffected by the underlying prevalence of disease in a population.

When a screening test identifies a patient as a positive (has the disease), most patients will ask, "Are you sure?" **Positive predictive value** of

Figure A.2. Standard 2 x 2 table comparing test results and true disease status (gold standard)

True Disease Status

		Yes	No	Total
Screening Tool Results	Yes	(a) True Positives	(b) False Positives	a + b All subjects with + screening
	No	(c) False Negatives	(d) True Negatives	c + d All subjects with − screening
	Total	a + b All subjects with disease	b + d All subjects without disease	a + b + c + d All subjects

a / (a + c) = Sensitivity
d / (b + d) = Specificity
b / (b + d) = False–Positive Error Rate (Alpha or Type 1 Error)
c / (a + c) = False–Negative Error Rate (Beta or Type 2 Error)
a / (a + b) = Positive Predictive Value
d / (c + d) = Negative Predictive Value

(a + c) / (a + b + c + d) = Prevalence

Example: 2 x 2 table for screening for hypertension

Hypertension

		Yes	No	
Screening Test	Positive	TP 90	FP 20	110
	Negative	FN 10	TN 80	90
		100	100	200

Sensitivity	=	$\dfrac{TP}{TP + FN}$	=	$\dfrac{90}{100}$ =	90%
Specificity	=	$\dfrac{TP}{TN + FP}$	=	$\dfrac{80}{100}$ =	80%
Positive Predictive Value	=	$\dfrac{TP}{TP + FP}$	=	$\dfrac{90}{110}$ =	81.8%
Negative Predictive Value	=	$\dfrac{TN}{TN + FN}$	=	$\dfrac{80}{90}$ =	88.8%
Accuracy	=	$\dfrac{TP + TN}{TP + TN + FP + FN}$	=	$\dfrac{170}{200}$ =	85%

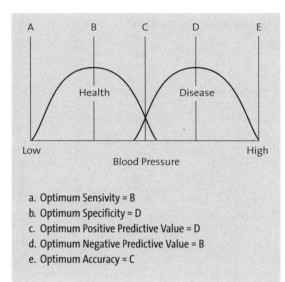

a. Optimum Sensivity = B
b. Optimum Specificity = D
c. Optimum Positive Predictive Value = D
d. Optimum Negative Predictive Value = B
e. Optimum Accuracy = C

Observational Study Designs and Comparative Risk

Risk factors identify who is more likely to develop a disease. However, individuals with risk factors do not necessarily develop the disease; in fact, often they do not. Being able to identify persons who are more likely to develop the disease allows prevention and monitoring efforts to be focused where they will do the most good. Risk factors are discovered by observation. Three basic types of observational research are cohort studies, case-control studies, and cross-sectional studies.

Cohort Studies

In a cohort study the researcher follows two samples of persons over time, those with and those without the risk factor to compare the onset of disease within these two groups. By comparing the incidence rate in people with the risk factor with the incidence rate in people without the risk factor, it is possible to estimate the relative importance of the risk factor as a precursor of the disease. The

the test answers this question. Positive predictive value is the percentage of all people who will test positive who actually have the disease. **Negative predictive value** is the degree to which a negative on the test identifies a person who is disease free. In a population with a high prevalence, a positive test is more likely to be accurate than a positive test in a population with a low prevalence. Conversely, in a population with high prevalence, a negative test is less likely to be true than a negative test in a population with a low prevalence of disease.

A researcher screened two populations, one with a prevalence of 1 out of 2 and one with a prevalence of 1 out of 1,000,000. Given a positive test from both samples, the researcher should feel more confident about the positive result from the 1 in 2 population because, just by random selection, any given person has a 50% chance of having the disease, compared to the 1 in a million chance for the positive test in the person from the other population.

Screening is only appropriate when attempting to detect a disease with relatively high prevalence. That is, screening for a disease with a prevalence of 1 per 100,000 would require screening approximately 100,000 people to detect just one case. This is not a good use of time or resources. Screening is also only appropriate when there is a clear action for those who are identified as having the disease (i.e., receiving treatment for an infectious disease).

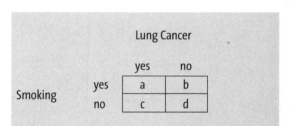

a. Cohort Study: Tracking incidence related to risk factor
   calculation = relative risk = (a/a+b) / (c/c+d)

b. Case-Control Study: Assessing retrospective occurrence of risk factor given existence of disease
   calculation = odds-ratio = ad/bc

c. Cross-Sectional Study: Measuring the association between disease and risk factor at a single point in time
   calculation = chi-square = $\chi^2 = \Sigma\ [(O-E)^2/E]$
   where O = Observed value for cell
   E = Expected value for cell

temporal sequence inherent in a cohort study helps to reveal any causal linkage between having the risk factor and developing the disease. The results provided by a cohort study are not subject to distortion due to biased recall because the outcome (i.e., the onset of disease) is assessed at the time it first appears.

The relative incidence of the disease between the two groups in a cohort study can be compared by calculating the **relative risk.** Relative risk is simply the ratio of the incidence rates of the two groups. This comparison yields the probability of acquiring the disease in one group compared to another. The difference between the two groups in terms of the actual number of persons who catch the disease can also be calculated. **Attributable risk** is computed by subtracting the incidence rate of the unexposed group from that of the exposed or at risk group. In more general terms, attributable risk is the incidence rate of one group subtracted from the incidence rate of the second group.

> If infant mortality in a given community is 14 per 1,000 live births for the African American population, and 6 per 1,000 live births for the white population, the relative risk of death in the first year of life for blacks compared to whites is 14/6 or 2.33. That is, an African American child has more than twice the chance of dying in the first year of life as does a white child. The results of cohort studies such as this alert epidemiologists to possible risk factors (e.g., socioeconomic status, or access to pre- and perinatal health care).

Case-Control Studies

A case-control study compares a sample of people who have a disease (cases) with a group of comparable people drawn from the same population who do not have the disease (controls). Historical features that distinguish the disease group from the control group can be identified as possible risk factors. An example of a case-control study would be selecting a sample of people who have lung cancer and a comparable group of people without lung cancer. From interviews with both groups, it would be possible to determine the percentage of each group who had smoked cigarettes (and how much) in the past.

Data from a case-control study are usually analyzed by calculating an **odds ratio,** or the odds of the risk factor appearing in the disease group divided by the odds of the risk factor appearing in the control group. The odds ratio provides an estimate of the likelihood that a risk factor is more common in the cases than in the controls. The larger the number produced by the odds ratio, the greater the difference between the two groups. Factors that significantly differ in incidence between the two groups can then be explored further to see how they contribute to the onset of disease.

Case-control studies are the research design of choice to study low frequency events such as suicide. For example, given a suicide rate of approximately 13 per 100,000, many hundreds of thousands of people would have to be followed prospectively in a cohort study to have a sufficient number of incidence cases to be analyzed. However, in a metropolitan area of 2.5 million people, 250 cases of suicide could be identified quickly. The only challenge would be to find 250 individuals each of whom ed one of the cases on certain selected variables (e.g., age, race, gender, socioeconomic class, education). The weakness of a case-control study is that recollections are subject to some decay over time. What participants recall at the time of the study may be different from what actually happened in the past.

Cross-Sectional Studies

The goal of a cross-sectional study is to establish the prevalence of disease and associated risk factors within a specific time frame. A sample, drawn from the population of interest, is analyzed to determine (1) who has the disease, (2) who does not, and (3) what characteristics distinguish the persons who have the disease from those who are disease free.

Because data regarding both disease prevalence and risk factors are collected at the same time, a cross-sectional study is not useful for determining cause and effect. In a cross-sectional study, it is impossible to determine whether the risk factors preceded the onset of disease, or whether they are the consequence of the disease. The results of a cross-sectional study are usually analyzed by means of a statistical test called a Chi-square (see Appendix B, Biostatistics) which determines if the patterns seen in the data collected are meaningful, or merely the result of random chance.

Reliability and Validity

The quality of a measure is judged in terms of its **reliability** (is it consistent?) and its **validity** (does it measure what it purports to measure?).

Reliability is a necessary but not sufficient condition for validity.

Types of Reliability

A measure given on two separate occasions should give consistent results if it has **test-retest reliability.**

If the items on an examination are randomly split into two groups and are scored separately but yield the same result, the examination has **split-half reliability.**

If a panel of observers watch the same event and all independently arrive at the same score, there is good **inter-rater reliability.**

Types of Validity

For an instrument to have **face validity,** individual items should appear to reflect the variable in question (e.g., to find out about depression, items would ask about mood).

Content validity requires that a measure directly assess the trait of interest (e.g., asking questions about heart sounds on a cardiology test).

Construct validity requires that the theoretical construct being assessed is consistent with the measurement (e.g., if schizophrenia is hypothecized to be genetic, items would not relate to child rearing practices).

Convergent validity stipulates that any new measure correlate positively with existing measures that purport to assess the same thing.

To establish **criterion-related validity,** the results of the measure must agree with some existing feature of reality (e.g., doing well on an examination that purports to assess knowledge in anatomy should be related to being ranked high in anatomy by an expert).

Predictive validity is criterion-related validity plus time (e.g., doing well on an entrance examination that purports to assess how well a student will do at a particular school should be correlated with rank in the graduating class four years later) (see Psychological Testing in Chapter 38, Introduction to Psychopathology).

Appendix B: Biostatistics

While epidemiology defines and measures the distribution of diseases and their risk factors, biostatistics enables the researcher to analyze the significance of these measures.

The Normal Curve

Distributions vary in size and shape, but the **normal distribution (Gaussian curve)** is the most common and is easily recognized by its **"bell shape"**. The frequencies of many things (e.g., height, weight, intelligence, blood pressure) are more or less "normally" distributed. When graphed, these distributions are generally balanced or symmetrical, with the bulk of cases in the middle (center) and relatively few at the extremes (tails) of the distribution. If split down the middle, the two resulting halves will generally match. The normal distribution serves as the central organizing element for a large number of statistical methods.

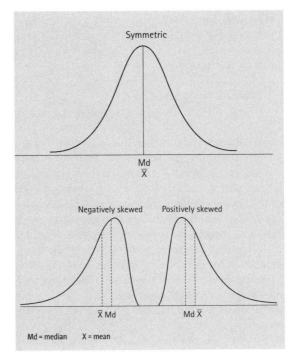

Md = median   X = mean

Measures of Central Tendency

A distribution can be summarized by two sets of parameters, central tendency and variability. **Central tendency** identifies the center of the distribution and its position along the dimension that defines it. **Variability** defines the degree to which the distribution spreads out from the center.

Central tendency is established by three parameters: the **mean,** the **median,** and the **mode.** The **mean** is the average, or the sum of the scores divided by the total number of scores ($Z(x)/n$). The **median** is the middle score or the score which has 50% of the scores below it and 50% above it. In the case of an even number of scores, the medi-

an is estimated by adding the middle two scores together and dividing by two [$(xm1 + xm2)/2 =$ median]. The **mode** is the most frequently occurring score regardless of its position with respect to the mean and the median.

In a normal distribution, the mean, median, and mode are all the same number. If the mean, median and mode are not all the same number, then the curve is skewed. A distribution can be skewed with the tail extending to the right (positive skew), or with the tail extending to the left (negative skew).

Measures of Variance

The variability of a distribution can be assessed by inspecting the range or the difference between the lowest and highest scores in the distribution. The range describes the width of the distribution, or how spread out the distribution is along the dimension of measurement.

The **standard deviation** (represented by a), provides a method for calculating a standardized

Given the following set of numbers [2, 2, 2, 3, 3, 4, 4, 6, 7, 7, 8, 8, 8, 8, 9], the mean is 5.4, the median is 6, and the mode is 8.

measure of the variance in any distribution. To compute a standard deviation, the mean is subtracted from each individual score of the distribution (x − mean). These differences, or deviations, are then squared $(x - mean)^2$, and the squared deviations then added, $\Sigma(x - mean)^2$. The sum of the squared deviations is then divided by the sample size minus 1 (n − 1) and the square root taken of the whole quantity.

$$\text{Standard deviation} = \sigma = \sqrt{\Sigma(x - mean)^2/(n - 1)}$$

A larger standard deviation signifies that the scores are more spread out. A smaller standard deviation means that the scores are more compact. In any normal distribution, approximately 68.0% of the cases lie between one standard deviation above the mean and one standard deviation below the mean. Approximately 95.5% of cases lie within plus or minus two standard deviations of the mean, and 99.7% of cases lie within plus or minus three standard deviations of the mean. These numbers are constants and will always apply for any normal distribution. Within two standard deviations of the mean, or 95.5% of the cases, is typically used to define **"within normal limits."**

Inferential Statistics

Descriptive statistics are useful for summarizing sample data. **Inferential statistics** permit drawing reasonable conclusions about a population based upon the sample data. The estimates generated from a sample are an approximation of the whole, but they are not exact. Statistical calculations enable the researcher to determine how good the approximation is likely to be.

Confidence Intervals

Confidence intervals provide a sense of how close estimates are to reality. Basically, a confidence interval begins with the number provided by the sample, and then adds and subtracts from that number to create a range within which the true parameter is believed to lie.

The formula for calculating the **confidence interval of the mean** is comprised of the **sample**

mean, which anchors the estimate, a **standard error,** which serves as an index of the quality of the sample, and a **standard score,** which indicates the degree of confidence the interval is to have.

The **standard error** is a measure of how far off the sample estimate of the population is likely to be. This error is estimated using two factors: the sample size and the standard deviation. The larger the sample, the better the estimate is likely to be. The standard deviation indicates how much variation there is in the sample. If there is little variation, then the cases are generally alike and any sample will offer a good approximation of the whole. If, on the other hand, the population is highly variable, then the chance of selecting unrepresentative cases in the sample rises, and the chance of error in the estimate increases. Thus, as the standard deviation increases, the standard error also increases.

If repeated random samples were taken from a population, 95% of the time the means computed from each of these samples would fall into the range defined by two standard deviations or the 95% confidence interval. The true mean is somewhere in the computed range. The confidence interval does not specify where in the given range it is most likely to be, only the likelihood that it falls somewhere within that interval.

Standard Score Distribution

Any normal curve distribution can be analyzed more easily by converting it to a **standard score** distribution. A standard score distribution is a normal distribution with a mean equal to zero and a standard deviation equal to one. Any number, in any distribution, whatever the computed mean and standard deviation, can be converted to a **standard score** by the simple formula:

$$\text{Standard score} = Z = (x - mean)/\sigma$$

Because the mean is equal to zero, any positive number is greater than the mean, and any negative number is less than the mean. By making the standard deviation equal to one, the basic unit on the z-**score** distribution becomes the standard deviation. The value of any score on the distribution tells us exactly how many deviations it is above or below the mean. This means that a z-score of 2.6 is exactly 2.6 standard deviations above the mean, and that a z-score of −1.3 is exactly 1.3 standard deviations below the mean.

In summary, the standard deviation is a measure of the variability or spread of the distribution; the standard error is an index of the quality of the parameter estimate (e.g., the mean) and is calculated using both the standard deviation and the sample size; and the standard score is a value taken from a normal distribution that has been standardized to have a mean equal to zero and a standard deviation equal to one.

Confidence Intervals for Relative Risks and Odds Ratios

Confidence intervals can be computed for **relative risks** and **odds ratios.** However, both the calculation and the interpretation will be different from that of a mean because these values are ratios. In any **ratio,** a value of one means that the numerator and the denominator are the same. Therefore, the number 1.0 is a critical value which implies no difference between the two populations being compared. Thus, when interpreting the significance of a confidence interval of a relative risk or odds ratio, if the value 1.0 falls within the confidence interval, the possibility exists that the groups being compared are the same.

The Null Hypothesis

Consider the example of a clinical trial testing a new anti-depressant drug against existing standard pharmacotherapy. How will it be determined if the new drug is more effective? The design involves the selection of two groups of comparably depressed patients one of which will receive the new drug and the other the standard approved therapy. The group treated with the new drug should show more or faster relief from their depressive symptoms if the drug is more effective. But how much more or faster relief would be needed to determine that the drug is better?

> Every statistical analysis begins with a question. What this question is and how it is framed are critical to determining the type of answer that will be found.

The question "Does the new anti-depressant drug work better than the standard therapy?" is transformed into the **null hypothesis:** "The group receiving the new drug will not show significant symptom reduction relative to the standard treatment group." Note that the null hypothesis is

Using Confidence Intervals

A researcher wishes to assess the efficacy of a new anti-hypertensive medication. Two groups of patients are randomly selected for this study. Both groups have the same level and severity of hypertension at the start of the study. One group is given the new anti-hypertensive medication over a 6 month trial, while the second group is given a placebo. At the end of 6 months, the blood pressures of both groups are assessed.

The results are shown below, plotted as means with bars representing the 95% confidence intervals. Note that the mean diastolic blood pressure for the treatment group is lower than that for the placebo group. Does the new anti-hypertensive drug work better than the placebo?

The best estimate of the effects of the medication in the population is defined by the confidence interval. An examination of the figure show that the bars overlap, that is the upper boundary of the treatment group is higher than the lower boundary of the placebo group. Because the true mean has a 95% chance of being within the confidence interval, and the intervals overlap, the true means could be the same. Therefore, as the graph shows, the best estimate is that if used in the population at large, the new anti-hypertensive will be no different from the placebo for lowering blood pressure over a 6-month trial.

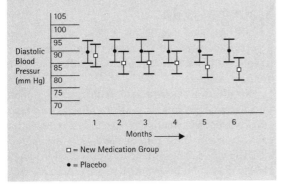

Diastolic Blood Pressur (mm Hg)

Months

□ = New Medication Group

● = Placebo

> The logic of statistics dictates that because nothing can be really proved, it is necessary to try to disprove its opposite.

stated exactly the *obverse* of the original question. To gain evidence that a given proposition is true, evidence is gathered to reject its opposite, in this instance, to disprove the null hypothesis.

The null hypothesis states that the results of the study are due to chance only and that any differences are the result of random variations within the data. Disputing this null hypothesis requires finding differences that are large enough that the researcher can be confident that they represent real differences. Statistical analysis provides information about just how large those differences must be to be interpreted as real at, for example, the 95% confidence level.

Probability

On what basis do we conclude that the null hypothesis can be rejected? The key to this decision lies in specific characteristics of the **p-value** (a probability ranging from 0 to 1.0), of which there are two of interest. The first, the **p-value criterion** is the standard against which the results of the statistical analysis will be judged. Most often the standard of $p < 0.05$ is used. This corresponds to the 95% confidence interval, just as $p < 0.01$ corresponds to the 99% confidence level. The second p-value is a **computed p-value**, generated by statistical analysis using data from the sample. The decision whether or not to reject the null hypothesis is made by comparing the computed p-value with the .05 or .01 criterion selected. If the computed p-value is less than the criterion, then statistical significance is achieved and the null hypothesis is rej ected. If the computed value is higher than the chosen criterion, statistical significance has not been achieved and the null hypothesis cannot be rejected. Thus, if the criterion is set at $p < 0.05$, then a computed p-value of $p = .03$ allows rejection of the null hypothesis while a computed p-value of $p = .09$ does not. Note that the null hypothesis is not accepted, it is either rejected, or "failed to be rejected". The distinction is similar to the difference between knowing that a person is innocent and not having enough evidence to prove guilt.

Type I (α) and Type II (β) Errors

If the cut-off for significance (criterion) has been set at $p < 0.05$, and a computed p-value is less than 0.05, the null hypothesis is rejected. However, because the data from the sample may not accurately reflect the real world population, rejecting the null hypothesis may be wrong. How likely is it to be wrong? If $p = 0.02$, the interpretation will be wrong 2% of the time, or 2 out of 100 times. This type of error, rejecting the null hypothesis when it is really true, is called a **Type I error.** Note that the researcher never knows if a Type I error was made, only the chance that one was made. A Type I error is only possible when the null hypothesis is rejected.

If the null hypothesis is not rejected, a Type I error is impossible. However, by failing to reject it, a **Type II error** may have been made. A Type II error is failure to reject the null hypothesis when it should have been rejected.

Returning to the example of the study of a new anti-hypertensive medication, the null hypothesis would be that the medication fails to relieve high blood pressure better than the placebo. A Type I error would occur if it were decided the drug is more effective, when in fact it is not. A Type II error would occur if it were decided the drug is not more effective, when in fact it is. Generally speaking, a Type I error is worse than a Type II error. A Type I error is an error of **commission** (the drug is said to be more effective when it is not), while a Type II error is an error of **omission** (failure to discover that the drug, in fact, is better). A computed p-value gives the chance of a Type I error. It does not indicate what proportion of the patients will benefit from the treatment, nor the probability that a single patient will benefit.

Scaling of Data

To conduct statistical analyses, things, events, and people must be converted into numbers. This is done by scaling.

Nominal or categorical scaling divides data into discrete groups that are mutually exclusive and exhaustive. Mutually exclusive means that each observation fits into one and only one category. Exhaustive means that every observation can be clearly classified into some category. A categorical or nominal variable contains two or more groups into which data can be classified. "Gender," a single nominal variable comprised of two groups, male and female, is one example.

Ordinal scaling organizes data along a given dimension. Ordinals provide information about the relative relationship between things (e.g., something is bigger, faster, or better). Although ordinal data give the order of things, the actual distance between them is not specified (e.g., how much bigger, faster, or better).

Interval scaling organizes data along dimensions with equally spaced gradations or intervals, which allows for more accurate comparisons (e.g., "He is twice as tall as she is"). Interval scales can provide means and standard deviations, which nominal and ordinal scales cannot. For example, "What is the mean of gender?"

A **ratio scale** has all the properties of an interval scale, plus one more: a true zero point. A true

These four types of scales, nominal, ordinal, interval, and ratio, form a hierarchy from the least specific information to the most specific information. Data can be degraded (e.g., interval data can be treated as ordinal data or ordinal data can be treated as nominal data) but cannot be upgraded. That is, interval data lack the information that ratio data provide and nominal data provide no information about the rank order necessary for ordinal data. For purposes of statistical analysis, ratio level data are generally treated as interval level data.

zero sets an absolute floor to the scale below which no lower values are possible. For example, when temperature is measured using the Fahrenheit scale, which is an interval scale, zero does not mean absolute zero. By contrast, when temperature is measured using the Kelvin scale, a ratio measurement is produced. Zero Kelvin means

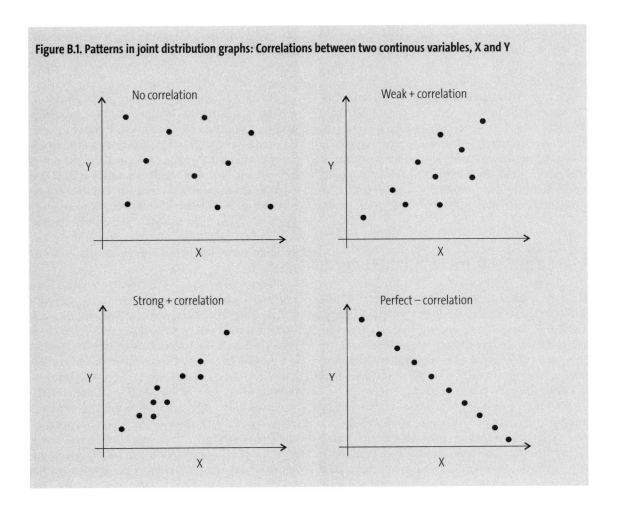

Figure B.1. Patterns in joint distribution graphs: Correlations between two continous variables, X and Y

absolute zero – no molecular movement. It cannot get any colder than zero degrees Kelvin.

Statistical Tests for Interval Data

The type of data determines which statistical test is appropriate to use. If data are measured on an interval scale, two basic statistical tests are available: Pearson correlation and regression analysis.

A **Pearson correlation** answers the question, "Is there a linear relationship between these two varables?" Pearson correlation tests the degree to which a line can be found to represent the data and is expressed as a number between -1.0 and +1.0. The further the value of the correlation is from zero, the stronger the linear relationship represented. Thus, a correlation of -.76 is a stronger correlation than a correlation of +.67. The plus or minus sign indicates the direction of the relationship; a plus sign indicates a positive relationship, a negative sign indicates an inverse relationship. A strong correlation says that two variables are associated and that they vary together, it does not say that one causes the other.

A **regression analysis** answers the question, "What exactly in the relationship between these two variables?" Regression analysis specifies the slope and the intercept that describe any linear relationship between two interval level variables. Regression analysis can be used to make predictions; that is, given a value for one variable, what is the expected value is for the other?

Statistical Tests for Nominal Data

If all the data in the study are nominal, three basic statistical tests are available: chi-square analysis, Fisher's exact test, and McNemar's test with matched pairs data. These statistical tests are sometimes referred to as non-parametric since the data are not measured in continuous parameters but rather discrete categories.

The most commonly used test statistic for the analysis of nominal level data is the **chi-square** (χ^2). A chi-square analysis tests whether two nominal sets of data are independent. For example, a chi-square analysis would be used to determine if there is any relationship in the data collected from a cross-sectional study between gender and hair color.

A **Fisher's exact test** does not derive a test statistic, but rather computes the p-value directly from the data. For this reason, a Fisher's exact test is used only when the sample size is less than 20 and when the nominal variables each have only two groups (2×2 design).

McNemar's test is used in those instances when the data in two of the nominal groups are joined or linked in some way.

Statistical Tests for Combined Interval and Nominal Data

If the study uses a combination of interval and nominal data, the basic statistical tests are either the student's *t-test (t-test)* or an analysis of variance (ANOVA). The **student's *t*-test** compares differences in the values of a single interval variable between two groups defined by a single nominal variable (e.g., a study comparing the heights of men with those of women).

If the nominal variable has more than two groups, a *t-test* is no longer possible. Instead, a one-way **analysis of variance (ANOVA)** would be used to determine if there are any differences among any of the groups that comprise the nominal variable. The test is called a **one-way ANOVA** because it uses only one nominal variable to analyze the included interval variable. For example, a study of differences in patient satisfaction ratings among five local hospitals (hospital is the single nominal variable) would make use of a one-way ANOVA.

A **two-way ANOVA** is used to analyze two nominal variables combined with a single interval variable. It yields three separate, independent statistical tests that answer the questions, what is the effect of each of the two nominal variables considered separately **(main effects),** and what is the effect of them both taken together **(interaction effect),** where the combined effect of the nominal variables may differ from either effect considered separately. A two-way ANOVA would be appropriate to assess whether men and women (1st nominal variable) from the north and south (2nd nominal variable) had different anxiety levels (interval level variable).

If the persons in the separate groups of a nominal variable were non-independent (e.g., siblings or husbands compared with wives) then a **matched-pairs *t-test*** would be used if there were only two groups and a **repeated measures ANOVA** would be used if there were more than two groups. Data from persons assessed repeatedly over time would be analyzed using one of these two techniques.

Statistical Tests for Ordinal Data

If all of the data in the study are ordinal, using a **Spearman's rank correlation** would be appropriate. Spearman's correlation is similar to Pearson's correlation except that it uses ordinal, rather than interval level data. Spearman's correlation would be used to answer the question, is there a relationship between students' class rank in college and their class rank in medical school?

Statistical Tests for Combined Ordinal and Nominal Data

The **Mann-Whitney** U test is a test for ordinal data that is similar to the students *t-test*. U designates the probability distribution.

The **Wilcoxon matched-pairs signed-ranks** test is a rank-order comparable to the paired *t-test*.

Table B.1. Statistical analyses

Data to be analyzed	Test statistic	Key features
Interval data only		
Pearson Correlation	r	Test for linear relationship only, be cautious about attributing causation
Basic Regression Analysis	b	Specifies exact nature of relationship, used for prediction
Nominal data only		
Chi-square	χ^2	For any size table, tests for independence
Fisher's Exact Test	p-value	For 2 x 2 table only, N<25 matched pairs
Interval and nominal data combined		
Student's *t*-test	t	Compares means of two groups
Analysis of Variance (ANOVA)	F	When a *t*-test will not do
One-way		Only one nominal variable
Two-way		Two nominal variables
Repeated measures		Assess subjects over time
Matched pairs *t*-test		Subjects are linked, or before and after design
Ordinal data only		
Spearman's Rank Correlation	rho	Tests for relationships within group
Ordinal and nominal data combined		
Mann-Whitney U	U	General
Wilcoxon's matched pairs		For matched pairs
Signed-ranks test		For matched pairs

Review Questions – Answer Key

Chapter 1
1. A
2. D
3. D

Chapter 2
1. E
2. D
3. D
4. C
5. A
6. B
7. C
8. D
9. D
10. A
11. E
12. B
13. B

Chapter 3
1. D
2. D
3. D

Chapter 4
1. A
2. E
3 B
4. A

Chapter 5
1. C
2. D
3. B
4. A

Chapter 6
1. A
2. B

Chapter 7
1. E
2. B
3. D
4. B

Chapter 8
1. B
2. B
3. E
4. C
5. A
6. E
7. E

Chapter 9
1. D
2. B
3. E
4. A
5. E

Chapter 10
1. C
2. E
3. A
4. C
5. D

Chapter 11
1. A
2. C
3. A
4. A

Chapter 12
1. A
2. E
3. E

Chapter 13
1. D
2. D
3. A

Chapter 14
1. D
2. C
3. A
4. E
5. E
6. A

7. E
8. C
9. D
10. B
11. E

Chapter 15
1. D
2. B
3. E
4. C

Chapter 16
1. A
2. C
3. D
4. E

Chapter 17
1. E
2. D
3. C
4. E

Chapter 18
1. A
2. A
3. B
4. E
5. C

Chapter 19
1. B
2. D
3. B
4. D
5. E

Chapter 20
1. C
2. C
3. E

Chapter 21
1. C
2. A

3. C
4. B
5. E
6. D
7. A

Chapter 22
1. C
2. D
3. B
4. E

Chapter 23
1. B
2. B
3. A
4. D
5. D
6. D

Chapter 24
1. D
2. B
3. D
4. B

Chapter 25
1. C
2. A

Chapter 26
1. D
2. A
3. D
4. C

Chapter 27
1. B
2. E
3. D

Chapter 28
1. A
2. E
3. C
4. C

Chapter 29
1. D
2. C
3. D
4. B
5. E
6. A
7. A
8. A

Chapter 30
1. D
2. D

Chapter 31
1. B
2. E
3. A

Chapter 32
1. A
2. C
3. B
4. B
5. D

Chapter 33
1. C
2. A

Chapter 34
1. E
2. C
3. C
4. B
5. B

Chapter 35
1. A
2. C
3. E
4. C
5. D

Chapter 36
1. D
2. C
3. B
4. B
5. C

Chapter 37
1. A
2. D
3. C
4. C

Chapter 38
1. A
2. B
3. C
4. E
5. D
6. A
7. B

Chapter 39
1. D
2. A
3. A
4. A
5. B
6. B

Chapter 40
1. B
2. A
3. E
4. D
5. C

Chapter 41
1. B
2. C
3 A
4. D
5. E
6. B
7. A

Chapter 42
1. E
2. A
3. A
4. E
5. D

Chapter 43
1. B
2. C
3. C
4. D

Chapter 44
1. D
2. A
3. B
4. B
5. C
6. D

Chapter 45
1. B
2. E
3. D
4. D

Chapter 46
1. C
2. B
3. B
4. C

Chapter 47
1. D
2. B
3. A

Practice USMLE Exam

Questions

All the following questions about aspects of behavioral science are presented in the same formats used by the USMLE. The answers are accompanied by in-depth explanations. Although some of the topics covered here reinforce information in the text, many questions provide an opportunity to learn about additional topics not found in the text.

1. A 35-year-old, chronically schizophrenic man is brought to the Emergency Department by his parents because of non-adherence to medication and an increase in symptoms. When interviewed by the social worker, the parents do not seem not to understand his illness. His mother says she is very aggravated by his laziness, and his father says he just doesn't seem to be trying to do anything. Both sound angry as they talk about him. This pattern of family response has been called
    A. help seeking, help-rejecting
    B. high expressed emotion
    C. parentification of an adult child
    D. splitting
    E. triangulation

2. A 55-year-old man drinks 4 or 5 ounces of alcohol every night and more on the weekends. He brags of his "strong head for liquor." He denies any serious health or legal consequences related to drinking and says that he plans to teach his 15-year-old son to drink responsibly. "If he does like I do, he should be fine, don't you think, doc?" he asks. What advice should the doctor give to this man about educating his son in the use of alcohol?
    A. Avoiding daily drinking will prevent the son from developing an alcohol problem.
    B. If he wants the boy to try alcohol, it should be at a meal with adults who do not condone drunkenness.
    C. The boy will be fine if he drinks only beer or wine and avoids hard liquor until he is at least 18.
    D. The safe limit of alcohol use for an adolescent is 4 ounces in a 24-hour period.
    E. The son is at low risk for alcoholism because high tolerance is genetic.

3. Case studies of physicians who seek care for problems in their intimate relationships suggest that distress is most commonly the result of

A. financial problems from the high cost of medical education
B. one partner being a physician and the other not
C. personality characteristics that affect communication or the capacity for intimacy
D. the particular specialty of the physician
E. the stress of the earlier phases of medical education (internship and residency)

4. The empathic way to present a patient or family with the option of agreeing to be treated under a "Do Not Resuscitate" order is to
    A. check in the chart for a previous advance directive, and avoid raising the issue if the patient's wishes are already known
    B. emphasize that the patient will not be abandoned and that all treatment, including palliative care, will be provided
    C. explain that "Do Not Resuscitate" only means refusal of external chest massage, assisted respiration, or electrical defibrillation
    D. explain that resuscitation does not generally improve or prolong the lives of patients with multisystem disease
    E. let the patient and family talk together privately and then accept the decision they reach without question

5. Mr. G has just been diagnosed with diabetes. His physician recommends changes in diet and once-a-day insulin injections, but is concerned that Mr. G will not remember the instructions he has been given. In this, and similar situations, patient recall of physician instructions is maximized when the
    A. most important information is given at the beginning of an interaction
    B. patient is allowed to fill in the specific details to adapt the instructions to his/her own situation
    C. patient is discouraged from interrupting by asking questions
    D. physician provides extensive information
    E. physician's instructions are all given completely in a single session

6. A 47-year-old, male, machine-tool operator drinks 2 six-packs of beer daily. He reports that he has recently become concerned that he might have an al-

cohol problem. He has not talked to anyone about it for fear that people will think that he is "being silly". According to the stages of change model he is most likely in which stage of change?

A. Pre-contemplation
B. Contemplation
C. Preparation
D. Action
E. Maintenance

7. Dr. J., a professor at UMC, is in the hospital after being diagnosed with colon cancer. During a recent visit by his physician, they only discussed non-medically related topics such as fishing and the trials and tribulations of watching one's children grow up. This description is an example of what type of awareness context?

A. Closed awareness
B. Delayed affectation
C. Mutual pretense
D. Open awareness
E. Suspicion awareness

8. A 35-year-old male patient calls the physician to be examined regarding "problems with my stomach." The patient reports nausea over the past week accompanied by some dizziness. During the physical examination, the patient reports substantial tenderness, but no difficulty with eating or defecation. The medical record shows that the patient has a history of a broad range of medical complaints for which no underlying cause can be determined. At this point the physician's best action would be to

A. ask the patient if the physician can speak to a family member
B. ask the patient to say more about his symptoms
C. gather a complete substance abuse history from the patient
D. tell the patient that he is fine and will feel better after a few days of rest
E. tell the patient that he may be a hypochondriac

9. Elisabeth Kübler-Ross has provided a much-used model for understanding patients' reactions to death and dying. When using this model, physicians should be aware that

A. Kübler-Ross adequately described the experience of dying for the average person.
B. patients must reach the final stage of acceptance before death can occur
C. the stages exist as Kübler-Ross described them, but most patients do not experience them all
D. the stages of experiencing dying occur only in patients with a lingering death trajectory

E. while the emotional states described are real, they do not represent distinct sequential stages

10. Patient adherence with treatment is facilitated by the formation of a partnership between physician and patient. The notion of "self-monitoring" has been used to facilitate patient involvement in this relationship. Physicians who try to teach their patients the self-monitoring technique should be aware that

A. patients should monitor behavior (e.g., dietary intake) rather than outcome (e.g., weight loss)
B. recording behaviors daily or weekly is more effective than recording throughout the day
C. self-monitoring alone can not increase adherence with treatment
D. self-monitoring does not improve patients' awareness of their adherence
E. self-monitoring works best when the patient is assertive

11. As attending physician, you have reviewed the histories obtained by first-year residents. This review reveals that many of the histories are incomplete. Among the items consistently absent are those regarding sexuality. Before discussing the results of this review with the first-year residents, you should realize that failure to obtain adequate sexual histories from patients is most often due to

A. the fact that most patients have no sexual issues
B. the patient's belief that sexual issues are private and should not be discussed
C. the patient's embarrassment about sexual topics
D. the patient's strong religious or moral qualms about sex that interfere with discussing the topic
E. the physician's discomfort with the subject of sex

12. A 33-year-old male married patient enjoys dressing in women's clothes. The patient states that this cross-dressing enhances sexual pleasure and that his wife cooperates with him by supporting this practice. This type of sexual behavior is most correctly described as

A. gender identity disorder
B. homosexuality
C. normal heterosexual behavior
D. transsexualism
E. transvestite fetishism

13. When passing the door of a patient on an oncology ward, a medical student overhears the patient

asking his physician, "Why is this happening to me? I've always tried to be a good person." The student realizes that this statement indicates that the patient is most likely in which one of the following stages of coping with dying as described by Kübler-Ross?

A. Anger
B. Bargaining
C. Confusion
D. Denial
E. Depression

14. You have been asked to create a template for patient education to be used by all of the physicians in your managed care group practice. When planning for patient education, it is most important to remember that

A. more disease information provided at the time of diagnosis leads to better adherence
B. patients perceived as intelligent by the physician typically remember significantly more information.
C. patients' level of education is positively correlated with adherence
D. patients' perception of the time spent giving information is positively associated with adherence
E. patients' recall of instructions is improved by warnings about the consequences of non-adherence

15. A young, heterosexual couple has been having sexual difficulties for about a year. The man complains of frequent impotence and woman has experienced anorgasmia. When approaching this problem, the physician should first evaluate for the presence of

A. anatomic structural disparity
B. autonomic nervous system abnormalities
C. endocrine disorders
D. performance anxiety
E. significant psychopathology in one or both of the partners

16. A 46-year-old, African American male confides to his physician that, although he used to enjoy the company of others, this holiday season he is reluctant to attend get-togethers. He states that he feels awkward and clumsy and that people are laughing at him behind his back. He is especially afraid that he will say the wrong thing, or spill his drink on someone. He seems agitated as he provides this account. Based on this patient's statements and presentation, the best preliminary diagnosis would be

A. agoraphobia
B. generalized anxiety disorder

C. histrionic personality disorder
D. narcissistic personality disorder
E. social phobia

17. Many families have a member who is considered the "health expert". This person often makes an initial health assessment and treatment plan and then decides whether a physician should be consulted. Although this role differs from family to family, this individual is most frequently the

A. best educated
B. oldest female
C. oldest female child
D. oldest male
E. oldest male child

18. Mr. S. reports that he consumes about 3 to 4 beers each evening to help him "settle down after a hard day of work". Using the CAGE questionnaire, you discover that: (1) he sometimes feels that he needs to reduce his drinking; (2) he feels bad some mornings about drinking the night before; (3) he becomes irritated when his wife "bugs him" about drinking every evening; and (4) he sometimes drinks in the morning. He says that he never "gets drunk". Based on this presentation, you should conclude that

A. because only 10% of the population is alcoholic, he probably does not have an alcohol problem
B. he is lying about never "getting drunk"
C. he most likely has alcohol abuse or dependence
D. he needs referral to an in-patient alcohol treatment center
E. laboratory studies are needed to confirm the diagnosis of alcohol abuse or dependence

19. A 28-year-old woman is concerned because she is no longer interested in sex, either with her husband or anyone else. Questioning reveals that she never has an orgasm during intercourse with her husband. She reports no symptoms of acute or chronic illness. When taking this patient's history, which one of the following questions is most likely to help you to select a treatment approach?

A. Are you satisfied with your sex life?
B. Do you have an orgasm with manual or other clitoral stimulation?
C. Does your husband have difficulty achieving or maintaining an erection?
D. What do you think your problem is?
E. What is the approximate frequency of your sexual activity?

20. A 50-year-old man with hypertension has responded well to the diuretic, hydrochlorothiazide

(HCTZ). On his last visit to your clinic, his serum potassium was found to be low. You believe your patient has adhered to the regimen prescribed (low salt intake, moderate exercise three times a week, daily diuretic). Of the several possible options for correcting the low potassium, which of the following would be best in terms of maintaining good adherence?

A. Change the HCTZ to a "potassium sparing" combination diuretic without changing the rest of the prescribed regimen.

B. Discontinue the low-salt diet until the serum potassium normalizes, then prescribe less intense sodium restriction.

C. Eliminate the diuretic until potassium levels return to normal.

D. Have the patient consult with a dietitian to plan an intensive potassium-enriched diet in addition to maintaining sodium restriction.

E. Supplement the diuretic with a daily potassium chloride tablet.

21. A 50-year-old male accountant develops diabetes mellitus that is not adequately controlled with diet and oral hypoglycemic treatment. The physician meets with him to discuss initiating insulin therapy. Saying that insulin is "poison", the patient declines the treatment. He, however, does not explain that his mother had to have her leg amputated one year after beginning insulin treatment. When reflecting on this situation, which of the following is most correct?

A. A family system problem is interfering with the treatment plan.

B. The patient and physician have differing belief systems about insulin.

C. The patient's passivity makes the probability of adherence poor.

D. The physician might gain acceptance of insulin by explaining treatment in more detail.

E. The physician should tell the patient he is being irrational.

22. A 10-year-old child is referred for assessment of difficulties in school. The child's developmental status would be best assessed by a focus on which of the following five domains?

A. Biologic, environmental, physical, language, and physiologic

B. Gross motor, fine motor, neurosensory, behavioral, and visual

C. Math, reading, spelling, the creative arts, and handwriting

D. Physical, neurologic maturational, cognitive, speech/language, and psychosocial

E. Sensory, gastrointestinal, physical, sexual, and psychological

23. A boy is observed bringing his hands to midline and is able to roll prone to supine. In response to voices, he begins to laugh and giggle. Medical record shows that the child's weight has doubled since birth. Assuming that the boy shows normal patterns of development, he is most likely what age?

A. 1 month
B. 3 months
C. 5 months
D. 7 months
E. 9 months

24. A girl is presented with a toy ball. After she plays with it for a moment, the ball is taken away and hidden. Even though it is completely out of sight, the child searches for the ball. Attainment of this degree of object permanence suggests that the child's age is closest to

A. 2 months
B. 4 months
C. 6 months
D. 8 months
E. 10 months

25. A young girl is tested for primitive reflexes such as the Moro, asymmetrical tonic neck, rooting, and palmar grasp. None is found to be present. The earliest age range at which this finding is expected is

A. 1–2 months
B. 3–4 months
C. 5–6 months
D. 7–8 months
E. 9–10 months

26. During the first months of life, the child's experience of the world is focused on sensations and movement, and learning how action and experience correspond. The child has not yet attained the realization of object permanence. Attachment to the primary caretaker is the dominant social dynamic. The developmental psychologist, Piaget, refers to this stage of life as the

A. action versus inaction stage
B. exploratory stage
C. oral stage
D. sensorimotor stage
E. trust versus mistrust stage

27. Mr. D. has been non-adherent with his treatment regime. His physician decides to make use of the goal-setting technique to increase his patient's adherence in the future. Published guidelines and clinical experience in the use of "goal setting" to increase patient adherence suggest that the technique will be most effective when

A. goals are defined by the physician to insure appropriate priorities

B. goals are graduated to maximize success experiences

C. goals are maintained consistently and may not be altered

D. goals are sufficiently broad to allow the patient leeway in meeting them

E. patients seek to "shoot for the moon" and achieve maximal results

28. Mr. J. has a documented history of alcohol abuse and symptoms consistent with alcoholism. Yet, he actively denies any drinking problem and distorts the amount, frequency, and consequences of his drinking. Using the stages of change model, the clinician's next best action would be to

A. encourage his wife or significant other to convince the patient to stop drinking

B. express concern and suggest the patient think about his drinking

C. recommend an in-patient treatment program

D. schedule a return appointment but make no comment at this point

E. send the patient to a local AA meeting

29. You must tell your 55-year-old patient that he has metastatic prostate cancer. After you have made the patient feel as comfortable as possible and ensured that you will not be interrupted, you begin speaking with him. In this conversation, you learn that the patient knows very little about his condition. The best next step would be to

A. check that you are communicating on the same level

B. discover how much information he would like to have

C. discuss what support systems the patient has

D. establish physical contact by patting his hand

E. give him information in small non-"Medspeak" chunks.

30. A 75-year-old man presents with a 1-month history of difficulty sleeping, loss of interest in his usual activities, feeling worthless, difficulty concentrating, and thoughts of suicide. Three months ago he suffered a stroke from which he has recovered, except for some gait disturbance and problems using his left hand, which appear to be permanent. He has lost four pounds in the last 2 months. Based on this information, it is most reasonable to conclude that

A. a careful history and physical is indicated to detect a probable occult malignancy

B. he is feeling a sense of letdown from lack of full recovery and requires brief counseling

C. he should be enrolled in a "stroke survivors" group to boost his spirits

D. screening for a substance abuse disorder is indicated

E. he will likely require treatment with antidepressant medication

31. You inform a 40-year-old man that his 75-year-old father has developed liver metastases from his colon cancer that was resected 1 year ago. The man's face becomes bright red and he angrily replies, "The surgeon said it was all removed. I am going to sue the pants off that goon." Which of the following would be your best response at this point?

A. Ask, "What do you know about the typical course of colon cancer?"

B. Reply, "I'm sorry, but it's not the surgeon's fault that your father's cancer recurred."

C. Sit quietly for a few minutes and then terminate the interview.

D. State, "You are too angry at the surgeon for apparently misleading you."

E. State, "You must be very upset that your father is ill from his cancer again."

32. A 55-year-old man reports to his primary care physician that he has been suffering from periodic impotence with his wife. The physician should tell him that the most common cause of periodic impotence in middle-aged men is

A. abnormalities of the urinary tract

B. excess intake of alcohol

C. marital infidelity

D. onset of diabetes mellitus

E. physiologic decline that accompanies aging

33. A terminally ill woman with heart disease says, "It's the doctor's fault that I got sick. She didn't take my blood pressure, and she never told me to watch my diet!" This behavior is most consistent with which of the following stages of coping with dying?

A. Anger

B. Denial

C. Depression

D. Fear

E. Guilt

34. Mrs. H. lost her husband of 50 years 6 months ago. Since that time she has stayed by herself, refused visitors, and cries frequently. Her daughter asks the physician how her mother "should be acting if she's all right". The physician should tell the daughter that normal coping with death often includes

A. feeling depressed for several months after the death

B. feelings of hopelessness lasting 2 or more years

C. profound guilt feelings lasting 6 months or more

D. sleep disturbances lasting 8 months after the death

E. threats of suicide during the initial weeks after the death

Items 35 and 36

During a routine physical exam, a middle-aged man reports recent stress in his marriage. He states that he and his wife rarely try to have sex, and the last time they tried, he was unable to maintain an erection. When questioned, he indicates that he commonly has morning erections. The medical record indicates no chronic illnesses and the patient is not currently taking any medications.

35. At this point the physician should
   A. order a nocturnal penile tumescence study
   B. recommend that his wife come in for a private session
   C. request a joint visit with the patient and his wife
   D. smile gently and tell him that this is bound to happen once in a while
   E. suggest trying a different position during intercourse

36. At a follow-up visit 1 month later, the patient reports trying intercourse once more but without success. At this point, the most appropriate intervention would be to
   A. indicate that this is a normal change with aging and encourage him to accept it
   B. recommend a penile implant
   C. recommend attempting intercourse with a different partner if his wife agrees
   D. refer for joint sex therapy with use of sensate focus
   E. suggest the use of the squeeze technique

37. When designing a program to assist "impaired" medical students, the organizers should remember that, compared to others in the population of the same age, medical students are most likely to abuse which one of the following drugs?
   A. Alcohol
   B. Barbiturates
   C. Cocaine
   D. Heroin
   E. Tobacco

38. Part of being a competent physician depends not only on knowing the right thing to say in a given situation, but also knowing when not to say anything. In which of the following difficult situations is physician silence most appropriate?
   A. A home visit is made to discuss changes in a cancer patient's pain medicine
   B. A man is concerned about impotence
   C. A recently diagnosed terminally ill patient is in the hospital
   D. A woman is anxious about her inability to experience orgasm
   E. Alcohol abuse is suspected in a patient being seen in the office

39. A 40-year-old patient whom you are seeing for an ear infection, smokes a pack of cigarettes a day. After discussing her ear infection, you tell her that smoking greatly increases her risk for heart disease. She responds, "Yes, I'd really love to quit. I'm planning to do it sometime". You ask her when. She replies "Oh, once I lose some weight I think I'll try." This patient most likely would be classified as being in which of the "stages of change?"
   A. Contemplation
   B. Maintenance
   C. Pre-contemplation
   D. Preparation
   E. Procrastination

40. You are talking with a 60-year-old man who has just been diagnosed with lung cancer. He has metastases to his lumbar spine causing back pain. He has no evidence of neurologic problems. When you ask him if he would like to know the biopsy results, he replies that he trusts you to care for him and that he would rather not hear the results. Which of the following is your best response at this time?
   A. "Even though you don't want to hear, we need to talk now so we can discuss treatment."
   B. "I understand. There's really no reason why you have to know anyhow."
   C. "I'll order some pain medication and come back tomorrow to see if you'd like to talk then."
   D. "Is there anyone in your family I can talk to?"
   E. "You must think I'm going to tell you bad news, and you don't want to hear it."

41. You are nearing the end of residency training and are looking at practice opportunities. You realize that there are numerous factors that will influence your decision regarding the practice you choose. Some are considered "intangible". One example of the intangible aspects to consider is the
   A. accountant who conducts annual audits of the practice income
   B. age and gender mix of the patients
   C. daily rituals of the office staff and physicians

D. design and age of the practice building
E. framed mission statement hanging in the waiting room

42. A faculty member is contemplating a career move to a new academic medical center. Based on the unique characteristics of organizations that are comprised of professional people, you would expect her to
A. accept that she has no latitude within the department to gravitate to those activities that she feels are most important
B. accept that she will need to sacrifice her own personal values and norms and give priority to organizational rules
C. anticipate that she will never find herself in conflict with the faculty she will be working with since they are all professionals
D. be able to create her own role within the department and negotiate for the resources she needs to accomplish that role
E. realize that power within the organization is relatively fixed and will not change while the university employs her

43. A new department is forming within an academic medical center. You have been asked to chair this new department and have been given the necessary resources to build a premier section for your specialty. From your medical school studies about organizations, you remember that the most important task in managing professional people is
A. dealing with reduced effectiveness
B. evaluating performance
C. hiring them
D. managing information
E. motivating them

44. Sally is just beginning to pull herself into an upright position by using the railings on her crib. Before she can learn to walk she, like any toddler, must first
A. develop leg muscles by crawling
B. develop sophisticated balance skills
C. master the mechanics of weight shifting
D. master object permanence
E. overcome separation anxiety

45. A 20 month-old-boy is playing while his mother watches. He moves a toy truck along the floor and then hands it to his mother. When communicating with this child, the physician should remember that at this age of development, a child's capacity for cognition is based on
A. formulation of internal mental symbols
B. movement and sensations
C. performance of actions to achieve outcomes

D. representation of reality through the use of words
E. what they see before them

46. The second year of life, sometimes called the "Terrible Twos", can be a trying time for parents and older siblings. The change in outlook on the world typical of this developmental stage is characterized by an ability to
A. adhere to rule-based play
B. create plans
C. distinguish unique facial features
D. imagine alternatives
E. recognize adult standards

47. The parents of a 1-year-old child ask their physician about potential risks to their child's health. The physician should tell them that the most significant health risk to children during the second year of life is
A. environmental poisons
B. failure to thrive
C. hearing loss
D. infection
E. injury

48. A monkey has learned that if he lifts his foot when a bell is sounded, he can avoid a painful electric shock. What biologic mechanism most likely makes this simple learning paradigm possible?
A. Protein kinase delays the action potential of the neuron by blocking neurotransmitter release.
B. Sequential stimulation of two adjacent neurons enhances the efficiency of their connecting synapse.
C. The cerebellum reduces motor reactivity under the influence of serotonin activity.
D. The hippocampus sends simultaneous sensory signals to relevant cortical storage areas.
E. The orbito-medial frontal cortex matches sensory input with the desired behavior.

49. Human behavior can be seen as a consequence of the interaction of heredity and learned behaviors. A key finding from research focused on this interplay tells us that
A. genetic and environmental influences interact across generations but not across individual developmental stages
B. genetic influences are easily distinguished from learned environmental adaptations
C. learned adaptive responses that contribute to survival are passed on to successive generations
D. learning influences individual development, but there is no evidence of an evolutionary effect

E. the capacity to learn, but not what was learned, is passed on genetically

50. Different types of learning have been identified and isolated in laboratory experiments. This allows research to be performed on the specific physiological substrates associated with particular types of learning. One type of learning has been called "implicit learning". This notion of implicit learning
A. involves the association of sensory stimuli with sequential motor system responses
B. is made possible by complex association mechanisms among diverse stimuli
C. occurs over a wide span of time
D. requires structures in the cortex for long-term information storage
E. requires the conscious participation of the individual

51. A 46-year-old homeless man appears at the free clinic complaining of GI distress and headache. He states that he has been living under the bridge of a local highway for the past 3 months. He has a spouse and two children, but has lost contact with them. When examining this individual, the physician should keep in mind that the most frequent health problems of the homeless are
A. HIV- and AIDS-related problems
B. mental illness and substance abuse
C. skin problems
D. upper respiratory infections
E. venereal diseases

52. A 45-year-old man is brought to the physician by his wife who complains, "he has always had his little quirks, but things are getting out of hand." She explains that her husband refuses to leave the house and has become increasingly terrified when forced to do so. Examination of the patient shows him to be in a highly anxious state characterized by sweating palms, shallow breathing and a rapid pulse. He sits slouched over, avoids eye contact and scans the room around him as if waiting for something to happen. Based on these findings, the physician is most likely to diagnose
A. agoraphobia
B. delusional disorder
C. dysthymia
D. paranoid personality disorder
E. social phobia

53. A 19-year-old man is brought to the local emergency room in a delirious state. The patient is calm, but communication with him is difficult. He is non-responsive to questions regarding time and place. Further examination is disrupted when

the patient begins to have seizures. This patient is most likely withdrawing from
A. amphetamines
B. benzodiazepines
C. hallucinogens
D. heroin
E. phencyclidine

Items 54 and 55

A 44-year-old woman is referred for evaluation by her employer because she has been increasingly difficult to deal with over the past week. When questioned by the physician, the woman is understandable but extremely talkative. In her conversation, she jumps from one topic to another. She reports that she recently embarked on a "great shopping spree" because she "deserves nothing but the best". After work she volunteers at four different community programs and says she is looking for additional activities to occupy her time. When asked how she finds the time for all of this, she reports that she needs only three hours of sleep per night

54. Based on this information, the most likely diagnosis for this woman is
A. bipolar disorder
B. hypothyroidism
C. narcissistic personality disorder
D. obsessive-compulsive disorder
E. vascular dementia

55. Long-term treatment of this woman would most likely include
A. chlorpromazine
B. clonazepam
C. diazepam
D. fluoxetine
E. lithium carbonate

Items 56 and 57

A mother brings her 5-year-old daughter to the pediatrician complaining that the child has recently developed enuresis. The girl seems shy at first when talking to the physician, but soon begins to make eye contact and answer the physician's questions. The physician discovers that the child has recently begun to attend kindergarten and that her mother gave birth to a baby boy in the past month.

56. The girl's enuresis is most likely the result of what defense mechanism?
A. Projection
B. Reaction formation
C. Regression
D. Sublimation
E. Undoing

57. The first intervention the physician should try is to
  A. advise the mother about helping the child cope with life transitions
  B. observe and follow-up in anticipation of spontaneous recovery
  C. prescribe a course of imipramine
  D. suggest that the child change to a different kindergarten class
  E. talk with the child about why enuresis is a bad thing

58. The physician asks Jennifer, a 2-year-old girl dressed in overalls and a baseball cap, whether she is a boy or a girl. The child seems confused by the question and looks at her mother while saying nothing. When given a set of toys to play with, the child selects a truck and proceeds to roll it around the room. This type of behavior suggests that the girl most likely
  A. has no siblings at home
  B. is at risk for developing a gender identity disorder later in life
  C. is showing developmental age and gender appropriate behavior
  D. will grow up to be relatively shy
  E. will grow up to have a sexual preference for women

Items 59 and 60

A 25-year-old woman with a history of depression and substance abuse is referred for additional evaluation following a suicide attempt. During the interview the woman reports that the suicide attempt occurred in response to her boyfriend of 3 months breaking up with her. She describes herself as feeling "empty" and says that the ex-boyfriend "was everything to me". Without him, she says she is "not sure who I am or why I'm here." She begins crying, saying that, "Everyone always abandons me." When asked what she is going to do now, the patient becomes suddenly very angry and says, "You can't wait to get rid of me either."

59. Based on this initial interview, you suspect this patient may have a personality disorder in addition to depression and substance abuse. The most likely type is
  A. borderline
  B. histrionic
  C. narcissistic
  D. paranoid
  E. schizoid

60. The most effective primary treatment for the personality disorder described here would be
  A. a 6-month course of alprazolam
  B. behavior modification

  C. family therapy
  D. group psychotherapy
  E. individual cognitive-behavioral therapy

61. A man is sitting in a corner by himself on the in-patient psychiatry unit. He suddenly bursts into loud laughter and then sits quietly giggling to himself as he picks at his fingernails. He is unkempt and malodorous. A nurse notices that the patient is sitting in his own feces and hurries over to clean the patient. As she approaches, the patient begins to wave his arms wildly, for no apparent reason. The most likely diagnosis is
  A. catatonic schizophrenia, excited type
  B. disorganized schizophrenia
  C. paranoid schizophrenia
  D. residual schizophrenia
  E. undifferentiated schizophrenia

62. A 55-year-old man who was diagnosed with schizophrenia at age 18 is asked to complete the Wisconsin Card Sort Test (WCST), a task that requires categorization and problem-solving abilities. Examination of the functioning of this patient's brain by means of a PET scan during the card-sorting task would most likely show that, when compared to non-schizophrenic individuals, the patient has decreased brain activity in the
  A. cerebellum
  B. frontal lobes
  C. occipital lobes
  D. parietal lobes
  E. temporal lobes

63. Culture affects almost all aspects of daily life, including medical care. When trying to gauge the impact of culture on day-to-day medical practice, the practitioner should remember that culture is
  A. a learned social phenomenon that has minimal impact on clinical encounters
  B. a learned social phenomenon that influences health, illness and therapy
  C. a social phenomenon that may be important to the patient but should not affect physician choices
  D. genetically determined but changeable through genetic engineering
  E. genetically determined and therefore unchanging

64. An overview of U.S. census data over the past 50 years reveals some strong and continuing secular demographic trends. In particular, these data show that in the near future the population will have
  A. a decrease in the number of Hispanics throughout the 21st century
  B. a lower average age for the white population

C. a steady increase in the size of ethnic minority populations
D. less concern about culture as a factor in the delivery of health care
E. zero population growth by the year 2020

65. One way to gain insight into an ethnic group's system of beliefs and practices regarding health and disease is to develop an awareness of the underpinnings of those beliefs. Research suggests that health beliefs are most closely associated with cultural beliefs about the
A. natural world, such as ideas about germs, stars, and the sun
B. social world, such as ideas about family members' relationships
C. supernatural world, such as concepts of spirits, death, and afterlife
D. natural and supernatural worlds
E. natural, supernatural and social worlds

66. During one day of working at a local health clinic, a physician encountered patients presenting with *empacho, mal de ojo, amok*, and a cold. All of these disorders are
A. conditions based on superstitious beliefs
B. culture-bound syndromes that describe a type of soul loss
C. ethnically recognized types of upper respiratory infections
D. illustrations of how people interpret bodily signs and symptoms in culturally specific ways
E. reflections of patients' lack of education

67. Mrs. L., an 82-year-old African American woman, complains to her physician that she has "high blood". At times, Mrs. L. says she can feel can feel her blood rising up to her head. She reports that when she drinks pickle juice and vinegar, she can feel her blood return to normal. Her physician tells her that she has hypertension and recommends a low-salt diet. The African American illness of high blood is an example of a folk illness. When treating Mrs. L., the physician should remember that
A. as a folk illness, high blood had no defined etiology, pathophysiology, or treatment
B. high blood and hypertension are different names for the same thing
C. high blood and hypertension are examples of how interpretations of body symptoms are culturally influenced
D. physicians need to eradicate folk illness beliefs that are contrary to conventional medical beliefs
E. the physician needs to guide the patient away from her incorrect understanding of her condition

68. Yesterday, it seemed to be a simple matter to explain to a woman from Pakistan that the diarrhea which her child was experiencing needed to be treated with antibiotics, and high fluid intake. Today, you learn that the child is not being given the medication as recommended, nor is the mother offering liquids as directed. At this point the most appropriate reaction on your part would be to
A. chastise the mother for endangering her child's well being by not following your directions
B. explore the possibility that the mother believes your recommendations will make the child worse
C. hospitalize the child whether or not the mother agrees
D. notify Child Protective Services that the child is not being well cared for
E. refer the mother to the nurse who is responsible for patient education

69. The attribution of individual involvement is a critical factor in understanding the subjective etiology of disease. Personal responsibility for disease is *lowest* in which of the following types of belief in disease etiology?
A. Individual etiologies
B. Intellectual etiologies
C. Natural etiologies
D. Social etiologies
E. Supernatural etiologies

70. A patient reports that he has been taking buffered aspirin and doing strengthening exercises to alleviate back pain. The patient further reports that this approach worked for a good friend who was having a similar problem. This patient got his medical advice from which sector of healers?
A. Folk
B. Paraprofessional
C. Pharmaceutical
D. Popular
E. Professional

71. According to Kleinman's categorization, an example of a healer from the popular sector would be a
A. chiropractor
B. nurse midwife
C. parent
D. physician
E. psychic palm reader

72. The concept of explanatory models is useful in helping to understand differences among the perspectives of patients, family members, and healers. Over the years, clinical experience has shown that almost all explanatory models

A. do not change once they are formed
B. eventually come to be shared among patients, family members, and healers
C. include the five concepts of pathophysiology, natural history, preferred treatment, etiology, and ethnic identity
D. include the three concepts of etiology, treatment, and ethnic identity
E. shared between a patient and a provider lead to fewer conflicts

73. One of the core functions of physicians is to provide societal recognition of the sick role. In any given community, the function of the "sick role" is to
A. allow estimates of the prevalence of various diseases
B. force the individual to seek medical care
C. legitimize withdrawal from regular activities and requests for assistance
D. permit collection of epidemiological data on disease incidence
E. require hospitalization

74. Cultural background and ethnic identity are key elements in patients' medical decisions. Strong identification with a particular ethnic group is most likely to influence their
A. choice of healers
B. desire for good health
C. response to physiologic effects of illness
D. type of health insurance
E. willingness to work

75. Mr. Schmidt has decided to seek complementary medical care for management of his Type I diabetes mellitus. He is a 34-year-old fifth generation European-American who regularly attends his local Episcopalian Church. He is a well-paid chemical engineer, who is married and has three children. For 24 years, he has followed physicians' recommendations regarding diet, exercise, weight control, and insulin injections with glucose monitoring. Despite his best efforts, his blood sugar and glycosylated hemoglobin levels have always been high. He now has multiple complications including decreasing eyesight, diminished kidney function, numbness in his legs, and a persistent sore on his foot. During the past year, he has sought assistance from a local holistic health center. He is taking vitamins and Chinese herbal medicines; receiving acupuncture; and doing meditation. He continues to take insulin and monitor his blood sugar. All in all, he feels better than he has for years.

Of all of the possible reasons why Mr. Schmidt decided to seek alternative therapies, which of the following reasons was probably *least* influential?

A. He agreed with the cultural and ideological underpinnings of Chinese medicine.
B. He felt alienated from health care providers because of philosophical differences.
C. He was dissatisfied with his physician's inattention to his personal struggles.
D. He was disillusioned with the results of medical therapies.
E. He was tired of the long waits and high costs associated with medical settings.

76. A colleague asks your advice about improving his capacity to work with patients from different ethnic and cultural backgrounds. He lists different options he is considering. Of all the options he presents, you tell him that the one *least* likely to result in improved multicultural patient-centered care is
A. adapting our style of communication to fit patients' preferred styles
B. being aware of our personal biases and prejudices
C. being our genuine selves with the expectation that patients will understand our meanings
D. learning about ourselves as cultural beings
E. learning culturally appropriate patient-centered communication skills

77. Non-verbal gestures communicate different messages depending on ethnic background. Misconceptions about what is communicated can lead to difficulties in the patient-physician relationship. Among the following, which generality about how non-verbal gestures are interpreted is correct?
A. Arab patients: offering things with the right hand is revolting
B. Asians: looking away is experienced as disrespectful
C. Asians: speaking loudly is experienced as an expression of eagerness to be understood
D. Europeans: Making direct eye contact is experienced as invasive
E. Native Americans: pausing less than a few seconds for a reply to a question conveys lack of interest

78. You are an ophthalmologist. An elderly Chinese Vietnamese man is accompanied by his daughter-in-law to your office. In response to your open-ended questions, the daughter-in-law explains that her father-in-law's vision in his right eye has slowly become worse, making him almost blind because he lost the vision in his left eye after an injury about 20 years ago. Now his vision is so bad that he is a danger to himself and others. For example, he recently lit the gas stove while there was a newspaper nearby that caught fire. The fam-

ily has tried traditional Chinese and Vietnamese treatments with no improvement and now the family wishes to obtain your opinion.

On your examination, you find there is a moderately dense cataract in the right eye and a dense corneal opacity in the left eye. You surmise that he might be afraid of surgery to repair the defects, so you take his hand, look caringly at him, lean forward, raise your voice a little so that he can hear you better, and say "Grandfather, you are going blind, but I can help you. We can operate on your eyes. We can use a plastic piece to replace your old lens on the right eye. And we can use part of another person's eye to replace part of your left eye that was damaged years ago. If you do not let us operate, however, you will go completely blind. If you sign this consent form, we can schedule the first operation next week." The daughter-in-law does not interpret for him, but says, "Thank you, doctor. I will tell my husband about your recommendations." Without looking at you, she leads her father-in-law away, but they never return.

Looking back over this exchange, you decide that the *least* likely reason for this outcome is that you

A. called him grandfather
B. did not ask them about their reactions to the operations
C. did not ask who would make the decision and sign the consent form
D. looked directly at him for a prolonged period of time
E. said he would go blind if he did not have the operations

79. Ms. Sanchez, a 62-year-old Afro-Cuban woman, has to make some choices about her treatment for a breast mass. She arrived in the U.S. 4 months ago after spending 3 years in a refugee camp on a military base. Through a U.S. government-sponsored program to promote refugee health, a physician discovered a lump in the patient's breast and performed a needle biopsy that revealed adenocarcinoma of the breast. In the last 2 months, the patient has missed several appointments with the surgeon to discuss various treatment approaches, including mastectomy, radiation therapy, and chemotherapy. Rather, she has sought assistance from Cuban healers who have been treating her with herbal medicines and performing Santeria religious rituals. Her youngest son (who has been in the United States for 20 years and is a Christian) has taken her to the healers and has paid for her treatments.

Which of the following is the *least* likely reason for Ms. Sanchez to consult traditional Cuban healers rather than allopathic physicians?

A. Cultural factors, such as interpretation of signs and symptoms, and beliefs about disease
B. Economic factors, such as the cost of medical treatment
C. Historical factors, such as familiarity with the healer and the success or failure of treatments
D. Social factors, such as the patient's and healer's social class, ethnic identities, and language abilities
E. Structural factors, such as distance to the healer and available transportation

80. A 4-year-old Cambodian child has a temperature of 39°C and linear bruises on the chest, back and upper arms. Her grandmother has brought her into the clinic because the child's parents are working. You do not have a Cambodian interpreter in the clinic and, instead, rely on the 8-year-old brother to help you communicate with the grandmother. What is the most likely cause of the bruises on this child?

A. Child abuse
B. Coagulopathy
C. Mongolian spots
D. Sepsis
E. Traditional health care practice

81. Recently you and other providers have been seeing a large number of patients from an immigrant community. These patients are presenting with a pattern of symptoms that does not fit any diagnosis with which you are familiar. Physical examination findings and all test results are normal. You and your colleagues should

A. ask the state health department to quarantine the entire community
B. assume that all patients from the community will present with the same syndrome
C. conclude that these individuals are trying to "work the system," perhaps to get pharmaceuticals to sell on the street
D. consider that the patients are maybe suffering from a culturally specific syndrome, perhaps related to the stress of immigration
E. tell the patients that they are not ill and should return home and resume all regular activities

82. One way of assessing families is to examine the family's structure or the way that it is organized. An outline of these structural components makes it easier to understand how family dynamics are likely to have an effect on the patient and the patient's care. Which of the following describes a structural element of a family?

A. Boundaries
B. Communication style

C. Family secret
D. Parentification
E. Scapegoating

83. Although various patterns of family systems exist, certain patterns are so common that they are given labels. Consider a patient whom a colleague tells you comes from a "disengaged" family system. Given this information, it is most reasonable to conclude that
A. boundaries around individuals within the system are closed
B. boundaries around the family system are closed
C. boundaries between the father and other family members are closed
D. emotional processes resonate quickly throughout the family system
E. interpersonal boundaries within the family system are diffuse

84. Sam and Ellen met several years ago in college and married recently. They seem somewhat apprehensive and ask their physician what they should expect in their interactions with their families during this early time in their marriage. The physician should tell them that most couples experience
A. being emotionally cut off from their families of origin
B. disengagement from parents
C. enmeshment with parents
D. the formation of a family subsystem with relatively closed boundaries around it
E. the formation of a family subsystem with relatively open boundaries around it

85. A task of adolescence is separation from parents. Some adolescents find this process easier than others do. Which of the following types of family system has the most difficulty adapting to the stage of adolescent separation?
A. Disengaged family
B. Enmeshed family
C. Extended family
D. Generational family
E. Overprotective family

86. Preventive intervention is critical for good health outcomes at any age. Of all of the areas that can be targeted for preventive education among adolescents, the one that would lead to the greatest reduction in the incidence of death to this age group is
A. homicide
B. motor vehicle accidents
C. physical abuse
D. sexually-transmitted disease
E. suicide

87. A mother brings her 10-year-old boy to see the physician, complaining that he has been "walking in his sleep". She reports that he walks up and down the stairs two or three times, and then, after letting out a low moan, returns to bed and is once again quiet. She asks what his actions mean and, specifically, what he is dreaming about while he is climbing the stairs. The physician's best response would be to tell her that the
A. best thing to do is wake him up and tell him to go back to bed
B. boy is probably not dreaming while he is walking in his sleep
C. boy is searching for something that he lost
D. boy will stop walking in his sleep if he goes to bed later
E. stairs are a symbol of the boy's drive to succeed in life

88. One way to think about families is in terms of constellations of interacting roles. Certain individuals assume or are given particular tasks or responsibilities. These responsibilities often reflect cultural expectations. In the traditional nuclear family, the father is usually assigned to what type of role?
A. Competitive
B. Functional
C. Instrumental
D. Socioemotional
E. Symmetrical

89. A family may be a household, but not all households are families. A survey conducted in the mid-1990s showed that the majority of non-family households consisted of
A. caretaker and patient
B. non-married couples
C. one-person households
D. roommates
E. same-sex couples

90. Family patterns and patterns of cohabitation change over time, affecting both the social position and the health status of people in the population. Based on U.S. government data, which of the following showed the largest increase among U.S. households during the last quarter of the 20th century?
A. Households below the poverty level
B. Households with three children
C. Kinship households
D. Married-couple households with children
E. Single-parent housholds

91. A 15-year-old girl is blamed by her parents for the problems in the family. She is continually getting into trouble and acting out at school. What type of

role is she most likely playing in her family system?
A. Disengaged
B. Emotionally cut off
C. Enmeshed
D. Parentified
E. Scapegoated

92. A 12-year-old patient is exhibiting some depressive symptoms. She is responsible for taking care of the household and caring for her younger siblings after school until her parents return from work. What type of role is she most likely playing in her family system?
A. Child-focused
B. Enmeshed
C. Instrumental
D. Parentified
E. Triangulated

93. A patient reports that there is emotional distance and many independent activities among members of the family. Even traumatic events involving family members evoke little response. What family dynamic best describes this family system?
A. Disengaged
B. Enmeshed
C. Parentified
D. scapegoated
E. triangulated

94. Each time a family member has a problem it resonates quickly throughout the family system. There is little individual autonomy in the family, and much emotional intensity. When describing this family, the most appropriate term would be
A. disengaged
B. child-focused
C. enmeshed
D. parentified
E. triangulated

95. An 18-year-old patient recently married as a way of leaving her parental home. Since her marriage, she has had no contact with her parents. What label best describes the dynamic between this woman and her parents?
A. Emotionally cut off
B. Enmeshed
C. Parentified
D. Scapegoated
E. Triangulated

96. In the traditional nuclear family in the U.S., the wife usually is the main caretaker and nurturer in the family. What term best describes the functional role fulfilled by this traditional wife?

A. Child-focused
B. Enmeshed
C. Instrumental
D. Parentified
E. Socioemotional

97. A 8-year-old child has been bed-ridden for the past week with an unidentified infection. The parents are anxious about the state of the child's health. During times of illness such as these, this child is most likely to have difficulty coping with
A. dependency on others
B. limitation of activity
C. loss of affection from parents
D. removal from friends
E. unexplained nature of events

98. A 17-year-old star on the high school football team is injured in an automobile accident. His injury is not life threatening, but will keep him bed-ridden for several months. When talking with this patient, the physician is likely to find that he is having the hardest time coping with
A. dependency on others
B. limitation of activity
C. removal from friends
D. the unexplained nature of events
E. the pain of his injury

99. A 27-year-old woman has been bed-ridden with the latest strain of influenza for the past 3 days. When visited by her family physician, she is most likely to complain about feelings of
A. anger
B. blame
C. guilt
D. helplessness
E. hopelessness

100. His physician has told Mr. P. that he has an elevated prostate-specific antigen (PSA) level but that before a definitive diagnosis can be made, the test must be repeated in a month. During this interval, Mr. P. becomes impatient. The most effective coping strategy for this and other medical problems requiring patience is
A. confronting the doctor
B. identifying the issues
C. practicing relaxation exercises
D. seeking information
E. venting frustration to others

101. Hypnosis may be a helpful adjunct to treatment in all of the following conditions EXCEPT
A. alopecia due to chemotherapy
B. management of chronic pain

C. reducing the frequency and duration of flare ups of genital herpes

D. relief of irritable bowel symptoms

E. smoking cessation

102. While recovering from surgery to treat her breast cancer, a woman is encouraged to attend a support group for breast cancer survivors. She seems uneasy about attending. The physician should tell her that one of the main benefits of attending an illness-specific patient support group is that it may help to

A. do active problem solving

B. forget about the illness

C. laugh at adversity

D. learn to accept negative outcomes

E. see that others are worse off

103. Mr. H. has just been diagnosed with an inoperable cerebral tumor. Although his prognosis is poor, he continues to be cheerful and to talk amicably with all who visit him. When faced with a patient who appears cheerful in the face of a poor prognosis, the physician should

A. continue to remind the patient of his grave prognosis

B. gently point out to the patient that he is in denial

C. refuse to care for the patient until he accepts his prognosis

D. speak with his family about his condition

E. understand that the patient may need more time to adjust

104. Ms. G., a new patient, tells you that psychological feeling and physical health have nothing to do with each other. A patient, such as this, who believes that mind and body are separate would be *least* likely to respond to which of the following treatments for pain?

A. Analgesics

B. Antidepressants

C. Relaxation training

D. Surgery

E. Trigger point injections

105. Mr. R., a patient with hypertension, stops taking his medication. When questioned about this nonadherence, he is evasive and avoids eye contact with the physician. Which intervention is most likely to help him resume his treatment?

A. Changing to a drug covered by his insurance plan

B. Explaining the health hazards of elevated blood pressure

C. Explaining the side effects of the medications

D. Increasing his medication to three times a day rather than twice

E. Signing him up for a hypertension support group

106. A 45-year-old man makes an appointment to see his physician because he has a mild cold. Many patients who see a physician for this type of minor self-limited problem are really seeking

A. a particular diagnosis

B. a prescription

C. an excuse to avoid work

D. help with a psychological problem

E. reassurance

107. How and by whom health care decisions are made affects both diagnosis and adherence with recommended treatment. Although individual variations exist, in Asia, Mexico, and the Middle East, the dominant cultural model puts the burden of health decisions on the

A. community

B. family

C. patient

D. physician

E. religious leader

108. Some stressful life events are associated with a negative impact on health, while others are not. The impact a stressful event will have on a given person's health is most dependent on

A. the magnitude of the event

B. the number of people involved

C. the subjective experience of stress associated with the event

D. the type of change involved

E. whether the event is positive or negative

109. Decisions about end of life care are some of the most difficult that patients and their families have to make. When discussing options, the physician should tell them that, compared with death in a hospice, death in a hospital is likely to be more

A. conducive to family visits

B. dependent on technology

C. likely to focus on the timing of death

D. likely to respect religious practices

E. palliative in nature

110. Three weeks after the death of her husband, a distressed widow visits her primary care physician. She tells him that 2 days ago she was sure that she saw her husband alive, strolling along the opposite side of the street. "I called to him," she says, "but he didn't turn around." The physician should tell her that

A a brief course of antidepressant medication is indicated

B. she is defending against her spouse's death
C. she needs to be hospitalized
D. she was having an hallucination
E. such experiences are common in grieving people

111. Coping with the death of a loved one is always difficult, but some deaths seem to be harder to deal with than others. The cause of death that seems to make grieving most difficult is death that involves
A. an automobile accident
B. cancer
C. heart attack
D. HIV/AIDS
E. suicide

112. Differentiating between normal grief and a psychiatric disorder is difficult because many of the defining diagnostic criteria are shared. Difficulty sleeping, anhedonia, appetite disturbance, and loss of energy are present in both grief and
A. anxiety
B. depression
C. panic disorder
D. personality disorder
E. psychosis

113. Examination of morbidity and mortality patterns of surviving spouses has shown that widows and widowers are at increased risk of death for how many months after the death of their spouse?
A. 6 months
B. 12 months
C. 18 months
D. 24 months
E. no set time period

114. A physician is conducting a history and physical examination on a 24-year-old single woman who is a new patient. When asked if she currently takes any non-prescription drugs, she confesses to using amyl nitrate about once a week. Her most likely reason for using this substance is to
A. calm down after work
B. ease her through a "bad trip"
C. enhance sexual experience
D. give her more energy
E. help her sleep

115. Mr. Jones is visiting his dentist who notices that his teeth are worn and ground down. When questioned, Mr. Jones reports that his wife has told him that he grinds his teeth in his sleep. "She says it really keeps her awake", he says. This teeth grinding most likely occurs during what stage of sleep?
A. Stage 1

B. Stage 2
C. Stage 3
D. Stage 4
E. REM Stage

116. H.G. is a 21-year-old referred for psychological evaluation by the local court system. He was arrested for a series of burglaries. During his arrest, he severely injured one of the arresting police officers. When interviewed, he is very pleasant, even charming. He answers all questions while smiling and looking directly in the eye of the examiner. When questioned about the injury to the policeman, he continues to smile and expresses no remorse. Past history reveals that he was placed in juvenile detention for a year at age 14 after being found guilty of vandalism and burglary. Based on this initial presentation, the physician makes a preliminary diagnosis of which of the following personality disorders?
A. Anti-social
B. Borderline
C. Histrionic
D. Paranoid
E. Schizotypal

117. A medical student is assigned to explain to a patient that he has a terminal condition. She researches the details and latest prognostic data about the patient's disease. In the morning, she makes a full and detailed presentation to the patient, citing the latest medical information including an in-depth explanation of the underlying biochemical mechanism of the illness. After the presentation, the patient confides to a nurse on the ward that he "really didn't get" most of what the student presented. The most likely defense mechanism being used by the student in this instance is
A. denial
B. intellectualization
C. isolation of affect
D. reaction formation
E. sublimation

118. Stressful life events can affect people's physical as well as psychological health. As measured by the Holmes and Rahe Stressful Life Events Scale, which of the following life events is associated with the greatest stress?
A. Death of a spouse
B. Divorce
C. Incarceration for more than 1 year
D. Loss of a job
E. Surviving an automobile accident

119. Neuronal development progresses through a series of defined stages as the child ages. Neuronal

migration, which provides the substrate for brain development, is generally completed by

A. birth
B. 2 months of age
C. 4 months of age
D. 6 months of age
E. 12 months of age

120. Pathology can be viewed as the failure or disruption of normal processes. The failure of "guidance cues" in human development is most likely to result in a person who

A. demonstrates no sense of right and wrong
B. fails to adhere to treatment recommendations
C. is unable to draw shapes from memory
D. lacks neuronal adaptation to environmental stimuli
E. loses control over peripheral physical movements

121. A patient is having difficulty sleeping. His physician advises him to listen to a relaxation tape every evening for ½ hour prior to going to sleep. Eventually, the patient reports that he falls asleep almost at once as soon as he hears the voice on the tape, even without going through the relaxation routine. This phenomenon is most likely due to the operation of

A. biofeedback
B. classical conditioning
C. inhibition
D. intermittent reinforcement
E. modeling

122. An overweight middle aged woman of average height and in good general health comes to the physician requesting advice about diet and weight loss. She says that she has dieted repeatedly throughout her life, and now she cannot lose weight even if she eats only 1400 calories/day. She is cold, constipated, and lethargic. She denies binging or purging, and she still has normal menstrual cycles. Her thyroid function tests are normal. The physician should

A. order a basal metabolic rate to investigate if she is hypometabolic
B. send her to Overeaters Anonymous for psychological support
C. suggest she try a very-low-calorie diet, or even a liquid fast, to restart the process of weight loss
D. suggest that people often underestimate dietary intake
E. try to motivate her to lose weight by emphasizing the health risks of obesity

123. Often, effective pharmacological treatments are identified before the mechanisms of action have been fully established. Recent research has shown that effective treatment of which one of the following conditions relies on the action of so called "second messengers?"

A. Bipolar disorder
B. General anxiety disorder
C. Huntington's disease
D. Schizophrenia
E. Tourrette's syndrome

124. A medication is prescribed for Mr. W. to help him cope with chronic generalized anxiety disorder (GAD). The general class of pharmacological agents most commonly used for the treatment of this anxiety disorder is believed to be effective because it

A. decreases norinepepherine in the locus ceruleus
B. increases acetylcholine in the temporal cortex
C. increases GABA diffusely throughout the brain
D. reduces available dopamine in the medial forebrain bundle
E. reduces serotonin available post-synaptically

125. Animal models are often used to predict the action of new pharmacologic agents in humans. A dog in a research laboratory is injected with a drug that imitates the effects of glutamate. Over the next hour, what behavior are you most likely observe from the dog?

A. Hiccups
B. Hypersomnolence
C. Manic-like hyperactivity
D. Seizures
E. Unusual quiescence

126. Evidence for the involvement of dopamine in the initiation of movement is most strongly found by monitoring the action of dopamine in which neuronal area?

A. Locus ceruleus
B. Mesolimbic-mesocortical tract
C. Nigrostriatal tract
D. Raphe nuclei
E. Tuberoinfundibular tract

127. One of the best indications of the level of serotonin activity in the brain can be found by monitoring 5-HIAA levels in

A. blood
B. spinal fluid
C. sweat
D. tears
E. urine

128. During rapid-eye-movement (REM) sleep, the words and images that provide the raw material for the mental representations called dreams originate in the
    A. amygdala
    B. basal ganglia
    C. cerebellum
    D. hippocampus
    E. reticular activating system

129. Following an automobile accident, Mr. S. presents with monotone speech that is devoid of emotional inflection. He evidences no difficulty understanding what is said to him. A CAT scan of the head is ordered. The results are most likely to show a lesion in
    A. Broca's area on the left side
    B. Broca's area on the right side
    C. Exner's area on both the right and the left sides
    D. Wernicke's area on the left side
    E. Wernicke's area on the right side

130. Animal models provide a method of understanding the functional importance of the brain and neurologic system. When observing the behavior of a rat that is receiving electrical stimulation of the orbital frontal cerebral region you are most likely to observe
    A. excessive aggression
    B. excessive fluid intake
    C. hypersexuality
    D. manic-like hyperactivity
    E. refusal of food by a hungry animal

131. A professional stock trader spends his days monitoring the changing process of the financial markets and buying and selling according to his observations of market activity. An examination of his record of trading shows that sometimes he makes money and sometimes he loses money. The trader complains that he is preoccupied with trading stocks and can not stop following the markets even when he is on vacation. The mechanism that most likely underlies his excessive attention to the financial markets is
    A. continuous operant reinforcement
    B. fixed interval operant reinforcement
    C. habituation
    D. stimulus generalization
    E. variable ratio operant reinforcement

132. Following a fall down the stairs, Mrs. F., a 77-year-old widow, is non-responsive to stimulation on the left side of her body. When asked to reproduce a presented figure, she is able to draw the right-hand side exactly, but neglects the left-hand

side of the figure entirely. Based on this initial evaluation, further physiologic examination of the patient is most likely to show a lesion in the
    A. dominant parietal lobe
    B. dominant temporal lobe
    C. non-dominant parietal lobe
    D. non-dominant temporal lobe
    E. orbital medial frontal cortex

133. Myelination of the anterior and posterior commissures and the corpus callosum allows improved communication between the right and left hemispheres. This process is most commonly completed during which Freudian stage of development?
    A. Oral
    B. Anal
    C. Phallic
    D. Latency
    E. Genital

134. You are tracking the cardiac functioning of Mr. B. over a 24-hour period. Mr. B. is a 45-year-old office worker who currently does not engage in regular exercise. Assuming that Mr. B. evidences normal biologic rhythms, you would expect to find the highest cardiac contraction rates
    A. just after awaking in the morning
    B. in the middle of the morning
    C. in the afternoon
    D. just before going to bed at night
    E. during REM sleep

135. Although used interchangeably by many people in day-to-day life, the concepts of illness and disease refer to different aspects of a person's perception of health. In contrast to illness, "disease" refers to
    A. chronic rather than acute medical problems
    B. contracted health problems rather than inherited health characteristics
    C. health from an epidemiological rather than a medical perspective
    D. objective pathology rather than subjective experience
    E. the impact of poor health on social functioning

136. The notion of the "sick role" encapsulates societal expectations for people with certain types of medical conditions. As generally applied, the concept of the sick role
    A. applies only to those with long-term chronic conditions
    B. defines the obligations of medical professionals to care for those who are ill
    C. places responsibility for having the patient get well on the medical professional

D. relieves the individual from responsibility during an illness
E. specifies a set amount of time to be devoted to illness recovery

137. Mrs. White receives a letter from her HMO informing her that she had abnormal cells on the Pap smear taken during her last visit. The letter requests that she call and schedule a follow-up appointment, which she does. When she appears for a follow-up visit 2 weeks later, she talks about a pain in her back but does not mention or seem to remember receiving the letter about her Pap smear. The defense mechanism that most likely accounts for Mrs. White's inability to remember the letter is
A. denial
B. intellectualization
C. rationalization
D. somatization
E. undoing

138. John, a patient with a long history of hypertension and cardiac problems, confides to his family physician that he is " feeling depressed" about the recent loss of his job. The physician's best response would be to
A. call John's wife to ask how he has been at home
B. explore the presence of depressive symptoms
C. refer John to a local psychiatrist for evaluation
D. tell John that his mood will pass in a couple of weeks
E. write John a prescription for an antidepressant

139. On the first day of kindergarten, the mother of a 5-year-old boy tells him that she will not leave right away when dropping him off at school. However, over the next few days, she finds that each day he insists that she stay a little longer and begins to cry when she starts to leave. Consequently, this morning she stayed with him for more than an hour. This change in the mother's behavior can be best explained as an example of the effects of
A. extinction
B. fading
C. negative reinforcement
D. positive reinforcement
E. secondary reinforcement

140. The mother of a 5-year-old child lingers for an hour after bringing her son to kindergarten. During this time the boy appears happy, but pays little attention to the teacher or the other children. Eventually the teacher convinces the mother to bring her son to the classroom, reassure him, and then leave.

After several days of crying and being fearful after his mother leaves, the boy becomes calmer, stops crying, and displays less fear. This change in the boy's behavior is most likely the result of
A. extinction
B. intermittent reinforcement
C. maturation
D. shaping
E. sublimation

141. Paul, a second year medical student, is angry at his professor for being late to an appointment. When the professor does appear, Paul tells him how angry he was with a physician he saw earlier in the day who made him wait for more than 30 minutes for no apparent reason. Paul is most likely using the defense mechanism of
A. conversion
B. displacement
C. projection
D. reaction formation
E. repression

142. Physical examination shows J.D. to have normal body strength, response to sensation, speech and comprehension. When engaged in conversation, he seems normal and communicates clearly. However, when asked to tie his shoelaces, he is unable to do so. This type of dysfunction is most commonly called
A. agnosia
B. anosognosia
C. aphasia
D. apraxia
E. aprosody

143. A 45-year-old man who exercises regularly and watches his diet admits to smoking a pack of cigarettes a day. He says that he has tried to quit repeatedly over the years. During his longest period of abstinence (three months) he gained 15 pounds. His father, an obese non-smoker, died of a heart attack at age 60. The patient believes that, for him, the risks of smoking are lower than the risks of obesity. The physician should
A. accept this assessment and focus on other aspects of the patients' life that may affect cardiovascular risk
B. confront the patient's rationalization of his addiction and suggest a 12-step program to help him quit.
C. examine his feelings about the early loss of his father as contributing to his smoking and suggest psychotherapy
D. explain that obesity has less of an impact on cardiovascular mortality than smoking, so he should quit again and accept the weight gain

E. if he did not use nicotine replacement or bu-proprion in his prior smoking cessation attempts, recommend these to reduce potential weight gain

144. When introduced to someone at a party, Sarah is able to converse in a normal manner. However, as the conversation progresses, it becomes evident that she is unable to recall any details from her remote past. She is able to remember the name of the person she had been talking to when questioned later in the evening. A deficiency of which of the following substances most likely accounts for this pattern of behaviors?
   A. Copper
   B. Niacin
   C. Potassium
   D. Thiamine
   E. Zinc

145. A 45-year-old man is placed on a narcotic-based pain medication following abdominal surgery. This medication is prescribed on a time-contingent basis. He is told that he can only take one pill every 5 hours, regardless of how much pain he feels. This type of prescription is an example of a reinforcement schedule generally referred to as
   A. continuous
   B. fixed interval
   C. fixed ratio
   D. non-contingent
   E. variable ratio

146. J.F., a 43-year-old office worker, has smoked two packs of cigarettes a day for the past 25 years. He tells his physician that he eats a lot of "junk food" and gets little exercise. The behavior that is most likely to significantly reduce J.F.'s risk of heart disease is
   A. modifying his diet to exclude high-fat foods
   B. signing up for "Weight Watchers"
   C. starting a rigorous weight-lifting program
   D. stopping smoking
   E. taking a cholesterol-lowering medication

147. H.Y., a 47-year-old woman, presents to her family physician feeling "a little out of sorts". In spite of feeling under the weather, she has made no changes in her daily routine as a legal secretary and mother. She only came to see the physician to have a rash evaluated so as not to expose her family and coworkers. Physical examination reveals a rash accompanied by a low-grade fever. A diagnosis of rubella is confirmed by tests. Based on this presentation, H.Y. has
   A. disability, without sick role
   B. disease, but not illness

   C. illness, but not disease
   D. infection, but not disease
   E. sickness, but not disability

148. Calvin, a 2-year-old boy, is brought to see the pediatrician for evaluation of an earache. One week before, a nurse in the physician's office had given Calvin an immunization shot that elicited a great deal of crying. When you enter the examination room, Calvin is playing happily with his stuffed tiger and interacting calmly with his mother. As the nurse enters the room, however, he begins to cry and tries to leave. Calvin's reaction to the nurse is most likely the result of
   A. classical conditioning
   B. fading
   C. negative reinforcement
   D. positive reinforcement
   E. shaping

149. A 3-year-old boy has recently begun to have major temper tantrums each morning when it is time to go to childcare. This causes considerable frustration for his mother who is then late for work. These temper tantrums are new. Previously, the boy had gone to childcare without incident. At her wit's end, the mother calls the pediatrician and asks for advice. The pediatrician recommends the use of a "sticker chart": the boy would get a sticker for each of three identified behaviors (eating breakfast, getting into the car, and walking into the childcare building). At the end of the day, the boy would be given a small treat if he has collected three stickers for that day. This strategy is an example of the use of
   A. biofeedback
   B. desensitization
   C. flooding
   D. shaping
   E. token economy

150. You are observing an emotional outburst from a patient who is upset for an unknown reason. A CAT scan of this patient would show that, during this emotional behavior, the part of the brain that is likely to be the most active is the
   A. cerebellum
   B. limbic system
   C. neocortex
   D. pineal body
   E. reticular activating system

151. A physician and his wife were invited to an early dinner party. However, office and hospital laboratory results had to be reviewed before the physician was able to leave work that night. As a result, the couple was unable to attend the dinner party

that evening. The physician's behavior exemplifies the ethical principle of

A. beneficence
B. fidelity
C. honesty
D. justice
E. trust

152. A physician has practiced in a rural area of Minnesota for over 30 years. In general, his relationships with patients can be considered paternalistic, a style he learned from his father who was his partner until he died 20 years ago. One of the core characteristics of the paternalistic physician is

A. mutual exchange of information between physician and patient
B. patient passivity during encounters with physicians
C. respect for patient autonomy
D. sharing of medical decision making by physicians and patients
E. valuing patients' moral integrity

153. Mr. E., a 75-year-old, long-standing patient recently visited his physician for his annual check-up. As part of that routine evaluation, the physician discovered that Mr. E. was suffering from metastatic lung cancer. This was surprising because he was asymptomatic, except for mild fatigue. The physician is struggling with whether she should inform the patient of his condition now or wait until he begins to deteriorate. The best course of action would be to

A. encourage Mr. E. to obtain life insurance before she informs him
B. immediately inform him of his condition
C. tell his relatives, but not the patient
D. tell the patient that he has a "tumor", but it can be easily treated
E. wait until he becomes significantly symptomatic before informing him

154. In the U.S., an effective physician-patient relationship is central to delivery of comprehensive health care services. Both patient satisfaction and positive care outcomes have been tied to maintaining a good relationship between physician and patient. One of the central characteristics of a good physician-patient relationship is

A. acknowledging differences in understanding of health-related issues
B. passive patient behavior when receiving medical services
C. patients' inability to make informed medical decisions
D. physician dominance in the relationship
E. the physician's superior moral integrity

155. A physician graduated from a combined Medicine-Pediatrics residency 5 years ago and began practice as the only physician in a rural county of her home state. In this role, she provides care to anyone who comes to her office, whether they are patients formally enrolled in her practice or not. Many of her patients are unable to pay their medical bills, but she continues to see them whenever they need her services. One of her regular patients, a community leader who always pays his bills on time, complained to her that he felt it was inappropriate for him to have to wait while she is caring for "deadbeats" who happened to show up at her office. The physician explained that because she is the only physician in the area, it is her obligation to ensure that medical services are available to all patients in the county. The physician's explanation is based on the ethical principle of

A. beneficence
B. fidelity
C. honesty
D. justice
E. non-maleficence

156. Informed consent is the basic underlying principle that governs medical decision making in the U.S. No medical decision should be made without it. This notion is best understood as the requirement that

A. all participating physicians concur before a medical procedure is performed
B. the patient have all necessary information before deciding to undergo medical treatment
C. the patient's family be advised before medical procedures are undertaken
D. the patient's primary care physician be informed before a sub-specialist performs a procedure
E. the physician be well-informed before consenting to perform a procedure

157. A first-year resident assumes the care of a woman who has had diabetes mellitus for many years. The patient was previously under the care of a recently retired faculty member noted for his authoritarian manner. She was notorious among office staff and clinic physicians for her lack of compliance with her physician's prescribed treatment regimens. When seeing the patient in the office for the first time, the resident noted that her diabetes was out of control despite multiple office visits, dietary counseling, large insulin doses, and a prescribed exercise regimen. To improve the patient's adherence to treatment recommendations, the first step the resident should take is to

A. explain the negative health consequences of non-compliance with recommendations

B. inform her that diabetes is incurable and improvement unlikely without good treatment

C. question the patient about her failure to follow treatment recommendations

D. show concern and ask what assistance she would like to help her manage the diabetes

E. tell the patient how she can best control her diet

158. A 52-year-old woman with metastatic breast carcinoma has been managed at her local community hospital since diagnosis. Her physicians have consulted with a renowned regional tertiary care center regarding all aspects of her care and have followed the consultants' recommendations meticulously. However, as the patient's condition gradually deteriorated, she requested transfer to the regional medical center. Although her treatment regimen was unchanged, shortly after arriving at the medical center the patient stated she "felt better" and was glad she was now under the care of "the famous specialists" at the center. The improvement in this patient's symptoms is likely due to

A. changes in nutritional supplements

B. natural history of the disease

C. nonspecific therapeutic effects

D. placebo effect

E. specific effects of treatment

159. Research studies designed to test the effectiveness of newly developed oral medications typically have two groups of study subjects, those who receive the drug being studied and those who receive an inert pill which looks identical to the study drug. The use of these two groups in the study design is intended to eliminate which of the following factors that might contribute to the drug's efficacy?

A. Investigator bias

B. Natural course of the disease

C. Nonspecific treatment effects

D. Placebo effect

E. Specific treatment effects

160. Adherence to treatment refers to active participation by patients in choosing to remain faithful to recommended treatment plans. High levels of adherence are associated with better medical outcomes. Physicians should remember that patient adherence to treatment is most likely to *decline* when

A. patient and physician negotiate the treatment plan

B. patient and physician openly share opinions about the problem

C. the patient's knowledge about the disease increases

D. the physician controls medical decision making

E. the physician provides additional information about the condition

161. The presence of empathy is crucial in the development of the physician-patient relationship. Without empathy, communication is more difficult and patients may feel that the physician does not care about them. One of the core skills required for establishing empathy is

A. avoiding excessive emotional detachment

B. displaying appropriate nonverbal behavior

C. listening actively or reflectively

D. maintaining calm self-control

E. using open-ended questioning

162. Ms. K is a 60-year-old woman with a history of diabetes and hypertension. Her son reports that, over the past month, she has become disoriented and confused: "One day she seems better, and then suddenly she seems worse." On the mini-mental status examination she is unable to correctly give the day of the week. Physical examination reveals muscle weakness on the left side of her body. Based on this preliminary examination, the most likely diagnosis for Ms. K is

A. Alzheimer's dementia

B. Creutzfelt-Jakob disease

C. Huntington's disease

D. Pick's disease

E. Vascular dementia

163. Before a physician can be empathetic with patients, he or she must first be clear what empathy means. Which of the following examples identifies an important behavioral manifestation of empathy?

A. Appearing relaxed and taking extra time

B. Minimizing nonverbal distractions

C. Remaining calm despite a patient's anxiety

D. Speaking in language that is similar to the patient's

E. Taking notes during a clinical interview

164. A family physician is counseling a patient concerning weight loss strategies to help relieve pressure and pain on arthritic knee joints. The patient becomes irate, stating that he feels criticized and put down. The physician reacts with amazement to what she sees as appropriate patient education. The patient's reaction is most likely the result of

A. a personality disorder

B. counter-transference by the physician

C. denial on the part of the patient

D. inadequate expression of empathy by the physician

E. transference by the patient

165. Unfortunately, increasing numbers of the disease states faced by physicians are iatrogenic in origin. Iatrogenesis is best defined as
    A. a hypnotic suggestion made by the physician to increase patient compliance
    B. a negative patient reaction to physician demeanor
    C. a premorbid condition leading to Muchausen Syndrome
    D. malingering or presenting false information to the physician
    E. the creation of additional problems or complications by the physician

166. Physician training requires basic socialization as well as the acquisition of basic medical knowledge. The acquisition of competence as part of this socialization process is best described as
    A. being able to judge whether a patient is able to act in his/her best interests
    B. combining technical expertise and effective human relations skills to be a "total" physician
    C. having the human relations skills to perform well as a physician
    D. having the mental capability to be responsible for one's behavior
    E. having the technical expertise to perform well as a physician

167. A medical student was spending a month with a physician in private practice in rural North Carolina. The physician had been in solo practice for 20 years and was on call whenever he was in town. He had a loving and supportive relationship with his wife and family, all of whom agreed with and were committed to traditional principles of physician professional behavior. The doctor and his wife were planning on a quiet dinner to celebrate their 25th wedding anniversary when he was called to the hospital for a difficult and prolonged obstetrical delivery. The physician missed the dinner and the medical student was amazed that his wife did not become angry because their plans for the evening were upset. The medical student asked his wife why she was not angry about not having the anniversary celebration. Based on the information above, her most likely answer was
    A. "he'll make it up to me next year"
    B. "patient come first when care is really needed"
    C. "people would talk if he didn't go to take care of a patient"
    D. "the kids are more fun to be with anyway"
    E. "when you've been married this long, you know your husband's job comes first"

168. A 24-year-old, cohabitating woman has come to the emergency room four times in six months, seeking treatment for severe headaches. An MRI of the brain done at the second visit was normal. The headaches are preceded by visual distortions and accompanied by nausea. They tend to occur premenstrually or after a stressful week. On questioning, she has chronic pelvic pain but a work-up for endometriosis was negative a year ago. She also has crampy abdominal pain, bloating and gas that, at times, keep her from going to work. She does not have a primary care physician. The astute ER clinician suspects this patient
    A. has a history of maltreatment or abuse by an intimate partner
    B. has conversion disorder
    C. has panic disorder
    D. is malingering and has an undiagnosed opiate addiction
    E. is suffering from hypochondriasis

169. A young physician was well known for allowing her patients sufficient opportunities to discuss all aspects of their medical care. She also respected their opinions and frequently negotiated management plans with them, deferring to their rights to determine what should be done for their bodies. The principle which best describes her behavior is
    A. beneficence
    B. justice
    C. moral virtue
    D. non-maleficence
    E. respect for autonomy

170. Expectations regarding the role of physicians in society are based on knowledge of traditional ethical principles and behaviors. Physician adherence to the majority of these principles and behaviors requires specific actions by the physician. Adherence to which of the following principles requires no action by the physician?
    A. Beneficence
    B. Justice
    C. Moral virtue
    D. Non-maleficence
    E. Respect for autonomy

171. Miss M., a 93-year-old woman with invasive esophageal carcinoma, has been in a nursing home for 6 months because of progressive disease. She has a single sibling, a sister, who visits her periodically. Her course in the nursing home has been marked by a 40% loss of body weight and, recently, several episodes of bleeding from her esophagus that required multiple transfusions. She is considered terminally ill with only a short time to live regardless of medical treatment. She has been mentally alert

at all times, and competent to make decisions. She has decided to forgo additional transfusions and to die comfortably at the nursing home. In planning for this course of action, the most essential component of her care will be

A. her insurance coverage
B. her relationship with her physician
C. her relationship with the nursing home director
D. her sister's feelings about the decision
E. regulations regarding blood transfusions

172. Mrs. S. was an 80-year-old widow who lived in a retirement home. She was mentally competent and very wealthy. All financial support for living and medical expenses until the time of her death was secure in an unbreachable trust fund. A second trust fund for discretionary use was available as she chose. Unfortunately, she was notorious for poor financial decisions and had lost considerable amounts from the second trust since the death of her financier husband. Her children approached her physician and asked that their mother be declared mentally incompetent so they could control the second trust fund and prevent further losses. The physician refused their request on grounds it would violate a key expectation of his role as a physician. Had he consented to their wish, he would have violated the patient's expectation for physician behavior consistent with

A. beneficence
B. justice
C. moral virtues
D. maleficence
C. moral virtues
E. patient autonomy

173. Research on the effects of the growing number of women entering medical practice has demonstrated a number of differences between the practice patterns of male and female doctors. This research has shown that

A. child-rearing is poorer than that of nonphysician mothers
B. female physicians show greater confidence in their interpersonal skills
C. female surgeons are less aggressive about performing invasive interventions
D. female surgeons have lower technical skills than male surgeons
E. rates of pay for male and female physicians have equalized

174. Many life decisions, including career choice, can be the result of transference. An example of transference in career decision making would be choosing

A. a career in health care after experiencing a significant childhood illness
B. a helping profession when a family member has a history of substance abuse
C. medicine based on a physician role model outside the family
D. medicine because a parent is a physician
E. medicine because of admiring a genial physician on television

175. When surveyed and asked to self-describe their personality, what proportion of physicians label themselves as "compulsive?"

A. 20%
B. 40%
C. 60%
D. 80%
E. 95%

176. Dual-physician marriages are becoming increasingly common as more women enter the practice of medicine. These marriages face unique challenges. Surveys of two-physician marriages have found that

A. female spouses consider family obligations when selecting practices
B. males and females have similar earning potential
C. marital partners choose practice sites regardless of spouse preference
D. marital partners take equal length of time in training
E. these marriages have a higher than average divorce rate

177. Diminished ability to carry out personal or professional responsibilities is referred to in the literature as "physician impairment." Which of the following examples would reflect physician impairment?

A. Completed rehabilitation for cocaine dependence 6 months ago
B. Compulsive gambling that only occurs on weekends
C. Heated, public verbal exchange with the nursing staff
D. HIV infection without current symptoms
E. Status post stroke with residual impairment of gait

178. An emergency department physician wants to identify a psychological assessment tool that will help her screen emergency room patients for suicide risk. She has identified several assessment tools, but wants to investigate them further to determine if they will be useful for her particular purpose. Therefore, when investigating these tests

she should pay special attention to information about their

A. administration
B. bias
C. consistency
D. reliability
E. validity

179. When applying for a position as a bank teller, John was surprised when he was asked to complete the Minnesota Multiphasic Personality Inventory (MMPI). He had recently learned about the test in graduate school and knew it was very useful with certain patient populations. However, he had serious doubts about its usefulness in selecting employees. John's doubts about the MMPI's use for employee selection reflect concerns about

A. bias
B. convergence
C. precision
D. reliability
E. validity

180. Universities and medical schools often use applicants' scores on tests such as the MCAT, GRE, and SAT as part of their admission decisions. These schools hope that these tests will help them determine which applicants will be successful in their programs. To be useful in this capacity, these tests must have strong

A. criterion-related validity
B. construct validity
C. content validity
D. face validity
E. predictive validity

181. A clinician is interested in assessing the trait of obsessiveness. To obtain information about how much of this or any other trait or attribute a person possesses, the clinician should be most concerned with

A. construct validity
B. content validity
C. criterion-related validity
D. face validity
E. predictive validity

182. Dr. Scott was considering giving the Benton Visual Retention Test to an 8-year-old patient who recently received a severe blow to the head in an accident. He tells you that this test has an interrater reliability coefficient of .95. You should advise Dr. Scott to

A. abandon the test since its reliability is extremely low
B. consider this test since its reliability is very strong

C. continue to investigate the test since its reliability is moderate
D. give the test on two separate occasions to confirm the results
E. look for a test with a reliability coefficient over 1.00

183. A patient was referred for outpatient psychotherapy after a recent emergency room visit when he was given several psychological assessments. The therapist wants to readminister the tests given in the emergency room to determine if there has been any significant change in the patient's condition. Since the therapist wants to be relatively certain that any changes in results reflect true changes in the patient's condition and not the change in environment, he needs to be most concerned about the tests'

A. adaptive capacity
B. bias
C. concurrent validity
D. content validity
E. reliability

184. Recent years have seen a lot of discussion in the popular press about intelligence and its assessment. After reading some of these accounts, one of your patients comes to you and, knowing that their child is about to be given an IQ test at school, asks you what the facts are. Which of the following statements about intelligence would you make, based on the current state of knowledge?

A. Intelligence tests are based on one agreed-upon definition of intelligence.
B. IQ and intelligence are the same thing.
C. Most differences in IQ scores are primarily due to environmental factors.
D. Race predicts what IQ score a particular individual will obtain.
E. Tests of intelligence generally attempt to measure ability not achievement.

185. The IQ score is norm referenced. This means that each individual's test score is compared to a normative range to derive the actual IQ. When looking at the distribution of IQ scores represented on the normal curve, approximately 68% of people score

A. > 130
B. > 100
C. $85–115$
D. < 100
E. < 70

186. J.G. is a 19-year-old man referred for evaluation by his college Dean. The Dean acted after reports from students that J.G. was "impossible to live

with" and was disrupting classes. At the initial interview, J.G. is dressed in mismatched clothing and seems anxious and suspicious of the physician. He giggles under his breath, and then laughs for no apparent reason. As the session progresses, J.G. confesses that he can hear what the physician is thinking. His speech is coherent, but characterized by odd choices of words that seem to hold some hidden private meaning for him. He reports no close friends other than his brother whom he sees once a month. Among the following types of personality disorder, which is the most likely diagnosis for this patient?

  A. Anti-social personality disorder
  B. Borderline personality disorder
  C. Narcissistic personality disorder
  D. Schizoid personality disorder
  E. Schizotypal personality disorder

187. Daniel, a 6-year-old boy, is brought by his mother to see his pediatrician. She reports that during sleep, he sits up in bed and screams for about a minute, and then lies back down to sleep again. In the morning he seems to have no recollection of these episodes. The physician should advise the mother that Daniel is most likely experiencing

  A. acute adjustment reaction
  B. bruxism
  C. hypnogogic hallucinations
  D. night terrors
  E. nightmares

188. A 55-year-old man with a history of hypertension is admitted to the hospital for removal of his gall bladder. He reports feeling anxious about his pending operation. His physician should keep in mind that the patient is most likely to recover sooner and request less pain medication if he

  A. has complete information about the surgical procedure and recovery
  B. has confidence in his surgeon's technical skill
  C. is given post-operative pain medication on demand
  D. is pleased with his nursing care
  E. likes his surgeon personally

189. The Minnesota Multiphasic Personality Inventory (MMPI) is a sophisticated test with a built-in check to determine whether a person's responses are genuine or merely an attempt to "look good." The validity scale on the MMPI that is used to assess the test taker's need to present himself or herself in a favorable or socially desirable light is the

  A. F or Infrequency Scale
  B. K or Correction Scale

  C. L or Lie Scale
  D. PY or Psychasthenia Scale
  E. SE or Self-Esteem Scale

190. During an assessment, a patient is asked to look at a picture and make up a story about it. The patient tells a story about two lovers who are fighting, but then make up. The patient is most likely being psychologically assessed with the

  A. Bender Visual Motor Gestalt Test
  B. Benton Visual Retention Test
  C. Minnesota Multiphasic Personality Inventory
  D. Peabody Picture Vocabulary Test
  E. Thematic Apperception Test

191. During assessment, a patient was administered the WAIS, MMPI, the Tactile Performance Test, the Speech Sounds Test, and the Categories Test. The patient is probably being evaluated for brain dysfunction with the

  A. Bender Visual Motor Gestalt Test
  B. California Personality Inventory
  C. Halstead-Reitan Neuropsychological Test Battery
  D. Luria Nebraska Neuropsychological Battery
  E. Thematic Apperception Test

192. A 10-year-old patient has been having academic difficulties at school. A psychologist suggests administration of a test that has confirmed validity in detecting brain damage, and also provides a nonverbal measure of personality. This test is frequently used to estimate intelligence and school readiness. The test most likely suggested by the psychologist is the

  A. Bender Visual Motor Gestalt Test
  B. Draw-A-Person Test
  C. Luria Nebraska Neuropsychological Battery
  D. Rorschach Test
  E. Wechsler Memory Scale

193. When individuals are forced to impose meaning on an ambiguous stimulus, it is assumed that responses will be reflections of their true feelings, thoughts, attitudes, desires, experiences, and needs. This assumption is an example of

  A. reaction formation
  B. subjective press
  C. the Gestalt laws of perception
  D. the law of effect
  E. the projective hypothesis

194. A physician suspects that a patient may have been a victim of childhood sexual abuse and requests that certain psychological tests be administered to see if any indicators of abuse appear in the patient's results. However, when requesting the test-

ing, the physician does not tell the patient or the psychologist administering the test that she wishes to screen for sexual abuse. She decided to do this to guard against

A. a placebo effect
B. bias
C. destroying the reliability of the test results
D. influencing the construct validity of the test
E. stigmatizing the patient

Items 195–197

Answer the following questions with reference to Table 1.

Table 1

		Actual Disease		
		Yes	No	Totals
Screening	Positive	a	b	a + b
Test	Negative	c	d	c + d
	Totals	a + c	b + d	a + b + c + d

195. Which of the choices below best represents the false-positive error rate?
    A. $a/(a + b)$
    B. $a/(a + c)$
    C. $b/(a + b)$
    D. $b/(b + d)$
    E. $d/(b + d)$

196. Which of the choices below best represents specificity?
    A. $a/(a + b)$
    B. $a/(a + c)$
    C. $b/(a + b)$
    D. $b/(b + d)$
    E. $d/(b + d)$

197. Which of the choices below best represents positive predictive value?
    A. $a/(a + b)$
    B. $a/(a + c)$
    C. $b/(a + b)$
    D. $b/(b + d)$
    E. $d/(b + d)$

198. You wish to determine the proportion of myocardial infarctions that are fatal within the first 24 hours after they occur. You decide to examine the records of all local emergency rooms and doctors' offices. Then, you will calculate the proportion of myocardial infarctions reported that resulted in death within 24 hours after the patient was seen

initially. You briefly discuss your plan with a local biostatistician who immediately points out that your study is particularly subject to

A. late-look bias
B. lead-time bias
C. measurement bias
D. observer bias
E. selection bias

199. An investigator is trying to determine whether medical screening programs using chest x-rays to detect lung cancer improve the survival time of the persons screened. She looks at the most recent year's data in the Connecticut Tumor Registry and discovers that the median survival time following the diagnosis of lung cancer is 6 months. She then performs a chest x-ray screening program in shopping centers and bowling alleys. She finds that in persons screened by this program, the median time from diagnosis to death is 9 months for the 95 cases of lung cancer discovered. The survival time difference is statistically significant. The investigator concludes that the screening program and subsequent treatment are adding an average of 3 months to the lives of lung cancer patients. You disagree on the basis of

A. late-look bias
B. lead-time bias
C. measurement bias
D. observer bias
E. selection bias

200. A 16-year-old boy, who describes himself as gay, comes for a physical exam so he can play tennis at school. He seems subdued in the office, and the examiner asks how he is doing. He describes feeling socially isolated and says that he switched to tennis because he felt bullied and teased when he played team sports like basketball and soccer. His grades have dropped from A's and B's to B's and C's over the past year. He denies drinking or the use of street drugs, but he admits to feeling apathetic and sad. On questioning, he says that, at times, he feels life is not worth living, and he has had some suicidal thoughts, especially since he has come out to his parents. They seem unperturbed but a few close friends have turned away from him saying they "can't deal with it." As someone who defines himself as homosexual, is he at higher or lower risk of suicide than heterosexual peers with this level of symptoms?

A. Higher, due to self hatred for his sexual orientation ("internalized homophobia")
B. Higher, due to the prejudice and discomfort he elicits in his peers
C. Lower, as he is less likely to consider violent means of suicide than heterosexual peers

D. Lower, because his openness suggests greater psychological maturity

E. Lower, since, as a homosexual male, his suicide risk is closer to that of a female

201. By definition, a woman is menopausal if she
A. has frequent hot flashes, disturbed sleep and irregular menses
B. has not menstruated in the past three months
C. has not menstruated in the past year
D. has noted a significant change in the pattern of her menstrual function (i.e., scantier or heavier periods, worsening or milder premenstrual symptoms)
E. is over 45, has unprotected sex, and has not conceived over the past year

202. A company concerned about productivity lost because of health problems instituted an intensive medical treatment and support program for the 10% of its workers with the most time lost due to illness during a certain year. The treated group had much better attendance and productivity the next year. You believe that the program actually had no effect. You explain that the the outcome is
A. effect modification
B. excessive power
C. random error
D. the statistical regression effect
E. type II error

203. When interventions are properly selected and performed by trained professionals, we refer to this kind of medical care as
A. acceptable
B. accessible
C. adequate
D. appropriate
E. available

204. When there is public disclosure of financial records and quality standards, we refer to this kind of medical care as
A. acceptable
B. accountable
C. adequate
D. appropriate
E. available

205. When the care provided is compatible with the patient's belief system, we refer to this kind of medical care as
A. acceptable
B. accessible
C. adequate
D. appropriate
E. available

206. A radiologist agrees to charge a reduced fee to all patients who are referred to him by a local hospital. Although now only collecting 60% of his usual fee, the radiologist hopes to make up the shortfall by an increased volume of referrals. This payment mechanism is most indicative of a(n)
A. DRG payment model
B. group model HMO
C. IPA model HMO
D. PPO
E. staff model HMO

Items 207 and 208
The following unpublished data concern the relationship between preventive treatment with chicken soup and the frequency with which colds develop. Assume that the data are from a randomized, double blind trial of chicken soup versus placebo (e.g., gazpacho) over the course of 1 year.

Outcome	Treatment		
	Chicken Soup	Placebo	Total
No Colds	21	11	32
1 or More Colds	36	35	71
Total	57	46	103

207. To make the data more comprehensible, you decide to use percentages for your analysis. Which of the following sets of percentages is a correct and meaningful representation of the data above and provides the most useful basis for comparing the relative number of colds between the two main groups of the research design?
A. 63% and 76%
B. 52% and 57%
C. 65% and 51%
D. 10% and 14%
E. 5% and 95%

208. Which of the following would be the most appropriate significance test for these data?
A. Analysis of variance
B. Chi-square analysis
C. Paired t-test
D. Pearson correlation coefficient
E. Student's t-test

Items 209–214
A test for the detection of politically incorrect tendencies is devised. It is applied to a population of 200 adults in the U.S. who insist they harbor no such tenden-

cies. Before the test was administered, however, 20 of the 200 are found to actually harbor politically incorrect tendencies based on a "gold standard" set by a panel of experts. The new test detects 12 cases of political incorrectness, of which 8 are positive by the findings of the gold standard and 4 are negative.

209. Based on these data, the sensitivity of the new test is
   A. 8%
   B. 12%
   C. 40%
   D. 80%
   E. 92%

210. The specificity of the new test is
   A. 1%
   B. 12%
   C. 40%
   D. 67%
   E. 98%

211. The positive predictive value of the new test in this population is
   A. 1%
   B. 12%
   C. 40%
   D. 67%
   E. 98%

212. The negative predictive value of the test is approximately
   A. 1%
   B. 12%
   C. 67%
   D. 94%
   E. 98%

Assume that the sensitivity and specifity of the new test remain unchanged but that the expert panel (i.e., the gold standard), after consulting with others, decides that instead of 20 cases of political incorrectness there are actually 150 cases.

213. The positive predictive value is now
   A. 1%
   B. 12%
   C. 67%
   D. 94%
   E. 98%

214. Given the revised prevalence of 150 cases of political incorrectness, the negative predictive value is approximately
   A. 1%
   B. 12%
   C. 35%

D. 67%
E. 98%

Items 215–218

You are the medical director of a company that manufactures plastic caps for the ends of shoelaces. You wish to screen the company's 1,000 workers for *capus plasticus pedo-reversilosus*, a condition that causes the worker to place caps for the laces of the right shoe on the laces of the left, and vice versa. The condition can be treated effectively with ice-water immersion and concomitant hypnosis, if it is detected early. From the literature on the subject, you determine that the sensitivity of the screening test is 94% and that the specificity is 90%. You estimate the prevalence of the condition to be 5%.

215. What percentage of positive screening test results will be false-positive results?
   A. 18%
   B. 23%
   C. 48%
   D. 67%
   E. 81%

216. What is the approximate positive predictive value of the screening test?
   A. 28%
   B. 33%
   C. 48%
   D. 67%
   E. 81%

217. How many cases of the disease will be missed if all 1,000 workers are screened?
   A. 3
   B. 16
   C. 18
   D. 47
   E. 95

218. Which of the following would be the most important information to know before deciding whether or not to implement the screening test?
   A. Cost of screening, follow-up, and treatment
   B. Disease incidence
   C. Genetic risk factors for the disease
   D. Prevalence of other diseases in the population
   E. Size of the population at risk

219. A screening test is applied to a population of 1,000 in which the prevalence of disease Y is 10%. The sensitivity of this test is 96%, and the specificity is 92%. The diagnostic work-up for each person found to have a true-positive result in the screen-

ing test would cost $50. A newer screening test has both a sensitivity and a specificity of 96% but costs $0.50 more per test than the older screening test. How much money would be saved or lost by choosing the newer test?

A. $500 lost
B. $500 saved
C. $1,300 lost
D. $1,300 saved
E. $1,800 saved

Items 220–223

A friend of yours thinks that she may be pregnant. She purchased a product to test for pregnancy and found the following data provided in the product brochure

True Status	Pregnancy Test Result		
	Positive	Negative	Total
Pregnant	253	24	277
Not Pregnant	8	93	101
Total	261	117	378

220. Turning to you for advice, your friend asks, "If the test says that I am pregnant, what is the probability that I really am pregnant?" Your answer is
    A. 67%
    B. 79%
    C. 85%
    D. 97%
    E. 100%

221. Your friend then asks, "If the test says that I am not pregnant, what is the probability that I really am not?" Your answer is
    A. 67%
    B. 79%
    C. 85%
    D. 97%
    E. 100%

222. Your friend is convinced that you actually know what you are talking about, so she asks, "If I really am pregnant, what is the probability that the test will discover that fact?" You confidently reply
    A. 57%
    B. 79%
    C. 88%
    D. 91%
    E. 97%

223. You caution your friend that the numbers that are provided in the product brochure might not apply to her because the
    A. false-positive error rate of the test is high
    B. prevalence in the population tested is unknown
    C. prevalence in the population tested may not match her prior probability
    D. test sensitivity is unknown
    E. test specificity is unknown

Items 224–226

A medical student is asked to assess the heart rate of a panel of 10 cardiac patients. The resting heart rates of these patients are 70, 68, 84, 76, 88, 66, 56, 60, 80, and 70 beats per minute.

224. Based on the measurements of this medical student, what is the modal heart rate for this set of data?
    A. 56
    B. 66
    C. 70
    D. 80
    E. 88

225. What is the median heart rate for this set of patients?
    A. 56
    B. 66
    C. 70
    D. 80
    E. 88

226. A trial of an antihypertensive agent is performed by administering the drug or a placebo, with a "washout period" in between, to each study subject. The treatments are administered in random order, and each subject serves as his or her own control. The trial is double blind. The appropriate significance test for the change in blood pressure with drug versus placebo is the
    A. ANOVA
    B. chi-square analysis
    C. paired t-test
    D. pearson correlation co-efficient
    E. regression analysis

Items 227 and 228

Two different groups of investigators perform separate clinical trials of the same therapy. The trials have approximately the same sample size. In the first trial, the investigators find more successes in the treatment group and report a p-value of 0.04. Based on these results, the investigators recommend the therapy. In the second trial, the investigators find more successes in the treatment group but report a p-value of 0.08. Based on these results, the investigators do not recommend the therapy.

227. As a clinician reviewing these studies, it is most important to keep in mind that
    A. data that are not statistically significant may still be clinically important
    B. if the data achieve statistical significance, the studies will be clinically important
    C. statistical significance has not been achieved because alpha has been set too high
    D. statistical significance has not been achieved because beta has been set too low
    E. if the data do not achieve statistical significance, the studies cannot be clinically important

228. An appropriate means for reconciling the conflicting recommendations would be to
    A. analyze the data using multi-variate methods
    B. conduct a case-control study
    C. obtain expert opinion
    D. perform intention-to-treat analysis
    E. pool the data

229. Both governmental programs and private insurance directives increasingly regulate relationships between physicians and patients. One such program, diagnosis-related groups (DRGs), is primarily used to
    A. assess the quality of subspecialty care in hospitals
    B. assign patients to appropriate hospital treatment
    C. provide support for patients following hospital discharge
    D. stipulate prospective payment to hospitals
    E. track epidemiological trends in the general population

230. A 15-year-old girl who was formerly a solid student with many friends and interests has become moody at home. She is irritable with her parents, and she constantly reacts to small frustrations with sobs and tears. She is often up late and then has trouble getting up in the morning. She seems to vary between lack of appetite and a tendency to eat lots of carbohydrates, especially chocolate. At times, she seems unusually animated around her friends, but she often refuses invitations to socialize, saying she is too tired, too fat, or that all her friends are "boring." Her grades have dropped over the past six months, and her mother overhears her say to a friend on the phone that she seriously wishes she were dead. This presentation is most consistent with

A. attention-deficit/hyperactivity disorder
B. body dysmorphic disorder
C. borderline personality disorder
D. major depression
E. normal puberty

231. A 4-year-old girl is admitted to the hospital to have her tonsils removed. Her father, who had been the sole financial support for the family, was injured over a year ago in a work-related accident and has been unable to work since that time. The father is depressed about his disability and worried about how he will pay for his daughter's surgery. Under these circumstances, the daughter's procedure is most likely to be covered by
    A. Blue Cross
    B. Medicaid
    C. Medicare
    D. the local physician-hospital organization
    E. the physician's resource fund

232. Dr. Hansen works in an office provided by the HMO that also refers all of her patients to her. Payments are made to the doctor, not based on how many patients she sees, but on how many patients consider her to be their physician. Recently, the HMO began to offer performance-based bonus payments that substantially increased Dr. Hansen's income. Dr. Hansen is most likely working for what type of medical delivery system?
    A. Group model HMO
    B. IPA model HMO
    C. Network model HMO
    D. PPO care delivery system
    E. Staff model HMO

233. The rising interest in preventive medicine in the U.S. is in part a byproduct of broader changes in the health care delivery system. Health care providers being compensated under which type of payment system are most likely to be supportive of a new program aimed at the primary prevention of disease?
    A. HMO
    B. Indemnity insurance
    C. Medicaid
    D. Medicare
    E. PPO

Items 234 and 235

A study was conducted to examine the relationship between exposure to stressful life events and the risk of myocardial infarction. 30,000 subjects were recruited and each completed the Holmes and Rahe Stressful Life Events Scale, indicating which events they had experienced in the past 6 months. The resulting scores were used to divide the subjects into three equal groups: Low events, Medium events, and High events. All subjects were then followed over the subsequent year and the incidence of coronary events recorded. Results of the study are presented in the table below in terms of relative risks accompanied by the appropriate confidence intervals.

Relative Risk of Myocardial Infarction by Experience of Stressful Life Events

Group	N	Relative Risk	Confidence Intervals
Low	10,000	NA	
Medium	10,000	1.3	(0.74 – 1.56)
High	10,000	1.5	(1.10 – 1.73)

234. This type of study is best referred to as a
    A. case-control study
    B. clinical trial
    C. cohort study
    D. cross-over study
    E. cross-sectional study

235. Based on the results presented, the conclusion most supported by this study would is
    A. any increase in experience of stressful life events increases the risk of MI
    B. because no *p*-values are given, no clear conclusions are possible
    C. no relationship can be demonstrated between stressful life events and subsequent MI
    D. only high levels of stressful life events are associated with increased risk for MI
    E. reducing exposure to stressful life events will reduce the number of MIs

236. Data examining the current trends for AIDS-related deaths in one of the midwestern states show a dramatic decrease in AIDS-related mortality, but little change in the incidence of AIDS. Given this information, we should also expect to find
    A. a decrease in AIDS-related medical care
    B. a decrease in survival rate following diagnosis
    C. an increase in AIDS prevalence
    D. an increase in HIV infections among family members
    E. an increase in the number of people practicing safe sex

237. The concept of homeostasis helps to explain long-term physiological reactions to stressful events and how these reactions mediate strategies for coping with stress. In this context, the notion of homeostasis refers to
    A. average physical reaction time to unexpected stimuli
    B. balancing interpersonal with psychological needs
    C. the ability of the body to metabolize food and convert it to energy
    D. the capacity to balance the sex drive and the aggression drive
    E. the tendency for the body to maintain a particular state

238. Certain types of behaviors, such as the Type A pattern, are associated with increased chances of disability and disease. The manifest behavior and subsequent liability for disease of a person with a Type A behavior pattern is believed to be most closely linked to the fact that these people
    A. are exposed to more stressful environments
    B. are socially withdrawn when faced with stressful events
    C. have greater ability to withstand stress
    D. have greater competence in problem solving
    E. have more psychological need for control over situations

239. For the past three months, a 36-year-old man reports suffering from heart palpitations, sweating palms, vague apprehension, difficulty concentrating, and difficulty falling asleep. He reports that nothing makes him feel better except taking long walks along the lakefront by himself or singing a special song to himself. His relationships with others have deteriorated during this time period and he fears being fired from his job. Based on this presentation, the most likely diagnosis for this man would be
    A. agoraphobia
    B. generalized anxiety disorder
    C. panic disorder
    D. obsessive-compulsive disorder
    E. social phobia

240. A student is apprehensive about the upcoming anatomy exam. On exam day, she is observed sitting in the exam room opening and closing both fists while breathing deeply. She is probably trying to control her anxiety by means of
    A. biofeedback
    B. meditation
    C. progressive relaxation
    D. self-hypnosis
    E. the stress response

241. On a cold day in January, a 40-year-old, well nourished man arrives at the emergency room wearing running shorts, a tank top, and new, very expensive running shoes. He was picked up running along a controlled access highway. He says he has started training for a marathon and needed a long unbroken course to run on. His demeanor is haughty, alternating between amused condescension and irritable impatience. His speech is rapid and he is difficult to interrupt. As the examiner challenges his story, the details keep shifting. He is convinced he will win the marathon in the spring, even though this is his first training run. Since recently losing his job, he feels he will have more than adequate time to pursue his athletic goals. He is oriented to person, place and time. He can recall 3 of 3 objects at 0 and 5 minutes. He does serial sevens rapidly to 44 with three unnoticed errors. Digit span is 6 forward and 3 in reverse. He interprets the proverb, "Do not judge a man until you have walked a mile in his shoes" as meaning, "The way to win a race is to be sure you know what the other guy has on his feet." He responds to the question, "What would you do if you found a stamped letter lying in the street?" by saying, "I'd think it was my lucky day!" This description is most consistent with
   A. delusional disorder
   B. histrionic personality disorder
   C. mania
   D. masked depression
   E. narcissistic personality disorder

242. Thinking can be usefully separated into a number of different processes, each appropriate to different types of problems and situations. The situation in which a physician, while examining a set of patients, categorizes a number of symptoms as sharing some features in common, is best regarded as an example of
   A. concept formation
   B. convergent thinking
   C. hypothesis testing
   D. insightful thinking
   E. stimulus discrimination

243. A person's experience of reality is not simply absorbed from the environment, but constructed by means of mental representations. Language plays a key role in this process. Language shapes the individual's perception of reality by
   A. assigning meaning to sounds
   B. defining how experiences are described and what is remembered
   C. limiting what the individual senses
   D. modifying the meaning of words through vocal intonation

   E. restricting perception to only what can be put into words

244. Different people see the world differently. Even people with the exact same experiences may recall and respond to them differently. These individual differences in the manner in which experiences are perceived, processed, and assigned meaning are called
   A. cognitive styles
   B. defense mechanisms
   C. delusional thoughts
   D. schemas
   E. sensations

245. Defense mechanisms can be thought of as cognitive processes, as well as affective controls. The re-conceptualization of an event or memory in sufficiently abstract terms in order to distance it meaningfully and emotionally describes the defense mechanism of
   A. denial
   B. intellectualization
   C. projection
   D. repression
   E. sublimation

246. Intelligence is one of the variables most predictive of human development and behavior. Over the past several years, there has been considerable debate about what intelligence is and how it functions. Based on a growing body of work, we can now say with confidence that
   A. intelligence is determined by heredity and is uninfluenced by experience
   B. intelligence is generally defined in terms of verbal ability and problem-solving skills
   C. measures of intelligence are usually based on divergent thinking
   D. rapid processing of information is a universal characteristic of high intelligence
   E. there are significant differences in intelligence between races

247. Choose the answer that ranks the signs of thought disorder from least to most severe.
   A. Cirumstantiality, loose associations, flight of ideas, tangentiality
   B. Circumstantiality, tangentiality, flight of ideas, loose associations
   C. Flight of ideas, circumstantiality, loose associations, tangentiality
   D. Loose associations, tangentiality, circumstantiality, flight of ideas
   E. Tangentiality, loose associations, cirumstantiality, flight of ideas

248. After hearing the description of a patient's illness, the physician repeats the essential symptoms to him and reflects back the patient's reaction to those symptoms. The physician receives confirmation from her patient that she, the doctor, understands the patient's description of his illness. In this example, the doctor has demonstrated
    A. accurate empathy
    B. clinical judgment
    C. concept formation
    D. divergent thinking
    E. paralinguistic communication

249. A woman decides she will give herself permission to buy a new dress after she loses 10 pounds. This procedure, in which the person plans rewarding consequences for attaining set goals, is best referred to as the technique of
    A. cognitive rehearsal
    B. cognitive restructuring
    C. problem solving
    D. self-control contracting
    E. skills training

250. A student is afraid that he will fail an upcoming examination. "I don't know what to do," he says, "I just keep telling myself that I'm so stupid and that there's nothing I can do." The student is encouraged to remind himself how much he studies and to remember that, "Hard work leads to good results." This technique, in which the student is encouraged to replace maladaptive cognitions with adaptive cognitions, is generally referred to as
    A. cognitive rehearsal
    B. cognitive restructuring
    C. problem solving
    D. self-control contracting
    E. skills training

251. A basketball player is trained to repeatedly visualize himself attempting and making a free throw in a game, with the fans yelling and the opposing players trying to distract him. The technique the athlete is using to visualize behaviors is an example of
    A. cognitive rehearsal
    B. cognitive restructuring
    C. problem solving
    D. self-control contracting
    E. skills training

252. Without the hippocampus, learning that is based on retention of long-term memories is impossible. What is the functional process by which the hippocampus and its associated structures of the limbic system facilitate this type of learning?

A. They act as a trainer and guide the learning of motor skills in the brainstem
B. They connect the various cortical storage sites to form combined memories
C. They directly stimulate the release of neurotransmitter hormones from the adrenal gland
D. They forward all incoming sensory information to the neocortex for permanent storage
E. They promote synaptic depolarization to facilitate neuronal transmission

253. Major neural pathways of the hippocampus use an excitatory amino acid called glutamate as their neurotransmitter. Upon neuronal excitation, glutamate binds with two types of protein receptors, NMDA and non-NMDA, on the cell membrane of the post-synaptic neuron. How do NMDA and non-NMDA activation contribute to learning?
    A. Because stimuli activating NMDA receptors are weaker than those activating non-NMDA receptors, the NMDA response becomes conditioned to non-NMDA stimuli
    B. Combined NMDA and non-NMDA activation blocks depolarization of the synapse
    C. Combined NMDA and non-NMDA activation releases magnesium in the cell body, facilitating transmission at the synapse
    D. Convergence of NMDA and non-NMDA receptor activation slows, prolongs, and increases the efficiency of the synapse, facilitating complex sensory learning
    E. Glutamate activation neutralizes the antagonistic actions of NMDA and non-NMDA, permitting the neuron to fire

254. A white rat is placed in a cage that contains a lever and a shute through which food can be dispensed. The rat presses the lever and receives a food pellet. After receiving the food, the rat again presses the lever. This type of learning is most influenced by
    A. emotionally intense responses
    B. genetically programmed reflexes
    C. simultaneously occurring stimuli
    D. specific stimulus cues at critical periods
    E. the consequences of behavior

255. Reinforcement is the key event in operant conditioning. The effect of reinforcement is well known, but less is known about what makes something a reinforcer. For example, the Premack Principle tells us that
    A. a high frequency behavior or reward can be used as a reinforcer for a low frequency target behavior
    B. a low frequency behavior can be used to punish an undesired high frequency behavior

C. a low frequency behavior, because of its higher value, can be used to reward a desired target behavior.

D. a moderate frequency behavior will have a more optimal effect than either a high or low frequency behavior.

E. if an individual seeks out and engages in an activity, it is because it is desirable and, therefore, a reinforcer.

256. When a behavior, symptom, or learned association ceases to be reinforced, it tends to weaken or decrease in frequency. This phenomenon is best described as

A. free operant behavior
B. negative reinforcement
C. positive reinforcement
D. response extinction
E. stimulus generalization

257. A 2-year-old girl is afraid of cats. To change this, she is put in a room with her favorite music playing while a friendly cat is gradually brought towards her. Finally, she is encouraged to pet the cat. This example is an illustration of which of the following principles of learning?

A. Aversive conditioning
B. Critical period learning
C. Negative reinforcement
D. Response extinction
E. The Premack Principle

258. A man learns to control his blood pressure by means of trial-and-error practice while watching a gauge that gives him feedback about the fluctuations in his blood pressure. The effectiveness of this technique is based on the operant principle that

A. a high frequency reinforcer will reward a low frequency target behavior
B. nehavior is controlled by selectively manipulating the consequences
C. consequences are controlled by controlling the stimuli
D. information about the consequences of behavior is reinforcing
E. motor performance is more easily reinforced than other forms of responses

259. There are several distinct forms of learning. Which of the following answers best describes the developmental order of forms of learning from most genetically influenced to most environmentally influenced?

A. Classical, operant, imprinting, reflex, one-trial, social
B. Classical, reflex, imprinting, one-trial, social, operant

C. Imprinting, reflex, one-trial, social, classical, operant
D. Reflex, imprinting, one-trial, classical, operant, social
E. Social, operant, classical, one-trial, imprinting, reflex

260. Social learning theory has expanded our understanding of how people learn and change their behavior beyond simple, animal-based models. The operation of social learning is most easy to recognize because it is

A. dependent on the reinforcement value of relationships
B. distinct from classical and operant learning
C. the least dependent on evaluative feedback
D. the least influenced by environmental conditions
E. unrelated to the individual's survival

261. Because of its ability to mount a prolonged response to sustained and intense stressors, which of the following systems has the potential to have the most detrimental effects on the body under chronic stress conditions?

A. Autonomic nervous
B. Endocrine
C. Immune
D. Limbic
E. Musculoskeletal

262. A physiologic state of arousal is induced. The emotional label (e.g., grief, anger, joy) that is given to this felt state of arousal is most likely to be dependent on

A. gender differences within the culture
B. sociocultural display rules
C. the context in which arousal occurs
D. the heredity of the individual
E. the intensity and quality of the arousal

263. You are observing the reactions of a husband and wife as they receive bad news regarding the health of their newborn child. Based on the type of gender differences in emotional reaction that have been documented cross-culturally, you would expect that, compared to a woman, a man will be more likely to

A. be less emotional
B. conceal his emotions
C. show happiness in public
D. show more anger when challenged
E. use different language to describe emotion

264. Theories improve our understanding of how the world works by providing models for the mechanisms of behavior. Which of the following theo-

ries of motivation is most closely associated with instinctual theory?

A. Arousal theory
B. Cognitive theory
C. Drive theory
D. Expectancy theory
E. Sociocultural theory

265. A student is preparing to take a 3-hour multiple-choice exam. This will be a timed test. To do his best under this time pressure, the student should remember that

A. arousal is unrelated to performance
B. arousal levels that vary as the task proceeds are associated with optimal performance
C. high levels of arousal are best for optimal performance
D. low levels of arousal are best for optimal performance
E. moderate levels of arousal are best for optimal performance

266. A 27-year-old woman reports that she often feels the urge to smoke after having sex or after eating. Which theory of motivation best helps to explain why she feels this impulse?

A. Arousal
B. Drive
C. Expectancy
D. Humanistic
E. Sociocultural

267. Many of the conflicts we feel in our day-to-day lives are explainable within the framework offered by behavioral psychology. For example, food that you find particularly tasty but that also may cause undesirable weight gain or cavities is an example of which type of conflict?

A. Approach-approach
B. Approach-avoidance
C. Avoidance-approach
D. Avoidance-avoidance
E. Oedipal

268. Patient adherence with medical prescriptions is influenced by a variety of factors, including the patient's motivation. The expectancy theory of motivation would most likely attribute a patient's adherence to medical treatment regimes to the patient's

A. belief system
B. cultural system
C. family history
D. homeostasis level
E. reinforcement experience

269. The notion that removing or avoiding an aversive stimulus can lead to behavioral change is most helpful in explaining

A. avoidance-avoidance conflict
B. cognitive dissonance
C. intrinsic motivation
D. secondary reinforcement
E. the opponent-process hypothesis

270. After he is discharged, Mr. G. reports that one of the nurses on the in-patient unit attempted to poison him. Although an investigation shows this allegation to be groundless, Mr. G. continues to insist that it is true. An examination of Mr. G. is most likely to find that he is experiencing

A. a delusional episode
B. an hallucination
C. an illusion
D. confabulation
E. sensory distortion

271. During the first month after the birth of his son, Harry awoke every night when the child cried. However, after the first month he no longer awoke, although his wife continued to do so. This change in behavior by Harry is most likely explained by the principle of

A. accumulated fatigue
B. adjustment reaction
C. habituation
D. just noticeable difference
E. threshold detection

272. A 54-year-old woman complains of pain in her lower back. During the subsequent history taking and physical examination, what variable will best tell the physician whether the patient's pain is acute or chronic?

A. Cause
B. Duration
C. Family history
D. Intensity
E. Site

273. Changes in disease patterns over time is one source of information about their contributing causes. Over the past 10 years, demographic and epidemiological data regarding suicide worldwide have shown that suicide rates are

A. generally constant over time
B. higher for Hispanics who immigrated to the U.S. than those in their country of origin
C. lower for people in their teens and early twenties
D. lowest among white men in the U.S.
E. lowest in industrialized nations

274. The overall suicide rate, per 100,000 general population in the U.S. in 1998, including all age, gender and ethic groups, was
    A. 0.09
    B. 4.0
    C. 12
    D. 20
    E. 33

275. A 22-year-old man with schizophrenia is hearing voices telling him to kill himself. In the emergency room, a urine toxicology screen is positive for cocaine and you smell ethanol on his breath. Appropriate management would include
    A. confrontation regarding the severity of his substance abuse problem
    B. discharge to home, once sober, with follow-up in 1 week
    C. psychiatric hospitalization with one-to-one monitoring
    D. referral to Alcoholics Anonymous or Narcotics Anonymous
    E. referral to out-patient psychotherapy

276. As part of answering questions on a mental status examination, a patient with schizophrenia describes the voices he hears as coming from the plumbing. Commonly called lack of insight, this answer more precisely illustrates
    A. deficient short-term memory
    B. dissociation
    C. disturbed source identification
    D. impaired concentration
    E. poor judgment

277. Rates of completed or successful suicides are substantially higher for the elderly than for the rest of the population. Clinical experience suggests that the elderly are more likely to complete suicide because they are
    A. less likely to communicate their intentions
    B. more experienced because they are older
    C. more likely to become clinically depressed
    D. more likely to choose overdose as the means
    E. more likely to live in poverty

278. A 70-year-old woman has been diagnosed with Alzheimer's dementia. Because she had to leave school when she was 15 to support her family, she never graduated from high school. She has made her living for more than 50 years by cleaning office buildings. When questioned, she has little insight about her memory deficits. During the past year, she has been well cared for by her daughter while enrolled in a protocol for a new experimental treatment. Unfortunately, the results of the trial have been poor. Now her daughter is concerned that her mother might be suicidal. Which feature of this patient's history would be most likely to place her at risk for committing suicide?
    A. A family member is a caregiver
    B. Enrollment in an experimental drug protocol with poor results
    C. Lower socioeconomic status
    D. Minimal schooling
    E. No insight about the memory deficits

279. During combat, a young soldier sees a live grenade on the ground next to his friend. He immediately covers it with his body and is killed in the explosion. According to Durkheim's theory of suicide, which type of suicide does this example illustrate?
    A. Altruistic
    B. Anomic
    C. Egoistic
    D. Fatalistic
    E. Heroic

280. A 55-year-old man has just committed suicide. A complete post-mortem examination is most likely to show
    A. atrophy of the adrenal glands
    B. decreased corticotrophin-releasing hormone
    C. higher than normal concentrations of serotonin in the raphe nuclei
    D. hyposecretion of ACTH by the pituitary
    E. low levels of 5-hydroindolacetic acid in cerebrospinal fluid

281. A chiropractor has applied to the local hospital for hospital privileges. Although the chiropractor is a long-time practitioner who has good referral relationships with several area physicians, there is considerable antagonism toward his application from within the hospital's Board of Directors as well as the general physician staff. A number of physicians are concerned that allowing a non-physician privileges will lead to other requests from "fringe" practitioners. At the same time, the Chief of Staff is aware of the successful 1990 antitrust suit brought against the AMA by three chiropractors, and that the AMA's Code of Ethics no longer prohibits physicians from consulting with chiropractors or teaching in schools of chiropractic. The Chief's dilemma is best addressed within which of the following theoretical perspectives?
    A. Conflict theory – adaptation
    B. Formal – implicit theory
    C. Goal attainment – structural functional analysis
    D. Symbolic interaction – latent pattern maintenance
    E. Utilitarianism – integration

282. In an effort to control costs, a hospital reduces the nursing staff by 20%. The decision about whom to terminate is based on seniority and degree status within the nursing hierarchy. Initially, the hospital enjoyed considerable savings. However, over the next several months, the number of hospital admissions decreased by almost 30%. A subsequent analysis found that the bulk of nurses terminated came from the ranks of "admitting nurses" who were responsible for timely and efficient processing of new patients. As a result, there was an unintended reduction in patient flow that was compounded by less patient satisfaction. Because patients chose to go elsewhere for care, the hospital found itself in worse financial condition than before the decision to reduce the number of nurses. The notion of "unintended consequences" and the observation that changes in one part of the system will have consequences for other parts of the system is best captured within which of the following theoretical perspectives?
    A. Conflict theory – adaptation
    B. Formal – implicit theory
    C. Goal attainment – structural functional analysis
    D. Symbolic interaction – latent pattern maintenance
    E. Utilitarianism – integration

283. While leading a tour for hospital executives from Third World countries, the tour guide is asked to explain why all of the patient rooms are either semi-private (two beds) or private. The guide gives a detailed explanation of sepsis, hospital infection rates, and clinical iatrogenesis, and, as an afterthought, mentions "patient preference" and the fact that insurance companies reimburse for both types of beds. No mention is made of the long-standing knowledge among the nursing staff that placing patients in private and semi-private rooms sharply reduces the number of patient requests for nursing assistance. Patient preference and reimbursement policies are examples of
    A. approximate causes
    B. implicit theory
    C. latent functions
    D. manifest functions
    E. secondary explanations

284. A patient admitted into the neurological ICU with a complete C5 transection is intubated, placed on a ventilator, and connected to electronic monitors. Every few hours, the staff rolls the patient over to prevent bedsores. However, nursing staff become concerned when they observe that the patient has not slept over the ensuing 2 days and seems to be increasingly agitated and distressed. Unable to communicate with the patient because of the intubation, the staff calls for a consultant who can read lips. The consultant discovers that the patient was forcing himself to stay wake because he thought the reason the nurses were turning him was: "If I fall asleep, I will die." It never occurred to the nursing staff that their actions might be so interpreted, and they quickly reassured the patient that this was not the case. The patient, now so informed, gratefully falls asleep. The difference in meanings held by the patient and nursing staff is best addressed within which of the following theoretical perspectives?
    A. Conflict theory – adaptation
    B. Formal – implicit theory
    C. Goal attainment – structural functional analysis
    D. Symbolic interaction – latent pattern maintenance
    E. Utilitarianism – integration

285. A manufacturing company offers its 10,000 employees several types of insurance coverage. Each has somewhat different benefits with respect to levels of co-pay, access to specialists, prescription drug coverage, and a variety of other dimensions. The rationale is that employees will assess their own needs, maximize their benefits, and choose the desired plan accordingly. Which one of the following theoretical perspectives best captures this model of employee decision making held by the company?
    A. Conflict theory – adaptation
    B. Formal – implicit theory
    C. Goal attainment – structural functional analysis
    D. Symbolic interaction – latent pattern maintenance
    E. Utilitarianism – integration

286. A 27-year-old woman comes to see her physician for a regular check-up. Examination reveals nothing out of the ordinary except for a general nervousness on the part of the patient. Finally, she reports that she is "beginning to feel old", and asks the physician what she should expect at her age. The physician should tell her that
    A. brain cell development peaks by 30 years of age
    B. her brain cells continue to grow in complexity until the late 40s
    C. she has passed the time of peak intellectual achievement
    D. she should cut back on athletic activity to avoid injury
    E. the human body is in its peak physical condition from 20 to 30 of age

287. On the Mini-Mental Status Examination, asking a person to name objects, repeat a sentence, and follow a verbal command all test for different types of
   A. agnosia
   B. amnesia
   C. aphasia
   D. apraxia
   E. executive function

288. Different things motivate people. For some people, the notion of "achievement need" helps to explain the life choices that they make in their adult years. Achievement need can be best understood as
   A. a desire to enhance cognitive development
   B. an outgrowth of Type A behavior patterns
   C. similar to innate cognitive ability
   D. the core motive fostering the desire to have children
   E. the desire for control over others

289. As people get older, their capacities change. Over the years, as a patient moves from adolescence to young adulthood, this transition will most likely be characterized by
   A. a decline in task oriented behavior
   B. decreased capacity to consider the consequences of impulsive action
   C. decreased narcissistic tendencies and increased capacity for interpersonal relationships
   D. increased difficulty with complex decision making
   E. increased focus on maintaining an independent self-identity

290. Although during young adulthood many people marry, a number of people remain single at age 30. Studies examining the lives of these unmarried singles have shown that
   A. approximately 20% of young adults choose long-term singlehood
   B. more than half of non-married individuals are homosexual
   C. most singlehood relationships survive for more than 5 years
   D. singlehood has disadvantages for career opportunities
   E. the proportions of sexually active single men and women are nearly equal

291. A well-educated, 75-year-old woman is brought by her family because of change in mental status. She has been treated in the past for depression, but has not been on medication for five years. She lives in an assisted living facility, where staff have noticed that she has rarely come to meals over the past three months. She seems sluggish and apathetic. On questioning, she describes feeling worthless and as though life has become meaningless. She formerly had many friends and enjoyed going on outings organized by the facility. When asked to answer questions on the mental status exam, she seems hesitant and self doubting, saying, "That's too hard," or "I am sure I won't be able to do that." She has to be prodded to finish tasks such as serial subtraction. Despite these findings, her final score is 28, well within the normal range for her age. This presentation suggests
   A. delirium
   B. dementia syndrome of depression
   C. generalized anxiety disorder
   D. senile dementia of the Alzheimer's type
   E. subcortical dementia

292. After several years of general clinical practice, you notice that, although individual variation exits, relationships of young adults with their parents share a number of common features. The most common relationship pattern you are likely to notice is that
   A. establishing a collegial relationship with parents typically begins during young adulthood
   B. most young adults resist financial help from their parents because they want to establish independence quickly
   C. most young adults seek to pattern their "sense of self" after that of their parents
   D. the process of raising questions about family or origin rarely begins before the age of 30
   E. young adults maintain relationships with parents similar to those set in place during childhood

293. You have been asked by a local community agency to address a group of young adults about common developmental issues for people their age. As you prepare your remarks, you should remember that, as a group, the young adults you are addressing most likely
   A. are striving to develop stable intergenerational relationships by seeking independence
   B. are working at being part of the adult culture
   C. generally disregard advice from older persons
   D. have dreams and aspirations that are mostly developed from the wishes of the family of origin
   E. occupy the majority of their time pursuing leisure activities and avoiding commitments

294. For most young adults, what event is most likely to be accompanied by a self-awareness of a transition into full-fledged adulthood?

A. Becoming a parent
B. Death of a parent
C. Getting married
D. Graduation from college
E. Starting a first job

295. Physical growth during puberty can be dramatic. Which of the following combinations of changes in height and weight is most commonly seen?

	Height	Weight
A.	+50%	+50%
B.	+25%	+50%
C.	+25%	+25%
D.	+10%	+25%
E.	+10%	+10%

296. During early adolescence, female children are generally taller than same-age male children. Among the following, which reason most likely accounts for this difference?
    A. Boys expend more energy in physical activity and so require more time to grow.
    B. Boys receive more familial attention than girls do.
    C. Boys show compensating advances in mental capacity compared to girls this age.
    D. Earlier height gain in girls reflects the body's adaptation to reproductive functioning.
    E. Girls are better nourished at the onset of puberty.

297. In the U.S. over the past century, the onset of puberty has been occurring earlier. Some children enter puberty as early as age 8 to 10. Current thinking suggests that the primary reason for this trend is an outgrowth of
    A. changes in the average age at first marriage
    B. decreases in chronic diseases of childhood
    C. global warming
    D. improved health and nutrition
    E. social needs for earlier reproductive maturity and childbearing

298. Along with the gonads, the two other organ systems primarily involved in regulating puberty for adolescents are the
    A. hypothalamus and the adrenal gland
    B. hypothalamus and the pituitary gland
    C. hypothalamus and the thyroid gland
    D. pituitary gland and the adrenal gland
    E. pituitary gland and the thyroid gland

299. An 11-year-old boy with diabetes is listening to his physician's explanation about appropriate care. The physician makes every effort to keep her explanation as simple as possible. The most important reason why children this age need sim-

ple explanations during a health care visit is that they
    A. are at the stage of concrete operations
    B. are highly distractible and do not listen well
    C. do not trust authority figures, including physicians
    D. have not achieved a high enough level of education
    E. have not attained their full level of intelligence

300. Adolescence is a period of development about which many myths and much misinformation exists. A set of middle-aged parents asks what they should expect regarding their son as he moves through adolescence. You should tell them that research examining the actual events that accompany this period strongly suggests that, for most adolescents,
    A. boys adjust to pubertal change more easily than girls
    B. development is necessarily filled with turmoil
    C. developmental struggles are relatively minor
    D. developmental struggles are rare to non-existent
    E. struggling with their transition to adulthood is psychologically traumatic

301. A 15-year-old girl comes to see her family physician for a checkup. At the end of her examination, she asks the doctor, with some embarrassment, if he would give her some advice on a problem that she is having. In counseling her, the physician should remember that this developmental period is typically characterized by
    A. a strong focus on one-on-one intimate relationships
    B. adjusting to the changes of puberty
    C. desires to stand out among one's peers
    D. goal formation related to career
    E. intense concern about social and peer relationships

302. The three leading causes of death for adolescents in the U.S. during the 1990s were
    A. accidents, suicide, and drug overdoses
    B accidents, suicide, and homicide
    C. cancer, accidents, and suicide
    D. cancer, congenital heart disease, and accidents
    E. suicide, accidents, and drug overdoses

303. S.G. is a 16-year-old who recently announced to her friends and family that she is gay. She was raised in a single-parent family and has a history of conflicts with her mother and her peers. During questioning, she reports that her mother keeps a

handgun in the house "for protection." Given this history, the strongest risk factor for suicide for S.G. would be

A. being brought up by a single parent
B. being female
C. being lesbian
D. handgun in the household
E. family and peer relationship problems

304. The timing of puberty has a number of identifiable social, psychological, and behavioral consequences for adolescent boys. A survey of adolescents in the U.S. has found that one of the more common behavioral correlates of late puberty in boys is

A. conduct disorders and delinquency
B. immature behavior and lower self-esteem
C. improved academic competitiveness
D. improved athletic competitiveness
E. improved musical abilities

305. The notion of a teenage subculture is a relatively new phenomenon. Historically, the transition between childhood and adulthood was seen as occurring directly, without this intermediate stage. The modern creation of a subculture is most likely due to

A. increased use of computer technology
B. increased use of illegal drugs
C. media influences such as MTV
D. pressure from adults to move into adult roles too quickly
E. society's moratorium on growing up

306. Different behavior patterns characterize different developmental stages. Children in Piaget's preoperational stage of development are most likely to

A. be able to put together simple picture puzzles
B. be able to use symbols to represent reality
C. explore their environment by physical manipulation of objects
D. have sophisticated mental processes
E. need the presence of an event to think about it

307. Piaget used a number of simple tasks to demonstrate children's capacities at different stages of development. The so-called "three mountain" experiment is used to demonstrate the concept of

A. categorical reasoning
B. centering
C. egocentrism
D. object constancy
E. precausal reasoning

308. A child's natural tendency to see life in non-living objects and assign them human feelings and motive is usually called

A. animism

B. artificialism
C. autism
D. magical thinking
E. symbolization

309. Children develop both language and conceptual abilities before they enter school. For example, a 6-year-old child already has a vocabulary of about how many words?

A. 1,000
B. 5,000
C. 10,000
D. 25,000
E. 50,000

310. According to Erikson's theory of social development, the developmental choice faced by a 5-year-old boy is most likely that of choosing between

A. autonomy versus shame
B. identity versus role diffusion
C. industry versus inferiority
D. initiative versus guilt
E. trust versus mistrust

311. Two soldiers are hospitalized after a motor vehicle accident in which a third soldier was killed. Both are being treated for compound fractures of one leg and the opposite arm. The soldier who was driving the vehicle and feels responsible for the accident asks for pain medicine more often and wants higher doses than the soldier who was the passenger. This situation illustrates that the degree of pain people experience from particular conditions is strongly influenced by the

A. availability of narcotics
B. location and extent of tissue damage
C. meaning of the pain
D. prior level of fitness
E. time of day

312. Much of our sense of self is socially determined. The stable conceptualization of being either a male or a female despite superficial features such as dress or mannerism is most often referred to as

A. gender identity
B. parental identification
C. sex role schema
D. sex role stereotype
E. sexual orientation

313. Medicine and health care providers contribute to both increased longevity and better quality of life. Over the past century, life expectancy in the U.S. has risen steadily. This increase in life expectancy at birth is largely due to

A. better nutrition with an emphasis on lower fat diets

B. higher levels of income and better health insurance
C. improved health and health care in older adults
D. reduced smoking among adults
E. reductions in infant mortality rates

314. Treatment of the elderly requires modification of general "rules of thumb" for therapeutic interventions. This is especially true when arriving at the correct dosing for medications. Lower medication doses are generally required for a comparable therapeutic effect in the elderly because of
A. age-related cardiovascular disease
B. drug interactions due to polypharmacy
C. lower tolerance of side effects
D. poorer absorption of oral medications
E. slower rate of metabolism

315. A 74-year-old woman presents with memory deficits and periodic loss of orientation to person, place, and time. Her family reports that deficits have appeared gradually over the past several years. When approached by her son, she fails to recognize him and asks for an introduction. She is able to converse about events from the distant past, but can not recall how or why she was brought to see the physician. Without any further information being given, the physician should assume that these symptoms are most likely the consequence of
A. Alzheimer's disease
B. cerebral brain tumor
C. cerebrovascular accident
D. iatrogentic effect of medication
E. normal senile changes

316. A physician suspects that a newly referred 85-year-old woman patient may be in the early stages of dementia. The most direct way for the physician to identify dementia in its early stages is to
A. administer a mini-mental status examination
B. administer the Wechsler Adult Intelligence Scale (WAIS)
C. ask a family member to describe the patient's recent behavior
D. do a CAT scan
E. observe the patient's behavior as she interacts with peers over a 2-day period

317. Assessment of Activities of Daily Living (ADL) in an elderly patient can be helpful in determining level of medical assistance needed. Included among the ADLs to be assessed are
A. ambulating, climbing stairs, and sitting
B. driving, using the phone, and watching TV
C. eating, bathing, and going to the toilet

D. shopping, cooking, and dressing
E. using the phone, driving, and cooking

318. A 64-year-old woman, who has been doing some reading about aging, comes to see her physician. Having just read Erikson and his stages of development, she decides that she is in the stage of *ego integrity vs. despair*. She asks the physician what this means. According to Erikson, the challenge of this stage of life is
A. adjusting to impending death and dying
B. balancing life's accomplishments and failures
C. coping with depression and loss
D. growing older with dignity
E. reviewing one's family life

319. Human development passes through a number of different stages across the lifespan. "Successful" development is most closely linked to
A. avoiding personal loss
B. economic status
C. educational attainment
D. maintaining good physical health
E. successful negotiation of transitions

320. Puberty is marked by a number of predictable physical and social changes. The hormonal changes that are most closely linked to puberty are
A. marked by estrogen increases in girls only
B. occuring at about the same age for 90% of children
C. seen as early as age 7 with increases in adrenal steroids
D. seldom observed during the middle childhood years
E. unrelated to increased subcutaneous fat during middle childhood

321. The social and psychological changes that characterize middle childhood are made possible by accompanying physical changes. Among these changes is a pattern of neurological development characterized by a significant increase in the
A. circumference of the head
B. complexity of synaptic connections
C. mechanism of neuronal processing
D. number of neurons
E. number of neurotransmitters

322. Although behavioral changes are the dominant means of tracking development in middle childhood, a number of physiological correlates have also been identified. During the middle childhood years, changes in EEG activity are most often characterized by
A. a decrease in function-specific activity

B. a lack of stabilization between the hemi-
spheres
C. a transition to primary delta activity
D. increases in alpha wave activity
E. the emergence of sleep-wake differences

323. An 8-year-old boy has recently been diagnosed
with Attention Deficit Hyperactivity Disorder
(ADHD). During an examination of the child, the
physician should check for what other behavioral
traits that are often associated with ADHD?
A. Deficits in executive functions
B. Enhanced ability in visual-spatial tracking
C. Increased ability to process verbal directions
D. Increased susceptibility to childhood infec-
tious diseases
E. Poor relationships with peers

324. Among the signs that a child has reached middle
childhood (ages 6 to 12) are changes in the child's
cognitive capacities. This cognitive development
allows the child to
A. consider how another person will feel in the
future
B. evaluate other people in terms of psychological attributes
C. form a self-generated philosophy of life
D. manipulate abstract concepts
E. predict behavior across differing social situations

325. A 10-year-old boy insists that the rules be followed
when playing his favorite board game and lectures
all participants about the importance of having
rules. This insistence that all participants follow
the rules is most likely because he wants to
A. avoid embarrassment
B. avoid punishment
C. be a replacement for his parents
D. be seen as good
E. give direction to others

326. You have been asked to arrange for play activities
for a group of 8-year-old children. When making
these arrangements, you should remember that
children at this age will prefer
A. anyone of the same age who likes the same
activities
B. playing in mixed-gender groups
C. simple fantasy games
D. structured games and sports
E. watching, rather than participating in sports

327. A 10-year-old boy was recently diagnosed with
insulin-dependent diabetes mellitus. When counseling the child and his parents, the physician must
remember that the child should be

A. encouraged to continue with school activities
such as team sports and physical education
B. encouraged to explain to teachers and peers
why his activities will be limited
C. exempted from family chores to attend to
managing his illness
D. expected to be absent from school periodically as a consequence of his illness
E. expected to have difficulty relating to peers as
he gets older

328. Physical changes during the middle years of adulthood set the stage for the later developmental
stage of old age. Experience with adults in this age
group has shown that
A. few people recognize changes in physical
health before the age of 50
B. physical changes are most closely tied to
chronological age and maturation
C. physical changes can be predicted from social
and interpersonal factors
D. the age at which facial wrinkles occur and hair
turns gray is fairly constant
E. the signs of aging appear in women earlier
than they do in men

329. A couple in their late 40s asks their physician what
changes they should expect with respect to their
sexual functioning as they age. Based on recent
research examining changes in sexual functioning for men and women, the physician should tell
them that
A. compared with women of color, Caucasian
women begin menopause early
B. over age 60, sexual activity is inversely related to how many children they have
C. the female menstrual cycle begins to change
during the 30s and 40s
D. The level of sexual desire for men is correlated with the level of sperm production
E. there is a "male climacteric" that corresponds
to the female "menopause"

330. A 28-year-old man has not gone to a social or
athletic event in three years. In the past, he had
friends and enjoyed sports. He works from home
in computer data entry. He is preoccupied with the
assymmetry of his eyebrows and, over time, he
has plucked out both eyebrows completely, trying
to equalize them. He now consults a dermatologist
about a hair transplant to repair the damage. This
presentation is consistent with
A. body dysmorphic disorder
B. delusional disorder
C. factitious disorder
D. malingering
E. social phobia

331. According to a report published by the University of Chicago on sexual behavior in the U.S.,
    A. marital status is an important predictor of sexual activity among older men, but not women
    B. sexual activity for both genders is most frequent in the 20s and declines with age
    C. sexual activity over a lifetime is positively correlated with socioeconomic status
    D. there is little interest in or desire for sexual activity after the age of 60
    E. women do not reach their sexual peak until their mid-50s

332. Although divorce patterns have fluctuated over the past 30 years, a number of age-related trends have been relatively stable. An examination of these age-related trends shows that
    A. a couple marrying before age 21 has a lower risk of divorce than a couple marrying after 30
    B. adults who divorce after age 50 are unlikely to remarry
    C. adults who remarry later in life have less stable marriages than those who remarry as young adults
    D. divorce is most common between the ages of 30 and 45
    E. less than 10% of divorced adults remarry within 5 years after divorce

333. Although much of traditional research on human development has focused on children, increasing attention has been paid in recent years to patterns of development across the life cycle, including the so-called "middle-aged." Research into patterns of relationships between middle-aged persons and their older parents have shown that
    A. although adult children ask their parents for financial support, they rarely ask for advice
    B. feelings of dependency on parents have been resolved prior to this age
    C. middle age is usually marked by increasing psychological distance from parents
    D. most adult children and their parents have positive feelings about each other
    E. relationships with siblings are more important than relationships with parents

334. Prematurity is a major risk factor for a number of developmental abnormalities. For the average woman of normal child bearing years who becomes pregnant, the chance of giving birth prematurely is closest to
    A. < 1%
    B. 5%
    C. 10%

D. 15%
E. 20%

335. A girl is born prematurely at 28 weeks gestational age. Based on current clinical experience, the best estimate of this girl's chance of surviving until her first birthday is closest to
    A. 25%
    B. 33%
    C. 50%
    D. 75%
    E. 90%

336. Low birth weight is associated with a number of physical and developmental problems. The percent of infants weighing 1000 grams or less at birth who survive and subsequently have major disability is approximately
    A. 15%
    B. 25%
    C. 33%
    D. 50%
    E. 66%

337. Pregnant women who use substances, either legal or illegal, risk damaging the fetus in a variety of ways. Maternal use during pregnancy of which of the following substances is responsible for the greatest number of cases of mental retardation in the infant?
    A. Alcohol
    B. Cocaine
    C. Lithium carbonate
    D. Opiates
    E. Tobacco

338. A 48-year-old man presents to his physician with complaints of clumsiness. Examination reveals a subtle, but apparent resting tremor accompanied by a "pill-rolling" gesture in his left hand. When walking, he moves slowly and shuffles his feet. A preliminary diagnosis of Parkinson's disease is made. Increased levels of which of the following neurotransmitters would best support this diagnosis?
    A. Acetylcholine
    B. Gamma-amino-butyric acid
    C. Norepinephrine
    D. Prolactin
    E. Serotonin

339. A student tells you that he seems to have an easier time cramming for an exam when he drinks coffee while he studies. This effect of coffee on learning ability is most closely linked to which of the following effects on brain activity?
    A. Decreased blocker cyclic-AMP response element binding protein activity

B. Increased activity in the reticular activating system
C. Increased serotonin activity
D. Reduced glutamate activity
E. Reduced prolactin activity

340. A 35-year-old woman is concerned that she has been gaining weight over the past few months. She reports that her appetite has increased for unknown reasons. At the biochemical level, this woman is probably experiencing increased serotonin activity at which receptors?
A. 5-HT1
B. 5-HT2
C. 5-HT3
D. 5-HT4
E. All of the above

341. A 50-year-old man with a history of schizophrenia reports to his physician that he has been feeling "uncomfortable" lately. When questioned more closely, the patient reports dry mouth, constipation, and infrequent urination; occasionally he has blurry vision and mild delirium. The physician suspects that these symptoms are a side effect of the medication the patient is currently taking. These symptoms most likely result from antagonism of which of the following receptors?
A. Dopamine
B. Histamine
C. Muscarinic
D. Norepinephrine
E. Prolactin

342. While flying to visit a relative for the holiday, you find yourself sitting next to a well-dressed woman in her late 20s. You make polite conversation with her at first, but then turn your attention to a book that you brought with you to read. Your reading is interrupted 15 minutes later when the woman begins to shake, hyperventilate, and sweat profusely. She is wild-eyed and her face is contorted in fear. Between great, gasping gulps of air she says that she is having a panic attack. At this point, what is the action you should take?
A. Ask her how frequently she has attacks
B. Give her a hard candy to suck on
C. Have her breathe into an airsickness bag
D. Hold her hand and tell her to calm down
E. Try to distract her by telling her a story

343. A first-time mother seeks advice from her physician as to how to care for her infant. She has been reading about Sudden Infant Death Syndrome (SIDS) and has been following the current medical recommendations for prevention. She asks if following these recommendations will alter her child's development in any way. The physician should advise her that her child will show
A. accelerated auditory discrimination
B. delays in developing a social smile
C. delays in learning to crawl
D. delays in speech acquisition
E. increased thumb-sucking behavior

344. A mother brings her 14-year-old daughter to the physician with concern that the girl "just doesn't seem to have much interest in anything." Examination shows the girl to be 5 feet 5 inches tall with a weight of 95 lbs. Enlargement of the parotid gland and halitosis are noted. Upon questioning, the girl confesses to binge and purge behavior, which she has kept carefully hidden from her parents. She reports feeling sad much of the time, and that she just does not fit in with others her own age. Continued physical examination of this girl is most likely to show which of the following additional signs?
A. A deep, red rash on the upper back
B. Elevated heart rate
C. Fine hair on the back and arms
D. Loss of tendon reflexes in the knees
E. Sensitivity to light

345. A 30-year-old woman seeks care for what she describes as "multiple chemical sensitivity." Since the age of 15, she has complained of headaches, body aches, fatigue, skin rashes, shortness of breath, unstable heart rate, and crampy abdominal pain. She also has painful menstrual periods and pelvic pain at mid cycle. Work-ups for endometriosis, asthma and allergy have been negative, except for mild seasonal rhinitis that responds to intranasal steroids. She seems to derive a sense of self worth from her interesting medical condition, having not been able to finish college, work consistently or establish a close, intimate relationship. This presentation is most consistent with
A. avoidant personality disorder
B. malingering
C. obsessive-compulsive disorder
D. panic disorder
E. somatization disorder

Answers

1. B. *high expressed emotion.* This is a well-defined variable in family research. High expressed emotion may be understood as the family's failure to grant a patient the sick role, resorting instead to blaming and accusing to explain the patient's behaviors. High expressed emotion has been shown to predict relapse in schizophrenic patients living at home. It adversely affects the outcome of other chronic medical and psychiatric disorders such as depression and adjustment to chronic renal failure. Help seeking/help rejecting is a pattern of patient behavior related to personality disorder and neuroticism. Parentification is a term used to describe the inappropriate caretaking roles that children or adolescents sometimes assume in troubled families. It may adversely affect the child struggling to meet age inappropriate expectations, but has not been related to schizophrenia. Splitting is a maladaptive, psychological defense mechanism, not a quality of family interaction. Triangulation, a concept from structural family theory, involves two family members communicating through a third person, usually crossing generational boundaries. Triangulation is a conflict ridden situation with negative implications. In this case, the parents have a single view of their son.

2. B. *If he wants the boy to try alcohol, it should be at a meal with adults who do not condone drunkenness.* Intermittent but otherwise unrestricted alcohol use can lead to binge drinking, which is no safer than chronic daily drinking. High tolerance is a risk factor for alcoholism, not a protective one. The safe limits for an adult male are no more than 2–3 ounces of hard liquor or 8 ounces (two 4-ounce glasses) of wine in 24 hours, or an average of no more than 14 drinks per week. The limits for adolescents are unknown, but, in general, adolescents progress more quickly to addiction than adults do. Since low potency alcohol-containing beverages are served in higher quantities than stronger ones, it is still possible to develop alcoholism from wine or beer at any age. Note: The legal drinking age is 21 years.

3. C. *personality characteristics that affect communication or the capacity for intimacy.* However, certain elements of physician identity (e.g., a desire to be in control, entitlement, inhibition of emotional expression, or expectations that the physician will be nurturing regardless of his/her own needs) may affect close relation-

ships. Although medical education and practice can be stressful, it is possible for physicians in any specialty to have satisfying or troubled relationships. Stress about time is more often a symptom than a cause of relational problems and, in fact, physicians often overcommit themselves at work to avoid problems at home, even though they may perceive the demands as externally imposed. Financial problems are real but need not destroy close relationships. Couples in which both partners are doctors are not necessarily more or less stable than those in which one partner is a physician and the other is not.

4. B. *emphasize that the patient will not be abandoned and that all treatment, including palliative care, will be provided.* People may hear the request for a Do Not Resuscitate (DNR) order as a statement that the case is hopeless and the staff have no real intention of caring for the patient. In fact, patients and families are often accepting of the possibility of death, as long as they know that care will be compassionate, attentive and appropriate. Advance directives must be revised at every stage of a patient's illness. A previous order either requesting or refusing resuscitation may not reflect the patient's current priorities or status. The statement that resuscitation does not prolong or improve life is true, but does not address the concerns of patients and families about abandonment and neglect. Giving a technical definition of the order similarly avoids addressing the emotional aspects of the decision. Respect for privacy is important, but letting the family discuss the matter with no input from the health care provider is a form of abandonment.

5. A. *most important information is given at the beginning of an interaction.* The first topic raised becomes the primary focus of attention and allows the patient time to consider the issues and to ask whatever questions he/she wishes. Giving extensive information or too many instructions all at once can overload the patient. Without patient questions and feedback the physician does not know if information is understood. Allowing the patient to fill in his/her own details may lead to drawing erroneous conclusions.

6. B. *Contemplation.* The patient is contemplating whether he has a problem or not before deciding to act. He has moved beyond pre-con-

templation but has not yet reached the level of preparing for action, taking specific action, or maintaining a plan of action.

7. C. *Mutual pretense.* Both patient and physician have tacitly agreed not to talk about the patient's disease. There is no indication of any level of awareness in the exchange.

8. B. *ask the patient to say more about his symptoms* as a way to facilitate differential diagnosis and to increase rapport with the patient. The presented symptoms are consistent with hypochondriasis, factitious disorder, malingering, or some as yet unidentified gastrointestinal problem. Telling the patient that he is a hypochondriac leaps to a diagnosis prematurely and is likely to anger him. Speaking with a family member is likely to leave the patient wondering why corroboration from others is necessary. The presented history contains no special indications for substance abuse. The patient is not "fine"; he is suffering. To simply send the patient home trivializes his symptoms, and abets the patient if the complaint is due to malingering.

9. E. *while the emotional states described are real, they do not represent distinct sequential stages.* A better way to think about these emotional states is as points along a continuous process; some points (e.g., anger) may be re-experienced several times. Different individuals assemble the pieces of the experience of dying in different ways. There is no "average" experience of death. Given enough time, most patients do finally accept death. Some, however, never appear to allow themselves to do so. Culture, religious beliefs, life experience and life satisfaction all play a part in a patient's reactions to death and dying. The pattern highlighted by Kübler-Ross is a useful guide, but every individual's experience is different.

10. A. *patients should monitor behavior (e.g., dietary intake) rather than outcome (e.g., weight loss).* The rule is to monitor what is under patients' control rather than something that may be affected by factors beyond their control. Self-monitoring does improve awareness of adherence and can, by itself, improve adherence. Paying close attention to behavior is most effective; therefore, recording throughout the day will increase awareness. Self-monitoring is dependent on awareness of one's behavior, not any specific personality trait (e.g., assertiveness).

11. E. *the physician's discomfort with the subject of sex.* Often, physicians employ the psychological defense mechanism of projection to think that this discomfort resides only in the patient; but this is not the case. Physicians must not allow their own discomfort to interfere with discussing sexual issues. A number of important medical issues, including sexually-transmitted disease prevention, require such discussions.

12. E. *transvestite fetishism.* Fetishism requires the inclusion of some object in the experience as part of sexual arousal or gratification. When this fetish involves a man dressing in women's clothing, it is termed transvestite fetishism. Note that transvestites, in general, are predominately heterosexual; that is, their preferred sexual partner is usually of the opposite sex. Male transvestites see themselves as male and therefore are not transsexuals or subject to a gender identity disorder.

13. A. *Anger.* The patient is angry at what is perceived as an unfair consequence. Depression would manifest itself more as despair and a sense of hopelessness. Bargaining would be trying to strike a deal with some higher power. Denial is the refusal to accept the reality of the impending death. Confusion is not one of the traditional Kübler-Ross stages for dealing with death and dying.

14. D. *patients' perception of the time their health care provider spent giving information is positively associated with adherence.* This supports the notion that one of the most potent forces in determining patient adherence is the relationship between the physician and the patient. In particular, In addition, if the exchange with the physician is positive, then the probability of adherence rises even further. Thus, although warnings are useful, the fear they induce can distract the patient from the details of the instructions. Too much information all at once can lead to information overload. Memory is dependent on attention and emotion as well as intelligence. Education is not related to adherence. In fact, highly educated patients may be equally as non-adherent as poorly educated ones, but for different reasons. For example, less educated persons may not understand; more educated persons may understand, but not believe or accept the information provided.

15. D. *Performance anxiety* is one of the more common reasons for impotence and anorgasmia. Although not a "disorder" as such, this anxi-

ety should be explored before investigating for either physical or psychological pathology. A simple counseling session with each partner in this couple may save time and expense. At the very least, it will rule out performance anxiety and justify more detailed examinations.

16. E. *Social phobia.* The recent onset, the fear of others making fun of him, and the conviction that he will do something shameful or stupid in public are all consistent with a diagnosis of social phobia. Personality disorders are lifelong, and so are ruled out by the recent onset. Agoraphobia is a fear of being exposed, but in a more general sense than merely in social situations. Although social phobia is a type of anxiety disorder, it is distinguished by the stimulus that triggers the anxiety. Generalized anxiety disorder is ruled out by the clear link between social situations and the anxiety.

17. B. *oldest female.* Although family dynamic and cultural patterns differ, in most family systems the role of the non-physician health expert is generally someone who is older and female (think, "grandmother.") Age is perceived as giving the experience required for expertise and females are more often in the role of caretakers. Education is not a key qualification in this informal network.

18. C. *he most likely has alcohol abuse or dependence.* The CAGE questions ask the patient if he/she ever 1) tried to Cut down alcohol intake but did not succeed, 2) been Annoyed about criticism concerning drinking, 3) felt Guilty about drinking behavior, and 4) had to take an Eye-opener in the morning to relieve anxiety and shakiness. Mr. S. gave positive answers to all four of the CAGE questions and, thus, most likely has alcohol abuse or dependency. Although some recent research has suggested that the CAGE questions must be used thoughtfully when evaluating certain ethnic populations, a full set of positive answers suggests that an alcohol problem exists. The positive predictive value of the CAGE questions is high enough that even though the prevalence of alcoholism is only 10%, the patient has a greater than 50% chance of having a problem. Not all alcoholics get drunk; many so-called "functional alcoholics" show few outward signs of a problem. Inpatient treatment is not indicated for patients who are able to function (e.g., hold a job), although counseling or attending AA meetings would be a reasonable course of action. It is likely that Mr. S. is in a state of denial, and may reject any suggestion that he has a problem. Alcohol problems are typically diagnosed by behavior, not by laboratory testing.

19. B. *Do you have an orgasm with manual or other clitoral stimulation?* This question helps to determine whether the woman is anorgasmic, or whether some other issue might be the root of her concern. A "yes" answer suggests that changes in sexual technique might make sexual intercourse more appealing. Asking about satisfaction and frequency misses the point; the patient has already expressed dissatisfaction and her concern about infrequency is her initial presentation. If her husband were impotent, it is unlikely that she would complain about her own lack of interest. Asking her what the problem is labels her feelings as a problem. A more targeted question will yield more specific and useful information.

20. A. *change the HCTZ to a "potassium sparing" combination diuretic without changing the rest of the prescribed regimen.* Although the answer may seem to hinge on pharmacological considerations, the real issue is maintaining the patient's routine so as to foster continued compliance with treatment. The patient is already adherent. Having the patient learn a new routine may reduce compliance and, by extension, lower the probability that the disease will be adequately managed.

21. B. *The patient and physician have differing belief systems about insulin.* The physician sees insulin as a good treatment while the patient sees it as a danger. The key issue here is that this difference in belief systems makes any communication about treatment options difficult. There is no evidence for family intervention here; although the family might share the patient's beliefs, the issue is not one of family dynamics. Nor would a detailed explanation of insulin treatment be effective if the patient rejects the idea in the first place. Beliefs that differ from those of the physician are not a sign of irrationality, just of different life experiences. Adherence would be poor, not based on passivity, but on the patient's active rejection of the treatment option offered.

22. D. *physical, neurologic maturational, cognitive, speech/language, and psychosocial* development comprise the cluster of domains usually assessed. Development is not a single dimension, but proceeds along several parallel dimensions. In certain circumstances, any of the

domains listed might be appropriate for evaluation. However, answer D provides a checklist of the classic five.

23. C. *5 months.* The physical behavior, level of responsiveness to external stimuli, and appearance of the ability to laugh combined with the child's weight gain all indicate a child of approximately this age. Recognizing what is normal behavior at each stage of development is critical for advising parents and detecting developmentally linked pathology.

24. D. *8 months.* The realization that objects out of sight continue to exist is a critical developmental milestone. On average, children gain this capacity shortly after 6 months of age. Note that we must infer this sense of object constancy from the child's searching behavior, as it is not yet possible to communicate with the child and receive verbal answers.

25. C. *5–6 months.* Each of these reflexes, present at birth, are lost as the child matures. The Moro and rooting reflexes disappear at about 3 to 4 months of age, tonic neck at about 4 to 6 months of age, and palmar grasp at about 5 to 6 months of age. Thus, 5-6 months of age is the earliest age at which these reflexes would be expected to have disappeared. Note that persistence of the Babinski and placing reflexes is expected until about 1 year of age.

26. D. *Sensorimotor stage.* This stage is the beginning of cognitive development. It is during this stage that the rudiments of assimilation and accommodation are first apparent. Schemas at this stage are combinations of movements and sensations, not objects with lives of their own. Freud called this same developmental period the Oral Stage. Erikson termed this age Trust vs. Mistrust.

27. B. *goals are graduated to maximize success experiences.* No one likes failure. Success in reaching a goal can, by itself, be reinforcing. Making goals incremental makes each step more attainable and helps to keep the patient motivated and on track. Goals that are too broad are ambiguous. Goals set by the provider without patient input may ignore difficulties of which the physician is unaware and typically do not have the level of "buy in" from the patient needed for success. "Shooting for the moon" may feel great if the moon is actually hit, but the chances of failure are too great, and the goal just looks unattainable (and, therefore, non-motivating) to

the patient. Goals must be flexible so they can be altered as circumstances change.

28. B. *express concern and suggest the patient think about his drinking.* The patient has not yet accepted the fact that there is a problem. Encouraging immediate corrective action (AA, in-patient treatment) is premature. Rather, the expression of concern helps to communicate the physician's perception that a problem exists. Failure to mention the problem and simply scheduling a follow-up visit will not assist the patient in realizing that a problem exists.

29. B. *discover how much information he would like to have.* Although patients have the right to know everything that you do about their medical condition, they also need to have some control over the level of detail with which facts are presented. For example, at what level of detail should the physician explain the physiology of the condition? Discussing support systems before giving any information about the disease would be premature. Prior to communicating about the patient's condition and gauging his reaction, physical contact may be misunderstood. Before you decide how to talk to the patient (e.g., in small chunks or laying all of the information out at once), ask the patient what he thinks would be most helpful. Every patient is different.

30. E. *he will likely require treatment with antidepressant medication.* The patient's symptoms, difficulty sleeping, loss of interest in his usual activities, feelings of worthlessness, difficulty concentrating, thoughts of suicide and weight loss, converge to support a diagnosis of depression, occult malignancy or substance abuse. His depression is unlikely to be successfully relieved by merely trying to boost his spirits through brief counseling or peer support. Depression is a condition that usually responds well to adequate pharmacological intervention, especially when it is coupled with psychotherapy. To fail to treat this patient's depression is to fail to relieve his suffering.

31. E. *"You must be very upset that your father is ill from his cancer again."* This statement focuses the conversation on the patient's reactions to his father's illness, not his reaction to the surgeon. Reflecting the patient's emotional state indicates that you have heard it, while reframing it in terms of his father. Sitting quietly leaves the patient wondering what you, the physician, are thinking. Defending the surgeon makes you

seem to be siding with him so that you now become the target of the patient's anger. Talking about his anger with the surgeon leads the patient away from the real source of his negative affect, namely, the return of his father's illness.

32.   E. *physiologic decline that accompanies aging.* The incidence of impotence in men rises with age. However, many men continue to be sexually active all their lives. Men who continue to be sexually active retain capacity. Men who attempt sexual relations only sporadically may find that they have more difficulty with sexual functioning. The main point is to realize that, although impotence may be the result of a pathological condition, a simpler explanation is most likely.

33.   A. *Anger,* the second of the five stages or emotional states of coping with death and dying as described by Kübler-Ross. Note that the patient blames someone else for her condition. Denial is a refusal to accept the reality of the impending death. Guilt, not one of Kübler-Ross's stages, is more likely to be felt by friends and relatives of the dying person, or anyone who feels that they should have done more. Depression means despair, a realization that the death is unavoidable, but not yet accepted. Not telling a patient what is happening is likely to produce fear. However, patients need to be told bad news in a way that they can tolerate. Coming to grips with news of impending death takes time. Kübler-Ross's five stages are: denial, anger, bargaining, depression, and acceptance.

34.   A. *feeling depressed for several months after the death.* This depressive reaction is called grief and is considered normal for months to about 1 year following the loss of a loved one. Patients need to know that grief is normal and takes time to resolve. Normal grief is self-limiting and most authorities agree that pharmacotherapy is rarely necessary. The other four symptoms listed as options, however, suggest complicated or prolonged grief. Some therapeutic intervention is likely to be required.

35.   C. *request a joint visit with the patient and his wife.* It is unclear whether the stress in the marriage is contributing to the lack of sexual activity, or whether the lack of sexual activity is contributing to the sense of stress within the marriage. A joint visit with both the patient and his wife will help to clarify this issue and provide additional information about the sexual expectations of both partners. Because the pa-

tient has erections in the morning, a nocturnal penile tumescence study is not necessary. The low level of sexual frequency and the report of impotence are unlikely to be resolved by a change in sexual position. Saying that this is bound to happen, does not address the patient's concern, and may miss some underlying issue that needs to be resolved. A joint visit will allow the physician to observe how the couple interacts together, something that is not possible by just interviewing the spouse separately.

36.   D. *refer for joint sex therapy with use of sensate focus.* Penile implant seems unnecessary given erection in the morning. The squeeze technique is used to treat premature ejaculation, which is not the problem presented by this patient. Other partners are less likely to help the couple function sexually together than they are to cause them to abandon their relationship. This level of dysfunction is not a normal part of aging. A middle-aged man should be able to continue to perform sexually for as long as he wishes to do so.

37.   A. *Alcohol* is the most abused drug for all ages and all occupational groups. Surveys of medical student populations suggest that medical students are more likely to abuse alcohol than are their peers in other educational programs. Less than 20% of medical students smoke, and anonymous surveys show that even fewer use the other drugs listed as options. Most physicians who abuse other drugs also abuse alcohol. In considering use rather than abuse, it appears that caffeine is the drug used most often by medical students.

38.   C. *A recently diagnosed terminally ill patient is in the hospital.* Silence in this setting allows patients time to collect their thoughts and to ask whatever questions they may have. Just being present can help to assuage the fears of abandonment felt by some terminally ill patients. Substance abuse always requires a response when identified; silence only allows the problem to get worse. During a home visit with a clear goal, silence does not attend to the task at hand. Silence, in the face of questions about sexual inadequacy, may be misinterpreted by the patient as embarrassment on the part of the physician.

39.   C. *Pre-contemplation,* she is not yet thinking about change, but she is thinking about thinking about it. This may seem like just putting it off, a type of procrastination, but procrastina-

tion is not recognized as a formal part of the stages of change model. To be in the stage of contemplation, she would be actively thinking about change. For preparation she would be making arrangements to facilitate change. For maintenance, she would be acting to keep changes in place once they have begun.

40. B. *"I'll order some pain medication and come back tomorrow to see if you'd like to talk then."* The patient needs to feel some control in this situation. Although the patient has the right to know everything, he also has the right to say he does not want to hear. Note that this does not mean that the physician will not tell the patient anything, only that the patient will be given time to prepare to receive the information. Going to a family member jeopardizes confidentially unless the patient requests this route of communication.

41. C. *daily rituals of the office staff and physicians* are important components of day-to-day practice. Because they are not things or people, they are considered intangible. These social norms and mores are real and influence workplace atmosphere. Buildings and framed mission statements are solid physical things. The types of patients in the practice and the accountant who audits the practice are identifiable, concrete individuals.

42. D. *be able to create her own role within the department and negotiate for the resources she needs to accomplish that role.* Professionals seek autonomy and the latitude to define their own goals and the methods for accomplishing those goals. Professionals generally seek careers and settings consistent with their sense of self and personally held values. Controls over professional behavior arise from internalized standards of conduct reinforced by the review of professional peers. Professionals can differ about acceptable standards of conduct, or the best way to achieve the collective goals of the profession.

43. C. *hiring them.* Because professionals expect to be able to define their own goals and the methods for achieving them, hiring decisions are critical. Whether or not a person gains entrée into an organization is the core control mechanism for managing professional conduct. Exclusion is the ultimate professional sanction. Professionals are expected to be self-motivated, to aspire to effectiveness, to gather the information they need, and to evaluate their performance by comparing themselves to their peers.

44. C. *master the mechanics of weight shifting.* Crawling is not a necessary preparation for walking. In fact, not all children learn to crawl. Object permanence is a milestone in cognitive development, not a prerequisite for the physical milestone of walking. Balance is important and continues to develop as children mature, but compared to the balance skills required to stand on tiptoes or bend to pick up an object, walking requires very unsophisticated mastery of balance. Separation anxiety is generally a stage of socio-emotional growth resolved by age 2; it is unrelated to walking.

45. A. *formulation of internal mental symbols is a hallmark of toddlerhood.* At this time, transition objects begin to appear. Having mastered object permanence, the child is no longer bound to full reliance on just what is before him. Although some language is present, it is not yet the organizing framework for mental representations. Instead, the child's representations are based on his experiences and relationships, not on concepts given to him linguistically by others.

46. B. The ability to *create plans* allows the child to plan how to gratify impulses. This is what makes the Two's so terrible. Not only are children this age impulsive, but they also can negotiate around simple impediments meant to protect and contain them. The ability to imagine alternatives does not become manifest until the child is 5 or 6 years old. Children can distinguish facial features from early infancy. Although 2-year-olds have some idea of the standards of good and bad conduct, these standards are not internalized; instead, a child of this age seeks simply to not get caught. Rule-based play is characteristic of middle childhood.

47. E. *injury,* as confirmed annually by epidemiological data. After age 1, injuries of all types are the number one cause of death among children. Automobile accidents account for a substantial proportion of these deaths, although fire-related death is also a prominent cause of mortality. Patterns of injury-related morbidity parallel those for mortality.

48. B. *Sequential stimulation of two adjacent neurons enhances the efficiency of their connecting synapse.* Protein kinase, the hippocampus, the orbito-medial frontal cortex, and even the cerebellum are all associated with higher order learning and memory functions.

49. C. *learned adaptive responses that contribute to survival are passed on to successive generations.* Better learning leads to better evolutionary survival. What is learned in one generation seems to be more easily learned in the next, suggesting that the learning is passed on. Genetic and environmental influences interact in complex ways that are difficult to separate. The interaction between genetics and environment changes as the individual moves through various developmental stages. This interaction is highlighted by the notion of so-called "critical periods" of development (e.g., brain growth spurt).

50. A. *involves the association of sensory stimuli with sequential motor system responses.* Implicit learning is felt by some to be the most primitive type of learning, and to form the foundation for all other learning. Implicit learning can occur below the level of the person's awareness. Implicit learning is comprised only of simple experienced associations, not higher level cognitive processes, and therefore does not require higher order cortical functioning. Finally, implicit learning occurs over a short span of time after the experience of a sensation, which is then followed by motor functioning.

51. B. *mental illness and substance abuse.* By some estimates, as many as 50% of all the homeless suffer from mental illnesses or substance abuse problems, including alcoholism. These problems may be the cause of the homelessness, or a result of coping with difficult conditions. Note that as a group, homeless individuals are more likely to suffer from all of the options listed, but are most likely to suffer from mental health issues.

52. A. *Agoraphobia.* The patient displays anxiety, which the history suggests is related primarily to leaving the safe confines of his home. Patients with social phobia are more likely to fear being shamed or doing something to embarrass themselves in public. Dysthymia is depressive symptoms lasting more than 2 years. The patient lacks the global mistrust of paranoid personality disorder and the clear, identifiable delusion of delusional disorder.

53. B. *benzodiazepines.* Abrupt withdrawal can produce delirium and seizures. Withdrawal from amphetamines produces fatigue and hunger and withdrawal from heroin results in flu-like symptoms including nausea and cramps. Hallucinogens and phencyclidine have no specific withdrawal effects.

54. A. *bipolar disorder.* This patient matches the DSM-IV criteria for bipolar disorder, manic phase. The distinguishing features are grandiosity, talkativeness, flight of ideas, distractibility, excessive involvement in activities, and decreased need for sleep for at least 1 week. A person with obsessive-compulsive disorder would manifest ritualistic behavior. Narcissistic personality disorder is characterized by a life-long pervasive pattern of seeing self as grandiose and the center of the universe. *Hyper*thyroidism is possible, but not *hypo*thyroidism which would be associated with decreased activity, sluggishness, and an increased need for sleep. The patient does not display characteristics of dementia and her age makes vascular dementia, in particular, unlikely.

55. E. *lithium carbonate,* treatment of choice for long-term control of bipolar disorder. Note that lithium must be taken consistently and at close-to-toxic levels to be efficacious. Fluoxetine is one of the selective serotonin reuptake inhibitors (SSRI), a common treatment for depression and obsessive-compulsive disorder. Chlorpromazine is an antipsychotic. Clonazepam and diazepam are anti-anxiety medications.

56. C. *Regression,* returning to an earlier level of functioning. The girl has lost the capacity to control her bladder as she returns to the wished-for infant state. Regression is common in children when siblings are born into the household. Reaction formation suggests a reversal, doing the opposite of what one really feels. Projection refers to experiencing one's own thoughts or emotions as coming from others in the external world. Undoing is a ritual reversal which "fixes" or repairs what is wrong in the sense that obsessive-compulsive hand washing fixes the feeling of being dirty. Sublimation is diverting unacceptable drives into personally and socially acceptable channels.

57. A. *advise the mother about helping the child cope with life transitions.* The regression response should abate as the girl learns other means of coping, such as feeling like a participant in her sibling's care, and receives positive reinforcement for attending school. Changing kindergarten classes is unlikely to resolve the issue. The source of the problem is separation from home, not problems with the school environment. A child at this age should not be enuretic; simply waiting does not address the problem. Imipramine would be a proper pharmacologic choice, but should not be given without an exploration

of the child's life circumstances. The child already knows that enuresis is "bad" and is probably embarrassed by it. Merely talking to a child about what is an unconscious response is unlikely to be effective.

58. C. *is showing developmental age and gender appropriate behavior.* The clothing is her parent's, not her, choice. She would not be expected to be able to identify herself by gender until about age 3. The truck does not have any gender-specific meaning for her, but is merely an object that can be moved in a fun way. This behavior does not suggest either a gender identity problem or a tendency towards homosexuality. Her social behavior gives no clues as to her level of shyness later in life, or the presence or absence of siblings at home.

59. A. *borderline* best matches the following DSM-IV criteria: unstable mood and self-image, self-detrimental impulsivity, unstable but intense interpersonal relationships, difficulty being alone, self-mutilation and suicidal gestures. Paranoid features a life-long patterns of pervasive mistrust of everyone and everything. Histrionic is preoccupied with being the center of attention. Narcissistic presents self as grand and omnipotent. Schizoid individuals just want to be left alone.

60. E. individual cognitive-behavioral therapy. A number of practitioners have reported significant improvement in people with borderline personality disorder when treatment is a combination of social skills training and cognitive reframing of emotional reactions. Group therapy is more appropriate for posttraumatic stress disorder, substance abuse recovery, and providing coping support. Alprazolam is an anti-anxiety medication often used to treat panic disorders. Family therapy might be a useful adjunct to individual therapy, but should not be the primary approach. Behavior modification is used to treat a wide range of disorders from autism to phobias but does not appear to be as effective as cognitive-behavioral therapy.

61. B. *disorganized schizophrenia,* matches DSM -IV criteria. This type of schizophrenia is accompanied by the most bizarre behavior, the most regression in capacities, and the most pronounced thought disorders. In paranoid schizophrenia, there is less loss of faculties and less pronounced symptoms. In addition, delusions of grandeur or persecution are common. Catatonia is manifested by either excessive excitement, or

pronounced decrease in movements, often with bizarre posturing. Undifferentiated is the classification used when the patient is schizophrenic, but does not fit any of the other classifications. Residual refers to situations where, although manifesting schizophrenic symptoms in the past, the patient is now symptom free, except for a few negative symptoms.

62. B. *frontal lobes.* Reduction in frontal lobe metabolism during the WCST is standard for schizophrenic people. The temporal lobes are involved in the production of schizophrenic symptoms, but are not the primary locus of the dysfunction for those who have schizophrenia. Parietal lobe dysfunctions center on agraphia, acalculia, and constructional apraxias. The occipital lobes are intimately involved with processing visual input. The cerebellum is involved in movement and certain types of memory.

63. B. *a learned social phenomenon that influences health, illness and therapy.* Culture is learned, not genetically determined. Furthermore, culture has a significant impact on ALL clinical encounters and should be taken into consideration by physicians when therapeutic options are being identified and evaluated.

64. C. *a steady increase in the size of ethnic minority populations.* The average age of the white population is increasing rather than decreasing. The population is projected to grow over the next century, although at a slower rate than in the past. Expected demographic changes include an increase in all minority populations to the point that whites will comprise less than 50% of the total population in the 21st century. The U.S. population is becoming increasingly ethnically diverse, and ethnic minority populations are increasing in size. Thus, culture will remain a highly significant factor in the delivery of health care.

65. E. *natural, supernatural and social worlds.* An ethnic group's cultural ideas about the natural, supernatural, and social worlds influence its system of maintaining health and treating disease. The natural realm includes ideas about the connections between people and the earth's elements of soil, water, air, plants, and animals. The social realm encompasses ideas about individuals and the appropriate interaction between people of different ages, genders, lineages, and ethnic groups. The supernatural realm includes religious beliefs about birth, death, afterlife, reincarnation, spirits, and interactions between

the spiritual world and the human world. To fully understand any ethnic group's perspective about health and disease, we must put it into context with other aspects of that culture such as beliefs about what a person is, the kinship system, and the meaning of suffering, life, and death.

66. D. *illustrations of how people interpret bodily signs and symptoms in culturally specific ways.* Entities that are recognized by certain ethnic groups but not others have been studied as folk illnesses or culture-bound syndromes. These entities are physical ailments. Each has a specified etiology, pathophysiology, and treatment. In some situations, they may also be expressions of mental or social distress, which have specific symbolic meanings. These folk illnesses and culture-bound syndromes are not separate categories of diseases but are examples of how all signs and symptoms are culturally interpreted. The use of culturally derived categories is not a sign of ignorance or lack of education.

67. C. *high blood and hypertension are examples of how interpretations of body symptoms are culturally influenced.* Folk illness or culture-bound syndromes are ailments that are explained by coherent, although generally non-European, concepts about etiology, pathophysiology, and treatment. When they are expressions of mental or social distress, they also have symbolic meanings. Folk illnesses and culture-bound syndromes are not a separate category of disease, but are examples of how all signs and symptoms are culturally interpreted. Biomedical concepts and folk illness concepts may be consistent or contradictory. In the case presented, two cultural systems have interpreted signs and symptoms differently, as hypertension and high blood. Regardless of how a conventionally trained physician views an illness, labeling other people's beliefs as superstitious is degrading. Working with patients' views of their own bodies is the most respectful, empowering, and productive approach to developing a treatment plan that is likely to be successful.

68. B. *explore the possibility that the woman believes that your recommendations will make the child worse.* Chastising the mother, notifying Child Protective Services, and hospitalizing the child are incorrect strategies because they do not take into consideration the possibility that the real problem is a failure to communicate across cultures. All of these approaches are likely to alienate the mother and make it less likely that

she will ever be receptive to negotiating therapeutic plans for her child or any other family member. Referring the mother for education may be appropriate at some time, but as an initial step, it is incorrect because it simply passes off the patient to someone else. Referrals allow the physician to conveniently extricate him/herself from a difficult situation, but the problem is not identified and addressed.

69. C. *Natural etiologies.* Individual, social, and supernatural etiologies all involve some degree of personal responsibility such as ignoring behavioral risk factors, causing conflict in social relationships, or offending or provoking the supernatural, respectively. Intellectual etiology is not one of the usual categories of etiology used to describe illness causation.

70. D. *Popular sector.* Folk sector refers to secular or sacred healers who have authority throughout a community. The professional sector refers to health care providers who are licensed and sanctioned by the government. The paraprofessional and pharmaceutical healers are not part of the usual categorization of healers according to the commonly cited Kleinman model.

71. C. *parent.* Kleinman's three sectors of healers are popular or lay; folk; and professional. The popular sector includes everyday people whose authority is acquired through experience, such as parents, neighbors, and community members. The folk sector includes sacred and secular healers whose authority is derived by inheritance, apprenticeship, religious position, or divine choice, such as ministers, astrologers, psychics, and lay midwives. The professional sector includes people whose authority is achieved by schooling and by licensure, both of which are determined by the profession's organizations and sanctioned by the government; medical doctors, homeopaths, chiropractors and nurse midwives are examples.

72. E. *shared between a patient and a provider lead to fewer conflicts.* Kleinman devised the notion of explanatory models (EMs) to describe people's ideas about a sickness event. EMs have five components: etiology of the condition, timing and mode of onset of symptoms, pathophysiologic processes, natural history, and appropriate treatments; ethnic identity is not one of the five components. EMs change over time as more information is gathered and as the disease unfolds. Different people hold different EMs about the same sickness

event, but Kleinman predicts that the more agreement there is between a provider's and a patient's EMs, the fewer conflicts there will be between them about diagnosis and management.

73. C. *legitimize withdrawal from regular activities and requests for assistance.* "Sick role" is a social notion and refers to the fact that others must agree that a person is sick before he or she is eligible for special treatment. The other options are incorrect because they refer only to medical or epidemiological illness.

74. A. *choice of healers.* This choice includes the ethnic background of the provider, how that provider is viewed within the patient's particular ethnic community, and how the provider understands and responds to the patient's belief system. Desire for good health and physiologic response appear to be applicable across ethnic groups. Type of health insurance and willingness to work are not typically culturally linked.

75. A. *He agreed with the philosophical and ideological underpinnings of Chinese medicine.* Given his ethnicity, gender, religion, socioeconomic class and language, he probably felt little social and cultural dissonance between himself and medical care providers. But he may have felt dissatisfied with his level of personal care, disillusioned with results, and tired of long waits and high costs; and he may have found that he disagreed with the philosophical beliefs behind the approaches to illness that are typical of conventional medical institutions. He may or may not have learned about or accepted the cultural and ideological underpinnings for the alternative approaches he was using. In fact, most people participate in complementary medicine regimens without knowing their derivation and without forsaking allopathic approaches.

76. C. *being our genuine selves with the expectation that patients will understand our meanings.* Effective education and skill development require that we learn about ourselves as cultural beings, which includes being aware of our personal biases and prejudices. It is vital to learn about patients as cultural beings, learn patient-centered communication skills, and be aware of potential abuses of power. Effective communication often requires giving up our preferred "genuine" selves in exchange for adapting our approach to fit patients' preferred styles.

77. E. *Native Americans: pausing less than a few seconds for a reply to a question conveys lack of interest.* Teaching that looking at someone in the eye communicates sincere interest probably has its roots in European culture. Other cultural groups, such as Asians, feel that direct eye contact is invasive and disrespectful; instead, intermittent eye-to-eye contact with periods of looking away communicates respect. Speaking loudly to Asians can be experienced as an expression of anger. For Arab patients, giving things with the left hand is revolting because the left hand is symbolically dirty, while the right hand is symbolically clean.

78. A. *called him grandfather.* You did do some things well, such as calling him by a family title respectful of his position (grandfather). Other things you did well were speaking in lay people's terms and asking open-ended questions about their perceptions of the problem early in the interaction. The remainder of your comments, however, could have caused problems. The non-verbal cues that were meant to improve communication could have the opposite effect. Direct eye contact can feel rude, as though you were staring. This is especially true among Asians who typically make only brief intermittent eye contact. Saying he will go blind unless he does as you suggest can sound as if you are placing a curse on him. Also, you did not ask how he would feel about receiving an organ transplant. To some individuals, regardless of culture, the idea of having the body part of someone else implanted in themselves is frightening and emotionally disturbing. At this point you also have no information about any religious or other prohibitions that might influence the patient's willingness to undertake such a procedure. Finally, rather than the patient, it is the family, particularly sons, who need to hear the information and who will make the decision. The son would probably want to sign the consent form as well.

79. B. *Economic factors, such as cost of medical treatment.* Economic factors are probably least significant because the patient is eligible for government refugee assistance funds. Structural factors may play a role, as she may not know how to drive and may be confused by the public transportation system, but her family has apparently helped her overcome these factors when she visits the Cuban healers. Cultural and social factors are probably playing the largest roles. The patient's interpretation of her breast lump, her experience of her bodily symptoms,

her concept of the word "cancer," and her experiences with cancer and cancer treatments in Cuba are potential major factors. In addition, her spiritual beliefs about the cause of the problem, her ethnic identity and newly-arrived refugee status, her acceptance or rejection of a "sick role," and her social network's assessment of her condition and recommendations for treatment may also be influencing her to choose traditional Cuban healing treatments over surgery, radiation, and chemotherapy.

80. E. *Traditional health care practice.* Traditional healing practices may take on forms that are unfamiliar to medical practitioners. Linear bruises on the back, chest, or extremities are most likely the result of the Southeast Asian practice of "coining". For illnesses caused by bad wind, or built-up pressure, rubbing the body with a mentholated cream followed by rubbing a silver coin vigorously over the area is believed to release the pressure, thus relieving the illness. Coining has been confused with child abuse, and parents have been reported to child protective services by physicians who are uninformed of the practice. Mongolian spots are congenital hyperpigmented areas, most often seen on the lower back or buttocks. The hyperpigmentation fades with age but may never disappear completely. Sepsis can present as petechiae which can progress to purpura, ecchymoses, and frank hemorrhage. Petechiae are usually distributed widely over the entire body.

81. D. *consider that the patients may be suffering from a culturally specific syndrome, perhaps related to the stress of immigration.* Telling symptomatic patients that they are not sick gives no consideration to the possibility that cultural and psychological factors may be a significant part of the problem. Making assumptions about working the system or that this may be a type of malingering represents negative stereotyping of the community. Quarantine is a drastic measure that is not warranted at this point.

82. A. *Boundaries.* The family structure consists of such arrangements or organizational characteristics as boundaries, triangles, and subsystems. Communication style, parentification, scapegoating, and family secret are components of family process or patterns of interaction, not structure.

83. A. *boundaries around individuals within the system are closed.* Disengaged families have more boundaries between individuals than normally

interactive families. Thus, other family members are less likely to be aware of and influenced by individual stresses or joys. The boundaries around the entire family system, however, vary and would not necessarily be closed. The term disengaged is more correctly applied to all the members rather than just the father. Answers D and E are descriptive of enmeshed families.

84. D. *the formation of a subsystem with relatively closed boundaries around it* is most common during the first months of a marriage. An open boundary around their relationship makes it difficult to establish their own identity as a couple. Most young married couples keep some connection with their parents and do not completely cut off or disengage from them unless there has been a major rift, such as around the choice of spouse. Enmeshment with parents would intrude on the couple's time together and their identity as a unit, and is developmentally inappropriate in young adulthood.

85. B. *Enmeshed family.* Enmeshed families are most likely to have difficulty with individuals separating and establishing their own identity. Disengaged families usually have less difficulty with independence. Generational and overprotective families may have some difficulty with separation, but not to the extent of an enmeshed family. Extended family refers to membership in a group rather than to how people in that group rely on each other.

86. B. *motor vehicle accidents.* Motor vehicle accidents account for approximately 50% of adolescent deaths. Successful educational interventions would include not driving while under the influence of alcohol or drugs, driving at safe speeds, and wearing a seat belt. Adolescents' sense of personal invulnerability ("It can't happen to me") makes them especially prone to recklessness and "death defying" behavior. This attitude also makes them vulnerable to sexually-transmitted diseases, homicide, suicide and various forms of abuse, but the incidence of mortality associated with these problems pales in comparison with motor vehicle accidents.

87. B. *boy is probably not dreaming while he is walking in his sleep.* Sleep walking (somnambulism) occurs in delta (Stage 4) sleep. Most dreams occur in REM sleep, a different stage of the sleep cycle. Assigning meaning to the somnambulism is strictly speculative, although it is likely that talking with the boy will reveal

that he has some anxiety when he is awake. If awakened while sleep walking, the boy will be groggy and have a difficult time waking up (deep delta sleep). There is no evidence that changing the time of going to sleep affects somnambulism.

88. C. *Instrumental.* In some approaches to family sociology, men are traditionally seen as performing more goal-directed task-oriented roles while women perform more socioemotional care-taking roles. In more recent times, familial roles have been in flux with a move toward more symmetry between gender roles. In some couple relationships, this change has been accompanied by increasing competitiveness between fathers and mothers who share bread-winning and child-rearing duties.

89. C. *one-person households.* Approximately 80% of the non-family households in the mid-1990s were persons living alone. Therefore, none of the other arrangements listed as options approach this percentage. It is important to note that some of the selections presented would be considered "family" by many professionals who work with families, but not as defined by the U.S. census.

90. E. *Single-parent households* comprised about 30% of all parent-child living arrangements in the mid-1990s compared to less than 15% in 1970. Families below the poverty level actually declined slightly in number over that same time period. The size of households dropped from 3.14 in 1970 to 2.67 in 1994. Kinship households decreased from 80% of total households to around 70% in 1994. The number of married-couple households with children decreased as well. Note that single-parent families headed by women are more likely to be below the poverty line, and that 25% of children in the U.S. live in poverty.

91. E. *Scapegoated.* When a person is scapegoated (identified as being the sole source of a problem), they help to dissipate the tension or stress in the family, usually by directing it outside the family. In the case presented, the girl and her difficulties at school become the focus of parental attention and frustration so that they do not have to deal with root problems such as a dysfunctional marital relationship. The term scapegoat is biblical in origin and refers to the archaic practice of symbolically placing the sins of a community on the head of a goat that was then driven into the wilderness.

92. D. *Parentified.* When a child is parentified, he or she is placed in the position of assuming parental authority over household decisions, especially those that include supervising and disciplining siblings. Typically, the oldest child, especially the oldest daughter, is given this role. Resentment from the other children in the family can lead to emotional isolation. Inability to spend time with peers because of home responsibilities can lead to social isolation. Depression is a common outcome.

93. A. *Disengaged.* The strength of disengaged families lies in fostering independence and autonomy. This is at the expense, however, of not teaching members how to work well together and nurture each other.

94. C. *enmeshed.* Enmeshed families are characterized by an unusually strong emotional connectedness. Because of this connectedness, family members have difficulty making autonomous choices and acting independently when necessary and appropriate. Exiting from the family, even briefly to attend kindergarten, for example, can produce exaggerated separation anxiety.

95. A. *Emotionally cut off.* Emotional cut off is more likely to create pseudo-independence rather than true independence. The need to completely abandon a relationship in order to exert autonomy suggests that the patient has learned an "all or none" approach (i.e., complete absorption vs. no contact) to interacting with others.

96. E. *Socioemotional.* In most cultures, women have been trained to take primary responsibility for raising and socializing children (i.e., teaching them how to behave acceptably within their community and larger society) and providing them with the emotional tools (e.g., good self-esteem) to become contributing members of their socioeconomic and political group.

97. E. *unexplained nature of events.* Young children view illness and associated noxious treatments as punishment. Many studies have shown that when they are provided with simple explanations about why they are sick and why certain therapies are necessary, they become less anxious and more cooperative, even when painful procedures (venipuncture, intramuscular injections) must be performed. Children who are sick fear separation from parents but usually do not fear loss of affection. Disappointments about limitation of activity and removal from

friends can be overcome by providing alternative distractions. People of any age usually enjoy the dependency on others allowed by being ill, if it is short term.

98. B. *limitation of activity.* In general, athletes are able to tolerate pain, removal from friends, and even short-term dependency better than inactivity. He is old enough to understand the cause-and-effect relationship between his accident and his injury.

99. D. *helplessness.* Helplessness ("I'm such a wreck I just can't do anything for anybody, including myself") is often the most difficult emotion for a patient to tolerate. It is easier to actively experience anger ("I'm so mad that I have to be sick during the holidays!"), guilt ("I should have gotten a flu shot"), or blame someone ("My sister gave this to me when she visited last week") than to feel there is nothing one can do. Hopelessness would be an unusual reaction to a short-term, self-limited illness.

100. C. *practicing relaxation exercises.* Relaxation is the most effective coping style for a problem requiring patience. The other styles are more likely to create or increase frustration and anxiety for the patient, the physician, and others, none of whom can change the circumstances. Some patients use waiting time to seek information. In the absence of diagnosis, this behavior can lead to erroneous conclusions and unnecessary worries.

101. A. *alopecia due to chemotherapy.* Hypnosis, a form of therapeutic communication in which patients learn to focus their attention on one area and reduce their focus on others, has a long history of usefulness in medicine. The systems most susceptible to psychological factors such as imagery, focus and suggestion are the autonomic nervous system, the endocrine system, and the immune system. The autonomic nervous system influences muscle tone, vital signs, and gastrointestinal function, making hypnosis helpful in irritable bowel syndrome and chronic pain, especially headaches and pain involving muscle spasm. Effects on the immune system may account for the impact of hypnosis on the course of herpes outbreaks. Smoking cessation is improved by reduction in anxiety, refocusing away from discomfort and imagining a positive outcome. Hypnosis may reduce pain, nausea and anxiety in patients receiving chemotherapy, but it does not affect hair loss.

102. A. *do active problem solving.* In discussion, the group shares methods that aid in coping and can offer each member suggestions about how to handle particular issues. Group members are unlikely to forget their illness, which is the major topic they are there to discuss. The group works together to maintain optimism, not to simply accept the worst. There is small comfort in learning that others are worse off, because the patient may get there eventually. The group aids the patient in confronting the problems of the disease realistically, and setting aside the façade of bravery which often seems to be necessary in the presence of others who do not have the disease.

103. E. *understand that the patient may need more time to adjust.* Denial may represent an important coping mechanism for the patient at this early stage of knowing about his diagnosis and prognosis. Stripping away the patient's coping mechanism at this moment can accentuate the patient's discomfort. Lastly, it will only alienate the patient to force him to "see the truth" until he is ready to do so.

104. C. *Relaxation training.* A patient who feels that the mind and body are separate is more likely to accept any kind of physical treatment (surgery, injections or pills, even antidepressants, if they are explained as affecting the body) than an obviously mind-oriented therapy such as relaxation training.

105. A. *Changing to a drug covered by his insurance plan.* Barriers to non-adherence include cost, side effects, and a complicated medical regimen. Exploring whether cost is an issue and changing to a drug covered by insurance would decrease the burden to the patient and would immediately make the treatment more attractive to anyone, regardless of financial status. Explaining the health hazards of elevated blood pressure and the side effects of the medication would be a good idea but will not, in themselves, change the patient's behavior. Increasing the number of pills he has to take each day complicates the regimen and will make him even less likely to take his medication.

106. E. *reassurance.* Many patients (sometimes called "the worried well") see a physician seeking reassurance. Their needs can often be met with periodic, scheduled office visits to give them a chance to discuss their health concerns without having to manufacture an illness. If this does not seem to solve the problem as expected, it

would be appropriate to probe for deeper psychological problems, which the patient may be reluctant to disclose or feel are outside the perview of "medical treatment." While some patients are seeking prescriptions and work excuses, this is less common than needing simple reassurance about their health status. Many patients with minor complaints are not particularly interested in a precise diagnosis for their problem.

107. B. *family.* In these family-centered cultures, the family is the primary decision-making body; lesser roles are played by the patient, the physician, and the community. In certain circumstances, a religious leader may be consulted but the family makes the decision. Physicians should be aware that decisions to seek care, who will be consulted, and adherence with treatment recommendations will be the result of collective, extended family discussions requiring more time and repeated explanations to achieve consensus.

108. C. *the subjective experience of stress associated with the event* is the major determinant of the degree of impact a stressor will have. The magnitude of the event will be experienced differently from person to person. Whether the event is positive or negative, how many people are involved (and so may have an opinion about how to handle the event, adding to the stress), and the type of change that accompanies the event all need to be taken into account, but their effects are dependent on the subjective interpretation of the person.

109. B. *dependent on technology.* A hospital death is more likely to involve "high technology," whereas a hospice death strives to involve friends and family, emphasizes pain control and palliation, and focuses on the process of death as a natural occurrence rather than as something to be fought and avoided. Religious practices should be equally respected in both settings.

110. E. *such experiences are common in grieving people.* People who are grieving often report the belief that they have seen the dead person or that they have heard the dead person speak to them. These experiences are usually comforting to the bereaved person. These events are neither hallucinations nor episodes of psychosis requiring hospitalization or further formal psychological intervention. Persons who are undergoing normal grief are not depressed and do not need to be medicated.

111. E. *suicide.* Suicide is the most difficult death to grieve because of the anger survivors feel toward the person who committed suicide for causing such pain. In addition, survivors can feel overwhelming guilt for not recognizing the depth of the person's despair or otherwise stopping the suicide. The other types of deaths do not involve the same feelings of abandonment or responsibility in the bereaved.

112. B. *depression.* Grief is actually the prototype for depression, and the typical signs and symptoms of grief resemble those of a major depressive episode. While some of these symptoms exist in the other options provided, they are most characteristic of depression.

113. A. *6 months.* The risk of death for the survivor after the death of a spouse is significantly increased within the first 6 months. Deaths due to cardiac problems are especially likely. Suicide is also prominent among older spouses who were married for many years. The suicide may take the form of inanition, or a lack of desire to continue living, manifested by not eating or not taking essential medications. Such a death may not be recognized as suicide.

114. C. *enhance sexual experience.* The hypoxia that accompanies using amyl nitrate ("poppers") is reported to increase the intensity of sexual experience. The mechanism appears to be the same as in autoerotic-asphyxiation, which is frequently achieved by masturbating while hanging.

115. B. *Stage 2.* Teeth grinding, or bruxism, occurs during Stage 2, the most common type of sleep. Bruxism is associated with waking time anxiety, which may not be recognized by the patient. When this anxiety is identified and resolved, the bruxism usually abates. Most other sleep disorders (somnambulism, night terrors, enuresis) are associated with stage 4 sleep. The pathology of narcolepsy is linked to the mechanisms that produce REM sleep.

116. A. *Anti-social* personality disorder. Although all of the formal criteria are not met by the information presented, the criminal background and lack of regret combined with the man's charming manner are suggestive of anti-social personality disorder (Cluster B). A borderline person is characterized by unstable affect and relationships. A person with paranoid personality disorder approaches the world and everyone in it with mistrust. Someone who is histrionic

tends to be flamboyant. People with schizotypal personality disorder are strange or eccentric and often avoided by others because of these eccentricities.

117. B. *intellectualization.* To deal with the personal distress and anxiety she feels, the student strips away the affect of this emotionally charged encounter and replaces it with academic content that is not emotionally relevant to the patient. Using different terms, the student substitutes cognition for affect and empathy. Simply removing the expression of affect would be isolation. Reaction formation entails acting the opposite of actual, but unconscious, feeling and desires. Sublimation refers to achieving gratification of an unacceptable impulse by acting in a socially acceptable manner. Denial refers to refusing to accept some clear feature of external reality.

118. A. *Death of a spouse.* The Holmes and Rahe scale lists events that are related to life changes. Those events that are most disruptive to important personal relationships seem to have the most negative effects on health. Although more true for men than women, one's spouse is often the primary source of social support and comfort. Of the life changes listed, this loss seems to be the hardest to bear, especially for men. Divorce is likely to produce high levels of anger, which can, under some circumstances, be mobilizing. Although surviving an automobile accident can be a very stressful event, it does not disrupt social support to the degree that death of a spouse does. Incarceration and loss of a job affect social status. Such stresses are typically easier to handle than the loss of a relationship.

119. A. *birth.* Although neuronal migration is virtually complete in the full-term newborn, the formation of dendrites and axons continues into childhood as the brain adapts to the environment. The number of dendrites peaks around puberty; after that, synaptic connections that are not used regularly disappear through dendritic pruning. New connections can be made until the time of death. Thus, contrary to the popular saying, you *can* teach an old dog new tricks!

120. D. *lacks neuronal adaptation to environmental stimuli.* Guidance cues are substances that provide a mechanism by which neuronal connections are made in response to sensory experience.

121. B. *classical conditioning.* The voice on the tape is similar to the bell used by Pavlov to induce salivation in a dog. The voice has become so closely associated with relaxation and sleep that it produces the reaction by itself without the need for the full relaxation routine. Inhibition is the mechanism by which an undesirable behavior is stopped from occurring. Intermittent reinforcement refers to providing a positive or negative consequence irregularly rather than each time the target behavior occurs. Modeling is demonstrating a behavior. Biofeedback is a self-regulation intervention typically relying on graphical representation of a physiological parameter that is linked to a particular behavior.

122. A. *order a basal metabolic rate to investigate if she is hypometabolic.* Persistent dieting may induce hypothalamic changes that down regulate the entire HPA axis. In such cases, both TSH (a pituitary hormone) and the thyroid hormones remain relatively balanced, and peripheral measurements of these hormones will be normal, but the patient is still hypometabolic. The test for this involves feeding the patient a standard carbohydrate load and measuring exhaled CO_2. Patients who are hypometabolic have symptoms resembling hypothyroidism. Paradoxically, increased intake may stimulate metabolism and allow for further weight loss. Patients do sometimes have trouble honestly estimating their intake of food (as they do with alcohol). Rather than confront the patient, however gently, it would be better to have her keep a detailed food record for a few days. In reviewing it with her, she may recognize the problem herself, rather than experiencing the humiliation of having it pointed out to her. Very-low-calorie diets are indicated primarily for people who are obese and need to lose weight quickly for medical reasons. Such diets must include behavioral and psychological support for patients to help them maintain their losses over time. Overeaters Anonymous is a useful support group, but is targeted mainly to people who either binge or describe themselves as emotional overeaters. The patient is already motivated to lose weight and discussing health risks is likely to merely increase her sense of frustration and helplessness.

123. A. *Bipolar disorder.* Treatment with lithium or other similar medications blocks inositol-1-phosphate. Schizophrenia, Tourette's syndrome, and Huntington's disease are influenced by dopamine, a first, or primary, messenger. General anxiety disorder is related to GABA.

124. C. *increases GABA diffusely throughout the brain.*
GABA is an inhibitory transmitter. GABA and its precursor, glutamate, are found in about 70% of all brain synapses. Benzodiazepines bind to GABA chloride receptors, making more GABA available post-synaptically. The increased availability of GABA reduces synaptic firing and reduces the felt sensation labeled as anxiety. Increases in norepinepherine are associated with a reduction in depressive symptoms. Excess dopamine is, among other things, associated with schizophrenia. Certain anti-anxiety medications, such as buspirone, reduce anxiety by raising serotonin levels. Acetylcholine levels are most closely associated with dementia, memory, and REM sleep.

125. D. *Seizures.* Excess glutamate has long been associated with seizures. Manic activity is associated with high levels of norepinepherine and serotonin. Quiescence is the result of benzodiazepines, barbiturates, or other agents that increase GABA; excessive amounts of these agents can lead to hypersomnolence. Severe hiccups are sometimes treated with neuroleptic medications to suppress spasms of the diaphragm, which produce the hiccups.

126. C. *Nigrostriatal tract.* Although three pathways are critical for dopamine activity (the meso-limbic-mesocortical, tuberoinfundibular, and nigrostriatal), control over movement is governed by the nigrostriatal tract. Action on the mesolimbic-mesocortical tract accounts for the anti-psychotic properties of neuroleptic medications. The tuberoinfundibular tract provides a neurosecretory pathway associated with activity in the anterior lobe of the pituitary gland. The locus ceruleus is typically associated with norepinepherine and depression. The raphe nuclei are the source of serotonin activity.

127. B. *spinal fluid.* Spinal fluid is a direct source of information about the central nervous system and so gives the best indication of serotonin levels in the brain.

128. D. *hippocampus.* The memories and images of REM sleep appear to originate in the hippocampus. Electrical activity in the hippocampus during REM sleep mirrors electrical activity in the cortex during the waking hours. The pons, lying above the cerebellum, is also active during REM sleep and seems to be critical for its initiation. The reticular activating system plays a critical role in sleeping and waking, but is not directly implicated in REM sleep. The amyg-

dala is concerned with emotions, not image-based memory. The basal ganglia coordinate sensorimotor activity.

129. B. *Broca's area on the right side* is involved in the production of expressive speech. Lesion of Broca's area on the left side would lead to idiosyncratic, non-grammatical speech. Wernicke's area lesions are associated with so called "fluent aphasias." There is no impairment in speech production, but the patient has difficulty comprehending what is said to him. A lesion in Exner's area is associated with agraphia or difficulty writing.

130. E. *refusal of food by a hungry animal.* This region of the brain plays s critical role in regulating all drives, including that of eating. Hypersexuality results from removal of the amygdala (the Klüver-Bucy syndrome). Excessive aggression may result from a variety of abnormalities including excessive norepinepherine and lesions of the temporal lobes. Excessive fluid intake suggests diabetes insipidus, which is caused by impaired functioning of antidiuretic hormone due to injury of the neurohypophyseal system. Manic-like hyperactivity is most likely to result form intoxication with amphetamines or cocaine, which affect dopamine along the nucleus accumbens pathway.

131. E. *variable ratio operant reinforcement.* Variable ratio reinforcement makes both learning and extinction more difficult. Although there has been no recent payoff, the patient believes that the next response (trade) may be the one that pays off. Because the patient does not know when the payoff is coming, the urge to trade again is overwhelming and irresistible. Note that for ratio schedules, the payoff is contingent not just on the passage of time, but on the quantity of the patient's actions. Variable ratio (random) operant reinforcement is the mechanism by which individuals become addicted to gambling. Winning occurs frequently enough to keep the person interested and hopeful. The randomness of winning makes it possible to believe that next time will be "the" time. Habituation refers to a developing insensitivity to repeated stimuli, such as when a person no longer attends to police sirens after living in the city for a while.

132. C. *non-dominant parietal lobe.* The constellation of clinical findings associated with a lesion in the non-dominant parietal lobe includes neglect of the left side and constructional apraxia. The

patient typically denies any problem. Lesions of the orbito-medial frontal cortex result in withdrawal, fearfulness, and explosive moods. Lesions of the dominant parietal lobe are accompanied by Gerstmann's syndrome (agraphia, acalculia, finger agnosia, and right-left disorientation). Temporal lobe lesions are characterized by general psychotic behavior if the lesion is on the dominant side, and dysphoria, irritability, and loss of visual or musical ability if on the non-dominant side.

133. C. *Phallic,* the third Freudian psychosexual developmental stage corresponding roughly to 4 to 6 years of chronological age. The myelination process is completed by about age 5.

134. C. *in the afternoon.* The combination of normal activity levels and internal biochemistry make this the time of highest contraction rates. Although heart rate would be greater during REM sleep compared with other stages of sleep, the heart works hardest when a person is awake.

135. D. *objective pathology rather than subjective experience.* Illness is the subjective label, or a self-description. Disease is a physiologic fact. Illness can exist without disease (e.g., PMS) and disease can exist without illness (e.g., hypertension).

136. D. *relieves the individual from responsibility during an illness.* The sick role incorporates two rights and two obligations. The two rights are to be excused from normal responsibilities and to not be blamed for the illness. Note that although patients may have certainly contributed to their condition (e.g., smokers with lung cancer), they are treated, not blamed for their condition. The two duties are to get well and to seek help to get well. Note that the sick role is about social relationships to other people and is distinct from the notions of illness (subjective label) and disease (objective pathology).

137. A. *denial.* She does not address the Pap smear information at all, as if this particular feature of reality does not exist for her. Intellectualization would be replacing affective reaction by excessive cognition (such as excessive information seeking). Rationalization implies justification, or saying why an unacceptable action or thought is acceptable in this case. Undoing suggests ritualistic action to reverse or repair something that is not acceptable. Somatization is having physical symptoms that have a psychological but not organic etiology.

138. B. *explore the presence of depressive symptoms.* Depression commonly accompanies long-term cardiac conditions and must be identified and managed along with any other health problems. Some studies have suggested that as many as one in five cardiac patients suffers from some identifiable form of depression. The added psychological burden of losing a job, especially if the loss is associated with the illness or due to downsizing, situations over which the patient has no control, magnifies the possibility that the patient presented is depressed. Referral to a psychiatrist is premature and may not be necessary. If a single physician can manage both the cardiac problems and depression, this places less burden on the patient and reduces the chance of missing negative synergies in the drugs that are prescribed. Giving medications, involving family members or telling the patient not to worry before exploring the full extent of the symptoms are never good ideas. Always complete the evaluation before recommending an intervention.

139. C. *negative reinforcement.* By lingering, the mother avoids the negative consequence of her son's crying and displeasure. Thus, she increases lingering to avoid the onset of the negative stimulus. Extinction signifies a reduction in an identified response. Positive reinforcement would mean that the mother get some benefit or pleasure which continues the behavior. Fading is gradual removal of the stimulus to below the level of the person's awareness while the behavior continues. A secondary reinforcer is something that, by itself, is not desired, but it changes behavior because of what can be done with it (e.g., a token economy).

140. A. *extinction.* The child's crying behavior stops or is extinguished. Intermittent reinforcement occurs when some, but not every, response is reinforced. Sublimation is a Freudian defense mechanism in which unacceptable impulses are satisfied by channeling them into socially acceptable avenues. Shaping is the process of shifting reinforcements to gradually eliminate all but the desired responses. Maturation suggests that behavior change results simply from a natural developmental process.

141. B. *displacement.* The student experiences his anger as directed at an unnamed physician, not the professor who just made him wait. The student is still angry, but the object receiving the anger has shifted. Reaction formation refers to overt action that is the opposite of what a person

unconsciously thinks or feels. Conversion is a type of somatization in which physical symptoms have a psychological etiology. Repression is pushing experience out of consciousness so that it is non-recoverable. Projection is a person perceiving his or her own thoughts and feeling as existing in the outside world.

142. D. *apraxia.* Loss of ability to do simple, specific coordinated movements, such as tying shoelaces or drinking from a straw. Aphasias are difficulties with comprehension or the production of language. Aprosody is the loss of the normal variations in stress, pitch, and rhythm of speech that convey emotional expression in human communication. Agnosia is the loss of the ability to recognize the import of sensory stimuli (e.g., tactile agnosia is the inability to recognize objects by touch). Anosognosia is unawareness or denial of a neurologic deficit despite the presence of a clear disability (e.g., hemiplegia).

143. E. *If he did not use nicotine replacement or buproprion in his prior smoking cessation attempts, recommend these to reduce potential weight gain.* Weight gain from smoking cessation is real, but not a valid reason not to quit. Increased exercise or the use of buproprion or nicotine replacement may reduce the amount of weight gain. No matter what the patient's genetic risk, smoking is the most serious, modifiable cardiovascular risk factor that he has. Obesity itself is not clearly a risk factor. If the patient's father was obese and had heart disease, the problem may have been related to hyperlipidemia, which can be modified by diet and drugs. The doctor's psychodynamic speculation may be valid, but addressing it in formal mental health treatment is not likely to be necessary or sufficient to induce habit change. Although the patient is rationalizing his addiction, support for smoking cessation is generally not built around 12-step programs. These target the social, interpersonal and spiritual consequences of addictions that have adverse effects on relationships. Nicotine addiction is more pro-social, and group support, for which there is limited evidence of efficacy, primarily involves education, behavioral techniques and encouragement.

144. D. *Thiamine.* Clinically manifested as Korsakoff's syndrome, the memory gaps associated with thiamine (vitamin B_1) deficiency are generally filled by confabulation. Korsakoff's syndrome is a result of long-term alcohol abuse and is only treatable if detected early, prior to neuronal damage. Wilson's disease is an autosomal-

recessive disorder, characterized by a deficiency in copper metabolism. Niacin deficiency results in pellagra, which is manifested as dermatitis, inflammation of mucous membranes, diarrhea, and psychic disturbances. Deficiencies in potassium are manifested as electrolyte imbalances that can lead to muscle cramping and cardiac conduction abnormalities. Zinc deficiency produces anemia, short stature, hypogonadism, impaired wound healing and geophagia.

145. B. *fixed interval.* The medication is taken on a preset, unchanging time schedule. Note that if the patient feels more pain, he cannot obtain more medication. A continuous schedule would be one where the patient takes medication whenever he feels in pain. Fixed and variable ratio schedules provide relief depending on how many times a behavior is done (e.g., pain is reported). Non-contingent suggests that reinforcement is not linked to behavior (e.g., feelings of pain) at all.

146. D. *stopping smoking.* Risk for heart attack returns to the level of people who have never smoked after 2 years of abstinence. Stopping smoking is difficult. The success rate of a single attempt to quit is below 10% without physician help and about 20% with help. Weight lifting may improve muscle tone, but will not provide the benefits of a cardiovascular workout. Losing weight and modifying diet are almost always good ideas, but the impact of stopping smoking will be more dramatic. Cholesterol-lowering medication is useful but must be combined with diet to be effective.

147. B. *disease, but not illness.* H.Y. has an objective physical health problem without the subjective self-label of illness. Sickness refers to the social role assumed by patients who are relieved of duties and responsibilities. She is performing all her tasks and so is not disabled.

148. A. *classical conditioning.* The child first cried when given the shot by the nurse. Now he cries when he sees the nurse, without any shot being involved. Thus, he has the same distress response, but it has become generalized to a new stimulus. Shaping, fading, negative reinforcement, and positive reinforcement all refer to operant conditioning.

149. E. *token economy.* This is an example of secondary reinforcement. The boy receives stickers that have no intrinsic value, but are reinforcing because of what they signify. Biofeedback

requires trial-and-error practice to modify an internal physiologic state by learning to change some proxy external stimulus (e.g. using a heart monitor to learn to control heart rate). Desensitization and flooding are treatments for phobias. Shaping involves reinforcing successively better approximations of desired behaviors (e.g., a child's putting away some toys, then most toys, then all toys).

150. B. *limbic system:* hippocampus, hypothalamus, anterior thalamus, cingulate gyrus, and amygdala. The limbic system constitutes the circuit through which the emotional response reverberates. The neocortex is a control mechanism and handles most higher level thought processes. The cerebellum is important for learning skills and for some memory functions. The reticular activating system helps control sleeping and waking. The pineal body is the site of melatonin synthesis.

151. B. *fidelity.* Fidelity refers to the ethical principle of faithfulness to one's duties and obligations as a physician. Justice in medicine is the fair administration of medical services, while beneficence is acting in the best interests of patients. Although the principle of beneficence might apply to the physician's behavior in this example, it does not apply as well as the principle of fidelity. The principle of medical honesty refers to truthfulness in physicians' dealings with patients. Trust is not an ethical principle.

152. B. *patient passivity during encounters with physicians.* Characteristics of a paternalistic physician role in physician-patient relationships include physician dominance, patients serving as passive recipients of medical information and services, and physician assumption that patients adhere to the physician's decisions about medical management. In contrast, the other choices offered are characteristics of a contractual, patient-centered relationship between physicians and patients.

153. B. *immediately inform him of his condition.* Studies have shown that terminally ill patients prefer to be told of their condition without delay. However, physicians may shy away from this discussion because it makes them feel uncomfortable. Being informed allows patients to make plans that can considerably benefit both patients and their survivors. Physician fears of patient decompensation and agony being precipitated by such knowledge have been unfounded. Mr. E. is the person responsible for telling relatives about his disease and only if he wants them to know. To encourage Mr. E. to buy life insurance before telling him about his disease is blatantly dishonest, toward both Mr. E. and the insurance company.

154. A. *acknowledging differences in understanding of health-related issues.* The preferred physician-patient relationship includes respect for the roles of physician and patient as provider of medical expertise and autonomous recipient of services, respectively. This relationship values mutual exchange of information, active involvement of patients in all aspects of their care, collaborative decision making, and respecting differences in background and understanding of health-related issues. The other options provided are concepts and beliefs consistent with traditional (but increasingly outdated) paternalistic physician-patient relationships.

155. D. *justice.* Justice refers to the fair administration of medical services and most closely applies to the case presentation. In contrast, fidelity is faithfulness to one's duties and obligations as a physician; beneficence is acting in the best interests of patients; non-maleficence is not harming patients; and honesty is truthfulness in dealing with patients.

156. B. *the patient have all necessary information before deciding to undergo medical treatment.* Informed consent focuses on the right of the patient to decide about a plan of care, after being provided with all relevant information. Informed consent does not allow the physician to withhold any information and does not pertain to providing all information to one or more family members unless the patient is incompetent to make decisions and has appointed a health care proxy.

157. D. *show concern and ask what assistance she would like to help her manage the diabetes.* The patient has a long history of diabetes mellitus and poor adherence to treatment recommendations. Although the patient may benefit from additional dietary counseling and information about the health consequences of poorly controlled diabetes, she has likely received this information during previous visits. Rather than confront the patient about her reasons for not adhering to the treatment plan or ensuring that she understands that the diabetes is her problem, the best first step is to demonstrate concern about her and that her opinions regarding her treatment are valued. An authoritarian phy-

sician-patient relationship has not produced the desired results in the care of this patient and a patient-centered approach should be emphasized in her future medical management.

158. C. *nonspecific therapeutic effects.* The patient's treatment regimen at the medical center was identical to the regimen at her local hospital. Therefore, symptom changes due to nutritional supplements, placebo effects, and specific effects of treatment are unlikely. Although symptom severity may fluctuate because of the natural history of the disease, significant fluctuations at this stage of metastatic breast cancer are not typical. The probable cause for improvement in the patient's symptoms is the nonspecific therapeutic effect associated with being treated at an impressive and renowned tertiary medical center. It is likely that this improvement is being mediated through a greater sense of hope, increased confidence in her health caregivers, and a diminished sense of anxiety.

159. D. *Placebo effect.* The placebo effect is a change in the patient's illness attributable to the symbolic import of a treatment. Patients in such studies are unaware if they are receiving the drug being studied or the inert pill. Assuming all other treatments are identical, the placebo effect should be the same (contribute equally to the findings in both groups) and, therefore be eliminated as a differentiating factor. Specific treatment effect refers to the therapeutic effect (e.g., antimicrobial action) of the new drug being studied and is usually what the study is intended to measure. Nonspecific treatment effects are effects due to factors unrelated to the drug being studied, such as how clinic staff treat the patients. Natural course of the disease refers to fluctuations in disease severity, which occur irrespective of treatment. Investigator bias refers to how preconceived ideas of research outcomes held by the investigators affect study results.

160. D. *the physician controls medical decision making.* Physician behaviors that decrease patients' involvement in their medical care and the decision-making process also decrease adherence to treatment. The other options provided are associated with *increased* patient adherence to treatment regimens.

161. C. *listening actively or reflectively.* While the other options provided represent components of empathy, it is the reflection of feeling as well as content that serves as the necessary and sufficient core element of empathy.

162. E. *Vascular dementia.* The age, history of hypertension and diabetes, relatively rapid onset, and lateralizing neurologic signs are all suggestive of vascular dementia. Alzheimer's dementia has a more insidious onset and lateralizing signs are not an associated feature. Huntington's is an autosomal dominant disorder that appears prior to age 40. Pick's disease is a rare dementia; clinical findings are similar to those of Alzheimer's dementia. Creutzfelt-Jacob disease is a rapidly progressive dementia that is fatal within two years.

163. D. *Speaking in language that is similar to the patient's* will facilitate relationship building. Asking questions and conveying responses at the patient's language level increases understanding and also allows the patient to discuss the illness without being overwhelmed with jargon or other confusing medical terminology. Empathy is best defined as understanding another person's thoughts and feelings. One of the most concrete ways to promote understanding is to use words that both parties understand.

164. E. *transference by the patient.* Transference is bringing into current life the experiences, beliefs, and perceptions of previous relationships. If the patient had experienced previous relationships that were hallmarked by criticism, then subsequent relationships (including the medical encounter) may be perceived in a similar fashion. While the behavior of people with personality disorders may be hard to understand, it is most appropriate to consider situational explanations before labeling a patient with a diagnosis that implies long-term pathology.

165. E. *the creation of additional problems or complications by the physician.* Iatrogenic effect is frequently applied to the negative consequences of drug therapy (e.g., superinfection following antibiotic therapy), but the broader concept applies to any adverse condition resulting from action by the physician (e.g., wound dehiscense following surgery). Iatrogenesis may also be present in elements of the medical interview such as the absence of empathic responses leading the patient to feel undervalued and, thus, impairing self-esteem.

166. B. *combining technical expertise and effective human relations skills to be a "total" physician.* Medicine is both an art and a science. The art of medicine is concerned with understanding human nature, how people perceive events,

and what motivates people's behavior. The science of medicine is understanding physiologic functioning, how to diagnose disease, and the pathophysiology of a variety of conditions in order to make judgments about appropriate treatment. Applying the art of medicine to the science of medicine permits the physician to interpret signs and symptoms in a given individual and negotiate a treatment plan that is most likely to be successful.

167. B. *"patients come first when care is really needed."* This physician's family has supported traditional principles of physician obligation in patients for 20 years. A key belief inherent in that obligation is that patients' needs must be placed ahead of physicians' needs in situations where medical services are necessary. While a spouse is an adult partner who can choose such a lifestyle and make a commitment to such principled behavior, a physician's children may feel hostage to disappointment such as lack of contact with the physician parent or feeling unable to rely on parent support or presence. Obligations as a physician and obligations as a parent typically conflict rather than overlap, making it essential that the physician be explicit about the motivation behind what may otherwise be felt as confusing and rejecting behavior.

168. A. *has a history of maltreatment or abuse by an intimate partner.* Epidemiological investigation has shown that a history of victimization is associated with both chronic pelvic pain and irritable bowel syndrome. Her headaches are classic migraines. Though the association of migraines with victimization is less clear, the fact that she does not have regular medical care despite having a recurrent, chronic illness is also a clue that she has been recently victimized in a relationship. The common thread is the effect of severe stress on various monoamine neurotransmitter systems, which control pain thresholds and autonomic nervous system activity. ER physicians often dismiss such patients as drug seeking, since their pain does not correlate with end organ damage or clear tissue injury. The diagnosis of malingering implies that she is only feigning symptoms, although in this case she has symptoms with a known pathophysiology, in a classic pattern, and with typical comorbidities. Malingering and drug seeking should not be the first hypothesis the clinician adopts. Hypochondria describes a conviction of severe illness in the face of contradictory evidence. The vignette does not de-

scribe the patient as magnifying her symptoms or being overly concerned about their implications. Conversion disorder describes patients with symptoms that do not have recognized pathophysiology and are associated with an identifiable psychological conflict, again possible but not likely here. Although panic disorder patients are intensely concerned about somatic symptoms, this patient's symptoms are not those of panic attacks, which by definition have acute onset and subside quickly. Pain is generally not a panic symptom.

169. E. *respect for autonomy.* The principles of nonmaleficence (not intentionally harming patients), beneficence (improving patients' welfare) and justice (assuring fair distribution of health care services) do not directly apply to the behavior described. Moral virtue refers to behaviors that conform to generally accepted moral standards.

170. D. *Non-maleficence* refers to not intentionally harming one's patients. Adherence to the other principles and behaviors requires specific action by the physician: justice, assuring fair distribution of health care services; respect for autonomy, encouraging patient involvement and self-rule in medical management decisions; beneficence, improving patients' welfare; and moral virtue, behaving according to moral standards.

171. B. *her relationship with her physician.* The patient's relationship with her physician will allow thoughtful discussion of all treatment options and decisions regarding her end-of-life care. Her physician will know her as a patient and person, aware not only of her medical history but also her philosophy of life and death. Given her competence (ability to make appropriate decisions regarding her medical management) and terminal medical condition, decisions regarding her care should not be unduly influenced by input from her sister, her insurance company, regulatory bodies, or the nursing home administration.

172. C. *moral virtues.* To consent to the children's wishes, the physician would have been blatantly dishonest. Since the first trust fund provided life-long living and medical care for the patient independent from the management of the second trust fund, the principles of nonmaleficence, beneficence, justice, and patient autonomy are not involved in the physician's decision.

173. B. *female physicians show greater confidence in their interpersonal skills.* However, significant stress factors continue to exist for females versus males. Lower pay or salaries, less confidence in business aspects of practice, and the demands of balancing family and child-rearing duties are examples often cited as unique stresses for female physicians. The old misconception that female surgeons would be likely to perform fewer operations has been repeatedly disproved.

174. B. *a helping profession when a family member has a history of substance abuse.* Transference refers to responses based on our own emotional needs from familial or developmental experiences. While choices A, C, and D may reflect important childhood issues, the emotional transference of familial substance abuse is likely unconscious and thus more accurately reflects this process. Wanting to be like a physician on television is a conscious choice, an imitation, not the unconscious attachment that transference implies.

175. D. *80%.* Compulsivity is a common trait in many physicians. It must be seen for both its positive as well as harmful qualities.

176. A. *female spouses consider family obligations when selecting practices.* While divorce rates in dual-physician marriages are lower than the general population, women physicians often place family and childbearing responsibilities in a higher priority. As such, interrupted training time, lower salaries, and part-time employment occur more frequently for female than male physicians.

177. B. *Compulsive gambling that only occurs on weekends.* While HIV infection reflects a controversial subject, physicians can practice in limited roles with HIV. Stroke recovery does not necessarily represent impairment depending on the location of the stroke. Physicians show a high level of successful drug rehabilitation. However, compulsive gambling represents an unaddressed addiction that often becomes progressive.

178. E. *validity* means that the test assesses what it is supposed to assess. In this case, that a test to identify suicidal people actually assesses suicidality. To have validity (accuracy), a test must first have reliability (precision or consistency), but having reliability tells us nothing about validity. Bias reflects a tendency of the test or

tester to produce skewed results. Administration refers to how the test will be given.

179. E. *validity.* Does the test assess qualities that are important to being a bank teller? Does it separate success from failure or help to predict who will be successful in this particular job? Reliability and precision refer to consistency, that is, does the test give the same result every time (test-retest reliability)? Bias is a deviation from truth and suggests a flaw in the test itself, or in its administration. Convergence is a type of validity, but not the type of interest here. For convergence, different tests that purport to assess the same thing would give the same result.

180. E. *predictive validity,* or that the validating criterion (success in school) will exist in the future. Content validity means that the items on the test seem related to the subject matter being assessed. Criterion-related validity means that the test matches some existing criterion, as when a person diagnosed as depressed tests as depressed on a depression inventory. Construct validity requires that the test's assessment be consistent with some underlying theoretical perspective. Face validity means that, on first impression, the items on the test seem to be about the subject being assessed.

181. A. *construct validity.* Does the test match the abstract theoretical notion represented by the trait of obsessiveness? Predictive validity refers to a match between the test results and validating criteria that will exist in the future. Content validity means that the items on the test seem related to the subject matter being assessed. Criterion-related validity means that the test matches some existing criterion, as when a person diagnosed as depressed tests as depressed on a depression inventory. Face validity means that, on first impression, the items on the test seem to be about the subject being assessed.

182. B. *consider this test since its reliability is very strong.* A number close to 1.00 is very good reliability. A number over 1.00 is not mathematically possible.

183. E. *reliability.* How likely is the test to give the same results on a consistent basis so that any change in results represents real change and not just random fluctuation? Adaptive capacity has nothing to do with evaluating how useful a test may be. Concurrent validity means that other, external criteria confirm the results of the test.

Bias is deviation from truth and reflects an inability of the test to give an accurate representation of reality.

184. E. *Tests of intelligence generally attempt to measure ability not achievement.* IQ tests measure capacity (how much is the child able to learn), not achievement (how much did the child actually learn). A number of different definitions of intelligence exist, and a number of different types of intelligence have been proposed (e.g., emotional intelligence). IQ is a derived measurement; intelligence is the inference from that measurement. A number of researchers have demonstrated some racial bias in IQ tests leading to the development of "culture-free" tests. A good test administrator should take these biases into account. Most differences in IQ scores are primarily due to heredity.

185. C. *between 85 and 115.* The IQ has a mean of 100 and standard deviation of 15. In an normal distribution, 68% of the scores will be within one standard deviation of the mean (plus and minus). 50% of the scores will be over 100 and 50% will be under 100. About 2.5% of the population will have scores under 70 or over 130. A score of 70 is the IQ criterion cutoff for mental retardation. However, social capacities, as well as IQ, are used for a diagnosis of mental retardation.

186. E. *Schizotypal personality disorder,* by DSM-IV criteria. J.G. evidences odd thinking, a belief in telepathy, suspiciousness, social anxiety, inappropriate affect, lack of close friends, and odd speech patterns. A narcissist sees the world and self in grand terms. The schizoid has no friends, but likes it that way and just wants to be left alone. Borderline people are in constant chaos with unstable mood, self-image and relationships. Anti-social personality disorder is the diagnosis applied to a person lacking a conscience.

187. D. *night terrors.* Night terrors are a Stage 4 (deep) sleep disorder that have the classical presentation described here. Night terrors tend to run in families and can be a precursor to temporal lobe epilepsy. In contrast, nightmares are called dream anxiety disorders. These are essentially bad dreams that occur in REM sleep. Hypnogogic hallucinations occur while falling asleep and are one of the symptoms of narcolepsy. Bruxism is teeth grinding and occurs in Stage 2 sleep. Acute adjustment reaction is a time-limited form of posttraumatic stress disorder.

188. A. *has complete information about the surgical procedure and recovery.* Knowing what is going to happen reduces stress and allows for faster recovery with less reported pain. Good relationships with hospital medical personnel are the best predictor of satisfaction with hospital stay, but has not been shown to shorten recovery time. Giving pain medication on demand tends to lessen the patient's fear of pain, but does little to reduce the need for the medication.

189. C. *L or Lie Scale.* The Lie scale reflects the tendency to answer in ways that are socially desirable but rarely practiced. The Infrequency scale measures the tendency to give statistically rare responses, and serves as a check on random responding. The Correction scale allows mathematical adjustment of MMPI scores to increase true positives. The Psychasthenia scale assesses liability to anxiety. A Self-esteem scale is not part of the MMPI.

190. E. *Thematic Apperception Test* or TAT. For the TAT, patients are presented with a number of ambiguous pictures and asked to create a story about what is happening in the pictures. Stories are scored for unconscious themes such as the need for power, need for intimacy, or need for achievement. The MMPI is a multi-dimensional, norm referenced test that provides a profile of the patient's personality. The other choices are tests that seek to diagnose neurologic or developmental impairment.

191. C. *The Halstead-Reitan Neuropsychological Test Battery* is a wide-ranging battery of standardized instruments seeking to generate a complete picture of the patient's neurologic functioning. The Luria-Nebraska Neuropsychological Battery provides a similar assessment, but makes use of different standardized tests. The Thematic Apperception Test is a way of assessing the patient's unconscious needs and preoccupations. The California Personality Inventory provides a profile of the patient in a manner similar to the MMPI. The Bender Visual Motor Gestalt Test looks at cortical functioning related to mental representation, retention, and reproduction of presented figures.

192. A. *Bender Visual Motor Gestalt Test* looks at cortical functioning related to mental representation, retention, and reproduction of presented figures. The Wechsler Memory Scale examines short-term memory and might be used to assess a patient with suspected Alzheimer's dementia.

The Rorschach and the Draw-A-Person tests are projective tests intended to assess a patient's unconscious content and preoccupations. The Luria Nebraska Neuropsychological Battery includes a wide-ranging group of standardized instruments seeking to generate a complete picture of the patient's neurologic functioning.

193. E. *the projective hypothesis* assumes that responses to ambiguous stimuli reveal information about the person responding. Subjective press is the perceived field of stimuli directing behavior. The Gestalt laws of perception focus on the role of context and mental set in governing what is perceived. Reaction formation is a Freudian defense mechanism in which real but unconscious feelings are hidden by acting in an opposite manner (e.g., love is manifested as hate).

194. B. *bias.* If the tester knows the hypothesized outcome, she may unwittingly act to confirm it. Stigma is a problem with most psychiatric diagnoses. Patients feel and can be treated with a level of shame not associated with illnesses considered strictly "physical". Construct validity refers to the degree to which the test matches a given theoretical concept. This is not the issue here. Reliability is the extent to which the test results are reproducible or consistent. A placebo effect is found when the patient shows improvement even though the intervention lacks any known therapeutic benefit.

195. D. $b/(b + d)$. In a 2×2 table, specificity is $d/(b + d)$, or the number of true-negative test results. Specificity is the ability of a test to exclude a disease when it is truly absent. Test results for those who do not have a disease can be either negative (i.e., true-negative results) or positive (i.e., false-positive results). The formula $(1 -$ specificity$)$ is the number of negative cases remaining after the true-negative cases have been subtracted (i.e., the false-positive results). This is shown as $1 - [d/(b + d)] = b/(b + d)$ or the false-positive error rate.

196. E. $d/(b + d)$. Specificity is the probability that the test correctly identified a healthy person. This is the proportion of all disease free people $(b + d)$ who are categorized as disease free by the test (cell d), or $d/(b + d)$.

197. A. $a/(a + b)$. The positive predictive value is the probability of disease in a patient with a positive test result. This is the proportion of all patients with positive test results $(a + b)$ who truly have the condition (cell a), or $a/(a + b)$.

198. A. *late-look bias.* Late-look bias is a tendency to detect only those cases of a serious disease that were mild enough to be identified prior to death. Many cases of massive myocardial infarction result in death before a patient can reach the doctor's office or emergency department. Consequently, your study might underestimate the probability of early death following an infarction. Other errors, such as classification error (i.e., the result of inconsistency in the diagnosis of myocardial infarction), could create bias in your findings as well. Selection bias is a problem when subjects are recruited for study participation or assigned to treatment in a nonrandom manner. Neither of these conditions is operative here. Observer bias or measurement bias occur when there is distorted interpretation of the outcome in study groups. In this case, the outcome is death, which is not usually subject to interpretive error. Lead-time bias is the detection of a disease by screening earlier in its natural history than it would have otherwise been detected, resulting in a measured increase in survival time after diagnosis when there is actually no change in real survival time.

199. B. *lead-time bias.* Screening for lung cancer with chest x-rays has proved to be generally ineffective, not because cases are never found, but because when they are, the natural history of the disease is not changed from what it would have been if the disease were found and treated after symptoms developed. Lead-time bias is the prolongation of survival time after diagnosis, not because death comes later, but because diagnosis comes earlier (i.e., when the patient is asymptomatic).

200. B. *Higher, due to the prejudice and discomfort he elicits in his peers.* Homosexual men have higher rates of suicidal behavior, especially in adolescence, compared to heterosexual peers. This appears to be related to the stigma and discrimination that they face, either due to the admission of their sexual orientation or to the effeminate behavior some homosexuals demonstrate, or both. Such discrimination disrupts the supportive peer relationships that are crucial to the well-being and self-esteem of teenagers. Although achieving the capacity for intimacy is thought to be a somewhat later developmental imperative, opportunities to imagine and experiment with sexual relations are also crucial to adolescent self-esteem and identity development. Homosexuality makes this developmental task more complex if there is little peer support. Additionally, the boy may have few opportuni-

ties to meet appropriate partners and a dearth of positive role models. Homosexuality is not clearly associated with cognitive maturity and, in fact, awareness of sexual orientation often predates adolescence. Non-violence and female patterns of suicidal behavior are not particularly associated with homosexuality in men. Internalized homophobia is not necessarily a feature of homosexuality. When homophobia is found, it is typically related to the degree of non-acceptance and discrimination that the person has experienced in his social environment growing up.

201. C. *has not menstruated in the past year.* Current research separates the perimenopause from menopause, which is diagnosed when the woman has not had a period for the past year. Hot flashes, disturbed sleep and irregular menses are common symptoms of perimenopause, a period of declining ovarian function that may last for years before cessation of menses. Perimenopausal women are less able to conceive than younger women, but women who do not wish to become pregnant should use contraception until they are fully menopausal, as pregnancy is still possible up to that point.

202. D. *the statistical regression effect.* When subjects with the most extreme values for any measure are observed over time, the values tend to become less extreme. This is the statistical regression effect, or "regression to the mean." This would be the most likely reason that moderation of extreme absenteeism is seen even though the treatment program has had no effect.

203. D. *appropriate.* Care is appropriate when the "right thing is done in the right way by the right person for the right reason." These are criteria for professional competency and comprehensiveness. Appropriateness is therefore defined by professional standards of care.

204. B. *accountable.* Accountability of care is the disclosure of standards of care to the public and an acceptance of responsibility by providers for the judgment of the public.

205. A. *acceptable.* Care may be accessible and available, but will not be utilized if it is unacceptable to patients. Acceptability requires that patients and providers communicate in the same language, that care is delivered with compassion, and that cultural beliefs and practices of patients are respected. If the quantity of available care is commensurate with need but the care is unacceptable to patients in the community, the care provided cannot be considered adequate.

206. D. *PPO* (preferred provider organization). A PPO is formed when an insurer establishes a network of contracts with independent practitioners. Practitioners agree to give discounts to patients of the insurer in exchange for increased volume of referrals. DRG (diagnosis-related groups) is a Federal prospective payment system that limits the amount the government will pay to treat specific diseases. All HMOs (health maintenance organizations) are prepaid group practices. In the situation presented, payment is fee-for-service at a discount or PPO.

207. A. *63% and 76%.* When data from a table are expressed as percentages, the percentage of the dependent variable is usually shown as a function of the independent variable. For this table, the assignment to either chicken soup or gazpacho is the independent variable and the frequency of colds is the dependent variable. To express the frequency of colds as a function of treatment assignment, the percentage of subjects in each group developing (or not developing) colds should be shown. The percentage of subjects in the chicken soup group developing one or more colds is 63% and in the gazpacho group is 76%. The only other meaningful fact that could be learned from the data is the percentage in each group that did not develop colds (37% and 24%, respectively). However, this was not among the choices provided.

208. B. *Chi-square analysis.* The chi-square analysis is the appropriate significance test for the comparison of two dichotomous data sets (all nominal data). The dichotomous outcome here is having a cold or not having a cold. The two groups are chicken soup or gazpacho. The *t*-tests are used for comparing means and require two groups of continuous, not dichotomous, data. The Pearson correlation coefficient is used to assess the strength of association between two continuous variables. The analysis of variance acts like a *t*-test, but compares more than two groups. The chi-square value for this table is 1.987 at 1 degree of freedom and is not statistically significant at an alpha level of 0.05.

209. C. *40%.* Sensitivity is the proportion of positive cases that also have a positive test result. We have been told that there are 20 cases. Of these 20, 8 had positive test results with the new test. The sensitivity is 8/20, or 40%. The

sensitivity can also be calculated by setting up the following 2×2 table

Test Status	True Status		
	Positive	Negative	Total
Positive	8 (a)	4 (b)	12
Negative	12 (c)	176 (d)	188
Total	20	180	200

The cells in the table contain the data we have been given. We know that there are 20 cases of political incorrectness, so the total for the first column in the table, the positive column, must be 20. Cell a shows the positive cases detected by the test; we know that there are 8 of these. If cell a is 8 and column 1 adds to 20, cell c must be 12. We know that there are 12 positive test results, representing the total in row 1 of the table. If cell a is 8 and the row 1 total is 12, cell b must be 4. The total for the table must be 200. Cells a, b, and c add up to 24, so cell d must be 176. The sensitivity is a/ (a + c) or 8/ (8 + 12), which is 40%.

210. E. *98%.* The specificity of a test is the proportion of negative cases that it identifies as negative cases. In the case presented, there are 180 negative cases in the population, according to the available gold standard. The test identifies 4 of these as positive and the remainder, or 176, as negative. The proportion of negative cases correctly identified as such by the test is 176/180, or approximately 98%. This can be verified from the table provided in the explanation above. Given that the specificity is d/ (b + d), this becomes 176/ (4 + 176), or 98%.

211. D. *67%.* The positive predictive value is the probability that the condition is present given a positive test result. This is the proportion of all positive results (cell a plus cell b) that are true-positive results (cell a). The formula for the positive predictive value is therefore a/ (a + b). In this case, the calculation is 8/ (8 + 4), or about 67%. Recall that the predictive value, which is calculated as a percentage of subjects with a particular test result, includes subjects with and without the condition and is therefore dependent on the prevalence. Neither sensitivity nor specificity is dependent on prevalence.

212. D. *94%.* The negative predictive value is the probability that a disease is absent given a negative

test result. This is the proportion of all negative test results (cells c and d) that are truly negative (cell d). The negative predictive value is therefore d/ (c + d), which here is 176/ (12+176). This is 93.6%, or approximately 94%. The negative predictive value is much higher than the positive predictive value in this instance because there are few cases of the condition in the population (i.e., the prevalence is low). The probability that anyone in the population has the condition is only 20 out of 200 or 10%. Therefore, the probability that a negative test result is correct is fairly high because of the specificity of the test and the low prevalence of the condition being studied.

213. E. *98%.* The positive predictive value is profoundly influenced by the prevalence, even when the operating characteristics of the test remain unchanged. The sensitivity of the new test is 40%, and the specificity is 98%; these values have not changed. We have now been told that there are 150 actual cases in the study population. Cell a in a new 2×2 table shows the number of true-positive results, or the sensitivity multiplied by the prevalence. This is 0.40×150, or 60. The total for column 1, the positive cases, must be 150, so cell c is 90. The number of non-cases is equal to the total population, or 200, minus the 150 cases, or 50. The number of true-negative cases is equal to the specificity, or 0.98, multiplied by the number of non-cases, or 50. This is 49, and this number is placed in cell d. Cells b and d must add up to 50, so cell b is 1. The table is as follows

Test Status	True Status		
	Positive	Negative	Total
Positive	60 (a)	1 (b)	61
Negative	90 (c)	49 (d)	139
Total	150	50	200

The positive predictive value is a/ (a + b), or 60/ (60 + 1), which is slightly greater than 98%.

214. C. *35%.* The negative predictive value is d/ (c + d). This is 49/ (90 + 49), or approximately 35%. The negative predictive value has fallen as the prevalence has risen. The probability that disease is absent, given a negative test result, declines as the overall probability of disease being absent declines.

215. D. *67%.* The easiest approach to this question is to construct a 2 × 2 table based on an arbitrary sample size. The prevalence is 5%. If the sample size is 1,000, then 50 workers will have the disease. The sensitivity of the test is 94%. Of the 50 workers, 94%, or 47, will be detected by the test. This is cell "a". Cells a and c must add up to the prevalence of 50, so cell c is 3. Of the 1,000 workers, 950 are disease-free. Since the test specificity is 90%, the test will correctly identify 90%, or 855, of these workers. This is cell d. Cells b and d must add up to 950, so cell b is 95. The table is drawn up as follows

Test Status	Disease Status		
	Positive	Negative	Total
Positive	47 (a)	95 (b)	142
Negative	3 (c)	855 (d)	858
Total	50	950	1000

The percentage of positive test results (cells a and b) that are false-positive results (cell b) is b/ (a + b), or 95/ (47 + 95). This is approximately 67%. The high percentage of false-positive results obtained despite the fairly good specificity of the test is the result of low prevalence.

216. B. *33%.* The positive predictive value is a/ (a + b). Based on the table shown, this is 47/ (47 + 95), or approximately 33%. Note that the false-positive error rate (the probability that disease is absent when the test result is positive) and the positive predictive value (the probability that disease is present when the test result is positive) add up to 100%, or 1.

217. A. *3.* The prevalence of the disease is given as 5% of the population, and we are told that the population is 1,000 workers. Therefore, we can expect 5% of 1,000, or 50 persons, to have the disease. Of these 50 cases, 94%, or 47 cases, will be detected by our test. This is what sensitivity tells us. Therefore, the positive cases not detected, or the remaining 3 cases, are the false-negative cases. The number of false-negative cases is (1 - sensitivity) multiplied by the prevalence. In this example, that is [(1 - 94%) × 50] or (6% × 50), which is the 3 cases in cell c of the table.

218. A. *Cost of screening, follow-up, and treatment.* We have already been told that the disease in question can be treated and we know the oper-

ating characteristics of our screening test. If the screening test is prohibitively expensive, we cannot implement it successfully. We need to consider the cost of follow-up testing because 67% of our positive test results will be false-positive results, and all of these subjects will need additional testing to demonstrate whether they do not, in fact, have the disease. Lastly, the cost of treatment for the true-positive cases must not be prohibitive or it will not be possible to provide therapy. The prevalence of other diseases in the population is not critical information, although if other diseases are considered more important and more prevalent, they might be a higher company priority. Disease incidence would be an important consideration in deciding how often to repeat the screening test after the initial round of testing. Once the prevalent cases have been detected, only incident cases remain to be found at subsequent screenings. The size of the population might influence the overall cost of screening, but of greater concern is the cost-effectiveness of the program for the company (i.e., whether the company profits by treating the disease and improving the work force.) If the company profits, the size of the population will not be a limiting factor, and if the company loses, the program will not be cost-effective in even a small population. Lastly, identifying a genetic risk factor is usually important only in an effort to prevent disease or to determine which persons are at increased risk for a disease, not in a program designed to screen for an established disease.

219. D. *$1,300 saved.* Regardless of which test is used, the entire population, or 1,000 people, will be screened. We do not know the cost of the original test, but we know that the new test costs $0.50 more per application. Therefore, screening the population of 1,000 will cost ($0.50 x 1,000), or $500 more with the new test than the old; however, the specificity of the new test (i.e., 96%) is higher than the specificity of the old test (i.e., 92%). We know that the prevalence of disease Y is 10%, so 90% of the population, or 900 people, are disease-free. The original test will correctly identify 92%, or 828, of these 900 subjects, and there will be 72 false-positive results. Each person whose test result is falsely positive will need the diagnostic work-up that costs $50 per person. The newer test will correctly identify 96%, or 864, of the 900 subjects who are disease-free, and there will be 36 false-positive results. Thus, there are 36 fewer false-positive tests with the new test than with the old test. The number of true-

positive results remains unchanged because the sensitivity of the new test is the same as that of the old test (i.e., 96%). All of the subjects that test positive will require the $50 work-up, and there will be 36 fewer of these with the new test. The savings resulting from not having to do the work-ups for 36 people is (36 x $50), or $1,800. When the $500 in additional costs associated with the new test is subtracted from $1,800, there is a net savings of $1,300 if the new test is used.

220. D. *97%.* The positive predictive value is equal to the true-positive results divided by all the positive test results. This table is shown with the true disease status in rows rather than columns. The positive predictive value is therefore 253/ (253 + 8), or 253/261, which is approximately 97%.

221. B. *79%.* This question is asking for the negative predictive value, or the proportion of all negative test results (24 + 93) that are truly negative (93). In this case, 93/ (24 + 93) yields a result of approximately 79%.

222. D. *91%.* The probability that a test will detect a condition when it is actually present is the sensitivity. This is equal to the true-positive test results (253) divided by the true-positive cases (253 + 24), or 253/277, which is approximately 91%.

223. C. *the prevalence in the population tested may not match her prior probability.* The predictive value, both positive and negative, is dependent on the prevalence. In the case of an individual, the prevalence is not applicable, but the probability of the condition in the individual, or the prior probability, is analogous to the prevalence. Both indicate the probability of the condition before testing and influence the probability after testing. The data in the product brochure are derived from a population in which the prevalence of pregnancy is 277 out of 378 women or about 73% of the population. If your friend is unlikely to be pregnant, perhaps because of consistent use of effective contraceptives, her prior probability of pregnancy may be much lower than 73%. If this were true, the estimates of positive and negative predictive value calculated above would not be applicable. All data should be assessed on the basis of both internal validity (i.e., correctness) and external validity (i.e., generalizability to people other than the study participants.) The data reported in the pregnancy test brochure are most likely correct, but whether or not they pertain to your friend is uncertain.

224. C. *70.* The mode is the most frequently occurring score. There are two 70's and only one of every other number.

225. C. *70.* The median is the middle number. Note that you must rank order the scores from highest to lowest first. If there is an even number of subjects, add the two middle numbers together and divide by two.

226. C. *paired t-test.* This is a before-after trial, so the data are paired. There are two groups (active treatment group and control group), so the independent variable is dichotomous. The outcome variable is blood pressure measurements, which are continuous data. The appropriate test for this situation is the paired t-test.

227. A. *data that are not statistically significant may be still clinically important.* When statistical significance is not achieved, the implication is that there is more than a 5% probability (if alpha is set at 0.05) that the outcome difference is due to chance. However, a p value of 0.08 still indicates a 92% probability that the outcome difference is not due to chance. In other words, failure to reject the null hypothesis does not mean that the null hypothesis is true. If a therapy is desperately needed and looks promising on the basis of trials that fail to show statistical significance, there are circumstances under which judicious use of the therapy would be appropriate. But a note of caution is warranted. With large samples, statistical significance may be achieved for outcomes that are not important clinically.

228. E. *pool the data.* The two studies show similar results, one with and one without statistical significance. If the studies were sufficiently similar, a quantitative meta-analysis would be appropriate. Pooling data effectively increases the sample size, providing greater power to detect a significant outcome difference. An alternative would be to recruit more subjects, but this approach is obviously more expensive. When sample sizes are small, power is reduced, and type II (false-negative) error increases.

229. D. *stipulate prospective payment to hospitals.* DRGs represent categories of diagnosis for which a standard hospital stay and resultant cost of care is anticipated. Hospitals are paid by insurers, such as Medicare, on the basis of the diagnos-

tic group rather than the actual care delivered. Efficient care results in a profit for the hospital. Complications result in hospital costs exceeding the DRG reimbursement and a potential financial loss for the hospital.

230. D. *major depression.* When depressed, children and adolescents are often more irritable than sad. Very brief upswings of mood are common, even when the child/adolescent is predominantly down. This vignette describes sleep disorder, changes in appetite, self loathing and lack of usual interests, along with suicidal ideation. Her social isolation and falling grades are signs that her problems are affecting general functioning, making depression the most appropriate diagnosis. Attention-deficit/hyperactivity disorder typically shows up earlier in life, although the diagnosis may be missed if the child is able to compensate in school. In any case, ADHD is not associated with changes in sleep, appetite and energy. Puberty can contribute to mood lability and intensification of moods but normal puberty is not associated with deteriorating general adjustment and suicidal ideation. In girls, the risk of major depression rises with puberty, and the hormonal changes of adolescence may be part of the pathophysiology of depression. However, it is a mistake to dismiss mood symptoms as "just hormones" when there are potentially serious consequences. Borderline personality disorder, by definition, is not diagnosed until after age 18. Some instability is expected during this stage of development, in which identity is being forged. Dissatisfaction with body image is common in both normal and ill adolescents, but body dysmorphic disorder implies that the person is completely preoccupied with some physical characteristic. In addition, concern specifically about weight is excluded from the criteria for this disorder.

231. C. *Medicare.* She is the dependent of someone who is disabled and, therefore, qualifies for Medicare. Medicaid provides payments for people who meet criteria of need as set by individual states. Blue Cross is an example of a large, private indemnity insurance company. A physician-hospital organization is a cooperative managed care arrangement in which physicians and hospitals share patients and financial risks. Most physicians do not have a special resource fund.

232. A. *Group model HMO.* The physician works in facilities run by the HMO and is paid on the basis of capitation and profit-sharing arrangements.

In a staff model HMO, physicians are employees paid a salary. In a network model HMO and the IPA model, physicians own the facilities in which they practice. A PPO is a fee-for-service system in which physicians agree to charge less in exchange for increased volume of patients.

233. A. *HMO.* Only prepaid health care, such as HMOs, benefit from keeping patients healthy. Prepay means the provider already has the money and benefits if the patient does not get sick and require the use of health care services. If patients stay healthy, the provider makes more money. Under fee-for-service systems, as in the other choices offered in this question, the provider only makes money when the patient accesses care.

234. C. *cohort study.* A cohort study is a type of prospective observational study. In this case, the groups were first identified and then followed forward in time. A cross-sectional study examines associations between events at a single point in time. A case-control study is generally retrospective. A clinical trial is an intervention study to test the relative effectiveness of a new treatment or procedure. A cross-over study exchanges the treatment and placebo groups at some predetermined point in the study. This means that everyone in the study will be in the treatment group for at least part of the study.

235. D. *only high levels of stressful life events are associated with increased risk for MI.* Answer this question by using the confidence intervals provided. The basic rule is that only those relative risk confidence intervals with do not include the number 1 (1.0) can be considered statistically significant comparisons indicating that different levels of risk exist for the two compared groups. Using this rule, only the HIGH group is significantly different from the baseline (LOW) group because only this confidence interval does not include 1.0.

236. C. *an increase in AIDS prevalence.* The conceptual formula is (prevalence = incidence x duration). Therefore, if mortality declines, then duration increases. This, in turn, leads to an increase in prevalence. No data are presented for infection rates among family members, changes in medical care, the number of people practicing safe sex, or the survival rate after diagnosis.

237. E. *the tendency for the body to maintain a particular state.* Homeostasis is an optimal state where demands on the body are balanced by

appropriate responses in terms of resources. Note that homeostasis is a dynamic state that changes over time with development and maturation. The central issue is a biological balance of the organism with the environment, not psychology versus physiology. Balancing sex and aggression drives is a core dynamic in Freudian psychology.

238. E. *have more psychological need for control over situations.* Type A or cardiovascular disease-prone behavior patterns feature greater anger, sense of time urgency, and need for control. The response to stress, not the exposure to stress, defines Type A. There is no relationship between Type A and problem solving or social withdrawal.

239. B. *generalized anxiety disorder.* The diagnosis requires that symptoms such as those described be present at least one month. Anxiety is a normal emotional response. The diagnosis of generalized anxiety disorder is made when the emotional state endures or rises to the level of dysfunction. Agoraphobia is fear of situations from which escape is difficult or help unavailable in the event of panic-like symptoms. Obsessive-compulsive disorder features obsessions (ideas that will not go away) or compulsions (actions a person feels compelled to perform). Social phobia is a fear of appearing inept or shameful in public, either in general, or limited to public speaking. The diagnosis of panic disorder requires three panic attacks within a 3-week period. No panic attacks are described by this patient.

240. C. *progressive relaxation.* The student is practicing a behavioral strategy to reduce physiologic arousal and allow for better concentration on the exam. Self-hypnosis is a technique for altering mental state and can include making suggestions to oneself about what to think, feel, or do in a given situation. Meditation is a systematic method of fixing attentional focus on a neutral stimulus that permits the control of physiologic responses. A stress response would entail the manifestation of reactions to stress. Biofeedback allows the altering of internal physiologic states by modifying an external stimulus that serves as a proxy to that internal state. For example, slowing the rhythm on a cardiac monitor to reduce the actual heart rate.

241. C. *mania.* Mania in this case is illustrated by poor judgment, unrealistic self appraisal, irritability, and pressured speech. The patient's recent loss is a soft clue that he is having a mood episode, since mania may be triggered by events that could just as well induce depression. His intact memory with poor concentration and his personalized and idiosyncratic interpretation of proverbs and judgment questions are also typical of mania. Delusional disorder is also associated with unrealistic thinking, but connotes a long-standing pattern of false belief, without disorganization of thought or impaired concentration. Manic patients often seem narcissistic (self absorbed, manipulative and grandiose), but narcissistic personality disorder does not imply an acute change in mental status, signs of cognitive impairment, or grossly poor judgment. In any case, personality disorders cannot be diagnosed based on a person's immediate state; by definition, they begin early in life and are evident across many situations. The patient's scanty clothing and labile mood could be considered histrionic (seductive and emotionally exaggerated), but these traits can also be seen in the context of acute mania. Finally, masked depression is not a well accepted term. When used, it connotes someone who denies feeling depressed and who may primarily complain of somatic symptoms. On systematic questioning, however, the person with masked depression will have depressive ideation (hopelessness, worthlessness, helplessness, suicidal thoughts) and neurovegetative signs (anhedonia, sleep problems, apathy, changes in weight or appetite, bodily anxiety).

242. A. *concept formation.* The physician is developing a classification scheme. This type of thinking is also called inductive reasoning. Insight suggests some sudden realization about a situation or relationship. Stimulus discrimination entails noting the difference between two or more experiences. Hypothesis testing involves seeking evidence that is consistent with, or that contradicts, a given proposition. Convergent thinking is the result of different reasoning processes that yield the same result.

243. B. *defining how experiences are described and what is remembered.* Reality is created as linguistic labels are assigned. The words we use to describe a situation help to give the context, and therefore the meaning, to events. Recent research suggests that humans are hardwired for language and that children can discriminate linguistic from nonlinguistic patterns from an early age. Sensation and perception are not limited by language, although recollection of them may be. Sound can have an associational

meaning that precedes language. The meaning of words is altered by the way they are pronounced or the intonation that accompanies them (prosody), but reality is linked to the linguistic labels, not to the particular form of their expression.

244. A. *cognitive styles.* Cognitive style denotes individual differences in taking in and coping with life experiences. Note that the emphasis here is on coping by the assignment of meaning. Cognitive styles, like computer programs, process incoming information in idiosyncratic ways depending on each person's past experience. Sensations are the result of physiologic perception. Defense mechanisms are Freudian concepts in which people cope with uncomfortable emotional states by means of unconscious mental processes. Schemas are the mental patterns or templates against which a person compares experiences and then categorizes them and assigns meaning to them. Delusions are false beliefs not shared by others of the same culture.

245. B. *intellectualization* cloaks an experience in abstract academic terms and removes it from the immediacy of emotional experience. That is, emotions are replaced by thoughts. Sublimation provides satisfaction by channeling unacceptable impulses into socially acceptable outlets. In repression, an event and any reactions to it are forgotten and generally not retrievable. Denial is the refusal to accept some clear feature of external reality. Projection entails seeing one's own thoughts or feelings as part of the external world.

246. B. *intelligence is generally defined in terms of verbal ability and problem-solving skills.* Most IQ tests assess intelligence by assessing these capacities. In some cultures, a slower, more reflective approach is seen as a sign of higher intelligence. Cross-cultural testing finds little to no differences in intelligence among races, if the tests are unbiased. Racial differences that appear within the U.S. disappear when people are tested in their countries of origin. Although as much as 70% of intelligence may be derived from heredity, the role of environment is critical to determining a person's ultimate functional capacity. Most measures of intelligence require convergent thinking (i.e., looking for preset solutions to the problems presented).

247. B. *Cirumstantiality, tangentiality, flight of ideas, loose associations.* Circumstantiality may be non pathological, especially in people who are anxious or trying to communicate by giving extra details. Tangentiality implies that the person is having trouble following a train of thought or suppressing associations, and unaware that he or she is not logical and goal directed. Flight of ideas is a more severe form of tangentiality, when the connections between ideas may be discernible, but off the point, pressured and idiosyncratic. As thought disorder becomes more severe, the logical connections between ideas are lost and people connect things by superficial rather than semantic qualities (e.g., by the sound of a word rather than the sense, clanging). With loose associations, the connections are random or arbitrary.

248. A. *accurate empathy* is the ability to understand the patient on the patient's terms and to have the patient confirm that understanding with the physician. Clinical judgment refers to decisions about diagnostic procedures and recommendations for treatment. Concept formation refers to gathering information to identify the common elements of a class of disorders. Divergent thinking is looking for creative, new, "out of the box" solutions to problems. Paralinguistic communication refers to the non-verbal cues that punctuate and give context to verbal communications.

249. D. *self-control contracting.* The patient contracts with herself that when a goal is reached, she gets a reward. Cognitive restructuring refers to relabeling or reframing the situation. Cognitive rehearsal is the process of visualizing action before actually attempting it. Problem solving refers to any cognitive routine to arrive at an acceptable solution to a presented dilemma. Skills training involves working with a person as an individual or in a group to help them learn and practice particular behaviors. Often this might be used to help people learn basic social skills such as greeting and conversing with others.

250. B. *cognitive restructuring.* The student is being urged to change the assumptions he has made about the outcome of future behaviors. Positive cognitions are more likely than negative cognitions to lead to productive behaviors. The mechanism behind this observation is unknown but may relate to feeling more relaxed, under control, and optimistic, three emotional states that enhance performance. Cognitive rehearsal is the process of visualizing action before actually attempting it. Problem solving refers to a cognitive routine to arrive at an acceptable solution to a presented dilemma. Skills train-

ing involves working as an individual or in a group to learn and practice particular behaviors. The target skill may be technical (learning how to do a certain job) or social (learning how to share). In self-control contracting, a person contracts with him or herself that, when a goal is reached, a reward will be received.

251. A. *cognitive rehearsal* is the process of visualizing action before actually attempting it. Like an actor, the player visualizes the task he must accomplish before attempting it. Cognitive restructuring involves changing the assumptions that are behind future behaviors. Problem solving refers to a cognitive routine to arrive at an acceptable solution to a presented dilemma. Skills training involves learning and practicing particular behaviors with the aid of an instructor or model. In self-control contracting, a person contracts with him or herself that, when a goal is reached, a reward will be received.

252. B. *They connect the various cortical storage sites to form combined memories.* Memories, themselves, are encoded all over the cortex. The hippocampus serves as an index or locator permitting them to be retrieved. The cerebellum serves as a trainer and guide for the learning of motor skills. The thalamus forwards incoming sensory input to the cortex.

253. D. *Convergence of NMDA and non-NMDA receptor activation slows, prolongs, and increases the efficiency of the synapse facilitating complex sensory learning.* This convergence signals that the stimuli are important and provides inducement for the structural changes required for long-term memory. Stimulation of the non-NMDA receptors triggers the depolarization that releases magnesium blockade of NMDA receptors. This results in a combined NMDA and non-NMDA receptor activation and produces a prolonged synaptic response.

254. E. *the consequences of behavior.* In this operant conditioning paradigm, what happens after the behavior is the key event. Anything that makes the behavior more likely to be repeated is called a positive reinforcer. Any stimulus event that makes the behavior less likely is called punishment. If stimuli occur spontaneously and are unconnected to behavior, they will have no effect, or can result in the unintentional conditioning of "superstitious" behavior. Genetics provides the substrate for behavior, but it is the appearance of stimuli in the environment that makes conditioning happen. The level of drive

can determine the intensity of responses, but not the learning of the actual response set.

255. A. *a high frequency behavior or reward can be used as a reinforcer for a low frequency target behavior.* A behavior that occurs frequently has high value and can, therefore, be used to reinforce other behaviors that are less common. The valance of low frequency behaviors is variable (i.e., they can be aversive or merely neglected) and so do not predictably influence behavior. Moderate levels of arousal are associated with optimum performance, but moderate frequency behaviors do not optimize learning. Individuals do seem to engage in behavior that they find desirable, but this is not a statement regarding the Premack Principle.

256. D. *response extinction.* When reinforcement stops entirely, the behavior tends to stop, although it may unexpectedly reappear in the future as spontaneous recovery. Note that if the reinforcer is not stopped completely, an intermittent reinforcement schedule is initiated, which will make the behavior even harder to stop in the future. Positive reinforcement is anything that, when applied, increases the chance of the behavior happening again. Stimulus generalization occurs when a similar, but not identical, stimulus elicits the same response. Negative reinforcement is anything that, when removed, makes a given behavior more likely in the future. Free operant behaviors are not associated with any clear conditioning regimen.

257. D. *Response extinction.* This is an example of systematic desensitization. Note that the fear is not attacked directly. Instead, the feared object is gradually introduced while another response (relaxation) is in place. While the new response (feeling relaxed) is in place, the old response (becoming fearful) can not occur and extinction results. A critical period (e.g., imprinting) is a time in a developmental sequence when specific (e.g., environmental) stimuli have especially great impact on subsequent learning and development. The Premack Principle holds that high frequency behaviors can be used as reinforcers for low frequency target behaviors. Negative reinforcement is anything that, when removed, makes a given behavior more likely to occur in the future. Aversive conditioning is the use of noxious stimuli to inhibit an already learned response.

258. D. *information about the consequences of behavior is reinforcing.* The vignette describes an

example of biofeedback in which an internal physiologic state is altered by using externally provided cues. In this instance, it is the information provided by the gauge, not the actual physiologic change, or a high frequency behavior, or motor performance, that is reinforcing.

259. D. *Reflex, imprinting, one-trial, classical, operant, social.* The sequence moves from lower level CNS to higher level cortical functioning.

260. A. *dependent on the reinforcement value of relationships.* Social learning involves our sense of and the value we place on other people and our relationships with them. The principles of classical and operant conditioning still apply. Social learning is a key part of individual survival and depends on the feedback of environmental cues like any type of learning. In this case, however, how we regard, and are regarded by, other people is the primary reward or motivation for behaviors.

261. B. *Endocrine* system. Neurologic responses to stress are electrochemical and instantaneous. In contrast, endocrine responses involve the release of endocrines into the blood stream. This produces a slower but more prolonged response due to reliance on the circulatory system for transportation of the active agents to the target organ.

262. C. *the context in which arousal occurs.* The context, and the individual's past experience with that context, will define the meaning and the labeling of the emotion. Whether arousal is felt as joy or anger depends on the cues available to us in the behaviors of others and our own cognitive attributions.

263. D. *show more anger when challenged.* Although emotional expressions can be different in different cultures, cross-cultural studies show that greater anger when challenged seems to be almost universal for males. The other options are more culture specific.

264. C. *Drive theory.* Drive theory concerns the motivational influences of survival instincts such as the need for, among others, food, water, air, and sex. Arousal theory focuses on the need of the organism to maintain an optimal, but idiosyncratic, level of activation. Expectancy theory frames motivation in terms of conditioned, expected associations. Cognitive theory focuses on the labeling of behavior and the mapping of activity within a perceived environment. Socio-

cultural theory points out that the impetus for many behaviors can be linked to the specific social and cultural milieu in which they occur.

265. E. *moderate levels of arousal are best for optimal performance.* The Yerkes-Dodson Law states that excessively high arousal (high anxiety) impedes performance, while low arousal (apathy) fails to provide the necessary motivation to do well.

266. C. *Expectancy.* The woman has come to expect (learned) that something (smoking) and gratification are associated. Drive theory focuses on the motivational influences of survival instincts such as the need for food, water, air, or sex. Arousal theory focuses on the need for the organism to maintain an optimal, but idiosyncratic, level of activation. Humanistic theory focuses on the desire for self-actualization and self-expression. Sociocultural theory points out that the impetus for many behaviors can be linked to the specific social and cultural milieu in which they occur.

267. B. *Approach-avoidance.* The taste of the food reinforces approach behavior, while the probability of unwanted weight gain serves as a negative reinforcer for avoidance behavior. In the conflict presented, the approach reinforcer (good taste), is more immediate and so may influence behavior more strongly. The long-term negative reinforcer (that it will make you fat in the unspecified future) is not only deferred to some later time but also is less certain to occur than the pleasure of the taste right now. The notion of an Oedipal conflict comes from Freudian, not behavioral, psychology.

268. E. *reinforcement experience.* Past experience with reinforcement determines what consequences are expected for present behaviors. The past is the best, although not always accurate, predictor of the future. Belief system refers to the patient's personal, culturally derived sense of how the world works. Family history is often a key indicator of susceptibility to particular diseases, but not of patient adherence. Cultural systems are the source for belief systems about how the world and disease states work. Homeostasis is a seeking of equilibrium both within the organism and between the organism and the environment.

269. E. *the opponent-process hypothesis* explains how a behavior that begins as a habit to achieve pleasure (positive reinforcement) needs to be sustained in order to avoid the pain of withdrawal

(negative reinforcement). This hypothesis underlies substance abuse and addiction behaviors. Avoidance-avoidance conflicts occur when one has to choose between the lesser of two evils. Cognitive dissonance occurs when a person performs a behavior contrary to an existing attitude and changes attitude to match the manifest behavior. Intrinsic motivation occurs when the very fact of doing the behavior is reinforcing in its own right. Secondary reinforcement refers to a stimulus that is not directly reinforcing, but that can be exchanged for something that is reinforcing (e.g., token economy).

270. A. *a delusional episode.* Delusion refers to a false belief that is not shared by others in the same culture. If we all believe that sacrificing a virgin will stop the volcano from erupting, that is a shared belief and therefore an aspect of culture. If I think this by myself with no support from others, we call it a delusion. An illusion is a misperception of an existing stimulus. An hallucination is a perception of a stimulus (e.g., seeing or hearing something) when such a stimulus does not exist. Sensory distortions, like illusions, involve misperceiving something. Gaps in memory can be filled in with fictitious content called confabulations.

271. C. *habituation* occurs when a stimulus loses its novelty and no longer evokes the same level of response. Threshold detection is the lowest level at which a stimulus can be perceived. Just noticeable difference is the smallest difference that can exist between two stimuli that allows them to be distinguished. Accumulated fatigue is the result of sleep deprivation over time and is a common problem among new parents. We do not have enough information about the parents' general activity level, however, to make this diagnosis. Adjustment reaction suggests difficulty coping with a new or stressful situation. The wife may be less likely to habituate because, for her, the child's cry is a cue for action. She is likely to become more, not less, attuned to it over time.

272. B. *Duration.* Chronic pain is generally defined as having duration beyond reasonable expectancy for the particular injury. Lasting more than 6 months is a typical threshold for the diagnosis of chronic pain. Intensity refers to the patient's level of discomfort. Family history will reveal any predisposing factors. The site and cause of the pain are useful in planning management and in establishing the probable level of residual disability.

273. B. *higher for Hispanics who immigrated to the U.S. than those in their country of origin.* Suicide rates tend to be higher in industrialized countries as a result of the *anomie* (a sense of normlessness or being unsure what rules govern behavior) referred to by Durkheim. Suicide rates are highest among white males. In fact, two of every three successful suicides is committed by a white male. Suicide rates shift over time. The rate for the elderly is in a long-term downward trend, while that for adolescents is on the rise. Currently, the suicide rate for people in their teens and twenties is similar to that of the population average, about 12 per 100,000. This makes suicide one of the leading causes of death among teenagers because their overall death rate is low.

274. C. *12* per 100,000 according to data from the Centers for Disease Control and Prevention, an agency of the U.S. government. The rate for the elderly is roughly twice as high as that of the general population, although much lower than it was 50 years ago. The rate for adolescents has risen over the past 30 years so that it is now at about the level of the general population.

275. C. *psychiatric hospitalization with one-to-one monitoring.* Because 50% of all schizophrenic patients attempt suicide and 10% are successful, precautions should be taken. The concomitant substance abuse raises the risk. Danger of suicide is the clearest reason to hospitalize a person for psychiatric reasons. Discharge, even with referral to a self-help program or out-patient therapy, gives the patient the opportunity to carry out the commands of the voices he hears. The immediate threat to life should be addressed before any treatment of the substance abuse problem is initiated.

276. C. *disturbed source identification.* Studies of memory and false memory have shown that the ability to correctly identify the source of a perception or belief may be manipulated or defective. For example, if a person watches an event and then hears a description with different details, the person may think that s/he witnessed something that never happened, not recognizing that the false memory came from the description. Schizophrenic hallucinations often seem to the person to be coming from outside, rather than from within the brain; another type of source misidentification. Not knowing whether one dreamed an experience or actually lived it is another common example of this phenomenon. Short-term memory is measured by giving the person unrelated ob-

jects to remember and asking him or her to say them after a period of distraction or delay. Dissociation is a state of trance in which some percepts are not registered or registered in a distorted fashion, and often not remembered accurately. Impaired concentration is measured by history and performance on serial sevens and digit span tests. Poor judgment is inferred from history and from the person's responses to conventional hypothetical situations.

277. A. *less likely to communicate their intentions.* Because they are less likely to give warning, preventive intervention is more difficult. The elderly, like the rest of the population, are most likely to use firearms as the method of choice for completed suicide. Being older does not connote more practical experience with suicide. The elderly have a lower incidence of clinical depression than other age groups in the population. Over the last three decades of the 20th century, government programs for the elderly and general prosperity in the country meant that the elderly were not more likely to live in poverty than people in other age groups.

278. B. *Enrollment in an experimental drug protocol with poor results.* Anything that might increase a sense of hopelessness increases the risk for suicide. If anything, her level of schooling and her lifetime job suggest that she is at less at risk for suicide. Suicide rates are higher among individuals with higher socioeconomic status (defined as a combination of education plus occupation). Having a family member as a caregiver means reduced isolation and, so, reduced suicide risk.

279. A. *Altruistic.* The soldier sacrificed himself to save a friend. Egoistic suicide is associated with a personal agenda, such as revenge on a loved one. The term anomic suicide stems from the term *anomie* which connotes a sense of normlessness and lack of social rules. Anomic suicides occur in situations of social upheaval and chaos, when normative rules are unclear. Fatalistic and heroic suicide are not part of Durkheim's typology.

280. E. *low levels of 5-hydroindolacetic acid in cerebrospinal fluid.* Decreased corticotrophin-releasing hormone suggests a lower level of physiologic arousal and, therefore, less energy to carry out suicidal ideation. Higher level of ACTH are associated with stress responses, but not suicide. Suicidal individuals have lower, not higher, levels of serotonin. No association

has been uncovered between suicide and adrenal functioning.

281. A. *Conflict theory – adaptation.* The hallmark of this situation is conflict about change. The question is whether or not the system will adapt to the new request, or will seek to maintain its current routine. Resolution will likely depend on the power of external influences and the perception of possible gains within the hospital organization.

282. C. *Goal attainment – structural functional analysis.* The tension in the scenario presented is between two goals of the hospital: (1) to take care of patients, and (2) to be profitable. More nursing staff provide the chance for better patient care, but at an economic cost. In a rush to control cost, the important functions of the admitting nurses in serving as a patient's first contact with the hospital and as the conduit for initiating the management plan accurately and quickly were overlooked. This led to unintended (and negative) consequences. Structural-functional analysis would examine both the manifest and latent functions of various individuals and groups within the organization. This analysis should uncover that the admitting nurses, although of junior status in the hospital hierarchy, fulfill a key function that allows the hospital to meet its intended goal of good patient care. When analyzing an organization, it is critical to assess both the intended and unintended consequences of organizational decisions.

283. D. *manifest functions.* Here, behavior is explained on the basis of readily apparent and often discussed "facts," suggesting that the reason for the use of private rooms is to better serve the patients. The question implies that the real reason may be the staff's needs, not the patient's, which would be a latent function. The explanation given is not intended to identify cause as much as to offer justification. Secondary explanations refer to alternative, but tangential, reasons for the presented events. Implicit theory is the internal subjective explanation from which we work that gives meaning to our world.

284. D. *Symbolic interaction-latent pattern maintenance.* Communication is possible when actions have a common meaning within a shared frame of reference. In this case, the assumptions about the meaning of the action (rolling the patient over) were different. The nurses rolled the patient over to prevent bedsores, but

the action prevented the patient from sleeping and communicated to the patient that sleeping would be fatal. Structural functional analysis examines how organizational and situational components work to allow the attainment of specific ends. Conflict theory examines the social structures and processes that emerge as the result of competition for dominance and other scarce resources. Integration maps the process by which the diverse components of a system are able to function together as a whole. Implicit theory refers to the subjective theory of action that organizes and gives meaning to the world in which a person moves.

285. E. *Utilitarianism-integration.* Integration and consensus are achieved by allowing choices in hopes of maximizing satisfaction for the greatest number of people. Structural functional analysis examines how organizational and situational components work to allow the attainment of specific ends. Conflict theory examines the social structures and processes that emerge as the result of competition for dominance and other scarce resources. Symbolic interaction focuses on the meaning of actions and the context that gives meaning to those actions. Implicit theory refers to the subjective theory of action that organizes and gives meaning to the world in which a person moves.

286. E. *the human body is in its peak physical condition from 20 to 30 years of age.* Patients often rely on their physician to tell them what is "normal" at every phase of life. "Feeling old" may be a sign of daily stress or perhaps the beginning signs of mild depression. The patient should be encouraged to elaborate on what she means by "feeling old". Athletic activity should be encouraged to foster cardiovascular fitness, maintain bone density and promote better mental health. Brain cell development peaks in utero, while complexity is highest during the teenage years. Peak intellectual achievement may occur very late in life, but is most common in the 40s.

287. C. *aphasia.* The most common type of aphasia (nominative, dysfluent or Broca's aphasia), results from lesions in Broca's area and compromises the ability to produce speech, although comprehension is intact. Receptive, fluent or Wernicke's aphasia implies lesions of Wernicke's area and describes problems of comprehension, with speech that may be fluent but syntactically and semantically imprecise. Conduction aphasia results from lesions of the

tract connecting the two brain areas. Such lesions damage the ability to repeat what one has heard, despite intact comprehension and speech production. Thus, these three aspects of the Mini-Mental Status Examination all relate to the concept of aphasia. Apraxia is the loss of a previously acquired ability such as tying one's shoes, putting on a shirt, drawing, or copying a drawing. Agnosia is the inability to recognize objects or parts of one's own body. Amnesia is loss of memory. Disturbance of executive function encompasses such things as problems doing things in sequence, suppressing impulses, or directing attention at will. The Mini-Mental Status Examination is a well standardized, bedside test that systematically assesses each domain, to aid in the recognition of both focal and diffuse brain pathology. The MMSE is especially helpful in dementia, a global brain state that may affect most or all of these abilities, depending on which areas are most affected.

288. A. *a desire to enhance cognitive development.* The need refers to the desire or impulse for cognitive growth and activity. Ability offers the potential for cognitive activity, but not the drive. The desire for dominance and control over others is separate from internal cognitive enhancement. The desire to have children does not spring from cognitive need. Type A behavior patterns are hard driving and competitive, but distinct from the desire for cognitive engagement and development.

289. C. *decreased narcissistic tendencies and increased capacity for interpersonal relationships.* The focus on the creation of an independent identity fades with maturation into young adulthood. Sense of self emerges from the reality of relationships and less from the idealization of self. Task oriented behaviors continue as career goals are identified, and are supported by increased experience with complex decision making. With experience, perspective increases and with it the capacity to manage and control impulsive behavior.

290. E. *the proportions of sexually active single men and women are nearly equal.* It is not true that, overall, there are more single women than there are single men. Less than 20% of young adults choose long-term singlehood. Most singlehood relationships last less than 3 years. Singlehood has career advantages in terms of the hours that can be spent working and can offer an increased sense of psychological autonomy. Overall, only 6% of males and 3% of females are homosexu-

al. Many of these individuals are married, and half of them have children. It is no more true to say that most single people are homosexual than to say that married people cannot be homosexual.

291. B. *dementia syndrome of depression.* The Mini-Mental Status Exam is particularly helpful for differentiating dementia of the Alzheimer's type from depression with reversible cognitive impairment or "pseudodementia", which is quite common in older depressed people. The cognitive problems of depression are mostly those of processing speed, effortful concentration and motivation to perform. Depressive ideation makes people overestimate their impairments. Demented patients, by contrast, may be unaware of their deficits. They tend to have problems that stem from different areas of brain cortex (marked deterioration of short-term memory, aphasias, apraxia, disorientation, and disturbance of executive functioning). Scores below 24 on the MMSE are a reliable indicator of dementia, if the patient has made a good effort. The maximum MMSE score is 30. Scores between 24 and 30 require careful assessment to distinguish early dementia from other forms of cognitive impairment. In this case, subacute onset, past personal history of depression and depressive ideation help corroborate the depression diagnosis. Subcortical dementia differs pathologically and clinically from Alzheimer's dementia. In later stages, both seem similar, but early in the course of illness, parietal lobe and hippocampal functions are more disturbed in Alzheimer's dementia, leading to amnesia, psychosis, aphasia and apraxia. In contrast, subcortical pathology preferentially disrupts the basal ganglia and frontal lobes, affecting motor activity, mood, executive functioning, social behavior and judgment. Although patients with any form of dementia may seem apathetic, self doubt and feelings of futility are associated more specifically with depression. Delirium connotes an acute change in mental status due to some metabolic, toxic or circulatory condition that does not permanently damage brain tissue but disrupts the function of the reticular activating system. Delirious patients may score very low on any form of mental status evaluation due to their fluctuating level of consciousness and global brain dysfunction, but a three-month course of illness is not consistent with delirium. Generalized anxiety disorder is associated with agitation, worry, bodily anxiety, and dread and by definition lasts at least six months.

292. A. *establishing a collegial relationship with parents typically begins during young adulthood.* Only as a young adult can the child begin to see the parent as a mutual participant in the adult world. Many young adults describe their sense of self by contrasting it with their parents. Financial assistance from parents to help pay for adult children's education, a first home, or having children is usually gratefully accepted. The process of questioning family origins and making commitments often begins in adolescence. Adult relationships are different from those between parents and their young children. Although old patterns can linger, the young adult's capacity for independence and self-determination alters the balance of dominance in the relationship.

293. B. *are working at being part of the adult culture.* Most young adults want to be a part of the adult world. Their dreams and aspirations flow from their life experience and the culture outside the immediate family. Seeking independence can make stable intergenerational relationships difficult. Young adulthood is a time for making commitments to intimate relationships and to career. Advice from older persons is sought and valued.

294. A. *Becoming a parent.* All of the options listed may give individuals pause to reflect on their identity and place in life, but nothing conveys the enduring meaning of becoming an adult as much as the advent of a child. Parenthood represents a psychological, social, and financial break from the past.

295. B. *25% increase in height and 50% increase in weight.* Weight increases more than height as physical development progresses. The period just before puberty is when the greatest growth spurt in height occurs.

296. D. *Earlier height gain in girls reflects the body's adaptation to reproductive functioning.* There is no evidence that the eating habits or nutrition of boys and girls differ appreciably. Most growth occurs during delta sleep and is unaffected by waking time or activity level. Nor is growth related to the attention that is paid to the child. Although boys and girls show slight differences on standardized tests (boys do better on mathematics and visual-spatial problems while girls do better on verbal tasks), this is more likely related to cultural mores and social roles than to height differences.

297. D. *improved health and nutrition.* Childhood diseases, in general, have little impact on the timing of puberty. Although many things have been cited as consequences of global warming, changes in the timing of puberty is not one of them. Given higher infant survival rates, later age at first marriage, and longer life expectancy, the social demand would be for later puberty, not earlier.

298. B. *hypothalamus and the pituitary gland.* The hypothalamus regulates the endocrine balance that is central for pubescent development. It also regulates eating, body temperature, and the sleep-wake cycle. Efferent pathways from the hypothalamus control the pituitary gland by both neural projection and a vascular link. The adrenal gland is composed of two parts. The medulla produces epinephrine and is responsible for the fight-or-flight response. The cortex produces both cortisol and aldosterone that are responsible for mobilizing nutrients, regulating the response to inflammation, and regulating salt and fluid levels. ACTH secreted by the pituitary gland regulates cortisol production. Thyroid hormone helps maintain the functioning of neuronal structures. Abnormalities in thyroid production have been linked with anxiety, depression, and bipolar disorder.

299. A. *are at the stage of concrete operations,* according to Piaget's theory of cognitive development. During this stage, children can abstract from their experiences, but have trouble reaching beyond those experiences to general abstractions such as hypothetical situations. This capacity is gained only with the transition to formal operations. Capacity for understanding in the situation presented is linked to development, not educational level. The measured IQ is remarkably stable from about age 5 onward. Although an infant may be distractible, a boy at this age should be able to pay attention long enough to hear what the physician has to say. In general, adolescents do trust those who care for them. Rebellion is manifested as symbolic struggles for identity, not rejection of everything related to the parents or other adults.

300. C. *developmental struggles are relatively minor.* Progression to adulthood follows a reasonably continuous pattern. The stresses and strains of adolescence make for good drama, but do not reflect the experience of most teenagers. Most adolescents derive their core values from those of their parents. Adjustment difficulties during adolescence are about the same for both boys and girls.

301. E. *intense concern about social and peer relationships.* Adjustment to the physical changes of puberty occurs at earlier ages (11–13 years). Although intimate relationships are become increasingly important during middle adolescence (14–17 years), peer relationships still predominate. This is the first age at which career preference is likely to be carried to action, but career preference is unlikely to be the girl's main preoccupation. The desire for conformity is likely to be stronger than the desire for recognition.

302. B. *accidents, suicide, and homicide.* These data are from the Centers for Disease Control and Prevention. This list reflects a pattern of risk-taking behavior. Risk-taking behavior reflects the lack of understanding of long-term consequences, feelings of invulnerability, impulsivity, and poor judgement seen in many adolescents.

303. E. *family and peer relationship problems.* Although there have been a few published studies linking homosexuality in male adolescents with suicide attempts, no such association has been found for girls. Having a handgun in the house offers a means, but not the motive. Children raised in single-parent families do have higher suicide rates, but these reflect dysfunctional relationships. Boys, not girls, have higher rates of successful suicide. Girls are more likely to attempt suicide and survive.

304. B. *immature behavior and lower self-esteem.* Boys who develop later are treated as if they are younger, and may feel deficient when they compare themselves to their peers. Athletic ability is more likely in those who experience early puberty due to the boost in muscle development provided by testosterone. No relationship has been found between timing of puberty and academic ability, delinquency, or musical ability.

305. E. *society's moratorium on growing up.* Pressure to grow into adult roles quickly would leave little social space for the subculture. MTV reflects the subculture, but did not create it. Drug use can be a part of adolescent exploration, but is not the force that created the subculture. The existence of the teenage subculture predates the age of computers.

306. B. *be able to use symbols to represent reality.* The preoperational stage lasts from about 2 to 6 years of age. During this stage, the child leaves

behind preoccupation with sensations and motion and represents the world to him or herself as composed of constant objects. Exploring the environment, manipulating objects, and needing to have an object present to trigger thought are more closely linked to the sensorimotor stage (ages birth to 2). Sophisticated, but inflexible, thought processes are the hallmarks of concrete operations (ages 6 to 12).

307. C. *egocentrism,* that is, the inability to see the world from another's point of view. In this classic demonstration, children are presented with a diarama of mountains and asked to describe what a person standing on the other side of the mountains would see. In early developmental stages, children can only respond in terms of what they see and can not imagine the perspective of the other person. Precausal reasoning sees events or objects that share similar properties as connected. Object permanence or constancy, the capacity to realize that objects out of sight continue to exist, is demonstrated by asking the child to find an object that has been covered. Attaining object constancy is an indication that the child has attained Piaget's preoperational stage.

308. A. *animism.* The child's tendency to understand all objects as living things is actually reinforced by fairy tales and other stories that attribute action and motives to non-human things. Magical thinking is believing that thought equals action, and that the child's desires actually cause events to occur. Autism is a psychiatric condition manifested as an inability to relate to other people, a preference for sameness in the environment, and lack of language development.

309. C. *10,000.* Most of these words are descriptive of things in the child's environment or are used to denote events in the child's life. Children at this age are, however, still mastering some of the finer points of grammar such as tenses.

310. D. *initiative versus guilt.* Trust versus mistrust is most important for the first 2 years of life, as children learn whether or not they can depend on their caretakers. Autonomy versus shame is the time of toilet training, generally encountered between ages 2 and 4. Industry versus inferiority corresponds with the Freudian latency period, ages 6 to 12. During this period children strive to display their competencies to themselves and others. Adolescence, ages 12 to 18, is the time when issues of identity are predominant.

311. C. *meaning of the pain.* A classic study done during World War II showed that soldiers with similar degrees of injury expressed different levels of pain, as measured objectively by how much narcotic they required for relief, depending on the meaning of their injuries. Those for whom the injury meant they would be sent home were in measurably less pain than those who expected to return to combat. Like any other subjective, conscious experience, pain is influenced by how much attention is paid to it, which, in turn, is a factor of what the pain means. The person's general state of morale (hopeful, cheerful, empowered vs. depressed, hopeless, helpless) also influences subjective pain, as shown by the efficacy of treatment for depression in helping people recover from painful states. Every other option presented (degree of tissue injury, availability of narcotics, general fitness and time of day) may influence pain but was matched between soldier groups. In research terms, these are controlled conditions that highlight the effect of the variable of interest.

312. A. *gender identity* refers to the psychological sense of self. Gender identity is more strongly determined by culture and parental assignment than by the physical genitalia with which the child was born. People with a mismatch between physical gender and psychological identity are termed transsexual. Sex role stereotypes reflect inflexible notions of what constitutes appropriate behaviors for males and females. Sexual orientation refers to the gender of a person's preferred sexual partner, either homosexual or heterosexual. Sex role schemas are mental templates or categories that help provide an understanding of the differences in male and female behaviors. Parental identification refers to the child's focus on and attachment to parental figures, and is one of the major contributors to gender identity.

313. E. *reductions in infant mortality rates.* Life expectancy at birth is defined as median survival time. Therefore, anything that results in loss of life at a young age has a disproportionate impact on life expectancy. All of the other options are associated with better health and reduced mortality, but occur too late in life to have the degree of impact on life expectancy that infant mortality has.

314. E. *slower rate of metabolism.* All of the other options presented are also naturally operative in any given individual. However, lower metabol-

ic rate and decreased clearance due to poorer liver and kidney function are issues for all elderly. Thus, among the options given, slower metabolic rate is the most important determinant of drug dosages.

315. A. *Alzheimer's disease* accounts for 65% of all dementias in the elderly. The patient's age and presentation argues against "normal senility." Loss of memory and failing to recognize family members is not a normal part of the aging process. The gradual onset tends to rule out tumor or stroke. The patient is not reported to be taking other medications, nor is the pattern of cognitive change described consistent with any particular medicine regimen.

316. A. *administer a mini-mental status examination,* which will give specific information about deficit areas. A CAT scan is likely to be normal at this stage. Family members' recollections and a 2-day observation lack structure and systematic data gathering. The WAIS is a test for assessing intelligence, not dementia.

317. C. *eating, bathing, and going to the toilet.* The other activities are frequently performed on a daily basis, but are not included in formal ADL listings and assessment. Ambulating and stair climbing are key components of the SF-36, a frequently used survey to assess the overall health status of people in the general population.

318. B. *balancing life's accomplishments and failures.* Maintaining ego integrity requires that one make reasonable decisions based on a fair appraisal of external life circumstances. The patient presented here has quite a bit of life to look back on. The issue now is does she feel a sense of accomplishment and purpose in this life that will carry herself forward in the coming years? Or does it seem to her that she has wasted life, and has more regrets than successes? Note that in the face of despair at this stage, Erikson's recommended therapeutic intervention is "regression in the service of the ego". This means mentally returning to a previous developmental stage and revisiting previous life-defining decisions. Once these earlier decisions are reviewed, the person can then move forward developmentally with a firmer ego foundation.

319. E. *successful negotiation of transitions* between life stages. This implies anticipating the need for change and making adjustments in activities and expectations to accommodate these changes. Accepting change means accepting new roles in both work and personal life, and learning to play these roles well. It is impossible to move through life without experiencing some loss. Coping with these losses, and arranging a new life pattern in the face of them is the key to successful development across the lifespan.

320. C. *seen as early as age 7 with increases in adrenal steroids.* Increases in adrenal steroids during middle childhood are the biochemical markers for the beginning of the process of puberty. The increase in these adrenal steroids precedes the hormonal changes in estrogen, testosterone, and progesterone seen in both girls and boys during adolescent development.

321. B. *complexity of synaptic connections.* More complex connections provide the neural substrate for increasingly sophisticated behavior and thought patterns. It is not the size of the brain as registered by head circumference that matters most, but the evolving interconnections within the brain that set the stage for development. It is the interconnections among the neurons, not their shear numbers, that allow for more complex social behavior. The mechanism of neuronal processing does not change nor do new neurotransmittors appear.

322. E. *the emergence of sleep-wake differences.* Sleep patterns, such as length of sleep cycle and differentiation among sleep stages, mature to adult-like patterns between 10 and 13 years of age. Hemispheric differentiation is established during infancy and is a central organizing principle for brain functioning. Function specific activity increases as certain areas of the brain become more adept at specialized tasks. Delta wave activity occurs in the deepest stages of sleep and is never primary in waking brain function. The amount of delta activity actually declines with age; as a result, the deepest stages of sleep do not occur in the elderly. Alpha wave activity suggests a disengagement from external stimuli and is most easily fostered by closing the eyes. As children explore and become more involved in their world, alpha wave activity is likely to decrease.

323. B. *Deficits in executive functions* such as reasoning and decision-making. Although ADHD children can be disruptive to teachers in the classroom, they are not more likely to have poor relationships with their peers. Some clinical experience suggests that they may concentrate more on peer

relationships to compensate for poorer academic performance. Deficits in attentional mechanisms make processing verbal directions more difficult, not easier. Persons with ADHD show no essential difference on visual discrimination tasks, although they may have difficulty adhering to the instructions of the testing situation. They may show deficits in visual-spatial tracking tasks. ADHD does not make children more susceptible to childhood infectious diseases.

324. B. *evaluate other people in terms of psychological attributes.* Children become less egocentric and are able to see the world from others' point of view as they mature. They are also able to classify these perceived differences and characterize people as having different "personalities." Manipulation of abstract concepts, anticipating the future, predicting in hypothetical situations, and having a personal philosophy are all characteristic of Piaget's stage of formal operations, which generally occurs after age 12.

325. D. *be seen as good.* At his stage of development, being good means following the rules. Knowing and following the rules is likely to garner approval of supervising adults, but also allows the child to generate self-approval by internalizing these standards. The issue here is not avoiding either embarrassment or punishment from others, but achieving a positively valued sense of self. The directions given by the child are the result of trying to adhere to the rules and not the result of a desire to dominate others. The child seeks rules, not to replace the parents, but to please them by being a "good boy."

326. D. *structured games and sports.* Between 6 and 12 years of age, play becomes truly interactive. To allow this interaction, children need structures and rules to govern their increasingly elaborate play. Competency is key. Children want to participate and show what they can do. To be relegated to the sidelines as one just watching is often taken as a sign of social shame. Same-gender play is generally preferred by both sexes. This is not a time for fantasy, but a time for doing in reality, a time for demonstrating that the child can make things happen. Children at this age also have preferred playmates and develop semi-exclusive play groups. Children do not seek to play with just anyone, but crave the company of their "friends."

327. A. *encouraged to continue with school activities such as team sports and physical education.*

The child has a medical condition, but one that, with proper attention, need not limit his quality of life. To encourage the child's withdrawal from normal activities risks stigmatizing him and reducing his chances of developing and maintaining supportive peer friendships. There is absolutely no reason for the child to take on the sick role and seek to be exempted from regular activities. To label the child as "unfit" risks harming him more than the disease will by itself. With proper management, the child can live a full, happy life without an increase in school absences or exemption from family chores.

328. C. *physical changes can be predicted from social and interpersonal factors.* People who have and enjoy social relationships early in life show less physical decline later in life. The exact reasons for this finding are unclear. It may be that generally healthy people have more interpersonal relationships, or that these relationships actually support physiological functioning over time, or that the presence of social relationships serves to buffer stressful life events, and so reduce physiological strain. Most individuals report signs of aging beginning in their 40s. However, different people manifest signs of aging at different times. Wrinkles and physical decline occur across a wide variety of ages. Women do not age sooner than men. In fact, life expectancy for women is, on average, 15 years longer than that for men.

329. C. *the female menstrual cycle begins to change during the 30s and 40s,* the beginning of the process that culminates in menopause. Men continue to produce sperm, although in declining quantity, throughout their lives. Sexual desire in males is neither the cause nor consequence of sperm production. Recent research has found no differences in the age of onset of menopause in different ethnic or racial groups. The number of children a couple has is not related to sexual activity in the elderly.

330. A. *body dysmorphic disorder.* Body dysmorphic disorder connotes undue preoccupation with some trivial or imagined physical defect. By definition, preoccupation with weight specifically is excluded. Everyone evaluates personal appearance differently from how others perceive it. In body dysmorphic disorder, the person's distorted image of a body part must cause distress and impair function. Social phobia may be associated with similar avoidance of social situations, but the root is fear of ridicule, humiliation or rejection. Factitious disorder describes someone who

induces illness in order to obtain the benefits of the sick role to gratify unconscious needs for attention, sympathy and relief from responsibility. Malingering involves feigning illness for conscious secondary gain, such as receiving opiates, escaping military duty, receiving compensation, or avoiding prison. Civilian malingerers may have antisocial personality traits. Delusional disorder typically involves more complex and pervasive false beliefs than preoccupation with a single physical trait. Delusions usually relate to interpersonal factors rather than physical ones, and the condition is typically associated with the seeking of medical care.

331. B. *sexual activity for both genders is most frequent in the 20s and declines with age.* However, this does not mean that sexual activity is confined to these ages. Sexual desire and arousal are experienced by many elderly people. The best predictor of whether an elderly person is having sexual relations is the availability of a partner, making marital status a good predictor for both genders. The University of Chicago study found that married people have more sex than single people. Although the sexual peak can differ for different woman, most woman report a peak in their 30s. The relationship between sexual activity and socioeconomic status (SES) is not linear. More sexual activity seems to occur in lower and very high SES groups.

332. D. *divorce is most common between the ages of 30 and 45.* Couples who marry young are at higher risk for divorce. More than 50% of adults remarry within 5 years after becoming divorced. Divorced people of any age tend to remarry, producing so-called "serial monogamy". Someone who is divorced once is more likely to get divorced again.

333. D. *most adult children and their parents have positive feelings about each other.* Older parents continue to be sources of help and advice for their adult children, and children of the elderly constitute their major support system during times of illness or other personal crises. Once they have their own children, adults tend to look at their parents differently, with a new understanding of the problems and dilemmas of parenthood. Feelings of dependency on parents continue throughout the lifespan, although the behaviors which express this dependency change over time. Child-parent, not sibling, relationships tend to hold the extended family together and provide a shared identity among family members even into middle age.

334. C. *10%.* One in ten children in the U.S. is born prematurely. The risk for prematurity is higher in African American mothers, teenage mothers, mothers from lower socioeconomic groups, and mothers who smoke.

335. E. *90%.* Some of the most dramatic advances in medicine at the end of the 20th century have been in the area of neonatal intensive care. Low birth weight infants who would have faced certain death in the 1960s and 1970s now routinely survive.

336. B. *25%.* Although survival rates for premature infants have improved dramatically over the past few decades, the child who survives is at higher risk of disabilities than a full-term infant. Long-term respiratory difficulties are common, as are a host of dysfunctions due to hypoxia.

337. A. *Alcohol.* Fetal alcohol syndrome is the leading prenatal cause of mental retardation. Convincing women who are pregnant, or are likely to become pregnant, to avoid alcohol consumption is the simplest known method for reducing the risk for retardation. Opiate (e.g., heroin, methadone) usage is associated with diffuse neurodevelopmental deficits, but not with mental retardation in particular. Women who smoke have a harder time becoming pregnant in the first place, and if they continue smoking after the child is born, increase the child's risk for asthma and sudden infant death syndrome (SIDS). Children of mothers who use cocaine may evidence withdrawal reactions following birth. Lithium carbonate, used to treat bipolar disorder, can cause Epstein's anomaly, a cardiac malformation of the tricuspid valve.

338. D. *Prolactin.* Parkinson's disease is characterized by reduced levels of dopamine in the substantia nigra. A number of treatments, including L-dopa, are available. Dopamine is a prolactin-inhibiting factor. Thus, prolactin levels can serve as a rough indicator of overall dopamine levels in the brain. Acetylcholine is more closely associated with Alzheimer's dementia. Norepinephrine is linked to mood disorders. Serotonin is implicated in a wide variety of disorders including mood disorders, anxiety and schizophrenia. Lower levels of GABA are associated with anxiety disorders.

339. A. *Decreased blocker cyclic-AMP response element binding protein activity.* Rolipram in coffee inhibits blocker CREB that allows cramming. Serotonin activity is linked to long-term

memories, but it is the pulsed application of serotonin, not the absolute amount, that fosters long-term memory. Glutamate in the hippocampus does allow for formation of long-term memories, but coffee does not act directly on glutamate. Prolactin is linked to sexual activity, not memory. The reticular activating system is important in regulating the sleep-wake cycle and general motivation, but not directly in memory acquisition or retention.

340. B. *5-HT2* activity works to modify appetite by means of phosphoinositide, a secondary messenger. Stimulation of the 5-HT1 receptors causes contraction of the gastrointestinal system and inhibits central nervous system activity. The action of the 5-HT3 receptors is not clear at this time. Stimulation of the 5-HT4 receptors increases adenylate cyclase activity. The answer of "all of the above" is incorrect because the action on appetite is specific to the 5-HT2 receptor.

341. C. *muscarinic.* The vignette presents a patient with symptoms of anticholinergic intoxication, a result of antagonism of the muscarinic receptors. Antagonism of histamine receptors is linked to central nervous system effects. Antagonism of the dopamine receptors produces anti-psychotic effects. Antagonism of norepinephrine receptors produces an anti-depressant effect. Antagonism of the prolactin receptors results in disruptions of sexual functioning.

342. C. *Have her breathe into an airsickness bag* as the most readily available way to control her hyperventilation and reduce the "air hunger" that is causing her gasping for breath. A panic attack is an overwhelming event that can not be controlled by simply trying to calm a person down or telling a story. Her acute symptoms must be addressed before trying to gather information about the frequency of attacks. Giving the woman a hard candy is unlikely to have an effect on the panic attack and might actually put her at risk for choking.

343. C. *delays in learning to crawl.* Infants who sleep on their stomach have a risk of SIDS two to three times that of infants who sleep on their back. Educating parents to place their infants to sleep on their back has been key to reducing the incidence of SIDS. However, children who spend more time on their back have less practice lifting and balancing themselves and, therefore, show delays in learning to crawl, which normally occurs at about 7 to 9 months.

Speech and social smile are not delayed by placing infants on their back, because this position allows for a broader visual field and may even facilitate these developmental tasks. Auditory discrimination has no known relationship to sleeping position. Thumb-sucking behavior occurs with relatively equal frequency whether the child is placed on the stomach or on the back.

344. C. *Fine hair on the back and arms,* or lanugo. The girl presented in the vignette most likely is suffering from anorexia nervosa. She is 20% below normal body weight for her height and within the usual age range for onset. Another classic sign is amenorrhea. Note that binge and purge behavior, a classic sign of bulimia, also occurs in about 50% of all anorexics. Sadness suggests the possibility of depression, a common accompaniment to anorexia nervosa. Anorexia is not consistently linked to rashes, loss of tendon reflexes, heart rate or light sensitivity. However, in the severest forms of the illness, idiosyncratic medical complications, such as bradycardia, may appear.

345. E. *somatization disorder.* Somatization is a term that generally connotes the expression of distress in physical rather than psychological terms. Somatization disorder describes a longstanding pattern of unexplained or excessively distressing physical symptoms in four domains: neurological, sexual, gastrointestinal, and pain. If a person develops fewer than the required criterion symptoms or if the symptoms start after age 18, then the diagnosis would be Somatoform Disorder NOS. While somatization disorder, rigorously defined, is a reliable diagnosis, it does not take into account our developing understanding of the neurophysiology of subjective distress. A proposed diagnosis that more closely relates to the phenomenon is "multiple unexplained physical symptoms" or MUPS. This diagnosis is not in the current DSM. How we experience our bodies is highly influenced by the balance between central norepinephrine, histamine, interleukins, acetylcholine, dopamine, and endogenous opiates, which are, in turn, regulated by serotonin, hypothalamic and pituitary hormones, and other neurological factors. The thresholds and stability of these neurological processes are, in turn, affected (sensitized or desensitized) by prior experience and elements of the current environment. Attributing somatic distress entirely to psychological processes is especially easy to do when a patient is convinced of an unproven

cause for the distress. Patients are "accused" of somaticizing when, in fact, they and their physicians lack a common language and a common framework for understanding the way in which they experience bodily sensations. There are many reasons people avoid social situations and cannot fill normal social expectations. Avoidant personality is only diagnosed if the patient expresses a desire for relationships but avoids them for fear of consequences such as rejection, humiliation or exploitation. Malingering is often invoked to explain why a distressed person with no objective signs of disease seeks attention, but it cannot be diagnosed without evidence the person is not actually in distress (or has purposefully inflicted distress) and is seeking secondary gain. Obsessive-compulsive disorder involves intrusive thoughts about contamination, danger, being harmed or doing harm to others associated with compulsions to try to control these thoughts. Panic disorder does present with multiple somatic complaints, but these come in acute bursts and follow a typical pattern related to peripheral autonomic arousal (pounding heart, air hunger, dizziness, restlessness) and are associated with overestimation of how dangerous the symptoms are.

Subject Index

A

abnormalities
- anatomical 350
- functional 350
abstinence syndrome, neonatal 82
abstraction 112
abuse 170
- child or elder 258
- elder 173, 191
- emotional 170, 171, 191
- environmental 170
- financial 191, 192
- partner 172
- physical 170, 171, 191
- psychological 170, 171, 191
- sexual 170, 172
- sibling 172
- social 170
access to health care 134, 141, 144
    145
accidents 99, 144
- motor vehicle 145, 152
accommodation 111
Accreditation Council for Graduate
    Medical Education (ACGME)
    223
acculturation 134, 142
accupressure 233
acetylcholine (ACh) 22
action potential 19
action stage 297
activities of daily living 108
acupuncture 233
- auricular 167
adaptability 63
adaptation 228
- diseases of 56
adaptive ability 111
adaptive behavior 110
adaptive experience 10
addiction 246
- neonatal 82
addictions, behavioral 279
address, manner of 136
adherence 279

adipose cellularity 160
adjustment 155, 234
adjustment disorders 320
adoption 201
adrenal steroids 94
adrenocorticotropic hormone 59
Adult Day Care 195
Adult Day Health Programs 195
adult family homes 221
advance directives 260, 261
advanced sleep phase syndrome
    (ASPS) 36
adverse outcomes, major 81
affect 77, 309
affective and social symptoms 351
affective disorders 181
affective instability 175
agency child care 153
aggravating factor 308
aging
- normal 279
- successful 194
AIDS, pediatric 82
alarm stage 56
alcohol 163, 192, 279
- abuse 164
- fetal alcohol effects (FAE) 82
- fetal alcohol syndrome 82, 164
- use 213
alcoholism 107, 144, 184
alertness 73
alleles 40
allopathic medicine 7
alpha-adrenergic receptor 21
Alzheimer's disease 103, 107,
    189
ambulatory care services 221
ambulatory surgery centers 221
amenorrhea 60, 317
American Psychiatric Association
    (APA) 318
amine neurotransmitter 23
amino acid 23
amnesia
- dissociative 345
- psychogenic 173

amnestic disorders 347
AMPA 21
amygdala 29, 57, 64
analysis of variance (ANOVA) 390
androgen 94
anger 173
angiogenesis 59
anorexia nervosa (AN) 60, 314
ANOVA
- one-way 390
- repeated measures 391
- two-way 390
anterior commissures 29
antidepressants 331
antipsychotics 247, 351
- atypical 341, 352
- typical 352
antisocial personality disorder 368
anxiety 107, 181, 191, 326
- anticipatory 61
- performance 204
- stranger 85
anxiety and depression 214
anxiety disorders 184
Apgar score 83
apnea 37, 38
apoptosis 59
appraisal abilities 62
arousal 77
- optimal degree of 56
arousal phase 198
art as therapy 236
articulation disorder 365
asphyxia 83
assault 170
- physical 173
assent 259
assessment 11
assimilation 111
assisted living 195
assisted living facility 153
association, principle of 63
astrocyte 18
atherosclerosis 60
attachment 85
attention 73

attention-deficit/hyperactivity disorder (ADHD) 367
attitudes 119, 310
aura 237
auscultation 289
authority 135
– unequal distribution of 126
authority figures, domineering/unjust 175
autism 366
autism spectrum disorders 366, 367
autoimmune disorders 59
autonomy 89, 152
avoidance 173
avoidance behaviors, learned 327
avoidance symptoms 330
avoidant person 357
Ayurvedic medicine 7

B

Ballard neonatal examinations 83
basal ganglia 27
basal metabolic rate 104
baseline 312
basic science 252
behavior modification 63
behavior therapy (BT) 68
behavior
– nonverbal 148
– reflexive 65
– social 123
behavioral changes 161
behavioral records 69
behaviors and roles, observable 101
beliefs 61, 119
Below Basic 270
beneficence 256, 265
benzodiazepines 247, 331
bereavement 153, 249
best methods 290
beta blockers 331
beta-adrenergic receptor 21
bilinear mode 368
biofeedback 69, 324
biologic functioning, changes in 106
biomedicine 8, 131, 133, 136, 236, 238, 239
biopsychosocial approach 317
biopsychosocial model 8, 9, 237
bipolar disorders 334, 336, 337

birth rate 144
birthweight 84
bisexual 206
bladder and bowel control, voluntary 88
blame 92
blind 284
board and care 195
bodily integrity, losing 278
body dysmorphic disorder 323
body image 97, 200
body mass index (BMI) 159
bonding 43, 44, 65, 85
boomerang effect 105, 152
borderline 356
boundaries
– closed 148, 151
– diffuse 148
brain 84
brain death 260
brain reward circuits 165
brainstem 26
Brazelton Neonatal Behavioral Assessment Scale 83
breast tenderness 200
breastfeeding 200
breathing training 70
British National Institute for Clinical Excellence (NICE) 318
Brodmann's areas 52
bulimia nervosa (BN) 60, 314
Bureau of Indian Affairs 143

C

caloric intake and energy expenditure, balancing 161
Campaign to Save 100,000 Lives 228
cancer 145, 185
– anal 213
– breast 213
– colon 213
– prostate 213
– testicular 213
capacity 258
capitation 224
carbamazepine 341
cardiac contractility 33
cardiac life support, advanced 262
cardiopulmonary resuscitation (CPR) 243

cardiovascular disease 44
cardiovascular impairment 164
care insurance, long-term 195
care services in the home and the community, long-term 195
care
– community-based 221
– continuity of 221
– custodial 153
– extended 195, 221
– home-based 221
– hospice 196, 262
– institution-based 221
– long-term 195, 222
– managed 226
– prenatal 144
– respite 153, 195
– supportive 166
career obligations 153
caregiving, apathetic 371
cataplexy 37
catastrophizing 76
catecholamine 21, 97, 338
caudate 27
cause-and-effect relations 91
cell processes, normal 59
Center for Epidemiological Studies Depression (CES-D) Scale 190
centering 91
cerebellum 26, 29
certification 223
chakras 237
chemoattractants 18
Cheyne-Stokes respiration 38
child maltreatment 171
childhood disintegrative disorder 367
chlorpromazine 373
cholecystokinin 23, 161
chromosomal bases for intrinsic deviations 81
chromosome 40
chronobiology 33
chronotherapy 36
circadian oscillator 35
circadian rhythm 33
circadian rhythm disorders 36
circumstantiality 309, 335
civil disobedience 113
civil law 257
climacteric 104

clinical guidelines 227
clinical programs 161
cocaine 82
cochlear nuclei 52
cognition 49, 60, 73, 307
Cognitive Behavioral Analysis System of Psychotherapy 342
cognitive differences 284
cognitive disorders 346
cognitive distortions 76
cognitive features 333
cognitive impairment 346
cognitive interpretation 77
cognitive rehearsal 77
cognitive restructuring 70, 77, 330
cognitive structure 61, 119
cognitive style 76
cognitive testing, type of 252
cognitive-behavioral therapy (CBT) 69, 307, 318, 324, 330, 331, 338
cohesion 148
coital activity 102
collaborative decision making 276
collaborative partnership 260
collective financing 219
coma 260
combination therapy 212
comfort care 262
comfort food 160
coming out 99
commercial programs 161
commissioning couple 155
common language 253
communicable disease 181
communicable infectious disease 92
communication 135, 148, 285
communication process between the patient and physician, open 277
communication, verbal 148
communities 123
community health program 11
community support 184
comorbidity 184, 323
companion animals 193
compensation 112
competence, personal 96
competency movement 251
competency, core 130
competency-based accreditation process 253

complex interaction 305
compulsion 330
computed tomography (CT) 30
concentrate, inability to 173
concentration 73
concept formation 73, 74
concepts 91, 111
concrete operational stage 95
conditioning 61
– aversive 68
– classical 43, 65
– operant 43, 66
conditioning therapy 68
condom 202
conduct disorder (CD) 368
cones 52
confidence interval 386
conflict theory 126
conflict
– interpersonal 175
– underlying 323
congregate care facilities 221
congregate housing 195
consciousness 73
consequences 125
conservation 95, 111
consolidation 74
construct validity 384
consumer price index 178
contemplation stage 297
content validity 384
context 308
– environmental 308
contextual cues 63
contingency management 69
continuation phase 338
continuous positive airway pressure (CPAP) 38
contraception 99
control, locus of 76
controlled substances 82
convergence 350
conversion disorder 323
co-payment 225
coping 44, 164, 184, 321, 323
coping response 76
coping skills 60, 62
coprolalia 368
cornea 51
Cornell Scale for Depression in Dementia 190
corpus callosum 29

cortex
– auditory 52
– cerebral 27
– medial prefrontal 28
– myelinization of the 94
– prefrontal 27
– premotor 27
– primary motor 27
– primary somatosensory 28
– ventral orbitofrontal 28
corticosteroids 338
corticotrophin-releasing hormone 59
cost benefit 289
cost to the patient 341
countertransference 278
crack/cocaine 164
crime 141
crisis, personal 184
criteria for diagnosis 322
critical periods 43
cultural appropriateness 130
cultural beliefs 134
cultural humility 130
cultural prejudice 210
cultural responsiveness 130
cultural sensitivity 130
culturally competent 130
culturally influenced 77
culturally sensitive treatments 193
culture-bound syndromes 131
curriculum 252
custody
– legal 155
– physical 155
customs 142
cutaneous nociceptors 50
cyclothymic disorder 336
cytomegalovirus (CMV) 82

D

danger to the patient or others 257
data
– objective 288
– subjective 288
death
– firearm 145
– of the spouse 153
– physician-assisted 191, 248, 263
– with dignity 196
decision balance 296

decision making, participatory 292
defense mechanism 76
defenses 59
degradation 19
deinstitutionalization 180
delayed sleep phase syndrome
    (DSPS) 36
delirium 247, 346
delusional disorders 352
delusions 350
delusions and/or hallucinations 349
dementia 106, 346
dendritic tree 64
denial 76, 173
dependent person 357
depersonalization disorder 345
depression 99, 107, 173, 191, 279
– double 334
– masked 191
– psychotic 339
depressive disorder not otherwise
    specified (NOS) 334
depressive disorders 333
derailment 309
desensitization 68, 331
desire phase 198
desire, disorder of 203
detachment 173
detoxification units 166
developmental coordination disorder
    365
developmental disfluencies 89
developmental disorders 181, 362
developmental milestones 81
developmental trajectories: continu-
    ous, surgent, and tumultuous
    98
developmentally arrested 110
deviance 307
diabetes mellitus (IDDM), insulin-
    dependent 60
diabetes mellitus (NIDDM), non-
    insulin dependent 60
diagnosis 312
Diagnostic and Statistical Manual of
    Mental Disorders (DSM) 305
dialectical behavioral therapy 358
diatheses 43
diencephalon 26
diet 90, 211
diet and lifestyle 161
diets, fad or quick-fix 161

differential diagnosis 289
disconnection, diseases of 315
discontinuation syndrome 339
discrimination 141, 179
disengagement 148
disorganized thought, speech,
    behavior 349
disparities in health status 140
display rules 77
dissociation 208, 344
– normal 344
– pathologic 344
dissociative disorder 346
dissociative fugue 345
dissociative identity disorder 345
distress 56
– cognitive and mental 173
– psychophysiologic 173
divorce 154
DNA 40
domestic violence 170
Do-Not-Intubate (DNI) 243
Do-Not-Resuscitate (DNR) 243,
    262
dopamine 21
dopamine hypothesis 349
dorsal prefrontal association area 27
double effect 263
drawback 225
dressing 214
drug history 200
drug interactions 341
drug use, intravenous 163
drugs 279
– illicit 99
– prescription 192
– recreational 213
Dubowitz neonatal examinations
    83
dyad 123
dyslexia 364
dyspareunia 205
dysthymic disorder 334

E

eating disorders 60, 314, 315
ecological factor 307
ecology 76, 121
education 145
– inadequate 141
– remedial 364

efficacy 341
– perceived 134
egg production 60
Ego 109
ego integrity vs. despair 107
egocentrism 88
ejaculation 107, 198, 200
– premature 60, 203, 204
– rapid 204
elastic nest 105, 152
electroacupuncture 233
electroencephalogram (EEG) 31,
    310, 347
electrolyte imbalances 317
eligibility criteria 226
emergency departments 221
emergency functions 57
emergency, life-threatening 258
emergent reaction (fight or flight) 57
emotional eating 160
emotional instability 173
emotional numbing 173
emotions 77
– primary 89
– secondary 89
empty nest 105, 152
encopresis 370
endocrine system 58
Engel, George 8
enmeshment 148
entitlement programs 225
entrainment 33
enuresis 370
environmental conditions 145
ependymal cell 18
epinephrine 21
episiotomy 200
erectile dysfunction 204
Erikson, Erik 85, 96, 98, 110
estradiol 97
estrogen 60, 94, 104
ethical principles 113
– universal 101
ethnic identity 134
etiologic factors 7
etiologies
– individual 132
– natural 132
– supernatural 132
eustress 56
euthanasia
– involuntary 263

– voluntary 263
evolution 63
examination, physical 347
exchange theory 127
exclusive provider organizations (EPO) 228
executive loop 27
exercise 104, 161, 211
exhaustion stage 56
expectations, unsubstantiated 76
experimental therapy 244
explanatory model (EM) 6, 134, 278
exposure 330, 331
– imaginal 70
– *in vivo* 70
– interoceptive 70
exposure therapy 68
expressive language 89
expressive language disorder 364
extinction 67, 111

F

factitious disorder 324
factitious disorder (Munchausen syndrome) by proxy 325
families, communal 150
family 147
– blended 149
– extended 147
– nuclear 147
– same-sex 150
– single-parent 149
– traditional 148
– two-career 153
family history 308, 310, 350
family members 137, 187
family of origin 147
family problems 165
family structure 148
fat/muscle ratio 189
fear 92
feeding tubes and intravenous fluids 247
fee-for-service 224
feeling 77, 310
fetishism 207
fight or flight 56
Fisher's exact test 390
fitness, physical 211
fixation 109

Flexner Report 8, 219
flight of ideas 335
focus exploration of a topic 283
focused interventions 187
folk healers 134
folk illnesses 131
folk treatments 133
follicle stimulating hormone (FSH) 60, 97
Folstein Mini Mental State Examination (MMSE) 310
forebrain 26
formal curriculum 124
formal operations 98
Freud, Sigmund 109
frontal lobe 27, 175
functional magnetic resonance imaging (fMRI) 31
functioning, intellectual 101

G

Galen 7
Gamblers Anonymous (GA) 360
gambling, pathological 360
game theory 127
gamma aminobutyric acid (GABA) 21
gastrointestinal motor activity 34
gender dysphoria 206
gender identity 85, 90, 210
gender role identification 92
gender role schema 92
general adaptation syndrome (GAS) 56
generalization 66, 95
generalized anxiety disorder (GAD) 328
generativity vs. stagnation 105
genes 40, 42, 43, 205, 306, 350
– dominant 40
– recessive 40
– regulatory 59
genetic bases for intrinsic deviation 81
genetic factors 160, 368
genetic transmission 326
genogram 148
genotype 40
gentrification 180
Geriatric Depression Scale (GDS) 190

germ theory of disease 219
gestational carrier surrogate 155
glia 18
global health program 11
globus pallidus 27
glucocorticoids 59, 60, 186
glucose 60
glutamate 21, 64
glycine 21
goal attainment 229
gonadotropin releasing hormone (GnRH) 97
Good Samaritan Law 257
G-protein-coupled receptors 19
grief 173
– anticipatory 248
– complicated 249
group 120
group model HMO 227
group practice 222
group values, maintaining 229
groups
– primary 120
– secondary 120
growth, bone and muscle 94
growth hormone 59
growth retardation, intrauterine 82
guilt 77, 92

H

hair pulling episodes 360
hallucinations 310
– auditory 350
– hypnagogic 37
Hamilton Depression Rating Scale 373
hardiness 76
harm reduction programs 167
health, public 224
Health Activity Literacy Scale (HALS) 272
Health Care Finance Authority (HCFA) 225
health care
– primary 220
– secondary 220
– tertiary 220
health care proxy 260
Health Insurance Portability and Accountability Act of 1996 (HIPAA) 282

health literacy 270, 271, 272
health problems 152, 220, 221
health program, regional 11
health savings accounts 127
health statistics 140, 141, 143
hearing impairment 53, 284
heart disease 145, 212
hedonism, native 96
helplessness, learned 44, 61, 76, 173
hemispheres, cerebral 26, 27
hepatic impairment 164
heritability 41, 160
heroin 164
herpes simplex virus (HSV), neo-
    natal 82
Heschl's gyri 52
heterogamy 151
high frequency stimulation 23
hindbrain 26
hippocampus 29, 58, 64, 186, 338
Hippocrates 7
Hippocratic Oath 276
histamine 21, 22
historical tradition, loss of 144
histories, social and developmental
    308
histrionic 357
HIV prevention programs 212
HIV/AIDS 185, 212
HMO 227
home health agencies 156
home health care services 195
home visit programs 240
homeopathy 232
homeostasis 7, 9, 55, 104, 124, 125
– ecological 307
– sociocultural 307
homicide 99
homicide-suicide 183
homogamy 151
homosexual experiences, explor-
    atory 99
homosexual fantasies 99
homosexual identity formation 99
hormone replacement therapy 201
hospice houses 240
hospice units, acute 241
hospice, home 240
hospital administration 222, 223
hospitalists 222
hospitalization
– medical 185

– psychiatric 187
human papillomavirus infections 99
Huntington's disease 103
hyperbilirubinemia 83
hypercortisolism 317
hypnosis 346
hypochondriasis 323
hypothalamic releasing hormones
    23
hypothalamus 27, 97, 175
hypothesis formation 113
hypothesis testing 74

I

Id 109
idealization, romantic 152
identity 153
– personal 98, 152
identity crisis 105
identity vs. role confusion 99
illness 5, 130
illness behavior 6
illusions 309
imaging, functional 31
imitation 68, 92, 111
immediate nervous system response
    57
immersion 69
immigrants 180
immune system 34, 59, 306
– heightened response 59
immune system suppression 59,
    164
impairment 279, 320
implicit personality theory 43
impotence 60
imprinting 43, 65
impulse control disorders 358
impulse control, impaired 175
incentive modification 63
incest 172, 208
income 144
incus 52
indemnity plans, managed 227
independent practice association
    (IPA) 227
Indian Health Service 143
indolamine 97, 338
infant mortality 141, 144
infectious disease 163
information processing 91

information, mutual exchange of
    276
informed assent 277
informed consent 256, 258, 277
inhalants 164
in-home supportive services 195
injuries, unintentional 145
inpatient care, acute 221
insomnia 36, 38
institutionalization 219
institution-based practices 222
insurance plans, private 219
Integrated Sciences Model 9, 12
integration of social and cultural
    factors 110
intellectualization 76
intelligence 73, 75, 104
– crystallized 104
– fluid 104
interaction, organism-environment
    43
intermediate care 195
internal capsule 26
International Statistical Classifica-
    tion of Diseases and Related
    Health Problems (ICD) 305
interneurons 18
interpersonal therapy 318
interpretation or meaning 29
interpreter 137, 284
interval scaling 389
intervention strategies 290
intimacy 100, 101, 102
intimacy vs. isolation 99, 102
iris 51
isolation 100, 102, 108

J

jargoning 88
jet lag 36
job relocations 154
jobs, low-paying 180
Joint Commission on Accreditation
    of Health Care Organizations
    (JCAHCO) 223
judgment 113, 310
justice 265

K

kainate receptor 21

karyotype 40
Kernicterus 83
kidney function 106
kinase 64
kleptomania 359
Kohlberg, Lawrence 113

L

lamotrigine 342
land laws 142
language 73, 142
latchkey children 153
law of effect 66
law of opposites 7
lay treatments 133, 134
learning 10, 49, 60, 61, 63
– critical period 65
– explicit 64
– implicit 64
– observational 68
– one-trial 43, 65
– social 43, 67, 111, 119
– vicarious 68
left hemisphere functions 30
lemniscal system 29
lens 51
leptin 161
Liaison Committee for Medical
    Education (LCME) 223
libidinal energy 109
libido, decreased 203
life changes 103
life expectancy 141
life experiences 61
life goals, reflection about 104
Life Review Therapy 193
like cures like 232
limbic loop 27
limbic system 28, 64, 77
listening
– attentive 282
– dichotic 31
literacy 269
– functional 269
lithium 341
litigation 154
living together 102
locus ceruleus 21
loose associations (derailment)
    351
LSD 164

lumbar puncture, 347
luteinizing hormone (LH) 60, 97

M

macula 52
magnetic resonance imaging (MRI)
    30, 310
main effects 390
maintenance phase 339
maintenance stage 297
major depressive disorder (MDD)
    334
major mood disorders 184
malingering 325
malleus 52
malpractice 257
marijuana 164, 213
marital rape 172
married couples with children 147
masturbation 99
mathematics disorder 364
maturational delays 365
McNemar's test 390
MDD 334
mean 385
mechanism of action 339
mechanoceptors 50
median 385
Medicaid 196, 220, 226
medical disorder, chronic 185
medical illness, chronic 185
medical practice, conventional 230
medicalization 126
Medicare 196, 220, 225
medications, prescribed 82
medicine as a social institution 124
medicine
– behavioral 8
– Chinese 7
– complementary 230
– evidence-based 254
– Greek 7
– "mind body" 237
– psychosomatic 8
Medigap insurance 225
medulla oblongata 26
memories 61
memory 73, 95
– anterograde 74
– episodic 74
– explicit 74

– implicit 73
– long-term or permanent 64
– personal 74
– procedural 73
– semantic 74
– sensory 73
– short-term 73
memory loss 344
menarche 94, 99
Mendel 41
menopause 104, 201
menstrual cycle 104
mental health hospital 222
mental illness 181
mental retardation (MR) 362
Mental Status Examination (MSE)
    288, 308
mental status, decreased 247
meridian 233, 237
mesolimbic-mesocortical tract 21
metabolic syndrome 373
metabolism of catecholamines,
    impaired 360
methadone 167
metrics for assessments, common
    253
MGN 52
microglial cell 18
midbrain 26
mid-life crisis 105, 152
mind reading 76
Mini-Mental Status Exam (MMSE)
    190, 347
mistrust 85
mixed model of inheritance 42
mobility, geographic 154
mood 309
mood change, pathological 333
Mood Disorder due to a General
    Medical Condition 337
Mood Disorder NOS 337
mood disorder, substance-induced
    337
mood disorders, other 333
mood stabilizers 341
moral behavior 91
moral judgment 91
moral reasoning, individual 114
morality 91, 98, 113
– conventional 113
– postconventional 113
– preconventional 113

mores 119
morning after pill 201
morpheme 76
mothering, surrogate 155
mothers, stay-at-home 153
motivation to change, building 298
motivational interviewing 70, 297
motives 310
motor activity 308
motor loop 27
motor movements, voluntary 91
motor or vocal tic disorder, chronic 369
motor skills 94, 101, 365
– fine 84, 88
– gross 84
movement empathy 236
movement, psychotherapeutic use of 236
multidisciplinary approach 318
multimodal approach 11
multimodal sensory association area 28
multiple personality disorder 345
Multiple Sleep Latency Test (MSLT), 37
multispecialty group 222
Munchausen syndrome 324, 325
musculoskeletal system 34

N

narcolepsy 37
National Adult Literacy Survey (NALS) 270
National Assessment of Adult Literacy (NAAL) 270
National Committee on Quality Assurance (NCQA) 223
National Family Caregiver Support Program 195
naturopathy 235
needle exchange programs 167
neglect 171, 173
neglect by caregivers 191
neocortex 64
neoplasms, malignant 145
nerve block 324
nerve cell response, individual 63
nerve fiber 50
network intervention 166
network model HMO 227

neural crest 18
neural tube 18
neurobehavioral development, impaired 180
neurobehavioral disorders 81
neuroblast 18
neurodevelopmental disorders 81
neuroendocrine system 104, 306, 326
neuroimaging 310, 347
neurological damage 164
neuronal pathways, degeneration of 103
neuronal soma 23
neurons 17
– bipolar 17
– cholinergic 18, 59
– dopaminergic 165
– motor 18
– multipolar 17
– norepinephrinergic 18
– projection 17
– sensory 18
– serotoninergic 18
– unipolar 17
neuropsychological testing 347
neuropsychology 32
neurosensory system losses 106
neurotensin 23
neurotransmitters 19, 306
neurovegetative features 333
nicotine 23, 192
night terrors 39
nightmare 38, 92
nigrostriatal tract 21
nitric oxide (NO) 23
NMDA 21
NMDA receptors 65
nociception 50
nominal or categorical scaling 388
noncompliance 186
nonmaleficence 256
non-NMDA receptors 65
non-REM sleep 34
nontomographic regional cerebral blood flow (RCBF), 30
nonverbal expressions 136
norepinephrine 21
normal distribution (Gaussian curve) 385
norms 95, 119, 201, 307
nucleus accumbens 27

nucleus basalis of Meynert 23
null hypothesis 387
nursing home 153, 222
nursing home hospice care 240
nutrient stores 60

O

obesity 159, 211
object permanence 85, 88, 111
observation 92, 111, 289, 308
obsession 330
obsessive-compulsive disorder (OCD) 329
obsessive-compulsive personality disorder 357
occipital lobe 27, 28
odds ratio 383, 387
odorants 53
Oedipal conflict 109
olfaction 53
oligodendrocyte 18
opioid peptides 23
oppositional defiant disorder (ODD) 368
ordinal scaling 389
organ system 305
organizational ability 111
orgasmic phase 198
origin, biologic 369
ossicles 52
osteoporosis 60
outcome criteria 291
outcome expectancy 298
outpatient clinic 240
outreach programs 222
ovulation 97

P

pain 45, 50
– acute 51
– chronic 51
– emotional 184
pain behavior 51
pain disorder
– psychogenic 322, 324
– sexual 203, 205
pain medication, scheduled 245
palliative care 240, 262
palliative care consult 241
palliative care team 240

palliative care, inpatient 240
palliative sedation 247
panic attack 327
panic disorder 184, 328
papillae 53
paraphilia 206
parental attitudes 85
parental discipline 171
parental modeling 371
parents' attention 164
parietal lobe 27
Parkinson's disease 103
patient autonomy 256
patient safety movement 254
Patient Self-Determination Act 277
patient sensitivity 192
Patient's Bill of Rights 277
patient's wishes, primacy of the
   260
PDD NOS 367
Pearson correlation 390
peer friendships 100
peer groups 95
peer review 227, 251
penetrance, incomplete 42
peptides 23
perception 73, 76
perceptual disturbances 309
percussion 289
period prevalence 379
personal experiences 61
personal standard 101
personality 43, 89, 355
personality disorder 355
personality inventories 312
personality state 345
personality traits, change in 43
personalization 76
pervasive developmental disorders
   365
pharmacotherapy 331
phenocopy 42
phenotype 40
phenylketonuria 82
PHO 227
phobia 309, 327, 328
– social 191, 327, 328, 329, 371
– specific 327, 328, 329, 331
phoneme 75
phonologic disorder 365
physical activity 161

physical and intellectual decline
   153
physical changes 98, 152
physical complaints 321
Piaget, Jean 84, 91, 95, 111
pica 369
play
– fantasy 95
– imaginary 90
– joint or associative 90
– parallel 90
– sexual 92
– symbolic 90
point prevalence 379
point-of-service (POS) plans 228
pons 26
Positive and Negative Symptom
   Scale 373
posterior commissures 29
post-structuralism 126
posttraumatic stress disorder
   (PTSD) 61, 174, 191, 330
potentiation, long-term 65
poverty 141, 144, 178
power dynamics 171
PPO 227
precontemplation stage 296
predictive validity 384
predictive value 289
– negative 382
– positive 380
predisposing factors 359, 360
pregnancy 102, 152
– unplanned 201
prejudice 142
preoperational stage 91
preparation stage 297
prevention 202
– primary 6, 176
– secondary 6, 176
– tertiary 176
prior authorization 226
prn (as-needed) analgesics 245
proband 41
problem list 289
problem solving 76
professional autonomy 251
professional dominance 251
professionalism 254
progesterone 60
projection 76
proprioceptors 50

prosody 76, 148
prostitution 207
provider competency 252
provider-based model 226
proxy 261
pseudoaddiction 246
pseudosuicide 183
psychiatric condition, diagnosable
   184
psychiatric evaluation 307
psychiatric illness 279
psychoeducation 330
psychogenic megacolon 370
psychogenic origin 369
psychological attributes 95
psychological make-up 124
psychometric properties 312
psychomotor change 333
psychopathology 306
psychosis 337
psychosocial factors 8, 321, 370
psychosocial interventions 318
psychosocial moratorium 98
psychotherapy 321, 342, 346, 358
psychotherapy and pharmacotherapy, combined 324
psychotic disorder
– brief 353
– primary 184
pubertal changes 94
public health agency, local 224
punishment 92, 96
putamen 27
p-value 388
pyromania 359

Q

Qi 233
quality of life 262
quality of services 252
questions, closed-ended 283

R

racism 179
rage 173
rape 170, 207
– date/marital 172
– statutory 207
rape centers 207
raphe nuclei 22

Rapid Estimate of Adult Literacy in Medicine (REALM) 272
rapid-eye-movement (REM) sleep 34
rapport 281
rates of illness and disability 144
ratio 387
ratio scale 389
reaction, short-term 320
reactive attachment disorder (RAD) 371
reading disorder 364
realism and compassion, balance of 242
rebound 155
receptive language 89
receptive language disorder 364
receptor, tactile 50
recovery readiness programs 167
recovery, spontaneous 67
re-experiencing the event 330
reference group 120, 123, 125
referral questions 287
reflex 65
refractory period 198
regression 76
regression analysis 390
rehabilitation program, short-term 166
reinforcement 61, 92, 111, 161, 359
– continuous 67
– intermittent 67
– negative 66
– positive 66, 322
reinforcers
– primary 67
– secondary 67
relapse prevention groups 166
relations, logic 91
relationship
– disturbances in interpersonal 173
– reciprocal emotional 89
– sexual 264
relatives, first-degree 41
relaxation training 70
reliability 310, 384
– inter-rater 384
– split-half 384
– test-retest 384
religion 184, 201, 259
Renaissance 7

representations 88
repression 76
reproductive system 101, 164
reserve, diminished 106
residential therapeutic community 166
resilience 44, 76
resiliency, loss of 173
resistance stage 56
resolution phase 198
resources, financial 153, 179
respiratory changes 34
respiratory infections, upper 181
respiratory pattern 84
response cost 69
response generalization 66
response prevention 331
responsibility to inform 276
resuscitation status 244
reticular system 29
retina 51
retirement 153, 194
retirement communities, continuing care 221
Rett's disorder 367
risk
– attributable 383
– financial 225
– genetic 350
– relative 383, 387
risk factors 249
risk for academic failure, increased 180
risk of harm 310
risk taking 152
risks to health
– direct 6
– indirect 6
rituals 96
RNA 40
role confusion 100
roles 95, 120, 148
– multiple 103
rules 95, 96
rumination 369

S

sadomasochism 207
safety 339
sample mean 386
sandwich generation 105

schema 74, 111
SCHIP 226
schizoaffective disorder 352
schizophrenia 181, 350
schizophrenic spectrum 356
scientific method 219
screening 312, 379
second opinion 226
segregation 142
selection, natural 63
selective mutism 371
selective serotonin reuptake inhibitors (SSRI) 187
selectivity 73
self 100
self, sense of 89, 102
self-care 161
self-control contracting 77
self-description 122
self-efficacy 61, 76, 298
self-help groups, esteem-building 162
self-image 152
self-management 322
self-monitoring 69
self-neglect 191
semantics 76
senior centers 195
sensate focus therapy 204
sensitivity 380
sensorimotor stage 84
sensory systems, losses in all 189
separation anxiety 85
separation anxiety disorder (SAD) 370
septal nucleus 29
serotonin 21, 22, 64, 186
sex practices, unsafe 164
sex reassignment 206, 214
sexual activity 100, 107
sexual desire, arousal, and orgasmic function, disorders of 203
sexual disturbance 202
sexual harassment 208
sexual identity 102
sexual intercourse 99
sexual orientation 102, 210
sexual response cycle 198
sexually transmitted diseases (STDs) 99, 152, 201, 258
shame 77
shaping 68, 69

shelter 179
shift work 36
sick role 5, 6, 133
SIGECAPS 334
signature energy waveform 232
significant other, socially 125
single parents 147
singlehood 102
single-specialty groups 222
situational context 77
skills
– attention 364
– linguistic 364
– perceptual 364
– performance 364
– social 96
– visual-motor 84
sleep (SWS), slow-wave 35
sleep apnea, obstructive 37
sleep architecture 35
sleep deprivation 200
sleep disturbances 189
sleep hygiene 35
sleep paralysis 37
sleep patterns 35
sleepiness, excessive daytime 37
slow tapering 339
smoking cessation programs 167
social approval 96
social class 120, 126
social cognition 95
social contract 101
social control 307
social development 89
social dissonance 134
social emotions 89
social etiologies 132
social experience 114
social factors 127
social impairment 349
social protocol 135
social referencing 89
social relations 89, 123
social structure 120, 123
social systems 120, 124
socialization 119, 307
societal stigma 211
society 110, 120, 123
sociocultural variables 305
socioeconomic status 120, 145
somatic complaints 173
somatic management 330

somatization 321, 324
somatization disorder 322
somatosensory system 50
Spearman's rank correlation 391
speech characteristics 309
speech therapy 365
sperm production 60
standard deviation 385
standard error 386
standard of living 179
standard score 386
standardized denominator 379
statistics 385–391
stepparents 149
stereotype 121
stereotypic movement disorder 369
stimulation, social and intellectual
    179
stimulus control 69, 162
stimulus discrimination 66
stimulus generalization 66
stress 7, 9, 12, 55, 73, 104, 173,
    322, 338, 346
– acute 57, 59
– chronic 56, 57, 59
– environmental 323, 327
– familial 323
– traumatic 344
stress disorders 55
stress management 323
stress response 55, 92, 326
stressed caregivers 195
stressful life events 320, 353
stressor
– duration of 56
– intensity of 56
stressors 190, 321, 323
– common 320
– interpersonal 327
– life 338
– sociocultural 327
strong opioids 247
structural/functionalism (SF) 125
stuttering 365
subluxation 234
substance abuse 152, 163, 181
substance dependence 163
substance intoxication 163
substance P 23
substantia nigra 27
subthalamic nucleus 27
suffering 51

suicidal ideation 173
suicide 99, 107, 152, 183, 191, 337
Superego 109
supernatural realm 131
support systems 104
support, social 60, 62, 179, 184
suspiciousness 173
symbolic interactionism 127
sympathetic nervous system, down-
    regulation 317
sympatho-adrenomedullary (SAM)
    axis 57
sympathy 278
symptom diary 322
symptoms, culturally determined
    expression of 190
synaptic links 64
syntax 76
system dynamics 124
systemic inflammatory conditions
    82

T

tachistoscopic viewing 31
tangentiality 309, 335
tantrum 90
tardive dyskinesia 373
taste 53
teeth, permanent 94
temperature regulation 84
temporal and spatial context 29
temporal lobe 27, 175
temporal sequence 308
terrible two's 90
territorial disputes 175
Test of Functional Health Literacy
    in Adults (TOFHLA) 272
testosterone 60, 97, 104
thalamus 26, 54, 64
therapeutic misconception 264
therapeutic touch 237
thermoceptors 50
thinking 73, 74
– convergent 75
– dialectical 101
– divergent 75
– magical 91
– precausal 91
– prelogical 91
– relational 114
thought content disorders 309

thought disorder 350
tic disorder, transient 369
tics 368
tobacco 99
tolerance 163, 246
tomographic functional imaging 30
Tourette's disorder 368
toxic substance 307
training sites, qualities of 252
trait 40, 43
transcutaneous electrical nerve
      stimulation (TENS) 324
transference 278
transgender 214
transient disturbances 98
transition periods 81
translator 284
transmitter-gated ion channels 19
transsexualism 206, 214
transvestitism 206, 214
trauma 83, 92, 181
– history of 345
– sexual 205
treatment
– futile 262
– goals of 337
– psychopharmacological 358
– somatic 338
treatment plans, principles for
      developing 165
Tribal Council Health Care Admin-
      istrations 143
trichomalacia 360
trichotillomania 360
trust 85

t-test
– matched-pairs 391
– student's 390
tuberoinfundibular tract 21
Type A personality 44, 76
Type A response 44
Type I error 388
Type II error 388

U

under-education 179
under-employment 179
unemployment 144
urgent care clinics (convenience
      clinics) 221
utilitarianism/rational choice theory
      127
utilization review 226

V

vaginismus 205
validity 310, 384
– convergent 384
– criterion-related 384
– face 384
valproic acid (VPA) 341
value conflicts 199
vascular depression 190
vegetative state 260
vested interests 126
vestibular system 51
Veterans Administration (VA)
      Health System 226

violence 99, 152, 170
– amily 170
– stranger-to-stranger 170
virtual reality 70
visceral fat deposition 160
visceral nociceptors 50
vision
– central 52
– peripheral 52
visual impairment 52
visual perception 84
vulnerabilities 60, 61
vulnerability factor 175

W

wealth, distribution of 179
weight loss, rapid 161
wellness programs 222
Wernicke's area 53
Wilcoxon matched-pairs signed-
      ranks 391
will, living 260, 261
withdrawal 83, 163, 166
work 98, 145
World Health Organization 305
written expression, disorder of 364

Y

Yerkes-Dodson Law 56

Z

zeitgebers 33
z-score 386